Imperfect C++

Imperfect C++

Practical Solutions
for Real-Life Programming

Matthew Wilson

⋏⋎Addison-Wesley

Boston • San Francisco • New York • Toronto • Montreal
London • Munich • Paris • Madrid
Capetown • Sydney • Tokyo • Singapore • Mexico City

The publisher offers discounts on this book when ordered in quantity for bulk purchases and special sales. For more information, please contact:

U.S. Corporate and Government Sales
(800) 382-3419
corpsales@pearsontechgroup.com

For sales outside of the United States, please contact:

International Sales
international@pearsoned.com

Visit Addison-Wesley on the Web: www.awprofessional.com

Library of Congress Cataloging-in-Publication Data is available for this book.

ISBN 0-321-22877-4
Text printed on recycled paper
1 2 3 4 5 6 7 8 9 10—MA—0605040302
First printing, August 2004

To Chris, for all the lessons
To Dad, for the inspiration and the resolve
To Grandma, for the pride
To James, for the brotherhood
To John, for the conviction
To Mum, for the wisdom and the facilities
To Sarah, for the support and the love (and the boys)
To Suzanne, for setting the targets and lighting the way

And to my boys: may you take only the blessings

Contents

Preface

Maybe I don't love C++ the same way I love my kids, nor even as much as climbing 10% smooth tarmac in 32° on the rivet,[1] although at times it does come close. But I do count myself blessed that I get to spend the parts of my life that are devoted to work in the practice of, to paraphrase Frederick P. Brooks, "creation by exertion of my imagination." I consider myself doubly blessed that I have at my disposal the singularly powerful, dangerous, and spellbinding language that is C++.

That all sounds very hearts and flowers, but you may have picked up this book because the title suggests that it will be a beat-up of C++. Indeed, you may be an aficionado of Java, or C, or another of the popular major languages, and have seized on a copy of *Imperfect C++* eager to find evidence to justify why you've given C++ a wide berth. If that is you, you may be disappointed, because this book is rather a critical celebration of C++. But stick around anyway; you might find some reasons why you should start looking towards C++ instead.

What You Will Learn

I wrote this book to empower fellow developers. It takes a critical, but constructive, look at C++ and its imperfections, and presents practical measures for avoiding or ameliorating them. When you've read it, I hope you'll have a better grasp of:

- How to overcome several of the deficiencies in C++'s type system
- The usefulness of template programming in increasing code flexibility and robustness
- How to survive in the realm of undefined behavior—that which is not addressed by the standard—including dynamic libraries, static objects, and threading
- The costs of implicit conversions, the troubles they bring, and the alternative of effective and manageable generalized programming via explicit conversions
- How to write software that is, or may more easily be made, compatible with other compilers, libraries, threading models, and the like
- What compilers do "behind the scenes" and how they may be influenced
- The tricky interoperability of arrays and pointers, and techniques by which they may be dissuaded from behaving like each other
- The power of C++ to support the *Resource Acquisition Is Initialization* mechanism and the variety of problem domains in which it can be applied
- How to minimize your effort by maximizing your compiler's ability to detect errors

You will certainly be equipped to write code that is more efficient, more maintainable, more robust, and more flexible.

It's my intention that even very experienced C++ practitioners will find new ideas and some new techniques with which to stimulate the mind and enhance their existing practice. Programmers with less experience will be able to appreciate the principles involved and to use the

---

[1]The cyclists among you will know of what I speak.

techniques within their own work, moving to fill any gaps in their understanding of the details of the techniques as their knowledge grows.

I don't expect any of you to agree with everything that I have to say, but I do expect even the most contentious material to stimulate your understanding of your use of this formidable language.

What I Assume You Know

Unless one wants to write a *very* large book, a good degree of knowledge must be assumed. It would be churlish to stipulate that you have read a precise set of texts, but I do assume that you have knowledge and experience sufficient to be comfortable with most of the concepts contained in Scott Meyer's *Effective C++* and Herb Sutter's *Exceptional C++* series. I also assume that you have a copy of the language bible: Bjarne Stroustrup's *The C++ Programming Language*. I don't assume you've read Stroustrup cover to cover—I haven't (yet)—but you should use it as the ultimate reference for the language, as there's a gem on every other page.

Imperfect C++ contains a fair amount of template code—which modern C++ book doesn't? —but I do not assume that you're a guru[2] or have advanced knowledge of meta-programming. Nonetheless, it's probably best if you're at least familiar with using templates, such as those that form the popular parts of the C++ standard library. I have tried to keep the template use down to a reasonable level, but it has to be acknowledged that the support for templates is the very thing that allows C++ to "self-repair," and it is that, therefore, which largely accounts for the existence of this book.

Since flexibility and practicality are big things with me, this is not a book whose code can only be used with a small minority of "bleeding edge" compilers; nearly everything in the book will work with just about any reasonably modern compiler (see Appendix A). Certainly there are good freely available compilers, and you can have confidence that your compiler will support the code.

Wherever possible, I've avoided reference to particular operating environments, libraries, and technologies. However, I do touch on several, so it would be useful, though by no means essential, to have some grounding in some of the following: COM and/or CORBA, dynamic libraries (UNIX and/or Win32), STL, threads (POSIX and/or Win32), UNIX, and Win32. The bibliography contains numerous references to good books on these and other subjects. It would also be useful to have familiarity with more than one machine architecture, though again this is not essential.

Since C remains the lingua franca of interlanguage and operating system development, it continues to be an extremely important language. Notwithstanding that this is a book about C++, there are many areas in which the common heritage of C and C++ comes into focus, and I make no apologies for addressing both languages in those circumstances. Indeed, as we see in Part Two, we need to fall back on C to support several advanced uses of C++.

There's one important assumption about you that I am making. I assume that you believe in doing quality work, and are motivated to finding new ways in which you can achieve this. This book cannot claim to be the sole source of such new ways of approaching C++. Rather it represents a practical, and in some cases heretical, look at the problems we all encounter with the language, and can at best form a part of your library of essential texts. The ultimate responsibility is yours. All the rest is just getting the best tools to back you up.

---

[2]There are several books listed in the Bibliography that can help you on the long journey to becoming one, if you're willing to invest the effort.

Organization

The main content of the book is divided into six parts. Each part is comprised of an introduction, followed by between five and seven chapters, each of which is further divided into relevant sections.

Inspired by the title of the book, I try to highlight the actual imperfections, so you will find them throughout the text. In the early parts of the book, the imperfections come thick and fast, reflecting the relatively straightforward nature both of the imperfections themselves and of their solutions. Each subsection refers to a particular feature of the language and generally describes an imperfection. Wherever possible, a specific technique and/or software technology is presented which either answers the problem, or provides the developer with control over it. As the book progresses, the imperfections become less discrete and more significant, with correspondingly lengthy and detailed discussions.

The book does not follow the modern "buffet" format, nor does it have a single contiguous thread requiring it to be read from front to back. Having said that, most of the later chapters are described in terms of, and will occasionally be built on, the content of earlier ones so, unless you're feeling perverse, you'll be better off reading it in order. However, once you've read it once, you should be able to come back to any point for reference without needing to read the whole thing again. Within the chapters, sections generally follow a sequential format, so I would recommend that you read each chapter in that vein.

In terms of difficulty, it's certainly the case that Parts One through Four follow a progression from reasonably straightforward to seriously demanding.[3] Although Parts Five and Six rely on some of the material from Parts Three and Four, they are considerably less challenging, and you should feel yourself cruising along to the appendixes.

Following the main content of the book are four short appendixes. Appendix A details the compilers and libraries used in the research for *Imperfect C++*. Appendix B regales you with some of the slack-jawed blunders of a young C++ engineer, taking his first steps in the land of the double crosses. Appendix C describes the Arturius project, a free, open-source compiler-multiplexer, which is also included on the CD. Appendix D describes the contents of the CD-ROM.

I have a very consistent, perhaps strict, coding style; you may well call it pedantic. Former colleagues and users of my libraries have certainly done so. But I do it the way I do because there are no unanswered questions as to where everything goes, which means I can come back to it years later and dive straight in. The downside is that I need a twenty-one-inch monitor and an industrial-strength laser printer.

In order to minimize the effects of my coding style on the readability of *Imperfect C++,* I've taken a few liberties in the code examples presented throughout the book. You'll see a lot of ellipses (. . .) in the examples, and this generally means something that's either been covered in a previous related example, or reflects boilerplate code that we all use (e.g., the proscription of methods from client code access—see section 2.2). Only the aspects of style that have manifest effects on reliability are discussed, in Chapter 17.[4]

---

[3]Parts of Parts Three and Four hurt my brain still.
[4]If you absolutely must sample the voluminous splendor of the rest of my coding style, there's plenty of exemplifying code in the libraries provided on the CD.

References

One of the things that irritates me when reading C++ books is when the author stipulates a fact but does not make reference to the relevant section of the standard. So in addition to including references to relevant articles and books, wherever I make a statement as to the behavior of the language I have attempted to provide references in the C (C99) or C++ (C++98) standards.

Supplementary Material

CD-ROM

The accompanying CD-ROM contains libraries, compilers (including many of the code techniques described in the book), test programs, tools, and other useful software, as well as a number of relevant articles from various publications. See Appendix D for more details on its contents.

Online Resources

Supplementary material will also be available online at *http://imperfectcplusplus.com.*[5]

Acknowledgments

In just about any book you'll ever pick up there are effusive acknowledgments to family and friends, and I can promise you they are heartfelt. Writing a book cannot be done without a huge amount of support.

Thanks to mum and Suzanne for enduring, financing, and raising the overstuffed cuckoo, who finally flitted the nest, to the other side of the world, at the overripe age of twenty-seven. Thanks to mum and Robert for helping said cuckoo and his family during a challenging but eventually fruitful couple of years. A special thanks goes to Robert for helping keep the mind at ease at a couple of important points during this time.

Thanks to Piker, for filling in the gaps in the extended family, and giving more than his share of babysitting, encouragement, and free lunches. Similar thanks to Dazzle, for always telling me he had ultimate confidence in me, and for tearing himself away from all those fascinating DBA-guru activities to put in a stalwart effort in helping with many of the boring review tasks; he'll never look at another Perl or Python script quite the same way again! Grunts of gratitude to Besso, for always showing interest, undue pride, and an encouraging perspective on my plans. And thanks to Al and Cynth (the in-laws!) for many free dinners and a limitless supply of free gourmet chocolate. (Now, where's that bike? . . .)

Essential thanks are due 808 State, Aim, Barry White, Billy Bragg, De La Soul, Fatboy Slim, George Michael, Level 42, Rush, Seal, Stevie Wonder, and The Brand New Heavies, without whom I could not possibly have survived being in "the bubble" for a year and a half.

---

[5]This site will also host an errata page, not that there'll be any errata, of course.

And most important, thanks to my beautiful wife, Sarah, who managed to suppress her reasonable concerns and doubts to present an almost unblemished veneer of support and confidence. A true star!

I'd like to recognize some remarkable people who've influenced my education and career thus far. Thanks are due (Professor) Bob Cryan for recognizing a fellow congenital overachiever and offering him the chance to dodge work (and ride his bike) for a further three years in postgraduate study.

I'd like to thank Richard McCormack for making me see beauty in the efficiency of code, not just elegance of concept. These days I'm sometimes accused of being too focused on efficiency; I say blame Richard! Also, Graham Jones ("Dukey") for `set -o vi`, and for six crazy months of friendship and good fun. Unrepeatable stuff!

Thanks also to Leigh and Scott Perry for introducing me to their "bolt-in" concept and other excellent techniques. They may wish to demur and instead confess to unabashed autogeneration of 16MB+ DLLs and a lamentable recent obsession with languages that run in virtual machines; I couldn't possibly comment.

Special thanks to Andy Thurling who showed generous faith in my potential when I hit the job market with Ph.D. in hand, and a level of software engineering skill in inverse proportion to my estimation thereof.[6] Andy taught me probably the single greatest lesson for anyone in this wonderful but scary profession: that we're all just "skegging it out."[7] Chuck Allison puts it more accessibly, with the ancient American Indian wisdom: "He who learns from one who is learning drinks from a running stream."

Crucial to the success of any book are the publishers, reviewers, and advisors. Thanks to my editor, Peter Gordon, who encouraged, calmed, and contained an ebullient and bullish author on the tortuously slow emotional rollercoaster that is a first book. Thanks also to Peter's able assistant Bernard Gaffney, who managed the process and endured multiple e-mails a day with patience and restraint, as well as the rest of the production and marketing staff at Addison-Wesley: Amy Fleischer, Chanda Leary-Coutu, Heather Mullane, Jacquelyn Doucette, Jennifer Andrews, Kim Boedigheimer, and Kristy Hart. Heartfelt thanks (and apologies) to my project manager, Jessica Balch, of Pine Tree Composition, who had the questionable pleasure of sifting through the text and weeding out all my poor grammar, weak attempts at humor, and British-English spelling (a myriad "ise"s instead of "ize"s). Also a special note of thanks to Debbie Lafferty for encouragement when *Imperfect C++* was nothing but a catchy phrase I dreamt up one night in 2002.

Thanks to my loyal band of reviewers—Chuck Allison, Dave Brooks, Darren Lynch, Duane Yates, Eugene Gershnik, Gary Pennington, George Frasier, Greg Peet, John Torjo, Scott Patterson, and Walter Bright—without whom I'd have a flat face from having fallen on it too many times. Some made me laugh, others made me question the sanity of the enterprise, but the feedback helped improve the final result no end. What a wonderful world we live in where friendships with people from a wide spectrum of countries, most of whom I've never physically met, can engender this level of helpfulness. Bravo!

---

[6] I didn't even know the difference between real mode and protected mode!

[7] This is a North Yorkshire term meaning "making the best of what information you have at the time."

Thanks also to the Addison-Wesley reviewers—Dan Saks, JC van Winkel, Jay Roy, Ron McCarty, Justin Shaw, Nevin Liber, and Steve Clamage—whose feedback was crucial in bringing the book in under 1000 pages, and not riddled with turgid prose and careless mistakes. Having been on the other side of the writing/review process, I know what it takes to do a thorough review, and I really appreciate the efforts.

Thanks to Peter Dimov, for graciously allowing me to use his superb quote in Chapter 26, and for providing some excellent feedback on the chapters of Part Five. Thanks to Kevlin Henney for casting his eye over Chapter 19 and some interesting discussions on smart casts, to Joe Goodman for helping me sift through my original dross to present a decent discussion of C++ ABIs (Chapters 7 and 8), and to Thorsten Ottosen for performing similar *denonsensisination* duties on the *Design by Contract* aspects of Chapter 1.

Special thanks to Chuck Allison, Herb Sutter, Joe Casad, John Dorsey, and Jon Erickson for great support and encouragement in a variety of activities over the last few years.

Thanks to Bjarne Stroustrup for subtle encouragements, and a little history lesson here and there. Oh, and for inventing this marvelous language in the first place!

Thanks to Walter Bright, for constantly improving his excellent Digital Mars C/C++ compiler throughout the writing of the book, for having such an amenable nature in the face of a constant barrage from the world's least patient man, and for graciously involving me in the D language development, which has been one of the many sources of inspiration for this book. Similar thanks to Greg Comeau, albeit that he didn't have much improving to do with the Comeau compiler: it is the most conformant in the business! As well as being great and responsive vendors, both these excellent fellows have provided repeated encouragement, advice, and input on a whole range of issues.

Thanks to CMP publishing, for letting me use material from some of my articles in the book, and include several original articles on the CD (see Appendix D).

Thanks to Borland, CodePlay, Digital Mars, Intel, Metrowerks, and Microsoft for providing me with their compilers to support my research, writing, and open-source library activities.

Special thanks to Digital Mars, Intel, and Watcom for granting permission to include their compilers on the CD (see Appendix D). And Greg Peet deserves several manly slaps on the back for his invaluable help in designing the CD and helping me with its contents.

Thanks to the readers of *C/C++ User's Journal, Dr. Dobb's Journal, BYTE,* and *Windows Developer Network* who have been kind enough to provide feedback and support for my articles and columns.

Similar thanks are also due to the C++ community at large and the kind people who give of themselves on various C++-related newsgroups (see Appendix A). These include Attila Feher, Carl Young, Daniel Spangenberg, Eelis van der Weegen, Gabriel Dos Reis, Igor Tandetnik, John Potter, Massimiliano Alberti, Michal Necasek, Richard Smith, Ron Crane, Steven Keuchel, Thomas Richter, "tom_usenet," and probably a whole lot more whom I've missed. Particular thanks to Ilya Minkov for putting in a request for me to implement Properties for C++ in the STLSoft libraries, something I'd not previously considered. Without that suggestion one of my favorite techniques (see Chapter 35) would never have been.

And finally, thanks to all the STLSoft users, without whose feedback many of the features of the library would not be, and parts of this book would have been all the harder to research and to write.

Prologue: Philosophy
of the Imperfect Practitioner

This book is about good practice as much as it is about C++ language techniques. It is not just about what is effective or technically correct in a specific situation, but what is safer or more practical in the long run. The message of the book is fourfold:

Tenet #1—C++ is great, but not perfect.

Tenet #2—Wear a hairshirt.

Tenet #3—Make the compiler your batman.

Tenet #4—Never give up: there's always a solution.

Together, these make up what I like to call the *Philosophy of the Imperfect Practitioner.*

C++ Is Not Perfect

I was taught very early, by a mother embarrassed by the overweening confidence of her youngest offspring, that if you're going to trumpet the good things to people, you'd also better be prepared to acknowledge the bad. Thanks, mum!

C++ is superb. It supports high-level concepts, including interface-based design, generics, polymorphism, self-describing software components, and meta-programming. It also does more than most languages in supporting fine-grained control of computers, by providing low-level features, including bitwise operations, pointers, and unions. By virtue of this huge spread of capabilities, coupled with its retaining a fundamental support of high efficiency, it can be justly described as the preeminent general purpose language of our time.[1] Nevertheless it is not perfect—far from it—hence the title of this book.

For very good reasons—some historical, some valid today—C++ is both a compromise [Stro1994] and a heterogeneous collection of unrelated, and sometimes incompatible, concepts. Hence it has a number of flaws. Some of these are minor; some of them are not so minor. Many come about as a result of its lineage. Others stem from the fact that it focuses—thankfully—on efficiency as a high priority. A few are likely fundamental restrictions to which any language would be subject. The most interesting set of problems comes about as a function of how complex and diverse a language it is becoming, things that no one could have anticipated.

This book meets this complex picture head on, with the attitude that the complexity can be tamed, and control wrested back to where it belongs, in the hands of the informed and experienced computing professional. The goal is to reduce the consternation and indecision that is experienced daily by software developers when using C++.

---

[1]Note that I'm not asserting that C++ is the best language in all specific problem domains. I wouldn't advise you to choose it over Prolog for writing Expert Systems, or over Python or Ruby for system scripts, or over Java for enterprise e-Commerce systems.

Imperfect C++ addresses problems that software developers encounter not as a result of inexperience or ignorance, but rather problems encountered by all members of the profession, from beginners through to even the most talented and experienced. These problems result partly from imperfections inherent in the language itself, and partly from common misapplications of the concepts that the language supports. They cause trouble for us all.

Imperfect C++ is not just a treatise on what is wrong with the language, along with a list of "do-nots"; there are plenty of excellent books available that take that approach. This book is about providing solutions to (most of) the flaws identified, and in so doing making the language even less "imperfect" than it is. It focuses on empowering developers: giving them important information regarding potential problem areas in the tools of their trade, and providing them with advice coupled with practical techniques and software technologies to enable them to avoid or manage these problems.

Hairshirt Programming

Many of the textbooks we read, even very good ones, tell you about the ways in which C++ can help you out if you use its features to their full extent, but all too often go on to say "this doesn't really matter" or "that would be taking [rigor] a bit far." More than one former colleague has engaged me in lively debate in a similar vein; the usual arguments amount to "I'm an experienced programmer, and I don't make the mistakes that XYZ would prevent me from doing, so why bother?"

Phooey!

This is flawed in so many ways. I'm an experienced programmer, and I do at least one stupid thing every day; if I didn't have disciplined habits, it would be ten. The attitude assumes that the code's never going to be seen by an inexperienced programmer. Further, it implies that the code's author(s) will never learn, nor change opinions, idioms, and methodologies. Finally, what's an "experienced programmer" anyway?[2]

These people don't like references, constant members, access control, `explicit`, concrete classes, encapsulation, invariants, and they don't code with portability or maintenance in mind. But they just love overloading, overriding, implicit conversions, C-style casts, using `int` for everything, globals, mixing typedefs, `dynamic_cast`, RTTI, proprietary compiler extensions, `friend`s, being inconsistent in coding styles, making things seem harder than they are.

Bear with me while I digress into some historical allegory. After being made Archbishop of Canterbury in 1162 by Henry II, Thomas À Beckett underwent a transformation in character, reforming from his materialistic ways and developing both a genuine concern for the poor and a profound sense of remorse for his former excesses. As his body was being prepared for burial, Beckett was found to be wearing a coarse, flea-infested hairshirt. It was subsequently learned that he had been scourged daily by his monks. Ouch!

Now, personally I think that's taking repentance and soul purging a tad far. Nevertheless, having in my earlier days made cavalier use of the power of C++ to create all manner of fell perversions (see Appendix B), these days I try to take a more temperate approach, and thus wear a bit of a hairshirt when programming.[3]

---

[2]It's hard to tell these days, when every vitae you see contains self-assessment matrices that are marked 10/10 for each metric.

[3]If the hairshirt analogy is too extreme for your tastes, you might like to think about yoga instead: tough, but worth the effort.

Of course, I don't mean I kneel on a gravel floor, or that I've punched nails through the back of my Herman-Miller, or have stopped blasting cooking dance music while I code. No, I mean I make my software treat me as harshly as I can whenever I try to abuse it. I like `const`—a lot of it—and use it whenever I can. I make things `private`. I prefer references. I enforce invariants. I return resources from where I got them, even if I know the shortcut is safe; *"Well, it worked fine on the previous version of the operating system. It's not my fault you upgraded!"* I've enhanced C++'s type checking for conceptual typedefs. I use nine compilers, through a tool (see Appendix C) that makes it straightforward to do so. I use a more potent `NULL`.

This is not done for a nomination for the "programmer of the year" award. It's simply a consequence of my being lazy, as all good engineers are wont to be. Being lazy means you don't want to find bugs at run time. Being lazy means you don't want to ever make the same mistake twice. Being lazy means making your compiler(s) work as hard as possible, so that you don't have to.

Making the Compiler Your Batman

A batman (as opposed to Batman) is a term derived from the days of the British Empire, and means an orderly or personal servant. If you treat it well, you can make the compiler your right-hand man, helper, conscience, your batman. (Or your superhero, if you prefer.)

The coarser your programming hairshirt, the better able your compiler is to serve you. However, there are times when the compiler, acting out of duty to the language, will stymie your intent, stubbornly refusing to do something you know to be sensible (or desirable, at least).

Imperfect C++ is also about allowing you to have the final choice by providing you with techniques and technologies to wrest control back from the compiler: getting what you want, not what you're given. This is not done blithely, or as a petulant thumbing of the nose from man to machine, but in recognition of the fact that it is the software developers who are the main players in the development process; languages, compilers, and libraries are merely tools that allow them to do their job.

Never Say Die

Despite most of my education being in the sciences, I'm actually much more of an engineer. I loved those early sci-fi books where the heroic engineers would "jury-rig" their way out of sticky situations. That's the approach taken in this book. There's theory, and we go with that first. But as often as not, when working on the borders of the language, most of the current compilers have problems with theory, so we have to code to their reality. As Yogi Berra said, "In theory, there's no difference between theory and practice. In practice, there is."

Such an approach can bring powerful results. Engineering effort, rather than academic induction, coupled with a stubborn refusal to live with the imperfections of C++, has led me (eventually) to a number of discoveries:

- The principles of explicit generalization via Shims (Chapter 20) and the resultant phenomenon of Type Tunneling (Chapter 34)
- An expansion of C++'s type system (Chapter 18), providing discrimination between, and overloading with, conceptually separate types sharing common implementation base types

- A compiler-independent mechanism providing binary compatibility between dynamically loaded C++ objects (Chapter 8)
- An incorporation of the principles of C's powerful NULL within the rules of C++ (Chapter 15)
- A maximally "safe" and portable `operator bool()` (Chapter 24)
- A fine-grained breakdown of the concept of encapsulation, leading to an expanded tool kit for the efficient representation and manipulation of basic data structures (Chapters 2 and 3)
- A flexible tool for efficiently allocating dynamically sized memory blocks (Chapter 32)
- A mechanism for fast, nonintrusive string concatenation (Chapter 25)
- An appreciation for how to write code to work with different error-handling models (Chapter 19)
- A straightforward mechanism for controlling the ordering of singleton objects (Chapter 11)
- A time-and-space efficient implementation of properties for C++ (Chapter 35)

Imperfect C++ does not attempt to be the complete answer to using the C++ language. Rather it takes the developer down the path of pushing beyond the constraints that exist to finding solutions to imperfections, encouraging a new way of thinking outside of the square.

I'm not perfect; none of us are. I do bad things, and I have a heretical streak. I have a poor habit of writing `protected` when I should write `private`. I prefer to use `printf()` when perhaps I should be favoring the IOStreams. I like arrays and pointers, and I'm a big fan of C-compatible APIs. Nor do I adhere religiously to the hairshirt programming philosophy. But I believe that having such a philosophy, and sticking to it wherever possible, is the surest and quickest way to achieve your aims.

The Spirit of *Imperfect C++*

As well as the tenets of *Philosophy of the Imperfect Practitioner,* this book reflects in general my own guiding principles in writing C++. These generally, though not completely, reflect the twin credos of the "Spirit of C" [Como-SOC]:

- *Trust the programmer: Imperfect C++* does not shy away from ugly decisions.
- *Don't prevent the programmer from what needs to be done: Imperfect C++* will actually help you achieve what *you* want to do.
- *Keep solutions small and simple:* most of the code shown is just that, and is highly independent and portable.
- *Make it fast, even if it is not guaranteed to be portable:* efficiency is given a high importance, although we do, on occasion, sacrifice portability to achieve it.

and the "Spirit of C++" [Como-SOP]:

- *C++ is a dialect of C with modern software enhancements:* We rely on interoperability with C in several important cases.
- *Although a larger language than C, you don't pay for what you don't use (so size and space penalties are kept to a minimum, and those that do exist must be put in perspective since what needs to be compared is equivalent programs, not feature X vs feature Y).*

- *Catch as many errors at compile time as possible: Imperfect C++* uses static assertions and constraints wherever appropriate.

- *Avoid the preprocessor when possible (inline, const, templates, etc. are the way to go in most cases):* we look at a variety of techniques for using the language, rather than the preprocessor, to achieve our aims.

Beyond these tenets, *Imperfect C++* will demonstrate an approach that, wherever possible:

- Writes code that is independent of compilers (extensions and idiosyncrasies), operating-systems, error-handling models, threading-models, and character-encodings

- Uses Design-by-Contract (see section 1.3) wherever compile-time error-detection is not possible

Coding Style

In order to keep the book to a manageable length, I've had to skip much of my normal strict—some might say pedantic—coding style in the examples given. Chapter 17 describes the general principles I tend to use in laying out class definitions. Other coding practices, such as bracing and spacing styles, are of less significance; if you're interested, you will be easily able to pick them up from much of the material included on the CD.

Terminology

Since computers speak the exact language of machine code, and human beings speak the various inexact languages of mankind, I'd like to define a few terms here that will be used throughout the remainder of the book:

Client code. This is code that uses other code, usually, but not limited to, the situation of application code using library code.

Compilation unit. The combination of all source from a source file and its entire dependent include files.

Compile environment. The combination of compiler, libraries, and operating system against which a given code set is compiled. Thanks to Kernighan and Pike [Kern1999] for this one.

Functor. This is a widely used term for Function Object or Functional, but it's not in the standard. I actually prefer Function Object, but I've been persuaded[4] that *Functor* is better because it's one short word, is more distinctive, and, most significantly, is more searchable, especially when searching online.

Generality. I've never properly understood the word *genericity,* at least in so far as a programming context, albeit that I sometimes bandy about the term with alacrity. I guess it means being able to write template code that will work with a variety of types, where those types are related by how they are used rather than how they are defined, and I restrict its use to that context. Generality [Kern1999] seems both to mean it better, and to apply the concept in a much broader sense: I'm just as interested in my code working with other headers and other libraries than merely with other (template parameterizing) types.

---

[4]Blame several of my reviewers for this.

In addition to these conceptual terms, I'm also including some specific language-related terms. I don't know about you, but I find the nomenclatural clutter in C++ more than a little confusing, so I'm going to take a small time out to drop in some definitions. The following are derived from the standard, but presented in a simpler manner for all our understanding, not least my own. Several of these definitions overlap, since they address different concepts, but all form part of the vocabulary of the accomplished C++ practitioner, imperfect or not.

Fundamental Types and Compound Types

The *fundamental types* (C++-98: 3.9.1) are the integral types (char, short, int, long (long long / __int64), the (signed and) unsigned versions thereof,[5] and bool), the floating-point types (float, double, and long double) and the void type.

Compound types (C++-98: 3.9.2) are pretty much everything else: arrays, functions, pointers (of any kind, including pointers to nonstatic members), references, classes, unions, and enumerations.

I tend not to use the term *compound types,* since I think the term implies things that are made up of other things, which can't really be said for references and pointers.

Object Types

Object types (C++-98: 3.9; 9) include any type that is "not a function type, not a reference type, and not a void type." This is another term I avoid, since it does not mean "instances of class types" which one might think. I use instances to refer to such things throughout the book.

Scalar Types and Class Types

Scalar types include the (C++-98: 3.9; 10) "arithmetic types, enumeration types [and] pointer types." *Class types* (C++-98: 9) are those things declared with one of the three class-keys: class, struct or union.

A structure is a class type defined with the class-key struct; its members and base classes are public by default. A union is a class type defined with the class-key union; its members are public by default. A class is a class type defined with the class-key class; its members and base classes are private by default.

Aggregates

The standard (C++-98: 8.5.1; 1) describes an *aggregate* as "an array or a class with no user-defined constructors, no private or protected non-static data members, no base classes, and no virtual functions." As an array or a class type, it means that there is a bringing together of several things into one, hence aggregate.

---

[5]Note that char comes in three flavors: char, unsigned char, and signed char. We see how this can be problematic in Chapter 13.

Aggregates may be initialized via a brace enclosed initializer clause, as in:

```
struct X
{
  int i;
  short as[2];
} x = { 10, { 20, 30 }};
```

Although aggregates are usually comprised of POD types (see the next section), they do not have to be. X's member variable i could be of a class type, so long as it had a non-explicit constructor (see section 2.2.7) taking a single integer argument and an available copy constructor.

POD Types

POD, which stands for plain-old-data (C++-98: 1.8; 5), is a very important concept in C++, but often misunderstood, and not least by this little pixie. It's also quite poorly defined. The standard gives two clues. In (C++-98: 3.9; 2) we are told that "for any complete POD type T . . . the bytes making up the object can be copied into an array of [bytes]. If the content of the array . . . is copied back . . . the object shall hold its original value." In (C++-98: 3.9; 3) we are further informed that "for any POD type, if two pointers to T point to distinct T objects obj1 and obj2, if the value of obj1 is copied into obj2, using the memcpy() function, obj2 shall subsequently hold the same value as obj1."

Wow! That's pretty slick, eh? Thankfully it does offer us a few—fifty-six to be precise— more crumbs dotted throughout its 776 pages in order to flesh out this definition.

In [Como-POD], Greg Comeau comments that most books (on C++) don't mention POD at all, and posits "most books are not worth buying." In a cynical attempt to improve saleability, I'm going to do my best here. It shouldn't be too hard, because in the same document, from which I've generously lifted here, Greg provides all the essential attributes of a POD-struct. Let's dig in.

The standard (C++-98: 3.9; 10) collectively defines POD types as "scalar types, POD-struct types, POD-union types, arrays of such types and [const and/or volatile] qualified versions of such types." That's all pretty clear, apart from POD-struct and POD-union.

A POD-struct is (C++-98: 9;4) "an aggregate class that has no non-static data members of type pointer to member, non-POD-struct, non-POD-union, or arrays of such types, or reference, and has no user-defined copy assignment operator and no user-defined destructor." A POD-union has the same definition, except it is a union rather than a struct. Note that an aggregate class can use either the class-key struct or the class-key class.

So far so good, but what's the point of POD? Well, POD types allow us to interact with C functions: they're the common currency between C++ and C, and therefore, by extension, between C++ and the outside world (see Chapters 7–9). Hence a POD-struct or union allows us to "obtain what a normal struct [or union] would look like and be in C" [Como-POD]. While you should certainly be aware of the various aspects of POD, the best short mnemonic for POD is *a type compatible with C.*

Other important aspects of POD are

- The type for which the macro `offsetof()` is defined shall be "a POD structure or a POD union" (C++-98: 18.1; 5). The use of any other type (see section 2.3.2 and Chapter 35) is undefined.
- A POD can be put in a union. This is used to constrain POD types (see section 1.2.4).
- A static object of POD type initialized with constant expressions is initialized before its block is entered, and before any objects (POD or otherwise) requiring dynamic initialization (see Chapter 11).
- Pointers to members are not POD types, as opposed to all other pointer types.
- POD-struct or POD-union types can have static members, member typedefs, nested types, and methods.[6]

---

[6]Naturally, none of these aspects may be visible to any C code, and must be elided from any C/C++ compatible code via conditional compilation.

Imperfections, Constraints, Definitions, and Recommendations

Imperfection: *C++ does not provide direct support for constraints.*   (p. 4)

Imperfection: *C++ does not provide suitable support for postconditions.*   (p. 15)

Recommendation: Use assertions to assert truths about the structure of the code, not about runtime behavior.   (p. 21)

Definition: *Resource Release Is Destruction* is a mechanism that takes advantage of C++'s support for automatic destruction to ensure the deterministic release of resources associated with an instance of an encapsulating type.   (p. 46)

Definition: *Resource Acquisition Is Initialization* is a mechanism that takes advantage of C++'s support for construction and automatic destruction to ensure the deterministic release of resources associated with an instance of an encapsulating type. It can be thought of as a superset of the RRID mechanism.   (p. 51)

Definition: *Encapsulated types* provide access to, and manipulation of, instance state via a robust public interface, and client code should not, and need not, have access to the internal member state of instances of such types. Encapsulated types provide a notionally complete separation between logical and physical state.   (p. 60)

Definition: *Value Type*   (p. 62)

Instances cannot polymorphically substitute, or be substituted by, instances of another type at run time.

Instances can be created as, or later made to be, copies of another instance.

Each instance has a logically separate identity. Any change to the logical state of one instance does not result in a change to the logical state of another. (Physical state may be shared according to implementation-specific design decisions, so long as such sharing does not invalidate the logical separation.)

Instances can be (in)equality compared with any other instances, and even with themselves. Equality (and inequality) is reflexive, symmetric, and transitive.

Imperfection: *The C++ standard does not define an ABI, leading to wholesale incompatibilities between many compilers on many platforms.*   (p. 92)

Imperfection: *C++ is not a suitable module-interface language.*   (p. 121)

Imperfection: *C and C++ say nothing about threading.*   (p. 132)

Imperfection: *C++ does not provide a mechanism for controlling global object ordering.*   (p. 158)

Recommendation: Don't rely on global object initialization ordering. Do utilize global object initialization ordering tracing mechanisms anyway.   (p. 161)

Recommendation: Don't create threads during global object initialization.   (p. 166)

Imperfection: *Function-local static instances of classes with nontrivial constructors are not thread-safe.*   (p. 171)

Imperfection: *The support for Empty Base Optimization (EBO) flavors is not universal, and varies significantly between compilers.*   (p. 183)

Imperfection: *C and C++ are missing a* `byte` *type.*   (p. 191)

Imperfection: *C and C++ need fixed-sized integer types.*   (p. 195)

Imperfection (reprise): *C++ needs fixed sized types that are different to, and not implicitly interconvertible with, its built-in integral types.*   (p. 196)

Imperfection: *C and C++ do not provide large fixed-sized integer types.*   (p. 200)

Imperfection: `bool` *should be the same size as* `int`.   (p. 205)

Imperfection: *C and C++ do not provide a* `dimensionof()` *operator (for array types).* (p. 207)

Imperfection: *Inability to distinguish between arrays and pointers can result in static array size determination being applied to pointers or class types, yielding incorrect results.*   (p. 211)

Imperfection: *C and C++ arrays decay into pointers when passed to functions.* (p. 214)

Imperfection: *C++'s array/pointer duality, combined with its support for polymorphic handling of inherited types, is a hazard against which the compiler provides no assistance.*   (p. 218)

Imperfection: *C++ does not support multi-dimensional arrays.*   (p. 224)

Imperfection: *C++ needs a* null *keyword, which can be assigned to, and equality compared with, any pointer type, and with no non-pointer types.*   (p. 229)

Imperfection: *Having more than one discrete value for the Boolean type is dangerous.* (p. 236)

Imperfection: *Specification of the size of integer types as implementation dependent in C/C++ reduces the portability of integer literals.*   (p. 238)

Imperfection: *C++ compilers do not agree on the syntax for suffixes of integer literals larger than those that will fit into* (unsigned) long.   (p. 239)

Constraint: *C and C++ do not guarantee to ensure that identical string literals will be folded within a single link unit, and cannot do so across separate link units.*   (p. 242)

Constraint: *Casting away* const *ness of a constant object is not legal, and will likely lead to unintended consequences.*   (p. 245)

Constraint: *Constants of class type are evaluated as immutable global objects, rather than as compile-time constants. Failure to be mindful of this distinction is hazardous.* (p. 246)

Recommendation: Avoid using enum values larger than those that will fit in an int. (p. 248)

Imperfection: *C++ does not support member constants of floating-point type.* (p. 249)

Constraint: *C++ does not support member constants of class type.* (p. 250)

Recommendation: Never attempt to simulate class-type member constants with function local static objects. (p. 251)

Imperfection: *C++ does not provide access control between types involved in a composition relationship.* (p. 257)

Imperfection: *The introduction of new keywords into the language requires contingency mechanisms to maintain portability.* (p. 268)

Imperfection: *Abuse of C++'s last-known access specifier mechanism leads to code that is hard to use and hard to maintain.* (p. 271)

Imperfection: *Implicitly interpreting non-Boolean (sub-)expressions leads to failure to be mindful of the values of certain types, with a consequent propensity to over-engineer user-defined types.* (p. 274)

Imperfection: *The implicit interpretation of scalar types as Boolean in conditional statements facilitates erroneous assignment caused by syntax errors.* (p. 275)

Imperfection: *The contradiction between the old and new* for*-statement rules results in non-portable code.* (p. 278)

Imperfection: for *statements requiring initializers of two or more types render the new* for*-scoping rule irrelevant.* (p. 279)

Definition: *Conceptual type definitions* define logically distinct types. (p. 289)

Definition: *Contextual type definitions* define types that correspond to well-known concepts, relative to specific contexts. Such types act as descriptions of the nature (type and/or behavior) of their host contexts. (p. 291)

Imperfection: *C++ provides no type-safety for the use of conceptual defined types, except where such types have incompatible underlying types.*   (p. 294)

Imperfection: *C++ does not support overloading on conceptually defined types, except where such types happen to have different underlying types on a particular platform.* (p. 294)

Recommendation: Avoid making conceptual typedefs that are comprised of contextual typedefs.   (p. 304)

Imperfection: *Logically related types in C++ can, and usually do, have incompatible interfaces and operations, rendering a generalized approach to type manipulation sometimes difficult, and often impossible.*   (p. 341)

Definition: *Attribute Shims*   (pp. 343–344)

Attribute shims retrieve attributes or states of instances of the types for which they are defined.

The names of attribute shims take the form `get_xxx`, where `xxx` represents the particular attribute being accessed (except where they form part of a composite shim concept).

The values returned from attribute shims are always valid outside the instance of the shim, in cases where the shim is implemented by the creation of a temporary object.

Definition: *Logical Shims*   (p. 346)

Logical shims are a refinement of attribute shims in that they report on the state of an instance to which they are applied.

The names of logical shims take the form of an interrogative coupled with the particular attribute or state being queried. Examples would be `is_open`, `has_element`, `is_null`.

Definition: *Control Shims*   (p. 347)

Control shims define operations that are applied to the instances of the types for which they are defined.

The names of control shims take the form of an imperative element coupled with the particular attribute or state being modified. Examples would be `make_empty`, `dump_contents`.

Definition: *Conversion Shims*   (p. 348)

Conversion shims operate by converting instances of the range of compatible types to a single target type.

The names of attribute shims take the form `to_xxx`, where `xxx` is the name of, or represents, the target type, for example, `to_int`.

The values returned from conversion shims may be provided by intermediate temporary objects, so must only be used from within the expression containing the shim.

Definition: *Composite Shims* (p. 350)

Composite shims are a combination of two or more fundamental shim concepts.

The names of composite shims do not have a fixed convention, but rather take a name indicative of their purpose.

Composite shims obey the most restrictive rule, or combination of rules, from their constituent shims.

Definition: *Access Shims* (p. 351)

Access shims are a combination of Attribute and Conversion shims, which are used to access the values of the instances of the types for which they are defined.

The values may have to be synthesised via conversion shims.

The values returned from access shims may be provided by intermediate temporary objects, so must only be used from within the expression containing the shim.

Definition: *Veneers* (p. 364)

A veneer is a template class with the following characteristics:

1. It derives, usually publicly, from its primary parameterizing type.
2. It accommodates, and adheres to, the polymorphic nature of its primary parameterizing type. This means that a veneer cannot define any virtual methods of its own, though it can override those defined by its primary parameterizing type.
3. It may not define any non-static member variables.

The consequence of 2 & 3 is that a veneer may not change the memory footprint of its primary parameterizing type, and this is achieved by virtue of the *Empty Derived Optimization* (EDO; see section 12.4), a very widely supported optimization. In other words, instances of a veneer composite have the same size as the primary parameterizing type.

Definition: *Bolt-ins* (p. 375)

Bolt-ins are template classes with the following characteristics:

1. They derive, usually publicly, from their primary parameterizing type.
2. They accommodate the polymorphic nature of their primary parameterizing type. Usually they also adhere to the nature, but this is not always the case, and they may define virtual methods of their own, in addition to overriding those defined by the primary parameterizing type.
3. They may increase the footprint of the primary parameterizing type by the definition of member variables, virtual functions and additional inheritance from non-empty types.

Imperfection: *The C++ template mechanism instantiates a template based on the arguments to it, and takes no account of how, or in what form, those arguments are subsequently used within the templates. This can lead to the generation of inefficient and/or erroneous code since temporary instances of class type may be created during the forwarding of arguments through the template.*   (p. 387)

Imperfection: *Overloading* `operator &()` *breaks encapsulation.*   (p. 425)

Imperfection: *Provision of implicit conversion operator(s) to pointer type(s) along with subscript operator(s) is non-portable.*   (p. 434)

Imperfection: *Some C++ compilers will substitute prefix increment/decrement overloaded operators at the call site in place of absent postfix equivalents.*   (p.440)

Imperfection: *Overloading the && and || operators for class types represents an invisible breaking of short-circuit evaluation.*   (p. 454)

Imperfection: *C and C++ make you choose between performance and flexibility when allocating memory.*   (p. 476)

Imperfection: *C/C++ does not support dynamically dimensioned multidimensional arrays.*   (p. 491)

Recommendation: An array size shim should always be used when determining the sizes of arrays, as all other approaches do not generalize for both built-in and user defined array types.   (p. 505)

Imperfection: *C++ does not support local functor classes (to be used with template algorithms).*   (p. 514)

Definition: *Type Tunneling* is a mechanism whereby two logically related but physically unrelated types can be made to interoperate via the use of *Access Shims.* The shim allows an external type to be *tunnelled* through an interface and presented to the internal type in a recognized and compatible form.   (p. 518)

Definition: A *Range* represents a bounded collection of elements, which may be accessed in an incremental fashion. It encapsulates a logical range—that is, a beginning and an end point, along with rules for how to walk through it (move from the beginning to the end point)—and embodies a single entity with which client code may access the values contained within the range.   (p. 521–522)

Imperfection: *C++ does not provide properties.*   (p. 531)

PART ONE

Fundamentals

In a cycling road race, the first hour or so of racing is generally pretty steady, with all the riders feeling their way into the race, warming up overtrained muscles, taking on board a last few calories, planning their strategies and tactics for the coming hours, and renewing acquaintances with friends and colleagues who they may not have seen for some time.

The first part of your journey with *Imperfect C++* will be in a similar vein. You'll meet several things that you already know, or at least have heard of, many of which will be important to remember in later parts of the book. The pace is measured, the tone is optimistic—we have the whole road ahead of us, after all—and there shouldn't be too many contentious bumps in the road at this point.

That's not to say that you'll not be expending energy in the reading, but things will seem calmer at least.[1] Indeed, there're only two imperfections defined in the six chapters in this part. Of course, there'll be lots of imperfect issues covered, but the focus is more about looking at some C++ fundamentals—the ontological issues in particular—in new ways.

Because this book is unashamedly about achieving quality in the context of the real world of work, we begin by looking at mechanisms for enforcing the design decisions we make in creating our classes, both at compile time and run time. After this, we go back to basics, and look at object lifetime, and the mechanisms for controlling client access to member data. Then we get all preachy on the virtues of using member initialization lists (section 2.3).

Next comes resource encapsulation. Since we don't have enough acronyms in computing, I introduce a new one, RRID (section 3.4), which is the half-brother of RAII (*Resource Acquisition Is Initialization*; section 3.5), arguably the most important feature of C++, and one that sets it head and shoulders above its C-language brethren.[2] The notion of a *value type* is examined, ranging from simple data structures right through to arithmetic value types, which are able to emulate the syntax of built-in operations for arbitrarily complex operations. We also look at *data encapsulation*, which goes swimmingly, until we look at just how difficult it can be to provide a truly encapsulated type in the real world.

There's a discussion of object access models to help clear up the terminological soup (in my head at least) concerning whether you share, copy, borrow, or take one object from another. Because C++ just does it so embarrassingly well, we end by really going to town on scoping

---

[1] You've got the rest of the race to run, in which there are going to be daunting climbs, precipitous descents, and some really tight corners, so make sure you save some energy for later.

[2] You may suggest templates, but I reckon we survived *reasonably* well without them; the same could not be said of RAII.

classes. We get to see just how far we can poke this marvelously simple language feature around the cobwebbed corners of the software engineering mansion, further relieving us of work that our helpful compiler will do for us.

There are six chapters: Chapter 1, *Enforcing Design: Constraints, Contracts, and Assertions*; Chapter 2, *Object Lifetime*; Chapter 3, *Resource Encapsulation*; Chapter 4, *Data Encapsulation and Value Types*; Chapter 5, *Object Access Models;* and Chapter 6, *Scoping Classes*. If you get to the end of this part and your response is "so what?" I can live with that. It means that you long ago embraced the power of RAII and apply it absolutely everywhere that it's suitable to do so (and that's a lot of possibilities). It also means that you've adopted the principles of the *Design by Contract* (see Chapter 1) philosophy, and are applying them in your work. That's great, because you'll be writing robust, clear, and maintainable code.

If you're not yet in that position, I hope this part gives you some food for thought. The result is the same for you, however: rejoice in the power of RAII, apply it everywhere suitable, and spread the message; everyone's life will be made that bit easier (not to mention that it's a great comeback when the proponents of other popular languages are banging on about robustness).

CHAPTER 1

Enforcing Design: Constraints, Contracts, and Assertions

When we design software, we want it to be used in accordance with our designs. This is not vanity. In most cases it is all too easy to use software in a way for which it was not intended, and the results of doing so are invariably disappointing.

As I'm sure you already know from personal experience, the documentation for most software is incomplete and/or out of date. That's when it's not plain wrong or missing: "if there is any situation worse than having no documentation, it must be having wrong documentation" [Meye1997]. Documentation is not needed when the components being used are simple, well used, and either standard or ubiquitous. For example, I'd be surprised if many programmers need to look up the usage for the C library function `malloc()` more than a couple of times. However, the number of such cases is very small. I've encountered many very experienced programmers who were not so familiar with the nuances of `malloc()`'s ostensibly simple brethren, `realloc()` and `free()`.

There are several answers to these problems. One option is to make all software components more error resistant by increased parameter validation, but this is generally unattractive since it damages performance and tends to breed bad habits. Making, and keeping updated, better documentation is certainly an important part of the answer, but, in and of itself, it is insufficient because it is optional. Furthermore, it is very difficult to write good documentation [Hunt2000], and the more complex software is the more difficult it is for its original authors to put themselves in the position of not understanding it or for independent technical writers to cover all the nuances. A better way of ensuring correct use of code is required in nontrivial cases.

It's preferable if the compiler can find our errors for us. In fact, a large part of the effort described in this book has been about encouraging and facilitating the compiler to choke on bad code. Hopefully you realize that a couple of minutes spent placating the compiler is better than a few hours spent inside the debugger. As Kernighan and Pike say in *The Practice of Programming* [Kern1999] "[W]hether we like it or not, debugging is an art we will practice regularly.... It would be nice if bugs didn't happen, so we try to avoid them by writing code well in the first place." Since I am no less lazy than any other engineer, I try to make the compiler do as much of my work as is possible. Programming by hairshirt is the easier option in the long run. But many causes of error cannot be policed at compile time. In such cases we need to look for runtime mechanisms. Some languages—for example, D, Eiffel—provide in-built mechanisms by which software can be ensured to be used according to its design via *Design by Contract* (DbC), a technique pioneered by Bertrand Meyer [Meye1997], which has its roots in the formal

3

verification of programs. DbC specifies contracts for software components, and these contracts are enforced at particular points during process execution. Contracts in many ways substitute for documentation, since they cannot be ignored, and are verified automatically. Moreover, by following a specific syntax contracts are amenable to automated documentation tools. We discuss these in section 1.3.

One mechanism for enforcement is assertions, both the commonly known runtime assertions, and the less well-known, but arguably even more useful, compile-time assertions. Both are used liberally throughout the book, so we will take a detailed look at this important tool in section 1.4.

1.1   Eggs and Ham

I'm no doubt teaching all you gentle readers about egg-sucking here, but it's an important thing to state nevertheless. Permit me to wax awhile:

- It's better to catch a bug at design time than at coding/compile time.[1]
- It's better to catch a bug at coding/compile time than during unit testing.[2]
- It's better to catch a bug during unit testing than during debug system testing.
- It's better to catch a bug during debug system than in prerelease/beta system testing.
- It's better to catch a bug during prerelease/beta system testing than have your customer catch one.
- It's better to have your customer catch a bug (in a reasonably sophisticated/graceful manner) than to have no customers.

This is all pretty obvious stuff, although customers would probably disagree with the last one; best keep that one to ourselves.

There are two ways in which such enforcements can take effect: at compile time and at run time, and these form the substance of this chapter.

1.2   Compile-Time Contracts: Constraints

This section is devoted to compile-time enforcements, commonly called constraints. Unfortunately, C++ does not provide direct support for constraints.

Imperfection: C++ does not provide direct support for constraints.

Because C++ is an extremely powerful and flexible language, many proponents (including some of the most august C++ thinkers in the business) consider that the implementation of such constraints as described in this section is sufficient. However, as a big fan both of C++ and of constraints, I must demur, for an eminently prosaic reason. I don't buy much of the criticisms

---

[1]I'm not a waterfaller, so coding time and compiling time are the same time for me. But even though I like unit-tests and have had some blisteringly fast pair-programming partnerships, I don't think I'm an XP-er [Beck2000] either.

[2]This assumes you do unit testing. If you don't, then you need to start doing so, right away!

espoused by proponents of other languages, but I do think there's no running away from the (sometimes extreme) difficulty in ploughing through the varying and often agonizingly esoteric messages produced by compilers when constraints are violated. If you're the author of the code that's "fired" the constraint, you are often okay, but understanding a many-level template instantiation that has failed from the messages of even very good compilers is next to impossible. In the remainder of this section we look at some constraints, the messages produced when they fail, and some of the measures we can take to make those messages a bit more understandable.

1.2.1   must_have_base()

This one is lifted, almost verbatim, from a comp.lang.c++.moderated newsgroup post by Bjarne Stroustrup, although he called his constraint Has_base. It's also described in [Sutt2002], where it's called IsDerivedFrom. I like to name constraints beginning with must_, so I call it must_have_base.

Listing 1.1

```
template< typename D
        , typename B
        >
struct must_have_base
{
  ~must_have_base()
  {
    void(*p)(D*, B*) = constraints;
  }
private:
  static void constraints(D* pd, B* pb)
  {
    pb = pd;
  }
};
```

It works by requiring that a pointer to the template parameter D can be assigned to a pointer to the template parameter B. It does this in a separate static function, constraints(), in order that it will never be called, so there's no generated code and no runtime cost. The destructor declares a pointer to this function, thereby requiring the compiler at least to evaluate whether the function, and the assignment within it, is valid.

In fact, the constraint is somewhat ill named. If D and B are the same type, then the constraint is still satisfied, so it should probably be called must_have_base_or_be_same_type, or something like that. An alternative would be to further refine must_have_base to reject parameterization when D and B are the same type. Answers on a postcard, please.

Also, if D is not publicly derived from B, then the constraint will fail. In my opinion, the problem here is one of naming, not an inadequacy in the constraint, since the only time I've needed this constraint is for publicly inherited types.[3]

---

[3]This smells like a circular argument, but I promise it's not.

Because this constraint attempts, within its definition, to perform an action directly representing the semantic of the constraint, the error messages produced by a constraint failure are reasonably straightforward. In fact, all our compilers (see Appendix A) provide quite meaningful messages on failure, either mentioning that the types in the constraint are not related by inheritance or that the pointer types cannot be interconverted or similar.

1.2.2   must_be_subscriptable()

Another useful constraint is to require that a type be subscriptable (see section 14.2), and it's a no-brainer:

```
template< typename T>
struct must_be_subscriptable
{
  . . .
  static void constraints(T const &T_is_not_subscriptable)
  {
    sizeof(T_is_not_subscriptable[0]);
  }
  . . .
```

In an attempt to help out with readability, the variable is called T_is_not_subscriptable, which should hopefully give a clue to the hapless victim of the constraint failure. Consider the following example:

```
struct subs
{
public:
  int operator [](size_t index) const;
}
struct not_subs
{};

must_be_subscriptable<int[]>   a; // int* is subscriptable
must_be_subscriptable<int*>    b; // int* is subscriptable
must_be_subscriptable<subs>    c; // subs is subscriptable
must_be_subscriptable<not_subs> d; // not_subs isn't: compile error
```

Borland 5.6 gives the incredibly dissembling: "'operator+' not implemented in type '<type>' for arguments of type 'int' in function must_be_ subscriptable<not_subs>::constraints(const not_subs &)". When you're fifteen levels deep in a template instantiation, you'd have precious little chance of surviving this without brain strain!

Digital Mars is more correct, but still not very helpful: "Error: array or pointer required before '['; Had: const not_subs".

Some of the others do include the variable name `T_is_not_subscriptable`. The best message is probably Visual C++, which offers: `"binary '[' : 'const struct not_subs' does not define this operator or a conversion to a type acceptable to the predefined operator while compiling class-template member function 'void must_be_subscriptable<struct not_subs>::constraints (const struct not_subs &)"`.

1.2.3   must_be_subscriptable_as_decayable_pointer()

In Chapter 14 we will take an in-depth look at the relationship between arrays and pointers, and learn that the arcane nature of pointer offsetting results in the legality of `offset[pointer]` syntax, which is entirely equivalent to the normal `pointer[offset]` syntax. (This may make Borland's perplexing error message for `must_be_subscriptable` seem that little bit less nonsensical, but that's going to be of much help to us in tracking down and understanding the constraint violation.) Since this reversal is not valid for class types that overload the subscript operator, a refinement of the `must_be_subscriptable` type can be made, which can then be used to constrain templates to pointer types only.

Listing 1.2

```
template <typename T>
struct must_be_subscriptable_as_decayable_pointer
{
   . . .
   static void constraints(T const &T_is_not_decay_subscriptable)
   {
     sizeof(0[T_is_not_decay_subscriptable]);
   }
   . . .
};
```

It is axiomatic that anything subscriptable by `offset[pointer]` will also be subscriptable by `pointer[offset]`, so there's no need to incorporate `must_be_subscriptable` within `must_be_subscriptable_as_decayable_pointer`. Where the constraints have different ramification, though, it can be appropriate to use inheritance to bring two constraints together.

Now we can discriminate between pointers and other subscriptable types:

```
must_be_subscriptable<subs>                     a; // ok
must_be_subscriptable_as_decayable_pointer<subs> b; // compile error
```

1.2.4   must_be_pod()

We'll see the use of `must_be_pod()` in a few places throughout the book (see sections 19.5, 19.7, 21.2.1, 32.2.3). This was my first constraint, and was written long before I ever knew what constraints were, or even what POD meant (see Prologue). It's very simple.

The standard (C++-98: 9.5;1) states that "an object of a class with a non-trivial constructor, a non-trivial copy constructor, a non-trivial destructor, or a non-trivial assignment operator cannot be a member of a union." This pretty much serves our requirements, and we could imagine that this would be similar to the constraints we've already seen, with a `constraints()` method containing a union:

```
struct must_be_pod
{
  . . .
  static void constraints()
  {
    union
    {
       T    T_is_not_POD_type;
    };
  }
  . . .
```

Unfortunately, this is an area in which compilers tend to have slightly strange behaviour, so the real definition is not so simple, requiring a lot of preprocessor effort (see section 1.2.6). But the effect is the same.

In section 19.7 we see this constraint used in conjunction with a more specialized one: `must_be_pod_or_void()`, in order to be able to check that the base types of pointers are not nontrivial class types. This relies on specialization [Vand2003] of the `must_be_pod_or_void` template, whose general definition is identical to `must_be_pod`:

```
template <typename T>
struct must_be_pod_or_void
{
    . . . // Same as must_be_pod
};
```

```
template <>
struct must_be_pod_or_void<void>
{
    // Contains nothing, so doesn't trouble the compiler
};
```

Once again, the messages produced by the compilers when the `must_be_pod` / `must_be_pod_or_void` constraints are fired vary considerably:

```
class NonPOD
{
public:
  virtual ~NonPOD();
};
```

```
must_be_pod<int>       a; // int is POD (see Prologue)
must_be_pod<not_subs> b; // not_subs is POD (see Prologue)
must_be_pod<NonPOD>    c; // NonPOD isn't: compile error
```

In this case, Digital Mars's customary terseness lets us down, since all we get is `"Error: union members cannot have ctors or dtors"` reported for the offending line in the constraint. Used in a significant project, it would be extremely difficult to track down the location of the offending instantiations. Arguably the most information for the smallest error message in this case was Watcom, with: `"Error! E183: col(10) unions cannot have members with constructors; Note! N633: col(10) template class instantiation for 'must_be_pod<NonPOD>' was in: ..\constraints_ test.cpp(106) (col 48)"`.

1.2.5 must_be_same_size()

The last constraint, `must_be_same_size()`, is another one used later in the book (see sections 21.2.1 and 25.5.5). The constraint class just uses the static assertion invalid array size technique that we'll see shortly (section 1.4.7) to ensure that the sizes of the types are the same.

Listing 1.3

```
template< typename T1
        , typename T2
        >
struct must_be_same_size
{
  . . .
private:
  static void constraints()
  {
    const int T1_not_same_size_as_T2
                        = sizeof(T1) == sizeof(T2);
    int       i[T1_not_same_size_as_T2];
  }
};
```

If the two sizes are not the same, then `T1_not_same_size_as_T2` evaluates to the constant value 0, which is an illegal size for the array i.

We saw with `must_be_pod_or_void` that we need to be able to apply the constraint in circumstances where one or both types might be `void`. Since `sizeof(void)` is not a valid expression, we must provide some extra compile-time functionality.

If they are both `void` it's easy, since we can specialize the template thus:

```
template <>
struct must_be_same_size<void, void>
{};
```

To make it work where only one of the types is void, however, is less straightforward. One option would be to use partial specialization [Vand2003], but not all compilers currently in wide use support it. Furthermore, we'd then need to provide the template, that is, one full specialization and two partial specializations—one where the first type is specialized to void, and the other where the second type is—and we'd also have to dream up some way to provide even a half-meaningful compile-time error message. Rather than resort to that, I decided to make void size_of-able. This is extremely easy to do, and does not require partial specialization:

Listing 1.4

```
template <typename T>
struct size_of
{
  enum { value = sizeof(T) };
};
template <>
struct size_of<void>
{
  enum { value = 0 };
};
```

All we now need do is use size_of instead of sizeof in must_be_same_size:

```
template< . . . >
struct must_be_same_size
{
  . . .
  static void constraints()
  {
    const int T1_must_be_same_size_as_T2
                = size_of<T1>::value == size_of<T2>::value;
    int      i[T1_must_be_same_size_as_T2];
  }
};
```

Now we can verify the size of any types:

```
must_be_same_size<int, int>   a; // ok
must_be_same_size<int, long>  b; // depends on arch/compiler
must_be_same_size<void, void> c; // ok
must_be_same_size<void, int>  d; // compiler error: void "is" 0
```

As with previous constraints, there is considerable equivocation between the compilers regarding the quantity of information provided to the programmer. Borland and Digital Mars strike out again, with little or no contextual information. In this case I think Intel provides the best output, stating that "zero-length bit field must be unnamed", showing the offending line and providing the two immediate call contexts including the actual types of T1 and T2, all in four lines of compiler output.

1.2.6   Using Constraints

I prefer to use my constraints via macros, whose names take the form `constraint_`
`<constraint_name>`,[4] for example, `constraint_must_have_base()`. This is useful in
several ways.

First, they're easy to search for unambiguously. To be sure, I reserve `must_` for constraints, so it could be argued that this requirement is already met. But it's also a bit more self-
documenting. Seeing `constraint_must_be_pod()` in some code is pretty unambiguous to
the reader.

The second reason is that using the macro form provides consistency. Although I've not
written any nontemplate constraints, there's nothing preventing anyone from doing so. Furthermore, I find the angle brackets don't add anything but eyestrain to the picture.

The third reason is that if the constraints are defined within a namespace, using them will
require tedious qualification. This can be easily hidden within the macro, saving any users of
the constraints from the temptation to use naughty using directives (see section 34.2.2).

The last reason is eminently practical. Different compilers do slightly different things with
the constraints, which can require a lot of jiggery-pokery. For example, depending on the compiler, the `constraint_must_be_pod()` is defined in one of three forms:

```
do { must_be_pod<T>::func_ptr_type const pfn =
                     must_be_pod<T>::constraint(); } while(0)
```

or

```
do { int i = sizeof(must_be_pod<T>::constraint()); } while(0)
```

or

```
STATIC_ASSERT(sizeof(must_be_pod<T>::constraint()) != 0)
```

Rather than clutter constraint client code with a lot of evil-looking nonsense, it's easier and
neater to just use a macro.

1.2.7   Constraints and TMP

One of my reviewers commented that some of these constraints could have been done via
template meta-programming (TMP) techniques,[5] and he's quite correct. For example, the
`must_be_pointer` constraint could be implemented as a static assertion (see section 1.4.7)
coupled with the `is_pointer_type` trait template used in section 33.3.2, as follows:

```
#define constraint_must_be_pointer(T) \
  STATIC_ASSERT(0 != is_pointer_type<T>::value)
```

---

[4]For the reasons described in section 12.4.4, it's always a good reason to name macros in uppercase. The reason I didn't
do so with the constraint macros is that I wanted to keep the case the same as the constraint types. In hindsight it seems
less compelling, and you'd probably want to use uppercase for your own.

[5]I've deliberately left TMP techniques out of this book as much as possible because it's a huge subject in itself, and is
not directly related to any of the imperfections I've been discussing. You can find plenty of examples in the Boost,
Rangelib, and STLSoft libraries included on the CD, as well as in several books [Vand2003, Alex2001].

There are several reasons why I do not take this approach. First, the codification of a constraint is always a straightforward matter, because a constraint is merely a simple emulation of the normal behavior to which the type is to be constrained. The same cannot be said of TMP traits, some of which can be exceedingly complex. So constraints are very easy to read.

Second, in many cases, though by no means all, it is easier to persuade compilers to produce moderately digestible messages with constraints than with traits and static assertions.

Finally, there are some cases in which a TMP trait is impossible, or is at least only definable on a small subset of compilers. Perversely, it can seem that the more simple the constraint, the more complex would be an equivalent implementation based on TMP traits—`must_be_pod` is an excellent example of this.

Herb Sutter demonstrates a combination of constraints and traits in [Sutt2002], and there's no reason why you should not do that in your own work for many concepts; I just prefer to keep them simple and separate.

1.2.8   Constraints: Coda

The constraints presented in this chapter in no way encompass the full range of constraints available. However, they should give you a good idea of the kinds of things that are achievable. The downside to the use of constraints is the same as it is for static assertions (see section 1.4.8), which is that the error messages produced are not particularly easy to understand. Depending on the specific mechanism of the constraint, you can have the reasonable `"type cannot be converted"` to the downright perplexing `"Destructor for 'T' is not accessible in function <non-existent-function>"`.

Where possible you can ameliorate the distress of unhappy erroneous parameterizers of your code by choosing appropriately named variable and constant names. We've seen examples of this in this section—`T_is_not_subscriptable`, `T_is_not_POD_type` and `T1_not_same_size_as_T2`. Just make sure that the names you choose reflect the failure condition. Pity the poor soul who falls afoul of your constraint and is informed that `T_is_valid_type_for_constraint`!

There's one very important aspect about this that can't be stressed too much: we have the latitude to upgrade the constraints as we learn more about compile time and/or TMP. You'll probably notice that I'm not exactly a guru of TMP from some of the components described throughout the book, but the point is that, by designing the way in which constraints are represented and used in client classes, we can upgrade the constraints seamlessly when we learn new tricks. I'm not ashamed to admit that I've done this many times, although I probably would be ashamed to show you some of my earlier attempts at writing constraints. (None of these appear in Appendix B because they're not daft enough—not quite!)

1.3   Runtime Contracts: Preconditions, Postconditions, and Invariants

"If all the routine's preconditions are met by the caller, the routine shall guarantee that all postconditions (and [any] invariants) will be true when it completes." —Hunt and Thomas, *The Pragmatic Programmers* [Hunt2000].

If we can't get compile-time enforcement, then the alternative is runtime enforcement. A systematic approach to runtime enforcement is to specify function contracts. A function contract defines exactly what conditions the caller must fulfill before calling the function (the preconditions of the function) and exactly what conditions the caller can expect upon return from the function (the postconditions of the function). The definition of contracts, and their enforcement, is the basis of DbC [Meye1997].

A *precondition* is what must be true in order for a function to fulfill its contract. It is the caller's responsibility to ensure that the precondition is met. The callee may assume that its precondition has been met, and has responsibility for correct behavior only in that case. This is a very important point, which is stressed in [Meye1997]. If the caller does not fulfill the terms of the precondition, the callee can legitimately do anything at all. Usually this involves the firing of an assertion (see section 1.4), which may terminate the program. This seems like a scary prospect, and programmers new to DbC often feel more than a little uneasy until you ask them what they would have a function do with conditions that violate its contract. The fact of the matter is that the more narrow the contract, and the more severe the response to a violation, the better quality the software. Making this leap is the most, and probably the only, difficult step when converting to DbC.

A *postcondition* is what will be true after the function has been called. It is the callee's responsibility to ensure the postcondition is met. The caller may assume that the postcondition has been met when the function returns control to it. The caller is not responsible for ensuring that the callee has fulfilled its contract. In the real world, it is sometimes necessary to hedge one's bets, for example, when calling into third-party plug-ins in live application servers. However, I think the principle still holds true. In fact, one can argue that a valid response to a contract-violating plug-in is to unload it, and send an e-mail to the managers of the hosting company and the third-party plug-in vendor. Since we can do anything in response to a violation, why not?

Preconditions and postconditions can apply to class member functions as well as free functions, which is a good thing for C++ (and object-oriented programming in general). In fact, there is a third component to DbC, which pertains only to classes: the *class invariant*. A class invariant is a condition, or set of conditions, which together always hold true for an object in a well-defined state. By definition, it is the role of the constructor to ensure that the instance is put into a state that conforms to the invariant, and the responsibility of the (public) member functions to ensure that the instance continues to be in such a state upon their completion. Only during construction, destruction, or the execution of one of its member functions may the invariant not hold true.

In some circumstances it is appropriate to define invariants that have wider scope than that of an individual object's state. In principle, an invariant can apply to the entire state of the operating environment. In practice, however, such things are very rare, and it is usual to simply deal with class invariants. Throughout the remainder of this chapter, and the rest of the book, when I speak of invariants, I am referring to class invariants.

It is possible to provide invariants for types that are partially, or not at all, encapsulated (see sections 3.2 and 4.4.1), which are enforced in the associated API functions (along with the function preconditions). Indeed, when using such types, invariants are a *very* good idea, since their lack of encapsulation increases the likelihood of their being abused. But the ease with which such invariants can be circumvented ably illustrates why such types should generally be avoided. Indeed, some [Stro2003] would say that if there is an invariant, public data make little sense in object-oriented programming; encapsulation is both about hiding implementation and protecting invariants. The use of properties (see Chapter 35) is one way in which we can have the semblance of public member variables, perhaps for reasons of structural conformance (see section 20.9), but still have the enforcement of invariants.

The action you choose to take upon the violation of preconditions, postconditions, or invariants is up to you. It may be logging the information to a file, throwing an exception, or sending the missus an SMS to let her know you'll be debugging late tonight. Commonly it takes the form of an assertion.

1.3.1   Preconditions

Precondition testing is easily done in C++. We've seen several examples of this already in the book. It's as simple as using an assertion:

```
template< . . . >
typename pod_vector<. . .>::reference pod_vector<. . .>::front()
{
  MESSAGE_ASSERT("Vector is empty!", 0 != size());
  assert(is_valid());
  return m_buffer.data()[0];
}
```

1.3.2   Post-conditions

This is where C++ stumbles badly. The challenge here is to capture the values of the out parameters and the return value at the epoch of function exit. Of course, C++ provides the singularly useful *Resource Acquisition Is Initialization* (RAII) mechanism (see section 3.5), which guarantees that a destructor for an object on the stack will be called when execution exits its defining scope. This means we can get some of the way toward a workable solution, in the mechanics at least.

One option would be to declare monitor objects, which take references to the out parameters and return value.

```
int f(char const *name, Value **ppVal, size_t *pLen)
{
  int             retVal;
  retval_monitor    rvm(retVal, . . . policy . . . );
  outparam_monitor  opm1(ppVal, . . . policy . . . );
  outparam_monitor  opm2(pLen, . . . policy . . . );
  . . . // The body of the function
  return retVal;
}
```

The policies would check whether the variable is NULL, or non-NULL, or is within a certain range, or one of a set of values, and so on. Notwithstanding the difficulties of getting just this far, there are two problems. The first one is that the destructor of rvm will enforce its constraint via the reference it holds to the return value variable retVal. If any part of the function returns a different variable (or a constant), rvm will inevitable report a failure. To work correctly we would be forced to write all functions to return via a single variable, which is not to everyone's taste and is not possible in all circumstances.

The main problem, however, is that the various postcondition monitors are unconnected. Most function postconditions are composite: the values of individual out parameters and the return value are only meaningful in concert, for example,

```
assert(retVal > 0 || (NULL == *ppVal && 0 == *pLen));
```

I'm not even going to start suggesting how the three individual monitor objects could be combined in such a way as to enforce a wide variety of postcondition states; such things might be an exciting challenge for a template meta-programmer doing postgraduate research, but for the rest of us we're *way* past the level at which the complexity is worth the payoff.

Imperfection: C++ does not provide suitable support for postconditions

---

In my opinion, the only reasonable, albeit prosaic, solution is to separate the function and the checks by using a *forwarding function*, as shown in Listing 1.5.

Listing 1.5
```
int f(char const *name, Value **ppVal, size_t *pLen)
{
    . . . // Do f() pre-conditions
  int retVal = f_unchecked(name, ppVal, pLen);
    . . . // Do f() post-conditions
  return retVal;
}
int f_unchecked(char const *name, Value **ppVal, size_t *pLen)
{
    . . . // The semantics of f
}
```

In real code, you may want to elide all the checks in builds where you're not enforcing DbC, and for this we'd need the preprocessor:

Listing 1.6
```
int f(char const *name, Value **ppVal, size_t *pLen)
#ifdef ACMELIB_DBC
{
    . . . // Do f() pre-conditions
  int retVal = f_unchecked(name, ppVal, pLen);
    . . . // Do f() post-conditions
  return retVal;
}
int f_unchecked(char const *name, Value **ppVal, size_t *pLen)
```

```
#endif /* ACMELIB_DBC */
{
    . . . // The semantics of f
}
```

It's anything but pretty, but it works, and is easy to incorporate into code generators. The issue gets more complex when working with overridden class methods, since you then have to face the question as to whether you enforce the pre- and postconditions of parent classes. That's something that must be determined on a case-by-case basis, and is outside the scope of this discussion.[6]

1.3.3   Class Invariants

Class invariants are almost as easy to do in C++ as preconditions. It's my practice to define a method is_valid() for classes, as in:

```
template<. . . >
inline bool pod_vector<. . .>::is_valid() const
{
  if(m_buffer.size() < m_cItems)
  {
    return false;
  }
  . . . // Further checks here
  return true;
}
```

This is then invoked in an assertion within all the public methods of the class, upon method entry, and prior to method exit. I tend to do the class invariant check just after the precondition check (as shown in section 1.3.1):

```
template< . . . >
inline void pod_vector<. . .>::clear()
{
  assert(is_valid());
  m_buffer.resize(0);
  m_cItems = 0;
  assert(is_valid());
}
```

An alternative strategy is to place the assertions within the invariant function itself. Unless you have a sophisticated assertion (see section 1.4), however, this leaves you with the choice of providing assertion information (file + line + message) on the offending condition or in the offending

---

[6]I confess to some self-serving cowardice on this point, but with good reason. Even in languages where the use of DbC is mature, there is equivocation on the usefulness of, and indeed the mechanisms for, relating contracts between levels of an inheritance hierarchy. Furthermore, the proposal to add DbC to C++ is, at the time of writing, only just about to be entered for consideration [Otto2004], so I believe it's inappropriate to discuss these details further here.

method. I prefer the latter, because invariant violations are rare. However, you may choose the former, in which case you'd wish to place the assertions inside the is_valid() member.

In fact, there's a reasonable half-way house, which I often use in environments where there's a well-known logging/tracing interface available (see section 21.2), which is to log the details of the invariant violation in the is_valid() member, and fire the assertion in the offending method.

Unlike out-parameter and return value checking, it's easy to use RAII (see section 3.5) to automate the class invariant check as part of the postcondition validation upon method exit, as in:

```
template< . . . >
inline void pod_vector<. . .>::clear()
{
  check_invariant<class_type> check(this);
  m_buffer.resize(0);
  m_cItems = 0;
}
```

The downside is that the enforcement is carried out within the constructor(s) and destructor of the check_invariant template instantiation, which means that simple assertion mechanisms that use the preprocessor to derive the _ _FILE_ _ and _ _LINE_ _ information (see section 1.4) may give misleading messages. However, it is not too challenging to implement macro + template forms that are able to display the appropriate location for the assertion failure, even incorporating the nonstandard _ _FUNCTION_ _ preprocessor symbol with those compilers that provide it.

1.3.4 Checking? *Invariably!*

In [Stro2003] Bjarne Stroustrup made the important observation that invariants are only necessary for classes that have methods, and not for simple structures that merely act as aggregates of variables. (The Patron type we look at in section 4.4.2 does not need an invariant, for example.) In my opinion, the converse is also true: I would say that any class that has methods should have a class invariant. In practice, though, there's a base limit to this. If your class holds a single pointer to some resource, then it is either going to have a NULL pointer, or a non-NULL pointer. Unless your class invariant method can use an external source of validity on the non-NULL pointer, there's not much for it to do. In that case, it's up to you whether you have a stub class invariant method, or don't bother. If your class is evolving, you're probably easing future refinement efforts by putting in a stub that'll be expanded later. If you use a code generator, then I would suggest that you simply generate a class invariant method, and calls to it, in all cases.

The benefits of using a class invariant method rather than individual assertions dotted around the class implementation are pretty obvious. Your code is easier to read, has a consistent look between the implementation of different classes, and is easy to maintain because you define the class invariant condition(s) in a single place for each class.

1.3.5 To DbC, or Not to DbC?

The picture of runtime contracts that I've painted thus far has contained the implicit assumption that one will create, after appropriate testing, a build of one's system that will have the DbC elements elided out by the preprocessor.

In fact, there is much equivocation as to whether any build ever should be made that does not enforce DbC [Same2003]. The argument is, to borrow a borrowed analogy [Same2003], that the contractual enforcements in DbC are equivalent to fuses in an electrical system, and one would not remove all the fuses from a sophisticated piece of electrical equipment just prior to deploying it.

The difference between assertions and fuses is that the assertions involve runtime tests, which have specific non-zero cost. Although the alloy in a fuse may have slightly different resistivity than the ambient characteristics of the system in which it serves, it is not reasonable to say that the costs involved are analogous. Striking the right balance is, in my opinion, something to be determined on a case-by-case basis. That's why the code examples shown in this section contain the `ACMELIB_DBC` symbol, rather than using `NDEBUG` (or `_DEBUG`), because the use of DbC should not be directly coupled to the binary notion of debug and release in your software. When you use it, and when you elide it, is an issue for you to determine for yourself.[7]

1.3.6 Runtime Contracts: Coda

Although we've seen that C++ is pretty broken for postconditions, it is reasonably well suited for precondition and class invariant testing. In practice, using these two together yields a great deal of the power of DbC. The absence of postcondition testing of return values and out-parameters, while disappointing, is not terribly inhibitive. If you *must* have it, you can resort to the preprocessor, as we saw in section 1.3.3.

For invariants, as with constraints, we make our lives easier by using a layer of indirection: a macro for constraints, a member function for invariants. It's thus simple to add support for new compilers, or to modify the internals of one's class, and we hide all the gunk of the mechanisms inside the class invariant method.

1.4 Assertions

I wouldn't call assertions a bona fide error-reporting mechanism, since they usually have profoundly different behavior in debug and release builds of the same software. Notwithstanding, the assertion is one of the most important of the C++ programmer's software quality assurance tools, particularly as it is widely used as the mechanism of enforcement of constraints and invariants. Any chapter on error-reporting mechanisms that did not include it would be decidedly *imperfect*.

Basically, an assertion is a runtime test that is usually only conducted in debug or testing builds, and tends to take the following form:

```
#ifdef NDEBUG
# define assert(x)  ((void)(0))
#elif /* ? NDEBUG */
extern "C" void assert_function(char const *expression);
# define assert(x)  ((!x) ? assert_function(#x) : ((void)0))
#endif /* NDEBUG */
```

---

[7]In ISE Eiffel 4.5 you cannot remove preconditions; presumably the rationale is that preconditions can react before program state becomes undefined and, therefore, it makes sense to continue the program by catching the violation exception.

It's used in client code to detect any conditions that you are sure should never happen:

```
class buffer
{
  . . .
  void method1()
  {
    assert((NULL != m_p) == (0 != m_size));
    . . .
  }
private:
  void    *m_p;
  size_t  m_size;
};
```

The assertion in this class reflects the class author's design assumption that if m_size is not 0, then m_p is not NULL, and vice versa.

When the condition of an assertion evaluates false, the assertion is said to "fire." This may mean that a message box is invoked if you're using a graphical environment, or it may mean that the program exits, or the process experiences a system-specific breakpoint exception.

However the assertion fires, it's nice to be able to display the text of the expression that failed, and, since they're primarily aimed at software developers, the file and line in which they occurred. Most assertion macros provide this ability:

```
#ifdef NDEBUG
# define assert(x)   ((void)(0))
#elif /* ? NDEBUG */
extern "C" void assert_function( char const *expression
                               , char const *file
                               , int         line);
# define assert(x)   ((!x) ?
                       ? assert_function(#x, _ _FILE_ _, _ _LINE_ _)
                       : ((void)0))
#endif /* NDEBUG */
```

Since the expression in an assertion is elided from release builds, it is very important that the expression have no side effects. Failure to adhere to this will lead to the curious and vexing situation whereby your debug builds work and your release builds do not.

1.4.1 Getting the Message

The nature of the action taken by the assertion can vary considerably. However, most assertion implementations make use of the stringized form of the expression. This is good as far as it goes, but it can leave the poor tester (who may be you) in a confused state, since all you'll get is some terse message like:

```
"assertion failed in file stuff.h, line 293: (NULL != m_p) == (0 != m_size));"
```

But we can take advantage of this simple mechanism to make our assertions that bit more meaningful. In the case where you might use an assertion in a switch case that you expect never to encounter, you can improve the message considerably by using a named 0 constant, as in:

```
switch(. . .)
{
  . . .
  case CantHappen:
    {
       const int AcmeApi_experienced_CantHappen_condition = 0;
       assert(AcmeApi_experienced_CantHappen_condition);
       . . .
```

Now when this assertion fires the message will be a lot more descriptive than

```
"assertion failed in file acmeapi.cpp, line 101: 0"
```

There's another way we can provide more information, and lose the unattractive underscores in the process. Because C/C++ can implicitly interpret pointers as Boolean (sub-)expressions (see section 15.3), we can rely on the fact that literal strings are non-zero to combine a readable message with the tested expression.

```
#define MESSAGE_ASSERT(m, e)  assert((m && e))
```

You'd use this as follows:

```
MESSAGE_ASSERT("Inconsistency in internal storage. Pointer should be null when
size is 0, or non-null when size is non-0", (NULL != m_p) == (0 != m_size));
```

Now we get a much richer failure information. And since the string is part of the expression, it is elided in release builds. All that extra information is free.

1.4.2   Inappropriate Assertions

Assertions are useful for debug-build invariant checking. As long as you remember that, you won't go far wrong.

Alas, all too often we see the use of assertions in runtime error checking. The canonical example of this, which one would hope is first-year undergraduate programming gotcha material, is that of using it to check against memory allocation failures:

```
char *my_strdup(char const *s)
{
  char *s_copy = (char*)malloc(1 + strlen(s));
  assert(NULL != s_copy);
  return strcpy(s_copy, s);
}
```

You might think that no one would do such a thing. If so, you might want to get busy with `grep` inside some of your favorite libraries, wherein you'll find such checks against memory, file handling, and other runtime errors.

Unfortunately, there's a kind of halfway house of badness here, which is that plenty of folks tend to use the assert *in addition* to a correctly written handling of the failure condition:

```
char *my_strdup(char const *s)
{
  char *s_copy = (char*)malloc(1 + strlen(s));
  assert(NULL != s_copy);
  return (NULL == s_copy) ? NULL : strcpy(s_copy, s);
}
```

I really can't understand this one. Given that just about everybody develops software on desktop hardware, with virtual memory systems, the only way you're ever likely actually to experience a memory system during debugging is when you've plugged in a low-stock allocation mechanism or stipulated low-stock behavior to your runtime library's debugging APIs.

But the ramifications are more significant when used with other, more commonly firing, conditions. When used with file handling, for example, this practice simply teaches you to put your test files in the right place, rather than to bulletproof your error-response functionality. This virtually guarantees that the response in deployment will be inadequate.

If the problem is a runtime failure condition, why would you want to catch the failure in an assertion? Wouldn't you want it to experience a crash if you'd failed to code it correctly, thereby being representative of the release mode behavior? Even if you've got a super smart assert [Robb2003], it still sets a bad example for yourself and anyone reviewing your team to see such things.

In my opinion, applying assertions to runtime failure conditions, even if accompanied by subsequent release-time handling code, is at best a distraction, and at worst bad practice. Don't do it!

Recommendation: Use assertions to assert truths about the structure of the code, not about runtime behavior.

1.4.3 Syntax and 64-Bit Pointers

Another issue[8] regards the use of pointers in assertions. On environments where an `int` is 32 bits and a pointer is 64 bits, using plain pointers in assertions can, depending on the definition of the `assert()` macro, result in truncation warnings:[9]

```
void *p = . . .;
assert(p); // Warning: truncation
```

---

[8] I know I'm throwing everything but the kitchen sink into this section, but I think it's all worth knowing.

[9] I've experienced this with Dec Alpha in the past, and I've seen newsgroup posts reporting similar experiences with other architectures.

Of course, this is just grist to my syntax mill of section 17.2.1, and is in fact the experience that started my obsession with all the bothersome issues of Boolean expressions. The answer is to be explicit in your intentions:

```
void *p = . . .;
assert(NULL != p); // Peachy now
```

1.4.4   Avoid `verify()`

A while back, I was chatting with someone about the definition of their own assertion macro, which they intended to call `verify()` to avoid conflict with the standard library macro. Alas, there are two problems with this.

First, the VERIFY() macro is a well-known part of Microsoft's Foundation Classes (MFC). It's used for the same thing as `assert()`, but its condition is not elided; it is executed under all circumstances, as in:

```
#ifdef NDEBUG
# define verify(x)   ((void)(x)) /* x still "is" */
#elif /* ? NDEBUG */
# define verify(x)   assert(x)
#endif /* NDEBUG */
```

If one was to define a `verify()` macro with `assert()` behavior, people accustomed to established verify behavior would be quite perplexed when well-tested debug mode code failed miserably in release mode. It'd be quite a while before they realized that the verify macro was eliding the expression from release mode builds, but only a few minutes thereafter they'd be chasing you through the parking lot with blunt instruments.

The second problem is that the word "assert" is only used for assertions. This is because you can use `grep` and similar tools to search for your assertions with almost no ambiguity, and because it stands out to the programmer. Seeing it in code, they are immediately mindful that some invariant (see section 1.3.3) is being tested. To start using assertions with different names will merely muddy this relatively clear picture.

Although in the past I've defined my own share of `verify()` macros—with the semantics of MFC's VERIFY()—I now consider them dangerous. An assertion expression must have no side effects, and it's not too hard to train yourself to adhere to this: I think it's several years since I made that mistake. But if you use a mix of assertion macros, some of which must have side effects, and others that must not, it's just too easy to get confused, and too hard to form unbreakable habits. I no longer use any form of `verify()` macros, and I'd advise you to do the same.

1.4.5   Naming Your Assertions

Since the issue of naming was raised in the last section, let's address it now. As I mentioned, an assertion macro should contain within it the word "assert." I've seen and used _ASSERTE(), ASSERT(), ATLASSERT(), AuAssert(), stlsoft_assert(), SyAssert(), and many others.

The standard assert macro for C and C++ is called `assert()`. In the STLSoft libraries I have `stlsoft_assert()` and a couple of others, all of which are lowercase. In the Synesis libraries the assert is called `SyAssert()`. In my opinion, all of these are wrong.

By convention, macros are all uppercase, and this is a really good convention, since they stand out from functions and methods. Although it's perfectly possible to write `assert()` as a function:

```
// Assume C++ compilation only
#ifdef ACMELIB_ASSERT_IS_ACTIVE
extern "C" void assert(bool expression);
#else /* ? ACMELIB_ASSERT_IS_ACTIVE */
inline void assert(bool )
{}
#endif /* ACMELIB_ASSERT_IS_ACTIVE */
```

This is not seen, as it would provide few of the benefits of current assertion macros. First, the compiler would not be able to optimize out the assertion expression. Well, to be strict, it would be able to do so in many cases, but not with all things, even with the best optimizing compilers. Whatever the precise differences between compilers, and projects, in principle there could be large amounts of wasted code involved.

Another problem would be that some types would not be implicitly convertible to `bool`, or `int`, or whatever you chose as your expression type. Since the canonical `assert()` macro incorporates the given expression within the `if` or `while` statements or the conditional expression of the `for` statement or the conditional operator (`?:`), then all the usual implicit Boolean conversions (see section 13.4.2 and Chapter 24) come into play. This is quite different from passing such conditional expressions to a function taking `bool` or `int`.

The final reason is that it would not be possible to display the expression as part of the assertion's error message at run time, since the stringizing is part and parcel of the preprocessor, and not the C++ (or C) language.

Assertions are now, and probably always will be, macros, so they should be uppercase. Not only is that a consistent coding standard, but they're also easier to spot which makes life simpler all round.

1.4.6   Avoid `#ifdef _DEBUG`

In section 25.1.4 I mention that the `default` condition is left out of the `switch` statement for performance reasons and that an assertion is used in its place. One of my esteemed reviewers, who's got a *much* more distinguished history than l'il ole me, queried this and suggested that I should have gone for the simpler:

```
switch(type)
{
  . . .
#ifdef _DEBUG
  default:
    assert(0);
```

```
      break;
#endif // _DEBUG
}
```

This just goes to show how easy it is for us all, even the most experienced, to become victims of the assumptions of our own development environment. There are several small things wrong with this. First, `assert(0)` can lead to some pretty uninformative error messages, depending on the given compiler's assertion support. This can easily be souped up:

```
  . . .
  default:
    { const int unrecognized_switch_case = 0;
    assert(unrecognized_switch_case); }
  . . .
```

but it's still unlikely to be more informative with most compilers than the original, more verbose, form:

```
assert( type == cstring || type == single ||
        type == concat || type == seed);
```

The main problem with the use of _DEBUG is that it may not be the definitive symbol instructing the compiler to generate an assertion. For a start, _DEBUG is, to the best of my knowledge, something that is only prevalent on PC compilers. For many compilers, debug builds are the default, and only the definition of the symbol NDEBUG causes the compilation to be release mode and assertions to be elided. Naturally, the correct way is to use a compiler-independent abstraction of the build mode, so you could get away with:

```
#ifdef ACMELIB_BUILD_IS_DEBUG
  default:
    assert(0);
    break;
#endif // ACMELIB_BUILD_IS_DEBUG
```

But even that's not the full picture. It's entirely reasonable to keep various subsets of debug functionality in the builds of prerelease versions of your product. You might use your own assertions, which may be active or inactive unrelated to the definition of _DEBUG, NDEBUG or even ACMELIB_BUILD_IS_DEBUG.

1.4.7 DebugAssert() vs int 3

Although this is a Win32 + Intel architecture specific point, it's worth noting because it's very useful and surprisingly little known. The Win32 API function `DebugBreak()` causes the execution of the calling process to fault with a breakpoint exception. This allows a standalone process to be debugged, or it causes the currently debugging process within your IDDE to halt, thereby allowing you to inspect the call stack or whatever other debugging delights take your fancy.

On the Intel architecture, the function simply executes the machine instruction `int 3`, which causes the breakpoint exception within the Intel processor.

The slight pain is that when control is given to your debugger, the execution point is inside `DebugBreak()`, rather than nicely with the code that caused the exception. The simple answer to this is to use inline assembler when compiling for the Intel architecture. The Visual C++ C run time library provides the `_CrtDebugBreak()` function as part of its debugging infrastructure, which is defined for the Intel architecture as:

```
#define _CrtDbgBreak() __asm { int 3 }
```

Using `int 3` means that the debugger stops exactly where it's needed, on the offending line of code.

1.4.8 Static/Compile-Time Assertions

So far we've just looked at runtime assertions. But catching bugs at runtime is a poor second best to catching them at compile time. In many parts of the book we've mentioned static assertions, also called compile-time assertions, so now's a good time to look at them in detail.

Basically, a static assertion provides a compile-time validation of an expression. Needless to say, for it to be validated at compile time, it needs to be capable of being evaluated at compile time. This reduces the scope of expressions to which static assertions can be applied. For example, you might use a static assertion to ensure that your expectation of the sizes of `int` and `long`, for your compiler, are adhered to:

```
STATIC_ASSERT(sizeof(int) == sizeof(long));
```

but note that they cannot be used to evaluate runtime expressions:

```
. . . Thing::operator [](index_type n)
{
  STATIC_ASSERT(n <= size()); // Compiler error - for real!
  . . .
```

The firing of a static assertion is an inability to compile. Since static assertions are, like most modern features of C and C++, not a feature of the language, but rather a side effect of a language feature, the error messages can be anything but obvious. We'll see how weird they can be momentarily.

The usual mechanism for a static assertion is to define an array, using the truth of the expression as the array dimension. Since C and C++ accord a true expression the value 1, when converted to an integer, and a false expression the value 0, the expression may be used to either define an array of size 1 or 0. An array dimension of 0 is not legal C or C++, so the compiler will fail to compile. Consider an example:

```
#define STATIC_ASSERT(x)    int ar[x]
    . . .
STATIC_ASSERT(sizeof(int) < sizeof(short));
```

An int is never smaller than a short (C++-98:3.9.1;2), so the expression sizeof(int) < sizeof(short) evaluates to 0. Hence, the STATIC_ASSERT() line evaluates to:

```
int ar[0];
```

which is not legal C or C++.

Clearly there are a couple of problems with this. The array ar is declared but not used, which will cause most compilers to give you a warning, and screw up your build.[10] Second, using STATIC_ASSERT() twice or more within the same scope will result in ar being multiply defined.

To obviate these concerns I define static assertions as follows:

```
#define STATIC_ASSERT(ex)    \
        do { typedef int ai[(ex) ? 1 : 0]; } while(0)
```

This works fine for most compilers. However, some compilers don't balk with an array of dimension 0, so there tends to be some conditional compilation to handle all cases:

```
#if defined(ACMELIB_COMPILER_IS_GCC) || \
    defined(ACMELIB_COMPILER_IS_INTEL)
# define STATIC_ASSERT(ex)    \
        do { typedef int ai[(ex) ? 1 : -1]; } while(0)
#else /* ? compiler */
# define STATIC_ASSERT(ex)    \
        do { typedef int ai[(ex) ? 1 : 0]; } while(0)
#endif /* compiler */
```

The invalid array dimension is not the only mechanism for providing static assertions. There are two other interesting mechanisms I'm aware of [Jagg1999], although I've not used either in anger.

The first relies on the requirement for each case clause to have a different value:

```
#define STATIC_ASSERT(ex) \
    switch(0) { case 0: case ex:; }
```

The second relies on the fact that bitfields must have a length of one or more:

```
#define STATIC_ASSERT(ex) \
    struct x { unsigned int v : ex; }
```

---

[10]You do set warnings to "high," and treat them as errors, don't you?

All three forms have similarly inscrutable error messages when they "fire." You'll see something like `"case label value has already appeared in this switch"` or `"the size of an array must be greater than zero"`, so it can take a while to comprehend the problem when you're in a nest of templates.

In an attempt to ameliorate this confusion, Andrei Alexandrescu, in [Alex2001], describes a technique for providing better error messages, and gets as far as is probably possible within the current limitations of the language.[11]

For my part, I tend to shy away from that level of complexity for three reasons. First, I'm lazy, and like to avoid complexity where possible.[12] Second, I write a lot of C code as well as C++, and I prefer wherever possible to have the same facilities available to me with both languages.

Finally, static assertions fire as a result of a coding time misuse of a component. This means that they're both rare and within the purview of the programmer who caused them to fire. Therefore, I figure it's only going to cost a given developer a couple of minutes to track the error (though not, perhaps, the solution), and they'll suffer this cost rarely.

Before we finish this item, it's worth noting that both the invalid index and the bit field forms have the advantage that they may be used outside of functions, whereas the switch form (and runtime assertions) may not.

1.4.9 Assertions: Coda

This section has described the basics of assertions, but there are many more interesting things that assertions can do that are outside the scope of this book. Two quite different, but equally useful, techniques are SMART_ASSERT [Torj2003] and SUPER_ASSERT [Robb2003], and I'd advise you to read up on both of them.

---

[11]You should check it out. It's quite nifty.

[12]I also think it's good to have your supporting techniques as simple as possible, although I admit that there have been sojourns to the land of a trillion brain cells in several parts of the book, so I can't seriously claim that as a good reason in this case. It's just laziness.

Object Lifetime

2.1   The Object Life Cycle

There are four phases in the life of every C++ object: nonexistence, partially constructed, instantiated, and partially destroyed [Stro1997]. Furthermore, the space that an object occupies must be acquired prior to its construction, and released after its destruction.[1]

Objects can be brought into existence in four standard ways:

- Global (global, namespace, and class-static) objects exist outside the scope of any functions. They are (usually) created prior to the execution of main(), and are automatically destroyed after it (section 11.1). The memory that they occupy is allocated by the compiler/linker.
- Stack objects exist in a local execution frame, within a function. They are created at their point of declaration—also their point of definition—and are automatically destroyed when they go out of scope. The memory that they occupy is allocated by adjusting the stack pointer, as determined by the compiler/linker.
- Heap objects exist on the heap/free-store [Stro1997]. They are created by using the new operator, and are destroyed by an explicit call to the delete operator. The memory that they occupy is acquired from the free-store, which may have insufficient resources, resulting in failure to create a new object. (See section 32.2 for a more detailed discussion on what can happen, and what we can do about it.) The language infrastructure ensures that the allocation of memory and the call of the constructor are effected together, and it does the same with the call of the destructor and the release of the memory.
- As part of another object. In this case, the composed objects have their lifetimes tied to that of their composing object (see Chapter 5).

2.1.1   In-Place Construction

In addition to the standard ways, you can explicitly control the memory and lifetime of instances by using placement new and explicit destruction, as in:

```
byte_t    *p = . . . // Correctly-aligned block for SomeClass
SomeClass &sc = *new(p) SomeClass(); // Create the instance
. . .
```

---

[1]Conceptually speaking, that is. The space that a former object occupied may be reused after its destruction without any actual release of memory. This happens in STL containers, for example.

```
sc.SomeMethod();

. . .

sc.~SomeClass(); // Explicitly destroy the instance; p remains
```

Naturally, this is hacky stuff. Apart from the implementation of containers (which store by value, rather than by reference), there are few legitimate reasons to use this technique.

2.2 Controlling Your Clients

One of the important and powerful features of C++ is its ability to enforce access control at compile time. By using the `public`, `protected`, and `private` [Stro1997] access specifier keywords, coupled with sparing use of the `friend` keyword, we can moderate the ways in which client code can use our types. These moderations can be extremely useful in a variety of ways, many of which we'll be using in the techniques described in this book.

2.2.1 Member Types

A powerful way to control the manipulation of your class instances is to declare members of the class `const` and/or of reference type. Because both constants and references (and `const` references) can only be initialized, and cannot be assigned to, using either in a class definition prevents the compiler from defining a copy assignment operator. More than that, however, it helps you, the original author, and any maintainers of your code by enforcing your original design decisions. If changes cannot be made to the class without violating these restrictions—which your compiler will help you out with—then that indicates that the design may need to change, and flags the importance of any changes that you may need to make to the class. It's classic hairshirt programming.

(Note that this is primarily a technique for enforcing design decisions within the class implementation, such decisions being "passed down" to future maintainers. It is not appropriate for users of your class to learn that it should not be used in copy-assignment from the compiler warning about const members. Rather they should glean this from your explicit use of copy assignment protection, as described below.)

2.2.2 Default Constructor

This gets hidden automatically if you define any other constructor, so you don't have to try too hard to hide it. This behavior makes sense if you're defining a class whose constructor takes parameters, then not having a default constructor (one that is not acquiring anything) is reasonable. Consider a class that acts to scope a resource (see Chapter 6): there'd be no sense having a default constructor. What would be released?

Hiding the default constructor in a class that has no other constructor defined prevents any instances of that class being created (apart from friends or static methods of the class itself), though it does not prevent their being destroyed.

2.2.3 Copy Constructor

Whether or not you define a default, or any other, constructor, the compiler will always synthesize a copy constructor if you don't explicitly provide one. For certain kinds of classes—

for example, those that contain pointers to allocated resources—the default member-wise copy
of a compiler provided copy constructor can result in two class instances thinking that they own
the same resource. This does not end happily.

If you do not want a copy constructor, you should render it inaccessible using the idiomatic
form [Stro1997]:

```
class Abc
{
    . . .
// Not to be implemented
private:
  Abc(Abc const &);
};
```

Only when your type is a simple *value type* (see Chapter 4), and has no ownership over any
resources (see Chapter 3), is it advisable to allow the compiler to supply you with a default implementation.

2.2.4   Copy Assignment

As is the case with copy constructors, the compiler will generate a copy assignment operator for your class if you do not define one. Once again, you should only allow this in cases
where simple value types are concerned.

If you have const/reference members, the compiler will not be able to generate a default
version, but you should not rely on this to proscribe copy assignment for two reasons. First, you'll
get lots of irritating compiler warnings, as it attempts to warn you of your presumed oversight.

Second, the use of const members is a mechanism for enforcing design that may reflect a
lack of copyability, but it more often reflects overall immutability. If you change the immutability assumption, you may still wish to proscribe copy assignment. Hence it is better to explicitly
declare it, using the idiomatic form [Stro1997]:

```
class Abc
{
    . . .
// Not to be implemented
private:
  Abc &operator =(Abc const &);
};
```

More often than not, proscribing copy assignment and copy construction go together. If you
need to have one without the other, using method hiding you can achieve this straightforwardly.

2.2.5   new and delete

These operators are used to create an element on the heap, and to destroy it. By restricting
access to them it means that instances of the class must be created on the frame (globals and/or
stack variables). The canonical form of hiding operators new and delete is similar to that for

hiding copy-constructor and copy-assignment operator. If you wished to hide the operators in a given class and any derived class (excepting those that redefined them, of course), then you would normally not provide an implementation, as in:

```
class Shy
{
  . . .
// Not to be implemented
private:
  void *operator new(size_t);
  void operator delete(void *);
};
```

In addition to controlling access, we can also usefully choose to implement our own versions of these operators, on a per-class basis [Meye1998, Stro1997] and also on a link-unit basis (see sections 9.5 and 32.3).

However, there are limitations to the use of access control with these operators, because they can be overridden in any derived class. Even if you make them `private` in a base class, there is nothing to stop derived classes from defining their own `public` ones. So restricting access of `new` and `delete` is really just a documentation tactic.

Notwithstanding this, one useful scenario can be to declare (and define) them as `protected` in a base class, thereby prescribing a common allocation scheme, and allowing any derived classes that are to be heap based to redefine their own `public` versions in terms of the protected ones they've inherited.

2.2.6 Virtual Delete

There's another interesting feature of delete, which is observed when you have a virtual destructor in your class. The standard (C++-98: 12.4;11) states that "non-placement operator delete shall be looked up in the scope of the destructor's class." Although providing a virtual destructor and hiding operator delete is a pretty perverse thing to do, if you do so you should be aware that you will have to provide a stubbed implementation to avoid linker errors.

2.2.7 explicit

The keyword `explicit` is used to denote that the compiler may not use the constructor of the class in an implicit conversion. For example, a function `f()` may take an argument of type `String`, and can resolve a call to `f("Literal C-string")` by implicitly converting the literal string to `String` if `String` has a constructor such as

```
class String
{
public:
  String(char const *);
  . . .
```

A missing `explicit` facilitates compilation of conversions that may not be desired and can be costly. Applying the `explicit` keyword to the constructor instructs the compiler to reject the implicit conversion.

```
public:
  explicit String(char const *);
```

This is a widely documented [Dewh2003, Stro1997], and well-understood concept. Use of the `explicit` keyword on such so-called conversion constructors is recommended except where the class author specifically wants to facilitate the implicit conversion.

2.2.8   Destructor

By hiding the destructor we forcibly prevent the use of frame/global variables, and we also prevent `delete` being applied to an instance to which we have a pointer. This can be of use when we have access to an object belonging to something else that we can use but not destroy. It is especially useful in preventing misuse of reference-counted pointers.

Another thing worth pointing out is that the destructor is the preferred place to locate in-method constraints (see section 1.2) for template classes. Consider the template shown in Listing 2.1.

Listing 2.1
```
template <typename T>
class SomeT
{
public:
  SomeT(char const *)
  {
    // Only constrained if this ctor is instantiated
    constraint_must_be_pointer_type(T);
  }
  SomeT(double )
  {
    // Only constrained if this ctor is instantiated
    constraint_must_be_pointer_type(T);
  }
  . . .
```

The constraint in any given constructor is only tested if that constructor is instantiated, and C++ only instantiates those template members that are needed. This is a good thing, as it allows for some seriously useful techniques (see section 33.2).

To ensure the constraint is applied, you would need to place the constraint in all constructors. However, there is only one destructor, so you can save yourself the typing and the maintenance headache by placing it there.

```
  . . .
  ~SomeT()
```

```
  {
    // Always constrained if instance of class is created
    constraint_must_be_pointer_type(T);
  }
};
```

Naturally, this also does not work if you don't actually create any instances of the type, and only call its static members. But in almost all cases you have your bases covered by exercising constraints in the destructor.

2.2.9   friend

Injudicious use of the `friend` keyword can serve to undo all the access control we may apply. It has its proponents, from whom I might be inviting powerful disagreement, but I think its use should be limited only to classes that share the same header file. Since it is a matter of good design [Dewh2003, Lako1996, Stro1997] that classes and sets of functions should exist in their own header files, only those that are intimately interdependent—such as a sequence class and its iterator class, or a value type and its free-function operators—should share the same header file. So give `friend`s a wide berth, they'll only cause you trouble in the long run.

If you follow the practice of defining free-functions, as much as is possible, in terms of class methods, the need for friendship can be dramatically reduced. A good example of this is defining the `operator +( X const &, X const)` free function in terms of `X::operator +=(X const &)`. We'll look at this in detail in Chapter 25.

In reviewing this section, I decided to bite the bullet and quantify my own (mis)use of the `friend` keyword. There are 41 uses of the keyword in the STLSoft libraries at the time of writing. Of these, 29 are sequence/iterator/value-type relationships and 8 involve the subscript subtypes of multidimensional array classes (see section 33.2.4). All of the other four involve same-file classes, sometimes with nested classes and their outer class. I was surprised to have so many instances of the keyword, but at least I haven't been transgressing my own advice.

2.3   MILs and Boon

There are seven different types of things that you might want to initialize from within a constructor body. They are:

1. Immediate parent classes.
2. Virtual base classes.[2]
3. Constant member variables.
4. Reference member variables.
5. Non-`const`, nonreference member variables of user-defined type that have nondefault constructors.

---

[2]But there's *no way* you'd ever have a virtual base that had any data or constructors, right? [Meye1998, Dewh2003, Stro1997].

6. Non-const, nonreference member scalar variables; we would think of these as "normal" member variables.

7. Array member variables.

Of these seven, only the last, array member variables, cannot be initialized in a member initializer list (or MIL), and the first five *must* be. Normal, non-const, nonreference, scalar member variables can be "initialized" within either the initializer list or within a constructor body. In fact, they undergo assignment, rather than initialization in this case. Although this may appear as initialization to client code of the class, and will not incur any additional instructions in the case of scalar types, the "initialization" will not be done in the same order as the members are declared. In rare cases where you might be relying on member declaration/initialization ordering—which is a bad thing to do (see section 2.3.2)—then you could be in for a nasty surprise. Irrespective of correctness issues in such border cases, there are good reasons to use the initializer list [Stro1997], since it is possible that you may be expensively assigning to something that has already had a nontrivial construction cost, thereby wasting speed for no gain whatsoever.

If you share my preference for const variables, you'll no doubt be making much use of initializer lists as it is, but I would advise everyone to do so at all times. Not only does it help you to avoid making inappropriate use of member variables of nontrivial types (i.e., costly default-construction-plus-assignment), but also it improves consistency: a much undervalued aspect of software development, albeit a distinguishing feature of well-developed software [Kern1999]. It also helps in the presence of exceptions, as we'll see in section 32.2.

In terms of hairshirt programming, MILs also facilitate our preference for const members, as described in the previous subsection. Furthermore, you can avoid code such as the example shown in Listing 2.2, based on a real code-base that I was given to "improve."

Listing 2.2
```
class Abc
  : public Base
{
// Members
protected:
  CString  m_str1;
  int      m_int1;
  int      m_int2;
  CString  m_str2;
  CString  m_str3;
  int      m_int3;
  CString  m_str4;
  int      m_int4;
  CString  m_str5;
  int      m_int5;
  int      m_int6;
  . . . // and so it went on
};

Abc::Abc(int i1, int i2, int i3, int i4, int i4
      , LPCTSTR pcsz1, LPCTSTR pcsz2
```

```
           , LPCTSTR pcsz3, LPCTSTR pcsz4)
  : Base(int i)
  , m_str1(pcsz1)
  , m_str2(pcsz2)
{
  m_str3 = pcsz3;
  m_int1 = i1;
  m_int2 = i2;
  m_int3 = i3;
  m_str2 = pcsz2;

  . . . // many lines later

  m_int3 = i3;
  m_str2 = pcsz4; // Eek!
  m_int2 = i2;
  m_int6 = i6;

  . . . // and on it went
}
```

There were over 20 redundant and potentially harmful assignments within the constructor body. In the remainder of the class's implementation, some of the member variables were never altered after construction. Changing them to const immediately found some of these issues. Having highlighted the problem, I then moved everything into the initializer list (using an automated tool), and the compiler nicely pointed out the duplicates. That took all of 10 minutes, and the class saved itself from a significant amount of accreted waste, not to mention a couple of errors.

2.3.1 Getting a Bigger Playpen

One argument against using member initializer lists is that it is a pretty small playpen within which to work. A regular complaint is that it is hard to carry out efficient and effective argument validation/manipulation within the restrictions of member initializer lists. This can be a justification for eschewing both initializer lists and const/reference members. However, I think this is largely incorrect, and with a little imagination we can provide robust, suitably constrained (i.e., we can wear our hairshirt), and efficient initialization. Consider the following class:

```
class String
{
// Construction
public:
  String(char const *s);

// Members
private:
```

```
    char *m_s;
};
```

In his book *C++ Gotchas* [Dewh2003], Steve Dewhurst distinguishes the following two possibilities for the implementation of this constructor (within a section where he otherwise broadly
espouses the preference of member initialization over assignment):

```
String::String(char const *s)
  : m_s(strcpy(new char[strlen(s ? s : "") + 1], s ? s : ""))
{}

String::String(char const *s)
{
   if(s == NULL)
   {
     s = "";
   }

   m_s = strcpy(new char[strlen(s) + 1], s);
}
```

Steve states that the first form is taking things too far—with which I think most would
agree—and favors the second. Frankly, I wouldn't write either. Why not put on our hairshirt (as
the first makes an attempt to do), but give ourselves a break while we're at it. The solution
(Listing 2.3) is very simple.

Listing 2.3
```
String
{
   . . .

// Implementation
private:
   static char *create_string_(char const *s);

// Members
private:
   char const *const m_s;
};

/* static */ char *String::create_string_(char const *s)
{
   if(s == NULL)
   {
     s = "";
   }
   return strcpy(new char[strlen(s) + 1], s);
}
```

```
String::String(char const *s)
  : m_s(create_string_(s))
{}
```

Rather than having an unintelligible mess of gobbledegook, or creeping into bad practice, we can achieve clarity of expression and correct initialization by placing the logic into a `private` `static` helper function. Seems simple now, doesn't it? Note also that the exception behavior of `String`'s constructor is not changed. This is an important aspect of using this technique.

The `String` instance may be constructed from either a pointer to a string, or a literal empty string. (As we will see in section 15.4.3, literal constants may or may not be folded—identical literals are merged into one by the linker—so this implementation is partial, and a fuller one would have to address this potential problem.)

Also note the change to the definition of m_s. Since Steve's example didn't show any mutating operations of his `String` class we can widen the scope of our "privations" to make m_s a constant pointer to a constant string. If we subsequently change the class's definition to including mutating operations to either the contained buffer, or to the buffer pointer, the compiler will remind us that we're violating our initial design decisions. That's perfectly okay; getting such an error doesn't mean we're doing something wrong, simply that we may be doing something that's challenging the original design decisions. The point is that we will be forced to think about it, which can only be a good thing.

There are two other advantages to the new form. A minor one is that it looks cleaner; we can plainly see the intent of the constructor, which is to "`create_string_()`."

A more significant advantage is that it centralizes the creation of the string contents, which could conceivably be used elsewhere in an expanded definition of `String`. (Indeed, in real string classes that I've written there are often several constructors that use a single `static` creation function. Naturally this increases maintainability and size efficiency, without affecting speed efficiency.) It is all too common to see the same logic appear in numerous constructors of the same class. This is sometimes centralized into an `Init()` method that gets called from within each constructor body, but that then misses the efficiency of initializer lists and reduces the scope for using `const`/reference members. Using this `static`-based helper function technique facilitates the centralization of constructor-common operations, while sacrificing neither efficiency nor safety. This technique in effect can be used to simulate the Java facility for calling one constructor from within another.

Note that the method does not have to be `static` in order for it to achieve the desired effect. However, if it is non-`static`, it opens the possibility of using member state in the method, such state being undefined because the instance is partway through construction. It is better, therefore, to use a little more hairshirt and always favor the `static` helper.

We will see some more sophisticated examples of its application in Chapter 11 when we look into adaptive code techniques.

2.3.2   Member-Ordering Dependencies

One of the caveats to using initializer lists is that member variables are initialized in the order of their declaration, regardless of their order in the list. Naturally, the advice ([Stro1997, Dewh2003]) is to list them in the same order to their declaration within the class. Indeed, you should expend diligent efforts in your maintenance work to ensure that changes in the declaration are reflected in the initializer list, and you should check those of other authors when asked to make changes. The possibilities for trouble are boundless [Dewh2003, Meye1998], and all guaranteed to bring unhappiness.

```
struct Fatal
{
  Fatal(int i)
    : y(i)
    , x(y * 2)
  {}
  int x;
  int y;
};
```

Despite the seemingly innocuous looking initializer list, instances of `Fatal` will have arbitrary garbage in their x members, because at the time x is initialized y has not been. You should avoid such dependencies as a rule. Only GCC detects this and issues a warning (when the -Wall option is used).

Notwithstanding that sound advice, this is a book about survival in the real world, wherein it is occasionally appropriate to do such dangerous things. What can the imperfect practitioner do to protect his/her code, when it must rely on the order of member variables, from dangerous changes in maintenance? The answer is to use compile-time assertions (section 1.4). An example of this protection of member ordering was to be found in the original implementation of the `auto_buffer` template, which we'll see in detail in section 32.2. The constructor contained the following protective assertion:

```
auto_buffer:: auto_buffer(size_type cItems)
  : m_buffer((space < cItems)
                  ? allocator_type::allocate(cItems, 0)
                  : m_internal)
  , m_cItems((m_buffer != 0) ? cItems : 0)
{
   STATIC_ASSERT( offsetof(class_type, m_buffer)
                  < offsetof(class_type, m_cItems));
   . . .
```

This code would not compile if the order of the m_buffer and m_cItems members were changed in the class definition. This means that the dubious practice of relying on member initialization order was rendered safe, and the class implementation robust and portable.

Alas, this particular class is not the best example of when it is appropriate to thumb our nose at the law, because it is achieves const member variables by using the offsetof macro, which is itself, in this circumstance, nonstandard, as we discuss in section 2.3.3.

The latest version of this class is resizable, so the advantage of the constness of the m_cItems is moot. Therefore it's probably better to rewrite the constructor as:

```
auto_buffer:: auto_buffer(size_type cItems)
  : m_buffer((space < cItems)
                  ? allocator_type::allocate(cItems, 0)
```

```
                   : m_internal)
{
  m_cItems = (m_buffer != 0) ? cItems : 0;
  . . .
```

Now there's no need to police a specific member ordering, and therefore no use of `off-setof()` in a less-than-legal guise.

2.3.3   offsetof()

The `offsetof` macro is used to deduce a compile-time constant representing the number of bytes offset of a structure member from the start of the structure. The canonical implementation is as follows:

```
#define offsetof(S, m)    (size_t)&(((S*)0)->m)
```

It's an extremely useful thing, and without it, we'd have all kinds of difficulty doing many clever and useful things, for example, the technique for providing properties in C++ (see Chapter 35) would not be as efficient as it is.

Alas, its use is only legal when applied to POD types: the standard states the type to which it is applied "shall be a POD structure or a POD union" (C++-98: 18.1). This means that, as with `auto_buffer`, using it in class types is not valid, and has potentially undefined behavior. Nonetheless, it is used widely, including several popular libraries, and its use with types such as `auto_buffer` is perfectly reasonable. The main reason that the standard says it may only be used with POD types is because it would be impossible to have it yield a correct compile-time value when used in multiple virtual inheritance. The current rules are probably overstrict, but even then it is up to an implementation as to how it lays out the memory of types.

Since I'm a pragmatist, I'll continue to use it where I think it's necessary and appropriate, although I'll make sure to take defensive measures: run time and static assertions (see Chapter 1) and testing. If you choose to do the same, just be mindful of the caveats, so that when a language lawyer trumpets your non-conformant code to your colleagues, you can disarm him with your acknowledgment of its non-conformance, and then bamboozle him with the rationale for your using it in the given instance and the list of tested environments on which you've proved your work correct.

2.3.4   MIL: Coda

Apart from cases where the degree of hoop jumping borders on the ridiculous, the advice is to prefer initializer lists wherever appropriate, which is, arrays aside, just about everywhere. I'm always astonished when engineers justify their inconsistent use of assignment over initialization by saying that they want to be consistent with their development-tool's (poorly written) wizard. It seems a great irony, and not a little sad, that a generation of software developers have grown up with a bad habit that has arisen out of a drawback in tools designed to simplify and enhance their practice.

## CHAPTER 3

Resource Encapsulation

Along with abstraction and polymorphism, encapsulation is one of the main tenets of object-oriented programming. Resource encapsulation is a refinement of encapsulation, insofar as the encapsulated data are actually references to allocated resources, albeit that resource is a broad term. A resource can be other class instances, allocated memory, system objects, API/library states, and object states.

Data encapsulation is the protection of an encapsulating type's inner state to ensure consistency of that type, or to abstract the public interface to it. Resource encapsulation, however, is the wrapping up of a resource reference in order to provide a more robust interface to that resource and to help in managing it; in other words it is a means of protecting the resource itself. The difference is subtle, and there's a lot of overlap in the real world between the two, to be sure, but it's worth being mindful of the distinction. This chapter and the next, Chapter 4, Data Encapsulation and Value Types, will cover both types of encapsulation.

Though most modern languages do very well at data encapsulation, C++ stands head and shoulders above its cousins in the C-language family in its support for resource encapsulation by virtue of the twin mechanisms of construction and automatic, deterministic destruction. In this chapter we look at the details of resource encapsulation and examine the different levels of encapsulation afforded by the language.

3.1   A Taxonomy of Resource Encapsulation

The classic texts [Stro1997] discuss resource encapsulation in terms of the *Resource Acquisition Is Initialization* (RAII) mechanism (see section 3.5). However, as with so many things in software engineering, there are several levels of resource encapsulation. The most basic level of resource encapsulation is, of course, no encapsulation at all. Beyond that, we need to consider the services that resource encapsulation provides

- Automatic acquisition of resource(s)
- Convenient interface for manipulation of resource(s)
- Automatic release of resource(s)

Given this list, we can postulate the following taxonomy of resource encapsulation:

1. No encapsulation
2. POD types (section 3.2)
3. Wrapper proxies (section 3.3)

4. RRID types (section 3.4)

5. RAII types (section 3.5)

We're going to use a couple of examples to take us through the journey into this concept in this chapter. Before we get into it, I should tell you that this chapter and the next took more thinking time (vs. writing time) than any others in the book. That's not because they're terribly complicated concepts, rather because the two concepts are so very similar that attempting to delineate cleanly between them was challenging, to say the least. As a consequence, you may find some of the examples in these chapters a bit contrived, but I ask you to bear with it and understand that the focus is on separating the concepts clearly.

3.2   POD Types

POD type encapsulation is the most basic form where some effort has been to increase robustness, by virtue of aggregating one or more resource references in a structure.

Let's imagine we have some notional network server that provides a selection of services based on different client requirements. Each service is represented by the following structure:

```
struct Service
{
  socket_t  txChannel;    // transmission socket
  socket_t  rxChannel;    // reception socket
  mutex_t   *lock;        // service mutual exclusion object
  byte_t    *txBuffer;    // transmission buffer
  size_t    txBufferSize; // # of bytes in transmission buffer
  byte_t    *rxBuffer;    // reception buffer
  size_t    rxBufferSize; // # of bytes in reception buffer
};
```

3.2.1   Direct Manipulation

The most primitive manner of manipulating a Service would look something like the following:

```
Service  service;

. . . // Initialize the service, and make some connections

pthread_mutex_lock(service.lock);
int i = recv( service.rxChannel, service.rxBuffer
            , service.rxBufferSize);
. . . // Many more lines of low-level coding
pthread_mutex_lock(&service.unlock);
```

This kind of coding is really hard to do, and doubly so to ensure quality and maintainability. If the definition of Service is changed, there can be thousands of lines of code that need to change. There are some well-known APIs that make you do a lot of this manually, but thank-fully most C APIs come along with many functions that help you out.

3.2.2 API Functions and Transparent Types

Naturally, if you were using the Service API you'd hopefully be using (or writing, if they didn't already exist) API functions to manipulate the `Service` structure at a higher level, such as:

```
int i = Service_GuardedReceive(&service, . . .);
```

This is one of the most common programming models around. It is very usable and reason-ably safe. Many an operating system has been built in this fashion. Nonetheless, there are still problems; it is insufficiently encapsulated. Since the client code has access to the structure, the temptation for users of the API to fiddle just here and there can be too great. Even if they only peek at the structures, and don't change anything, a reliance on the format of the structure still represents a brittle code set, and can make maintenance a big challenge.

3.2.3 API Functions and Opaque Types

If the client code has no need of access to the structure, or the risk of direct access is too great, the API function model is enhanced markedly by making the structures opaque. There are several ways to do this; it usually takes the form of declaring a structure, but not defining it publicly.

```
// ServiceAPI.h

struct Service;

int Service_Create(. . . init parameters . . . , Service **svc);
int Service_Open(. . . init parameters . . . , Service **svc);
int Service_Destroy(Service *svc);
int Service_GuardedReceive(Service *svc, . . . );
```

Only in the API implementation is the `Service` structure defined, and so client code nei-ther knows nor cares about its actual structure. And, more important, it cannot peek at the struc-ture contents and introduce breakable dependencies.

There's a slight refinement of this, allowing for a greater syntactic opacity, which is help-ful, albeit that it has no deeper significance.

```
// ServiceAPI.h

struct ServiceInternal;
typedef struct ServiceInternal *Service;

int Service_Create(. . . init parameters . . . , Service *svc);
int Service_Open(. . . init parameters . . . , Service *svc);
```

```
int Service_Destroy(Service svc);
int Service_GuardedReceive(Service svc, . . . );
```

Now `Service` is not a structure, to which one must manipulate pointers, but rather an opaque type. For those who like a bit of syntactic sugar, this might be called `HService`, to denote that it is a handle to a service.

3.3   Wrapper Proxies

A small, but often useful, step up from POD types is wrapper proxies. Such types do nothing to address the automatic acquisition or release of resources; they merely make it easier to use the types that they wrap.

Consider that you're working with a source-parser plug-in product, whereby you register a dynamic library (see Chapter 9) that receives notifications from a parsing engine in response to certain events. The entry point might look like Listing 3.1:[1]

Listing 3.1
```
enum SPEvent { . . . };

struct ParseContext
{
// Callback functions
  void *(*pfnAlloc)(size_t cb);
  void (*pfnFree)(void *p);
  void *(*pfnRealloc)(void *p, size_t cb);
  int (*pfnLookupSymbol)( char const *name, char *dest
                        , size_t *pcchDest);
// Data members
  . . .
  char const *currTokBegin;
  char const *currTokEnd;
  . . .
};

int SrcParse_LibEntry(SPEvent event, ParseContext *context);
```

Clearly, dealing with the `ParseContext` structure is going to be messy, as in Listing 3.2.

Listing 3.2
```
// MyPlugIn.cpp

int SrcParse_LibEntry(SPEvent event, ParseContext *context)
{
  switch(event)
```

---

[1]The callback API will most likely be in pure C, for the reasons we discuss in Part Two.

```
  {
    case SPE_PARSE_SYMBOL:
      MyPlugIn_ParseSymbol(context);
  . . .
}


void MyPlugIn_ParseSymbol(ParseContext *context)
{
  size_t  tokLength;
  char    *tokName;
  size_t  cchDest;
  tokLength = 1 + (context->currTokEnd -context->currTokBegin);
  tokName = strncpy( (char*)(*context->pfnAlloc)(sizeof(char)
                 * tokLength), context->currTokBegin, tokLength);
  size_t  cchDest   = 0;

  int  cch = (*context->pfnLookupSymbol)(tokenName, NULL, &cchDest);
  . . .
}
```

Not pretty is it? As well as being a royal pain to deal with all that code, we're messing around with raw pointers in our logic code, and the handling of errors and exceptions is sketchy at best. All these things are what C++ positively excels at, so surely we can improve it.

The answer is that most of the complexity can be easily encapsulated within a wrapper proxy

Listing 3.3

```
class ParseContextWrapper
{
public:
  ParseContextWrapper(ParseContext *context)
    : m_context(context)
  {}

  void *Alloc(size_t cb)
  {
    return (*m_context->pfnAlloc)(cb);
  }

  string CurrentToken()
  {
    return string(m_context->currTokBegin, m_context->currTokEnd);
  }

  string LookupSymbol(string const &token)
  {
    . . .
```

```
  int OnParseSymbol();

private:
  ParseContext *m_context;
};
```

which leads to considerably simpler user code.

Listing 3.4

```
int SrcParse_LibEntry(SPEvent event, ParseContext *context)
{
  try
  {
    ParseContextWrapper        cw(context);

    switch(event)
    {
      case SPE_PARSE_SYMBOL:
        return OnParseSymbol();


    .  .  .
  }
  catch(ParseException &x)
  {
    .  .  .
```

APIs such as this represent the stereotypical wrapper proxy case. `ParseContextWrap-`
`per` does not in any way own the `ParseContext` pointer it is given, it merely enables client
code to work with a simpler, and presumably well-tested, interface over the base API. Note that
I've made the `m_context` member private out of habit; you could arguably leave it public,
since the client code has access to the raw `ParseContext` anyway, but old habits die hard.[2]

3.4   RRID Types

The previous mechanisms are the domain of the C programmer [Lind1994]. Even where we've
used C++ to help us out with wrapper proxies, the encapsulation was an enhancement to usability. When we need to manage the lifetimes of resources, C++ offers programmers better options.

While I was explaining the veneer (see Chapter 21) class `sequence_container_`
`veneer`, which I'll discuss in a moment, to my friend Scott Patterson, he observed that what I
was describing didn't really fit the RAII (see section 3.5) idiom, since there was no acquisitional component to the class—just release upon destruction. He then suggested the derivative
term *Resource Release Is Destruction* (RRID). I like it, if for no better reason than that it is just
as hard to say or to understand as its more complete elder brother.[3]

---

[2]Be thankful I didn't go really paranoid and take a pointer reference in the constructor, and then set the raw pointer to
`NULL`, so nothing else could use it.

[3]Personally, I think they should both change the *Is* to *At*, and they'd make a lot more sense, but they're not my phrases.

Definition: *Resource Release Is Destruction* is a mechanism that takes advantage of
C++'s support for automatic destruction to ensure the deterministic release of resources
associated with an instance of an encapsulating type.

Despite RRID not having an acquisitional component, it can still be most useful. This is because it is the destruction of an object, and the release of its allocated resource(s), that can be
lost in premature or inappropriate exiting of a scope and that we therefore wish to bind into the
compiler's clean-up infrastructure.

```
{
  int device;

  if( . . . ) // Some selection criteria
  {
    device = open(. . .);
  }
  else
  {
    device = socket(. . .);
  }

  . . . // If you return, or throw exception, here then device remains open

  close(device);
}
```

Before an object is constructed there is nothing to lose, so there is no need to automate the
construction.

So RRID types are characterized as providing built-in destruction semantics. However, it's
not just a simple case of omitting all initialization; a destructor acting upon uninitialized data
would exhibit undefined behavior, which means it will mostly likely crash in your first important demo—you know, the one your employer is relying on to bring in the contract that'll keep
the company afloat. No pressure, or anything.

The presence or absence of (default) initialization characterizes the two flavors of RRID
discussed in the following subsections.

3.4.1   Default-Initialized: Lazy Initialization

The default-initialized form of RRID involves setting the resource reference in the encapsulating type to some null value that will result in correct destruction behavior, usually to do nothing at all. The minimal form of a default-initialized RRID type would look like the following:

```
struct DeviceCloser
{
  DeviceCloser() // Default initializtion
    : m_device(NULL)
```

```
  {}
  ~DeviceCloser() // Destruction
  {
    close(m_device); // Close the device handle
  }
  int m_device;
};
```

This can be inserted into the code shown above, and will plug the memory leak. If you wish, you can make `device` a reference to the `DeviceCloser` instance's pointer, to minimize the code changes:

```
{
  DeviceCloser  dc;
  int           *&device = dc.m_file;

  if( . . . ) // Some selection criteria
  {
    device = open(. . .);
  }
  else
  {
    device = socket(. . .);
  }
  . . . // Whatever happens here, the device will be closed
} // Device closed here
```

`DeviceCloser` has a constructor that initializes its `m_device` member to a valid state, but it acquires no resources, so it's not RAII (see section 3.5). (I've made it a `struct` because all members are `public`.)

Naturally, it's preferable to initialize the resource handler in its constructor, but this is not always possible, or convenient at least. Consider the case where we might need to perform some other actions on the conditional branch where we open the device from a socket. These other actions might cause an exception to be thrown. One option is to move all that branch's code out into a separate function which itself will either return the opened socket, or will catch the thrown exception, close the socked handle, and rethrow the exception. But that's not necessarily always preferable.

Classes such as `DeviceCloser` can be useful (generalized in template form, of course), but in the majority of cases we're better served by a higher level of encapsulation, as we'll see shortly.

3.4.2   Uninitialized

The second form of RRID is where there is no initialization performed at all. Naturally this is quite dangerous, so this form is of very limited appeal. Because no initialization is performed, the costs of initialization are avoided. However, this is only valid when the initialization that would be performed in the client code is guaranteed to happen. If it's not, then an execution path that leads to the destructor of the RRID instance before it's been set to a valid state will cause a crash. This is so rarely the case that this technique should have a big red warning sign over it: "Bridge out!" There is only one case where I've ever used it, which I'll describe in Chapter 21, when we look at veneers. In that case it is in the form of the `pod_veneer` template, which takes two policy classes that stipulate initialization and uninitialization semantics for a given parameterization of the template.

Having said all that, there's a twist on this technique when it concerns the layering of another type around an existing type whose resources are well managed. In such cases it is not dangerous at all, and therefore eminently usable.

One thing that has always irked me about the standard library's container classes is that they do not clean up after themselves properly. Actually, I am not being fair; they clean up after themselves perfectly insofar as they correctly control the lifetime of the instances that they manage. The problem is that when the instances that they manage are pointers, they don't do anything with the pointed-to objects, just the pointers, and the destructor for a pointer is the same as it is for any nonclass type: a no-op.

Of course, such a fantastic blend of genericity and efficiency could not account for such special cases, but it is vexing nonetheless. This is especially so when one cannot use certain lifetime-managing classes in the containers. Unless the pointed-to object is of a type that is reference-counted, or can be adapted to be reference-counted,[4] we are left with manipulating the container contents as raw pointers.

Despite the portents, this can actually be fine in many cases, and when explicitly removing elements from a container, it is not too onerous to remember to destroy the element once its pointer has been erased from the container. This can always be simplified with a specific method on the class using the container, as shown in Listing 3.5:

Listing 3.5

```
class Resource;

class ResourceManager
{
  . . .
// Members
private:
  typedef std::vector<Resource*> Resources_t;
  Resources_t m_resources;
};

void ResourceManager::EraseResource(size_t index)
{
  delete m_resources[index];
  m_resources.erase(&m_resources[index]);
}
```

The one issue that is hard to deal with in this manner is the erasure of elements from the container in its destructor, which will leave all still pointed-to elements dangling in hyperspace:

---

[4]The Boost `shared_ptr` can be used to provide nonintrusive reference-counting.

a memory (and who knows what else) leak! To avoid this, the author of `ResourceManager` would have to include the following code in the destructor for that class.

```
void del_Resource(Resource *);

void ResourceManager::~ResourceManager()
{
  std::for_each(m_resources.begin(),m_resources.end(),
              del_Resource);
}
```

This doesn't seem too bad, but this is a trivial example, after all. I've seen examples of this in the real world involving up to ten managing containers within a single class. Putting aside the issue of whether such coding indicates a design problem, this is a maintainer's nightmare, and is virtually guaranteed to end in unhappiness.

The `sequence_container_veneer` is a template that takes as its parameters the container type to be wrapped, and the type of a functor that will be used to clean up the outstanding resources (see Listing 3.6).

Listing 3.6
```
template< typename C
        , typename F
        >
class sequence_container_veneer
  : public C
{
public:
  ~sequence_container_veneer()
  {
    // delete all remaining elements with F()
    std::for_each(begin(), end(), F());
  }
  . . .
};
```

The only method it defines is the destructor; hence it is pure RRID. It relies on its parameterizing sequence type, from which it derives, being correctly constructed itself. A simple change to the design of `ResourceManager` can relieve the maintenance developer from some headache, as shown in Listing 3.7:

Listing 3.7
```
struct RelResource
{
  void operator ()(Resource *r)
  {
    del_Resource(r);
  }
```

```
};

class ResourceManager
{

// Members
private:
    typedef std::vector<Resource*>        Resources_t;
    typedef sequence_container_veneer< Resources_t
                                     , RelResource
                               >
                                       Resource_vec_rrid_t;

    Resource_vec_rrid_t m_resources;
};

void ResourceManager::~ResourceManager()
{
    // Nothing to do now
}
```

Now the container automatically does what you would want in the destructor, saving you from the manual and error prone boilerplate. We've been able to leverage the automatic destruction support provided by C++ of the parameterized `sequence_container_veneer` class to effect desired behavior, rather than having to create a specific class to do our task.

It is important to note that the destruction of the outstanding `Resource` instances is as a result of parameterizing with the `RelResource` type, rather than an artifact of the `sequence_container_veneer` class per se. A useful alternative scenario would be where the `Resource` instance lifetimes are managed elsewhere in the application with `Resource Manager` fulfilling a dispenser function, and a log trace is required when it terminates in order to determine which resources have not been used by the application logic. Indeed, anything you can think of to do with an outstanding `Resource` can be applied during the destruction of `ResourceManager` via the `sequence_container_veneer` template.

Before we finish this topic, I'd like to point out that if you want to use a standard library container to own resources, rather than just refer to them, there are sometimes better approaches than using a component such as `sequence_container_veneer`, depending on your needs. For example, if your objects are reference counted, then you can use a reference-counting class to manage them. Alternatively, you may be able to apply external reference counts to these objects.

3.5   RAII Types

The term *Resource Acquisition Is Initialization* (RAII[5]) is about the best tongue twister in the business, but it is a remarkably simple concept. All it means is that the initialization (via a call to one of the constructors) of an object involves the acquisition of the resource that the object

---

[5]I think the pronunciation of this one is open for debate: "rah-ee," "rye," and "ray" are all recognized, but I go for the full glottis-confronting "R-A-I-I."

will manage. The implicit complement is that the uninitialization (via a call to the destructor) of the object will (automatically) result in the resource being released (see Resource Release Is Destruction).

Definition: *Resource Acquisition Is Initialization* is a mechanism that takes advantage of C++'s support for construction and automatic destruction to ensure the deterministic release of resources associated with an instance of an encapsulating type. It can be thought of as a superset of the RRID mechanism.

It is this mechanism that allows objects to clear up after themselves—actually it's the compiler, the author of the class and, sometimes, the machine itself who do it—rather than you having to do it. This is the essence of the power of C++'s RAII support. However the object comes to be destroyed, its destructor will be called.

Objects allocated on the stack, as automatic variables, are destroyed automatically when they go out of scope. Furthermore, the order of destruction is the reverse of the order of construction. Objects allocated on the heap are destroyed when they are explicitly deleted (via invocation of `delete` or by explicit destruction).

The destruction of automatic variables happens irrespective of the manner in which the scope is exited. This may be because execution has reached the end of the scope, or because a return statement was encountered, or because an exception was thrown, or as a result of a `goto` statement; in all cases the destructors are executed. Clearly this requires a little housekeeping work from the compiler, but this is highly optimized and very efficient. The point is that this guaranteed and deterministic destruction of objects presents an extremely powerful tool, which will feature strongly throughout the book. We'll now look at different flavors of RAII.

3.5.1   Immutable / Mutable

For some RAII types, the resource is acquired in the constructor and released in the destructor, and no manipulations of the encapsulating instance between these two times cause the encapsulation relationship to be altered. This is immutable RAII and is, in my opinion, the best form of resource encapsulation, as it provides the simplest semantics to the writing of such types and to their use, as shown in Listing 3.8.

Listing 3.8

```
template <typename T>
class scoping_ptr
{
public:
  scoping_ptr(T *p)
    : m_ptr(p)
  {}
  ~scoping_ptr()
  {
    delete m_ptr;
  }
  T &operator *();
```

```
  T *operator ->();
private:
  T *const m_ptr;
private:
  scoping_ptr(scoping_ptr<T> const &);
  scoping_ptr &operator =(scoping_ptr<T> const &);
};
```

The resources for the type are allocated and passed to the constructor, and they are uninitialized and deallocated in the destructor. During the rest of the lifetime of the instance, its contents cannot be changed. Note that hiding the copy constructor and copy-assignment operators enforces immutability (see section 2.2); m_ptr is defined to be a constant pointer just as an extra constraint for safety junkies.

Scoping classes (see Chapter 6) are generally immutable RAII types, but the concept is a bit restrictive for most uses one would wish to make of value types.

Conversely a mutable RAII type provides mechanisms so that it can be set to encapsulate another resource, or no resource at all. std::auto_ptr<> is a good example, since it provides a reset() method and assignment operators to change the managed pointer.

```
std::auto_ptr<int>    api(new int(1)); // Manage an int

api.reset(new int(2));   // Manage a new int

api.reset();             // Manage nothing
```

Mutable RAII is very useful, but it does lead to complications in the semantics of such types—an ordered sequence of any number of individual allocate/deallocate cycles within the lifetime of an instance has to be supported. At first glance, this seems like an unnecessary complication, but it is often necessary from a logical point of view. Furthermore, it can be more efficient when the managed resource is expensive to create and/or destroy, and instances of it are often unused.

3.5.2   Internally/Externally Initialized

As we just saw with the auto_ptr and scoping_ptr classes, the resource is created externally, and is passed to the constructor of RAII instance, which then assumes ownership of it. This is external initialization. The converse type is internal initialization, wherein the class is responsible for both resource acquisition and destruction (see Listing 3.9).

Listing 3.9

```
class mem_buffer
{
public:
  mem_buffer(size_t size) // Allocate the buffer
    : m_size(cb)
```

```
      , m_buffer(new byte_t[size])
    {}
    ~mem_buffer()                 // Release the buffer
    {
      delete [] m_buffer;
    }
public:
    operator byte_t *();     // Access the buffer
    size_t size() const;

private:
    size_t  m_size;
    byte_t  *m_buffer;
};
```

3.5.3   RAII Permutations

Naturally the four permutations of mutability and initialization represent different kinds of classes. For example, immutable, internally initialized types represent the purest form of RAII: easiest to code, easiest to understand, and inflexible (which can be a good thing). There's no need to worry about bad initialization values, but the constructor must take account of failure to allocate the resources. Simple utility classes often fall into this category, for example, the `auto_buffer` (see section 32.2).

Immutable, externally initialized types are similarly easy to code and understand, and exchange allocation failure handling for the increase in complexity by having to deal with null, and invalid, resource references. Most scoping classes (see Chapter 6) fit into this category.

The mutable types represent considerable increases in complexity over their immutable brethren. Indeed, in many cases the increase is needless, and represents one of the common ways in which C++ is abused by overeager object-oriented enthusiasts. For now, we can say that such types represent a great deal more flexibility, but have to pay the cost of more complicated implementations, dealing with copy semantics, and having to eschew useful constraints such as `const`/reference members (section 2.2.1). The more powerful your class, the more likely it will fall into this category.

We see examples of all these types of classes throughout the book.

3.6   RAII Coda

There's not much more to say about the fundamentals of the concept of RAII,[6] but there are myriad uses to which it can, and should, be put, some of which are examined in Chapter 6. There are two things I'd like to point out before we leave the subject.

---

[6]There's a lot more to be said about the details, though, such as sub-objects, member initialization, and exception-safety—all of which we'll get to in later parts of this book.

3.6.1   Invariants

The first pertains to class invariants (section 1.3), which feature throughout the book. Simply speaking, an invariant is a condition that must hold true for any instance of a class throughout its lifetime. In C++, the invariants are assessed either through dedicated member functions, or through individual testing, and may result in either an assertion or an exception being thrown.

An invariant should hold from the point at which a constructor is complete, until the point at which the destructor commences. The only times that the invariant may temporarily not hold is during state change in a member function. Hence assessments are done at the end of constructors, the beginning of the destructor, and at the start and end of any member functions, especially non-`const` ones.

The level of resource encapsulation impacts on the efficacy of invariants. If your class fully encapsulates its resources, instances can enforce invariants throughout their lifetimes. The degree to which your class breaks encapsulation corresponds to the degree to which invariants can be applied, which crudely corresponds to the level of confidence you can have in the correctness of your code. RAII classes can apply invariants throughout the lifetime of the instances. RRID classes can only really enforce invariants during the destruction of instances. POD types cannot have invariants, since they don't have access via methods, so there's nowhere to plug in the tests. Actually, this is not entirely fair. Insofar as POD types (open or opaque) are manipulated via API functions, the functions can (and should) test invariants, but it is an incomplete solution, nonetheless.

3.6.2   Error Handling

The last point to make regarding RRID and RAII is that they represent, to a degree, the debate between construction initialization and the dreaded "create function" (see section 6.3.1).

What can be said now is that internally initialized immutable RAII types are appropriate for use in exception-aware environments if the resource allocation can fail. Otherwise, we're in the realm of the nasty create and test idiom (section 6.3.1).

## CHAPTER 4

Data Encapsulation and Value Types

In the last chapter we looked at resource encapsulation as distinct from data encapsulation. Where resource encapsulation is more about mechanism than meaning, data encapsulation can be said to be the opposite (though the distinctions do blur from case to case).

Data encapsulation provides the classic object-oriented encapsulation benefits:

1. Coherence of data. Object instance state can be initialized to a meaningful whole, and subsequent manipulations of the instance via its interface methods are done atomically; the instance will have consistent members before a method is called and after the method call is complete.

2. Reduction of complexity. Client code manipulates a straightforward public interface to the object instances, and does not know of, or care about, the level of internal complexity.

3. Immunity to change. Client code is insulated from changes to the internal implementation of the type, as well as supporting generic techniques operating on several types with similar public interfaces but differing internal representations.

Classes that implement data encapsulation may also implement resource encapsulation— strings are a great example—but the resource encapsulation is the "how" and we're going to focus on the "what" here.

Further to the issue of data encapsulation is the notion of value types. In this chapter we're going to distinguish the difference between value types and entity types and examine in detail what it means to be a value type. We also examine how differing levels of encapsulation affect the definitions of value types.

4.1   A Taxonomy of Data Encapsulation

We saw in the last chapter that there were various levels of resource encapsulation from open structures with API functions to manipulate them through to fully encapsulated classes.

The breakdown of data encapsulation is reflected in C++'s access specifiers. Unencapsulated data, which is defined in a `public` section of a `class` (or the default section of a `struct` or `union`), is accessible to any other context. (Fully) encapsulated data is defined in a `private` or `protected` section of a class type.

With a small set of sample types, it can seem that the level of encapsulation and the degree to which the value type concept is represented are closely related. However, this is not always the case, and there is not necessarily any direct correlation between the two. Naturally, this is just one more permutation to confuse us all, and we should remain mindful of the distinction.

4.2   Value Types and Entity Types

From a simplistic point of view—this is my own definition—we can characterize value types as things that "are," and entity types as things that "do."

Bjarne Stroustrup provides a great definition of value types—he calls them concrete types:[1] "The intent . . . is to do a single . . . small thing well and efficiently. [They do not usually] provide facilities to modify [their] behaviour."

Langer and Kreft [Lang2002] provide more detailed definitions. Value types are "types that have content, and whose behaviour depends vitally on this content. For example, two strings behave differently when they have different content, and they behave in the same way (and compare equal) if they have the same content. Their content is their most important feature." They stress that equality is more important than identity, which I think is a very important aspect of the value type concept.

Langer and Kreft define entity types as those "whose behaviour . . . is largely independent of their content. [Their] behaviour is their most important feature." Comparing equality of entity types is generally meaningless. I confess to liking the simplicity of my own definition (a surprise, to be sure!), but the qualification provided in the Langer-Kreft definition is important.

The notion of an entity type encompasses a great spectrum of characteristics—at the least it covers concrete types, abstract types, and polymorphic and nonpolymorphic types—but in the context of this chapter I'm considering them as one. Many of these concepts are referenced and some elucidated further later in the book.

The remainder of this chapter examines the concept of value types, looking in detail at whether there's a single grade of value type. As is my wont, I'm going to assert that there's not.

4.3   A Taxonomy of Value Types

In [Stro1997] Bjarne Stroustrup defines value semantics, as opposed to pointer semantics, as being the independence of copied entities. This is a great foundation, but we need more, I think.

One of the *Imperfect C++* reviewers, Eugene Gershnik, has a language-independent definition of value types. A type is a value type if:

1. Instances can be created as, or later made to be, copies of another instance.
2. Each instance has a separate identity. Any change to one instance does not result in a change to another.
3. Instances cannot polymorphically substitute or be substituted by instances of another type at run time.

This is an appealing definition, but it is very broad: too broad for my tastes. We'll refine this later in the chapter.

One way to look at value types is whether, and by how much, they behave in sensible ways. For example, what should I expect given the following expressions?

---

[1]To me concrete types are those that are instantiable, in other words complete (you can see the definition) and not abstract (no pure virtual methods left to be filled). Perversely, there are even different definitions of what an abstract type is. Aargh! Brain hurts.

```
String      str1("Original String");
String      str2("Imperfect");
String      str3("C++");
char const  *cs1 = str1.c_str();

str1 = str2 + " " + str3; // 1
if(!str3) { . . . }       // 2
str2.Empty()              // 3
++str;                    // 4
```

I would say that expression 1 would concatenate `str2`, `" "` and `str3`, in that order, placing the result into `str1`, either overwriting, extending, or replacing the storage used to represent `"Original String"` when `str1` was constructed.[2] I would also say that at the point of completion of expression 1 the pointer `cs1` is no longer valid, and cannot be used subsequently without undefined behavior. (Of course, if `String::c_str()` was `temporary` [see section 16.2], this wouldn't be a problem, since the assignment would not be allowed.)

Expression 2 would likely be interpreted to mean if `str3` is "not" then the contents of the block should be executed. Note that what it means to be "not" is up for debate: It may mean no contents, or that the contents contain the empty string `""`, or both. It could even mean that the string contains `"false"`! Such an expression is ambiguous, and ambiguity is the enemy of both correctness and maintainability. Sadly, I've seen this very thing in production code.

The third expression could mean: empty `str2` of its contents. However, it could also mean: return a value indicating whether or not `str2` is empty. Given the choice, I would always go for the former. (Types and variables are nouns; methods and functions are verbs.) Alas the standard library disagrees, and it can be hard to disagree with the standard library.[3] Expression 4 is meaningless. I cannot think of a sensible way in which a string in C++ can be incremented.[4] (See Appendix B to see evidence of a time long, long ago in a galaxy far, far away when this was not the case.)

For built-in types, expected behavior is easy, as it is already prescribed and inviolable. It is our responsibility, therefore, to ensure that our types operate as expected with the operators for which they are defined. If you write an extended-precision integer type whose `operator -=()` performs modulus division, you'll be hunted down. Types intended to be treated as values should, as much as is possible, behave "as the `int`s do" [Meye1996].

In the remainder of the chapter, we investigate what I see as a spectrum of value type concepts. I suggest there are four levels:

1. Open Types: plain structures + API functions
2. Encapsulated Types: partially or fully encapsulated class types, manipulated via methods

---

[2]Although it's convenient, using the + operator for strings is a misuse. Addition is an arithmetic operation, and applying it to character strings is the first step down a long scary road (see Appendix B). Notwithstanding these misgivings, I still sell out my principles for glory in Chapter 25.

[3]With the STLSoft libraries I've had to swallow my principles and go with the flow: lowercase, underscores, `empty()`, etc.

[4]In Perl, and some other scripting languages, a string may be increment by making a best interpretation of it as a numeric type, then incrementing that value, and then converting back to a string. That's fine for Perl, but I don't think that's a good thing for C++ code to be doing.

3. Value Types: fully encapsulated class types, including assignment and (in)equality operators

4. Arithmetic Value Types: for numerics, and includes all arithmetic operators

Depending on your point of view, they are all value types, or only the last two. Whichever way you look at it, however, they're in there because they represent recognized steps in the spectrum and are used in the real world.

4.4   Open Types

4.4.1   POD Open Types

Open types are simple types whose member data are publicly accessible, and usually have no methods at all: aggregate types (C++-98: 8.5.1;1) in other words. Consider the `uinteger64` type:

```
struct uinteger64
{
  uint32_t  lowerVal;
  uint32_t  upperVal;
};
```

This structure is very simple indeed. However, it's not in the least bit usable, and is, therefore, a perfect example of an open value type since such types are, by and large, pretty unusable.

Attempting to use open types as value types is taxing, to say the least. They cannot take part in simple comparison expressions, and manipulating them arithmetically is only possible using manual manipulation of their constituent parts.

```
uinteger64   i1 = . . .;
uinteger64   i2 = . . .;
bool         bLess   = i1 < i2;  // Compiler error!
bool         bEqual  = i1 == i2; // Compiler error!
uinteger64   i3      = i1 + i2;  // Compiler error!
```

We should be grateful that C++ rejects all of these operators by default, since at least that affords us protection at compile time. Doing a memberwise comparison would be very dangerous. It might work in most cases for (in)equality, but how would the compiler know which order to prioritize the member variables in a less than comparison? (Note, however, that for backward compatibility with structs, copy construction and copy assignment [see section 2.2] are accepted by the compiler.)

Despite the serious usability issues, there are times when we have to use types such as this, usually because we're interfacing to an operating system or library API, for example, to get extended precision arithmetic [Hans1997]. For illustrative purposes, we're going to assume that we've got good reasons for proceeding with our 64-bit integer types, and define an API to deal with them.

```
void    UI64_Assign( uinteger64 *lhs, uint32_t higher
                   , uint32_t lower);
```

```
void     UI64_Add( uinteger64 *result, uinteger64 const *lhs
                 , uinteger64 const *rhs);
void     UI64_Divide( uinteger64 *result, uinteger64 const *lhs
                    , uinteger64 const *rhs);
int      UI64_Compare(uinteger64 const *lhs, uinteger64 const *rhs);
#define UI64_IsLessThan(pi1, pi2)     (UI64_Compare(pi1, pi2) < 0)
#define UI64_IsEqual(pi1, pi2)        (0 == UI64_Compare(pi1, pi2))
#define UI64_IsGreaterThan(pi1, pi2)  (0 < UI64_Compare(pi1, pi2))
```

Using the API, the previous code can be implemented legally:

```
uinteger64  i1 = . . .;
uinteger64  i2 = . . .;
bool        bLess  = UI64_IsLessThan(i1, i2);
bool        bEqual = UI64_IsEqual(i1, i2);
uinteger64  i3;


UI64_Add(&i3, &i1, &i2);
```

But it's horrible stuff. Naturally C++ let's us do a lot better than this.

4.4.2   C++ Data Structures

Before we all go rushing to our source databases to convert every `struct` to a `class` in an object-oriented blooding frenzy, it's important to emphasize that the open types we've been talking about so far are those where the individual members together represent some logical whole, and whose independent manipulation therefore represents a manifest risk to the logical condition.

There are also those open types that are quite safely manipulated in this fashion and that cannot be represented as being a danger. The important distinction is whether individual manipulation of the constituent fields leads to a significant breaking of meaning.

Consider the following currency type:

```
struct Currency
{
  int majorUnit; // Dollars, pounds
  int minorUnit; // Cents, pence
};
```

This is a dangerous open type, since it is possible to add a value to the `minorUnit` that will make the logical value of a `Currency` instance invalid. However, the following is an eminently reasonable open type:

```
struct Patron
{
  String    name;
  Currency  wallet;
};
```

The name and wallet fields are not intrinsically linked, and a change to the `name` and/or the `wallet` fields does not result in a prima facie breaking of the logical coherence of a `Patron` type. Such types are referred to as (C++) data structures [Stro1997].

Naturally, there's a gray area in these matters, but the two cases above are both clear-cut: one's black and the other's white.

4.5 Encapsulated Types

POD open value types are fragile types, and their usefulness is limited to circumstances in which using a higher concept is demonstrably damaging to other requirements, such as performance, language-interoperability, or coupling. It is evident that most types are not useful and/or robust until they correspond at least to our next level: the encapsulated type. (Note that this definition can equally be applied to entity types.)

Definition: *Encapsulated types* provide access to, and manipulation of, instance state via a robust public interface, and client code should not, and need not, have access to the internal member state of instances of such types. Encapsulated types provide a notionally complete separation between logical and physical state.

Encapsulated types will generally hide the implementation details to a greater (usually complete) and, importantly, safe degree, and provide methods to safely access the representation of the value. For example, the `uinteger64`'s `lowerVal` and `upperVal` members would be manipulated by `Add()`, `Assign()`, and similar methods on the class. And because methods are used to arbitrate access to, and manipulation of, the instance internal state, class invariants (section 1.3) can be enforced, significantly improving code quality.

Types may also provide additional methods so that client code will not have to hand-code common or expected operations. Unfortunately, this can be an open set of possibilities, even when we are being good citizens and maintaining orthogonality. This can be ameliorated by preferring free functions to class methods wherever possible [Meye2000].

Hence, our `classified` implementation might look like the class `UInteger64` (see Listing 4.1), which aggregates a `uinteger64` as a member variable (so that it may reuse the `UI64_*()` API).

Listing 4.1

```
class UInteger64
{
public:
  UInteger64();
  UInteger64(uint32_t low);
  UInteger64(uint32_t high, uint32_t low);
#ifdef ACMELIB_COMPILER_SUPPORTS_64BIT_INT
  UInteger64(uint64_t low);
#endif /* ACMELIB_COMPILER_SUPPORTS_64BIT_INT */
  UInteger64(UInteger64 const &rhs);

  . . .
```

```
// Comparison
public:
  static bool IsLessThan(UInteger64 const &i1, UInteger64 const &i2);
  static bool IsEqual(UInteger64 const &i1, UInteger64 const &i2);
  static bool IsGreaterThan(UInteger64 const &i1, UInteger64 const &i2);

// Arithmetic operations
public:
  static UInteger64 Multiply(UInteger64 const &i1, UInteger64 const &i2);
  static UInteger64 Divide(UInteger64 const &i1, UInteger64 const &i2);

private:
  uinteger64  m_value;
};
```

4.6   Value Types

From the encapsulated types, it is a small step up to what I would call actual value types. In my opinion, the distinguishing characteristic of a value type is that it is *EqualityComparable* [Aust1999, Muss2001]: it provides meaningful responses, bearing in mind the Langer-Kreft [Lang2002] definition (see section 4.2), to equality and inequality tests. Since the compiler does not provide these operators for class types by default, we need to provide them.

Fundamentally, we need types that do sensible things. The problem with encapsulated types is that they cannot be used in code that makes use of equality comparison. An important use for value types is to be placed in by-value containers, which includes those containers provided by the standard library. Although we can declare and manipulate instances of std::vector <UInteger64>, because it places no restrictions on the uniqueness of the elements it stores, we cannot search for a given type using the standard std::find<>() algorithm:

```
std::vector<UInteger64>   vi;

vi.push_back(i1);
vi.push_back(i2);
vi.push_back(i3);

std::find( vi.begin(), vi.end()
        , UInteger64(1, 2)); // Error! No op == for UInteger64
```

(Remember that std::vector<> maintains unordered sequences, so there's also no ordering comparison, and so no < operator, needed either.)

Converting the type to be a full value type is very simple. Since the previous definition of UInteger64 provided an IsEqual() method, we can implement the (in)equality operators in terms of that, as in:

```
inline bool operator ==(UInteger64 const &i1, UInteger64 const &i2)
{
```

```
    return UInteger64::IsEqual(i1, i2);
}
inline bool operator !=(UInteger64 const &i1, UInteger64 const &i2)
{
    return !operator ==(i1, i2);
}
```

The advantage here is that we've "promoted" the type to be a full value type by the addition of nonmember functions [Meye2000]. Since these functions were previously unavailable, there can be no extant code that depends on their presence (or absence), so we've achieved the enhancement with no maintenance connotations whatsoever. (Author's carp: it is the thoughtless eagerness to push everything into classes that lies behind a great many fat frameworks and C++'s undeserved reputation for inefficiency.)

So, we can now look again at our value-type definition, and propose the following:[5]

Definition: *Value Type*

   Instances cannot polymorphically substitute, or be substituted by, instances of another type at run time.
   Instances can be created as, or later made to be, copies of another instance.
   Each instance has a logically separate identity. Any change to the logical state of one instance does not result in a change to the logical state of another. (Physical state may be shared according to implementation-specific design decisions, so long as such sharing does not invalidate the logical separation.)
   Instances can be (in)equality compared with any other instances, and even with themselves. Equality (and inequality) is reflexive, symmetric, and transitive.

4.7   Arithmetic Value Types

The last step on the ladder is to move on and provide support for other operators, so that our types can participate in natural expressions, such as:

```
uinteger64   i1 = . . .;
uinteger64   i2 = . . .;
bool         bLess   = i1 < i2;   // Ok
bool         bEqual  = i1 == i2;  // Ok
uinteger64   i3      = i1 + i2;   // Ok

i3 %= i1;
i1 = i2 *= i3;
```

The first operator we're going to be concerned with is the less-than operator (operator <()), since it is this that will allow types to be ordered. A type that can enter into a less-than

---

[5]Eugene insists that the *EqualityComparable* aspect is unnecessary, so we can't christen it the Gershnik-Wilson Value Type Definition, however much that might mellifluously trip off the tongue.

comparison is called *LessThanComparable* [Aust1999]; this is an essential characteristic of types that are supported by the STL. Indeed, in the standard, this is the only ordering operator required. I must admit that I've a tendency to stick to using this one exclusively, even when it causes me to write less clear code such as `assert(!(size() < index))`, rather than `assert(index <= size())`; I'm not sure that's to be advised.

Given the definition of `UInteger64`, we can follow the example of the (in)equality operators, and supply this as a nonmember function. Now we can add `UInteger64` instances into a `std::set` or a `std::map`, if we choose.

There are many other arithmetic operators that can potentially be provided. Whether we do so depends on the type. For our `UInteger64` type it is likely that we'd want to provide all of them, +, -, *, /, %, ~, <<, >>, &, |, ^ and all the corresponding assignment operators, because our type is an integer. (We'll look at the best ways to implement such things in Chapter 29.) We see a great example of the provision of free operators in the `true_typedef` template class (section 18.4), where all the arithmetic operators are provided for the class as free functions, and we can do the same for other types.

The important thing is to define only those operators as are appropriate. If we had a currency type we would certainly want to be able to add and subtract two `Currency` instances using the + and − operators, but not be able to multiply them: What is $6.50 × £2.93? Conversely, we'd want to be able to multiply a numeric value and a `Currency` instance together, but not be able to add or subtract them.

Of course, C++ allows you to define any operators for any class types and have them do anything. This is open to considerable abuse (see Appendix B). Indeed, we saw at the start of the chapter that the `String` class had defined the + and ++ operators. Use of + to concatenate strings is wrong[6] since it does not perform an arithmetic sum on its operands. However, this is of such utility that we all, almost to a man, gloss over the immorality and revel in the convenience. (Convenient it may be, but it's not efficient. We'll see how to make it a *lot* more efficient in Chapter 25.)

Despite operator abuse being sanctioned at the highest levels, it is sick and you should not be tempted to do it. I know: I've been bad. Very bad (see Appendix B).

4.8   Value Types Coda

It's interesting to note how this spectrum of value types is analogous to that of the STL iterator concepts. The most difficult iterator concept to emulate in user-defined types is the random access iterator, but it is the one supported by pointers, which are the simplest to implement insofar as the language already does that for us.

Similarly, the most difficult of the value type concepts to emulate is the arithmetic value type, which again is the default value type of the fundamental integral types. We see how powerful C++ is to let us do such things, and how arcane it is that the syntax of the fundamental types is the high-bar of our achievement.

---

[6]This is another of those "contentious" statements that are going to buy me a lot of flak. Just remember that just because something is widely accepted, and even useful, does not necessarily make it right. There're plenty of examples of that in this book.

4.9   Encapsulation Coda

We've now looked at the value type concept from a theoretical perspective, but the question remains as to how such types are to be encapsulated. In instructional texts, we are directed to be good object-oriented citizens and fully encapsulate our types. However, in the real world, things are rarely so clear.

At this time I'll suggest seven possible implementation of the UInteger64 type, only three of which use full encapsulation. In order to select the appropriate form, there are several salient questions we need to ask ourselves:

Do we need to interoperate with, or be implemented in terms of, an underlying C API? If so, we'll want to contain (form 2), or inherit from (form 3), an existing structure, as otherwise we will not be able to pass the appropriate parts of the internal structure of the class to the C API.[7] If we don't, then we can simply contain the basic members (form 1).

Listing 4.2

```
// form #1
class UInteger64
{
    . . . // Value type methods and operators

private:
    uint32_t  lowerVal;
    uint32_t  upperVal;
};


// form #2
class UInteger64
{
    . . . // Value type methods and operators

private:
    uinteger64  m_value;
};


// form #3
class UInteger64
    : private uinteger64
{
    . . . // Value type methods and operators
};
```

Remember that I've deliberately chosen 64-bit integers because I can cheat in the actual implementation by using conversions to and from real 64-bit integers, which are used to realize the actual arithmetic operations. If we wanted to provide integers of arbitrary size layered over C APIs (as in [Hans1997]), we have no choice but to work with C structures.

---

[7]Well, not without a lot of packing pragmas, casting, and other inexcusable hacks. Better to just use the C structure.

Can all operations be encapsulated within the type? If so, then we can probably provide full encapsulation by making the internal implementation `private` (forms 1–3) If not, then we are going to have to leak out some internal state in order to interact with other functions and/or types, although `friendship` (section 2.2.9) can be used with the latter. There are several related questions that determine whether we will need to expose implementation details to the outside world.

Is the type we are creating the "one true type" or rather just one of many? The classic miscreant in this regard is the handling of time. There are `time_t`, `struct tm`, `struct timeval`, `DATE`, `FILETIME`, `SYSTEMTIME`, to name a few. And those are just C time types. If we include C++ classes, the list is potentially limitless. Who's not implemented their own date/time type? If it is one of many, we must consider the need to interact and intercovert with other types.

Do we need to interact with a C-compatible interface? Of course, the ideal answer to this is always no, but unfortunately the real answer is often yes. If we consider a date/time class, we're going to base it on one of the C-types, because to do otherwise would require that we rewrite all the complex, tedious, and error-prone calendar manipulation code. Leap years, Gregorian time, orbital corrections, anyone? No thanks. Given this, how can we be sure we've encapsulated all the necessary functionality?

It is the case that the C++ community as a rule ignores the issues that inform on this particular question, which I personally believe is a great disservice to the development community.[8] Vendors are complicit in this deception, since the more locked-in a developer is to some "really useful class," the less likely he/she is to seek alternatives. And the ramifications of being locked-in can be greater than just preferring one application framework to another. I'm sure we've all known projects that have been locked-in to a particular operating system because the developers were not comfortable, or able, to escape the confines of their application framework. This is a big fat imperfection in C++, which we'll deal with in no small way in Part Two.

It's clear that in many practical circumstances we are forced to use only partial encapsulation. There are several ways of doing this. The simple way is to change the access specifier from `private` to `public` (forms 4–6), but this is, in effect, leaking out everything.

Listing 4.3

```
// form #4
class UInteger64
{
    . . . // Value type methods and operators
public:
    uint32_t   lowerVal;
    uint32_t   upperVal;
};

// form #5
class UInteger64
{
```

---

[8]Indeed, several reviewers for this book frequently complained that I should not be including any examples of C-compatible code in a book ostensibly about C++.

```
    . . . // Value type methods and operators
public:
   uinteger64   m_value;
};


// form #6
class UInteger64
   : public uinteger64
{
    . . . // Value type methods and operators
};
```

There are ways of being a bit more circumspect about how much is given out. An effective, but thoroughly inaesthetic, way is to provide accessor functions.

```
// form #6
class UInteger64
   : private uinteger64
{
    . . . // Value type methods and operators
public:
   uinteger64 &get_uinteger64();
   uinteger64 const &get_uinteger64()const; // Ugly!
};
```

There's another way to make this ugly stuff a bit nicer: explicit_cast, which we examine in more detail in sections 16.4 and 19.5.

Listing 4.4
```
// form #7
class UInteger64
   : private uinteger64
{
    . . . // Value type methods and operators
public:
   operator explicit_cast<uinteger64 &>();
   operator explicit_cast<uinteger64 const &>() const;
};
```

Implicit access to the internals is denied, but explicit access is achievable. The alternative is to add methods to the class for each new feature in the underlying API that you wish to make available to users of the superior class form.

Closely related to this are two final questions, which can further inform on our choices:

Will efficiency concerns require us to break orthogonality? Some desirable operations on our types could be the logical combination of two simpler operations, but combining them into one operation can give significant efficiency benefits. Worse, sometimes this is done simply for convenience. Either way is the first step on the path to fat classes with a woeful number of methods (e.g., std::basic_string<>). The decision here must be on a case-by-case basis, but remember to only put a lot of stall by efficiency for methods that genuinely represent bottlenecks, through extent and/or frequency of use, and based on measurement rather the often fallible (in this regard) instinct.

Are we confident that we can avoid (link-time and compile-time) coupling? Again, this is a much underdiscussed aspect of class design. If the entire implementation of the type can be efficiently expressed in an inline definition then we don't have to worry at all about link-time coupling—the linking to function implementations, either compiled in a separate compilation in the current link-unit, or in external static/dynamic libraries. Either way, we still have to worry about compile-time coupling—the number of other files that must be included in order to compile our class. It's a cruel irony that often the reduction of link-time coupling can increase compile-time coupling.

Unfortunately, avoiding compile-time coupling is hard to achieve, and ironically the more you try for portability, the more compile-time coupling you introduce. This is because you'll have to handle nonstandard types (section 13.2), compiler-features, calling-conventions (Chapter 7), and so on. Such things are sensibly factored out into common, well-tested, header files, which necessarily grow as they mature, in order to centralize architecture/compiler/operating-system/library discrimination.

As you can see, data encapsulation is not a straightforward matter, and, as with so many other issues we examine in this book, the only real solution is to be mindful of all the issues. Your classes need to care about more than just the specific environment in which you create them, and since they're not clever, you have to be.

## CHAPTER 5

Object Access Models

We've talked a lot about what the lifetime of an object means, both in terms of what actions are performed by the compiler on our behalf (with our functions), and in terms of the details of the mechanisms involved. Now I'd like to talk about lifetime issues as they pertain to the relationships between object instances, in particular between container objects and the client code that uses their contained objects. (Note that when I refer to a container in this section, I mean both containers in the standard sense—list, vector, map—and any composite types that "contain" their member variables.)

5.1 Vouched Lifetimes

This is the simplest and most efficient manner in which one object can allow another access to the objects that it contains. Put simply, it is part of the documented semantics of the type that it guarantees that the objects that it contains will not live outside its lifetime. This is obvious in the case of composition, as shown in Listing 5.1.

Listing 5.1

```
class EnvironmentVariable
{
// Accessors
public:
  String const &GetName()const
  {
    return m_name;
  }
  String const *GetValuePart(size_t index) const
  {
    return index < m_valueParts.size() ? &m_valueParts[index] : NULL;
  }
// Members
private:
  String          m_name;
  Vector<String>  m_valueParts;
};
```

This is the most efficient access model, because the caller is given a direct reference (or pointer) to the instance to which it wants access. In the above example, the member variable m_name and a string from the m_valueParts collection are both accessed in the same sense, via vouched lifetime.

However, this model is vulnerable to undefined behavior in situations where the client code maintains and attempts to use a pointer (or reference) that it acquired after the container has ceased to exist. But as long as the client code is written correctly in respect of this constraint, it is a perfectly respectable access model and is one of the most commonly used.

5.1.1   Checkout Model

A twist on the vouched lifetime model, which has a bit more overhead, but helps to ensure that callers behave themselves, is the checkout model. This can aid in the implementation of the container, since it can use the checkout count as a reference count, or as a supplement to any reference counting it may already employ. It can allow exclusive access to the contained instance (either by rejecting subsequent calls, or by blocking), or it can allow the instances to be shared, as appropriate to the situation.

The checkout model works by returning a token to the client code if the requested resource can be accessed and which must be used to "check-in" the resource once it is no longer needed. This is a bit like valet parking: the resource you use is the parking space, and the token is the little slip of paper you receive as a promise that no one's going to go joyriding in your car while you're having your meal. Naturally, something that has been checked out has to be checked in or all will not be right with the world, and of course these checkouts can usually be protected via scoping classes (see Chapter 6), so that the ticket's destructor will ensure the resource is checked in without requiring an explicit call.

Sometimes the accessed value can do double-duty and serve as the token, which can make for a simpler situation all round. The Synesis BufferStore API provides efficient fixed-size fixed-number block containers—useful in multithreaded high-speed network communications systems that efficiently acquire, and optionally share, memory blocks from a preallocated pool. It has a C++ wrapper that looks something like that shown in Listing 5.2.

Listing 5.2

```
class BufferStore
{
// Construction
public:
  BufferStore(Size siBuff, UInt32 initial, UInt32 maximum);
// Operations
public:
  // Acquire one or more buffers
  UInt32 Allocate(PVoid buffers[], UInt32 cBuffers);
  // Share many buffers. Each buffer MUST be already acquired
  UInt32 Share(PCVoid srcBuffers[], PVoid destBuffers[]
            , UInt32 cBuffers);
  // Release one or many buffers
  void Release(PVoid buffers[], UInt32 cBuffers);
  . . .
```

In this case, the buffer pointer values are void*, and also serve as the tokens to return to the store for release, from which they may be subsequently acquired by other client code. Whether you have to check out instances or not, use of the vouched lifetime access model requires the usual mature approach: read the documentation, code in accordance to the documentation, test, level a custard pie at any developer who changes the semantics and not the documentation.

5.2   Copied for Caller

The access model taken by the standard library containers is to give out copies to the caller. Changing our previous Container example to this model would look like Listing 5.3.

Listing 5.3

```
class EnvironmentVariable
{
// Accessors
public:
  String GetName()const
  {
    return m_name;
  }
  String GetValuePart(size_t index) const
  {
    return index < m_valueParts.size() ? m_valueParts[index] : String();
  }
// Members
private:
  String          m_name;
  Vector<String>  m_valueParts;
};
```

This model has some appeal: it's simple to understand and it doesn't have the concerns with respect to the relative lifetimes of the container and the client code. However, returning anything other than fundamental types or simple value types can involve a nontrivial amount of code, with a consequent performance cost.

5.3   Given to Caller

A simple model, where applicable, is to give the instances to the caller. It isn't widely useful, but it does find appeal in some circumstances. An example would be when implementing a container that is seldom traversed more than once, and whose elements occupy a large amount of memory and/or other resources. Maintaining copies in these circumstances is likely to be a wasted effort, so they can just be given to the caller. This model is therefore more efficient than the vouched-lifetimes model (see Listing 5.4).

Listing 5.4

```
class EnvironmentVariable
{
// Accessors
public:

    . . .

  String const *GetValuePart(size_t index) const
  {
    String *item;
    if(index < m_cParts)
    {
      item = m_store.Load(index);
    }
    else
    {
      item = 0;
    }
    return item;
  }
// Members
private:
  int        m_cParts;
  DiskStore m_store;
};
```

5.4   Shared Objects

Where it is suitable, this is my favorite access model and is based around reference counting (see Listing 5.5). The container holds a reference count on the contained items and provides reference-counted pointers to the items upon request.

Listing 5.5

```
class EnvironmentVariable
{
public:
  typedef ref_ptr<RCString>  String_ref_type;
// Accessors
public:

    . . .

  String_ref_type GetValuePart(size_t index)
  {
    return index < m_valueParts.size()
             ? m_valueParts[index]
             : String_ref_type(0);
  }
// Members
private:
```

```
    Vector<String_ref_type> m_valueParts;
};
```

With a suitably competent reference counting smart-pointer class, which we'll assume our notional `ref_ptr` to be, it's ridiculously easy. The semantics of the `ref_ptr` ensure that when copies are taken, the reference count is increased, and when instances are destroyed, the reference count is decreased. When the reference count reaches 0, the `RCString` instance deletes itself.

This does incur a performance cost, which is generally low, but not so low as to be insignificant in very high-performing systems. Herb Sutter reports in [Sutt2002] on the results of performance tests of strings that implement reference counting and copy-on-write, which demonstrate that the reference counting can often end up being a pessimization [Sutt2002]. The scenario I've shown here is a little different, whereby it's the string object itself that is reference counted, so the performance effects may differ, but it's important to be aware of the costs of the different access models.

Despite these caveats, this model is a very powerful technique, and needn't be hindered by performance concerns. I have used a reference-counting scheme on a high-speed data parser that runs on several platforms, and outperforms the previous version by an order of magnitude.[1]

This solution can even work for types that have not been built for reference counting by using a smart pointer type that brings reference-counting logic with it, such as Boost's `shared_ptr`. Furthermore, a reference-counted approach can be used to remove the dependency of a contained object's lifetime on that of its (original) container. For example, consider you have a component that enumerates the contents of the file system. If it uses reference counting for the data objects it uses to represent file-system entries, client code would be able to hold on to these objects for as long as they need them, rather than having to take copies of all particular file attributes they potentially need before the enumerating component is destroyed. This can have substantial cost savings.

---

[1] I must be honest and admit that this was the same system that I mention in section 22.6 whose first version spent 15 percent of CPU on doing nothing due to an "oversight" on my part.

CHAPTER 6

Scoping Classes

In section 3.5 we looked at the definition of *Resource Acquisition Is Initialization* (RAII), and in this chapter we're going to demonstrate some of the different ways in which it can be applied.

RAII is singularly potent when it comes to resource management. We expect that when a `vector<string>` goes out of scope, its destructor is called and it releases its contents. As part of this process, all the contained `string` instances are also destroyed and release their resources, after which the memory block that the vector used to store the `string` instances is released back to the free store. You get all that functionality just by typing a `}`.

The treatment here is pure RAII: a scoping instance acquires a resource in its constructor and faithfully releases it in its destructor. Nevertheless, what is perhaps not widely considered is that the mechanism can support a very wide definition of "resource." In this chapter I hope to demonstrate that RAII is suitable, indeed desirable, to be applied to things other than memory blocks and file-handles. We will see how such resources can include values, states, APIs, and even language features.

6.1 Value

Occasionally we would like to change the value of a variable for a defined period, and then change it back. It can look like this:

```
int     sentinel = . . .;

++sentinel;
. . .   // Do something significant
--sentinel;
```

This can be used to mark a quantum of resource use, or the depth in a recursion, or even the (internal) state of an object. I've seen (and written[1]) code such as the little horror shown in Listing 6.1.

Listing 6.1
```
class DatestampPlugIn
{
  . . .
```

---

[1] My excuse was that it was in an internal development tool, so no one's ever going to see it. We all know that internal development tools never get refined and released to the world, so I'm quite safe, eh?

```
private:
  int m_saveCount;
};


HRESULT DatestampPlugIn::OnSave(. . .)
{
  HRESULT hr;
  if(m_nSaveCount != 0)
  {
    hr = S_OK;
  }
  else
  {
    ++m_nSaveCount;
    . . . // Do something inside the file as its being saved!
    --m_nSaveCount;
  }
  return hr;
}
```

The `OnSave()` handler is used to update the contents of the file while its being saved. In order to do this within the framework of the IDE (integrated development environment) for which `DatestampPlugIn` operates, it has to update the corresponding document's contents and cause a save to be effected again. In order to prevent infinite looping, it uses `m_nSaveCount` as a sentinel to indicate whether the program flow is already within `OnSave()`, in which case the update step is skipped. (This outrageous strategy is caused by the constraints of the IDE and anyone using it should blush while they do so.)

Naturally, neither of these code examples is either exception-safe, or multiple return statement-safe. If the code between the changing of the sentinel variable throws an exception, or executes a return from the function, then all bets are off. Obviously this calls for RAII, plain and simple. Just as obvious is that a template (see Listing 6.2) will do nicely.

Listing 6.2

```
template <typename T>
class IncrementScope
{
public:
  explicit IncrementScope(T &var)
    : m_var(var)
  {
    ++m_var;
  }
  ~IncrementScope()
  {
    --m_var;
  }
private:
```

```
    T &m_var;
};
```

It should seem pretty obvious that you'd want to generalize further and facilitate the functionality that a complimentary `DecrementScope` class would provide by means of policy classes. We'll see how this is done shortly, along with some further refinements and some valid usage scenarios.

You may be thinking that the situation seems a little artificial, and perhaps it does at first glance. However, I had need of just such a facility when implementing a high-throughput multi-threaded network server a couple of years ago. I wanted to be able to monitor a number of characteristics of the server with minimal intrusion into the performance (which was at a high premium), and initially came up with the two classes shown in Listing 6.3.

Listing 6.3

```
class AtomicIncrementScope
{
public:
   AtomicIncrementScope(int *var)
     : m_var(var)
   {
      atomic_inc(&m_var);
   }
   ~AtomicIncrementScope()
   {
      atomic_dec(&m_var);
   }
// Members
private:
   int   *m_var;
   . . .

class AtomicDecrementScope
{
public:
   AtomicDecrementScope(int *var)
     : m_var(var)
   {
      atomic_dec(&m_var);
   }
   ~AtomicDecrementScope()
   {
      atomic_inc(&m_var);
   }
   . . .
```

Using these classes allowed for modification of system counters in a thread-safe and exception-safe manner. Since debugging was impossible, using this technique meant that I could peek into the current values of important system variables from within a lowest-priority thread that woke up once a second, and printed the data into a logging console. This *dramatically* helped with honing the application, since it simplified the morass of threads, sockets, and shared-memory blocks into a manageable set of statistics.[2]

    Naturally, the next time I wanted to use these classes it wasn't in a multithreaded scenario, so that was the appropriate time to derive a more general solution, as shown in Listing 6.4.

Listing 6.4

```
template <typename T>
struct simple_incrementer
{
  void operator () (T &t)
  {
    ++t;
  }
};

template <typename T>
struct simple_decrementer
{
  void operator () (T &t)
  {
    --t;
  }
};

template< typename T
        , typename A = simple_incrementer<T>
        , typename R = simple_decrementer<T>
        >
class increment_scope
{
public:
  explicit increment_scope(T &var)
    : m_var(var)
  {
    A()(m_var);
  }
  ~ increment_scope()
  {
    R()(m_var);
  }
private:
  T &m_var;
  . . .
```

---

[2]And helped me fix some glaring oversights.

Sometimes it's not increment (or decrement) that you're after, it can be distinct value change(s). In this case, our previous template can't be used, however general we make the modifications. But we can easily fulfill our requirements, as shown in Listing 6.5:

Listing 6.5

```
template <typename T>
class ValueScope
{
public:
  template <typename V>
  ValueScope(T &var, V const &set)
    : m_var(var)
    , m_revert(var)
  {
    m_var = set;
  }
  template <typename V1, typename V2>
  ValueScope(T &var, V1 const &set, V2 const &revert)
    : m_var(var)
    , m_revert(revert)
  {
    m_var = set;
  }
  ~ValueScope()
  {
    m_var = m_revert;
  }
private:
  V &m_var;
  V m_revert;
  . . .
```

There are two constructors, so that you can opt to have the managed variable revert to its original value in the destructor, or to be changed to some other value.

An example would be:

```
string s1 = "Original";
cout << "s1: " << s1 << endl; // Prints "s1: Original"
{
  ValueScope<string>  vs(s1, "Temporary");
  cout << "s1: " << s1 << endl; // Prints "s1: Temporary"
}
cout << "s1: " << s1 << endl; // Prints "s1: Original"
```

6.2 State

The safety that comes with scoping classes can be invaluable when acquiring resources that represent program state.

A classic application of this is to scope the acquisition of synchronization objects [Schm2000]. Failure to release an acquired synchronization object has pretty obvious consequences—deadlock, crash, unemployment—so it's as well to make sure you're safe. A simple template definition would be like that shown in Listing 6.6:

Listing 6.6

```
template <typename L>
class LockScope
{
public:
  LockScope(L &l)
    : m_l(l)
  {
    m_l.Lock();
  }
  ~LockScope()
  {
    m_l.Unlock();
  }
protected:
  L &m_l;
};
```

This constrains the lockable type L to have the methods Lock() and Unlock(). Seems a reasonable first assumption, but there're plenty that don't have these method names, so we might generalize further (see Listing 6.7).

Listing 6.7

```
template<typename L>
struct lock_traits
{
public:
  static void lock(L &c)
  {
    lock_instance(c);
  }
  static void unlock(L &c)
  {
    unlock_instance(c);
  }
};

template< typename L
        , typename T = lock_traits<L>
        >
class lock_scope
{
```

```
public:
  lock_scope(L &l)
    : m_l(l)
  {
    T::lock(m_l);
  }
  ~lock_scope()
  {
    T::unlock(m_l);
  }
// Members
private:
  L &m_l;
  . . .
```

For brevity I've skipped a step here, which is a practical measure to cope with the fact that you might want to use the template on types from other namespaces. We could have just provided a degenerate version of lock_traits which would call, presumably, lock() and unlock() methods on the instances to which it was applied. But if we had a lock class in another namespace, we'd have to specialize back into the lock_scope's namespace, and that's a pain (as described in the coverage of Shims in chapter 20). So lock_traits is defined in terms of the functions lock_instance() and unlock_instance(). Rather than specializing, with all the potential junk and effort that goes along with that, you can just define lock_instance() and unlock_instance() along with your class and Koenig lookup[3] (see sections 20.7 and 25.3.3) which will handle the resolution, as can be seen with the thread_mutex class implemented for the Win32 platform (see Listing 6.8).

Listing 6.8

```
class thread_mutex
{
// Construction
public:
  thread_mutex()
  {
    ::InitializeCriticalSection(&m_cs);
  }
  ~thread_mutex()
  {
    ::DeleteCriticalSection(&m_cs);
  }
public:
  void lock()
  {
```

---

[3]This is the mechanism whereby the compiler will lookup a function in the namespace of the instance to which it's being applied, rather than your having to specify it yourself explicitly; think of std::string's free function == and != operators, which are automatically referenced when you compare instances

```
      ::EnterCriticalSection(&m_cs);
  }
  void unlock()
  {
      ::LeaveCriticalSection(&m_cs);
  }
private:
  CRITICAL_SECTION      m_cs;
    . . .


inline void lock_instance(thread_mutex &mx)
{
    mx.lock();
}
inline void unlock_instance(thread_mutex &mx)
{
    mx.unlock();
}
```

Now you can use your own synchronization class with ease.

```
thread_mutex   s_mx;
    . . .
{ // Enter critical region, guarded by s_mx
   lock_scope<thread_mutex>   scope(s_mx);
    . . . // Do your thread-critical stuff here
} // Guard is released here.
```

So that's kind of nice, you say, I can scope critical regions of my code with any synchronization object I choose. However, the flexibility we've built into the model can take us further.

In analyzing the performance of the threaded server I mentioned previously, it transpired that there were some critical regions that were too broad. Where this is the case, and the cost of effecting the exclusion locks is low compared with the cost incurred in contention (as is often the case of intraprocess locks), it can help performance by breaking up the single critical regions into smaller ones. Naturally, this has to be valid from a logical point of view. If you break the coherence of your application, it doesn't really matter how fast it is.

The following monolithic critical region:

```
typedef lock_scope<MX_t>    lock_scope_t;

{ // Enter scope: either a function or an explicit block
   lock_scope_t    scope(m_mx);
    . . . // Costly operation #1
    . . . // thread-neutral operations #1
    . . . // Costly operation #2
    . . . // thread-neutral operations #2
```

```
    . . . // Costly operation #3
} // release here
```

can be broken into the three separate ones (see Listing 6.9):

Listing 6.9
```
typedef lock_scope<MX_t>    lock_scope_t;

{ // Enter scope: either function or explicit block
  lock_scope_t    scope(m_mx);
  . . . // Costly operation #1
} // release here
. . . // thread-neutral operations #1
{ // Enter scope: either function or explicit block
  lock_scope_t    scope(m_mx);
  . . . // Costly operation #2
} // release here
. . . // thread-neutral operations #2
{ // Enter scope: either function or explicit block
  lock_scope_t    scope(m_mx);
  . . . // Costly operation #3
} // release here
```

Danger lurks here, however. First, from a practical point of view it is all too easy for you—or rather, for a colleague, since you've not had chance to document the rationale for your changes and disseminate in triplicate around the development team—to insert code that needs to be protected into the code that lies between the three protected regions. CDIFOC![4]

Second, from a more theoretical point of view, what we are trying to effect is a temporary release of the locking for a defined period, followed by its reacquisition. Well, call me a didactic popinjay, but this sounds a lot like a situation in dire need of some RAII.

The answer is as simple as it is elegant: `lock_invert_traits<>` (see Listing 6.10).

Listing 6.10
```
template<typename L>
struct lock_invert_traits
{
  . . .

// Operations
public:
  static void lock(lock_type &c)
  {
    unlock_instance(c);
  }
  static void unlock(lock_type &c)
```

---
[4]Core Dump In Front Of Client.

```
  {
    lock_instance(c);
  }
};
```

In this class, the locking is inverted by simply swapping the semantics of lock() and unlock(). Now we can change the critical region code back into one, and insert noncritical regions within it (see Listing 6.11).

Listing 6.11

```
typedef lock_scope<MX_t>    lock_scope_t;
typedef lock_scope< MX_t
                 , lock_invert_traits<MX_t>
                 >         unlock_scope_t;

{ // Enter scope: either function or explicit block
  lock_scope_t    scope(m_mx);
  . . . // Costly operation #1
  { // release here
    unlock_scope_t    scope(m_mx);
    . . . // thread-neutral operations #1
  } // Re-enter main scope
  . . . // Costly operation #2
  { // release here
    unlock_scope_t    scope(m_mx);
    . . . // thread-neutral operations #2
  } // Re-enter main scope
  . . . // Costly operation #3
} // release here
```

There are countless other state-scoping classes. We'll see a glimpse of a personal favorite, a current directory scope class, in section 20.1. I've written a few of these in my time, and they're immensely useful. File processing tools use them for descending into subdirectories to process the files there, and then ascending back to the starting position. The scoping is not without issue, however, since current working directory is usually an attribute of the process, rather than the thread, so it is possible for multithreaded use to cause nasties, although this is a function of the program's behavior rather than of the directory scope class. Furthermore, changing directory is something that is ripe for failure as it's all too easy to get an invalid path (user input, changing file-system, etc.). As with most things, consultation of the documentation prior to judicious use is called for.

6.3   APIs and Services

6.3.1   APIs

As we'll see in Chapter 11, the only reliably portable way to use a C-API is to call its initialization function before using any of its facilities, and then to call the uninitialization function after you have finished with it. This has the following form:

```
int main(. . .)
{
  Acme_Init(); // May or may not fail. Must test if it can!
  . . . // The main processing of the application, using Acme API
  Acme_Uninit();
}
```

This is a clear example of the need for RAII. Such APIs often have a reference-counted implementation, such that `Acme_Uninit()` must be called once for each call to `Acme_Init()`.
It is only at that point that the API ensures that any API-specific resources are released. If the
call count is not balanced, then the release will not happen, and the result will be anything from
certain resource leaks to possible process failure.

When dealing with such C-APIs from C++, this balance can usually be achieved in a really
simple way. Where the API initialization function does not have a failure condition, it is trivial,
as shown in Listing 6.12.

Listing 6.12
```
#ifdef _ _cplusplus
extern "C" {
#endif /* _ _cplusplus */

 void Acme_Init(void);
 void Acme_Uninit(void);

#ifdef _ _cplusplus
} /* extern "C" */

class Acme_API_Scope
{
public:
  Acme_API_Scope()
  {
    Acme_Init();
  }
  ~Acme_API_Scope()
  {
    Acme_Uninit();
  }
// Not to be implemented
  . . .
};

#endif /* _ _cplusplus */
```

It's not quite so simple when the initialization function can fail, as is most often the case.
Because some APIs may need to be initialized before other services, including those that support C++ features, it is not always appropriate to throw exceptions. Conversely, an API failure

is indeed an exceptional circumstance [Kern1999], and where supportable it seems more appropriate to have an exception thrown. You can either implement a testable scoping class that implements `operator bool() const` and `operator !() const` or equivalent operators (see chapter 24), or always throws a specific exception. We'll look at the trade-offs between these two approaches now.

If the Acme API initializing function could fail, then you may choose to code the scoping class as shown in Listing 6.13:

Listing 6.13

```
int Acme_Init(void); // Returns 0 if succeeded, non-0 otherwise


class Acme_API_Scope
{
public:
  Acme_API_Scope()
    : m_bInitialised(0 == Acme_Init())
  {}
  ~Acme_API_Scope()
  {
    if(m_bInitialised)
    {
      Acme_Uninit();
    }
  }
public:
  operator bool () const
  {
    return m_bInitialised;
  }
private:
  bool m_bInitialised;
};
```

and use it in the following way:

```
int main(. . .)
{
  Acme_API_Scope  acme_scope;

  if(acme_scope)
  {
    . . . // Do the main business of the program
  }
}
```

This is fine, but it's not hard to imagine how painful it can become when there are many different APIs to initialize. Checking each and every scoping instance leads to a lack of detailed error information:

```
{
  scope_1_t scope_1(. . .);
  scope_2_t scope_2(. . .);
  scope_3_t scope_3(. . .);
  scope_4_t scope_4(. . .);

  if( !scope_1 ||
      !scope_2 ||
      !scope_3 ||
      !scope_4)
  {
    . . . // only a generic "something failed"
```

or tedious and verbose code:

```
{
  scope_1_t scope_1(. . .);
  scope_3_t scope_3(. . .);
  scope_4_t scope_4(. . .);

  if(!scope_1)
  {
    . . . // log/signal error, or terminate, or whatever
  }
  else
  {
    scope_3_t scope_3(. . .);

    if(!scope_2)
    . . . // log/signal error, or terminate, or whatever
    }
    else
    {
      . . . // ad infinitum
```

This can get seriously tiresome, and is close to the canonical form of "good reason to use exceptions." In these circumstances it is much easier to use throwing exception-scoping initializer classes, with the following client-code form:

```
int main(. . .)
{
  try
  {
    scope_1_t scope_1(. . .);
    scope_2_t scope_2(. . .);
    scope_3_t scope_3(. . .);
    scope_4_t scope_4(. . .);
```

```
    . . . // Do the main business of the program
  }
  catch(std::exception &x)
  {
    . . . // Do something with the exception
  }


  . . .
```

However, some APIs have to be set up independently of exception-handling mechanisms, so the given form isn't always achievable and/or desirable. Hence, the third, and probably best, option is to use a policy-based approach, which we'll see in section 19.8.

Whichever way you (have to) play it, using scoping classes for keeping APIs alive for the period that you need increases safety and reduces coding. Do it!

6.3.2   Services

As well as scoping API active lifetimes, scoping classes can be used to temporarily alter API states. For example, Microsoft's C run time library has a debugging API, which can be tuned using the `_CrtSetDbgFlag()` function. Sometimes it is useful to alter the debugging information that the library is providing for a short period, and again this is classic scoping class territory:

```
  {
    . . .
    { // Suspend block release to stress memory system
      CrtDbgScope       scope(_CRTDBG_DELAY_FREE_MEM_DF, 0);
      . . . // Stressful section of code
*   } // return to normal
```

6.4   Language Features

I'm sure you're a bit over scoping classes by now, but I'm going to give you just one last interesting example before we drop the subject.

The C++ language allows you to customize the way in which memory exhaustion is handled, by means of your calling the free function `std::set_new_handler()` (C++-98: 18.4). You pass a function with the signature defined by the type `new_handler`, as follows:

```
typedef void (*new_handler)();
```

`set_new_handler()` returns the currently registered handler, or the null pointer if one wasn't previously registered. When `operator new()` cannot satisfy a request to allocate memory, it calls the new handler if one's been registered, or throws an instance of `std::bad_alloc` otherwise. The new handler function should either succeed in acquiring more memory to satisfy the request, or should throw an instance of `std::bad_alloc`[5] itself.

---

[5]Or a class derived from `std::bad_alloc`.

By specifying your own handlers, you can customize the behavior of the heap in low memory conditions, or provide extended error responses, such as logging the condition (as long as that action does not itself require allocation from the heap, of course).

The problem here is how to make sure our code behaves consistently. For example, if we wish to plug in a new new-handler, how/where/when do we do it? If we do that in main(), it's quite likely that we'll have missed the execution of a fair amount of code—such as the constructors of globals (global, namespace, or class-static objects; see section 11.1)—that saw a different new-handler. Potentially a memory exhaustion condition could occur and result in behavior that we did not intend, and may not be prepared to handle. But how do we ensure that our new-handler gets plugged in before anything happens? And how do we decide which bit of code has the responsibility of setting the new-handler?

Well, the answer involves scoping classes, of course. For example, the Synesis libraries' root header contains code like that shown in Listing 6.14.

Listing 6.14

```
#ifdef __cplusplus

void custom_nh(void); // The customized handler

class NewHandlerInitiator
{
public:
  NewHandlerInitiator()
     : m_oldHandler(set_new_handler(custom_nh))
  {}
  ~NewHandlerInitiator()
  {
     set_new_handler(m_oldHandler);
  }
private:
  new_handler_t    m_oldHandler;
// Not to be implemented
  . . .
};
static NewHandlerInitiator    s_newHandlerInitiator;
  . . .
#endif /* __cplusplus */
```

NewHandlerInitiator is a scoping class that scopes the setting of a new-handler. In the constructor it sets custom_nh() as the new new-handler, and remembers the previous handler in m_oldHandler. In the destructor it does the courteous thing and switches it back.

The significant part of this is the following line, in which a static instance of the class is defined. This causes s_newHandlerInitiator to have internal linkage[6] (C++-98: 3.5.3; and

---

[6]It uses static rather than an anonymous namespace (C++-98: 7.3.1.1) due to its age, and backward compatibility. This is an anachronism, and use of anonymous namespaces should be preferred [Stro1997], as shown in section 11.1.2.

see sections 11.1.2 and 11.2.3), which means that every compilation unit in which this definition appears will see a unique instance of it.

Since this code is in the root header, every C++ compilation unit that uses the Synesis libraries will contain an instance of the `NewHandlerInitiator`. Hence, it doesn't matter which one is linked first (and therefore has any globals constructed first), because the `s_newHandlerInitiator` ensures that the setting of the new-handler is performed. Of course, this doesn't apply to any code that is not created by "us," such as third-party source and/or static libraries. But this doesn't matter, because they're not going to be expecting our special new-handler to activate if they cause memory exhaustion, even if they happen to link first and hence have global/namespace/class-statics constructed before the change of handler.

Of course, all this would be of minor significance if people would avoid globals as we all know that they should, but I leave it to others to write code for an ideal world; we've got to deal with this one.

This technique of declaring static instances in headers is a very powerful technique—open to abuse of course—and we will look at it again in Part Two when we learn just how perilous the use of globals really is.

PART TWO

Surviving the Real World

As is the case with C, C++ leaves the definition of a great many of its features open. In the parlance of the standard (C++-98: 1.3), a conformant implementation may have features that are *implementation-defined*, or are *unspecified*. Both of these terms mean that such features can be implemented as the compiler vendor deems fit and/or the operating environment mandates. The difference between them is that implementation-defined behavior has to be documented, whereas unspecified behavior does not. For the sake of clarity, I'm going to refer to all of this as implementation defined, since there are precious few unspecified things that you genuinely will not care about. Note that this is quite different from *undefined behavior*, which customarily means a nasty crash in full view of management.

In some cases there are valid reasons for the freedom of implementation; in others, the language has failed to adequately address modern techniques. In either case, these issues can cause huge headaches in the real world of C++ programming.

What we will see throughout much of the book are imperfections, techniques, and strategies that largely pertain to individual source files or to individual classes. However, the chapters in this part cover matters that pertain to whole programs, consisting of multiple source files and, potentially, binary components. The programs have to interface with their operating environment in a safe and predictable fashion, and, in some cases, have to be robust in the presence of other processes or threads of execution.

Hence, these chapters address some of the most significant imperfections in C++. It's not that there aren't techniques for dealing with the imperfections—there are—rather, the failure to handle the imperfections can have very serious ramifications, and the techniques themselves can be both difficult to understand and difficult to apply. It is in these areas that critics of the language acquire much of their ammunition.

Although these issues are notionally separate, they all tend to affect each other, so I would recommend that you read the chapters in order, and keep in mind that some issues may not be fully addressed until a later chapter.

We start with a discussion about the lack of a binary standard for C++ component interaction, which places serious constraints on the development of large systems and severely limits the ability to provide reusable software components in C++. Next, the issue of providing polymorphic behavior in a compiler-independent fashion is examined, including a discussion of the object layout strategies taken by several compilers and techniques for obviating these differences.

The use of dynamic linking to build executables for modern operating systems is also not addressed by C++, and complicates the experience of most practitioners. Similarly, multithreading is a big area in which C++ proves to be deficient, and in fact it provides virtually no support for this popular and powerful technique. These two issues form the next two chapters.

Then the issue of static objects is discussed, illustrating the problems encountered when using both local statics and nonlocal statics. Though the two are closely related, there are some significant differences, particularly when one considers multithreading and multimodule development.

After spending time showing things that are seriously wrong with the language, we finish with a bit of informative light relief and a look at optimization; what compilers take away (often without asking).

There are six chapters: Chapter 7, *ABI;* Chapter 8, *Objects across Borders;* Chapter 9, *Dynamic Libraries;* Chapter 10, *Threading;* Chapter 11, *Statics;* and Chapter 12, *Optimization.* Naturally one part of one book cannot hope to provide a complete picture of all the issues involved, but I hope that this will help you be better prepared when you encounter these imperfections in your work.

After Part One, I expect you came out with a warm, happy sensation, seeing C++ in an almost entirely positive light. You'll need to hold on to those feelings as you read this part (and the next), as we'll be giving the old girl a bit of a savaging. Several of the issues highlighted are those where C++ does not generally distinguish itself well with respect to other languages. The upside is that there are practical answers to most of the problems highlighted.

ABI

7.1   Sharing Code

Suppose that you've implemented a library of some useful classes, and want to make it available for other programmers to use. Furthermore, let's say that some of these other programmers are using different operating systems and/or different compilers than the one used to develop the software. How do you do it?

Well, the most obvious solution, although not necessarily the most desirable, is to simply let them have all the source code, and build it themselves. In theory, that should work fine, since all the compilers should be able to deal with your C++ code, right? Unfortunately, as you have probably already experienced, or at least gleaned from this book, the complexity of C++ is such that compilers have their own dialectical differences, and the chances are that your source code will require some nontrivial persuasion to work with other compilers: this is especially so when dealing with very modern techniques, such as template meta-programming (TMP). If your code is to be used on another operating system, it is overwhelmingly likely that you'll need to port it—modify various calls, algorithms, even whole subsystems—to the new platform, so the issue of binary compatibility becomes moot. Let's put these matters aside, however, for the moment, and stipulate that sharing at the source-code level is, in principle, a relatively straightforward concept, even if in reality it is sometimes less so.[1]

The advantages of supplying binary-only are not solely the protection of intellectual property, but also that you retain control of any fixes or updates to the code. The downside is that in order to avail themselves of improvements users need to obtain new copies of the libraries, and relink their projects. Conversely, when you supply source, there is nothing stopping your clients effecting their own fixes or enhancements (or sometimes the opposite). However, unless they take care to apprise you of the fixes and you take care to incorporate them into the future versions, the next time they upgrade your software their fixes will be overwritten and need to be reapplied.

For whatever reason—paranoia, protection of intellectual property, convenience, shame—you don't want to expose the internals of your library to the outside world, and wish to provide it in binary form. In an ideal world, you'd compile your implementation files into a binary library and supply it, along with the appropriate header files, to your clients. They would `#include` the headers in their client code and link to your binary library. What could be simpler?

Alas, this rosy picture does not reflect reality. For it to work there would need to be an agreed representation for the compiled forms and mechanisms of the types, functions, and

---

[1]Reality can be harsh: one of my friend's development teams spent four months porting code that worked correctly on three variants of UNIX to a fourth. Ouch!

classes that are described in your headers. Such a thing is called an *Application Binary Interface*, or ABI, and C++ does not have one!

Imperfection: The C++ standard does not define an ABI, leading to wholesale incompatibilities between many compilers on many platforms.

In recent times there have been moves to standardize ABIs for C++, notably the Itanium C++ ABI [Itan-ABI]. But in general the above imperfection holds.

Since C++ is a compiled-to-machine-code language, there is no requirement to run binaries built for one platform on a different one, so it's more accurate to speak of C++ lacking ABI for specific platforms, that is, combinations of architecture and operating system. In this chapter we're going to look at the issues encountered on the Win32-Intel x86 platform. In some senses Microsoft represents a de facto standard for Windows development, since compilers must, at a minimum, be able to interact with the C functions provided in the Win32 system libraries. But this hardly represents a true ABI, and there are a great many incompatibilities between compiler vendors on this one platform.

For a language as complex as C++, there are many aspects that would have to be standardized to support an ABI. These include object layout (including base classes), calling conventions and name mangling, the virtual function mechanism, static object instantiation, C++ language support (e.g., `set_unexpected()`, `operator new[]()`, and so on), exception handling and run time type information (RTTI; C+-98: 18.5), and template instantiation mechanisms. There are also less obvious issues, such as run time library memory debugging facilities, which are not part of the language per se, but which nevertheless have significant practical impact.

Left without direction or control, different compiler vendors have inevitably come up with different implementations of C++ (and C) run time formats, behavior, and infrastructure; whether the result of a natural diversion, or deliberate commercial tactics, is outside the scope of this book. But whatever the reason is we can say that this is a big problem. A good friend of mine[2] summarizes it thus:

> The biggest fault in C++, for my money, is the lack of a standard for the ABI. As a direct consequence C++ code compiled with GCC won't work with C++ code compiled with MSVC *unless* you provide a 'C' interface (using extern "C" linkage). This forces all C++ providers looking to provide generic, reusable code to use 'C' linkage at some point.

He's right, up to a point. If I provide a binary library built with one compiler, there is a good chance that it will not be compatible with code compiled with another compiler. In other words, I cannot deliver a single binary version of my library; rather I may need to provide versions for all possible compilers used by potential clients.

Naturally, the commercial sway of some compiler vendors has caused there to be some coalescence of compatibility. So it is possible for me to build C++ libraries in, say, CodeWarrior and Intel, and link the binary form into an executable built with Visual C++. But a partial solu-

---

[2]Sadly, he's not much of a friend of C++ anymore, for this and several other important imperfections. *Splitter!*

tion is no solution unless you're prepared to restrict yourself to a single compiler or a small set of compilers.

Until the movements toward unified per-platform ABIs such as the Itanium project become the norm, we are faced with the thorny problem that my erudite friend identifies. This chapter and the next acknowledge the problem, but do not acknowledge the complete defeat that he implies. Let's look at the measures we can take to ease our discomfort.

7.2 C ABI Requirements

Since C++ is an almost complete superset of C, any C++ ABI would encompass a C ABI. A natural first step in examining C++ ABI issues, therefore, is to look at C-specific issues.

C is a much simpler language than C++, in line with the spirit of C (see Prologue). It does not have classes, objects, virtual functions, exception-handling, run time type information, and templates.

However, several of the issues identified above are relevant to C. C has structures, which compilers are free to align according to their own criteria, unless we intervene with our own packing dictates via compiler-specific options and pragmas (see section 8.2).

Even the way functions are called at run time and named at link-time can vary. All functions in C are expressed according to one or more calling conventions which, depending on platform, may or may not be compatible between compilers. Similarly, the names of compiled functions—symbol names—may vary between compilers. It is the case that these two issues are more varied with compilers on the Win32 operating system than, say, UNIX operating systems, which is one of the reasons why I've chosen to focus on Win32 compilers in this chapter. Those of you from exclusively UNIX backgrounds can probably breathe a sigh of relief that the extent of these problems is lessened on your operating system of choice. Hopefully you'll spare a moment to have a care for the poor Win32 programmer trying to achieve C++ (and C) binary interoperability.

Although vastly simpler than those of C++, C does have issues with its language support—such as the reentrant semantics of `atexit()` [Alex2001]—and this means that a C ABI is dependent on common interpretation of such library functionality between compilers.

7.2.1 Structure Layout

The layout issues in C are pretty straightforward to understand. Consider the following structure:

```
struct S
{
  long  l;
  int   i;
  short s;
  char  ch;
};
```

The size of this structure is entirely implementation defined. In practice it depends on a given compiler's packing conventions, which invariably operate on a simple algorithm. If the structure is packed to an alignment of one byte, then the four members will be packed contiguously. Assuming sizes of 8, 4, 2, and 1 byte(s) respectively for `long`, `int`, `short`, and `char`, the size of S will be 15 bytes. However, for a packing alignment of 2 bytes the size will be 16. For an alignment of 4 it will be 24 and for an alignment of 8 or more it will be 32 bytes.

If two compilers use different packing alignments then the binary components that they build will not be binary compatible. In fact, packing alignment can generally be set by a compiler option, so it's quite possible to build different binary components of a single application by a single compiler and still have incompatibilities.

7.2.2   Calling Conventions, Symbol Names, and Object File Formats

Where compilers have, or are persuaded to use, the same structure packing alignment, the next problem comes when linking binary components together. This comes down to two issues: symbol names and calling conventions.

In the early days of C on UNIX [Lind1994], all compilers used the same calling convention, which is known as the C calling convention, whereby arguments are pushed onto the stack right to left, and the caller clears up the stack.[3] More recently, other compilers, especially on the Windows platforms, have provided other conventions, known as `stdcall` (standard call), `pascal`, and `fastcall`, among others. On such environments, the C calling convention is known as `cdecl`. If two compilers are using different calling conventions, then the binary components they generate will not be compatible.

A related issue is that of the names given to symbols in the object files, the binary files produced by compilation corresponding to the compilation units (see Prologue 0.4). Symbol names are the names given to functions and variables with external linkage in object files in order that when the program is linked the various symbols can be located and linked together. Classically, the format is simply to use the function name itself [Kern1999]. Many compiler vendors define their own symbol naming schemes for C++, and this is one factor why C++ compatibility is poor (see section 7.3.3). This is further complicated by the fact that some compilers provide different names for symbols based on the threading model used for a given build.

Finally, object files may have different formats, which is another source of incompatibility on the Win32 platform. Several different formats exist—that is, OML, COFF, and so on—and they are generally incompatible, although most compilers support more than one format.

7.2.3   Static Linking

In practice, some compilers are able to share the same static libraries. Table 7.1 shows the compatibilities in the building and use of simple C static libraries for some popular Win32 compilers. As you can see, there are a few combinations in which compatibility is achieved, but the overall picture is not terribly encouraging. I've generally gone along with the default code generation options for each compiler in gathering this information. There do exist a few additional tailoring measures, but there is certainly no way to ensure full interoperability.

---

[3]This is how variable argument list functions—`int printf(char const *, ...);`—are supported, because the calling context "knows" how many arguments have been passed, whereas the function itself would have no chance in the general case.

Table 7.1 Static linking compatibility (C code) on Win32; # represents a compatible combination.

Compiler Making the Library	Compiler Using the Library					
	Borland	CodeWarrior	Digital Mars	GCC	Intel	Visual C++
Borland	#					
CodeWarrior		#				
Digital Mars			#			
GCC		#		#	#	#
Intel		#		#	#	#
Visual C++		#		#	#	#

Clearly, the lack of an ABI prevents the provision of a single statically linked version of your library, on the Win32 platform; similar incompatibilities exist on other platforms, although the Itanium standardization means that GCC and Intel can cooperate on Linux. There is a prosaic solution to the problem. For each compiler your clients may wish to use, you need to have access to that compiler, or a compatible one, and produce target libraries aimed at it. Thus, you might create `mystuff_gcc.a` (`mystuff_a.lib` for Win32), `mystuff_cw.a` (`mystuff_cw.lib` for Win32), and so on. The practical impediment is that you are unlikely to have access to all the compilers you may need, especially if you want to support several operating systems. Even if you do, it is an odious task to maintain all the makefiles/project files—more like hard labor than software engineering. It may be considered reasonable for small projects, but it's unacceptable for any large project: you can't imagine writing operating systems in this way!

7.2.4 Dynamic Linking

Modern operating systems, and many modern applications, make use of a technique known as dynamic linking, which we look at in detail in Chapter 9. In this case, you link against the library in a similar way, but the code is not copied into the finished executable. Rather, entry points are recorded, and when an executable is loaded by the operating system, the dynamic libraries on which it depends are also loaded and the entry points altered to point into the actual code within the library as it now resides within the new process's address space. On Win32 systems, the creation of a dynamic library is usually accompanied by the generation of a small static library, known as an import library, which contains the code that the application will use to fix up addresses when the dynamic library is loaded. Executables are linked against such import libraries in the same way as they are with normal (static) libraries.

From the library side, the functions that are made available for dynamic linking are known as export functions. Depending on the compilers and/or operating system, all the functions in the library may be exported, or only those that you explicitly mark in some way, for example, selection via mapfile on Solaris or using `__declspec(dllexport)` modifiers for Win32 compilers.

An advantage of dynamic linking is that demands on disk space and operating system working sets are reduced, because there aren't duplicated blocks of code spread throughout sev-

Table 7.2 Dynamic linking compatibility (C code, cdecl) on Win32; # represents a compatible combination.

Compiler Making the Library	Compiler Using the Library					
	Borland	CodeWarrior	Digital Mars	GCC	Intel	Visual C++
Borland	#	#	#	#	#	#
CodeWarrior	#*	#	#	#	#	#
Digital Mars	#*	#	#	#	#	#
GCC	#*	#	#	#	#	#
Intel	#*	#	#	#	#	#
Visual C++	#*	#	#	#	#	#

eral executable files or in several concurrently executing processes [Rich1997]. It also means that bug fixes and enhancements can be deployed without requiring any rebuilds of dependent executables. Indeed, where the libraries are part of the operating system, such updates can be done without the program vendors, or even the users, being aware of it, as a side effect to the installation or update of other software or to the operating system itself.

Naturally, there are downsides to using shared libraries, the so-called "DLL Hell" [Rich2002] whereby updated versions of dynamic libraries can, if they contain bugs, break previously well-functioning (and often essential) programs. The other side of DLL Hell is the all too common problem of fixes to libraries breaking programs that depended on the bugs. Naming no names, you understand. Notwithstanding these very real problems, the advantages generally outweigh such concerns, and it is hard to conceive of a move back to pure static linking.

The impact of dynamic linking on our compatibilities is significant, as can be seen in Table 7.2. Each client program for a given compiler was built against the import library built by that compiler, and the compatibility tested by switching the DLLs with those built using the other compilers and attempting execution.

There is almost perfect compatibility here, apart from using other compilers' libraries by Borland (marked *). This is due to the fact that Borland prefixes any symbols using the C calling convention with a leading underscore in dynamic libraries, as the Win32 convention requires for static linking. Most other Win32 compilers omit them, probably due to the fact that Microsoft's Visual C++ does so. (Working around this with Borland can be a bit of a pain, hence the *. I'll leave it to the reader to delve into this subject. Hint: check out the -u- option, and the IMPLIB and IMPDEF tools.) On UNIX systems these prefix naming issues do not occur.

If you think about it, this full compatibility makes perfect sense. Whether you're on Win32 or on Solaris, you have to be able to interface to dynamic system libraries. If you weren't able to do so, then your compiler would not be able to generate code for that system, and there'd be little point in producing it for that environment.

7.3   C++ ABI Requirements

There are several aspects of C++ that complicate the challenge of a unified ABI far beyond that seen for C. C++ has classes that, although they share much in common with structures, are more complex, since a particular class may have one or more base classes.

C++ provides runtime polymorphism via the virtual function mechanism. Although compilers use a common mechanism—virtual function tables—many of them have mutually incompatible schemes. C++ compilers employ much more complex, and proprietary, symbol-naming schemes, almost rendering it impossible to call a C++ binary component built with one compiler from C++ client code built with another.

On top of the symbol naming issues of C, C++ compilers use name mangling in order to provide for the overloading of functions and the policing of type-safety during linking.

Because C++ supports static objects, the language must support the construction and destruction of global and function-local static objects. We'll see in Chapter 11 that different compilers employ different schemes, resulting in different initialization orders for global objects. Clearly this is another inhibition to a C++ ABI.

C++ also has exception handling, run time type information (RTTI), and various C++ standard language functions, all of which must have the same, or compatible, formats, and the run time behavior must be consistent.

7.3.1   Object Layout

In C++, all the C structure layout issues (see section 7.2.1) still hold, but the matter is much complicated by the layout of inherited classes, templates, and virtual inheritance [Lipp1996]. The layout of inherited classes has much in common with the packing issues that are seen in C with nested structures; virtual inheritance is another of those implementation-defined (C++-98: 9.2;12) issues that adds to this complex picture.

The way in which templates are implemented also has an effect. Sections 12.3 and 12.4 cover aspects in which templates may affect object layout through inheritance.

7.3.2   Virtual Functions

The C++ standard describes the effects of the virtual function mechanism, upon which C++ run time polymorphism is based, but does not prescribe the way in which the mechanism should be implemented. It is the case that all modern commercial compilers use the virtual function table mechanism [Stro1994], whereby an instance of a class defining virtual functions (or which inherits from such a class) contains a hidden pointer—the *vptr*—to a table of function pointers—the *vtable*—which refer to the virtual functions. This commonality gives some cause for optimism, but different vendors employ different conventions. This issue is explored in detail in Chapter 8.

As well as the format of the *vtable*, compilers must also agree on when objects of a given class have *vtable*s, or when they "reuse" those of a base class.

7.3.3   Calling Conventions and Mangling

One of the most obvious of the flies in the ABI soup for C++ is name mangling, which is a must to support one of C++'s fundamental mechanisms: overloading. Consider the code in Listing 7.1.

Listing 7.1

```
class Mangle
{
```

```
public:
  void func(int i);
  void func(char const *);
};

int main()
{
  Mangle  mangle;
  mangle.func(10);
  mangle.func("Hello");
  return 0;
};
```

I've deliberately omitted definitions for `Mangle`'s methods, so that we can sneak a look at the mangling. If you build this with Visual C++ 6.0, you will get no compilation errors, but the linker will report.

```
error: unresolved "void Mangle::func(char const *)" (?func@Mangle@@QAEXPBD@Z)
error: unresolved "void Mangle::func(int)"          (?func@Mangle@@QAEXH@Z)
```

The funny squiggles are there to support overloading. In C, there can only be a single definition of a given function within an executable, so the binary name, known as the symbol name, is given as a simple variant of the function name on a system specific basis. But in C++, functions (free functions, class methods, and instance methods) can be overloaded. If several functions with the same name can be defined, there has to be a way of providing a distinct symbol name to each overload. The same applies to same-named methods in different classes, or within same-named classes within different namespaces. The result is that all compilers perform what is called mangling, a very apt term, since moderately readable function names are mangled into indecipherable spaghetti in order to guarantee uniqueness.

Since C++ piggybacks on top of operating system APIs—which are written for handling C-compatible APIs—for loading symbols, the C++ symbol identifiers need to be converted to a single-name form. Without such a scheme, the linker would not know which overload to link to calls in client code, and the program would not function. It's conceivable that in a complete integrated environment built for C++, the linker would understand overloading and the squiggles would not be necessary. However, there'd still need to be some form of encoding, and you need look no further than the Java Native Interface (JNI) [Lian1999] to see how such things, however "pure" in implementation, are still pretty unreadable. In any case, an integrated C++ operating environment would require a C++ loader, so we're almost in circular argument territory.

But since we've got linkers to handle that, why should we care? Mangling schemes are perfectly reasonable in and of themselves, so what's the problem? It's very simple. Different compiler vendors use different mangling schemes, so it is impractical to dynamically load and call into C++ libraries built by one compiler from code built by another. We see more of this in section 9.1.

7.3.4   Static Linking

If we look now at static linking compatibilities between a simple C++ library and a simple client program, produced with different Win32 compilers,[4] we see (in Table 7.3) that the picture is even bleaker than it is with C.

7.3.5   Dynamic Linking

We've discussed that the problems of clash from mangling schemes in static linking can be avoided by providing compiler-specific variants of our libraries against which clients can build their executables. But this is not a solution for the dynamic linking case. Dynamic libraries are potentially shared at run time between several executables, which may or may not have been built with different compilers. If the symbol names in the dynamic library are mangled with a convention not understood by the compiler used to create another process, that process will not load.

Once again, in practice several Win32 compiler vendors use compatible schemes, including mangling conventions, as can be seen in Table 7.4.[5]

It's clear that there is a greater degree of compatibility with dynamic libraries than is the case with static linking. However, it should be equally clear that there remains a significant degree of incompatibility. This is clear proof that C++ does not have a respectable ABI to speak of on the Win32 platform.

Once again, we might consider producing several dynamic libraries, each with the appropriately mangled names. We could envisage shipping compiler-specific versions of our dynamic libraries: `libmystuff_gcc.so`; `mystuff_cw_dmc_intel_vc.dll`. (We'd still have to make more import libraries, corresponding to the static linking compatibilities shown in the previous section, but that's a minor issue.)

However, there are several problems with this approach. First, it defeats both purposes of DLLs, in that more libraries will be resident on disk and in memory, and updates to the library must be consistently built and installed in all forms. Also, some dynamic libraries act as more

Table 7.3   Static linking compatibility (C++ code) on Win32; # represents a compatible combination.

Compiler Making the Library	Compiler Using the Library					
	Borland	CodeWarrior	Digital Mars	GCC	Intel	Visual C++
Borland	#					
CodeWarrior		#				
Digital Mars			#			
GCC				#		
Intel		#			#	#
Visual C++		#			#	#

---

[4]The Intel compiler now has static C++ linking capability with GCC on Linux.

[5]The Intel compiler now has dynamic C++ linking capability with GCC on Linux.

Table 7.4 Dynamic linking compatibility (C++) on Win32; # represents a compatible combination.

Compiler Making the Library	Borland	CodeWarrior	Digital Mars	GCC	Intel	Visual C++
Borland	#					
CodeWarrior		#	#		#	#
Digital Mars		#	#		#	#
GCC				#		
Intel		#	#		#	#
Visual C++		#	#		#	#

than just code repositories. Dynamic libraries are allowed to contain static data (and we touch more on the ramifications of this in the next chapter), which can act to provide program logic, for example, a custom-memory manager or a socket-pool. If several compiler-specific versions of the same logical library exist, things could get very hairy.

So although it is feasible to get around the dynamic-library C++ ABI problem on a limited scale by supplying multiple compiler-specific dynamic libraries, it is fraught with problems, and I am not aware of any systems that actually do this. It seems pretty clear that to achieve portability within a given operating system we have to stick to C linkage. The significant downside is that this rules out mangled names, so we cannot export/import overloaded functions, or any class methods.

So far, we seem to be agreeing with the portents of doom outlined by my friend. Thankfully there's some help at hand, we just have to get a little retro.

7.4 I Can C Clearly Now

Having looked at static and dynamic linking for both C and C++, it's pretty clear that the only thing that we could reasonably call compiler-independent entails dynamic linking to code with a C interface.

We're now going to look at a way we can have our objects in a compiler-independent fashion, but first we should do a quick recap of C and C++ compatibility.

7.4.1 extern "C"

As a near superset of C, there naturally has to be a way for C++ to interact with C functions. Since C++ mangles every function, in case it is overloaded, there needs to be a mechanism to tell it not to mangle functions that are implemented in C. This is done using extern "C" as in:

```
void cppfunc(int);
extern "C" void cfunc(int);
```

Now you can use cfunc() in your C++ source, and the compiler and linker will ensure that the references will be resolved to an unmangled symbol (e.g., _cfunc). Uses of the C++

function `cppfunc()` will resolve to the symbol `?cppfunc@@YAXH@Z` for Visual C++ compatible compilers/linkers.

Naturally, once a function has been declared to have C linkage, it is illegal to overload it with another of C linkage:

```
void cppfunc(int);
extern "C" void cfunc(int);
extern "C" void cfunc(char);   // Error: "more than one instance of "cfunc" has
"C" linkage"
```

But—and this surprises a lot of interview candidates[6]—you can overload a function declared as `extern "C"` as many times as you like, as long as none of the overloads is also declared `extern "C"`. This can actually be very handy. Consider that you have a set of overloaded C++ functions, of which all but the first are forwarding functions for the user's convenience, as shown in Listing 7.2.

Listing 7.2
```
// ConnApi.h
struct conn_info_t *conn_handle_t;
conn_handle_t CreateConnection( char const *host
                              , char const *source
                              , int flags, unsigned *pid);
conn_handle_t CreateConnection(char const *host, int flags);
conn_handle_t CreateConnection( char const *host, int flags
                              , unsigned *pid);


// ConnApi.cpp
conn_handle_t CreateConnection( char const *host
                              , char const *source
                              , int flags, unsigned *pid)
{
  . .
}
conn_handle_t CreateConnection(char const *host, int flags)
{
  return CreateConnection(host, host, flags, NULL);
}
conn_handle_t CreateConnection(char const *host, int flags
                              , unsigned *pid)
{
  return CreateConnection(host, host, flags, pid);
}
```

In order to house this API in a compiler-agnostic dynamic library, you could simply declare the first variant of the function `extern "C"`, and define the others as overloads within the C++ compilation units only, as shown in Listing 7.3.

---

[6]And a few interviewers, at that!

Listing 7.3

```
// ConnApi.h
struct conn_info_t *conn_handle_t;
#ifdef __cplusplus
extern "C" {
#endif /* __cplusplus */
conn_handle_t CreateConnection( char const *host
                              , char const *source
                              , int flags, unsigned *pid);

#ifdef __cplusplus
} /* extern "C" */

inline conn_handle_t CreateConnection( char const *host
                                     , int flags)
{
  return CreateConnection(host, host, flags, NULL);
}
inline conn_handle_t CreateConnection( char const *host
                                     , int flags
                                     , unsigned *pid)
{
  return CreateConnection(host, host, flags, pid);
}
#endif /* __cplusplus */

// ConnApi.cpp
conn_handle_t CreateConnection(char const *host, char const *source, int flags,
unsigned *pid)
{
  . .

}
```

A nice side effect is that this is now usable by C programmers. Since there are still a lot of them out there, it's nice to be able to increase the potential user-base of your code.

Obviously, this only works when your library is using functions, and where all its types are expressible in C, or at least have an identical layout in all the potential C++ compilers for the given operating system.

Types that are expressible in C essentially mean POD types (see Prologue), which are defined in C++ in order to allow interconvertibility between C and C++. When using C-linkage, one normally tends to restrict one's parameter types to POD types. However, extern "C" really only means "no mangling"; it does not mean "C only." Thus it is quite feasible to define the following:

```
class CppSpecific
{
```

```
    int CppSpecific::*pm;
};
extern "C" void func(CppSpecific const &);
```

Even though it is feasible to build your shared library around C linkage functions that manipulate C++ classes, it is dangerous to do so, because many compilers have different object layout models [Lipp1996], as we'll see in Chapter 12. In practice, it is wise to stick to POD types.

However, that's not the end of the portable C++ story, as we'll see later in this chapter.

7.4.2   Namespaces

When I mentioned earlier that we're not able to portably export overloaded functions or class methods, I didn't mention namespaces. That was not an oversight.

In [Stro1994] Bjarne Stroustrup discusses the restriction of a maximum of one instance of `extern "C"` functions per name in a link unit, irrespective of any namespace context. He describes it as a "compatibility hack," and indeed it is. However, it is a hack we can be thankful for, since it provides us with a degree of flexibility when defining portable functions.

Basically, if an `extern "C"` function is defined within a namespace, the namespace is omitted from the symbol name. Hence the following still has the symbol name `ns_func`:

```
namespace X
{
  extern "C" void ns_func();
}
```

This is how the standard library can place C standard library functions in the `std` namespace without breaking linkage to it from C++ programs.

We can turn this to our advantage, since we can define our portable functions within a namespace to be good C++ citizens, and yet still use them from within C code. However, it's a double-edged sword, since there can only be one binary form of a function with C linkage. In other words, if you're defining portable functions and you link to something that has done the same thing, you will have a linker clash, irrespective of whether you defined your functions in different C++ namespaces.

In practice, I've never encountered this problem, but it's not to be dismissed. It's better to opt for some C-style disambiguation in the form of the API_Function naming convention, for example, `Connection_Create()`.

7.4.3   extern "C++"

A curious converse to `extern "C"`, seldom used, is `extern "C++"`. This declares a function, or a block of functions as being of C++ linkage. Since this is only valid within C++ code, you might wonder when you'd ever have cause to use such a thing.

Consider the following header file:

```
// extern_c.h
#ifdef __cplusplus
```

```
extern "C" {
#endif /* __cplusplus */
  int func1();
  int func2(int p1, int p2, int p3 /* = -1 */);
#ifdef __cplusplus
} /* extern "C" */
  inline int func2(int p1, int p2)
  {
    return func2(p1, p2, -1);
  }
#endif /* __cplusplus */
```

func2() has a third parameter that, when not specified to a meaningful value, should be defaulted to −1. Since C does not support default parameters, the appropriate thing to do is to provide a C++-only overload, which we do by overloading the function for C++ compilation (inside the second #ifdef __cplusplus block).

Now consider another header file, written purely for use by client code:

```
// no_extern_c.h
int func1();
int func2(int p1, int p2, int p3);
```

If this file provides the declarations for files compiled in C, then they will have C linkage, and be unmangled in the object/library file. Using them from within C++ would therefore result in a linker error, as the compiled code would tell the linker to look for mangled names. In order to guard against this, the advice [Stro1994] is to surround the inclusion with extern "C", as in:

```
// cpp_src.cpp
extern "C"
{
#include "no_extern_c.h"
}
int main()
{
  return func2(10, 20, -1);
}
```

Unfortunately, if you do the same with a file such as extern_c.h, you'll be informed that you cannot have a second overload of func2() with C linkage. Hence, it's not good enough to simply declare your C++-only overloads outside the extern "C" block; you also need to enclose them within an extern "C++" block, which tells the compiler to give them C++ linkage (i.e., to use mangling), as in Listing 7.4.

Listing 7.4

```
// extern_c.h
#ifdef __cplusplus
extern "C" {
```

```
#endif /* __cplusplus */
  int func1();
  int func2(int p1, int p2, int p3 /* = -1 */);
#ifdef __cplusplus
  extern "C++"
  {
    inline int func2(int p1, int p2)
    {
      return func2(p1, p2, -1);
    }
  } /* extern "C++" */
} /* extern "C" */
#endif /* __cplusplus */
```

Etiquette requires one to refrain from enclosing any pure C++ headers (sometimes denoted by having .hpp or .hxx extensions, or all those daft no-extension standard library headers). But mixed headers are almost always given the .h extension, and so if you have C++ code in there, you should protect it accordingly. That's the way to write robust headers to be compatible with both C and C++.

There are occasions when you want to declare, and even define, C++ functions in contexts that are going to be surrounded with extern "C" automatically. A good example of this is when using COM IDL. It is not uncommon to define some C++ helper functions, or simple classes, inside the IDL, since in this way the separation between your code and the types and interfaces it uses is minimized. In this case, wrap the code inside a conditionally defined extern "C++" in an order that they will survive the MIDL compiler, which surrounds the entire translations of the interface definitions in extern "C".

There's a related side note I should make before we finish this topic. Several old compilers have problems instantiating template parameterizations made inside functions that are declared extern "C", giving confusing error messages:

```
extern "C" void CreateSomeObject(SomeObject *pp)
{
  *pp = new Concrete<SomeObject>(); // Error: template Concrete cannot be
defined extern "C"
}
```

The simple answer here is to provide forwarding functions:

```
SomeObject *makeSomeObject()
{
  return new Concrete<SomeObject>();
}
extern "C" void CreateSomeObject(SomeObject *pp)
{
  *pp = makeSomeObject();
}
```

7.4.4   Getting a Handle on C++ Classes

Thus far we've got a fair degree of portability, but at a severe sacrifice of C++ expressiveness. Thankfully that's not the end of the story. Few of us want to implement our client code in C. Having the option is nice, as there are plenty of C programmers out there who may want to use our libraries, even if it is written in that inefficient, new-fangled object-oriented stuff. But we want C++ on the client side, if only for our RAII (see section 3.5), so what can we do to make our portable code more C++-friendly?

Well, just as we can deconstruct the public interface of a class behind a C API we can reconstruct it on the client side, in the form of a wrapper class, which conveniently can handle our resource management for us via RAII. Of course, this will rankle the efficiency instincts, but it's often a sacrifice worth making. The wrapper class can also handle the initialization and release of the library, so it can be entirely self-contained.

In some circumstances you can enhance the technique to genuinely, albeit circuitously, export classes. Let's look at one of my favorite classes, the Synesis `BufferStore` class, which is implemented according to the technique I'll be describing. Logically, it has the following form:

```
class BufferStore
{
public:
  BufferStore(size_t cbBuffer, unsigned cBuffers);
  ~BufferStore();
public:
  unsigned Allocate(void **ppBuffers, unsigned cBuffers);
  unsigned Share( void const **ppSrcBuffers
                , void **ppDestBuffers, unsigned cBuffers);
  void Deallocate(void **ppBuffers, unsigned cBuffers);
};
```

It creates a set of shareable buffers, which it can then allocate, deallocate, and share in a highly efficient manner. It's ideal for implementing networking services. It is made portable behind a C API as follows:

```
// MLBfrStr.h
__SYNSOFT_GEN_OPAQUE(HBuffStr); // Generates a unique handle
HBuffStr BufferStore_Create(Size siBuffer, UInt32 cBuffers);
void     BufferStore_Destroy(HBuffStr hbs);
UInt32   BufferStore_Allocate( HBuffStr hbs, PPVoid buffers
                             , UInt32 cRequest);
UInt32   BufferStore_Share( HBuffStr hbs, PPVoid srcBuffers
                          , PPVoid destBuffers, UInt32 cShare);
void     BufferStore_Deallocate( HBuffStr hbs, PPVoid buffers
                               , UInt32 cReturn);

. . .
```

This API is implemented by translating `HBuffStr` handles to pointers to an internal class `BufferStore_`,[7] as in:

```
// In MLBfrStr.cpp
UInt32 BufferStore_Allocate( HBuffStr hbs, PPVoid buffers
                           , UInt32 cAllocate)
{
  BufferStore_ *bs = BufferStore_::HandleToPointer(hbs);
  return bs->Allocate(buffers, cAllocate);
}
```

This is a lot of brain dead boilerplate, and it also has a slight cost in efficiency. But it allows us to implement the class in C++, while maintaining a portable C interface. We can also use it in C++ form, because the header file also contains the code shown in Listing 7.5.

Listing 7.5
```
// MLBfrStr.h
#ifdef __cplusplus
extern "C++" {
#endif /* __cplusplus */

class BufferStore
{
  . . .
  void  Deallocate(PPVoid buffers, UInt32 cReturn)
  {
    BufferStore_Deallocate(m_hbs, buffers, cReturn);
  }
  . . .
private:
  HbuffStr m_hbs;
};

#ifdef __cplusplus
} /* extern "C++" */
#endif /* __cplusplus */
```

Now we have C++ on both sides, communicating across a portable C interface. It's actually the Bridge pattern [Gamm1995], so you can convince yourself that you're being terribly modern if it makes up for the drudge of implementing it.

The cost is a small time penalty due to the indirection of the external class holding a handle to the internal class. However, in the main this technique is reserved for meatier classes, and therefore that small cost is not significant. (I accept that this may be a self-fulfilling prophecy; I

---

[7] It would be better named as `BufferStoreImpl`, but I'm an underscore addict. Don't copy me!

must confess that the ABI issue has percolated a lot of my thinking on C++ over the last decade.)

7.4.5 Implementation-defined Pitfalls

So far, the picture painted is reasonably rosy, but there are still a couple of things that can spoil the party.

First, on some operating systems, there can be different calling conventions. A full discussion of these calling conventions is outside the scope of this book, but it should be clear that if a function has a different binary name, or uses the stack in a different way, that it will break the ABI techniques that we've developed. Therefore, where necessary, the function calling conventions must form part of the ABI specification. Thus, you'd expect to see something like that shown in Listing 7.6.

Listing 7.6
```
// extern_c.h
#ifdef WIN32
# define MY_CALLCONV  __cdecl
#else /* ? operating system */
# define MY_CALLCONV
#endif /* operating system */

#ifdef __cplusplus
extern "C" {
#endif /* __cplusplus */
  int MY_CALLCONV func1();
  int MY_CALLCONV func2(int p1, int p2, int p3 /* = -1 */);
#ifdef __cplusplus
} /* extern "C" */
. . .
#endif /* __cplusplus */
```

A similar situation exists with respect to the sizes of the types used by your ABI functions. You have no guarantee that the sizes of types in one compiler will be the same as those for another. If you use a type, say long, that is interpreted differently by different compilers for the same operating system, you are in trouble. This is where fixed-sized types (see Chapter 13) are very useful, and my policy is to only use fixed-sized types in ABI functions.

In practice, this problem is rare with integral types, but it is very common for compilers to differ with respect to floating-point or character types. For example, there is considerable disagreement between compilers on the size of the long double type. Some (e.g., Borland, Digital Mars, GCC, and Intel) conform to the IEEE 754 standard [Kaha1998] and define it as an 80-bit type, whereas others define it to be 64-bits (and thus the same size as double). In the absence of a guarantee, you are strongly advised to err on the side of caution.

A related problem which you're much more likely to fall foul of is the packing of structures. Since different compilers can have different default packing behaviour, we must explicitly stipulate the packing size for any structures that will be shared across our ABI. As with the calling conventions, this can involve a lot of pre-processor gunk, using common, but non-standard, packing #pragmas, as shown in Listing 7.7.

Listing 7.7

```
#if defined(ACMELIB_COMPILER_IS_ABC)
# pragma packing 1
#elif defined(ACMELIB_COMPILER_IS_IJK)
# pragma pack(push, 1)
#elif . . .
   . . .
struct abi_struct
{
  int   i;
  short s;
  char  ar[5];
};
#if defined(ACMELIB_COMPILER_IS_ABC)
# pragma packing default
#elif defined(ACMELIB_COMPILER_IS_IJK)
# pragma pack(pop)
#elif . . .
```

A good way to get around this, if all compilers are suitably similar in packing semantics, is to define the pushing and popping pragmas in their own include files, which can help maintainability and readability:

```
#include <acmelib_pack_push_1.h>
struct abi_struct
{
  . . .
};
#include <acmelib_pack_pop_1.h>
```

There are certainly a lot of practical problems when trying to get our ABI, but we're imperfect practitioners, and we're not going to lie down in the face of a bit of adversity. In the next chapter we're going to see how we can support more of C++ in a portable fashion.

Objects Across Borders

We've seen how we can get a workable ABI if we restrict ourselves to C functions and how to provide a modest enhancement to this in the provision of overloaded functions for use in C++ compilation units. For all that that seems restrictive, a lot can be achieved with this API-based approach. We've also seen how we can portably emulate non-polymorphic classes by using a handle-based approach.

But we're still not up to passing objects around, and both of these techniques have restrictions on the types that can be manipulated by their functions. Conspicuous by its absence is one of C++'s most important features: run time polymorphism. Can we do better?

8.1   Mostly Portable *vtables*?

Anyone who has done any COM programming is certain to know that polymorphism in a compiler-independent fashion is feasible. Indeed, COM is a language-independent technology, and it's common to write COM components in C++, D, VB,[1] and even C. Doing it in C is the hard way, and can get you extra points in interviews as well as a "very good" for understanding how COM (and C++) works, but in the real world you're better off letting your compiler synthesize your virtual function tables (*vtables*) [Stro1994] if you can.

Without any further preamble, I'll just show you how easy it can be to pass C++ across C ABIs:

```
#define OBJ_CALLCONV  . . . // consistent within each OS

struct IObject
{
  virtual void       OBJ_CALLCONV  SetName(char const *s) = 0;
  virtual char const *OBJ_CALLCONV GetName() const = 0;
};

extern "C" int make_Object(IObject **pp);
```

Let's look at some client code (Listing 8.1):

Listing 8.1
```
int main()
{
```

---

[1]Not that one would choose to use VB, you understand.

```
  IObject  *pObject;

  if(make_Object(&pObject))
  {
    pObject->SetName("Reginald Perrin");
    std::cout << pObject->GetName() << std::endl;
  }
  return 0;
}
```

Dynamic libraries containing an implementation of the factory [Gamm1995, Sutt2000] function `make_Object()` and executables containing `main()` were created for each of our six compilers. In this case there's no need of a compiler comparison table, because all 36 permutations ran perfectly. How's *that* for some C++ ABI?

It would appear that we are able to support runtime polymorphism by using an object via a fully abstract class: an interface. The extension of this is to select different `make_Object()` functions, or to have it return instances of different types dependent on arguments, or other criteria.

8.1.1   *vtable* Layouts

You're probably looking at the code and wondering about the assumptions on which it relies regarding the C++ object-model, and you'd be right to do so. There is no stipulation in the C++ standard as to how a class's *vtable* is accessed with respect to a given instance. This is not a problem, so long as we restrict ourselves to interfaces that contain no member data; whether the pointer to the *vtable* goes at the front or the back is immaterial since it will be the only member.

More significantly, there is no stipulation as to how a class's *vtable* is represented itself. In fact, the standard does not even stipulate that virtual functions are to be implemented using a *vtable*. It's just that all compilers use them. There's nothing stopping some brilliant person inventing a completely different implementation. The issue seems clearer if we look at it expressed in terms of C structure layouts. The equivalent of `IObject` in C might look that shown in Listing 8.2.

Listing 8.2
```
struct IObject;
struct IObjectVTable
{
  void (*SetName)(struct IObject const *obj, char const *s);
  char const *(*GetName)(struct IObject const *obj);
};


struct IObject
{
  struct IObjectVTable *const vtable;
};
```

If you're not experienced with COM, this may look pretty foreign to you, but it's actually quite straightforward. It works because fundamentally a class is just a structure, and if it defines virtual functions (or inherits from one that does), then it contains a hidden member called a *vptr*. The *vptr* is a pointer to a table (usually shared between all instances of the class) that contains pointers to all the class (virtual) member functions, called a *vtable*. In this case, the *vtable* is of type struct IObjectVTable, which contains pointers to the SetName() and GetName() methods. It's like any function pointer table except that the first parameter to all functions is a pointer to the interface structure—the this pointer in C++. The interface structure struct IObject has a single member vtable which points to its *vtable*—an instance of struct IObjectVTable.

As I said, there is perfect adherence among our six Win32 compilers to this layout. It's probably not a coincidence that Win32 compilers support this layout, since that is the layout that COM uses, and no Win32 compiler is going to very popular these days unless it can support COM.

While we can accept that this is certainly an obvious and efficient object layout model, there are compilers that choose to do things differently. One Win32 compiler that does not support this is GCC 2.95 (version 3.2 was used in the tests). A lot of messing around using unprintable techniques reveals that it uses a *vtable* layout like the following:

```
struct IObjectVTable
{
    uint32_t     v1;   /* Always 0 */
    void         *v2;  /* Some unknown function */
    uint32_t     v3;   /* Always 0 */
    void         (*SetName)(struct IObject *, char const *s);
    uint32_t     v4;   /* Always 0 */
    char const   *(*GetName)(struct IObject const *);
};
```

The values of v1, v3, and v4 are zero, so I presume this is a packing issue. v2 appears to be a function whose actual address is very close to that of SetName() and GetName(), but I don't know its precise nature. GCC 2.95 is not the only compiler to differ. Sun's C++ compiler[2] uses a layout along the lines of:

```
struct IObjectVTable
{
    void         *v1; /* Some unknown function */
    void         *v2; /* Some unknown function */
    void         (*SetName)(struct IObject *, char const *s);
    char const   *(*GetName)(struct IObject const *);
};
```

So we have a somewhat unpleasant choice. One option would be to accept this partial solution, at least on Win32, since every modern compiler appears to support it. Working on other platforms might reveal similar uniformities of representation, in which case we could take the same position.

---

[2]Many thanks to Gary here for being my Solaris avatar.

Flummery! We're imperfect practitioners, and this just doesn't cut the mustard. We need to find a complete solution.

8.1.2   Dynamic Manipulation of *vtables*

Before we try to work out our fully portable solution, I want to play the irresponsible host for a moment, and show you some dodgy-but-informative techniques for messing around inside the C++ object layout.

You may be looking at all this stuff in horror, worrying about whether you have to define those C *vtables* yourself. Normally you don't. That's one of the things that the C++ compiler takes care of quite nicely.

It's a very bad thing to go messing around with the *vtables* of any C++ compiler-generated classes, since any changes are likely to be reflected in all instances of that class for the duration of your process, but there's nothing stopping you from manipulating your own *vtables* in C. This can, in *very* rare circumstances, be used to change the nature of objects at run time. It's not something I'd recommend, and it's mainly useful for learning about C++ implementations rather than a technique one would wish to use in production software, but it's good to know how to do it.

Basically, you need three things. First, you have to allocate your own *vtable*. That's done from within C, and is simply a matter of allocating memory to hold the *vtable* contents. Second, you need to copy an existing *vtable* from a valid object. This is done from within C, but on an object created in a C++ compilation unit. Finally, you can change the members of your new *vtable*, and set it onto the object you wish to mess around with. This is done from within C, but it can be done on an object that was created from within a C++ compilation unit. This can all be wrapped up in one function:

```
void AlterObject(Thing *thing)
{
  typedef struct ThingVTable  vtable_t;
  vtable_t *vt  = (vtable_t*)malloc(sizeof(vtable_t));
  *vt           = *thing->vtable;
  vt->Method    = someOtherFunction;
  thing->vtable = vt;
};
```

I'll leave it as an exercise for your coding skills to fill in the error handling and the cleanup of the *vtable*, and an exercise for your judgment to determine whether you'd ever want to do such a thing. I do know of one vendor that uses these techniques to efficiently push dynamic behavior on variant types by switching *vtables* and *vtable* entries, but you didn't hear it from me!

8.2   Portable *vtables*

Okay, that's enough dubious hackery. Let's get back to trying to find a portable *vtable* approach. The problem with the approach developed so far is that there is equivocation on the definition of the members and packing of *vtables* between compilers. This basically renders the technique platform-specific at best, useless at worst, since it is subject to any change in compilers' *vtable* representation schemes.

Fortunately, in one of those Eureka "why-didn't-I-think-of-that-five-years-ago?" moments, I worked out a simple way around this: instead of deducing the format of *most* compilers' *vtable*s and working around that, why not define our own *vtable* format and make *all* compilers work with that? The result doesn't look too much different from what we've already seen, but it works for all compilers for a given platform. I should warn you, though: even though it's conceptually nice, it's not pretty to look at. Consider the fully portable version of our `IObject` interface in Listing 8.3.

Listing 8.3

```
#include <poab/poab.h>
#include <poab/pack_warning_push.h>
#include <poab/pack_push_ambient.h>
struct IObject;
struct IObjectVTable
{
  void (*SetName)(struct IObject *obj, char const *s);
  char const *(*GetName)(struct IObject const *obj);
};
struct IObject
{
  struct IObjectVTable *const vtable;
#ifdef __cplusplus
protected:
  IObject(struct IObjectVTable *vt)
    : vtable(vt)
  {}
  ~IObject()
  {}
public:
  inline void SetName(char const *s)
  {
    assert(NULL != vtable);
    vtable->SetName(this, s);
  }
  inline char const *GetName() const
  {
    assert(NULL != vtable);
    return vtable->GetName(this);
  }
private:
  IObject(IObject const &rhs);
  IObject &operator =(IObject const &rhs);
#endif /* __cplusplus */
};
#include <poab/pack_pop_ambient.h>
#include <poab/pack_warning_pop.h>
```

Irrespective of whether the compilation unit is C or C++, the interface and its *vtable* are defined as C-compatible structures. This is where we gain control over the packing. The formats of the structures are precisely packed via the inclusion of the files `<poab/pack_push_ambient.h>` and `<poab/ pack_pop_ambient.h>`. These files contain compiler-specific packing pragmas, for example, `#pragma pack(4)` for Borland. The two other warning inclusions are there to suppress and re-express some compilers' warnings about including files containing packing pragmas. These warnings are pretty important, so it's unwise to just switch them off wholesale. The solution is to surround such included files with warning suppressions. Naturally, the warning suppressions/expressions cannot be inside the "offending" files, as they would not then operate in the included file.

There are three significant aspects to note. First, the interface is given a protected constructor. Since the C++ compiler will not be setting up our *vtable*, we need to do it ourselves. Naturally, this is something only a derived class can do, so the constructor forces the derived class to provide one. Note that the copy constructor and copy assignment operator are private. You might wonder why we would not provide a copy constructor like the following:

```
IObject(IObject const &rhs)
  : vtable(rhs.vtable)
{}
```

If the instance being copied lived in another module (i.e., a dynamic library) that might be subsequently unloaded during the lifetime of the copy, you could end up with a correctly constructed object that pointed to code that no longer existed in the process address space. Not pretty! This issue of disappearing code is dealt with in more detail in Chapter 9.

Second, the destructor is defined `protected`, to prevent client code from calling `delete` on an instance of the interface. It is also non-`virtual`. Both of these issues are discussed in more detail in section 8.2.6.

Third, as a convenience to C++ client code, there are two inline methods defined on `IObject`. This means that C++ client code can use a normal syntax, as in:

```
IObject *obj = . . .
obj->SetName("Scott Tracy");
```

Since it is usually the case that there is more client code than server implementation in such infrastructures, this is an important boon to usability. This is also important for another reason, which we'll see in the next section.

8.2.1 Simplifying Macros

The downside of this approach is that it's very verbose. *Very* verbose. In a sense, that's just hard luck; you play the cards you're dealt. Nonetheless, a practical objection to this is that it's too verbose to use. Frankly, I think that's a furphy.[3] This stuff is not complex, and easily

---

[3]I'm always attempting to broaden my skills in the language of my adopted country: *furphy* is an Australian word meaning "an absurd or false report, or rumor."

cranked out by a code generator, or a wizard plug-in to your favorite IDDE. There are plenty frameworks out there that require more complex and arcane necromancy than this. Furthermore, all the complexity lies on the server side. On the client side the code looks exactly as it would when using a normal C++ class virtually.

Nonetheless, as an aid to acceptance, you can, if you choose, wrap this all up in macros.[4] I've done an example in the code available on the CD, which looks like:

```
#include "poab_gen.h"

STRUCT_BEGIN(IObject)
  STRUCT_METHOD_1_VOID(IObject, SetName, char const *)
  STRUCT_METHOD_0_CONST(IObject, GetName, char const *)
STRUCT_END(IObject)
```

8.2.2 Compatible Compilers

We know that the *vtable* format we're using reflects that used by some compilers for their *vtable* implementations. For those compilers it is possible to refine the interface definition as:

Listing 8.4
```
#if defined(__cplusplus) && \
    defined(POAB_COMPILER_HAS_COMPATIBLE_VTABLES)
struct IObject
{
  virtual void SetName(char const *s) = 0;
  virtual char const *GetName() const = 0;
};
#else /* ? __cplusplus */
. . .   // The previous definition (Listing 8.3)
#endif /* C++ && portable vtables */
```

When using such a compiler, the interface is a C++ virtual class. When using another compiler, it uses the portable definition. This is the case on client and/or server sides. This can also be encapsulated within the macros.

Now we can see why providing the convenient inlines in our interface is more than just a convenience. It enables client code to be written for compatible and incompatible compilers alike.

8.2.3 Portable Server Objects

We've seen the portable interface and some simple client code. Obviously the bulk of the complexity of this technique is going to lie on the server side, so let's look at just how bad it is. Listing 8.5 shows the first half of the implementation of a class `Object`, which implements the interface `IObject`.

---

[4]It also relies on some funky inclusion recursion, so you might check it out just to amuse yourself with the arcane nature of it all.

Listing 8.5
```
class Object
  : public IObject
{
public:
  virtual void SetName(char const *s)
  {
    m_name = s;
  }
  virtual char const *GetName() const
  {
    return m_name.c_str();
  }
#ifndef POAB_COMPILER_HAS_COMPATIBLE_VTABLES
  . . . // POAB gunk
#endif /* !POAB_COMPILER_HAS_COMPATIBLE_VTABLES */
private:
  std::string m_name;
};
```

For compilers that have a *vtable* layout that is compatible with our portable *vtable* format, that's the entirety of the implementation. Note that SetName() and GetName() are both defined virtual; we'll see why in a moment.

For compilers that require portable *vtable*s we need to use the code between the pre-processor conditionals, which is shown in Listing 8.6.

Listing 8.6
```
#ifndef POAB_COMPILER_HAS_COMPATIBLE_VTABLES
public:
  Object()
    : IObject(GetVTable())
  {}
  Object(Object const &rhs)
    : IObject(GetVTable())
    , m_name(rhs.m_name)
  {}
private:
  static void SetName_(IObject *this_, char const *s)
  {
    static_cast<Object*>(this_)->SetName(s);
  }
  static char const *GetName_(IObject const *this_)
  {
    return static_cast<Object const*>(this_)->GetName();
  }
  static vtable_t *GetVTable()
  {
```

```
      static vtable_t s_vt = MakeVTable();
      return &s_vt;
   }
   static vtable_t MakeVTable()
   {
      vtable_t vt = { SetName_, GetName_ };
      return vt;
   }
#endif /* !POAB_COMPILER_HAS_COMPATIBLE_VTABLES */
```

The first thing to note is that both default constructor and copy constructor initialize the *vtable* member by calling a static method `GetVTable()`. This method contains a local static instance of the `vtable_t` member type, for `Object` it is `IObjectVTable`. The initialization of the static instance is by copying the instance of `vtable_t` returned by another static method `MakeVTable()`. As we'll see in Chapter 11, such local static objects are a pretty bad idea, especially in multithreaded contexts. However, in this case there are no issues, because the pointer returned from `GetVTable()` will always be the same within any link unit (see Chapter 9). Because `SetName_()` and `GetName_()` have fixed addresses within a link-unit, the return value from `MakeVTable()` will always contain the same values. Any way the concurrency works out, therefore, the static *vtable* s_vt will always have the same values; the only side effects from any race conditions will be that it may be initialized more than once, and this will be vanishingly rare.

The virtual methods themselves are actually the static methods `SetName_()` and `GetName_()`. They each take the `this` pointer of the given instance as their first argument, `this_`.[5] It's important to note that this is then downcast to type `Object`. If this were not done, we'd find ourselves in an infinite loop, as they would call the `inline` methods defined in `IObject`.

Let's look now at the reason why the `SetName()` and `GetName()` accessor methods are defined `virtual` in the class. With compatible compilers, which basically inherit from the bona fide C++ abstract class, these methods would be `virtual`, since `Object` would inherit from an `IObject` that would define them as `virtual`. Failure to make them `virtual` for *all* compilers could represent a serious inconsistency, if you are deriving subclasses from `Object`, which are then passed to out to client code via the `IObject` interface. By having them virtual, we can implement the external `virtual` behavior—what the client sees—in terms of internal `virtual` behavior.

The downside is that if the compiler cannot determine whether optimizing out the virtual call of the accessor method into the static method is applicable, we pay the cost of two indirections rather than one. I think that in most cases it's a cost worth paying to get our compiler-independence. If it concerns you, you are free to implement your servers using a compatible compiler, or you can, based on your own judgment, make the accessor methods nonvirtual in which case the efficiency of the method call is identical to that of a normal virtual method.

---

[5] I know, I know. Underscore crazy. Again. (I'm not being very "Chapter 17".)

8.2.4 Simplifying the Implementation of Portable Interfaces

The main problem with the approach so far outlined, as least in my opinion, is the appearance of the infrastructure gunk in the concrete classes implementing the portable interfaces. Thankfully, this is easily rectified by placing it in a related class, which is then used as the base for any concrete class implementations. Hence, we can define a class `IObjectImpl` in the same header file as `IObject`, which contains the functions and *vtable* code that we have placed in `Object`. For compatible compilers, `IObjectImpl` will just be a typedef to `IObject`. Now the whole picture is far more attractive:

Listing 8.7

```
// In IObject.h
struct IObject
{
 . . .
};
#if defined(__cplusplus) && \
    defined(POAB_COMPILER_HAS_COMPATIBLE_VTABLES)
typedef IObject IObjectImpl;
#else /* ? __cplusplus */
 . . . The previous definition (Listing 8.3)
class IObjectImpl
   : public IObject
{
   . . . // function definitions and vtables
};
#endif /* C++ && portable vtables */
```

Now the definition of any derived class is simple and uncluttered by infrastructure, as in:

```
class Object
  : public IObjectImpl
{
public:
  virtual void SetName(char const *s);
  virtual char const *GetName() const;
private:
  std::string m_name;
};
```

Since interfaces are very important things that are designed and implemented with care, and take considerable time, I personally don't think there's an issue with crafting an associated "impl" class, or enhancing your code generator to build one for you, so I think this represents an eminently practical technique.

8.2.5   C Client Code

Just as we saw in the last chapter with the handle (API + wrapper) approach, with the *Objects across Borders* technique we can allow C client code to manipulate our servers. There are a great many C programmers out there, and that picture's not likely to change for a very long time. Thus, anything that broadens the appeal of your libraries can't be a bad thing.

If you're a C++ type of person,[6] it's pretty rare you'd need to call your interfaces from C, although it can happen. You may be enhancing some existing C code, and want to use a particular C++ library.

Whatever the reason, calling your C++ ABI from C is very straightforward, although it's not terse:

```
// C client code
IObject *obj;

obj->vtable->SetName(obj, "Archie Goodwin");
printf("Name: %s\n", obj->vtable->GetName(obj));
```

8.2.6   OAB Constraints

So far I've painted a rosy picture, albeit that it's a non-trivial amount of effort. But before you dash off to take a sharp knife to all your existing projects, I need to confess the several drawbacks to the technique.

Naturally there's a raft of C++ features that are not covered. Since cooperating link-units in your executable may be built with different compilers, any aspects of C++ that are not explicitly covered in the technique are very likely to have different characteristics. For a start, any run time type information (RTTI) mechanism [Lipp1996] will probably be different. The same goes for exception throwing/catching, which relies on the RTTI mechanism. You cannot use `typeid` on a pointer to a portable interface, nor can you throw an exception from a call on a portable interface method.

Non C++-specific constraints regarding resource handling between link-units (discussed in detail in Chapter 9) all apply here. For example, if your interface allocates some memory for the client from its internal heap, say via `operator new`, then it is not valid for the client to delete it. It must be returned via some deallocation method on the same interface or on another object acquired via that interface. This is all standard resource-consumer good citizenship stuff.

The interface does not contain a virtual destructor. There is actually no problem with providing a virtual destructor method in and of itself. To do so in a portable way is eminently simple:

```
struct IObjectVTable
{
  void (*Destructor)(struct IObject *obj);
};
```

---

[6]As I guess most of you are; I can't imagine many "++-ophobes" will have made it through the previous deferential chapters, to get to the C++ bashing herein.

The problem comes when it is used. First, there is no way to provide an "inline" destructor method, so you have no means of calling it from the client side as part of a `delete` statement, except for compatible compilers that are seeing the interface as a C++ abstract class. But this is no bad thing really: We would not want `delete` to be able to be called in any circumstances anyway, because it is unlikely that the client code and the server code would share the same `new`/`delete` operator implementations and a crash would follow. So we don't want a destructor as part of the interface.

A further point is that we don't want a virtual destructor at all, whether client code can access it or not. The reason is that we may want to derive from a given interface,[7] and having a virtual destructor would mean that the layouts for compatible and incompatible compilers would differ. We'd be required to insert a stub field (like those `void*`s in the Solaris *vtable*, from section 8.1.1) in order to keep them aligned.

Speaking of inheritance, you can't have multiple inheritance with this technique. However, that rarely presents a problem, given the other C++ privations one must bear.

There are other issues with the specific example I've used. For instance, the notion of ownership is not specified, but these are merely the result of the simplicity of the example, rather than flaws in the portable *vtable*s technique. The fundamental basis of the technique is sound, and you can use it to build any required level of complexity.

Regarding ownership, there are two approaches generally used. Both use a factory function, such as `make_Object()`. In one, a corresponding `destroy_Object()` function is called to return the instance when it is no longer needed. This is a simple and workable model, but it lends itself more to single-use/large-object scenarios, for example, a compiler plug-in. The other approach is to use reference counting. Generally, this is the best technique to go with the portable *vtable*s.

8.3   ABI/OAB Coda

I'd now like to revisit the imperfection from Chapter 7 and rephrase it. I hope there's no ambiguity in the message from most of this book that C++ is a superb language in many respects, and it is almost always my first choice for the implementation of libraries. But for codifying the interfaces between binary modules, especially between dynamically linked modules, it is just not up to the task.

Imperfection: C++ is not a suitable module-interface language.

It's not possible here to go through the full gamut of problems I've encountered when trying to use mangling across borders, but I am comprehensively convinced through my own experiences, and those of many clients, that C++ is not an appropriate module-interface language. We'll see more ramifications of this in other chapters in this part.

I won't try to pretend for a second that the techniques described are trivial to use. They require a degree of effort, and one must accept serious constraints. I've not gone into them all here because we'll be discussing them in forthcoming chapters as they pertain to other techniques in C++, as well as making an ABI.

---

[7]Yes, that's right. You can also have inheritance in your C++ ABI, albeit that it's only single inheritance.

Nor can I claim that they represent a full ABI by any stretch of the imagination. For example, you cannot use multiple or virtual inheritance, cannot throw exceptions through ABI barriers, or directly delete objects acquired through them. If you're writing code that needs to work only with other code written by the same compiler vendor (and version, as that can often need to remain constant), then you're best off not buying into these techniques.

There are efforts in the industry to support the full range of C++ language facilities [Itan-ABI], but they are neither mature nor broadly applicable. What I have presented is a useful and broadly applicable technique that, although constraining, can be used on a wide variety of existing compilers and operating systems.

But don't let the constraints and complexities make you think that this is nothing but a theoretical solution that couldn't be practically applied; nothing could be further from the truth. Once the infrastructure is set up, using such systems is easy and straightforward.[8]

Indeed, the best example I have of the manifest usefulness for this technique was on a project I worked on a few years ago. I was brought in as a C++ specialist[9] on a project that had a little bit of time pressure. The development lead and I had to take a parsing system developed, over several years, for the U.S. market and apply it to the Australian market, and it had to be ready within a month. After one day on the existing system, we got a serious case of NIH (*Not Invented Here* syndrome), and started on a total rewrite. Three weeks later, we had an extensible parsing architecture, along with several Australia-specific parsing modules, that was working on Win32, Linux and UNIX (DEC Alpha). It was subsequently ported to several other operating systems, including Solaris and VMS. It was faster, and achieved higher levels of input data recognition, than any previous system for the company, and soon became their world standard.

The point of all this is not to regale you with one of my occasional successes but rather to assure you that the *Objects across Borders* approach is very powerful and widely applicable; it is not just useful for COM on Win32.

One last thing: there's no doubt that my perspective on this matter is colored by my own experience and prejudices. I am not a single-language person, and I relish working at the borders between one language and another.[10] I've done a lot of COM in the last decade, and I like many, though by no means all, aspects of that technology. Finally I am not a huge fan of exceptions,[11] and I can't remember the last time I used RTTI, so the absence of these mechanisms from the C++ ABI does not represent much of a loss to me. You will undoubtedly have different experiences, and may well have different views. If that's the case, then I hope that you can at least take from these two chapters a deeper understanding of the C++ object model, and ABI issues in general, even if you do not utilize these techniques in your own work.

---

[8]I've used it to good effect in the Arturius compiler multiplexer (see Appendix C).

[9]A specialist is a euphemism for an expert, and that's always a dangerous thing. I probably know twice as much about C++ now as I did then, and the more I learn the less (I realize) I know. In fact, you should probably put this book down now, and go read some Sutter!

[10]I write a column for *C/C++ User's Journal* called "Positive Integration" which is all about integrating C++ with other languages. (There are some installments included on the CD.)

[11]Don't get me wrong here. Exceptions are the absolute best mechanism for several problems in C++, such as constructor failure, out-of-memory conditions, and deep semantic processing such as parsing. I just think they're much overused in other circumstances.

Dynamic Libraries

In the last chapter we touched on some aspects of dynamic libraries, but the full picture is considerably more complex. There are several areas in the use of dynamic libraries that can catch the unwary and especially affect the use of C++.

Most of the issues discussed in this chapter aren't specific to C++, or even to C/C++, but they *do* have relevance to all our day-to-day development experiences, and also inform on C++ specific issues that are discussed in later chapters.

There are four main problems one encounters when working with dynamic linkage: identity, lifetime, versioning, and resource ownership.

9.1   Calling Functions Explicitly

Before we delve into those three important issues, I want to talk a little more about C++ functions and dynamic linking. This is not something you'd often want to do in the real world, but working it through will inform on several issues we're going to cover, as well as add a little more to the ABI picture.

Operating environments that support dynamic linking generally support the two different-but-related mechanisms of implicit and explicit loading. Your compiler/linker and the operating environment handle implicit loading, and you can basically treat it all as automatic. Essentially, your executable has records placed within it that indicate the symbols it requires and which dynamic libraries they reside within. When the executable is loaded prior to execution all its dependencies are resolved. If any libraries are missing, or if any functions are missing from those libraries, the execution is halted.[1]

With explicit loading, your code issues a system call, for example, dlopen(), requesting that a given library is required. The operating system will then attempt to locate that file using its particular set of rules. For example, on Linux, it looks in the paths listed in the LD_LIBRARY_PATH environment variable, the system library cache, and the system library directories. Win32's LoadLibary() function has a considerably more convoluted algorithm, incorporating the application directory, the current directory, several system paths, and the paths listed in the PATH environment variable; it even involves the registry! [Rich1997] If the library is located and determined to be of a recognized executable format, it is then loaded into the address space of the calling process.

Once the operating system has loaded a library, you need to get access to the functions within. This is done by calling a search function, for example, dlsym(), passing the handle of

---

[1]Actually, some APIs allow for on-demand resolution of symbol fixups, which has the obvious pros and cons.

the library, and a descriptor for the function you want to acquire. Such search functions generally return an opaque type, for example, `void*`, from which you cast to your desired function type. Clearly, it is your responsibility to know the signature of the function you intend to call.

Once you've finished with the function(s) from the library, you can tell the operating system to unload it, for example, by calling `dlclose()`.

9.1.1   Calling C++ Functions Explicitly

The use of explicit loading of dynamic libraries is an area where C++'s piggybacking on C comes into sharp focus. When we wish to load and use a C function (from C or C++), it's really pretty simple (error-handling elided):

Listing 9.1
```
// To call the function
//   char const *find_filename(char const *fileName);
// located in libpathfns.so

void print_filename(char const *fileName)
{
  char const * (*ffn) (char const *);
  void     *hLib = dlopen("libpathfns.so", RTLD_NOW);
  (void*&)(ffn) = dlsym(hLib, "find_filename");
  printf("%s => %s", path, find_filename(fileName));
  dlclose(hLib);
}
```

However, if `find_filename()` was a function with C++ linkage, we'd have to pass its mangled name to the call to `dlsym()`. With GCC on my Linux box, this is `_Z13find_file-namePKc`. Not too memorable, is it?

When you are dealing with class methods, the picture is a bit more complex. Consider the following class:

```
class Thing
{
public:
  void PublicMethod(char const *s);
private:
  void PrivateMethod(char const *s);
};
```

To load and execute `PublicMethod()` you would do something like the following:

```
Thing thing;
void  *lib = dlopen(. . .);
void  *pv = dlsym(lib, "_ZN5Thing12PublicMethodEPKc");
void  (Thing::*pubm)(char const *);
(void*&)pubm = pv;
(thing.*pubm)("Ugly ...");
```

This leaves much to be desired in terms of usability. Since different compilers operate different mangling schemes, we'd have a *lot* of conditional compilation, even if we stayed with one compiler for all link-units in our application.[2] This stuff is altogether too much of a pain to be a workable solution for anything but exceptional cases.

9.1.2 Breaking C++ Access Control

Even though it's almost never the case that you do, let's assume for a moment that you have a good reason to call `Thing`'s private method `PrivateMethod()`. Within the normal bounds of C++ you're pretty much out of luck. You can't do it via a derived class, since it's `private`, rather than `protected`. Moderately sneaky things like taking the address of it won't work either.

```
void (Thing::*pm)(char const*) = &Thing::PrivateMethod; // Error
```

However, if the implementation of `Thing::PrivateMethod` is in a dynamic library, you can call it via explicit loading, as in the following code compiled with Visual C++:

```
Thing      thing;
HINSTANCE lib = LoadLibrary(. . .);
void  *pv = dlsym(lib, " _ZN5Thing13PrivateMethodEPKc");
void (Thing::*prim)(char const *);
(void*&)prim = pv;

(thing.*prim)("Evil ...");
```

This is one of those techniques that you could be keelhauled for using without buy-in from someone higher up the food chain, but it can be a lifesaver if you're working with some truly truculent technology, and you have no way of recompiling its source, or insufficient masochism to do so.

9.2   Indentity: Link Units and Link Space

9.2.1   Link Units

Static libraries are, by definition, incomplete. If they weren't, they'd be executables. This means that there exist some unresolved symbol references in the static library, or that it does not contain an executable entry point conformant to the operating system or virtual machine for which it resides, or both. It's the same for objects (with external linkage): they need only be declared.

---

[2]I know of a chap who spent huge amounts of (his employer's) time and (his own) effort working on a multiplatform library that deduced the mangled names for various mangling schemes, and would, for a given platform, try several known schemes in order to try and locate a symbol. As with all such "good ideas," it had an unceremonious end for the usual reasons: no one had asked for it, no one needed it, and no one was prepared to use something so hideously complex.

By contrast, a dynamic library, like an executable, is complete. There exist no unresolved symbols, save for those that refer to system libraries and/or other dynamic libraries. And any referenced objects must be defined within the link unit.

In the minutiae this distinction is a bit wavy—for example, a dynamic library may not always contain an entry point—but conceptually it is quite clear.

9.2.2   Link Space

The significance of the link unit is more salient when we consider the link space. For the classic standalone executable model, the link space is the combination of all the object files and static libraries. Within the link space there can be only one instance of each symbol and each object (variable with external linkage). Whether we are talking about just plain old C objects, such as arrays, or C++ first-class objects, any static objects in the link unit are resolved when the link unit is built. The same applies to all link units, including dynamic libraries. Within each dynamic library exists one copy of all the functions and objects from which it is comprised.

(Note that I'm glossing over the fine details regarding dependencies of link units on other link units. For example, an executable may depend on a dynamic library, and therefore will not contain within itself the actual functions on which it will rely. However, it will contain information enabling the operating system loader to fix up those dependencies, so it can be thought to be notionally complete. Further, dynamic libraries can export objects as well as functions, and so a link unit may share an object with another by this mechanism. Again, this is a detail that you should be aware of, but that does not detract from the main point about link spaces.)

This notion of multiple copies is crucial to the successful use of dynamic linkage, and it is especially significant for C++ and the use of static objects. Whenever code within a given link-space references an object by name, it references the one within the same link space.

9.2.3   Multiple Identities

Let's consider a simple case to illustrate what this means. A classic example for the use of statics is the instance counter, whereby each constructor of the class increases the instance counter. In that way, you can monitor the total number of instances of your class that were used in the application. But if you have defined the static member within each link unit, you will only get a reading for the number of instances created within the link unit from which you are calling. If you're sharing such classes between link units, this kind of thing does not represent a problem, but if you're not, you need to be aware of it.

Another area in which you can't escape it is where you have inline code (whether class methods or free functions) that contains function-local static objects. In this you most certainly will end up with different instances in different link units, irrespective of any code sharing. We saw an example of this in the last chapter, when synthesizing compiler-independent *vtable*s. In that case, the separate instances per link unit were actually required, but most uses of function-local statics do not require it and some may assume its absence. We'll see more regarding the care required for function-local statics in the remaining chapters of this part.

9.3 Lifetime

The lifetime problem involves things—code and objects—that can disappear while they are still needed. (See Chapter 31 for the comparable problem of *Return Value Lifetime*.)

When using implicit loading, this is usually not a problem. The operating system loader keeps all the libraries on which the link unit depends in process memory until the process terminates. Hence, it is rare for the code for a link unit to disappear before it is needed, and the only time I've experienced this was when a dynamic library was implicitly loaded as a result of a dependent library being explicitly loaded. When the latter was unloaded, references to code in the former were left around in the executable, and when they were called, the process bombed. However, this is still explicit loading, just indirectly.

There is another problem, however, with explicit loading, regarding the issue of the lifetimes of C++ objects. Since objects undergo construction prior to coming into existence, and destruction to remove them from existence, if some code references such an object before it's alive, or after it's dead, undefined behavior results. This is the classic static ordering problem, and does not, in and of itself, pertain to dynamic linking; it's just that dynamic linking can exacerbate it. This issue is important enough to deserve its own treatment (see section 11.2) so we'll not discuss it further here.

When using explicit loading, making ghosts of loaded code is remarkably simple to do. If you are using explicit loading to extract symbols from a dynamic library, you must ensure that you do not cache the function address and later use it after you have released the library. The canonical example looks like:

```
void *lib = dlopen(. . .);
void *pfn = dlsym(lib, ". . .");
dlclose(lib);
((void (*)())pfn)();
```

Naturally, you'd not get this past your peer-programming partner, never mind the thorough code review your manager had scheduled in the time that the considerate senior V.P. of marketing had granted for the project. However, there are subtle ways in which this can come up. Any time you store a pointer to a function in an explicitly loaded library, you need to ensure that the library will not be unloaded prior to any potential call of that function. This is not as easy as it sounds in the real world, so this issue also gets a bigger coverage in the next chapter when we talk about *Thread-Specific Storage*.

By the way, I experienced one gotcha several years ago on a UNIX system—it wasn't Linux—that did not do reference counting on its dlopen()/dlclose(). Our program used dynamic libraries within which one or more plug-ins to the application could reside. The program made independent calls to dlopen() for each registered plug-in and, like a good resource-consumer, made the equivalent number of calls to dlclose(). Alas, the first one of these unloaded the library, and subsequent calls to those functions resulted in undefined behavior. Thankfully this kind of thing is reasonably easy to spot, and not too hard to fix. Given that you're probably abstracting the dynamic library loading behind a platform-independent API, this can be catered for, and that's the solution we used.

9.4   Versioning

The second major sources of dynamic linking problems come about as a result of version changes. Some of these are obvious, others much less so, but they can all end up breaking your executables, and others if you're really unlucky.

In bad cases, changes you've made can leave you in the situation whereby you need an older version of a given dynamic library for some of the applications on a system and a new version for some of the other. This is "DLL Hell" [Rich2002].

9.4.1   Lost Functions

The first, and perhaps most obvious, versioning problem is where a newer version of a dynamic library is deployed with a missing function from a prior version. In this case, any dependent link units will not load, and your executable will not load. The simple solution is to never remove any functions from your dynamic libraries, and operating systems mandate this as part of their ABIs.

Some vendors take a more detailed approach, and assign APIs stability levels, which indicate to developers how the API will evolve, or not, in future versions. The developers use this information to inform on their use of the APIs and plan strategies for evolution of their software consistent with that of the vendors.

9.4.2   Changed Signatures

When using C linkage, the symbols in dynamic libraries contain no information as to the function's arguments. This applies both to C code and to C++ code using `extern "C"`. The danger here is that if the function's signature is changed, the client code in any dependent link units will still be linked to the new form of the function at load time, with the obvious consequences to the robustness of your executable and the gloss on your resume. With mangling, this does not happen, since a different function signature results in a different mangled name.

Naturally, one of the main principles of a good software engineer is to avoid changing the signature of functions that have been "released," that is, where client code may exist that is outside the control of the programming team effecting the change. In practice, once you've been through a release cycle, you should refrain from changing functions even when you're "sure," since surety is an ephemeral notion in computing. If you need to provide a function with changed semantics, add a new one and deprecate, but do not remove, the old one.

There's another aspect of this that's worth highlighting. On most systems, the load-time fixing up for dynamic library imports and exports is done based on names. On Win32, however, exported symbols can either be represented in the export table via their name or an ordinal number. Using ordinals can make your dynamic libraries smaller, and it can also be used to hide function names from overeager reverse engineers. The downside is that client link units rely on the ordinal for a given function being immutable. Removing the ordinal from a Win32 DLL almost guarantees that client executables will not load. Reusing an ordinal for a new function will simply mean that caller and callee are expecting different things, and you'll have a nasty crash. As reported in [Rich1997], Microsoft favors export by function name, and the Win32 system DLLs mostly follow this convention.

There's one nice, but perverse, use of ordinals, which is that it does allow you to rename APIs without breaking client code, as long as the function signatures stay the same. However, doing this without taking a misstep can be tricky, so I wouldn't recommend it.

9.4.3   Behavioral Changes

The most significant part of all software engineering activity is maintenance [Glas2003], and you will inevitably have to modify the behavior of existing functions. These changes can be bug fixes, or can be semantic enhancements. When making enhancements, you must retain backward compatibility. This is often only achievable if you've planned for forward compatibility in the original design. For example, you may provide flags for one of the parameters that stipulate what behavior you want from the function. In that case, you can enhance the function by adding new flags.

In principle, you are free to change any behavior of your software that is not defined in its published interface documentation. However, in practice, you still have to be careful. Even if you're fixing a bug, sometimes you need to be aware that some client code may be dependent on the buggy behavior. For example, you may have a function that writes some data into a caller-supplied buffer. The first version always fills out the remaining part of the buffer with 0s. This is not part of the original design, and no client code had a problem with it, initially. Eventually, you come across a requirement that needs the unused remainder to be left intact. Unfortunately, there are now client applications that have been written to rely on the 0 padding.

Your actions in these cases will depend on real-world factors, no doubt factoring in issues of the number of clients, your support resources, and so on and so forth. For example, operating system vendors, with huge user bases, usually opt to preserve such undocumented "features" because of the likely hit to their business. In this case, the only option is to introduce a new function with the correct semantics, and leave the old one around for old client link units.

9.4.4   Constants

If you've got an enum, or a set of flags, for a dynamic library function, it's obvious that you must not change any of the values of the enum members or the flags, or you run the risk of breaking extant clients. However, where you have a constant—whether #define, const, or a class member constant—things can be a bit trickier. Any changes to the constant will only be reflected in code compiled and deployed after the constant has been changed.

One way around this is to define the constant in a function in a core library, and all the dependent libraries call that function to elicit the constant at run time. Obviously this will only work for values that do not need to be evaluated at compile time.

The C++ version of this is to declare a class constant and to define it within one library. To affect the behavior in all dependent libraries, one need only ship an updated version of the core library. Naturally, the dependent libraries must have been written to be able to work with different values of the constant, and your testing infrastructure must exercise this.

9.5   Resource Ownership

Good resource consumers should always return a resource whence it came. In general, if fn1() in link unit A allocates a resource, and returns it to its caller fn2() in link unit B, then fn2()

should return that resource to a function in link unit A. If it does not, then it is likely that the program will fail.

This issue is of particular importance when dealing with dynamic libraries, since any static resource manager objects will be local to the dynamic library's link space. Thus, calling delete on some memory in one library that was allocated in another can be as nonsensical as returning an un-liked birthday present from your mother-in-law to your next-door neighbor.[3]

There are two solutions to this problem.

9.5.1 Shared Pools

The first is to ensure that all the dynamic libraries used by the executable use a shared pool in a single dynamic library. There are two ways of doing this, but both boil down to the same thing. Let's consider the issue of memory.

One way to provide safe memory allocation and deallocation between dynamic libraries is to have all libraries themselves depend on a single dynamic library that provides operators new & delete and/or the functions malloc()/free(). The Visual C++ runtime library uses this model in the form of MSVCRT.DLL, and other vendors offer similar facilities.

A variant of this is to provide a per-link-unit implementation of these functions, but implement them in terms of a shared allocation function. This is the approach I use in the Synesis shared libraries on Win32, whereby there is a local new/delete that depend on functions (Mem_Alloc(), Mem_Free(), etc.) in the core dynamic library.

This is the most straightforward manner of sharing C++ implementations in your resource-handling dynamic libraries.

9.5.2 Return to Callee

The better general solution is always to return your resources to the callee who gave them to you, but it can be made difficult by the use of C++ classes. If your class's implementation is in one shared library, and all others share it, then it all works fine. But if some of the implementation is built into each link space—for example, by use of inline function definitions—then something constructed in one dynamic library and destroyed in another will be passing through different code, even though it's using the same class.

In practice, the use of classes obliges one to use the shared pools approach for most resources, especially the more ubiquitous and granular: if it's memory you're likely already using shared pools anyway courtesy of your compiler vendor. However, for other resources the pools may not be shared. If so, you could be in trouble if you're maintaining separate pools in separate dynamic libraries.

9.6 Dynamic Libraries: Coda

If you want to talk C++ across link units, you must stick with one compiler, and the same C/C++ run time libraries, or compilers that are mutually compatible in this regard, for example, Intel and Visual C++. Given what we learned in the previous two chapters, this seems like kind

---

[3]Unless your mother-in-law is your next-door neighbor, that is. But this is a tale of dynamic linking, not a horror story!

of a tautology. But the significance is that if we now look back at the C++ ABI issue, we can see that if a compiler had a compatible mangling scheme but had incompatible RTTI, object mode, and so on, it would be straightforward to produce programs whose correctness could never be verifiably asserted. That wouldn't be nice.

In practice, many (perhaps most?) programs are produced with C++ spanning link-units. However, the vast majority that do are done by a single compiler or by compilers with a shared C++ ABI. Conversely, interfacing with operating system and third-party link units is done via C.

CHAPTER 10

Threading

The subject of multithreading is a pretty big one, and worthy of several books all to itself [Bute1997, Rich1997]. In an attempt to simplify, I intend to stipulate that the challenges of multithreaded programming all pertain to synchronization of access to resources. The resources may be a single variable, a class, or they may even be some product of one thread that is to be consumed by another. The point is that if two or more threads need to access the same resource their access needs to be made safe. Alas, both C and C++ were developed before multithreading became as popular as it now is. Hence:

Imperfection: C and C++ say nothing about threading.

What does that mean? Well, in no part of the standard will you find any reference to threading.[1] Does this mean that you cannot write multithreaded programs with C++? Certainly not. But it does mean that C++ provides no support for multithreaded programming. The practical consequences of this are considerable.

The two classic concepts [Bute1997, Rich1997] one must be wary of when writing multitasking systems are race-conditions and deadlocks. Race-conditions occur when two separate threads of execution have access to the same resource at the same time. Note that I'm using the term "thread of execution" here to include processes on the same system and threads in the same process or in different processes in the same host system.

To protect against race-conditions, multitasking systems use synchronization mechanisms, such as mutexes, condition variables, and semaphores [Bute1997, Rich1997], to prevent concurrent access to shared resources. When one thread of execution has acquired a resource (also called locking the resource), other threads are locked out, and go into a wait state until the resource is released (unlocked).

Naturally the interaction of two or more independent threads of execution is potentially highly complex, and it is possible to have two threads each holding a resource and waiting for the other to release. This is known as a deadlock. Less common, but just as deadly, is *livelock*, whereby two or more processes are constantly changing state in response to changes in the others and so no progress can be made.

Both race conditions and deadlocks are hard to predict, or test for, which is one of the practical challenges of multithreaded programming. Even though deadlocks are very easy to detect—your executable stops—they are still hard to diagnose, since your process (or a thread within it) has hung.

---

[1]The only occurrence of the word *thread* is (C++-98: 15.1;2) when discussing threads of control in exception-handling.

10.1   Synchronizing Integer Access

Since the contents of the processor registers are stored in the thread context each time a process experiences a thread switch, the most basic form of synchronization is that which ensures that access to a single memory location is serialized. If the size of the memory to read at that location is a single byte, then the processor will access it atomically. Indeed, the same would apply to the reading of larger values according to the rules of the given architecture. For example, a 32-bit processor would ensure that accessing a 32-bit value was serialized, so long as the value was aligned on a 32-bit boundary. Serialization of access to nonaligned data may or may not be provided by any given processor. It's hard to imagine a workable architecture where such atomic operations were not provided.

The processor's guarantees are fine if you want to read or write platform-sized integers atomically, but there are many operations that you would wish to have atomic that are not so because they are actually several operations in one. The classic one of these is incrementing or decrementing variables. The statement

```
++i;
```

is really only a shorthand for

```
i = i + 1;
```

The increment of i involves a fetch of its value from memory, adding 1 to that value, and then storing the new value back in i's memory location, known as *Read-Modify-Write* (RMW) [Gerb2002]. Since this is a three-step process, any other thread that is concurrently attempting to manipulate the value of i can cause the result in either or both thread(s) to be invalidated. If both threads are attempting to increment i, it is possible for the threads to be out of step, as in:

```
Thread 1                    Thread 2
load i from memory
                            load i from memory
                            increment value
increment value
                            store new value to i
store new value to i
```

Both threads loaded the same value from memory, and when Thread 1 stores the incremented value, it writes over the result of Thread 2. The effect is that one of the increments is lost.

In practice, different processors will have different operations for conducting these steps. For example, on the Intel processor it could be implemented as follows:

```
mov eax,dword ptr [i]
inc eax
mov dword ptr [i], eax
```

or, more succinctly, as

```
add dword ptr [i],1
```

Even in the second form, where there is a single instruction, the operation is not guaranteed atomic on multiprocessor systems, because it is logically equivalent to the first, and a thread on another processor may interleave in the manner described above.

10.1.1   Operating System Functions

Since atomic increments and decrements are the cornerstone of many important mechanisms, including reference counting, it is very important that there are facilities for conducting these operations in a thread-safe manner. As we will see later, atomic integer operations can often be all that is required to make nontrivial components thread safe,[2] which can afford considerable performance savings.

Win32 provides the `InterlockedIncrement()` and `InterlockedDecrement()` system functions, which look like the following

```
LONG InterlockedIncrement(LONG *p);
LONG InterlockedDecrement(LONG *p);
```

These implement preincrement and predecrement semantics. In other words, the return value reflects the new value, rather than the old. Linux provides analogous functions [Rubi2001]: `atomic_inc_and_test()` and `atomic_dec_and_test()`. Similar functions may be available on a platform-specific basis.

Using such functions we can now rewrite our initial increment statement in a thoroughly thread-safe manner

```
atomic_inc_and_test(&i); // ++i
```

The implementation of such a function for the Intel processor would simply incorporate the LOCK instruction prefix, as in:[3]

```
lock add dword ptr [i], 1
```

The LOCK instruction prefix causes a LOCK# signal to be expressed on the bus, and prevents any other threads from affecting that memory location for the duration of the ADD instruction. (Naturally, it's a lot more complex than this, involving cache lines and all kinds of magic jiggery-pokery, but logically it makes the instruction atomic with respect to any other threads/processors.[4])

---

[2]The Synesis BufferStore component that I mentioned in Chapter 7 is one example, deriving its high speed from the avoidance of any kernel object synchronization.

[3]This is not the actual instruction(s), but I'm trying to be brief!

[4]On multi-CPU machines, or machines with hyperthreading/multiple-core CPUs, threads may really be running in parallel, whereas on single CPUs threads only appear to execute simultaneously. In single-CPU machines, interrupts may interrupt instructions (except for atomic ones).

The downside to applying locking semantics is a cost in speed. The actual costs will differ for different architectures: on Win32 the cost can be roughly 200–500% that of the nonlocked variant (as we'll see later in this chapter). Thus, it is not desirable simply to make every operation thread safe; indeed, the whole point of multithreading is to allow independent processing to take place concurrently.

In practice, therefore, one normally determines whether to use atomic operations dependent on a build setting. In UNIX, one tends to use the _REENTRANT preprocessor symbol definition to indicate to C and C++ code that the link unit is to be built for multithreading. In Win32 it is _MT or _ _MT_ _ or similar, depending on the compiler. Naturally, such things are abstracted into a platform/compiler-independent symbol, for example, ACMELIB_MULTI_THREADED, which is then used to select the appropriate operations at compile time.

```
#ifdef ACMELIB_MULTI_THREADED
  atomic_increment(&i);
#else /* ? ACMELIB_MULTI_THREADED */
  ++i;
#endif /* ACMELIB_MULTI_THREADED */
```

Since this is ugly stuff to be dotted around, it's also common practice to abstract the operation into a common function within which the preprocessor discrimination can be encapsulated. Plenty of examples of this exist in common libraries, such as Boost and Microsoft's Active Template Library (ATL).

I should point out that not all operating systems provide atomic integer operations, in which case you may need to resort to using an operating system synchronization object, for example, a mutex, to lock the access to the atomic integer API, as we'll look at later in the chapter.

10.1.2 Atomic Types

We've seen how we can simply use – – and ++ on the integer types for single threaded contexts, but for multithreading we need to use operating system/architecture primitives. The downside of this approach is that even when we abstract the differences into a common function, say integer_increment, it relies on all uses of the integer being done atomically. It's not terribly difficult to forget one, in which case you could have a race condition in your application that's very difficult to diagnose.

C++ is a language that aims to provide uniformity of syntax by allowing user-defined types to appear as built-in types. So why not make atomic types that look like built-in types, except that they operate atomically, in all respects? There's no reason why not, and it's actually very simple to do:[5]

Listing 10.1
```
class atomic_integer
{
```

---

[5]The volatile qualifiers facilitate the use of volatile as a qualifier on the declaration of any such variables, which is a reasonably common practice in multithreaded code, since it prevents the compiler from manipulating variables in its internal registers, thus failing to synchronize the value with the actual memory location of the variables. We'll look at it in more detail in section 18.5.

```
public:
  atomic_integer(int value)
    : m_value(value)
  {}
// Operations
public:
  class_type volatile &operator ++() volatile
  {
    atomic_increment(&m_value);
    return *this;
  }
  const class_type volatile operator ++(int) volatile
  {
    return class_type(atomic_postincrement(&m_value));
  }
  class_type volatile &operator --() volatile;
  const class_type volatile operator --(int) volatile;

  class_type volatile &operator +=(value_type const &value) volatile
  {
    atomic_postadd(&m_value, value);
    return *this;
  }
  class_type volatile &operator -=(value_type const &value) volatile;

private:
  volatile int m_value;
};
```

This is a clear area in which C++ makes threading easier and simpler. However, there is a question as to how much of the natural semantics of integer types are made available. The code above shows how easy it is, given a library of atomic integer functions, to implement increment/decrement, and addition and subtraction. However, doing multiplication, division, logical operations, shifting, and other operations are considerably more complex, and most atomic integer libraries do not provide such operations. If you want them in your code, that'll have to be the author's get-out-of-jail-free card: an exercise for the reader.

The Boost atomic operations components take just this approach, providing platform-specific versions of a type, `atomic_count`, which provides only `++` and `−` operations (`atomic_increment`/`atomic_decrement`), along with implicit conversion (`atomic_read`), so if you choose to opt out of anything much more complicated, you'll be in good company.

10.2   Synchronizing Block Access: Critical Regions

For most synchronization requirements, a single atomic operation is not sufficient. Such cases require exclusive access to what is known as a critical region [Bulk1999]. For example, if you have two variables to update atomically, you must use a synchronization object to ensure each thread is granted exclusive access to the critical region, as in:

```
// Shared objects
SYNC_TYPE    sync_obj;
SomeClass    shared_instance;
    . . .
// Somewhere in code called by multiple threads
lock(sync_obj);
int i = shared_instance.Method1(. . .);
shared_instance.Method2(i + 1, . . .);
unlock(sync_obj);
```

The two operations `Method1()` and `Method2()` must be conducted in an uninterrupted sequence. Hence, the code wherein they are called is encapsulated within calls to acquire and release a synchronization object. In general, the use of all such synchronization objects is very expensive, and so ways in which their costs can be minimized or avoided are desirable.

There are two causes of the high-costs of synchronization objects to secure critical regions. The first is that the costs of using the synchronization objects themselves can be high. For example, consider the timings (in milliseconds) shown in Table 10.1, for 10 million acquire-release cycles of four Win32 synchronization objects, and a control scenario consisting of two empty function calls. The results plainly show that the cost of using synchronization objects is considerable, up to 150 times that of a normal function call.

The second cost associated with synchronization objects for protecting critical regions is that incurred by any threads that are blocked from entering the critical region. The longer the critical region, the more likely this cost is to be incurred, and therefore it is good to keep critical regions as short as possible or to break them into subcritical sections, as was discussed in section 6.2. However, because the costs of the acquire and/or release calls can be very high, the balance between breaking critical regions and the causing long waits for pending threads is a delicate one. Only performance profiling can give you definitive answers on a case-by-case basis.

10.2.1   Interprocess and Intraprocess Mutexes

Mutexes are the most common form of synchronization object for guarding critical regions and, depending on the operating system, can be two kinds: interprocess and intraprocess. An interprocess mutex is one that may be referenced in more than one process, and can therefore provide interprocess synchronization. On Win32, such a mutex is normally created by calling

Table 10.1

Synchronization Object	Uniprocessor machine	SMP machine
None (control)	117	172
CRITICAL_SECTION	1740	831
Atomic inc	1722	914
Mutex	17891	22187
Semaphore	18235	22271
Event	17847	22130

`CreateMutex()` and naming the object. Other processes may then access the same mutex by specifying the same name to `CreateMutex()` or `OpenMutex()`.[6] With PTHREADS [Bute1997], the UNIX POSIX standard threading library, a mutex may be passed to its child via a process fork, or can be shared via mapped memory.

Intraprocess mutexes, by contrast, are only visible to threads within a process. As they do not need to exist across process borders, they can partially or completely avoid the costly trips to the kernel, since their state can be maintained within process memory. Win32 has such a construct, known as a `CRITICAL_SECTION`, which is a lightweight mechanism that keeps most of the processing out of the kernel, only making kernel calls when the ownership is to be transferred to another thread. There are considerable performance gains to be had by using intraprocess mutexes where suitable, as can be seen in Table 10.1, whose results were obtained by an executable with a single thread. We'll see later how the `CRITICAL_SECTION` performs when the application is multithreaded.

10.2.2   Spin Mutexes

There's a special kind of intraprocess mutex, which is based on the ordinarily bad practice of polling. Simply, polling is waiting for a condition to change by repeatedly testing it, as in:

```
int g_flag;

// Waiting thread
while(0 == g_flag)
{}
. . . // Now do what we've been waiting for
```

This kind of thing chews up the cycles, as the polling thread is often[7] given equal priority with the thread that will be changing the flag to enable it to proceed. Polling is one of those *bad ideas* that ordinarily mark one out as a multithreading neophyte, suitable for apple-pie desks or unlooked-for severance pay.

However, there are circumstances in which spinning is eminently suitable. Let's first look at an implementation of a spin mutex, the imaginatively named UNIXSTL[8] class `spin_mutex`, shown in Listing 10.2.

Listing 10.2

```
class spin_mutex
{
public:
  explicit spin_mutex(sint32_t *p = NULL)
    : m_spinCount((NULL != p) ? p : &m_internalCount)
    , m_internalCount(0)
  {}
```

---

[6]An unnamed mutex handle may also be passed to a child process through other IPC mechanisms, but naming is the most straightforward mechanism.

[7]Depending on respective thread priorities and on any external events on which other threads may be waiting.

[8]The STLSoft subproject that maps UNIX APIs to STL.

```
  void lock()
  {
    for(; 0 != atomic_write(m_spinCount, 1); sched_yield())
    {}
  }
  void unlock()
  {
    atomic_set(m_spinCount, 0);
  }
// Members
private:
  sint32_t  *m_spinCount;
  sint32_t  m_internalCount;
// Not to be implemented
private:
    spin_mutex(class_type const &rhs);
    spin_mutex &operator =(class_type const &rhs);
};
```

The mechanism of a spin mutex is very simple. When `lock()` is called, an atomic write is performed to set the spin variable `*m_spinCount` (an integer) to 1. If its previous value was 0, then the caller was the first thread to set it, and has "acquired" the mutex, so the method then returns. If its previous value was 1, then the caller was beaten to it, by another thread, and thus does not own the mutex. It then calls the PTHREADS function `sched_yield()` to yield to another thread, and when it wakes up again, it tries again. It repeats this until it succeeds. Thus it is locked out of ownership of the mutex.

When the thread that acquired the mutex calls `unlock()`, the spin variable is set back to 0, and another thread may then acquire it. The slight complication with the constructor and the `m_internalCount` is that this class can be constructed on an external spin variable, which can be very useful in certain circumstances (as we'll see in Chapters 11 and 31).

Spin mutexes are not a good solution where there is a high degree of contention, but where the likelihood of contention is very low and/or the cost of acquiring/releasing the synchronization mechanism must be low, they can be an effective solution. Given their potential high cost, I tend to use them only for initialization where contention is exceedingly rare, but theoretically possible, and must be accounted for.

10.3   Atomic Integer Performance

Before we and move on to multithreading extensions (section 10.4) and *Thread Specific Storage* (section 10.5), I want to take a look at the performance aspects of various atomic integer operation strategies.

10.3.1   Atomic Integer by Mutex

Where your atomic integer operations are not provided by your operating system, you may need to resort to using a mutex to lock the access to the atomic integer API, as shown in Listing 10.3.

Listing 10.3

```
namespace
{
  Mutex s_mx;
}
int atomic_postincrement(int volatile *p)
{
  lock_scope<Mutex>    lock(s_mx);
  return *p++;
}
int atomic_predecrement(int volatile *p)
{
  lock_scope<Mutex>    lock(s_mx);
  return --*p;
}
```

The problem here is performance. Not only do you pay the sometimes considerable cost of going to the kernel in the acquiring and release of the mutex object, but you also have contention from several threads wanting to perform their atomic operations simultaneously. Every single atomic operation within your process involves the single mutex object, which naturally leads to a bottleneck.

I once witnessed a tragic attempt to ameliorate this cost by having a separate mutex for each atomic function. Unfortunately, this proved very successful in reducing waiting times. As I'm sure you've guessed, this was thoroughly tested on a single-processor Intel machine. As soon as the application was run on a multiprocessor machine, it fell in a heap.[9] Since each mutex protected the function, rather than the data, it was possible to have some threads incrementing a variable while another was decrementing it. All that was achieved was to prevent two threads doing the same thing to the same integer at the same time. As with so many things in multithreading, you cannot have confidence in your code until you've tested it on a multiprocessor machine.

Despite that abject failure, there is a way to share the contention between more than one mutex in order to reduce the bottleneck. What is required is to base the mutex selection on a property of the variable being manipulated. Well, there's only one attribute we know about it: its address. (We can't very well know its value, since that is going to be changing.)

This looks something like the following:

```
namespace
{
  Mutex         s_mxs[NUM_MUTEXES];
};

int __stdcall Atomic_PreIncrement_By(int volatile *v)
{
  size_t             index = index_from_ptr(v, NUM_MUTEXES);
```

---

[9]It would suffer the same fate on modern hyperthreading single processor machines.

```
    lock_scope<Mutex> lock(s_mxs[index]);
    return ++*(v);
}
```

The function `index_from_ptr()` provides a deterministic mapping from an address to an integer in the range `[0, NUM_MUTEXES-1]`. It would not be suitable simply to perform modulo division of the address, since most systems align data on boundaries of 4, 8, 16, or 32 bytes. Something like the following might be suitable:

```
inline size_t index_from_ptr(void volatile *v, size_t range)
{
    return (((unsigned)v) >> 7) % range;
}
```

In testing on my own Win32 machine, I found 7 to give better performance than other values, but that's unlikely to translate to other platforms, so you'd have to optimize this for your platform.

10.3.2 Run Time Architecture Dispatching

I'd like to show you a little trick for enhancing performance of atomic integer operations for the Intel platform. As we've learned, the Intel processor will conduct a single-instruction RMW operation (such as ADD, XADD) uninterrupted, so on single processor machines a bus lock is not required. Conversely, the bus must be locked for these operations on multiprocessor machines. Since it's much easier to build and ship a single version of code, it would be nice for our code to only pay the performance cost of bus locking when necessary. Since the number of instructions in either case is very small, we'd need a very efficient way of doing this, otherwise the test would cause more latency than the savings gained. The solution looks like the simplified form[10] shown in Listing 10.4, which is compatible with most modern Win32 compilers.

Listing 10.4

```
namespace
{
    static bool s_uniprocessor = is_host_up();
}


inline __declspec(naked) void __stdcall
    atomic_increment(sint32_t volatile * /* pl */)
{
    if(s_uniprocessor)
    {
        _asm
        {
            mov ecx, dword ptr [esp + 4]
            add dword ptr [ecx], 1
```

---

[10]The full implementations for these functions are included on the CD.

```
        ret 4
      }
    }
    else
    {
      _asm
      {
        mov ecx, dword ptr [esp + 4]
        lock add dword ptr [ecx], 1
        ret 4
      }
    }
}
```

Even if you're not familiar with the Intel assembler, you should be able to understand how simple the mechanism is. The `s_uniprocessor` is true for uniprocessors, and false for multiprocessor machines. If it's true, the increment is effected without a lock. If it's false, the lock is used. Any possible race conditions in the instantiation are unimportant, since the default case is to apply the lock, which is benign.

In the performance tests below, this is the mechanism used by the Synesis Atomic_ API and the WinSTL atomic functions.

10.3.3 Performance Comparisons

I've done a lot of talking about the various mechanisms available for atomic integer operations, so let's look at some facts. Before we do so, I'd like to stress that the figures in this section reflect the performance of Win32 operating systems on (single- and multi-) processor Intel architecture only. Other architectures and/or operating systems may have different characteristics.

I've examined seven strategies. For each there is a common global variable which is either incremented or decremented by the thread. The first strategy—Unguarded—does no locking, and simply increments or decrements the variable via the ++ or – operators. The next two use the architecture-dispatching techniques: the Synesis `Atomic_*` library functions and WinSTL's inline functions. The fourth calls the Win32 `Interlocked_*` system functions. The final three use a synchronization object—the Win32 CRITICAL_SECTION, the WinSTL `spin_mutex` and the Win32 mutex kernel object—to guard access to the critical region, within which the ++ or – operator is used to modify the variable. The results are shown in Table 10.2, which includes the total times for 10 million operations for 31 contending threads for each strategy. Since these were measured on different machines, the relative performance figures are also obtained.

Deliberately, the test program that exercised the various locking mechanisms spawned an odd number of threads, such that when all threads were complete the manipulated variables should have a large non-zero value equal to the number of iterations. This was a quick validation that the operations were indeed atomic. All of the cases shown, including the Unguarded manipulation on the uniprocessor machine behaved correctly. Verifying what we know about the nonatomic nature of some single instructions on multiprocessors, the Unguarded/SMP case

Table 10.2

Synchronization Scheme	Uniprocessor Machine		SMP machine	
	Absolute (ms)	% of unguarded	Absolute (ms)	% of unguarded
Unguarded ++ / − −	362	100%	525 (incorrect)	100%
Synesis Atomic_* API	509	141%	2464	469%
WinSTL atomic_* inline functions	510	141%	2464	469%
Win32 Interlocked* API	2324	642%	2491	474%
Win32 CRITICAL_SECTION	5568	1538%	188235	35854%
WinSTL spin_mutex	5837	1612%	3871	737%
Win32 MUTEX	57977	16016%	192870	36737%

produced wildly different values on each run, indicating that threads were interrupting each other's RMW cycles.

In terms of the performance, several things stand out. First, the relative cost of all mechanisms is higher on the multiprocessor machine, which indicates that multiprocessor caches are things that don't like being disturbed.

Second, as far as the architecture dispatching mechanism—the Synesis Atomic_ API and the WinSTL atomic_* inline functions—is concerned, it's fair to say that it does a very good job on the uni-processor system, being only 22% the cost of the Win32 Interlocked_* system library functions, and only being 141% the cost of the unguarded ++/−− operators. On the multiprocessor machine the additional cost over and above the LOCK for the processor test is very acceptable, being only an additional 1%. I would say that if you're writing applications that need to work on both single and multithreaded architectures, and you want to be able to ship a single version, you're likely to see significant benefits from using this dispatching technique.

The results show the well-known fact that mutexes, as kernel objects, represent a *very* costly way of implementing atomic operations, and you'd be crazy to use them for that purpose on Win32 systems.

Somewhat different from the mutex is the CRITICAL_SECTION. I don't know about you, but much of the wisdom gleaned as I was learning multithreaded programming on the Win32 platform advocated the use of the CRITICAL_SECTION as a much better alternative to the mutex. Indeed, it appears to be about 10 times as fast on the uniprocessor system. However, it has about the same performance on the multiprocessor machine. Once again, you need to test your code on multiprocessor systems, in this case to verify your assumptions about the efficiency of the mechanisms you are using. I would say that the CRITICAL_SECTION is not a valid mechanism with which to get atomic operations; unlike the mutex I've actually seen a lot of use of it in clients' code bases.

You may wonder why anyone would use a spin mutex to implement atomic operations. Well, the atomic operations provided in Linux's <asm/atomic.h> are only guaranteed to provide a range of 24 bits. Furthermore, on some flavous of Linux, functions with the correct semantics—increment the value and return the previous value—are not available. By using the conceptually simpler write/set functions the full-range atomic operations can still be provided, without incurring too high a performance penalty.

I hope these results give you some pause for thought in your implementations. Remember that this is Win32-specific; other architectures may have significantly different performance behaviors. But the main lesson is to profile, and to question your assumptions.

10.3.4   Atomic Integer Operations Coda

I've focused a great deal on atomic operations in this chapter, and I make no apologies for doing so. There are three reasons for this. First, they are something that I think could be incorporated directly into C++, which probably cannot be said for other multithreading and synchronization constructs, due to too-great differences or lack of broad availability.[11]

Second, they are an extremely useful construct, whose power is in inverse proportion to their simplicity. Using atomic integer operations only, one can achieve most or all the required thread safety in a significant number of C++ classes, as is shown in later chapters.

Last, the level of discussion of atomic operations in the literature is scant, to say the least. Hopefully by providing some focus here you'll think of them more often.

Atomic operations are available on many platforms, either as system library functions, or as nonstandard libraries, or by writing your own assembler versions. (I'm aware of the irony in promoting the use of assembler in a book largely dedicated to showing advanced C++ techniques; we live in a strange world.)

Even when we elect to use a (usually PTHREADS) mutex to implement our atomic operation, there are measures available to increase efficiency. The one thing to watch out for is not to use spin-mutexes in such cases. You'll be using several instances of a mutex class that are implemented in terms of an atomic integer API that is implemented on one, or a few, global mutexes. In such a case, you should use some preprocessor discrimination to make your chosen mutex a plain (PTHREADS-based) mutex, otherwise you'll be impacting negatively on performance, which won't be what you'll want or expect.

This is actually a good example of a broader truth to be found in multithreaded development. In practice we really need to consider the details of our synchronization needs and the facilities of the host system(s) on which our applications will run. It would be great if C++ did indeed stipulate atomic operations, but it's my personal opinion that providing standard higher-level synchronization primitives[12] and maintaining maximum efficiency over different architectures is a lot harder to do. As often the case, you are best served by being aware of all the multithreading tools at your disposal ([Bute1997, Rich1997]).

10.4   Multithreading Extensions

Now that we've looked at a few issues pertaining to multithreading, it may have occurred to you that it would be useful for the language to provide built-in support for multithreading operations. Indeed, several languages do provide multithreading constructs. The C++ tradition is to

---

[11]Having said that, there are some libraries, such as the excellent PThreads-Win32 (see Appendix A), which go some way to unifying the threading experience.

[12]There are moves afoot to make this happen in a future version of the standard, at which point I hope all the foregoing will be irrelevant. I doubt it, though.

favor the addition of new libraries rather than new language elements. We'll take a look at a couple of potential areas, see how the language might provide them, and how we can implement them using libraries (and a little bit of preprocessor trickery).

10.4.1   synchronized

D and Java have the `synchronized` keyword, which can be used to guard a critical region, as in:

```
Object obj = new Object();
. . .
synchronized(obj)
{
    . . . // critical code
}
```

One way to incorporate a `synchronized` keyword into the language would be to automatically translate the above code as follows:

```
{ __lock_scope__<Object> __lock__(obj);
{
    . . . // critical code
}
}
```

The `__lock_scope__` would be to all intents similar to the `lock_scope` template described in section 6.2. This would be pretty easy to do, and having an associated `std::lock_traits` template would enable an instance of any traits-able type to be synchronized in this way, which would not necessarily translate to a synchronization object lock.

This one is not a really strong contender for language extension, however, since with a modicum of macros we can achieve the same thing. Basically, all that is needed is the following two macros:

```
#define SYNCHRONIZED_BEGIN(T, v) \
    {                            \
    lock_scope<T> __lock__(v);
#define SYNCHRONIZED_END() \
    }
```

The only slight loss is that the type of the object would not be deduced for us, and also that the code looks somewhat less pretty:[13]

```
SYNCHRONIZED_BEGIN(Object, obj)
{
```

---

[13]It could be argued that the uglification is actually a benefit, since it increases the profile of the synchronized status of the critical region, which is a pretty important thing for anyone reading the code to take notice of.

```
    . . . // critical code
}
SYNCHRONIZED_END()
```

If you don't like the `SYNCHRONIZED_END()` part, you can always get a little bit trickier with your macro and define `SYNCHRONIZED()` macro as follows:

```
#define SYNCHRONIZED(T, v)                                    \
   for(synchronized_lock<lock_scope<T> > __lock__(v);    \
        __lock__; __lock__.end_loop())
```

The `synchronized_lock<>` template class is only there to define a state[14] and to terminate the loop, since we can't declare a second condition variable within the `for` statement (see section 17.3). It is a bolt-in class (see Chapter 22) and looks like:

Listing 10.5
```
template <typename T>
struct synchronized_lock
   : public T
{
public:
   template <typename U>
   synchronized_lock(U &u)
      : T(u)
      , m_bEnded(false)
   {}
   operator bool () const
   {
      return !m_bEnded;
   }
   void end_loop()
   {
      m_bEnded = true;
   }
private:
   bool  m_bEnded;
};
```

There's another complication (of course!). As was described in section 17.3, compilers have different reactions to `for`-loop declarations, and if we were to have two synchronized regions in the same scope, some of the older ones would complain.

```
SYNCHRONIZED(Object, obj)
{
```

---

[14]It doesn't really define an `operator bool()`. We'll see why they're not used, and how to do them properly, in Chapter 24.

```
    . . . // critical code
}
    . . . // non-critical code
SYNCHRONIZED(Object, obj) // Error: "redefinition of __lock__"
{
    . . . // more critical code
}
```

Thus, a portable solution needs to ensure that each `__lock__` is distinct, so we have to get down and dirty with the preprocessor.[15]

```
#define concat__(x, y)          x ## y
#define concat_(x, y)           concat__(x, y)
#define SYNCHRONIZED(T, v)                      \
  for(synchronized_lock<lock_scope<T> >         \
      concat_(__lock__, __LINE__) (v);          \
      concat_(__lock__, __LINE__);              \
      concat_(__lock__, __LINE__) .end_loop())
```

It's ugly, but it works for all the compilers tested. If you don't need to be concerned with anachronistic `for` behavior, then just stick to the simpler version. The full versions of these macros and the classes are included on the CD.

10.4.2   Anonymous synchronized

There's a twist on the object-controlled critical region, which is that sometimes you don't have an object that you want to use as a lock. In this case, you can either just declare a static one in the local scope or, preferably, one in (anonymous) namespace scope in the same file as the critical region. You could also build on the techniques for the `SYNCHRONIZED()` macro, and produce a `SYNCHRONIZED_ANON()` macro that incorporates a local static, but then you run into a potential race condition whereby two or more threads might attempt to perform the one-time construction of the static object simultaneously. There are techniques to obviate this, as we'll see when we discuss statics in the next chapter, but it's best to avoid the issue. The name-space scope object is the best option in these cases.

10.4.3   atomic

Getting back to my favorite synchronization issue, atomic integer operations, one possible language extension would be to have an `atomic` keyword to support code such as the following:

```
atomic j = ++i; // Equivalent to j = atomic_preincrement(&i)
```

or, using the XOR exchange trick,[16]

```
atomic j ^= i ^= j ^= i; // Equiv. to j = atomic_write(&i, j);
```

---

[15]I'll leave it up to you to do a little research as to why the double concatenation is required.

[16]This is an old hacker's delight [Dewh2003], and frequent interview question. Test it out—it works, although I think it's not guaranteed to be portable!

It would be the compiler's responsibility to ensure that the code was translated into the appropriate atomic operation for the target architecture.[17] Unfortunately, the differences between processor instruction sets would mean that we'd either have to live with nonportable code, or that only a very few operations would be eligible for `atomic` decoration. We certainly would not want the compiler to use lightweight measures where it could and silently implement other operations by the locking and unlocking of a shared mutex: better to have these things expressly in the code as we do now.

It would be nice to have the `atomic` keyword for C and C++, for the limited subset of atomic integer operations that would be common to all architectures. However, using the `atomic_*` functions is not exactly a hardship, and it's certainly as readable—possibly more so—than the keyword form. Their only real downside is that they're not mandatory for all platforms; hopefully a future version of the C/C++ standard(s) will prescribe them.

10.5 Thread Specific Storage

All the discussion in the chapter has so far focused on the issues of synchronizing access to common resources from multiple threads. There is another side to threading, which is the provision of thread-specific resources or as it is more commonly known, *Thread-Specific Storage* (TSS) [Schm1997].

10.5.1 Re-entrancy

In single-threaded programs, the use of a local static object within a function is a reasonable way to make the function easier to use. The C standard library makes use of this technique in several of its functions, including `strtok()`, which tokenizes a string based one of a set of character delimiters:

```
char *strtok(char *str, const char *delimiterSet);
```

The function maintains internal static variables that maintain the current tokenization point, so that subsequent calls (passing NULL for `str`) return successive tokens from the string.

Unfortunately, when used in multithreaded processes, such functions represent a classic race-condition. One thread may initiate a new tokenization while another is midway through the process.

Unlike other race-conditions, the answer in this case is not to serialize access with a synchronization object. That would only stop one thread from modifying the internal tokenization structures while another was using them. The interruption of one thread's tokenization by another's would still occur.

What is required is not to serialize access to thread-global variables, but rather to provide thread-local variables.[18] This is the purpose of TSS.

---

[17]Note that I'm suggesting the keyword would apply to the operation, *not* the variable. Defining a variable atomic and then 50 lines down relying on that atomic behavior is hardly a win for maintainability. The clear intent, and grepability, of `atomic_*` functions is much preferable to that.

[18]And modern C and C++ run time libraries implement `strtok()` and similar functions using TSS.

10.5.2   Thread-Specific Data / Thread-Local Storage

Both the PTHREADS and Win32 threading infrastructures provide some degree of TSS. Just for consistency, the PTHREADS [Bute1997] version is called *Thread-Specific Data* (TSD), and the Win32 [Rich1997] version is called *Thread-Local Storage* (TLS), but it all amounts to the same thing.

They each provide the means to create a variable that will be able to contain different values in each thread in the process. In PTHREADS, the variable is known as a key; in Win32 an index. Win32 refers to the location for a key's value in each thread as a slot. I like to refer to keys, slots, and values.

PTHREADS' TSD works around the following four library functions:

```
int pthread_key_create(     pthread_key_t  *key
                      ,     void (*destructor)(void *));
int pthread_key_delete(     pthread_key_t  key);
void *pthread_getspecific( pthread_key_t  key);
int pthread_setspecific(    pthread_key_t  key
                      ,     const void     *value);
```

`pthread_key_create()` creates a key (of the opaque type) `pthread_key_t`. The caller can also pass in a cleanup function, which we'll talk about shortly. Values can be set and retrieved, on a thread-specific basis, by calling `pthread_setspecific()` and `pthread_getspecific()`. `pthread_key_delete()` is called to destroy a key when it is no longer needed.

Win32's TLS API has a similar quartet:

```
DWORD   TlsAlloc(void);
LPVOID TlsGetValue(DWORD dwTlsIndex);
BOOL    TlsSetValue(DWORD dwTlsIndex, LPVOID lpTlsValue);
BOOL    TlsFree(DWORD dwTlsIndex);
```

The normal way in which these TSS APIs are used is to create a key within the main thread, prior to the activation of any other threads and store the key in a common area (either in a global variable, or returned via a function). All threads then manipulate their own copies of the TSS data by storing to and retrieving from their own slots.

Unfortunately, there are several inadequacies in these models, especially with the Win32 version.

First, the number of keys provided by the APIs is limited. PTHREADS guarantees that there will be at least 128; Win32 64.[19] In reality, one is very unlikely to need to break this limit, but given the increasingly multicomponent nature of software it is by no means impossible.

The second problem is that the Win32 API does not provide any ability to clean up the slot when a thread exits. This means that one has to somehow intercept the thread's exit and clean up the resources associated with the value in that thread's slot. Naturally, for C++ folks, this is a

---

[19]Windows 95 and NT 4 provide 64. Later operating systems provide more (Windows 98/ME: 80, Windows 2000/XP: 1088), but code that must be able to execute on any Win32 system must assume 64.

painful loss of the automatic destruction that the language provides for us, and can be next to impossible to work around in some scenarios.

Despite PTHREADS providing a means for cleanup on thread termination, it still presents an incomplete mechanism for easy and correct resource handling. In essence, PTHREADS provides us with immutable RAII (see section 3.5.1). Although this is a great improvement on Win32's absence of any RAII, there are occasions when it would be desirable to be able to change the slot value for a given key. It's possible to manually clean up the previous values, but it'd be a lot better if that is done automatically for us.

The fourth problem is that PTHREADS assumes that the cleanup function is callable at the cleanup epoch. If, at the time that any of the threads exit, an API has been uninitialized, then it may no longer be valid to call a cleanup function that may call that API directly or indirectly. Similarly, and even more likely in practice, if a cleanup function is in a dynamic library, the cleanup function may no longer exist in the process's memory, which means it will crash.

10.5.3   _ _declspec(thread) and TLS

Before we look at handling those challenges, I'd like to describe one TSS mechanism that is provided by most compilers on the Win32 platform in order to ease the verbosity of using the Win32 TLS functions. The compilers allow you to use the _ _declspec(thread) qualifier on variable definitions, as in:

```
_ _declspec(thread) int  x;
```

Now x will be thread specific; each thread will get its own copy. The compiler places any such variables in a .tls section, and the linker coalesces all of these into one. When the operating system loads the process, it looks for the .tls section and creates a thread-specific block to hold them. Each time a thread is created a corresponding block is created for the thread.

Unfortunately, despite being extremely efficient [Wils2003d], there's a massive drawback to this that makes it only suitable for use in executables, and not in dynamic libraries. It can be used in dynamic libraries that are implicitly linked, and therefore loaded at process load time, since the operating system can allocate the thread-specific block for all link units loading at application load time. The problem is what happens when a dynamic library containing a .tls section is later explicitly loaded; the operating system is unable go back and increase the blocks for all the existing threads, so your library will fail to load.

I think it's best to avoid _ _declspec(thread) in any DLLs, even ones that you're *sure* will always be implicitly linked. In the modern component-based world, it's entirely possible that the DLL may be implicitly linked to a component that is explicitly loaded by an executable produced by another compiler, or in another language, and that does not already have your DLL loaded. Your DLL cannot be loaded, and therefore the component that depends on it cannot be loaded.

10.5.4   The Tss Library

Having been bitten too many times by the four problems associated with the TSS mechanisms of PTHREADS and Win32, I got on the ball and wrote a library that provides the functionality I needed. It consists of eight functions, and two helper classes. The main functions, which are compatible with C and C++, are shown in Listing 10.6:

Listing 10.6

```
// MLTssStr.h - functions are declared extern "C"
int     Tss_Init(void);      /* Failed if < 0. */
void    Tss_Uninit(void);
void    Tss_ThreadAttach(void);
void    Tss_ThreadDetach(void);
HTssKey Tss_CreateKey( void (*pfnClose)()
                     , void (*pfnClientConnect)()
                     , void (*pfnClientDisconnect)()
                     , Boolean bCloseOnAssign);
void    Tss_CloseKey(    HTssKey  hEntry);
void    Tss_SetSlotValue( HTssKey  hEntry
                        , void     *value
                        , void     **pPrevValue /* = NULL */);
void    *Tss_GetSlotValue(HTssKey  hEntry);
```

Like all good APIs it has Init/Uninit[20] methods, to ensure that the API is ready for any clients that need it. It also has two functions for attaching and detaching threads that I'll talk about in a moment.

Manipulating keys follows the convention in providing four functions. However, these functions offer more functionality. For providing cleanup at thread termination, the Tss_ CreateKey() function provides the optional callback function pfnClose; specify NULL if you don't need it. If you want that cleanup function to be applied to slot values when they are overwritten, you specify true for the bCloseOnAssign parameter.

Preventing code from untimely disappearance is handled by the two optional callback function parameters pfnClientConnect and pfnClientDisconnect. These can be implemented to do whatever is appropriate to ensure that the function specified in pfnClose is in memory and callable when it is needed. In my use of the API I have had occasion to specify the Init/Uninit functions for other APIs, or to lock and unlock a dynamic library in memory, or a combination of the two, as necessary.

Tss_CloseKey() and Tss_GetSlotValue() have the expected semantics. Tss_ SetSlotValue(), however, has an additional parameter, pPrevValue, over its PTHREADS/ Win32 equivalents. If this parameter is NULL, then the previous value is overwritten, and subject to the cleanup as requested in the key creation. However, if this parameter is non-NULL, then any cleanup is skipped, and the previous value is returned to the caller. This allows a finer-grained control over the values, while providing the powerful cleanup semantics by default.

Being a C API, the natural step is to encapsulate it within scoping class(es), and there are two provided. The first is the TssKey class. It's not particularly remarkable—it just simplifies the interface and applies RAII to close the key—so I'll show only the public interface:

Listing 10.7

```
template <typename T>
class TssKey
```

---

[20]A little tip for all those who use British spelling out there: you can avoid pointless arguments about Initialise vs Initialize with your U.S. friends by using a contraction.

```
{
public:
  TssKey( void (*pfnClose)(T )
        , void (*pfnClientConnect)()
        , void (*pfnClientDisconnect)()
        , Boolean bCloseOnAssign = true);
  ~TssKey();
public:
  void  SetSlotValue(T value, T *pPrevValue = NULL);
  T     GetSlotValue() const;
private:
  . . . Members; hide copy ctor and assignment operator
};
```

The implementation contains static assertions (see section 1.4.7) to ensure that `sizeof(T)` == `sizeof(void*)`, to prevent any mistaken attempt to store large objects by value in the slot. The values are cast to the parameterizing type, to save you the effort in client code.

The next class is a fair bit more interesting. If your use of the slot value were to create a single entity and then to reuse it, you'd normally follow the pattern in Listing 10.8:

Listing 10.8
```
Tss key_func(. . .);
. . .
OneThing const &func(Another *another)
{
  OneThing *thing = (OneThing*)key_func.GetSlotValue();
  if(NULL == value)
  {
    thing = new OneThing(another);
    key_func.SetSlotValue(thing);
  }
  else
  {
    thing->Method(another);
  }
  return *thing;
}
```

However, if the function is more complex—and most are—then there may be several places where the slot value may be changed. Each one of these represents the possibility for a resource leak due to a premature return before the call to `SetSlotValue()`. For this reason the scoping class `TssSlotScope`, shown in Listing 10.9, is provided. I confess I have a perverse affection for this class, because it's a kind of inside-out RAII.

Listing 10.9
```
template <typename T>
class TssSlotScope
{
```

```
public:
  TssSlotScope(HTssKey hKey, T &value)
    : m_hKey(hKey)
    , m_valueRef(value)
    , m_prevValue((value_type)Tss_GetSlotValue(m_hKey))
  {
    m_valueRef = m_prevValue;
  }
  TssSlotScope(TssKey<T> key, T &value);
  ~TssSlotScope()
  {
    if(m_valueRef != m_prevValue)
    {
      Tss_SetSlotValue(m_hKey, m_valueRef, NULL);
    }
  }
private:
  TssKey   m_key;
  T        &m_valueRef;
  T const m_prevValue;
// Not to be implemented
private:
  . . . Hide copy ctor and assignment operator
};
```

It is constructed from a TSS key (either `TssKey<T>`, or an `HTssKey`) and a reference to an external value variable. The constructor(s) then set the external variable to the slot's value, via a call to `Tss_GetSlotValue()`.

In the destructor, the value of the external variable is tested against the original value of the slot, and the slot's value is updated via `Tss_SetSlotValue()` if it has changed. Now we can write client code much more simply, and rely on RAII to update the thread's slot value if necessary.

Listing 10.10
```
OneThing const &func(Another *another)
{
  OneThing               *thing;
  TssSlotScope<OneThing*> scope(key_func, thing);

  if( . . . )
    thing = new OneThing(another);
  else if( . . . )
    thing = . . .;
  else
    . . .

  return *thing;
} // dtor of scope ensure Tls_SetSlotValue() is called
```

So we've seen how to use the Tss library, but how does it work? Well, I'm going to leave you to figure out the implementation,[21] but we do need to have a look at how the thread notifications are handled. This involves the two functions I've so far not described: `Tss_Thread Attach()` and `Tss_ThreadDetach()`. These two functions should be called when a thread commences and terminates execution, respectively. If possible, you can hook into your operating system or run time library infrastructure to achieve this. If not, then you will need to do it manually.

On Win32, all DLLs export the entry point `DllMain()` [Rich1997], which receives notifications when the process loads/unloads, and when threads commence/terminate. In the Synesis Win32 libraries, the base DLL (MMCMNBAS.DLL) calls `Tss_ThreadAttach()` when its `DllMain()` receives the `DLL_THREAD_ATTACH` notification, and calls `Tss_Thread Detach()` when it receives `Tss_ThreadDetach()`. Since it is a common DLL, all the other members of any executable can just use the Tss library, without being concerned with the underlying setup; it all just works.

Listing 10.11
```
BOOL WINAPI DllMain(HINSTANCE, DWORD reason, void *)
{
  switch(reason)
  {
    case DLL_PROCESS_ATTACH:
      Tss_Init();
      break;
    case DLL_THREAD_ATTACH:
      Tss_ThreadAttach();
      break;
    case DLL_THREAD_DETACH:
      Tss_ThreadDetach();
      break;
    case DLL_PROCESS_DETACH:
      Tss_Uninit();
      break;
  }
  . . .
```

On UNIX, the library calls `pthread_key_create()` from within `Tss_Init()` to create a private, unused key whose only purpose is to ensure that the library receives a callback when each thread terminates, which then calls `Tss_ThreadDetach()`. Since there is no mechanism for a per-thread initialization function in PTHREADS, the Tss library is written to act benignly when asked for data for a nonexistent slot, and to create a slot where one does not exist when asked to store a slot value. Thus, `Tss_ThreadAttach()` can be thought of as a

---

[21]Or to take a peek on the CD, since I've included the source for the library. Take care, though, it's old code, and not that pretty! It's probably not that optimal, either, so it should be taken as a guide to the technique, rather than the zenith of TSS library implementations.

mechanism for efficiently expanding all active keys in response to a thread's commencement, rather than doing it piecemeal during thread processing.

If you're not using PTHREADS or Win32, or you're not happy to locate your library in a Win32 DLL, you should ensure that all threads call the attach/detach functions. However, even if you cannot or will not do this, the library is written such that when the final call to `Tss_Uninit()` is received, it performs the registered cleanup for all outstanding slots for all keys.

This is a powerful catchall mechanism, and the only problem you'll have relying on this—apart from tardy cleanup, that is—is if your cleanup function must be called from within the same thread to deallocate the resource that was used to allocate it. If that's the case, and you can't ensure timely and comprehensive thread attach/detach notification, then you're out of luck. What do you want—we're only protoplasm and silicon!

10.5.5 TSS Performance

So far I've not mentioned performance. Naturally, the sophistication of the library, along with the fact that there is a mutex to serialize access to the store, means that it has a nontrivial cost when compared with, say, the Win32 TLS implementation, which is very fast indeed [Wils2003f]. In one sense, there's not an issue, since if you need this functionality, then you're going to have to pay for it somehow. Second, the cost of a thread switch is considerable, potentially thousands of cycles [Bulk1999], so some expense in TSS will probably be a lesser concern. However, we cannot dismiss the issue. Measures you can take to minimize the costs of the Tss library, or any TSS API, are to pass TSS data down through call chains, rather than have each layer retrieve it by itself and thereby risk precipitating context switches due to contention in the TSS infrastructure. Obviously this cannot be achieved with system library functions, or other very general or widely used functions, but is possible within your own application implementations.

Further, for the Tss store it's good to use the `TssSlotScope` template, since it will only attempt to update the slot when the value needs to be changed.

As usual, the choice of strategies is yours, representing a trade-off between performance, robustness, ease of programming, and required functionality.

CHAPTER 11

Statics

Static objects are distinguished from stack variables and heap variables in that their storage is fixed and allocated by the linker, and their lifetimes are (largely) independent from the execution flow of the process. Static objects fall into three categories.

1. Function-local static variables are those that are defined within function scope.
2. Global and namespace-global static variables—also known as nonlocal statics—are those that are defined in the global namespace or within a named or anonymous namespace.
3. Static member variables are those that are shared between instances of the class within which they're defined.

This chapter looks at the problems inherent in the use of static objects and suggests some measures to ameliorate them.

It's important to realize that the initialization of static objects is a two-phase operation. First, the memory they occupy is zero-initialized by the "implementation." The standard (C++-98: 3.6.2;1) states that "the zero initialization of all local objects with static storage duration is performed before any other initialization takes place." In practice this is usually carried out by the operating system process loading mechanism because the variables are placed in the `.data` (or `.bss`) segment of the link unit (executable or dynamic library), which is simply copied into a read-write memory segment [Lind1994]. In Listing 11.1, the variables `i1` and `i2` would both be initialized to zero.

Listing 11.1

```
extern int SomeOtherModulesFunc();

namespace StaticsAbound
{
  inline int LocalFunc()
  {
    return 10;
  }
  struct Thing
  {
    Thing()
      : i(SomeOtherModulesFunc())
    {}
    int i;
  } thing;
```

```
    int i1 = 0;
    int i2;
    int i3 = 1;
    int i4 = LocalFunc();
    int i5 = ::SomeOtherModulesFunc();
}
```

When static objects are of POD type (see Prologue) and are initialized from constant expressions, their values can be written into the executable by the compiler, and therefore do not require any run time initialization, that is, i3 would be given the value 1 during compilation/linking. Furthermore, it is legal (C++-98: 3.6.2;2) for an implementation to make optimizations and apply static initialization in circumstances where it can determine that the dynamic initialization would result in an identical value. Hence, it would be legal for compilers to static initialize i4 to the value 10.

Zero and constant initialization are collectively known as *static initialization*: this is the first phase. All other initialization is known as *dynamic initialization*; the second phase. Dynamic initialization is required for anything that cannot be completely determined at compile time, which includes the initialization of POD types to dynamic values, as well as the construction of nonlocal static class type objects: i5 and thing in Listing 11.1.

All static initialization is carried out before any dynamic initialization. Furthermore, it is usual for all dynamic initialization of nonlocal static objects to be carried out before main() is executed, although this is not mandated by the standard. As described in (C++-98: 3.6.2;3), a nonlocal static object must be initialized before the "first use of any function or object defined in the same translation as the object to be initialised." In practice, such late initialization is rare, and the compilers with which I'm familiar do this prior to the entry of main().[1] Tellingly, (C++-98: 3.6.1;1) states that, in a free-standing environment, "start-up contains the execution of constructors for objects of namespace scope with static storage duration," which could lead one to believe that the expectation of the standards body is that dynamic initialization of nonlocal static objects is completed prior to main().

11.1 Nonlocal Static Objects: Globals

Despite the fact that the language clearly defines the relationships between the initialization phases and the mainline execution, the use of nonlocal static objects has several pitfalls (see section 15.5) and is generally not recommended [Sutt2000, Dewh2003]. The main problem with their use relates to ordering, and we'll look at this now.

The ordering problem is comprised of two closely related issues. The first problem is that it is possible to have cyclic interdependencies between two or more static variables. This is a fundamental engineering issue, and there's no solution to it, but there are ways in which it can be made more detectable.

The second problem is that it is possible to reference a nonlocal static variable before it is initialized, or after it has been uninitialized. This is a constant source of consternation for developers, and a constant topic of conversation on newsgroups, and may be said to be an imperfection of C++.

---

[1]Presumably this is implementation defined to cater for embedded or other non-run-of-the-mill environments.

Imperfection: C++ does not provide a mechanism for controlling global object ordering.

11.1.1   Intracompilation Unit Ordering

Within a given compilation unit, the lifetime of global objects obeys the same ordering as do stack objects: they are constructed in the order of their definition, and destroyed in reverse order (C++-98: 3.6.2;1). Note that it is the order of definition, not declaration, that is important. In Listing 11.2, the order of construction is o1, o2, o3, o4, and the order of destruction is o4, o3, o2, o1.

Listing 11.2

```
class Object;

extern Object o2;

Object  o1("o1");
Object  o2("o2");

int main()
{
  Object   o3("o3");
  Object   o4("o4");

  return 0;
}
```

When the static objects are in the process's compilation unit, they are constructed prior to the entry to main() and destroyed after main() returns.

It is entirely legal and proper to have one global object dependent on another that has already been defined within the same link unit. Hence o2 could have been defined as a copy of o1.

```
extern Object o2;

Object  o1("o1");
Object  o2(o1);   // This is fine
```

However, though the compiler will let you do so, it is not valid to have a dependency on another that has not yet been defined, even if it has been declared. The following leads to undefined behavior:

```
extern Object o2;

Object  o1(o2);   // Undefined!
Object  o2("o2");
```

Since the space for global objects is preallocated and zero initialized, `o1` is passed the correct address of `o2`, but the members of `o2` are all zero. Depending on the definition of `Object`, this may cause a crash or merely result in a silent error. In some circumstances it will produce correct behavior, but it is still a serious mistake to rely on it.

11.1.2   Intercompilation Unit Ordering

When it comes to the issue of ordering of globals between compilation units, we're firmly in implementation-defined territory. In practice this comes down to the linker. For most linkers, the global objects are ordered according to the order of linking of the compilation units. Consider Listing 11.3.

Listing 11.3
```
// object.h
class Object { . . .};
extern Object o1;
extern Object o2;
extern Object o3;

// main.cpp
#include "object.h"
Object o0("o0");
Object o1("o1");
int main() { . . . }

// object2.cpp
#include "object.h"
Object o2("o2");

// object3.cpp
#include "object.h"
Object o3("o3");
```

Stipulating the object files for `object1.cpp`, `object2.cpp`, and `object3.cpp` in that order to the linker, the ordering for several compilers is shown in Table 11.1:

Table 11.1

Compiler/Linker	Order
Borland C/C++ 5.6	o0, o1, o2, o3
CodeWarrior 8	o0, o1, o2, o3
Digital Mars 8.38	o3, o2, o0, o1
GCC 3.2	o3, o2, o0, o1
Intel C/C++ 7.0	o0, o1, o2, o3
Visual C++ 6.0	o0, o1, o2, o3
Watcom C/C++ 12	o3, o2, o0, o1

Evidently these compilers operate two clear, but opposing, strategies. Borland, CodeWarrior, Intel, and Visual C++ cause global objects to be constructed in the order corresponding to the object file link order. Digital Mars, GCC, and Watcom do the reverse.

This inconsistency causes a problem. If all compilers/linkers supported a standard global object ordering mechanism, it would be possible to rely on a predictable global object ordering in your application.

Doing so is a fragile thing, to be sure, since the correctness of your code depends on something external to it: the ordering of object files in the makefile/project-file. It would take very little "effort" in a large project to break such dependencies, and such breakage could be very difficult to diagnose, or even detect.

Nonetheless, relying on linker-controlled object file ordering is, in principle, a way of achieving static object ordering. If you are sufficiently confident of your development team, and the stability of your tools, you may choose to employ this technique. The difficulty remains, however, of validating that your build project(s) continue to reflect the required linker ordering through the lifetime of your product.

One practical measure of this is to insert debugging code into each compilation unit, in debug builds at least, to trace out the initialization order. Since we know that the order within a given compilation unit is fixed, and that the objects are either all initialized prior to `main()`, or prior to the first use of any one of them, all we need to do is to inject a tracing, nonlocal, static object at the beginning or end of each compilation unit, and we will be able to unambiguously determine the linker ordering.

Let's look at how this can be done. `CUTrace.h` contains the declaration of the function `CUTraceHelper()`, which prints the file being initialized, a message, and some optional arguments. It might be something like `". . . cu_ordering_test.cpp: Initialising."` The other function is `CUTrace()`, which simply takes the message and arguments, and passes them, along with the file, to `CUTraceHelper()`:

```
// CUTrace.h
extern void CUTraceHelper(char const *file, char const *msg, va_list args);

namespace
{
  void CUTrace(char const *message, ...)
  {
    va_list args;
    va_start(args, message);
    CUTraceHelper(__BASE_FILE__, message, args);
    va_end(args);
  }
  . . .
} // namespace
```

There are two important features of this. The first is that `CUTrace()` is defined in an anonymous namespace, which means that each compilation unit gets a copy of the function (see section 6.4). However, this is not a concern, since compilers can easily optimize it down to the call to `CUTraceHelper()`. In any case, such a thing would likely only be used in debug and test versions, rather than the full release. Without the `static`, the linker would complain about multiple definitions, whereas using `inline` would just result in all but one version being elided by the linker.

The second feature is the use of the nonstandard symbol `__BASE_FILE__`. Digital Mars and GCC both define this symbol as the name of the primary implementation file for which the compilation is taking place, generally the file named on the command-line. Thus, even though `CUTrace()` is defined in the header `CUTrace.h`, it will pass the name of the primary implementation file through to `CUTraceHelper()`.

Naturally, since this symbol is nonstandard, this technique does not work in its current form for other compilers. The answer is to provide `__BASE_FILE__` for other compilers. Admittedly it's verbose, but it works, and it's easy to insert it with a Perl, Python, or Ruby script.[2] And let's be honest: if you're going to the extreme measure of relying on linker ordering, this extra bit of code in each source file won't be the top of your list of concerns.

```
// SomeImplFile.cpp
#ifndef __BASE_FILE__
static const char __BASE_FILE__[] = __FILE__;
#endif /* __BASE_FILE__ */
#include "CUTrace.h"
. . .
```

The last part of the picture uses internal linkage again, this time to ensure that we get a single copy of the class `CUTracer`.

```
// CUTrace.h
. . .
namespace
{
    . . .
    static CUTracer    s_tracer;
} // namespace
```

Note that this also works if you declare `CUTrace()` and `s_tracer static` (see section 6.4), but the anonymous namespace is the better option as long as you don't need to support any old compiler relics.

Even if you wisely don't want to get into linker ordering as a means of developing your program—and let's be frank: who wants to write code whose correctness depends on observed behavior?—this technique can still be a very useful diagnostic aid, so I'd recommend your including it on big projects, even if I wouldn't recommend that you rely on linker ordering in your work.

Recommendation: Don't rely on global object initialization ordering. Do utilize global object initialization ordering tracing mechanisms anyway.

---

[2]I've included a reasonably competent one on the CD.

11.1.3   Avoid Globals, in the main()

Obviously, one can avoid all these problems by simply not having any global variables, but there are just some times when you cannot avoid the need for them. A simple, albeit inelegant, way to avoid them is to change your global objects into stack objects within main(), from where you can explicitly control their lifetimes, and give out pointers to them to the other code in your executable. Listing 11.4 shows how this can be achieved.

Listing 11.4

```
// global1.h
class Global1
{
  . . .
};
extern Global1 *g_pGlobal1;

// global2.h
class Global2
{
  . . .
};
extern Global2 *g_pGlobal2;

// main.cpp
#include "global1.h"
#include "global2.h"

int main(. . .)
{
  Global1  global1;
  g_pGlobal1 = &global1;

  Global2  global2;
  g_pGlobal2 = &global2;

  return g_pGlobal2->Run(. . .)
}
```

The obvious drawback to this is that you have to use all the global variables by pointer, which can lead to a small loss of efficiency to go along with the small syntactic inconvenience. A more insidious drawback is that if any of the client code of the objects somehow itself makes use of global variables and uses the main()-based, faux-global variables outside of main(), your program will crash in a heap. But where it is manageable you get full control over your static objects' lifetimes and ordering, so it's sometimes worth the effort.

11.1.4 Global Objects Coda: Ordering

In the general case, managing global object ordering in a predictable and portable fashion is very difficult, if not impossible. However, we'll see in the next section that things are a little bit more tractable when dealing with singletons (see section 11.2). It is possible to adapt one of the solutions to the singleton ordering problem—the counted-API solution—to the issue of global objects if each global object of a given type can be associated with a unique compile-time identifier, but that's getting outside the scope of this chapter. Indeed, to solve that problem requires so many leaps through burning hoops that it's better to step back and consider whether the right questions were asked at the design stage.

11.2 Singletons

The notion of the singleton pattern [Gamm1995] is that for a given type there exists only a single instance of it. In C++, the implementation of a singleton generally relies on a static object. Since C++ lets you shoot your leg off,[3] if a type relies on singleton semantics the author of the type should ensure that only a single instance *can* be created. There are several mechanisms available, all of which rely on the `static` keyword in one form or another.

11.2.1 Meyers Singleton

In [Meye1998] Scott Meyers describes what has come to be known as the Meyers Singleton. Basically, it looks like this:

Listing 11.5
```
class Thing
{
public:
  Thing &GetInstance()
  {
    static Thing s_instance;
    return s_instance;
  }
private:
  Thing(Thing const &);
  Thing &operator =(Thing const &);
};
```

This uses lazy-evaluation [Meye1996] to create the single instance on demand, via the `GetInstance()` method. Hiding copy constructor and copy assignment operator ensure that no other instances can be made.

---

[3]Bjarne Stroustrup is widely reputed to have said something like: "C makes it easy to shoot yourself in the foot; C++ makes it harder, but when you do it blows your whole leg off" [Stro-Web]. I think this book demonstrates that I'm in agreement with that sentiment.

There are several problems with this. First, it uses local static objects, which we look at in detail in section 11.3, and therefore represents, in its current guise, a race condition in multi-threaded execution.

Second, you have no control over the lifetime of the instance, beyond the fact that it is created the first time it is used, and will be destroyed during the process shutdown mechanisms, along with all other static objects (local and nonlocal). If something—probably another static object's destructor—calls `Thing::GetInstance()` after the destruction of `s_instance`, it will be talking to an uninitialized object, and bad things will happen. This is known as the Dead Reference problem [Alex2001].

11.2.2   Alexandrescu Singleton

A sophisticated solution to the dead-reference problem is provided in the form of the Alexandrescu Singleton [Alex2001], which hooks into the language cleanup mechanisms for singleton objects and ensures that they are destroyed according to a relative longevity rating.

Each type's single instance is created on the heap, and the logical nature of the type would be similar to the following:

Listing 11.6
```
class Thing
{
public:
  Thing &GetInstance()
  {
    if(NULL == sm_instance) // The real one would be thread-safe
    {
      sm_instance = new Thing();
      SingletonInfrastructure::Register(sm_instance, . . .);
    }
    return *sm_instance;
  }
private:
  static Thing *sm_instance;
  . . .
};
```

The destruction of `Thing` is then scheduled in a manner according to a programmer-supplied grading of its "longevity." Although the actual implementation is quite complex, it would be churlish of me to shy away from complexity if it helps overcome an imperfection, and I'm sure you'd be the first to point that out, gentle reader.

Using this technique would actually result in your code containing something like the following:

```
class ThingImpl { . . .};
class AnotherImpl { . . .};
```

```
inline unsigned GetLongevity(ThingImpl *) { return 3; }
inline unsigned GetLongevity(AnotherImpl *) { return 1; }

typedef SingletonHolder<ThingImpl, . . .>       Thing;
typedef SingletonHolder<AnotherImpl, . . .>     Another;
```

The GetLongevity() functions provide a relative longevity, which the infrastructure then uses to arbitrate destruction ordering to ensure that Thing lives longer than Another.[4]

There are some really interesting and informative concepts bound up in this implementation, and I heartily recommend that you familiarize yourself with it, but the problem I have is that the solution is based on the programmer providing the ranking values for all global objects in the system. This seems to be easy to get wrong, and potentially hard to diagnose, since there's no reason that an erroneous ranking would show up within an arbitrary test sequence. Furthermore it could require a considerable amount of effort if new types/singletons need to be added into the mix. My solution, which we'll meet shortly, is much less sophisticated, but also requires less foresight from the programmer.[5]

11.2.3 Just-in-Time Schwarz Counters: A Nifty Idea

There's a really simple solution to the global object ordering issue known as the Schwarz Counter—also called the "Nifty Counter"—which was described by Jerry Schwarz [Lipp1998], as a mechanism for ensuring that static objects within the IOStreams library are available before mainline execution begins, and before they are used by any other static objects.[6]

We've seen an example of this already, in section 6.4, for ensuring timely new handler installation. The technique is to define an initializer class, and inject an instance of it into every compilation unit that includes the header of the class or API to initialize. When applied to the Thing class, it would look like the following:

Listing 11.7
```
class Thing
{
public:
  Thing &GetInstance();
  . . .
};


struct ThingInit
{
  ThingInit()
```

---

[4]These functions are actually attribute shims, which we meet in Chapter 20.

[5]You might suggest that this may be a reflection of my own limitations; I couldn't possibly comment.

[6]This technique is one of the most widely "invented" in C++. Being more doer than reader, I had my own private *Eureka!* moment on this issue, only to subsequently realize that smarter people had been there before me.

```
    {
        Thing::GetInstance();
    }
};
static ThingInit s_thingInit;
```

Now the static[7] instance `s_thingInit` will acquire the instance in each compilation unit. The first one in gets the worm, and the assumption is that it will also be the last one to need it. The Schwarz counter works really well for independent static objects that merely serve other "client" objects or mainline code. However, there are still two problems with this approach.

First, if you are brave enough to be starting threads from within global object initialization, then it's possible to have a race condition in the `GetInstance()` method. In general it's not a desirable thing to be starting threads before you enter `main()`, for a variety of reasons, not the least of which is that its possible to deadlock the process since some run time libraries use dynamic library initialization functions, which are internally serialized, to activate global object constructors and provide thread attachment notifications.

Recommendation: Don't create threads during global object initialization.

The second problem is that it is still possible to have ordering problems. If the order of inclusion is different in different compilation units, it is still possible to get things created and destroyed in the wrong order. Say you have two classes A and B, in files `headerA.h` and `headerB.h`, that also contain initializer objects `initA` and `initB`, respectively. Now we have two implementation files `X.cpp` and `Y.cpp`, as follows:

```
// X.cpp
#include <headerA.h> // brings in initA
#include <headerB.h> // brings in initB

// Y.cpp
#include <headerB.h> // brings in initB
#include <headerA.h> // brings in initA
```

The designers of A and B have nicely used forward declarations, so if A depends on B, its header merely declares `class B;` rather than including `headerB.h`, and vice versa.

But, again, we are subject to the vagaries of linker order. If the objects in `X.cpp` are link ordered before those in `Y.cpp`, we will have the initialization order of `initA`, `initB`, `initB`, `initA`, which will create the A singleton before the B singleton. If the link ordering is reversed, the singleton creation is reversed.

---

[7]As I've said before (see sections 6.4 and 11.1.2), anonymous namespaces are the preferred mechanism of achieving internal linkage. I'm using `static` here because the code shown in the next section uses it. In any case, I'm not frightened of looking like a crusty old duffer.

Although this ordering fragility is rare in practice, it can still happen, so this solution is not good enough.

11.2.4 Counting on APIs

In C, the unit of functionality above the function is the library, as represented by the set of functions, or API, that provide access to it. Some libraries are simply a set of related, but unbound, functions. A good example of this would be the C standard library's string functions.[8] We can call these *stateless libraries*.

Other libraries, however, maintain internal state that supports some or all of their functions. These are *stateful libraries*. We saw an example of this with the Tss library from section 10.5.

A library may itself be stateless, but might use other stateful libraries for the implementation of its functionality. Since it will rely, indirectly, on the state of the underlying libraries, we'll regard them as stateful for the purposes of this discussion.

It is a requirement of stateful libraries that they be initialized prior to their use, and uninitialized once they are no longer needed. This initialization can take several forms. It may be that the initialization function should be called once only. This would usually be done within the process `main()`. Another form may be that the initialization function ignores all but the first call. Either of these forms may come with an uninitialization function, but that's not always the case.

Both of these forms represent a problem when used in applications consisting of multiple link units. A better form allows multiple calls of the initialization function, and a corresponding collection of multiple calls of the uninitialization function—so-called reference-counting APIs.

Although it's not often discussed, all general purpose, and most specific, libraries should be able to be multiply initialized/uninitialized, such that each component of client code within a greater whole can be made as independent as possible. The unappealing alternative is having to rely on the author of the applications within which they reside to provide the initialization for them.

As long as clients of such APIs faithfully initialize and uninitialize them correctly, and as long as the APIs reference count the APIs that they themselves use, then it all works without a hitch.

For example, the initialization and uninitialization functions for the Tss library (see section 10.5) look like the following (with error-handling elided):[9]

Listing 11.8
```
int Tss_Init(void)
{
  CoreSync_Init();  // Initialise synch objects API
  Mem_Init();       // Initialise the memory API
  {
```

---

[8]With one or two minor exceptions, e.g., `strtok()`.
[9]I can't show you the unprintable contents of _sg_tsslib() here, but it's on the CD if you really must torture yourself.

```
    Scope_CoreSync  lock(sg_cs);
    _sg_tsslib(1); // Create the tss singleton
  }
  return 0;
}
void Tss_Uninit(void)
{
  {
    Scope_CoreSync  lock(sg_cs);
    _sg_tsslib(-1); // Close the tss singleton
  }
  Mem_Uninit();
  CoreSync_Uninit();
}
```

Thus the Tss library cannot possibly be used when the libraries on which it depends—Core-Sync and Mem—are not initialized. So the ordering problem does not raise its ugly head.

A great side effect of this approach is that any cyclic interdependencies are detected immediately, since the initialization will go into an infinite loop. Although we don't like infinite loops, they are very useful if their occurrence is deterministic, as it is in this case. If your initialization function returns to you, you have no cyclic interdependencies; if it does not, then your code's not ready to ship.

There's one final minor point. Some libraries require that the first call to the initialization function be (manually) serialized, that is, the user of the library must ensure that the first call is made from the main thread before any other threads have a chance of calling it. This is usually because the synchronization primitives used to ensure thread-safe access are themselves created within the first call. While in most cases this does not represent a problem, it is self-evident that libraries that can handle multithreaded initialization are more robust and easier to use.

11.2.5   Counted APIs, Wrappers, Proxies: Ordered Singletons at Last!

This whole issue bugged me for several years, until I realized that taking what some might term a step back actually represents a (simple) step forward. I recognize that I may be accused of teaching grandma to suck eggs by C programmers, or of being anachronistic by C++ programmers, but I'm afraid a solution is all I want here, and that's what we've got. Simply put, a multiply-initializable stateful library is logically equivalent to a singleton. Given that we've seen that we can provide correct ordering for such libraries, it's but a small leap to represent ordered singletons as thin wrappers over them. All that needs to be done is to throw a little Schwarz counter and #ifdef exclusion into the mix, and we're there.

Using the Tss library as an example, the singleton form would look like Listing 11.9.

Listing 11.9
```
class Tss
{
public:
  Tss()
```

```
  {
    if(Tss_Init() < 0)
    {
      . . . // Throw an appropriate exception
    }
  }
  ~Tss()
  {
    Tss_Uninit();
  }
  HTssKey CreateKey( void (*pfnClose)()
                   , void (*pfnClientConnect)()
                   , void (*pfnClientDisconnect)()
                   , Boolean bCloseOnAssign = false);
  . . . // other Tss API functions as methods
private:
  . . . Hide copy ctor and assignment operator
};
#ifndef ACMELIB_BUILDING_TSS_API
static Tss  tss; // The Schwarz counter
#endif /* ACMELIB_BUILDING_TSS_API */
```

First, each compilation unit that includes the header gets the Schwarz counter, and so every compilation unit that needs it is guaranteed that the Tss "singleton" exists. Second, the ordering dependencies between the "singletons" is handled within the Init/Uninit functions of the APIs—any library that itself relies on the presence of the Tss library will call Tss_Init/Unit within its own initialization functions; that's the dead reference problem handled. Finally, the Schwarz counter is elided from the compilation unit(s) in which the Tss library itself resides, since we don't want it to have a dependency on itself.

This technique discards, at least in plain form, the lazy evaluation of most C++-based singleton techniques. However, it is pretty simple to dissociate the initialization of the API from the creation of the underlying state, and lazily create the state on demand. Since it is the API, and not the instance, that is reference counted, the creation of the state can be deferred until needed but yet deterministically destroyed when the API reference count goes to 0.

There's an implicit assumption in all this, which is that the library state can be resurrected if, after an uninitialization, it can be reinitialized. In practice, I've never encountered any problems in making this possible, or in having it happen, but it's only fair to mention it, since you may run into a situation in which that's not feasible and/or desirable.

The only real penalty of this approach is that there is an efficiency cost in the use of the singleton. It's very likely that there'll always be one function call per singleton method call that is not inlined (except where using whole-program optimizations). However, since a singleton is usually a big thing, doing big important things, this is probably not going to be noticeable. In any case, correctness is more important than efficiency.

Whether you choose to use simple wrappers over the library API, or whether you incorporate the portable *vtable*s technique to actually be manipulating bona fide C++ objects is up to you; in either case you're working with a singleton!

11.3   Function-Local Static Objects

In the last two sections we looked at nonlocal static objects. In this one we'll look at local-static objects, which are those defined at function-scope, such as

```
Local &GetLocal()
{
  static Local local;
  return local;
}
```

The crucial difference between nonlocal and local static objects is that local static objects are created when they are needed, that is to say the first time the function is called. Subsequent calls simply use the already-constructed instance. Naturally there needs to be some mechanism to record that an instance has been constructed, and so an implementation will use an unseen initialization flag.

Although the mechanism of flagging the initialization is not specified by the standard, the implication is pretty clear. Section (C++-98: 6.7;4) states that "an object is initialized the first time control passes through its declaration; . . . If the initialization exits by throwing an exception, the initialization is not complete, so it will be tried again the next time control enters the declaration. If control re-enters the declaration (recursively) while the object is being initialized, the behaviour is undefined." Hence, the previous function actually looks much like the following, under the covers:

Listing 11.10
```
Local &GetLocal()
{
  static bool  __bLocalInitialized__  = false;
  static byte  __localBytes__[sizeof(Local)];
  if(!__bLocalInitialized__)
  {
    new(__localBytes__) Local();
    __bLocalInitialized__ = true;
  }
  return *reinterpret_cast<Local*>(__localBytes__);
}
```

The problem with this situation is that in multithreaded environments it is subject to a race condition. Two or more threads could come in and see that __bLocalInitialized__ is false, and simultaneously go on to construct local. This could result in a leak, or it could crash the process, but whatever does happen it's undesirable.

One might naively[10] suppose that using the volatile keyword on the static declaration might help. After all, the C standard says (C99-5.1.2.3;2) that "accessing a volatile object, modifying an object, modifying a file, or calling a function that does any of those operations are

---

[10]I'm talking about myself here. Ah, bittersweet memories. . . .

all side effects, which are changes in the state of the execution environment. . . . At certain specified points in the execution sequence called sequence points, all side effects of previous evaluations shall be complete and no side effects of subsequent evaluations shall have taken place. (A summary of the sequence points is given in annex C.)" The C++ standard says much the same thing in (C++-98: 1.9;7).

Alas, the fact that the standards say nothing about threading means that one cannot rely on an implementation supporting our presumption. In practice, the use of `volatile` does nothing to ensure that the use of an object is thread safe. Thus, `volatile` is essentially a mechanism for dealing with hardware, although it's occasionally useful for other things (see section 12.5).

Imperfection: Function-local static instances of classes with nontrivial constructors are not thread-safe.

11.3.1 Sacrifice Lazy Evaluation

One way to obviate this risk is to use the Schwarz counter to ensure that all local static instances are initialized prior to going into multithreaded mode (with the caveat being that threads are not initiated in any global object constructors, as mentioned in section 11.1). This is effective, but it does negate most of the purpose of having the object local. Furthermore, it is quite possible that some functions containing local statics would behave inappropriately if called too early; we could be back to the global object problems again.

11.3.2 Spin Mutexes to the Rescue

The race condition inherent in the initialization of thread-local objects is very important, so it cannot be ignored. However, it is also very rare. We can trade on this rarity and use a wonderfully elegant solution,[11] based on spin mutexes, which are themselves dependent on atomic operations, both of which were examined at length in Chapter 10.

```
Local &GetLocal()
{
  static int             guard; // Will be zeroed at load time
  spin_mutex             smx(&guard); // Spin on "guard"
  lock_scope<spin_mutex> lock(smx);   // Scope lock of "smx"
  static Local           local;
  return local;
}
```

This all works because the static `guard` variable is set to zero during the zero-initialization phase of the process initialization. The non-`static` `spin_mutex` instance `smx` operates on `guard`, and is itself locked by a parameterization of the `lock_scope` template, also non-`static`. Therefore, the only way to get to the test of the unseen initialization flag for `local`, and to `local` itself, is guarded by the efficient guard mechanism of the spin mutex.

---

[11]Reader hint: Anytime I refer to a solution as wonderfully elegant, you can be sure it's one that I *think* I've invented.

There's a cost to this, to be sure, but, as we saw in section 10.3, spin mutexes are very low cost except where there is a high degree of concurrent contention around the guarded section, or the guarded section is long, or both. Since in all but the first case the guarded section will consist of one compare (of the unseen initialization flag) and one move (returning the address of `local`), the section itself is very low cost. And it is hard to conceive of any client code where several threads will be contending for the `Local` singleton with such frequency that the likelihood of them wasting cycles in the spin will be appreciable. Therefore, this is a very good solution for guarding local statics against races.

11.4   Static Members

It would be churlish to leave a chapter on statics without covering static members, so let's do that now. Some of the issues in this section are new; others are a look at issues raised in earlier chapters.

11.4.1   Heading Off Linker Issues

Sometimes, you will be coding to library classes or functions that never change for the life of the process, or for the life of the current user or system session, or even for the life of the system installation. In such cases, it is undesirable to call into these components each time you want to access the constant information, especially when the information is itself potentially quite expensive.

A good example of this is the Win32 high performance counter API, which consists of two functions:

```
BOOL QueryPerformanceCounter(LARGE_INTEGER *);
BOOL QueryPerformanceFrequency(LARGE_INTEGER *);
```

Each takes a pointer to a 64-bit integer. The first returns the current value of the system's hardware high-performance counter. The second returns the counter's frequency, which cannot change during the lifetime of the system session and, in practice, is constant for a given processor. The frequency is used to translate the machine specific epochs returned by `Query PerformanceCounter()` into actual time intervals.

Naturally, my C++ instincts bristle at using a naked API such as this, so a wrapper class got written the second time I had to use it.[12] The `high_performance_counter` class maintains two integers that represent a measured interval (acquired by calls to `start()` and `stop()` methods), and provides methods to interpret the interval in seconds, milliseconds, or microseconds. The problem is that both these API functions have quite a large call cost in and of themselves [Wils2003a], so it's prudent to avoid the unnecessary repeated calls to `QueryPerformanceFrequency()` by caching the value. This is the classic static member situation. However, since one of the guiding principles of STLSoft is to be 100% header-

---

[12]Robert L. Glass [Glas2003] makes a compelling case for avoiding premature generalization by deferring the conversion of code from specific to reusable until the *second* time you need it, and I tend to agree.

only,[13] this represents a challenge. The way to provide it is to use a function-local `static` instance, from within a `static` method, as in:

```
class high_performance_counter;
{
  . . .
private:
  static LARGE_INTEGER const &frequency()
  {
    static LARGE_INTEGER s_frequency;
    return s_frequency;
  }
  . . .
```

But that's only half the picture; it's not yet initialized. The answer is to initialize s_frequency with a call to another `static` method to retrieve the frequency value, as in Listing 11.11.

Listing 11.11
```
class high_performance_counter;
{
  . . .
  static LARGE_INTEGER const query_frequency()
  {
    LARGE_INTEGER freq;
    if(!QueryPerformanceFrequency(&freq))
    {
      freq = std::numeric_traits<sint64_t>::max();
    }
    return freq;
  }
  static LARGE_INTEGER const &frequency()
  {
    static LARGE_INTEGER s_frequency = query_frequency();
    . . .
```

Note that if the system does not support a hardware performance counter, and `Query PerformanceCounter()` returns `FALSE`, then the value is set to the maximum value, so that subsequent division of the interval will not result in a divide by zero error, but will just return `0`. I chose this approach because these performance measurement classes are intended for code profiling rather than as part of application functionality; you might wish to have it throw an exception.

---

[13]I should come clean and admit that I have a personal, and probably dogmatic, bias against implementation files that are needed only for static members. In calm moments, I wonder whether this is rationale, but I just can't seem to shake my love of the unfettered "atomic" `#include`. Whether rationale or not, it serves to provide much material for this chapter that (I hope) is germane to the topic of statics.

But we're not quite there yet, since we're using a function-local static, and they are generally subject to races. In this case, the worst that can happen is that the `query_frequency()` may be called multiple times in extremely rare circumstances. Since it always returns the same value, and we need the performance counter class itself to be as low-cost as possible, I chose to risk the very rare, but benign, multiple initialization.

11.4.2 Adaptive Code

Before we finish the subject of static members, I'd just like to show you a final sneaky trick,[14] which allows you to write classes that can adapt their own behavior to the circumstances in which they find themselves.

The performance counter class described in the last section had a problem in that if the hardware counter were unavailable the user of the class would be left with useless timings all reading 0. In fact, Win32 supports other timing functions, one of which, `GetTickCounter()`, is available on all platforms, but has much lower resolution [Wils2003a]. Hence, another class, `performance_counter`, attempts to provide the high-resolution measurements where possible, and the low-resolution ones where not.

To do this, it eschews direct calls of `QueryPerformanceCounter()` in favor of calling a static method `measure()`, defined as shown in Listing 11.12.

Listing 11.12

```
class performance_counter
{
  . . .
private:
  typedef void (*measure_fn_type)(epoch_type&);
  static void performance_counter::qpc(epoch_type &epoch)
  {
    QueryPerformanceCounter(&epoch);
  }
  static void performance_counter::gtc(epoch_type &epoch)
  {
    epoch = GetTickCount();
  }
  static measure_fn_type get_measure_fn()
  {
    measure_fn_type fn;
    epoch_type      freq;
    fn = QueryPerformanceFrequency(&freq) ? qpc : gtc;
    return fn;
  }
  static void measure(epoch_type &epoch)
```

---

[14]I don't show these things to encourage the arrogant, rebel-without-a-cause attitude that far too many software engineers wear with pride. But I don't believe that hiding complex and dangerous things from people helps much either; look at Java! I show you these things to inform, and because seeing a wrong way can often be as valuable in learning as seeing a right way.

```
  {
    static measure_fn_type  fn  =  get_measure_fn();
    fn(epoch);
  }
// Operations
public:
  inline void performance_counter::start()
  {
    measure(m_start);
  }
inline void performance_counter::stop();
  . . .
```

The `frequency()` and `query_frequency()` methods are the same as before, except that failure from `QueryPerformanceFrequency()` causes the frequency to be set to 1,000, to reflect the fact that `GetTickCounter()` returns millisecond units and gives valid interval divisions.

Once again, race conditions are benign, so they're ignored in favor of keeping the normal call costs of the counter class as low as possible.

11.5   Statics Coda

When you boil it all down, the problems of statics are ordering, identity, and timing. It's not hard to imagine how the language came to be vulnerable to these three issues. Ordering is really only an issue when you have several global objects which accrete interdependencies: this would not have been an issue in the early days of their use, since there simply would not have been many at all, just the odd `cout` and `cin`. Identity is really only a problem when you have multiple link units within an executable; dynamic linking, while not exactly a new technology, is not so old as to have been of prime importance during the original design of C++. Timing is only an issue in multithreaded scenarios; as with dynamic libraries, multithreading is something that has become prevalent after the original designs of C++.

That's not to say that all these problems could have been avoided had the original designers of the language only had sufficient foresight or a time machine. Later languages still fail to address these issues convincingly: sometimes by disallowing the problematic construct—requiring all objects be heap based; sometimes not addressing them any better (and often worse) than C++. What new language is efficient, and yet immune to threading issues?

So, I'll trot out my well-worn advice. The only true solution is to be aware of the issues, and use the techniques for obviating, or at least ameliorating, the problems where appropriate. Most of these techniques are conceptually very simple, even if the implementation of them can be tedious (i.e., API-based singletons).

Before we leave this chapter, don't you think it's kind of nice that the answers to most of the problems of the various uses of `static` rely on the `static` keyword itself? And then, of course, there's the old spin mutex. . . .

Optimization

The compilers giveth, and the compilers taketh away; in the end we are just bits twiddling in the jaws of the virtual machine; waiting to execute our little nuggets of logic on an always too-slow meta processor.

— George Frazier, esteemed software engineer and part-time space cadet, 2003

In Chapter 2 we looked at various things that the C++ compiler adds in implicitly if you do not specify your own, such as constructors, copy operators, new and delete operators, and so forth. In this chapter, I want to look at the other side of the coin, and discuss some of the things the compiler takes away for you. Naturally, this is not a full discussion of optimization per se—for that you should look at several good books listed in the bibliography ([Bulk1999, Gerb2002, Meye1998]). It focuses on optimizations that can impact on C++ features, rather than just the performance of your executable.

Note that we do not cover library optimizations—such as the small string optimization [Meye2001], variable automatic buffers (see Chapter 32), or the fast concatenation optimization (see Chapter 25)—here, only language-level optimizations.

12.1 Inline Functions

In a sense, this section is not about optimization as much as it is about borrowing an optimization keyword for other means. The inline keyword was introduced to enable the "programmer to help" [Stro1994] direct the compiler in its optimizations. Although many modern compilers pay as much attention to the command-line optimization options as they do to inline specifiers, it still has a role to play in optimizations.

Incidentally, inline is also featured in C as of the C99 standard. It is also available with many compilers as an extension: _ _inline_ _ for GCC, _ _inline for most other Win32 compilers.

12.1.1 Beware Premature Optimization

Premature optimization is something that we are frequently warned against [Stro1997, Dewh2003, Sutt2002, Meye1996, Meye1998], and the use of inline is included in the list of things not to do. There are several reasons why you should avoid premature inlining. First, time spent optimizing before you have identified performance problems with your application represents time not spent on ensuring robustness, flexibility, maintainability, and all the other important aspects of good coding.

Second, if you inline, say, a class method, then you tie the client code of that method to the class's implementation more closely than would be the case if the method's implementation resided in an implementation file not visible to the client code. Any changes you make to the method will require a recompilation of the client code, and in medium-large projects this can prove expensive [Lako1996]. It can also represent a genuine hazard to your popularity in your team.

Third, you cannot set debug breakpoints in inlined code. Compilers and IDDEs help out here, in inhibiting inlining for debug builds, so most of the time this doesn't crop up. But remember in that case that you will be debugging code paths that do not precisely correspond to what's going to happen in release builds.

Finally, indiscriminate use of `inline` can actually make your code larger, since the compiler may—remember `inline` is an advisory—insert the body of the function at each call site. Large code, coupled with modern pipelining architectures, where instructions are cached in blocks, can actually cause a reduction in speed.

The best thing to do is to listen to the gurus, profile your code, and make informed adjustments accordingly.

12.1.2   Header-Only Libraries

Notwithstanding the caveats described for its use as an optimization measure, `inline` also has other uses. These may not have been in the original intent of its inclusion into the language, but we should not discount them.

When one is writing libraries, it is far easier to distribute and use them if they can be reasonably contained in header files only. Even when a function marked `inline` cannot be inlined, being so marked obliges the compiler/linker to handle any duplicates (C++-98: 3.2;5) without issuing an error message, and usually means that a single definition of the function resides within the link unit.

Hence, `inline` buys the freedom from having to define a single version of a function and to provide it in an implementation file. This is a great benefit when writing libraries. Furthermore, you'll be in good company when doing so, since it's also used throughout the standard library. Of course, much of the standard library is template code, and so *must* be inline, and also expected to perform well, so it's not the only reason it's inline. But it's still a factor, and a significant one at that.

Note that when your functions are templates, you do not need to use the `inline` keyword to guarantee this duplicate coalescence, unless you want your code to be portable to very old compilers (e.g., Visual C++ 4.2).

12.2   Return Value Optimization

The *Return Value Optimisation* (RVO) is widely documented [Dewh2003, Meye1996], so I'm not going to dwell on it too deeply. Basically, if the return value from a function is a call to the constructor of the returned type, the compiler is able to optimize the notional intermediate instance and construct directly into the instance that will receive the return value in the client code. In the following example, the temporary inside `CreateString()` is not created, and the construction occurs directly into the memory occupied by `s1`:

```
String CreateString(char const *s)
{
```

```
    return String((NULL == s) ? "" : s);
}
String  s1 = CreateString("Initialization via Assignment syntax");
```

As long as you write code that uses an explicit constructor, you can pretty well rely on any modern compiler applying this optimization. Given the following client code, the results for several modern compilers can be seen in Table 12.1, which shows the number of object constructions for each case.

```
1 CreateString("1");
2 String  s2 = CreateString("2");
3 String  s3(CreateString("3"));
```

However, there are a couple of weird little nuances in some implementations. If you use the assignment syntax, as shown in case 2 in the table, then the copy constructor must be available in the calling context, even though it's not used. The standard (C++-98: 3.2;2) says "a copy constructor is [considered] even if it is elided by the implementation." So, if your class has hidden the copy constructor (see section 2.2.3), or it cannot be generated by the compiler (see section 2.2.1), you will not be able to use RVO.

Well, that's the theory anyway. If the copy constructor of String is explicit, then only CodeWarrior, Comeau, GCC, and Visual C++ (7.1) pick it up; the others optimize it out anyway. If it is declared private, all the compilers except Digital Mars pick that up. In either case, the application of the optimization absent of an accessible copy constructor is illegal and should not be relied upon.

If you write your code using the function call syntax, you still need the accessible copy constructor, even though, again, it is not used.

```
String s2(CreateString("Init via function call syntax"));
```

In this guise, the compilers are still prone to break the law. The same effects are seen when the copy constructor is declared private or explicit, as with the assignment syntax. But

Table 12.1   The values represent the number of instances
                created for each case.

Compiler	Case 1	Case 2	Case 3
Borland (5.6)	1	1	2
CodeWarrior 8	1	1	1
Comeau 4.3.0.1	1	1	2
Digital Mars 8.38	1	1	1
GCC 3.2	1	1	1
Intel 7.0	1	1	2
Visual C++ 7.1	1	1	1
Watcom 12.0	1	1	1

the strange thing is that several compilers are less able to apply the optimization than with the assignment syntax. As you can see from Table 12.1, Borland 5.6, Comeau 4.3.0.1, and Intel 7.0 all fail to apply RVO in the function call syntax case, whereas all compilers examined applied RVO in the case of the assignment syntax. I can only surmise that their testing has focused on the assignment syntax.

12.2.1 Named Return Value Optimization

The *Named Return Value Optimization* (NRVO) is a slight modification of the RVO, that's almost as widely supported and just as easy to comprehend. Sometimes we might want to manipulate a variable before returning it in a way that is not commensurate with a reasonable class interface. The standard example is in the implementation of addition operators. The last thing we'd want to do is have our class provide a constructor to facilitate concatenation, as in:

```
String operator +(String const &lhs, String const &rhs)
{
  return String(lhs, rhs);
}
```

We might just be able to live with it[1] for strings, since there are not other binary operations returning evaluated results for `String`. But consider how you work with such a strategy for numeric types? What about subtraction, multiplication, division? And don't say that you can have a third parameter to the constructor defining the operation, or I'll tell the publisher to leave the second half of the book blank and charge you double!

Anyway, the canonical implementation of a string concatenation is as a free function, implemented in terms of the += instance method on a copy of the first argument:

```
String operator +(String const &lhs, String const &rhs)
{
  String result(lhs);
  result += rhs;
  return result;
}
```

But since we're not returning an already constructed instance of the type, we lose the facility of RVO. Thankfully, this is where NRVO steps in. It basically does RVO for named instances. As long as the compiler can deduce that the return values from all possible code paths refer to the same variable, it can apply the construction and all subsequent manipulation of the named return value into the return context.

Just as with RVO, there is varying support for NRVO throughout the range of compilers. If we take the same client code from the RVO case, and just change `CreateString()` a little we can test out our compilers for NRVO.

```
String CreateString(char const * s1, char const * s2)
{
```

---

[1] I couldn't live with it. It is daft, ugly, and just plain wrong.

Table 12.2   The values represent the number
of instances created for each case.

Compiler	Case 1	Case 2	Case 3
Borland (5.6)	2	2	3
CodeWarrior 8	2	2	2
Comeau 4.3.0.1	1	1	2
Digital Mars 8.38	1	1	1
GCC 3.2	1	1	1
Intel 7.0	2	2	2
Visual C++ 7.1	2	2	2
Watcom 12.0	1	1	1

```
String result(s1);
result += s2;
return result;
}
```

The results are quite interesting. Table 12.2 shows the number of objects constructed in each of the three cases.

Of course, for both optimizations, it is possible that we are skewing the results by placing a `printf()` statement in to trace the execution. However, even if this is the case, there are two reasons why this does not concern us. First, these optimizations are not there to elide code with no side effects. In the real world, most code where we will care about these optimizations will have such non-zero execution costs. That's the whole point. It wouldn't be a terribly useful optimization otherwise, would it? Second, several of the compilers fully employ the optimizations in the tested form in several cases, and there are not reports of erroneous installations buzzing round the C++ development world.

Notwithstanding the legality issues, there are ramifications for the semantics of your software, not just its performance. If you develop software using a compiler that successfully employs these optimizations in all guises, and your application employs some kind of instance tracking mechanism as a metric on the process's health, you could be in for some unpleasant moments if you port to another compiler, until you realize what's going on.

12.3   Empty Base Optimization

The *Empty Base Optimisation* (EBO) is an optimization that compilers can implement to enable a class derived from an empty base—for example, `class EmptyBase {};`—to occupy no extra space for the base, which makes sense, since it's empty. In other words, the address of the derived part and base part for a given instance is the same. This can be useful when base classes are used for providing member types, as with the standard library `unary_function` and `binary_function` template classes,[2] and also when one is providing policy-based implementation reuse.

---

[2] It is customary to derive your functors (see sections 20.2 and 34.3) from these in order that certain necessary member types are available to standard library algorithm adaptors [Aust1999, Muss2001].

The canonical form of EBO is shown thus:

```
class EmptyBase
{};

class Child
  : EmptyBase
{};

// Child should be same size as any empty class, e.g. EmptyBase
STATIC_ASSERT(sizeof(Child) == sizeof(EmptyBase));  // form 1
```

But this form (which we'll call EBO-1) is scarcely the full picture of the situations in which the optimization can be applied. There are seven forms I can think of. Four of these, involving single inheritance, are shown in Figure 12.1, where the circles represent empty classes, and the squares represent classes with members. P stands for parent, C for child, and G for grandchild.

The second form (EBO-2) is identical to the first, except that the child has one or more member variables, and is, therefore itself of non-zero size. The third (EBO-3) and fourth (EBO-4) forms determine whether the optimization is carried down to children of the optimized derived class. To be honest, it would be hard to conceive of an implementation that would not carry down the optimization, but we constantly learn that implementation-defined behavior leads to surprises.

The last three forms, shown in Figure 12.2, evaluate the application of the optimization to multiple inheritance situations. This is important, since many modern template techniques rely on being able to inherit from a primary nontrivial type, and to inherit additional mixin[3] classes that merely supply type or policies.

Figure 12.1   Single inheritance EBO relationships.

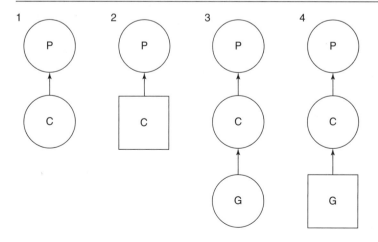

---

[3]One of the nicest bits of C++ terminology. It stems from the term for cookies, cheesecake pieces, and other goodies mixed into deliciously stodgy gourmet ice creams.

Figure 12.2   Multiple-inheritance EBO relationships.

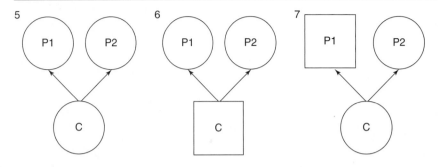

Form five (EBO-5) is where an empty child derives from two empty base classes. Form six (EBO-6) is the same, except that the child is nonempty. Form seven (EBO-7) involves derivation from one empty base class, and one nonempty class; this is much like the situation with some containers implementations that inherit (`private` or `protected`) from an implementation class, and also inherit from an empty allocator mixin class.

Table 12.3 shows the support for a range of Win32 compilers. The results show that most of the compilers support all forms, which is good to know. However, the only forms fully supported by all compilers are the simplistic EBO-1 and EBO-3. Since it's a good bet that most classes for which we would want to take advantage of EBO will have non-zero size themselves, this is not terribly useful.

The only compiler that has a problem with any of the single inheritance forms is Borland 5.6, which can be made to behave by specifying the nondefault flags –Ve and –Vl, which stipulate zero-length base classes and "old Borland class layout," respectively. I'm not sure how usable this will be in a production scenario; we can hope that the next version of the Borland compiler will catch up with the rest.

Anyway, I think that's enough Borland bashing. The only case that presents any kind of problems for any of the other compilers is the case where we have two empty bases from which a nonempty base is derived. Although not the most common inheritance layout, the increasing

Table 12.3   Support for EBO forms. # indicates support.

Compiler	EBO-1	EBO-2	EBO-3	EBO-4	EBO-5	EBO-6	EBO-7
Borland (5.6)	#	–Ve –Vl	#	–Ve –Vl			–Ve –Vl
CodeWarrior	#	#	#	#	#		#
CodePlay	#	#	#	#	#	#	#
Comeau	#	#	#	#	#	#	#
Digital Mars	#	#	#	#	#	#	#
GCC	#	#	#	#	#	#	#
Intel	#	#	#	#	#		#
Visual C++	#	#	#	#	#		#
Watcom	#	#	#	#	#		#

use of policy-based template parameterization mixed with inheritance means that this is a conceivable inheritance relationship.

Imperfection: The support for EBO flavors is not universal, and varies significantly between compilers.

Sure, it's not an imperfection of the C++ language itself, since it's a difference between implementations of an optional optimization. But it does impact the performance of your code, sometimes quite dramatically (see section 32.2.5). So what do we do about it? In one sense, there's very little that can be done. Obviously an important measure is to pick your compiler. Most modern compilers support the optimization in most or all its guises. As for Borland, it's possible that by the time you reach this they will have released their new compiler (to accompany their new C++BuilderX product) and that it implements this optimization.

Second, if you must have broad compilation compatibility, try to use techniques that do not rely on EBO, and learn to live with the space hit when you're using a compiler that does not support it.

There's one slightly bogus trick you can use when the EBO you require is for standard library allocators, which we'll look at in section 32.2.5.

12.4   Empty Derived Optimization

So EBO is about empty bases. What about empty child classes? Consider the following:

```
class X
{
  int i;
};

template <typename T>
class Y
  : T
{};

std::cout << sizeof(Y<X>); // What is the size of Y<X>?
```

Since Y does not provide any more member variables, and does not introduce any virtual members, to its parameterizing type, we'd ideally like to see it adding no additional memory requirements. Hence, `sizeof(Y<X>)` should equal `sizeof(X)`. We could call this *Empty Derived Optimization* to mirror its more widely recognized older brother. So the question is, how do our compilers handle EDO?

As with EBO, there are several situations in which an empty child class can appear, as shown in Figures 12.3 and 12.4. Again P is the parent and C is the child. Note, however, that the use of template child classes is also evaluated, denoted by the angle braces.

But why should we care about this? Well, as we'll see in several examples in Part Four, the use of template classes that derive from their parameterizing types is the basis of some powerful

Figure 12.3   Single inheritance EDO relationships.

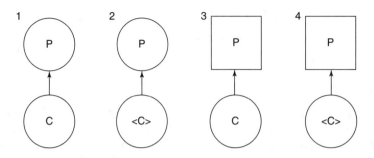

techniques. When we're using such techniques we would never want to waste space, and occasionally being a different size can render a technique invalid (see Chapter 21).

So how do our compilers go with this optimization? Table 12.4 shows that they do a fair bit better. In fact, only Borland has any problem with this optimization.[4] It does not support forms 5–8. However, when using the −Ve and −Vl flags together it does support forms 7 and 8.

Table 12.4

Compiler	EDO-1	EDO-2	EDO-3	EDO-4	EDO-5	EDO-6	EDO-7	EDO-8
Borland (5.6)	#	#	#	#			−Ve −Vl	−Ve −Vl
CodeWarrior	#	#	#	#	#	#	#	#
Comeau	#	#	#	#	#	#	#	#
Digital Mars	#	#	#	#	#	#	#	#
GCC	#	#	#	#	#	#	#	#
Intel	#	#	#	#	#	#	#	#
Visual C++	#	#	#	#	#	#	#	#
Watcom	#	#	#	#	#	#	#	#

Figure 12.4   Multiple-inheritance EDO relationships.

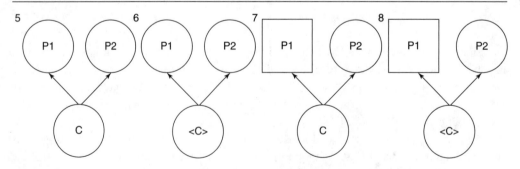

---

[4]By the time you read this, the new Borland C++ compiler for C++BuilderX may be available, and we can hope it will fall into step with the others.

So once again, if you wish to have efficient use of this facility, you have to select your compiler.

12.5   Preventing Optimization

As programmers we spend so much time and effort on facilitating optimization that it can seem strange to want to prevent it. Why would we want to do such a thing?

There are two reasons. First, you may have global optimization settings for your build that are not appropriate for a given compilation unit, or even for a given block of code within a compilation unit. A good example of this is when you are optimizing for space, but you have a particular block of code that you wish to be optimized for speed.

The other reason for disabling optimizations is that in order to increase the efficiency of your code, you sometimes have to disable certain optimizations so that you can actually measure them. Sounds kooky, of course, but some modern compilers are getting so good at optimization that they can hinder your working to increase the efficiency of your own code.

When a whole compilation unit is to be optimized differently, you can simply specify different settings for your compiler(s) in the makefile/project files. However, when the specific settings are required on a subcompilation unit basis, you will have to resort to compiler-specific optimization features. For example, the following code prevents the function `slow()` from being optimized for speed under Intel and Visual C++ irrespective of the optimization settings defined for the compilation unit.

```
// functions.cpp
. . .
# pragma optimize("gt", off)
void slow()
{
  for(int i = 0; i < std::numeric_limits<int>::max(); ++i)
  {}
}
# pragma optimize("", on)
. . .
```

Perversely, some compilers are actually so good at optimization, they are in a sense too good. A program such as the following will be optimized out to nothing by several compilers.

```
int main()
{
  for(int i = 0; i < std::numeric_limits<int>::max(); ++i)
  {}
  return 0;
}
```

Nothing terribly surprising there, apart from the fact that a number of compilers don't actually optimize this one. Of course, in practice you'd be unlikely to be interested in profiling such empty loops. However, you might be attempting to measure the performance of some inline functions, and be contrasting the cost of your functions with equivalent ones that have no actual implementation, as in Listing 12.1.

Listing 12.1

```
template <typename T>
inline T const &func1(T const &t)
{
   . . . // Actual manipulation of t
}
template <typename T>
inline T const &func2(T const &t)
{
  return t; // Stub function. Just return t
}

int main()
{
  performance_counter counter;

  counter.start();
  for(int i = 0; . . .)
  {
    func1(i);
  }
  counter.stop();
  cout << "func1: " << counter.get_millisecond() << endl;

  counter.start();
  for(int i = 0; . . .)
  {
    func2(i);
  }
  counter.stop();
  cout << "func1: " << counter.get_millisecond() << endl;
```

If you run loops to compare the costs of the two functions, some compilers are able to deduce that the second form does nothing, and actually elide the entire loop for the func2() case. CodeWarrior 8 and Visual C++ 7.1 can both do this.

We've already seen that volatile is not useful in multithreading, since the standard does not say anything about threading at all, and it is implementation defined whether a given implementation will respect volatile with respect to threading. However, volatile can be useful in regard to preventing optimization when it's not wanted. Indeed, the standard (C++-98: 7.1.5.1;8) says that "volatile is a hint to the implementation to avoid aggressive optimization involving the object because the value of the object might be changed by means undetectable by an implementation."

So where do we apply it? Well, you might think that you could change the definition of func2() to make its argument type and return type T const volatile &. That actually works for CodeWarrior 8, but Visual C++ 7.1 is just so modern that it can't be fooled so easily. The answer is to apply it to the loop indexer `i`, in which case all the compilers I've tried respect this code.

```
for(int volatile i = 0; . . .)
{}
```

Notwithstanding this, I think we're very much in implementation-defined territory here. I guess we'd be surprised if an implementation didn't respect `volatile` given the wording in the standard, but it's always possible. On a modern operating system that uses virtual memory, the only way a `volatile` variable of such limited scope as our loop indexers could be modified would be via some incredibly clever injection of code from another process. It's certainly conceivable, therefore, for an implementation to just optimize away `volatile`, when it's very sure that it can: the keyword is only a hint, after all.

If you're feeling really paranoid, a very safe option is to call an external system function from within your loop. Since the compiler cannot, in principle, know the internal workings of a system function at compile/link time, it cannot optimize it away. A simple one would be to call `time()`. The downside is that you cannot know that the cost of such calls may not be constant, so you may be skewing your results. The way to get around this is to use a local static, as in Listing 18.2, and so the system call is done once, but your compiler still cannot optimize it all away.

Listing 12.2

```
time_t inhibit_optimization()
{
  static time_t t = time(NULL);
  return t;
}

int main()
{
  int                  ret;
  performance_counter counter;

  counter.start();
  for(int i = 0; . . .)
  {
    . . .
    ret = static_cast<int>(inhibit_optimization());
  }
  . . .
  return ret;
}
```

Anyway, I'm sure you get the idea. `volatile` appears to be able to suppress optimization, but if you want to be really sure you need to have the compiler think that something is variable, even though you know it's constant.

PART THREE

Language Concerns

The new author's almanac of good writing principles advises that the first sections of a book should represent a gentle introduction to the overall subject matter, covering basic concepts and laying firm foundations for later material. They should provide the reader with an opportunity to get a feel for the author's writing style and way of thinking, and should make them comfortable with the material. Later chapters should build on this knowledge, gently steering the reader through the increasing complexity in an incremental fashion.

Well, I've got most of that right. The material in these six chapters covers several fundamental issues, and, though more complex than previous chapters, does not make huge leaps into daunting territory.[1] Nonetheless, I can't promise that you're going to be entirely comfortable: some of the imperfections in this part are best taken with a bar of chocolate and a lie down.

In a bike race, we'd be entering territory with many short, steep foothills. There's nothing to do but grin and bear it, keep up with your teammates, and keep telling yourself that the pain in your legs is necessary to get them properly warmed up for later.

Many of the imperfections described in this part identify "imperfections in the small." In other words, the imperfections are discrete and relatively minor in nature and in the problems that they cause, and the solutions are consequently reasonably straightforward and modest in scope. But almost all highlight important issues that we will return to later in the book, as we move toward some "imperfections in the large" in Parts Four and Five, and look at extending C++ in Part Six.

Several items touch on contentious issues. We cover the virtues of expression layouts, criticisms of the `bool` type and the handling of Boolean values, issues with literals, and problems with "implementation-defined" behavior. I suggest that there are missing keywords, the new `for`-scoping is broken at best, and recommend the use of a reinvigorated NULL. I even have the temerity to suggest that C++ needs a whole new *cv*-qualifier! I hope you'll bear with me as we look at issues that may raise your eyebrows, or your blood pressure; reading a book called *Imperfect C++* must mean you're prepared for *some* controversy, anyway, don't you think?

There are six chapters: Chapter 13, *Fundamental Types;* Chapter 14, *Arrays and Pointers;* Chapter 15, *Values;* Chapter 16, *Keywords;* Chapter 17, *Syntax;* and Chapter 18, *Typedefs.* I hope you learn several new things, are challenged at times, and gain a new appreciation for the subtleties, the flaws, and the underlying strength of C++. The perspective in all cases concerns how best to write code that is correct, efficient, and robust in the face of maintenance. When you've made it through, I expect that you'll want to see how the imperfections and solutions highlighted here will affect the remainder of our journey into C++'s dark corners.

---

[1]I'm saving that for Part Four.

Fundamental Types

Conceptually, a type is defined by a set of values and the operations that may be performed on those values. This is a widely accepted notion of type, and represents the minimum strict definition.

In practice, however, the correct manipulation of types depends not just on a balance between suitability—fitness for purpose—and expressiveness, but also on safety and even "human" factors such as its name. It is important that a type provides you with enough power and flexibility to enable you to clearly and efficiently represent and manipulate the concept you require, but equally important that the range of operations is restricted to a safe and predictable set.

The fundamental types (see Prologue) provided by C++ come from C [Kern1988]. Apart from the `bool` type, which has been added to C++ (the C++-98 standard) and to C (as of the C99 standard), this list has remained largely unchanged from the early days of the language [Stro1994]. As such, there are several subtle hazards associated with the use of these types. Furthermore, the list is a little dated, and there are a number of types that could usefully be added to it.

This chapter looks at some new types that could be useful enhancements to the language and the ways in which they may be provided within the bounds of the current language. We'll also take a look at some problems that we can encounter when using fundamental types, including `bool` which is often more trouble than it's worth (as we discuss in sections 13.4.2 and 15.3).

13.1   May I Have a byte?

Computers use the byte as their fundamental unit of memory storage,[1] so it would seem natural to have a type with which to access and manipulate bytes. Most of the time in C++, and in C, we are interested in dealing with specific types, for example, `char const*`, `Person&`, and so on. However, there are times when we need to manipulate opaque blocks of memory, such as in data compression. In such cases, we are dealing with chunks of bytes, where the content of individual bytes has no meaning.

Imperfection: C and C++ are missing a `byte` type.

Unfortunately, there is no `byte` type in C/C++, and so the common practice in such cases is to use `char`. This makes sense, since the size of `char` is always one byte. The (C++-98) standard does not say this directly, but it does say (C++-98: 5.3.3) that "the `sizeof` operator yields the number of

---

[1]Modern architectures allow individual bytes to be addressed (though there are caveats; see section 10.1), but there have been architectures where pointers of different sizes were used to address different types (e.g., 16-bit pointers for 16-bit words and 24-bit pointers for bytes).

bytes in the object representation of its operand" and "sizeof(char), sizeof(signed char) and sizeof(unsigned char) are 1." Clearly, then, sizeof(char) == sizeof(*byte*) must always be true. (Note that a byte is not necessarily 8 bits, just that it is "large enough to fit the basic character set" [C++-98: 3.9.1.1]. Irrespective of the bit size, however, sizeof(byte) == 1 is an axiom.)

However, there are problems with this approach.

13.1.1   Look for a Sign

The first problem is that the "signedness" of the char type, when not qualified with signed or unsigned, is implementation dependent. This leads to problems when the char-as-byte variable is used in arithmetic conversions where we need to interpret its meaning as a number. If char is signed, then assigning it to a larger type will sign-extend the value [Stro1997]. If an 8-bit char's value were 0xff, then when it is involved in an integer promotion, say to a 32-bit integer (whether signed or unsigned), the result would be 0xffffffff, which is −1 for signed or 4294967295 for unsigned. If char is unsigned, the same assignment will result in a value of 0x000000ff, which is 255 irrespective of integer sign.

The answer to this issue is very simple: always specify the sign. In my opinion the better option is to use unsigned to avoid the sign extension, since this fits my notion of a byte as a collection of bits, though I concede that this is not unequivocally superior to choosing signed; some argue that signed is preferable for finding underrun bugs. The important thing is to make an explicit choice and remove the ambiguity.

13.1.2   It's All in the Name

The second problem is that the names of types carry semantic significance: they suggest their intended use. Of course, the names of types don't matter in the least to a compiler, but they are extremely important to human writers *and* readers of code. Using (un)signed char for a byte is misleading.

Using a type char indicates to the reader that the variable represents a character; if it's a byte, it should be called byte, or byte_t or something similarly obvious. Given Robert L. Glass's [Glas2003] assertion that 60 percent of software engineering is maintenance, it seems prudent to keep your code's maintainer(s)—which may be you in 18 months' time—as informed as possible.

The answer here is to provide a suitable typedef for a byte type, as in:

```
typedef unsigned char byte_t;
```

Consider the following two variable declarations:

```
unsigned char    v1;
byte_t           v2;
```

v2 is unambiguously a byte, with all the semantic significance that conveys. v1 may or may not connote "byte" as opposed to character, depending on the experience and instincts of the developer reading this code. Unfortunately, the APIs for multibyte character set (MBCS) encoding schemes in the very widely used Visual C++ libraries use `unsigned char (const) *` for MBCS character strings, which pretty much nullifies these instincts for developers who use these libraries. Even when `unsigned char` always says "byte" to all the readers of such code, it is all too easy to leave off the sign qualifier, either in your code or in your mind.

Another benefit of the explicit stipulation of sign is that compilers will reject statements like the following:

```
signed byte_t   x;
unsigned byte_t y;
```

This further emphasizes the (logical) independence of bytes from sign.

13.1.3   Peering into the Void

An important use for a `byte` type is to be able to represent pointers to bytes. A common practice is to use `void*`, which certainly primes the reader to think in terms of "pure memory." Using `void*` has the advantage that the compiler will pick up on any attempts to use pointer arithmetic, which it otherwise performs automatically for us with other pointer types. However, it presents its own difficulties in that pointer arithmetic involves casts to and from byte-sized type pointers, with the consequent potential for mistakes.

Some APIs express pointers to bytes as `unsigned char (const) *`. The problem from a human point of view is that seeing a parameter of type `char*` inclines the reader to think of the recipient of a writable string buffer or of a single character, and a parameter of type `char const*` to think of a null-terminated string. Explicitly qualifying with `(un)signed` helps in this regard, of course, but it only takes a couple of slips of the sign qualifier to propagate throughout the code base and you're at 300kph on the autobahn to unmaintainability. In any case, we've seen that some libraries use `unsigned char` to represent a character.

A slightly better solution might be to use the C99 type `uint8_t (const) *` (see next item), but this is not (yet) part of standard C++, and it still says "integer" (number) rather than "byte" (opaque value).[2]

Using `byte_t (const)* s` means that we can express pointers to opaque bytes in a simple, readable way, and we don't have to resort to any casting with pointer arithmetic, so the code is immune to pointer-type mismatch and offset problems.

13.1.4   Extra Safety

There's one more step that can be employed to eke out a little extra type safety. I've used the approach shown in Listing 13.1 in several libraries.

Listing 13.1
```
#if defined(ACMELIB_COMPILER_IS_INTEL) || \
    defined(ACMELIB_COMPILER_IS_MSVC)
```

---

[2]And on those very rare architectures where a byte is not 8 bits, it would be very misleading!

```
 typedef unsigned __int8          byte_t;
...
#else
 typedef unsigned char            byte_t;
#endif /* compiler */
```

The `__int8` type is an 8-bit integer defined by the Intel and Visual C++ (and a few other) compilers. There is a feature (maybe it's a bug?) of the Visual C++ 6.0 compiler, which is emulated in the Intel compiler,[3] which means that `int8` and `char` are not considered as simple aliases of each other (see section 18.3). Rather they represent distinct types.

We can turn this to our own advantage by defining `byte_t` to be `unsigned __int8` when compiling with these compilers, which allows us to write functions with greater type safety. (Naturally, the fact that we're defining byte in terms of a specifically 8-bit integer would run aground on a platform where a byte might contain 9 bits, but on such a platform we'd adjust the definition of `byte_t` accordingly.)

Consider the following class, which is written to work with memory but not characters.

```
class NoCharsPlease
{
public:
  NoCharsPlease(byte_t *);
// Not to be implemented
private:
#ifdef ACMELIB_CF_DISTINCT_BYTE_SUPPORT
  NoCharsPlease(char *);
  NoCharsPlease(signed char *);
  NoCharsPlease(unsigned char *);
#endif /* ACMELIB_CF_DISTINCT_BYTE_SUPPORT */
};
```

Now if you try to pass a pointer to a `char`-based block of memory, the compiler will reject it.

```
byte_t         *pc   = new byte_t[10];
unsigned char *puc  = new char[10];
NoCharsPlease  ncp1(pc);  // Ok
NoCharsPlease  ncp2(puc); // Compile error
```

Since this only works on a small (and aging) subset of compilers, and relies on nonstandard compiler features at that, it is arguable as to whether you would want to use this technique. It can be helpful when you are using several compilers to maximize your information, however (see Appendix C). Since I tend to do that, I use this technique.

A portable and future-proof alternative, for C++ compilation only, is to use the True Typedef technique (see chapter 18), thereby making conversions between the byte type and any other integral type invalid.

---

[3]When used in Visual C++ 6.0 compatibility mode.

13.2   Fixed-Sized Integer Types

In most C and C++ code, the integer type used is `int`. There are good reasons for this. For one thing, in the very early days of C, the `int` was the only type. Of more than historical relevance is that `int` is usually the most efficient integer type to use, because it is defined to be the "natural size [of] the architecture" (C++-98: 3.9.1.2). It would be silly to use a 32-bit type on current 32-bit machines if, when your code was ported to a 64-bit architecture, it performed suboptimally. By using `int`, you protect your code against such issues in the face of the future.

However, the potential variation in size between different architectures can also cause problems if your code relies on a particular capacity. A variable providing unique keys that may hold 0-4294967295 on one environment could run into some trouble on another where it may hold only 0-65535. This is especially important with embedded software: hardware people need fixed-sized types. The answer is to provide fixed-sized type definitions that correspond to the appropriate fundamental type for the given target environment, using similar techniques as we saw for bytes.

Imperfection: C and C++ need fixed-sized integer types.

The C99 standard provides just such a set of types, called `int8_t`, `int16_t`, `uint32_t`, and so on albeit that they are typedefs rather than built-in types. (It also provides minimum-sized integers, e.g., `int_least64_t`, and fastest integers of a minimum size, e.g., `sint_fastt16_t`.) Most libraries that need to be portable employ similar techniques: ZLib defines `uLong`, `Byte` and so on; STLSoft has `uint16_t`, `sint8_t` and so on; Boost imports the C99 types into the `boost` namespace if available, otherwise it defines them itself.

This seems like the full picture, but unfortunately the C++ language's fascination for `int`, its favored firstborn type, can lead to problems. The problem relates to overloading and type resolution of functions overloaded on some, but not all, the integral types. (To be strictly correct, it's not always `int`: it is possible that this can occur for any of the fundamental integral types that share a size in a particular environment. It's just that the problems raise their ugly heads most often with `int`.)

13.2.1   Platform Independence

Let's imagine we're writing a component to provide serialization in a cross-platform communications architecture. We want to be able to write the values of variables at one end, and have them read at the destination in the same types in which they were written. Barring the minor complexities of byte-ordering—which we'll assume are taken care of inside our component using `ntohl()`, `htonl()` or similar functions—this is straightforward and meaningful for the sized types, because they always have the same size on whatever machine they may be received. However, it is not in the least bit reasonable to write an `int` to such a stream, since it could be 64 bits on the source and 32 bits on the receiver, resulting in probable loss of information.

Consider the `Serializer` class and some client code shown in Listing 13.2.

Listing 13.2

```
class Serializer
{
```

```
    . . .
// Operations
public:
  void Write(int8_t i);
  void Write(uint8_t i);
  void Write(int16_t i);
  void Write(uint16_t i);
  void Write(int32_t i);
  void Write(uint32_t i);
  void Write(int64_t i);
  void Write(uint64_t i);
    . . .
};

void fn()
{
  Serializer  s    = . . .;
  int8_t      i8   = 0;
  int64_t     ui64 = 0;
  int         i    = 0;

  s.Write(si8);
  s.Write(ui64);
  s.Write(i);       // ERROR: Ambiguous call
  s.Write(0);       // ERROR: Ambiguous call
}
```

In environments where `long` is 32 bits, we may define 32-bit types in terms of `long`. In such environments where `int` is also 32 bits, `long` should still be used. (This is a deliberate decision, as we'll see.) In such an environment, the above definition of `Serializer`'s overloaded `Write()` methods do not contain an entry matching either the variable `i` or the literal constant `0`, both of which are of type `int`. The conversions from `int` to any of the eight specific (non-`int`) integrals are all equivalent in priority (see section 15.4.1), so the compiler balks with the ambiguity.

This is a sticky situation. In another environment, it may be the case that `int` is 32 bits and `long` is 64 bits, in which case there would be no ambiguity and the above code would compile correctly. One way to deal with this inconsistency is to restrict yourself to using the specific-sized types wherever you may have formerly used `int` (or `short`, or `unsigned long`, etc.). This can be (very) inconvenient, and it means you have to cast literals (which are `int`s or `long`s; see section 15.4.1), and you can't be certain that using `short`, `int`, `long` (, `long long`) with such overloaded functions will be portable.

Imperfection (reprise): C++ needs fixed sized types that are different to, and not implicitly interconvertible with, its built-in integral types.

There are a few solutions to this, as we'll see shortly.

13.2.2 Type-Specific Behavior

Consider another case, where we may want to convert integers to (C-style) strings (see Chapter 31), and cater for all the fundamental numeric integral types, including the nonstandard ones, such as `long long`[4]`/__int64`. Because `signed` and `unsigned` integers will naturally convert differently (i.e., signed conversions will prefix a `'-'` if the value is less than 0), we need to provide two separate functions to cater for sign. We also need to provide 64-bit versions for (`unsigned`) `long long`, in addition to those for (`unsigned`) `int` (this assumes a 32-bit architecture, where `int` is 32 bits). So now we have explicitly catered for `int`, `unsigned int`, `long long`, and `unsigned long long`.

```
char const *integer_to_string(int );
char const *integer_to_string(unsigned int );
char const *integer_to_string(long long );
char const *integer_to_string(unsigned long long );
```

But there are four more numeric integral types: `signed char`, `unsigned char`, `short`, and `unsigned short`. Well, that's okay, isn't it? These types will undergo implicit, benign promotion (C++98: 4.5) to (`unsigned`) `int`, so they can reuse those two functions. Unfortunately, there are several problems here. By relying on integer promotion, we also allow `bool`, `char`, and `wchar_t`[5] to be converted. What if we want `bool` to be converted to (in an English locale) `"true"` or `"false"` rather than `"1"` or `"0"`? What if it's not meaningful/appropriate for `'A'` (whether `char` or `wchar_t`) to be converted to `"65"`?

The answer here is to define explicitly only the conversion functions that we want, as follows (using C99 types):

```
char const *integer_to_string(int32_t );
char const *integer_to_string(uint32_t );
char const *integer_to_string(int64_t );
char const *integer_to_string(uint64_t );
char const *integer_to_string(bool ); // return "true" or "false"
```

and these inline ones:

```
inline char const *integer_to_string(int8_t i)
{
  return integer_to_string(static_cast<int32_t>(i));
}
char const *integer_to_string(uint8_t i)
{
  return integer_to_string(static_cast<uint32_t>(i));
}
```

---

[4]`long long` is part of C99, and will undoubtedly feature in the next C++ standard.

[5]Some older, nonstandard compilers don't define `wchar_t` as a native type, in which case libraries `typedef` it from another type, usually `unsigned short`. Naturally, this flies in the face of this and any other code that needs to discriminate between character and numeric types.

```
char const *integer_to_string(int16_t i)
{
  return integer_to_string(static_cast<int32_t>(i));
}
char const *integer_to_string(uint16_t i)
{
  return integer_to_string(static_cast<uint32_t>(i));
}
```

Unfortunately, this will only work for compilers where int32_t is defined as a type other than int and that is not intrinsically treated as int; most compilers which use, say, __int8/16/32/64 in their definitions of the C99 fixed sized types treat them as equivalent to the corresponding standard types, rather than being a peer integer type of the same size (on 32-bit platforms, that is). Where the types are not distinguished, your unwanted conversions from char / wchar_t will proceed unhindered. There are two solutions here: the wicked and the long-winded.

The wicked one is to declare the char / wchar_t functions, but to have them return an incompatible type, as in:

```
void integer_to_string(char );

char ch = 'A';
puts(integer_to_string(ch)); // Compiler error
```

That works, but can you imagine the error message, as the poor old compiler tries to fulfil puts()'s requirement for a char const* with a void? It'll hardly be very useful. We can make this a bit more palatable by borrowing a neat compile-error naming technique from Andrei Alexandrescu [Alex2001], as follows:

```
struct wchar_t_cannot_convert_as_integer {};
wchar_t_cannot_convert_as_integer integer_to_string(wchar_t );

wchar_t ch = L'A';
puts(integer_to_string(ch)); // Error, with a hint 'twixt the noise.
```

Digital Mars gives the error "Error: need explicit cast for function parameter 1 to get from: wchar_t_cannot_convert_as_integer to: char const *."

It's still not really something one could be proud of, though, is it? The long-winded solution is to use a class to proscribe the unwanted conversions via its access control specifiers, as in:

```
class integer_convert
{
// Conversions
public:
  static char const *to_string(int8_t );
```

```
    . . .
    static char const *to_string(uint64_t );
    static char const *to_string(bool );
#if !defined(ACMELIB_INT_USED_FOR_FIXED_SIZED_TYPES)
    static char const *to_string(int );
    static char const *to_string(unsigned int );
#endif /* !ACMELIB_INT_USED_FOR_FIXED_SIZED_TYPES */
// Proscribed conversions
private:
    static char const *to_string(char );
    static char const *to_string(wchar_t );
};

int32_t i  = 0;
char    ch = 'A';

puts(integer_convert::to_string(i));  // Ok
puts(integer_convert::to_string(ch)); // Compiler error
```

The messages this time are a lot more on the ball, such as (Intel C/C++): "`error #308:`
`function "integer_convert::to_string(char)" is inaccessible.`" Note that
because we've specifically hidden the `char` / `wchar_t` overloads, we can now safely cater for
the (`unsigned`) `int`, via the preprocessor discrimination, in the case where they are not used
in the definition of the C99 fixed-sized types for the given compiler.

The third option is to use True Typedefs, which we look at in detail in Chapter 18, where
we will also revisit the `Serializer` component described in section 13.2.1. Despite being a
little inconvenient to use, they represent a full solution to such problems.

13.2.3   Fixed-Sized Integer Types: Coda

Hopefully, now you can see why we should define sized integral types, where possible, in
terms of types other than `int`. It is interesting to note that of the compilers to which I have access that provide `cstdint` / `stdint.h`, all but one—GCC—either define the C99 fixed-sized
types in terms of proprietary fixed-sized types, or they use `short` and `long` and eschew `int`.
Both approaches fall down if you do not have another type of the same size as (`unsigned`)
`int` to use in their place, or if your compiler vendor uses them in its definition of the C99 types.
In that case, you either live with the potential subtle errors, or you must use True Typedefs (see
section 18.4).

For myself, I choose to either proscribe the (`unsigned`) `int` types, or to go for True
Typedefs solution, since I prefer the hairshirt to these possibilities for implicit conversions: typing more is fine now, if that means I get to type less later.

But none of it's particularly pretty, is it? It's clear that there are at least two problems with
the fundamental integer types: variable size between environments, which is pretty obvious, and
the preference for integer conversion of literals, which is subtle, surprising, and, perhaps, the
more troublesome. It's also clear that (at least the first) problem has wide recognition, as evi-
denced by the C99 move to introduce fixed-sized types. We've seen how it is better to avoid the

int type in the definition of such types, but also how this may not be achievable in all environments. The answers, then, are:

- Always use fixed-sized types if you are using the type in a sense that pertains to its capacity.
- When overloading functions to support multiple integral types, overload for *all* the types you want, and *none* of the ones you don't.
- Specify literals sparingly, and be prepared to cast them when dealing with overloaded functions. It is a concession to the problem that this is a real, albeit minor, pain.
- Be aware that these steps are *not* a complete answer, so you must keep the issues in mind.
- Compile your components on as many compilers as you can practically manage, and listen to all their warnings.
- When you absolutely *must* have full control, use True Typedefs (section 18.4). (This is rare, and inconvenient, hence the stress on "must.")

13.3 Large Integer Types

The built-in integer types provided by C/C++ are often entirely sufficient for one's programming needs. However, as machine architectures and disk sizes have grown, the need for larger integer types has grown. A 32-bit signed integer has a range of $-2,147,483,648$ => $2,147,483,647$, an unsigned one of 0 => $4,294,967,295$. So a 32-bit number can represent, say, a file offset only if the maximum size of the file is ~4GB. On 64-bit operating systems, it is essential to have 64-bit types to represent the full-sized data word, as well as to represent pointers that can manipulate a 64-bit address space. Modern C/C++ compilers provide 64-bit integers, and while there is currently an inconvenient lack of standardization—some provide the C99 standard long long type, others __int64—it is pretty straightforward to harness the preprocessor to create compiler-independent typedefs, for example, int64_t.

But sometimes we want larger types than those provided by our compilers.

If the requirement is for arbitrarily large integer types, then this is something that should be provided by a library [Hans1997], as some other languages, such as Python and Ruby, do. Such types are very flexible, but representation and manipulation use complex, and comparatively slow, techniques.

Some applications require large fixed integer types, for example, cryptographic analysis. If we need more than 64 bits, or we're dealing with compilers that don't have 64-bit integers,[6] we do not have the support of the language?

Imperfection: C/C++ do not provide large fixed-sized integer types.

In and of itself, this is not really a serious flaw, since the demand for such types is reasonably low, and the minimum acceptable range of fixed-sized types would always be a matter for subjective debate. You can sear your eyeballs just imagining the flame wars. Furthermore, the difficulties of providing integer arithmetic without direct support from the processor hardware

---

[6]I know of no modern (32-bit) compilers that do not provide 64-bit integers, but it's possible.

are nontrivial. Walter Bright, author of the Digital Mars C/C++/D compilers, states [WB-Email], "To do it inefficiently is pretty simple: just turn it into BCD[, but to] do it efficiently requires dealing with the Carry flag, which is not accessible from [C/C++]. Hence it would need to be done with assembler."

Just as with arbitrarily large types, the answer for C++ (and C) is to create user defined types that represent such types. Indeed, one of C++'s most powerful features is the fact that it supports the definition of user-defined types.

The natural technique to adopt is to define a structure that contains suitable fundamental integers, such as the `uinteger64` type we saw in section 4.4 and its signed equivalent:

```
struct integer64
{
  uint32_t  lowerVal;
  int32_t   upperVal;
};

struct uinteger64
{
  uint32_t  lowerVal;
  uint32_t  upperVal;
};
```

As we saw in section 4.4, using such types is anything but straightforward. They lack encapsulation (see section 4.5), since `lowerVal` and `upperVal` can be manipulated independently in client code. They are not *value types* (see section 4.6) since the following is not supported:

```
integer64 i1;
integer64 i2;

if(i1 == i2) // Error - integer64 does not define this operator
{
```

They do not support the natural syntax and semantics (see section 4.7) of integers:

```
integer64 i2 = i1 + i2; // Error. integer64 does not define this operator
```

We're going to study the `uinteger64` type, and how it can be made to support the syntax and semantics of *arithmetic value types* (see section 4.7) in detail in Chapter 29. As we'll see, C++ allows us to transform it into a near-perfect 64-bit user defined type. But it is the "near" aspect of this transformation that represents the real imperfection and validates the imperfection presented earlier.

13.4   Dangerous Types

We've commented on some of the dangers of integer truncation and sign extension. Now it's time to look at what other dangers the C/C++ type system has for us.

13.4.1   References and Temporaries

In Steve Dewhurst's *C++ Gotchas* [Dewh2003], Gotcha #44—"References and Temporaries"—highlights the danger of mixed use of built-in and `typedef`'d integer types, when it comes to references. (Actually, it doesn't really have anything to do with typedefs, just that it's more likely to slip under the programmer's radar when using them.) Consider the following code:

```
int main()
{
  long       l   = 2222;
  short const &s  = l;

  l = 0;
  printf("%ld, %d\n", l, s);
  return 0;
}
```

As Steve points out, because the types are different (perhaps because of the sizes), the compiler will synthesize a temporary whose lifetime will last at least as long as that of the reference (C++-98: 8.5.3), and copy in the value of its intended *rvalue* (l in this case). Thus, when l is subsequently set to 0 the temporary is unaffected. Hence, "0, 2222" is printed, rather than "0, 0". Steve states that this "change in meaning will occur [, and will do so] silently." Table 13.1 shows the responses to this code from several popular compilers. Only Borland flags the erroneous behavior by default, Comeau, CodeWarrior, Intel, Visual C++, and Watcom all require a higher than default warning level to flag the potential hazard. Digital Mars and GCC present an interesting case, since they actually provide the intended behavior. However, they are wrong,

Table 13.1   Compiler warnings for mixed-type references

Compiler	Warn at default warning level?	Required warning level	Output
Borland C/C++ 5.6	Yes	-	"0, 2222"
CodeWarrior 8.3	No	-warn implicit	"0, 2222"
Comeau 4.3.0.1	No	--remarks	"0, 2222"
Digital Mars C/C++ 8.34	No	-	"0, 0"
GCC 3.2	No	-	"0, 0"
HP 11.00 aCC 3.39	No	-	"0, 2222"
Intel C/C++ 7.0	No	-W4	"0, 2222"
Sun Solaris 2.7 Forte 6.0	No	-	"0, 2222"
Visual C++ 6.0	No	-W3	"0, 2222"
Visual C++ 7.0	No	-W3	"0, 2222"
Visual C++ 7.1	No	-W3	"0, 2222"
Watcom 12.0	No	-wx	"0, 2222"

since the standard states (C++98: 8.5.3) that "a temporary . . . is created and initialised [, and] the reference is bound to the temporary." This is a good demonstration that no individual compiler can be treated as an ultimate source of language correctness.

The solution in this case is straightforward: don't do it. A corollary to making this abstinence solution workable is to (1) set your compiler warnings high, and (2) use multiple compilers. That's a combination of advice that you're going to hear from me many times throughout this book.

13.4.2 bool

This may be the single most unpopular item with C++ aficionados in this whole book. My position is that `bool` is a highly desirable type, and useful in the internal implementation of classes and functions but, as it is currently defined in the standard and implemented by compiler vendors, it is a useless type in the specification of functions and the public interfaces of classes. The size of `bool` type is "implementation defined" (see C++-98: 5.3.3), albeit all of our compilers (see Appendix A) implement it as a single byte (see Table 13.2).

Although conditional expressions are notionally converted to `bool`, inspection of the generated code of our compilers reveals that they do not do a conversion to their (1-byte) `bool` type first; they simply test the "truth" of the expressions as is. For example, in the expression `if(p)`, where p is of pointer type, p is evaluated as not being equal to 0. On a 32-bit architecture, with 32-bit pointers and integers, it would clearly be inefficient to convert to a Boolean with logic such as `((p & 0xFFFFFFFF) != 0) ? true : false` or similar. Regrettably, when one wishes to assign the truth of an expression to a variable of type `bool` just such a conversion must be performed. Users of CodeWarrior or Visual C++ will be used to receiving warnings (because you all set warnings to max, right?) regarding the inefficiency of this conversion, and perhaps avoiding precipitating them wherever possible. What is unnerving is that none of the other compilers I use warn about the performance loss at any warning level (see Table 13.2).

We might presume that the C++ standard leaves this decision to compiler implementers because it is prone to do so, which is, in the main, a well-founded strategy. One can further

Table 13.2 Compiler warnings for `bool` truncation

Compiler	sizeof(bool)	Warn at default warning level?	Required warning level
Borland C/C++ 5.6	1	No	-
CodeWarrior 8.3	1	No	-warn implicit
Digital Mars C/C++ 8.34	1	No	-
GCC 3.2	1	No	-
Intel C/C++ 7.0	1	No	-
Visual C++ 6.0	1	No	-W3
Visual C++ 7.0	1	No	-W3
Visual C++ 7.1	1	No	-W3
Watcom 12.0	1	No	-

assume that compiler implementers choose to implement `bool` as a 1-byte type because of space-efficiency concerns.

The number of instances of `bool`s in containers compared with those where it serves as return values or arguments to functions would be low, and if you care about space efficiency in the containment of Boolean values, you should check out Chuck Allison's `bitset` and `bit-string` [Alli1993, Alli1994] and their derivative classes.[7]

But the conversion issue does not pertain to correctness, only efficiency, and depending on how you write your code, it is one not encountered especially often anyway. The real problem with `bool` is its lack of *predictable* size, especially in terms of interacting with other languages.

Even if you don't ever implement your source in C, you'll no doubt use C as the exchange language between your dynamic libraries; if you don't, you learned some good reasons to do so in Part Two. C compatibility is something that, whether you like it or not, is here to stay in C++, and it is this that is the root of the `bool` problem. It is hard to conceive of a C/C++ compiler providing different sizes in C and C++ for types that are defined in both languages, so one can mix C and C++ with little concern for these types. But `bool` has been provided by some (C/C++) compilers for C++ for longer than it has for C (where `bool` is a `#define` for the C99 type `_Bool`), and for some is still not provided in C, so one must synthesize a `typedef` for it. There is a profusion of such things out there in the real world: `BOOL`, `BOOLEAN`, `Boolean`, `boolean_t`, `Bool`, and so on. Frequently these are defined as `int`, or as `enum`s, and in many cases were done so long before `bool` entered the C++ vocabulary, when the choice of `int` was eminently sensible.

The problem is that if one defines data structures or API functions that use Boolean types for operation with both C and C++, it is all too easy to do something like:

```
#if defined(__cplusplus) || \
    defined(bool) /* for C compilation with C99 bool (macro) */
 typedef bool    bool_t;
#else
 typedef BOOL    bool_t;
#endif /* __cplusplus */
```

This is an accident waiting to happen, and I've seen this in the software of more than one client. I've also done this myself, once. A fair proportion of the APIs in the Synesis common libraries are implemented in good old C, and so the Synesis `Bool` type was a commonly used type. The problem was that in one function implemented in C the `Bool` return was efficiently derived from a called function that returned a 32-bit unsigned integer, which represented a path length. When path lengths stayed within the range 1 -> 255, everything worked swimmingly. However, the function eventually got recycled to work with URLs, and once a path length was longer than 255 and an exact multiple of 256, the whole thing came crashing down.

Because the offending part of that function was its return type, and symbol-naming schemes tend to ignore return types if they incorporate function signatures at all (see Chapter 7), there was no detection of the mismatch at compile/link time.

---

[7]You could use `std::vector<bool>`, but it's dishonestly named and tramples over the standard namespace, so I'd suggest you steer well clear of that one.

Naturally, I concede that such a mistake doesn't need a genius to spot, and I was seriously embarrassed to have made it. However, I'm someone who thinks about these things a lot, and that mistake had lain dormant in well-used code for several years before an error was precipitated! Once the error occurred it still took me the best part of two days of debugging before the lights went on.

There are two seemingly conflicting views here. On the one hand I am berating the lack of fixed size for a `bool` type, and on the other hand I am arguing for a speed-efficiency based size, which, for me, translates to wanting it to be the same size as `int`. I contend that if `bool` was defined by the standard to have the same size as `int`, the "natural size of the architecture," then both requirements would be satisfied in one go. Thus code using `bool` could rely on its having a predictable size for any given architecture (actually we must say operating environment, since some operating systems can be virtually implemented on others, sometimes of a different word size), which would only restrict its being run on different architectures. All the other fundamental types prevent any such cross-execution anyway, so this is a nonproblem.

Imperfection: `bool` should be the same size as `int`.

The solution to this imperfection is, as it so often is, abstinence. I never use `bool` for anything that can possibly be accessed across multiple link units—dynamic/static libraries, supplied object files—which basically means not in functions or classes that appear outside of header files. The practical answer, such as it is, is to use a pseudo-Boolean type, which is the size of `int`. The Synesis Software public library headers define a type `Boolean` that does just that, and the use of `bool` is restricted to automatic variables and exclusively C++-specific compilation units.

Arrays and Pointers

An array is "a fixed collection of same-type data . . . [logically] stored contiguously and . . . accessible by an index" [Sedg1998a], and is one of the fundamental data structures [Knut1997]. While most languages have arrays, many modern ones do not have pointers because they are deemed too dangerous. Pointers allow direct access to the memory locations of the instances to which they point, but they can, and often do, lead to memory corruption. Nonetheless C and C++ provide pointers because they afford such power and opportunity for efficiency, in keeping with the "Spirit of C" (see Prologue).

In this chapter, we look at some issues where the language(s) leave something to be desired, including the issues of array sizes, array/pointer duality, and the uniquely C++ problem of passing pointers to arrays of inherited types.

14.1 Don't Repeat Yourself

In *The Pragmatic Programmer*, Andrew Hunt and David Thomas describe their DRY, or *Don't Repeat Yourself*, principle. In essence, this stipulates that you should only define anything once, since more than one definition will inevitably lead to inconsistencies when one definition is updated without the other(s). This is a basic code quality measure, and can be readily seen in the definition and manipulation of arrays:

```
char   ar[23];

strnset(ar, ' ', 23);
```

If we change the dimension of `ar` without making a corresponding exact change to the third argument in the call to `strnset()` then, the program would fail to fill the entire array, or possibly worse, overwrite objects other than the array. The usual advice in such situations is to declare a constant (via `#define` in C, or `const` in C++), from which both points are derived, and only a single change is necessitated,[1] as in:

```
#ifdef __cplusplus
 const size_t DIM_A = 23;
#else
# define DIM_A       (23)
#endif /* __cplusplus */
```

---

[1] Actually, there are two if you are, like the example shows, providing C and C++ compatible forms, as is often the case in library headers. Notwithstanding this, the principle of one change is well founded.

```
char   ar[DIM_A];

strnset(ar, ' ', DIM_A);
```

Now a change to the size of `ar` is effected by a change to `DIM_A`, which will be reflected in the argument passed to `strnset()`, and any other places where the constant is used. This is a good solution, but it is still fragile to erroneous changes in the code. Perhaps the maintainer wants to add space for a null terminator, and mistakenly changes the wrong line

```
char   ar[DIM_A + 1];
```

```
strnset(ar, ' ', DIM_A); // What about ar[DIM_A] ?
```

Naturally code reviews can pick this up, but as we all know, reviews are conducted far less regularly than they should be.[2] It would be really nice if arrays in C++ had, as they do in other languages, a `length` property, as in:

```
char   ar[DIM_A];

strnset(ar, ' ', ar.length);
```

C and C++ have the `sizeof()` operator, but this returns only the size in bytes. In this case we could use `sizeof()` because `sizeof(char) == sizeof(byte)` (see section 13.1). However, if the example used `wchar_t` and `wcsnset()`, then using `sizeof()` would result in only a half or a quarter (depending on the number of bytes in a `wchar_t`) of `ar` being acted upon by `wcsnset()`. What we need is an operator that will yield the number of elements in an array, rather than the number of bytes.

Imperfection: C and C++ do not provide a `dimensionof()` operator (for array types).

This is a well-trodden path, and the classic[3] solution (that works for C and C++) takes a macro form, as with the `NUM_ELEMENTS()` macro,[4] which is defined as:

```
#define NUM_ELEMENTS(x)    (sizeof((x)) / sizeof((x)[0]))
```

The number of elements is calculated by dividing the total number of bytes by the number of bytes in a single element. Our example becomes:

```
char   ar[DIM_A];

strnset(ar, ' ', NUM_ELEMENTS(ar));
```

---

[2] In any case, if you let ten reviewers review the same piece of code, they will come with ten different sets of problems. So the problem is not just frequency, but also the "findability" of problems like these.

[3] Until recently many compilers were unable to provide the newer form, which we meet in section 14.3.

[4] This is the only bit of code that survives from my postgraduate research days in the early nineties. Everything else has been jettisoned in embarrassment long ago. I'm given to understand that the Solaris kernel development uses pretty much the same thing.

This is a workable general solution, but it still has a flaw, which we deal with in section 14.3, after a brief detour.

14.2   Arrays Decay into Pointers

For reasons of efficiency, convenience, and, perhaps, historical accident [Lind1994], C and C++ have a somewhat blurred distinction between pointers and arrays. A pointer is a single storage location, whose value refers to some point in the addressable memory space. An array is a contiguous block of one or more instances of a particular type. A pointer of the same type as an array's element type may be set to point to any element in the array, and dereferencing the pointer yields the same value as would indexing the array. (Actually, there's a little too much flexibility in the interconvertibility between pointers and arrays, which leads us to another problem. See section 14.6.) Hence:

```
int ar[5];
int *p = ar;
```

ar is an array of int, which has five elements. p is a pointer to int. Since an array is convertible to a pointer (C++-98: 4.2), it is perfectly legal to assign ar to p, but what that actually means is that p points to the address of the first element of ar.

```
int *q = &ar[0];
assert(p == q);
```

It is also legal, and quite common, to apply the indexing operator to p, so the following two are semantically equivalent.

```
int v1 = ar[3];
int v2 = p[3];
assert(v1 == v2);
```

14.2.1   Subscript Operator Commutativity

The reason that a pointer can be indexed just as well as an array has to do with the way C and C++ interpret indexing expressions. A compiler interprets the expression ar[n], at compile time, to be *(ar + n) [Lind1994]. Since pointers can enter into arithmetic, p can substitute for ar to form *(p + n), and thus p[n] is valid. An interesting quirk [Dewh2003, Lind1994] is that the built-in subscript operator is commutative, and so both array and pointer subscript expressions can have the reverse form, as in n[ar] and n[p]. It's sometimes remarked [Lind1994] that this is nothing more than an amusing piece of arcana with which to confuse novices, or win an obfuscated C Code Contest, but it does have a practical benefit in one of the most modern of C++ activities, generic programming. Indeed, as mentioned in [Dewh2003], because it only occurs for the built-in subscript operator, it can be used to constrain a piece of code to only work with array/pointer types, and reject class types with an overloaded subscript operator, as in:

```
template <typename T>
void reject_subscript_operator(T const &t)
{
  sizeof(t[0]); // Compiler will balk here if T is not subscriptable
  sizeof(0[t]); // Compiler will balk here if T only has user-defined subscript
  operator
}


void reject_subscript_operator(void const * const)
{}


void reject_subscript_operator(void * )
{}
```

The overloads for `void` are there because it's illegal to dereference a `void` (`const`) pointer. These functions are used to reject a user-defined type with a subscript operator. Consider the code in Listing 14.1.

Listing 14.1

```
struct Pointer
{
  operator short *() const;
};


struct Subscript
{
  int operator [](size_t offset) const;
};

  void        *pv = &pv;
  void const  *pcv = pv;
  int         ai[100];
  int         *pi = ai;
  Pointer     ptr;
  Subscript   subscr;

  reject_subscript_operator(pv);
  reject_subscript_operator(pcv);
  reject_subscript_operator(ai);
  reject_subscript_operator(pi);
  reject_subscript_operator(ptr);
  reject_subscript_operator(subscr); // This one fails to compile!
```

You're probably wondering why we'd want to detect, and reject, a user-defined type with a subscript operator. Well, it's always nice to discover new ways to detect and enforce character-istics (see Chapter 12); generic programming's here now, and it's not going away. Looking back at our definition of NUM_ELEMENTS(), we see that if we reverse the subscript operator we can reject its application to user-defined types, which the previous definition did not.

```
#define NUM_ELEMENTS(x)     (sizeof((x)) / sizeof(0[(x)]))


template <typename T>
struct vect
{
  T &operator [](size_t index);

  . . .

};


vect<int>  vi;
int        ai[NUM_ELEMENTS(vi)]; // Compiler rejects when using new
NUM_ELEMENTS
```

14.2.2 Preventing Decay

I don't wish to say that this decay from arrays into pointers is a full-fledged imperfection, as without it code would be a great deal less terse, and a lot of flexibility would be lost. Nonetheless, it can be irksome, as we note throughout this chapter and in Chapters 27 and 33.

For built-in arrays, there is nothing that can be done to prevent the assignment of an array to a pointer. When passing them to functions, one can declare the functions to take pointers or references to arrays, rather than a pointer, but there's still nothing preventing the code inside the function from converting them to a pointer.

You're probably wondering why you should care. Well, the very fact that arrays do decay into pointers has led to the ubiquitous use of the decay form p = ar, rather than the more precise p = &ar[0]. While this is convenient, it can have a negative effect on coding for genericity. If you define a class type that acts, in some respects, as an array, you would usually provide subscript operators, as in

```
class IntArray
{
  . . .
  int const &operator [](size_t offset) const;
  int       &operator [](size_t offset);
  . . .
```

This is, in general, preferable to providing an implicit conversion operator. (We talk about this more in Chapters 32 and 33.) Although this class now supports arraylike subscript syntax, it does not provide implicit conversion to a pointer. If you attempt to use such a type with code that uses the decay form it will fail.

There's a similar issue with random access iterators [Aust1999, Muss2001] provided by sequence containers. Since it is legal for iterators to be implemented as class types, you can get into scrapes by relying on decay form syntax. For example, the pod_vector container (see section 32.2.8) implements insertion operations via memmove(), as in:

```
memmove(&first[0], &last[0], . . .
```

If you assume, as I did myself when writing it, that the iterators are pointers, rather than types that act like pointers only to the degree prescribed by the STL *Iterator* concept [Aust1999, Muss2001], then you might write the following:

```
memmove(first, last, . . . // Iterators won't convert to void *
```

which does not compile when used with those standard libraries that define class-type iterators. Thus, it's worth your while to refrain from using the incorrect array-to-pointer syntax. Even when you don't run foul of such things, it's still a good way to remind yourself what's happening behind the syntax.

14.3   dimensionof()

The definition of `dimensionof()` (in the form of `NUM_ELEMENTS()`) given in section 14.1 relies on textual substitution by the preprocessor, and as such it contains a serious flaw. If we apply it to a pointer, to which we now know we can apply subscripts, the substituted code will be wrong.

```
int     ar[10];
int     *p = ar; // or = &ar[0]
size_t  dim = NUM_ELEMENTS(p); // sizeof(int*) / sizeof(int) !
```

The result yielded will be the integer division of the size of a pointer to `int` divided by the size of `int`, which would be 1 on most platforms. This is wrong (except in the case where the dimension of the array to which `p` points happens to be 1) and quite misleading.

Just as bad is the case where the operator is applied to a user-defined type with an accessible index operator (`operator []`). In such a case, the size yielded can be anything from 0 where the size of the instance is larger than the type it returns from the index operator, to a large number where that size relationship is reversed. It is even conceivable that the number yielded can be correct during an interactive debugging session, giving an entirely false sense of security to the author of the code! Far better for the compiler to balk at our application of the (pseudo-)operator and refuse to compile the expression. Thankfully, if we take the advice of section 14.2.1, and use the reversed form of `NUM_ELEMENTS()`, this problem goes away. But even if your equivalent macro does this—and most don't—we've still got the problem with pointers, since they can work just as well as an array name in either subscript operator form.

Imperfection: Inability to distinguish between arrays and pointers can result in static array size determination being applied to pointers or class types, yielding incorrect results.

The answer here is to distinguish between arrays and pointers. Until recently this was not possible, but most modern compilers support a technique that can do so. It relies on the fact that array-to-pointer conversion (decay) does not occur in the resolution of template arguments that are of reference type (C++-98: 14.3.2; [Vand2003, p58]). Thus we can define a macro—let's call it `dimensionof()`—with the same definition as `NUM_ELEMENTS()` for older compilers, but for modern ones use the following combination of a macro, a structure, and a function:

```
template <int N>
struct array_size_struct
{
  byte_t  c[N];
};

template <class T, int N>
array_size_struct<N> static_array_size_fn(T (&)[N]);

#define dimensionof(x)      sizeof(static_array_size_fn(x).c)
```

Basically it declares, but does not define, a template function `static_array_size_fn()` that takes a reference to an array of type `T` and dimension `N`, its two template parameters. That gets rid of the pointers and user-defined types, but it's not yet got us to `dimensionof()`. The function returns an instance of the template structure `array_size_struct`, which is parameterized on the dimension passed to `static_array_size_fn()` and contains an array of bytes of that dimension. The macro `dimensionof()` simply applies the `sizeof()` operator to the array within the returned structure instance, thereby yielding the dimension of the array.[5]

A `dimensionof()` expression (whether `NUM_ELEMENTS()` or our new `dimensionof()` macro + function) is evaluated at compile time, and so may be used wherever any other constant value can, for example, in template parameters, in array dimensions, `enum` values, and so on. Because the standard (C++-98: 5.3.3) states that the operand to a `sizeof()` operator is not evaluated, there is no need to define `static_array_size_fn()`, so all this utility comes at absolutely no price. There's no run time cost, and no code bloat; in fact there's no code generated at all! Attempting to apply `dimensionof()` to any type other than an array causes a compilation error.

```
int        ai[23];
int        *pi = ai;
vector<int> vi(23);

size_t cai = NUM_ELEMENTS(ai); // Ok
size_t cpi = NUM_ELEMENTS(pi); // Compiles, but it is wrong!
size_t cvi = NUM_ELEMENTS(vi); // Compiles, but it is wrong!

cai = dimensionof(ai); // Ok
cpi = dimensionof(pi); // Error - good!
cvi = dimensionof(vi); // Error - good!
```

---

[5]Note that compilers are free to layout members of structures according to whatever criteria they choose, so a full implementation must surround the definition of `array_size_struct` with an appropriate packing pragma(s), such as `#pragma pack(1)`, to be certain that the structure size is equal to N.

14.4   Cannot Pass Arrays to Functions   213

I should point out there's a slightly shorter (albeit harder to decipher) way to implement `dimensionof()`, as follows:

```
template<typename T, int N>
byte_t (&byte_array_of_same_dimension_as(T (&)[N]))[N];

#define dimensionof(x)        sizeof(byte_array_of_same_dimension_as((x)));
```

Unfortunately this is recognized by fewer compilers[6] so I recommend the first form.

14.4   Cannot Pass Arrays to Functions

What would you expect the code in Listing 14.2 to print?

Listing 14.2

```
void process_array(int ar[10])
{
  printf("[");
  for(size_t i = 0; i < dimensionof(ar); ++i)
  {
    printf("%d ", ar[i]);
  }
  printf("]\n");
}

int main()
{
  int ar1[10] =
  {
    0, 1, 2, 3, 4, 5, 6, 7, 8, 9
  };
  process_array(ar1);
  return 0;
}
```

If you said `"[0 1 2 3 4 5 6 7 8 9]"`, you'll probably be very surprised to learn the actual result. In fact, this program prints `"[0]"`. This behavior, of both C and C++, can be very surprising when you first learn about it. We have declared an array of 10 integers, given them a sequence of values, and passed them to a function declared to take an array of 10 integers. So what's the problem?

Well, C and C++ cannot pass arrays to functions! But you've been passing arrays to functions for as long as you can remember, haven't you? Alas, it's a big fib. Arrays are always converted to pointers when passed to functions in C, blithely ignoring any attempts at dimensioning on your part, and C++ has (almost completely) followed along for compatibility. In the example

---

[6]Visual C++ 7.0 recognizes the first but not the second.

above, we could have declared `process_array` as any of the following, and the behavior would be the same:

```
void process_array(int ar[20]);
void process_array(int ar[]);
void process_array(int *ar);
```

Now I've brought it up you'll probably recall seeing `main()` declared with both `char **argv` and `char *argv[]`. I'm not going to delve into the history of this situation, as it's dealt with in great depth in Chapter 9 of the excellent *Deep C Secrets* by Peter van der Linden [Lind1994], but I am going to suggest that:

Imperfection: C and C++ arrays decay into pointers when passed to functions.[7]

This flexibility is very useful in many circumstances, but it can be a real source of problems. C++ (and C, in this regard) provide a tight type system, so we cannot pass a pointer to (or array of) `double` to something expecting a pointer to `float`. Yet we can pass an array of any length to a function expecting (in the form of a pointer) an array. So what can be done?

The real problem is that the size of the array is lost, so if we can find a mechanism for passing the size through to the function as well as the (pointer to the base of the) array, we'll be pretty content. Unsurprisingly, this is done via a template, which I've imaginatively called `array_proxy` (shown in Listing 14.3).

Listing 14.3

```
template <typename T>
class array_proxy
{
// Construction
public:
  template <size_t N>
  explicit array_proxy(T (&t)[N])
    : m_base(t)
    , m_size(N)
  {}
  explicit array_proxy(T *base, size_t size)
    : m_base(t)
    , m_size(size)
  {}
// State
public:
  T *base()
  {
    return m_base;
```

---

[7]Actually, there are some cases where this is not true, as we see in the last section of this chapter (section 14.7).

```
    }
    size_t size() const
    {
      return m_size;
    }
// Members
private:
    T *const      m_base;
    size_t const  m_size;
// Not to be implemented
private:
    array_proxy &operator =(array_proxy const &);
};
```

There are also forwarding functions defined (which we see in action in section 14.6.5), that allow us to create an `array_proxy` instance without having to specify the type.

```
template <typename T, size_t N>
inline array_proxy<T> make_array_proxy(T (&t)[N])
{
    return array_proxy<T>(t);
}
template <typename T >
inline array_proxy<T> make_array_proxy(T *base, size_t size)
{
    return array_proxy<T>(base, size);
}
```

This template is featured throughout this chapter as it is refined to assist in some other array/pointer problems, so don't worry too much about its lack of polish for now.

We can now pass our array as an array:

```
void process_array(array_proxy<int> const &ar)
{
    printf("[");
    for(size_t i = 0; i < ar.size(); ++i)
    {
        printf("%d ", i[ar.base()]); // Just messing with ya!
    }
    printf("]\n");
}
```

Now this produces the desired result. Obviously, we'd like to have some nicer interface to the proxy than to have to specify `base()` in indexers. Hold that thought: more `array_proxy` coming up.

14.5   Arrays Are Always Passed by Address

As described in detail in [Lind1994], variables of nonarray type in C are passed in function arguments by value, and those of array type are passed by address. The same applies by default in C++, except that one can also pass nonarray types in C++ by reference by decorating the argument with the address-of operator &. There's no built-in mechanism in either language for passing arrays by value.

```
int i;
int ar[10];

void f(int x, int y[10])
{
  x = x + 1;          // i is not affected
  y[0] = y[0] + 1;  // ar is affected
}

f(i, ar);
```

Though the need is rare, so it can't be considered an imperfection, it can sometimes be desirable to pass an array by value. Thankfully it's ridiculously easy. The contents of structs (and unions and, in C++, classes) are copied by value, so you simply define a struct containing your array and pass that.

```
int i;
struct int10
{
  int values[10];
}   ar;

void (int x, int10 y)
{
  x = x + 1;                          // i is not affected
  y.values[0] = y. values [0] + 1;  // ar is not affected
}

f(i, ar);
```

Naturally, in C++ you would generalize, for both type and dimension, in a template

```
template <typename T, size_t N>
struct array_copy
{
  T values[N];
};
```

That's it. The C++ compiler will generate default constructor (section 2.2.2), destructor (section 2.2.8), copy constructor (section 2.2.3), and copy assignment operator (section 2.2.4) according to whether T can support those methods on a per-instance basis.

Naturally, the size of any such copyable array is fixed at compile time. If you want a variable sized copyable array, you're best to use `std::vector` (see section 14.6.4).

14.6 Arrays of Inherited Types

This well-documented pitfall [Meye1996, Stro1997, Dewh2003] is one of C++'s most problematic imperfections. If you have a parent class `Base` and a derived class `Derived`, and they are different in size (i.e., instances of `Derived` are larger than those of `Base`), then passing a pointer to an array of `Derived` to a function that takes a pointer to an array of `Base` will result in unpleasant consequences, since all but the item at index offset 0 will be misaligned. The best that can be hoped for in such circumstances is a quick and obvious crash. Consider the code in Listing 14.4.

Listing 14.4
```
struct Base
{
  Base()
    : m_i0(0)
  {}
  int m_i0;
};


void print_Base(Base &b)
{
  printf("%d ", b.m_i0);
}


class Derived
  : public Base
{
  Derived()
    : m_i1(1)
  {}
  int m_i1;
};


void print_array(Base ab[], size_t cb)
{
  for(Base *end = ab + cb; ab != end; ++ab)
  {
    print_Base(*ab); // Process each element
  }
}
```

```
int main()
{
  Base    ab[10];
  Derived ad[10];
  print_array(ab, 10); // Ok
  print_array(ad, 10); // Compiles and runs, but badness awaits!
  . . .
```

In the example, the first call to `print_array()` will correctly yield "0 0 0 0 0 0 0 0 0 0", but the second will yield "0 1 0 1 0 1 0 1 0 1". This is actually worse than a crash, since the bug can go unnoticed when the symptomatic behavior is as "benign" as this. Thankfully most real cases of this do crash.

It can be argued that this is not an imperfection at all,[8] merely an artifact of the C++'s object model [Lipp1996]. But it is so often overlooked and/or misunderstood, it is so dangerous, and compilers are unable to provide any defense against it, so it adds up to a serious imperfection in my estimation.

Imperfection: C++'s array/pointer duality, combined with its support for polymorphic handling of inherited types, is a hazard against which the compiler provides no assistance.

In the remainder of this section, we look at several partial solutions and avoidance techniques and a fully effective alternate representation of array parameters.

14.6.1   Store Polymorphic Types by Pointer

Since a derived class pointer *is* a base class pointer, the standard recommended approach [Meye1996, Dewh2003, Sutt2000] to our problem is to store pointers to the instances in an array (or `std::vector`), and process that. It obviates the problem entirely, and is the preferred solution in many cases.

However, this only covers those cases where you wish to manipulate types via (virtual) functions. This is not always appropriate, since it's often desirable to provide simple wrapper classes for C-API structures (see sections 3.2 and 4.4). Also, it can sometimes be desirable (although this is rare; see Chapter 21) to inherit from non-*vtable*-polymorphic types.

One final disadvantage is that it imposes costs both on the algorithm manipulating the code due to the extra indirection incurred for each element, and on the calling code in allocating and instantiating the array and the item references in the array independently, as in Listing 14.5.

Listing 14.5

```
void process_array(Base *ab[], size_t cb)
{
  for(Base **end = ab + cb; ab != end; ++ab)
  {
    print_Base(**ab); // Process each element. Might also need
                      // to test *ab is not null!
```

---

[8]As several of my reviewers did!

```
    }
}

int main()
{
  Derived ad[10];
  Base    *apb[dimensionof(ad)];
  for(int i = 0; i < dimensionof(ad); ++i)
  {
    apb[i] = &ad[i];
  }
  process_array(apb, 10); // Ok, but was it worth the effort?
  . . .
```

Since we're in the business of exploring all our options, we'll proceed to look at the alternatives.

14.6.2   Provide Nondefault Constructors

The first thing one can do is to prevent any arrays from being created. Arrays of class types may only be declared when the class type provides an accessible default constructor, one with defaulted arguments, or no constructor at all. If one can ensure that derived classes do not contain default constructors, then the problem is avoided. However, since there is no way to define a base class such that its derived classes may not contain default constructors, this is barely a solution when all classes are written by a single author, or within a team or by a development organization that is subject to thorough code reviews. It has no hope in other circumstances.

14.6.3   Hide Vector new and delete

It is possible to influence the array nature of derived types by hiding the vector new and delete operators—operator new[]() and operator delete[]()—in the base class:

```
class Base
{
  std::string  s;
private:
  void *operator new [](size_t);
  void operator delete [](void *);
};

int main()
{
  Base    *pbs = new Base[5];    // Illegal - inconvenient
  Derived *pds = new Derived[5]; // Illegal - good
  Base    ab[5];                 // Still legal - good
  Derived ad[5];                 // Still legal - bad!
  . . .
```

Hiding the vector `new` and `delete` operators only proscribes the allocation of arrays from the heap. It does not prevent one from declaring a stack-based array of derived instances and then passing that to a function expecting an array of parent instances.

Furthermore, there is nothing to stop the authors of derived classes from providing publicly accessible vector `new` and `delete` operators. Hence, the primary effect of this method is to prevent us from creating a heap array of `Base`; since it doesn't prevent the things we want to avoid, it's pretty useless!

14.6.4   Use std::vector

As I said in the previous section, when it comes to storing and manipulating variable sized arrays, I believe there are very few reasons (see section 32.2.8 for one such reason) to look past `std::vector`, and that is certainly the advice from the experts [Sutt2000, Stro1997, Meye1996, Dewh2003].

Most C++ afficionados would suggest that using `std::vector` would represent the solution to our array processing problem:

```
void process_array(std::vector<Base> &ab)
{
  std::for_each(ab.begin(),ab.end(), . . .); // Process all elements
}


int main()
{
  std::vector<Base>      ab(10);
  std::vector<Derived>   ad(10);
  process_array(ab); // Ok
  process_array(ad); // Compile error

  . . .
```

However, what you might use in your client code is a different matter from what a library function should be able to handle. This solution is certainly type-safe, since `std::vector<Base>` is an entirely different beast than `std::vector<Derived>` and the two cannot interoperate (without some sledgehammer casting). But despite this, I think that the advice is flawed.

First, there are circumstances where arrays are required—for example, when of static storage—and `std::vector` (or any other arraylike container) simply will not suffice.

Second, the elements may already be stored somewhere else, perhaps as part of a larger range within another `vector`. If we want to pass a subset of that `vector`'s contents to our function, we must copy them out, pass them, and, for non-`const` manipulation, copy them back in again.[9] This is because `vector`, like all standard library containers, stores and manipulates elements by value. Even if we could somehow guarantee the consistency in a real system during

---

[9]At this point you may well be suggesting that such copying might also be necessary for built-in arrays. Fear not—that will be taken care of in the solution.

this process, imagine the performance implications! (And don't even start to ponder the exception-safety ramifications!)

14.6.5 Ensure That Types Are the Same Size

None of the previous suggested mechanisms represent an optimal or appropriate mechanism to defend us against the inappropriate use of derived-type arrays of inherited types. Before we look at the solution, we should consider the cases where, for all its dangers, using array algorithms on inherited types may be desirable. What if we could enforce the restriction that any derived class types used by the array processing functions have the same memory footprint as their base and are, therefore, safe to use in this context? If they're the same size, then the slicing issue is moot (see Chapter 21), and since a derived type *is* a base type, it's perfectly valid to treat it as such in the processing function.

So we allow arrays of inherited types when the sizes are the same. The question, then, is how do we ensure that they are the same size? Expert reviewers may have the skills to determine this in code reviews for limited cases, but the variety of factors that can influence this effect—template derivation (see Chapters 21 and 22), structure packing (see Chapters 13 and 14), derived class overhead (see section 12.4)—conspire to make this unrealistic in practice. Even where reviews are conducted—which is all too rarely—they are not guaranteed to catch all errors and are only part of the verification armory [Glas2003].

We could have assertions (see section 1.4) in the code, but run time assertions may not be fired (i.e., incomplete coverage of code paths, release build testing). Compile-time assertions are a lot better, but do not provide obvious error messages and their omission from a particular derived class may slip under the reviewing radar. A better way is to use a constraint (see section 1.2). A constraint is a special piece of code, usually a template class, which serves to enforce a design assumption. This enforcement usually takes the form of a compile-time error, such as the inability to convert one type to another. Since we want our types to be the same size, we use the imaginatively named `must_be_same_size` constraint (see section 1.2.5).

Now we have the tool to detect inappropriate derived-type arrays, but where do we use it? In fact the answer is suggested by the `std::vector` solution, in that the parameterization of templates by inheritance-related types results in unrelated types. Our final solution takes the form of an enhanced version of the `array_proxy` template that we saw in section 14.4. Listing 14.6 shows its full form, incorporating the constraint and some extra member template constructors.

Listing 14.6

```
template <typename T>
class array_proxy
{
public:
  typedef T                value_type;
  typedef array_proxy<T>   class_type;
  typedef value_type       *pointer;
  typedef value_type       *const_pointer; // Non-const!
  typedef value_type       &reference;
```

```
    typedef value_type       &const_reference; // Non-const!
    typedef size_t           size_type;
// Construction
public:
    template <size_t N>
    explicit array_proxy(T (&t)[N]) // Array of T
      : m_begin(&t[0])
      , m_end(&t[N])
    {}
    template <typename D, size_t N>
    explicit array_proxy(D (&d)[N]) // Array of T-compatible type
      : m_begin(&d[0])
      , m_end(&d[N])
    {
        // Ensures that D and T are the same size.
        constraint_must_be_same_size(T, D);
    }
    template <typename D>
    array_proxy(array_proxy<D> &d)
      : m_begin(d.begin())
      , m_end(d.end())
    {
        // Ensures that D and T are the same size.
        constraint_must_be_same_size(T, D);
    }
// State
public:
    pointer            base();
    const_pointer      base() const;
    size_type          size() const;
    bool               empty() const;
    static size_type   max_size();
// Subscripting
public:
    reference          operator [](size_t index);
    const_reference operator [](size_t index) const;
// Iteration
public:
    pointer            begin();
    pointer            end();
    const_pointer begin() const;
    const_pointer end() const;
// Members
private:
    pointer const m_begin;
    pointer const m_end;
// Not to be implemented
private:
```

```
      array_proxy &operator =(array_proxy const &);
  };
```

The first constructor sets the member pointers m_begin and m_end to the start and (one past) the end of the array to which it is applied.

Using the array_proxy we can rewrite process_array():

```
void process_array(array_proxy<Base> ab)
{
    std::for_each(ab.begin(), ab.end(), . . .); // Process all elements
}
```

In this case, process_array() was written to take a non-const array_proxy by value, because the processing of the elements may want to change them. If your function requires only read only access, it is potentially slightly more efficient to declare it as passing array_proxy<T> const &, though the difference in performance is unlikely to show up on any profiler you can use, given the likely relative cost of the internals of process_array() itself.

We can expand the example, to include a Derived_SameSize type that derives from Base but does not change the memory footprint (see section 12.4). It is now valid to pass arrays of Derived_SameSize to process_array(), and the new array_proxy facilitates that via its other two template constructors.

```
Derived_SameSize
  : public Base
{};

void main()
{
    Base               ab[10];
    Derived            ad[10];
    Derived_SameSize   ads[10];
    process_array(make_array_proxy(ab));    // Ok
    process_array(make_array_proxy(ad));    // Compiler error. Good!
    process_array(make_array_proxy(ads));   // Ok - very smart
}
```

This is a complete solution to the problem. It is efficient (there is no cost on any decent compiler), it is type safe, and it completely empowers the designer of functions to defend themselves (or rather their code) against potential misuse by derivers of their types. Furthermore, it is smart enough to facilitate the case where the inherited types are of the same size as the parent type and to allow them to be proxied!

One final advantage is that it is now not possible to pass the wrong array extent to process_array, as it certainly was with the original two-parameter version, allowing us to adhere to the DRY principle.

This technique does not impose protection on hierarchies of types, so one could argue that it fails to adequately guard against passing around arrays of inheritance-related types. But I believe that that's the wrong way to look at it. It is the functions—free functions, template algorithms, member functions—themselves that need protecting from being passed arrays of the wrong type. Since it is within the purview of the author of any such functions to stipulate `array_proxy<T>` rather than `T*`, he/she can have all the protection considered necessary.

14.7   Cannot Have Multidimensional Arrays

This one's an overt part of the language, so I'm not going to try and soften you up before declaring:

Imperfection: C++ does not support multidimensional arrays.[10]

Okay, okay, I've done a tabloid-journalism-101 on you, omitting some of the truth for a good headline. To be precise, both C and C++ do support multidimensional arrays. The standard (C++-98 8.3.4.3) states, "[W]hen several array . . . specifications are adjacent a multidimensional array is created." However, it also says, "[T]he constant expressions that specify the bounds . . . can be omitted only for the first [dimension]," so all but the left-most dimensions must have a constant (at compile-time) extent. Hence:

```
void process3dArray(int ar[][10][20]); // Ok
void process3dArray(int ar[][][]);     // Error! Confused compiler
```

For me, this is a bona fide imperfection, since I don't think I've ever wanted to use a multidimensional array in a serious application where I didn't want flexibility in more than the most significant dimension. In such cases, one either has to find workarounds (manual pointer calculation hackery, in other words), or stipulate maximum fixed dimension extents within which the actual dynamic extents must lie, or use multidimensional array classes.

Built-in arrays in C and C++ use a contiguous layout scheme whereby the storage allocated for each element of a given dimension contains the elements of the next most significant dimension in ascending order. An array `a3[2][3][4]` actually has the following shown in Figure 14.1.

Figure 14.1

```
Subscripts        Address
a3[0][0][0]       a3 + 0
a3[0][0][1]       a3 + 1
a3[0][0][2]       a3 + 2
a3[0][0][3]       a3 + 3
a3[0][1][0]       a3 + 4
a3[0][1][1]       a3 + 5
```

---

[10]The C99 standard introduced *Variable Length Arrays* (VLAs) into the C language, which support multidimensional arrays whose dimension extents can be determination at run time. We look in detail at the reasons why VLAs are not terribly useful for C++ in section 32.2, not the least of which is that they are not part of the standard.

```
a3[0][1][3]     a3 + 7
a3[0][2][0]     a3 + 8
a3[0][2][1]     a3 + 9
a3[0][2][2]     a3 + 10
a3[0][2][3]     a3 + 11
a3[1][0][0]     a3 + 12
a3[1][0][1]     a3 + 13
a3[1][0][2]     a3 + 14
a3[1][0][3]     a3 + 15
a3[1][1][0]     a3 + 16
a3[1][1][1]     a3 + 17
a3[1][1][2]     a3 + 18
a3[1][1][3]     a3 + 19
a3[1][2][0]     a3 + 20
a3[1][2][1]     a3 + 21
a3[1][2][2]     a3 + 22
a3[1][2][3]     a3 + 23
```

This contiguous layout[11] is very useful, because it allows array slices (subarrays) to be passed simply by taking the address of the requisite part. For example, some code that manipulates a two-dimensional array of dimensions [3][4] can also manipulate a3[0] or a3[1], as shown in Listing 14.7.

Listing 14.7

```
void print_array(int (*pa2)[3][4]);

int    a3[2][3][4]; // A 3-D array of extents (2,3,4)
int    a2[3][4];    // A 2-D array of extents (3,4)
int (*pa2)[3][4];   // Ptr to a 2-D array of extents (3,4)

pa2 = &a2;          // Point to the 2-D array
pa2 = &a3[0];       // Point to a slice of the 3-D array

print_array(pa2);        // passing pointer-to-array
print_array(&a2);        // a2
print_array(&a3[0]);     // A slice of a3
print_array(&a3[1]);     // Another slice of a3
```

This example shows one case where an array does not break down into a pointer when being passed to a function (see section 14.4), but that's because the function parameter is defined as a pointer to an array rather than an array that, as we now know, can be treated as a pointer. Confused yet?

The array layout scheme explains why multidimensional arrays must have all but the most significant dimension fixed: the compiler needs to know the sizes of all other dimensions, so

---

[11]Note that this ordering is incompatible with Fortran ordering, which uses right-most-significant ordering. (See section 33.2.3.)

that it can generate the correct offsets when translating from the subscript form (see section 14.2.1) to calculate the actual location to manipulate. For example, the address of element `a3[1][0][3]` is actually decomposed as follows, where the notional constants D1 and D2 represent the extents of the two least significant dimensions:

```
a3[1][0] + 3
(a3[1] + 0 * D2) + 3
((a3 + 1 * D1 * D2) + 0 * 4) + 3
```

Unless the values of these extents are known to the compiler, it cannot calculate the actual offset, which in this case is:

```
a3 + 15
```

We saw in section 14.2 that arrays decay into pointers. We need to refine that rule somewhat. The most significant dimension of an array is almost always interpreted as a pointer by the compiler. I grant you this is a bit chicken-and-egg, but that's our funky language(s).

Okay, so the most significant dimension decays, hence we can rewrite the first form as:

```
void process3dArray(int (*ar)[10][20]);
```

which says that `process3dArray()` takes a pointer to a two-dimensional array of dimensions 10 and 20. The compiler clearly still knows the dimensions of the second and third dimensions, and can use that array without getting confused. However, the second, illegal, form decays into:

```
void process3dArray(int (*ar)[][]);
```

which equally clearly contains no information about the extents of the two least significant dimensions. The compiler would have to be clairvoyant to be able to deduce the calling context's array dimensions and to manipulate `ar` appropriately. The only way to make use of it as a three-dimensional array is to provide `process3dArray()` with the extents of the three (or at least two, anyway) dimensions. This can be done at compile time, with constants, but then one might as well just use the first form with the explicit dimensions. Alternatively, it can be supplied by global variables, which is very poor form, so we'd use additional parameters, as in:

```
void process3dArray( int *ar, size_t extent0, size_t extent1
                   , size_t extent2);
```

Hardly succinct is it? Nor is it respectful of encapsulation, or particularly maintainable. Thankfully, it's reasonably straightforward to come up with a very nice solution. I won't say it's easy, because balancing expressiveness, flexibility, and efficiency for such things is no mean feat. Naturally, we'll define a template class. The details are to be found in Chapter 33—I've got to keep some powder dry for now, or you'll never make it to the back cover—but it's worth pointing out here that it relies on the ability to meaningfully take N dimensional slices from N+1 dimensional arrays, as shown earlier.

CHAPTER 15

Values

15.1 NULL—The Keyword That Wasn't

In the C programming language, the macro NULL, located in `stddef.h`, is used to represent a null pointer. By using this specific symbol to denote a null pointer, its meaning is obvious to the reader. Furthermore, because it is defined to be of type `void*`, it can help to avoid potential problems. Consider the following C API for generating and managing some kind of identified tokens:

```
struct Token *lookup(char const *tokenId);

void fn()
{
  struct Token *token = lookup(NULL);

  /* use token here */
}
```

`lookup()` will return a matching existing token, or will create a new one if `tokenId` is the null pointer. Because the `tokenId` parameter is of type `char const*` (to which `void*` is convertible in C), the author of the client code (who may or may not be the author of the Token API) passes NULL to create a new `Token`. Suppose that once the API reached a certain level of maturity, its author decided to speed up the system by changing the lookup mechanism to be based on an integer index.[1] Naturally, the index would be a 0-based, with the sentinel value of -1 used to request a new token. Now we get a compile error (or at least a warning) if we use NULL:

```
struct Token *lookup(int tokenId);

void fn()
{
  struct Token *token = lookup(NULL); // error

  /* use token here */
}
```

---

[1] In the ideal world, such breaking changes are never made; a new function or a new API is born. However, the real world is seldom ideal.

227

227

This is great news. Had the client code author used 0 instead of NULL, we could be heading for all kinds of trouble. The 0 would be happily converted into an int as it was to char const*, and fn would do who-knows-what as token receives an invalid or null pointer rather than a newly created Token instance.

In C++, the picture is very different. Ironically, it is C++'s tightening of the type system over C that causes it to actually lose type strength in such cases. Because in C a type void* can be implicitly converted to any other pointer type, it is feasible to define NULL as ((void*)0) and achieve interconvertibility with any pointer type. However, because C++, for good reasons, does not allow an implicit conversion from void* to any other pointer type without use of a cast (usually static_cast), it means that NULL can no longer be usefully defined as it is in C.

In C++, 0 may be converted to any pointer type, so the C++ standard (C++-98: 18.1;4) stipulates that "The macro NULL is an implementation-defined C++ null pointer constant. . . . Possible definitions include 0 and 0L, but not (void*)0". But 0 can, of course, also be converted to any integral type (including wchar_t and bool, and floating point types), which means that the type checking we saw in the C version would not happen if it were compiled in C++, and we'd be heading down Trouble Boulevard with not even a warning of our impending doom.

Though it does confer useful meaning to code maintainers,[2] it is clear that using NULL instead of 0 in C++ is a bit like putting your head under the sheets to keep the monsters away; hence nearly everywhere you look the advice is to use 0 rather than the "arcane" NULL. But apart from not being lulled into a false sense of (pointer) security, this is not really much better, and you can end up in a similar mess because the literal 0 is always preferentially matched to an int. Imagine that you have a string class like the following:

```
class String
{
   explicit String(char const *s);
};
```

Unlike the standard library string, you decide to make the constructor have valid semantics when passed a null pointer, so you expect to see expressions such as

```
String  s(0);
```

All well so far. However, you then decide to add a constructor to initialize the String's underlying storage based on an estimate of the number of characters that may be used.

```
class String
{
   explicit String(char const *s);
   explicit String(int cch, char chInit = '\0');
};
```

---

[2] Except where it is erroneously used for integers, in which case it is positively harmful

Without a change to your client code, or to the function it was originally calling, a recompilation will result in an entirely different constructor being called. That can't be good, surely? Perversely, if you change the type from `int` to `size_t` (or `short`, or `long`, or any built-in other than `int`), the compiler will no longer have a preference for either conversion, and you will get an ambiguity error. It seems like C++ has managed to get hobbled with respect to null pointers such that it is less safe than C.

Imperfection: C++ needs a `null` keyword, which can be assigned to, and equality compared with, any pointer type, and with no nonpointer types.

So what's to be done? In [Dewh2003] Steve Dewhurst states, "[T]here is no way to represent a null pointer directly in C++." He also says that use of NULL marks one as being "hopelessly démodé." Well, I always like a challenge. This being a book about how to get what you want from the language, and make the compiler your best friend, I do of course have a remedy.

We want a fully fledged null pointer keyword, with the semantics described in the imperfection above. The solution, unsurprisingly, relies on templates.

Alas, a good part of the solution was already spelled out, a good five years previously, in Scott Meyers's *Effective C++*, Second Edition [Meye1998], which I own, but had not read.[3] I only came across it while checking on something else during the writing of this book.

Once the solution dawned on me—a member template conversion operator—I was almost there with the first attempt:

```
struct NULL_v
{
// Conversion
public:
    template <typename T>
    operator T *() const
    {
        return 0;
    }
};
```

Now we can write.

```
String    s(NULL_v());
```

Because `NULL_v` is a nontemplate class that has a member-template conversion operator, it can be applied anywhere, without any qualification or restriction. Now it is entirely in the purview of the compiler to resolve the correctness of its application, which is what we're after. (Note that it has to be given an `operator T *() const`, in order to force conversions only to pointer types. If it was just `operator T() const` it would convert to numeric types as well, and we'd have a very elegant mechanism for doing precisely nothing.)

---

[3]I'd read a friend's copy of the first edition, and purchased it on the strength of that. I don't recall the NULL issue being in the first edition, but of course it may have been, making me a witless plagiarist, as well as an incompetent researcher.

So we have our "way to represent a null pointer . . . in C++". The picture is far from complete, though. There are two problems. First, while it is possible to write expressions such as

```
double *dp;

if(dp == NULL_v())
{}
```

converse expressions such as the following will fail

```
if(NULL_v() == dp)
{}
```

This is where the modest originality in my solution begins. The treatment so far is incomplete, since it only works in statements and on the right-hand side of expressions. We see in section 17.2 that in conditional expressions, we should prefer *rvalue*s on the left-hand side in order to prevent erroneous assignment.

In fact, there is a surprising amount of equivocation between the compilers on which this was tested. (This, in and of itself, suggested more work was needed.) Some work fine with both expressions, some with neither.

To fully support these comparisons for the broad spectrum of compilers, we must expand the definition of NULL_v, to include the equals() method and four free functions. It also includes a pointer-to-member conversion operator.

Listing 15.1
```
struct NULL_v
{
// Construction
public:
  NULL_v()
  {}
// Conversion
public:
  template <typename T>
  operator T *() const
  {
    return 0;
  }
  template <typename T2, typename C>
  operator T2 C::*() const
  {
    return 0;
  }
  template <typename T>
  bool equals(T const &rhs) const
  {
```

```
      return rhs == 0;
  }
// Not to be implemented
private:
  void operator &() const;
  NULL_v(NULL_v const &);
  NULL_v &operator =(NULL_v const &);
};

template <typename T>
inline bool operator ==(NULL_v const &lhs, T const &rhs)
{
    return lhs.equals(rhs);
}
template <typename T>
inline bool operator ==(T const &lhs, NULL_v const &rhs)
{
    return rhs.equals(lhs);
}
template <typename T>
inline bool operator !=(NULL_v const &lhs, T const &rhs)
{
    return !lhs.equals(rhs);
}
template <typename T>
inline bool operator !=(T const &lhs, NULL_v const &rhs)
{
    return !rhs.equals(lhs);
}
```

The `equals()` method compares the rhs to 0, and is called in the two overloaded `operator ==()` free template functions. These two functions facilitate the two expressions that were troubling us. For completeness, two corresponding `operator !=()` functions are also provided.

`NULL_v` purports to represent the null pointer value, so the copy constructor and copy assignment operator are hidden: Since we would not assign `NULL` to `NULL` it makes no sense to allow `NULL_v` to be able to assign to itself. Now a default constructor is also required, since we are declaring, but not defining, the copy constructor. (Note that I've borrowed Scott's `void operator &() const`, since taking the address of something that is purely a value makes no sense. An excellent point!)

So we have our solution, `NULL_v` with `operator T *() const` and `operator T2 C::*() const`, and four (in-)equality free functions. `operator T2 C::*() const` handles pointers to members.

```
class D
{
public:
```

```
    void df0()
    {}
};
```

```
void (D::*pfn0)() = NULL_v();
```

There are no <, <=, and so forth operators, since that is meaningless for the null pointer. Now we just have to slot in NULL_v() everywhere we'd formerly used NULL. It's still not really a keyword, and unfortunately, human inertia and forgetfulness being what it is, this would likely be nothing but a nice theoretical treatment that gets put on the shelf. On cosmetic grounds alone we would never get this accepted by the C++ community: It's too many characters, and something that looks like a function call will always look inefficient, even if it's not. I know I certainly wouldn't use it!

But we're imperfect practitioners, and we are sworn to never say die. My original thought was to have a new preprocessor symbol, perhaps null. But defining a small preprocessor symbol for oneself that will be exposed in a header is fraught with danger. Without the power of a mega-large software corporation, one cannot hope to introduce anything as indistinguishable as null[4] into the global preprocessor namespace. So what's to be done?

I don't like the idea of having a more unique macro such as null_k, and there's still no guarantee against its being defined by someone somewhere else. We need a preprocessor symbol that no one's ever going to redefine, but how can we guarantee that? Maybe it's staring us in the face.

By now you may have guessed, so I'll just lay it straight out. The STLSoft header file stlsoft_nulldef.h contains the following:[5]

Listing 15.2

```
#include "stlsoft_null.h" // whence stlsoft::NULL_v
#include <stddef.h>

#ifndef NULL
# pragma message("NULL not defined. This is potentially dangerous. You are
advised to include its defining header before stlsoft_nulldef.h")
#endif /* !NULL */

#ifdef __cplusplus
# ifdef NULL
#  undef NULL
# endif /* NULL */
# define NULL    stlsoft_ns_qual(NULL_v)()
#endif /* __cplusplus */
```

---

[4]If I admit that I once did exactly this (with a different definition) before I'd taken off the training wheels, do you promise to not mention it until we get to the appendixes?

[5]There's actually a bit more in there to ensure that #pragma message is not presented to compilers that do not understand it. Those that do include Borland, Digital Mars, Intel, and Visual C++.

Seems kind of obvious now, doesn't it? We hijack NULL! We can safely do this because no one would ever redefine it, would they? Now we have a plug-and-play null pointer type-safety-enhancer that we can activate with nothing more than a single #include.

This file is never included in any other STLSoft header files, because that would be too arrogant an assumption. It also guards against the naivety in assuming people will respect the inviolability of NULL. But if you wish to use it, you simply include it somewhere high in your application header hierarchy, and you'll get all the null safety you can handle. I don't use it as a matter of course, but I do have it on the checklist of prerelease tests: "—a build with NULL++". Now the advice can be turned on its head, and you should prefer NULL to 0 for null pointers. It will mark you as *très moderne*.

But you may still be skeptical, and not buying the motivating example I gave. You may be fortunate to work in a development environment whose procedures ensure that APIs are never changed in the way I described. There're two more reasons to consider NULL. The first, eminently prosaic, one is that it aids the search and replace (to null) when porting algorithms from C++ to one of its (less object-oriented) cousins. The second one is that it makes a great sniffer dog for detecting shoddy implementations. If you don't believe me, try including stlsoft_nulldef.h at the head of your application inclusion hierarchy, and wait for the fireworks. I've run it over several popular libraries—no names, no pack-drill—and I can tell you there's a lot of dodgy code out there. If people are using NULL for integral types, it makes you question what other little oversights are creeping in.

Before I conclude I should address a point Scott Meyers makes in his treatment of the subject. He states that using such a NULL is of limited use because it is something that protects the writer of the calling code, rather than the called code. But I see this as being exactly what is called for, since it is changes to libraries that one needs to protect against in this case.

I would suggest that if library code also needs to be protected in this way, it simply declares short, long, char const * versions, and declares a private int version. Given our established preference (see section 13.1) for avoiding int and going with sized types, this fits nicely. Anyway, I don't think this is a problem for saving library code from client code, rather that it is the other way round. The users of libraries can now protect themselves against changes in the libraries' public interfaces.

15.2 Down to Zero

We saw in the previous item how to protect our client code from changes (from pointer to integer) in library code. What about the opposite situation? Suppose we had client code using the newer lookup(int).

```
// library.h
struct Token *lookup(int tokenId);

// client.cpp
struct Token *token = lookup(0);
```

Let's now imagine the requirements have changed again, and the API is to migrate back to using char const*. Now our client code will be changed with no warning, potentially for the worse. What we need is an equivalent to NULL_v for 0 literals.

Given the lessons learned with NULL, we can skip straight to the solution, shown in Listing 15.3.

Listing 15.3

```
struct ZERO_v
{
// Conversion
public:
  operator sint8_t () const
  {
    return 0;
  }
  operator uint8_t () const;
  operator sint16_t () const;
  operator uint16_t () const;
  operator sint32_t () const;
  operator uint32_t () const;
#ifdef NATIVE_64BIT_INTEGER_SUPPORT
  operator sint64_t () const;
  operator uint64_t () const;
#endif /* NATIVE_64BIT_INTEGER_SUPPORT */
#ifndef INT_USED_IN_STDINT_TYPES
  operator signed int () const;
  operator unsigned int () const;
#endif /* ! INT_USED_IN_STDINT_TYPES */
  operator float () const;
  operator double () const;
  operator long double () const;
// Not to be implemented
private:
  void operator &() const;
  ZERO_v(ZERO_v const &);
  ZERO_v const &operator =(ZERO_v const &);
};

/// operator == for ZERO_v and integral types
bool operator ==(ZERO_v const &, sint8_t i)   { return i == 0; }
bool operator ==(ZERO_v const &, uint8_t i)   { return i == 0; }
. . .
bool operator ==( ZERO_v const &
                , long double const &i)       { return i == 0; }

/// operator == for an arbitrary type and ZERO_v
bool operator ==(sint8_t i, ZERO_v const &)   { return i == 0; }
```

. . .

```
/// operator != for ZERO_v and an arbitrary type
bool operator !=(ZERO_v const &, sint8_t i)   { return i != 0; }
```
. . .

```
/// operator != for an arbitrary type and ZERO_v
bool operator !=(sint8_t i, ZERO_v const &)   { return i != 0; }
```
. . .

Note that there is no operator T() const, since that would also convert to pointers as well as integers. This means that we must supply individual conversion operators for all numeric fundamental types. Furthermore, there is a deliberate omission of conversion operators for char, wchar_t, and bool types. In the same way that NULL is defined to be NULL_v() in stlsoft_nulldef.h, so ZERO is defined to be ZERO_v() in stlsoft_zerodef.h.

For me, however, this is a step too far. Though I've implemented this in the STLSoft libraries, it's not become a part of my day-to-day tool kit, unlike NULL_v, for a couple of reasons:

1. I'm uncomfortable with the potential for clashes with macros defined in third-party and client code. As I said, the assumption that there will be no perverse redefinitions of NULL (other than ours, of course) is reasonable, and I've certainly not encountered one. However, the same cannot be said of the symbol ZERO. I've seen several of these in the past, so the likelihood of a clash is considerably greater.

2. It's plain ugly. Naturally this is merely an artifact of experience—we are used to seeing NULL, and not used to seeing ZERO—but programmers are notoriously churlish about ugliness being foisted on them. In this case I churl with the best of them.

Nonetheless, it's worth knowing about. If you have a "clean" application development where you can be pretty sure that ZERO is not already used, and you want every last drop of type safety that C++ can provide, you are most welcome to use it.

Furthermore, using ZERO_v() directly is useful as a straightforward way to constrain a template to be applied to numeric types only, as in:

```
template <typename T>
bool is_zero(T const &t)
{
  return ZERO_v() == t; // Won't compile if T is not numeric!
}
```

15.3 Bending the Truth

Boolean logic is based on the notion of two states, 0 and 1. Correspondingly, the C++ bool type is similarly defined (C++-98: 3.9.1.6) to hold values of true or false. What could be simpler, or better? Those of us that had to program C++ before bool was introduced certainly yearned for such a type, and many Boolean pseudotypes have been created. They've been based on enums, constants, and #defines, but none had all the features and support that a fully fledged type would provide, hence bool was introduced in C++-98.

Alas, even in the standard (C++-98: 3.9.1.6; note 42), it is noted that "using a bool value in a way described . . . as "undefined" . . . might cause it to behave as if it was neither true or false." This would never happen to you, right?

Well, it's very easy to synthesize an example:

```
reinterpret_cast<char&>(b) = 128;

if(b != false)
{
  printf("b != false\n"); // This is printed, ...
}
if(b != true)
{
  printf("b != true\n"); // as is this, ...
}
if(b)
{
  printf("b is implictly true\n"); // and this.
}
```

Of course, this is an artificial and deliberate sabotage of the type system, from which good programming practice will protect you 99 percent of the time, but there are still times when it can "byte" you. Commonly this is when using unions, and when interacting with other languages, such as C, as we saw in section 13.4.2.

In *The Gods Themselves*, Isaac Asimov said there are no meaningful numbers other than 0, 1, and infinity [Asim1972].[6] The bool type purports to support two values, which violates this rule, and the practical effect is that it supports a theoretically infinite (albeit practically bounded by its bit-size representation) number of values.

Imperfection: Having more than one discrete value for the Boolean type is dangerous.

Three solutions are possible. First, the language could dictate, or compiler vendors could opt to assume, that any conditional statement involving the literal true be rewritten in the obverse using the literal false. In other words, the following expression:

```
if( i &&
    b1 == true &&
    ( j < 3 ||
      b2 != true))
```

---

[6]Mind you, I bet he never had a fuzzy-logic rice cooker.

would be interpreted as

```
if( i &&
    b1 != false &&
    ( j < 3 ||
      b2 == false))
```

Since neither language nor compilers do this at the moment—and probably never will—the second, practical, measure is for you to ensure that you never compare against the literal `true` in your code.

Third, we'll see in section 17.2 that there are good reasons to ensure that all conditional subexpressions are Boolean. Since `bool` types are, by definition, Boolean, it is appropriate to avoid comparison with the literals altogether, and use the variable itself to test for truth, and its logical negation to test for falsehood, as in:

```
if( i &&
    b1 &&
    ( j < 3 ||
      !b2))
```

This is the accepted way of programming with Booleans, is undoubtedly more attractive, and most programmers do this without thinking about it. If that's not you, then maybe you should think about it: you can avoid the problems by simply getting rid of `true` (and, perhaps, `false`) from all conditional expressions in your own code.

15.4   Literals

We saw in the previous example how we can get into trouble by relying on variables having the precise value of literals. This section looks at the situation from the other way round. In other words, it deals with the nature of literals themselves and various inconsistencies and cautions.

15.4.1   Integers

"The type of an integer literal depends on its form, value and suffix" (C++-98: 2.13.1.2). That seems pretty plain. This section of the standard goes on to explain how the suffix affects the type of an integer literal. Basically, if it has no suffix then it will be `int` or `long int` if its value would not fit into an `int`. If it has the suffix `l` or `L`, it will be `long`. If it has a suffix of u or U, then it will be `unsigned int`, or `unsigned long int` if `unsigned int` is not large enough. If it is any combination of U (or u) and L (or l), then its type is `unsigned long int`.

As we mentioned in the item on NULL, interpretation of which overloaded function call is selected by the compiler can be quite a muddied concept. Consider now that you may have written a set of overloaded functions/methods and client code such as the following:

```
void f(short i);
void f(long i);
```

```
int main()
{
  f(65536);


  . . .
```

If you'd written this code on a compiler where `int` was a 16-bit quantity, then this would compile fine, because `65536` exceeds the limits of the 16-bit signed (or unsigned, for that matter) integer capacity and so would be interpreted as a `long`. The second overload takes a `long` argument so the function call resolves without issue. However, if you now attempt to compile this on a modern 32-bit compiler, where the size of an `int` is 32 bits, you'll find that the compiler interprets `65536` as being of type `int` and therefore cannot select between the ambiguous conversions required to use either `short` or `long` overloads.

Imperfection: Specification of the size of integer types as implementation dependent in C/C++ reduces the portability of integer literals.

To be frank, I'm not exactly sure that this warrants being an imperfection. I understand, and largely agree with, the need for the sizes of at least some of the fundamental types to be implementation dependent. Being general-purpose languages C and C++ need to run them on all sorts of architectures, and the only realistic way to have the constant space bound is to shoot for the lowest common denominator if we want compile-time checking. Given that, one cannot fail but to understand the cause for this issue. Nonetheless, it does present a problem, and we must be aware of it. There are two possible solutions.

The first solution is to eschew the use of literal integers in your code in favor of using constants. Since C++ constants should (and these days must) have an explicit type, then the problem pretty much disappears, at least as far as the constant definitions, where it is much more visible and likely to receive more "informed" maintenance attention than when lurking in bits of code. If you don't want to pollute the local namespace—a good instinct to have—and you are certain that the literal is of meaning to the current context only, then you can use a function-local constant.

```
void f(short i);
void f(long i);

const long THE_NUMBER = 65536; // Namespace-local constant, or

int main()
{
  const long THE_NUMBER = 65536; // ... function-local constant, or
  f(THE_NUMBER);
  if(. . .)
  {
    const long THE_NUMBER = 65536; // block-local constant

    . . .
```

In those rare circumstances where you feel you must have literals in your code, the second solution is to explicitly type-qualify your literals in situ. This may be by any of the following forms

```
f(long(65536));                // "Constructs" a long - looks elegant
f((long)65536);                // C-style cast - nasty!
f(static_cast<long>(65536));   // static-cast - not pretty
f(literal_cast<long>(65536));  // Funky custom cast - good for code searches
```

For fundamental types, the first form, known as function-style cast [Stro1997], is identical to the second C-style cast.[7] C-style casts are rightly deprecated in most circumstances (see Chapter 19, and [Meye1998, Meye1996, Sutt2000, Stro1994, Stro1997]; also see section 19.3 for the very limited cases where C-style casts are preferred). Even in this case, where their use (in either guise) is generally harmless, the possibility for error still exists in casting to a type that is too small for the given literal. However, the exact same problem exists when using static_cast. In either case, the solution is to raise your compiler's warning levels and to use more than one compiler. The static_cast form is preferred, because it is easier to search for, and because it is ugly [Stro1994], which reminds you that you probably shouldn't be using literal integers in your code in the first place.

If you want to make your code more amenable to automated code quantification, or you just like being flash, or both, you can take the ugliness to a higher level and implement a literal_cast operator (we learn about how to do such things in Chapter 19), but you may be pushing the bounds of reason (and modesty) if you do.

Whichever approach you choose, it is important to be mindful of the problem and as much of the minutiae of the rules that cause it as you can bear. This awareness will aid you no end when you come across code that has not taken care with its literals.

15.4.2 Suffixes

We've just seen how the type of integer literals is assessed. What I didn't mention was the ominous sentence that constitutes the next clause: "A program is ill-formed if one of the translation units contains an integer literal that cannot be represented by any of the allowed types" (C++-98: 2.13.1.3). In other words, literals for types larger than long are not a defined part of the language.

It's not surprising to learn, therefore, that 32-bit compilers equivocate on the manner in which they will understand the representation of 64-bit integer literals. Some need LL/ULL, others L/UL; still others accept both. Needless to say, this is quite a hassle when trying to write portable code.

Imperfection: C++ compilers do not agree on the syntax for suffixes of integer literals larger than those that will fit into (unsigned) long.

---

[7]This is a bit of an imperfection in itself, since when used in templates it will do strong checking, à la static_cast<> for most type, but C-style cast for fundamental types, with the consequent problems of potential conversion losses and inefficiencies.

The solution to this is as mundane and unattractive as the problem: macros. The Synesis Software numeric limits header contains the following ugly macros:

```
#define __SYNSOFT_GEN_S8BIT_SUFFIX(i)    (i)
. . .
#define __SYNSOFT_GEN_U32BIT_SUFFIX(i)   (i ## UL)
#if ( __SYNSOFT_DVS_COMPILER == __SYNSOFT_VAL_COMPILER_DMC || \
        __SYNSOFT_DVS_COMPILER == __SYNSOFT_VAL_COMPILER_DECC || \
        . . .
        __SYNSOFT_DVS_COMPILER == __SYNSOFT_VAL_COMPILER_XLC)
# define __SYNSOFT_GEN_S64BIT_SUFFIX(i)   (i ## LL)
# define __SYNSOFT_GEN_U64BIT_SUFFIX(i)   (i ## ULL)
#else
# define __SYNSOFT_GEN_S64BIT_SUFFIX(i)   (i ## L)
# define __SYNSOFT_GEN_U64BIT_SUFFIX(i)   (i ## UL)
#endif /* compiler */
```

and the following symbol definitions:

```
/* 8-bit. */
#define __SYNSOFT_VAL_S8BIT_MAX  \
    (+ __SYNSOFT_GEN_S8BIT_SUFFIX(127))
. . .
#define __SYNSOFT_VAL_U32BIT_MAX  \
    ( __SYNSOFT_GEN_U32BIT_SUFFIX(0xffffffff))
#define __SYNSOFT_VAL_U32BIT_MIN  \
    ( __SYNSOFT_GEN_U32BIT_SUFFIX(0x00000000))
/* 64-bit. */
#define __SYNSOFT_VAL_S64BIT_MAX  \
    (+ __SYNSOFT_GEN_S64BIT_SUFFIX(9223372036854775807))
#define __SYNSOFT_VAL_S64BIT_MIN  \
    (- __SYNSOFT_GEN_S64BIT_SUFFIX(9223372036854775807) - 1)
#define __SYNSOFT_VAL_U64BIT_MAX  \
    ( __SYNSOFT_GEN_U64BIT_SUFFIX(0xffffffffffffffff))
#define __SYNSOFT_VAL_U64BIT_MIN  \
    ( __SYNSOFT_GEN_U64BIT_SUFFIX(0x0000000000000000))
```

Yuck! If you are confident that you can avoid name clashes with fewer characters in your macros (or you're more reckless than me), then feel free to define something like S64Literal() and U64Literal(), which would make it a lot more manageable. Whatever macro you use, you can achieve portability (though not beauty) in the following way:

```
int64_t  i = __SYNSOFT_GEN_S64BIT_SUFFIX(1234567891234567891);
uint64_t i = U64Literal(0xDeadBeefDeadBeef);
```

15.4.3   Strings

Literal strings are expressed in C and C++ within the two double-quotes, as in `"this is a literal"` and `L"so is this"`. A literal is simply a null-terminated contiguous number of `char` or `wchar_t` (when prefixed with L) items. Hence, the literal `L"string"` is an array of the seven characters (of type `wchar_t`) `'s'`, `'t'`, `'r'`, `'i'`, `'n'`, `'g'` and `0`. The null terminator enables the literals to be interpreted as C-style strings, and passed around by a pointer. (Without null termination a length would also have to be included.)

Some languages ensure that all equivalent literal strings are "folded" into the same storage, which means that meaningful comparisons can be made between the pointers (or the language equivalent to a pointer) to the strings, rather than having to compare the string contents. For eminently sensible practical reasons (see section 9.2), C++ does not do this, and so code such as that shown in Listing 15.4 is neither correct C++ syntax, nor semantically valid.

Listing 15.4

```
enum Type
{
    abc
  , def
  , unknown
};

void interpret(char const *s)
{
  switch(s)
  {
    case "abc":
    case "ABC":
      return abc;  ,
    case "def":
    case "DEF":
      return def;
    default:
      return unknown;
  }
}
```

However, since some compilers can, and do, ensure that all identical strings within a link unit are "folded" into one instance, it is possible to do something such as shown in Listing 15.5.

Listing 15.5

```
Type interpret(char const *s)
{
  if(s == "abc")
  {
    return abc;
```

```
    }
    else if(s == "def")
    {
      return def;
    }
    else
    {
      return unknown;
    }
}
```

However, this is still not a sensible thing to do, for two reasons. First, if the executing process consists of more than one link unit (see section 9.2), which is very common, then it is possible for s to be a pointer to "abc" but fail to match the "abc" in the first conditional subexpression. Second, programs often deal with character strings that are generated, copied, and built up from pieces of others. It is likely in many scenarios that s will point to a character string that is not a literal created by the compiler, but rather one generated within program execution. In either case, the plain pointer comparison fails to correctly identify logical equivalence of the strings to which they point.

Constraint: C and C++ do not guarantee to ensure that identical string literals will be folded within a single link unit, and cannot do so across separate link units.

The advice is, of course, to effect string comparison by value, using strcmp() or similar functions, or to use string objects and use their operator ==() overloads for char/ wchar_t const*. However, you should not completely discount the pointer testing. Indeed, there are circumstances wherein a substantial number of the string pointers passed to interpret() would be literals (perhaps because they were handed out from a translation table). In such cases the following code may be appropriate.

```
enum Type
{
    abc
  , def
  , unknown
};

Type g(char const *s)
{
  if(s == "abc")
  {
    return abc;
  }
  else if(s == "def")
  {
    return def;
```

```
  }
  else
  {
    if(0 == strcmp(s, "abc"))
    {
      return abc;
    }
    else if(0 == strcmp(s, "def"))
    {
      return def;
    }
  }
  return unknown;
}
```

Please bear in mind that the circumstances in which this technique is appropriate are few and far between, and you should only evaluate whether this "enhancement" is beneficial when you've determined through *quantitative* performance analysis that the `interpret()` function is a source of significant latency. In other words, listen to the legions of esteemed engineers [Kern1999, Sutt2000, Stro1997, Meye1996, Dewh2003, Broo1995] who warn of premature optimization!

We know that equivalent non-empty literal strings are not guaranteed not to be different, but I wondered whether the standard dictated that the empty string — `""` — would be a special case. I could find nothing[8] in the standard that said that they are treated as one, so I conducted a simple test on a selection of compilers, which amounted to the following code:

```
int main()
{
  char const  *p1 = "";
  char const  *p2 = "";
  printf("%sequal\n", (p1 == p2) ? "" : "not-");
  return 0;
}
```

It seems that with Borland, Intel (in debug mode), and Watcom `p1` and `p2` are different. With CodeWarrior, Digital Mars, GCC, Intel (in release mode), and Visual C++ they are the same. I expect all of these compilers have flags to enforce folding (or "duplicate string merging" as it's also called) of literals but despite that, there's enough variation to make us be very wary of making assumptions.

You're probably wondering why I'm giving this issue such attention. Well, it could be convenient to use the empty string — `""` — as a sentinel value. For example, you may implement a string class `String` and use the empty string for empty (e.g., default constructed) instances rather than allocate an array of one character (with the value `'\0'`). The `String` destructor

---

[8]Of course, absence of evidence is not evidence of absence.

would then compare with the empty string literal and skip deallocation when it was "containing" the empty string.

With such a technique instances would always be able to render a non-null pointer to a string—as decreed by the *String* model (C++-98: 21.3)—while eliminating the costs of allocating those single character arrays for each empty string class instance. There's an example of this in the string class discussed in section 2.3.1.

However, we've learned that this is not prescribed by the standard, is only partially provided by the compilers, and is practically impossible when dealing with dynamic libraries. So the simple advice is, don't ever rely on equivalent literal strings *always* having the same address, but you can optimize for it happening *some* of the time.

15.5   Constants

15.5.1   Simple Constants

Constants in C++ take the following straightforward form:

```
const long  SOME_CONST  = 10;
```

The value of SOME_CONST is fixed, thus SOME_CONST can be used wherever an integer literal may be used, such as in specifying the dimensions of arrays, in enum values, and in the integer parameters of templates.

```
int ai[SOME_CONST];                              // ok
enum { x = SOME_CONST };                         // ok
frame_array_d2<int, SOME_CONST, SOME_CONST> ar; // ok
```

All fundamental types can be used in the definition of constants, although floating-point constants can only be used where floating-point literals can, for example, they cannot be used to define the bounds of arrays. The compiler assigns the values of such constants at compile time and, except where their addresses are taken, the constants occupy no storage in the linked module.

That's all straightforward and pretty obvious. Where the problems come in is when engineers get a bit slap happy with casts. Consider the following code:

```
const int W = 10;

int main()
{
  int &w = const_cast<int&>(W);
  int const    *p = &W;
  w *= 2;
  int const    *q = &W;
  int i[W];
  printf("%d, %d, %d, %d, %d\n", W, NUM_ELEMENTS(i), w, *p, *q);
  return 0;
}
```

It's not a reasonable thing to do, and the standard (C++-98: 5.2.11,7 & 7.1.5.1,7) tells us that such behavior is undefined. Hence, there is the expected disagreement between the compilers. Digital Mars gives `10,10,20,10,10`. Borland, CodeWarrior, Intel, and Watcom give `10,10,20,20,20`. Arguably the most useful behavior, from the perspective of the maintainer at least, is that of GCC and Visual C++ (from version 4.2 all the way up to 7.1), which both crash on the assignment to w.

Constraint: Casting away `constness` of a constant object is undefined, and will likely lead to unintended consequences.

The "answer" to this is simple: don't cast away the `constness` of anything that you don't know to be actually non-`const`, otherwise chaos will rain down upon you!

15.5.2 Class-Type Constants

It is possible to define constants of class type, as in

```
class Z
{
public:
  Z(int i)
    : z(i)
  {}
public:
  int z;
};

const Z g_z = 3;
```

However, in such cases the constant instance may not be used in place of integer literals.

```
int ai[g_z.z];                      // error
enum { x = g_z.z };                 // error

frame_array_d2<int, g_z.z, g_z.z);  // error
```

Furthermore, the constant objects are not created at compile time rather at run time.[9] Since they have static scope (i.e., they exist outside the scope of any particular function), they must be constructed (and destroyed) during program execution. You need to be aware that there are three potential drawbacks to their use in this regard:

First, the constructors and destructor for the particular type may have significant run time cost. This is borne at application/module start-up and shutdown, where such costs are usually, though not always, of concern.

---

[9]That's not to say that some cannot be (and are not) elided in the optimization steps in compiling and/or linking.

Second, there is the potential for one global object to depend on another. Consider the following (admittedly contrived) situation:

```
const Z g_z = 3;

extern const Z g_z3;

const Z g_z2 = g_z3;
const Z g_z3 = g_z;

int main()
{
  printf("%d %d %d\n", g_z, g_z2, g_z3);
  . . .
```

I trust you realize that it's not going to print 3, 3, 3. You actually get 3, 0, 3. The reason is that g_z2 is copied from g_z3 before g_z3 is initialized. Since global objects reside in global memory, which is guaranteed to be 0-initialized (see chapter 11), all the member of g_z3 are, preconstruction, 0, whence the value of g_z2. Rare, but nasty.

Third, if (non-extern) class-type constants are shared (i.e., by being declared in a shared header) between compilation units, then each compilation unit actually receives a separate copy of the constant instance. Obviously, if the definition or use of such constants relies on a singleton nature, it is broken.

Constraint: Constants of class type are evaluated as immutable global objects, rather than as compile-time constants. Failure to be mindful of this distinction is hazardous.

The simple answer to these hazards is to avoid using such constants if possible, or to proceed with caution[10] if not.

15.5.3   Member Constants

As well as declaring constants at global and function scope, they may also be declared within the scope of classes, as in the following:

```
class Y
{
public:
  static const int  y = 5;   // member constant
  static const int  z;       // constant static member
};
```

---

[10]Some companies actually have strict policies regarding the use of statics in this vein, especially when a value is to be changed.

These member constants are declared with very similar syntax to (`const`) static members, except that they have the form of a variable declaration and initialization statement, and they are limited to integral or `enum` (C++-98: 9.4.2,4) type. By using the initialization syntax, you declare that the compiler is free to interpret the member as a literal constant. In this case they differ from static members because you can use them in compile-time expressions, and you do not have to separately define them.

Well, actually, that last part is only sort of true. The same paragraph (C++-98: 9.4.2 in the standard) says, "The [static] member shall still be defined . . . if it is used in the program." This implies that we do indeed need to provide a definition, just as we would for any other static member. However, this is theory, and we'll see that in practice (see Table 15.1) none of our compilers require the definition in order to make use of the constant in a linked and functioning program. Nonetheless, if you take the address of a member constant, or make a reference to it, it will need to be given a definition:

```
int const *p = &Y::y;
int const &r = Y::y;

/* static */ const int     Y::y; // Define here
```

Despite the need for the definition, you do not initialize here, as the compiler does that for you. This helps to avoid different definitions of the same constant in different link units. Naturally, if your application code sees the constant with one value, and your dynamic library sees another, things are not likely to run swimmingly for very long. However, this modicum of safety can easily be subverted (deliberately or accidentally) since dynamic libraries are usually loadable without rebuilding. Still, it's better than nothing, and if your development procedures are up to scratch, you should avoid such clashes until you get into deployment.

While member constants are a nice feature, there are a couple of imperfections. First, not all compilers currently support them, as shown in Table 15.1.

Table 15.1 Support for integral and floating-point member constants.

	Supports Member Constants		
Compiler	Integral	Requires Definition	Floating Point
Borland 5.6.4	Yes	No	No
CodeWarrior 8	Yes	No	No
Comeau 4.3.3	Yes	No	No
Digital Mars 8.40	Yes	No	No
GCC 2.95	Yes	No	Yes
GCC 3.2	Yes	No	Yes
Intel 8	Yes	No	No
Visual C++ 6	No	-	No
Visual C++ 7.1	Yes	No	No
Open Watcom 1.2	No	-	No

There is a pretty straightforward workaround for this, which suffices for most cases: use enums. The downside is that this may not work for integral types that are larger than the range of enum, since the standard provides a very open definition of how much space an enum occupies. It says the "underlying type shall not be larger than an int unless the value of an enumerator cannot fit in an int or unsigned int." Note that it does not say that the type *will* be larger, and in practice most compilers do not allow enumerators to have values larger than their int type. The following enumeration provokes a wide range of behavior in our compilers:

```
enum Big
{
  big = 0x1234567812345678
};
```

Borland, CodeWarrior, Comeau, GCC (2.95), and Intel all refuse to compile it, claiming it's too large, and they have a perfect right to do so. Digital Mars, GCC (3.2), and Open Watcom all compile it and are able to print out its correct value (in decimal): 1311768465173141112. Visual C++ (6 and 7.1) compiles and prints out a value, but we only get the correct value if big is first assigned to an integer and we use printf() rather than the IOStreams. I think the answer regarding defining enum values larger than int is simple: don't.

Recommendation: Avoid using enum values larger than those that will fit in an int.

Notwithstanding this aspect, using enum for contants this is a very well-used technique, and quite successful where applicable. Indeed, I would say that it should be the preferred approach for anyone who has to maintain even a minimal degree of backward compatibility. (Note that the Boost libraries use macros to select between one option and the other, which is perfectly reasonable. You may be like me[11] though and prefer to dodge macros wherever possible.)

The second issue is that member constants cannot be floating point type.

```
class Maths
{
public:
  static const double pi = 3.141592653590; // Member constants must be integral
};
```

This is a strange inconsistency given that they are valid as members of a namespace.

```
namespace Maths
{
  const double pi = 3.141592653590; // Ok
}
```

I must confess I don't really know why member constants cannot be floating point, when it is legal to define nonmember constants of floating point types. [Vand2003] states that there is no serious technical impediment to it, and some compilers do support them (see Table 15.1). It

---

[11]MFC battle-hardened, that is.

may be because a floating-point variable of a given size, on a given platform, could vary in its precise value between compilers, which is not the case for integers. But then, nonmember constants are subject to this same potential behavioral inaccuracy, so it seems an arbitrary choice. It may also have been influenced by the fact that floating-point literal constants may not take part in compile-time evaluation of constant expressions—such as defining the extent of an array dimension—that integral constants can, and therefore it was deemed less important to support them. However both these reasons are subject to the counter that nonmember constants have the same issues, so it is inconsistent.

Imperfection: C++ does not support member constants of floating-point type.

If your compiler does not support member constants and the values you wish to use are too large for enum, or your constant needs to be of floating-point type, you can use an alternative mechanism based on static methods. This is simply achieved by use of static methods, as in:

```
class Maths
{
public:
  static const double pi()
  {
    return 3.141592653590;
  }
};
```

Thus calling Maths::pi() provides access to the constant value. This is the approach used in the numeric_limits<> traits type in the standard library. Note, however, that this is a function call; it is likely that your compiler will optimize out all instances of the actual call, but it is still the case that the value is evaluated at run time and cannot participate in compile-time expressions, as in:

```
class X
{
  static const int i1 = std::numeric_limits<char>::digits; // Ok
  static const int i2 = std::numeric_limits<char>::max();  // Error
};
```

The member constant digits may be used, because it is itself a compile-time constant, but the result of max() may not because it is a function, even though it may well be optimized out because it always returns the same constant value.

15.5.4 Class-Type Member Constants

We saw with all constants of fundamental type that they are true constants in the sense of being evaluated at compile time, but that if you wish to take the address of such constants they must have a single, separate definition to provide their storage. We saw with class-type constants that they must be initialized at run time, which means there is a potential for using them before they're initialized (or after they're uninitialized), and also that they may not partici- pate in compile-time expressions. This latter restriction also applies to static member functions that aim to provide member constants of types not supported by the language.

These limitations come together when we look at class-type member constants, which are not supported by the language, and largely for good reason, as we'll see.

```
class Rectangle
{
public:
   static const String  category("Rectangle"); // Not allowed
};
```

Constraint: C++ does not support member constants of class type.[12]

There are two reasons for this: identity and timing. With normal static class members, the member is declared in the class declaration, and the storage is defined elsewhere, usually in an accompanying implementation file, as in:

```
// In Rectangle.h
class Rectangle
{
public:
   static const String  category;
};


// In Rectangle.cpp
/* static */ const String Rectangle::category("Rectangle");
```

As we saw in section 9.2, within a given link unit (executable or dynamic library), there is a single definition, residing in `Rectangle.cpp`. This instance is constructed by the language run time support, when the link unit is loaded into a running state (i.e., when the process starts exe- cuting or when the dynamic library is loaded into the process). It is destroyed when the link unit is unloaded from its running state. Thus there is a single entity, and the timing of it is defined.

Having said that, though, the real world can come along and bite us. In multimodule devel- opment there are several problems with timing and identity, for example, instances can be brought into a process in more than one dynamic library link unit (see section 9.2.3). It should be clear that if the member constant form was allowed for class types then the compiler would have to make even more decisions on our behalf than it already does. For example, the com- piler/linker would have to work together outside of the purview of the developer in order to pro- vide an implicit definition of the static instance. Which compilation unit would it insert it into? How would that affect potential ordering issues?

---

[12]Well, in a sense it does, insofar as a member of `const` type can be declared in a class, and defined elsewhere. How- ever, this is not the same as a constant. Anyway, this hair-splitting is ruining my point.

If you want the whole of the class in a header file and/or you want the definition visible within the class declaration, you could provide the constant via a static method, as in:

```
class Rectangle
{
public:
  static const String  category()
  {
    static const String   s_category("Rectangle");
    return s_category;
  }
};
```

The static method `category()` uses a local static instance of String, `s_category`, which is initialized once the first time that `category()` is called, and that instance is then returned to all subsequent callers of the method. A by-product of this is that `s_category` is only initialized when needed; if `category()` is never called, then the initialization cost is not incurred. This is known as lazy evaluation [Meye1996].

This is perfectly fine if the class is only ever used in single-threaded processes, but, as we saw in section 11.3, it is not thread safe in its current guise, and therefore *must not* be used in multi threaded environments, or in any library that has an outside chance of being used in such environments in the future. In most nontrivial applications, you can be better off reading such things, for example, a String, from configuration information (file, Web-based token, registry key) associated with the application.

The problem is that one thread could have just in-place constructed `s_category` but not yet have set the hidden flag variable. At this point a second thread (or several) may come in and carry out the in-place construction of `s_category` again. The least amount of badness that would happen in such a circumstance is that whatever resources the first construction would have allocated would be lost. Of course, two threads could both be partway through the construction, and the inconsistent state may very well lead to a crash.

The really nasty part about this issue is that it will so *very* rarely cause a problem, and even when it does it may be a benign effect. That's because once any thread completes step 2, any subsequent thread entering the function for the entire duration of the process will have well-defined behavior. You could run millions of instances of a process containing such code,[13] and never find this, but there still remains the possibility that the program will behave correctly, that is, according to your "design," and yet still crash.

We could use some of the magic of spin mutexes (see section 10.2.2) to efficiently render function-local static objects safe, much as we did in section 11.3.2, but that is only half the problem. It still leaves the "constant" with an identity crisis. If it is an entity type (see section 4.2) rather than a value type (see section 4.6), we're still in the soup. So I'll just say once more: *never* use this technique!

Recommendation: Never attempt to simulate class-type member constants with function local static objects.

---

[13]Perhaps running a Web server, a heart monitor, a nuclear power station!

C H A P T E R   1 6

Keywords

It's easy to define new types in C++ (see Chapter 13), since that's one of the prime features of C++. It's harder to define values (see Chapter 15), but still eminently feasible. But it's pretty much impossible to introduce or effect new keywords in a safe manner. The only way to do this is with macros, which we all know are the last resort of the competent practitioner, even an imperfect one. So, into the breach we go. . . .

16.1   interface

The word `interface` has found common use in the Common Object Request Broker Architecture (CORBA) and the Component Object Model (COM), taking the meaning of a fully abstract class, that is, one in which every member is pure virtual. It is such a great thing to denote—from the perspective of a reader of code at least—that it has found a fully fledged role as a keyword in several newer languages, including D, Java, and C#/.NET. In the COM headers, `interface` has been defined using `#define`; Microsoft exhibited their customary disregard for the preprocessor namespace, albeit one is inclined to forgive them in this case.

At first glance, with COM spectacles on, the absence of this keyword seems like an imperfection that could easily be amended by adding it to the language. But there are three objections. First, it would serve no use with current COM headers, since it would be redefined to `struct` as it is now. Second, it might break existing COM-independent code, which may be "legitimately" using the word as a variable name. Finally, and most compellingly, there is no reasonable definition.

As we see in section 19.8, there are good reasons for flouting good C++ idioms when implementing reference-counting interfaces. COM interfaces (and those of other reference-counted infrastructures) are concerned only with the methods `QueryInterface()`, `AddRef()`, and `Release()` or their equivalents along with the additional interface-specific methods.

```
interface ICompress
  public : IUnknown
{
  // IUnknown methods
  virtual HRESULT QueryInterface(REFIID riid,  void **ppvObject) = 0;
  virtual uint32_t AddRef() = 0;
  virtual uint32_t Release() = 0;

  // ICompress methods
```

252

```
     virtual HRESULT Compress( byte_t    *pyin
                             , uint32_t  cbIn
                             , byte_t    *ppyOut
                             , uint32_t  *pcbOut
                             , int32_t   *pdwFlags) = 0;
};
```

They specifically do not contain constructors or destructors, since the rules of the reference-counting architecture prohibit an interface client of an object from deleting it, and a virtual destructor would interfere with binary layout and thus language interoperability. Even if destructors were not proscribed by the rules of the architecture, the fact that COM is language neutral (to the degree that an implementing language is able to formulate the appropriate calling conventions and parameter types), any provision of a C++ destructor would be meaningless to other languages.

Note that it is perfectly reasonable, and fairly common, to have a reference-counting architecture with similar characteristics (i.e., no destructors) to COM, which has nothing to do with COM. Indeed, I wrote one that worked on various UNIX flavors and VMS (see Chapter 8).

In other interface-based scenarios that are purely C++ and do not use reference counting, it is common to see that an interface *does* contain a pure-virtual destructor to ensure that there will not be incomplete destruction [Meye1998]; sometimes this is the only member.

```
interface IRoot
{
public:
  virtual ~Root() = 0;
};


inline IRoot::IRoot() // Implementation required for pure dtor
{}
```

Both of these flavors of "interface" imply lifetime control (see Chapter 5): one uses reference counting and the other uses explicit deletion. However, when we're not causing our client code to be concerned with the lifetime of the interface (or, rather, the implementing instance) then the model can be very simple and concerned entirely with the functionality provided. This is the model of interface used in D, Java, and .NET:

```
interface IIdentity
{
  virtual int GetId() = 0;
}
```

So should interface be used solely for reference-counting interfaces, for destructible interfaces, or reserved for "regular" interface classes? Should its meaning be implementation dependent? It's not an answerable question, since C++ (thankfully) supports all these techniques.

Perhaps we could compromise with a weakened definition that mandates that all `interface` methods be pure virtual? But this would also fail, since (as we see in section 8.2) it is actually useful to insert nonvirtual methods into an interface definition, at least when it is visible in C++ compilation units.

The only worthwhile definition of `interface` I can think of is that it has the following characteristics:

- Its default access is public, as is the case with struct.
- It may contain nonvirtual functions (and their implementations).
- It may contain pure virtual functions.
- It may *not* contain any nonpure virtual functions (and their implementations). The only definition for a virtual function allowed is that for any pure virtual destructors, since they are required by the C++ object-model. However, such pure virtual destructor implementations must be strictly empty (as shown in the earlier example).
- It may not inherit from any class-key type (i.e., `struct/class/union`; C++-98: 9.1) except another `interface`.

Of course, all the behaviors facilitated by this definition are already expressible with the existing language, so it's hardly likely that there will be serious interest in adding this keyword. Nonetheless, I think it's worthwhile to have highlighted the issues, since they are often used but little discussed. In section 8.2.7 we looked at a related keyword that would be much more useful to have, `pinterface`.

16.1.1 pinterface

Although I may think that there's probably no good way of defining an `interface` keyword, I would suggest there's a pretty strong case for some other keyword, for example, `pinterface`, by which all the effective but incredibly verbose gunk of the portable *vtables* technique (see Chapter 8) could be encapsulated. In other words, a `pinterface` would be a `struct` that could contain only pure virtual methods or nonvirtual methods, and no member data, and would have a common prescribed layout (a contiguous packing of architecture-sized pointers) for itself and its *vtable* for a given architecture. Then we could have portable polymorphism with ease.

16.2 temporary

It is generally a bad thing to use implicit conversion operators (see Part Four, and [Meye1996, Sutt2000, Sutt2002]), and a class such as the following will bring howls of derision upon its author these days:

```
class String
{
public:
  operator char const *() const;
};


String s("Little Nose");
puts(s); // Uses implicit conversion operator
```

Hence the standard string class does not provide an implicit conversion operator. Instead it provides the `c_str()` method, which returns a pointer to `const char` (or `wchar_t`). Let's change `String` to correspond to the standard.

```
class String
{
   . . .
public:
   char const *c_str() const;
};


String s("Little Nose");
puts(s.c_str()); // Uses method - better
```

It is also generally a bad thing to assign raw pointers to return values. Consider the following potentially dangerous code:

```
String     s("Little Nose");
char const *p = s.c_str();
puts(p);
```

`p` holds a pointer to the internal buffer of `s`,[1] but that pointer is valid only so long as `s` remains unchanged. As soon as `s` is manipulated in any modifying, or potentially modifying, manner, it may reorganize its internal storage in such a way as to invalidate `p`.

This is not a problem with pointers, per se. It's actually an instance of a broader problem whereby client code may be holding onto a reference, pointer, iterator, and so on that becomes invalidated. We look in detail at this problem in Chapter 31, *Return Value Lifetime*.

```
String     s("Little Nose");
char const *p = s.c_str();

s[0] = 'L'; // May cause s to reallocate its storage

puts(p);    // May or may not be valid. Could work; could crash!
```

Imagine that we had a `temporary` keyword that would, when applied to a method, require that the values returned by that method could not be assigned to variables. We would decorate the `c_str()` method with it, as in:

```
class String
{
```

---

[1]Actually it holds a pointer to an internal buffer managed by `s`. A conformant implementation may provide a separate buffer for the `c_str()` method from its actual internal storage, and implementations that do not zero-terminate their storage will necessarily do so.

```
. . .
temporary char const *c_str() const;
. . .
```

Now the compiler will be able to reject the offending statement

```
String     s("Little Nose");
char const *p = s.c_str(); // Error - cannot assign result of a temporary method
```

and the undefined behavior is avoided. Naturally, that wouldn't stop someone from writing something such as the following:

```
void steal_temp(char const *p, char const **pp)
{
  *pp = p;
}

String     s("Little Nose");
char const *p;
```

```
steal_temp(s.c_str(), &p); // Nasty!
```

However, if we refine the definition of temporary to have a similar propagation as do const and volatile (known as the cv-qualifiers; C++-98: 3.9.3), the temporary nature of the pointer can be enforced right down to the C run time library.

```
char *strcpy(char *dest, char const temporary *src);
char *strdup(char const temporary *src);

void steal_temp(char const temporary *s, char const **pp)
{
  *pp = s; // Illegal: implicit cast from temporary pointer
}

void copy_temp(char const temporary *s, char **pp)
{
  *pp = strdup(s); // Ok, since strdup() takes temporary ptr
}

String     s("Little Nose");
char const *p;
char       *copy;
```

```
steal_temp(s.c_str(), &p);    // Will not compile. Good!
copy_temp(s.c_str(), &copy);  // Ok
```

Since it's only an idea—I've not written a compiler-extension for this yet, as I've been busy writing this book—it might be that applying temporary would stop potentially legitimate uses of assigning such a pointer to a variable, but it would be nice to have the choice; there's always `const_cast` to give the ultimate power back to the programmer.

Language specifiers (and compiler writers, too) don't like adding new keywords and I know that Beelzebub will be the Olympic ice dancing champion before this idea is adopted, but I think it would be a significant strengthening to C++'s type system and would represent a material increase in code safety. Of course, all the extra typing wouldn't make it (or me) popular.

There's a school of thinking that suggests that returning a pointer from a function is always a no-no, and that this is therefore a nonissue. However, there are plenty of instances where efficiency can overrule such concerns; in any case you must go to the C run time library and/or the operating system C APIs at some point. From a more fundamental point of view, the Shims concept (see Chapter 20) provides a generalizing mechanism that is a highly useful alternative to traits, and shims for certain types do indeed return pointers. Also, certain user-defined cast operators (see section 19.4) may also use a similar mechanism. As the incidence of these "advanced" techniques increases, there may be more impetus to add `temporary` support to the language. This issue is dealt with in depth in Chapter 31.

Conversely, people from the other side of the C++ debate may suggest that `const_cast`-ing `const`, `volatile`, and `const volatile` are bad enough and that the prospect of four more permutations involving `temporary` is ample evidence that C++ has grown too complex and/or that garbage collection should be the only way of doing things.

These two viewpoints are too extreme in my opinion. One suggests that we rely on volition and good practice to restrict ourselves to a subset of possible constructs. The other suggests that the language should have large parts of its flexibility removed. Both are perfectionist points of view, and we're "imperfectionists," are we not? What I would like to see is a middle ground where I still have the power to do as much (or more) as I can now, but with more help from the compiler. That's what it's there for, after all.

16.3 owner

The three access control flavors are `private`, `protected`, and `public`. The semantics of `private` and `public` are pretty clear: `private` means that nothing outside the class (apart from any `friends`) can see or use the given members (variables or methods); `public` means that the members are accessible to any other code.

`protected` means that only things within the class (or `friends`) or derived classes can see or use the given members; it provides access to parts of a *base* class type to a *derived* type where the types are related in an inheritance relationship. Occasionally, it would be useful to allow access to otherwise inaccessible parts of an *inner* type to a separate *outer* type where the types are involved in a composition relationship. We see a perfect example of this when we look at how to provide properties in C++ in Chapter 35. Unfortunately C++ does not support this type of access control.

Imperfection: C++ does not provide access control between types involved in a composition relationship.

What we'd like to see is something like the following, where the new access specifier `owner` grants composing types access to the constructor of `Inner`:

Listing 16.1

```
class Inner
{
owner:
  Inner(Resource *r)
    : m_r(r)
  {}
public:
  ~X();
  . . .
};

class Outer
{
public:
  Outer( . . . )
    : m_inner(GetResource(. . . ))
  {}
private:
  Inner m_inner;
};
```

If you are coding a specific type, which will be owned by one specific type, or a few specific types, the class can be coded granting the owning type(s) as friend(s). However, this is very specific and highly coupled.

```
class Inner
{
private:
  friend class Outer; // Coupling: brittle!
  Inner(Resource *r)
    : m_r(r)
  {}
```

Each time you need to allow Inner to be composable in a new type, its class definition will need to be amended, and therefore all code involving existing composable types will have to be recompiled. This is not a solution, merely an intensive way of making new problems for oneself. Clearly the only usable form of this technique is going to be a generic one, and there are two ways to achieve this.

The first is that one can define as protected the members that are to be owner accessible, and then derive private member classes within each composing class.

Listing 16.2

```
class Inner
{
protected:
  Inner(Resource *r);
```

```
    . . .
};

class Outer
{
public:
  Outer( . . . )
    : m_inner(GetResource(. . . ))
  {}
private:
  class OuterInner
    : public Inner
  {
  public:
    OuterInner(Resource *r) // Forwarding constructor
      : Inner(r)
    {}
  };
  OuterInner m_inner;
};
```

This effectively grants owner access, but the downside is that there's still a finite amount of coding to be done for each case in tiresome constructor forwarding (see Chapter 23). Further, it only works to provide access for methods; it cannot grant direct access to fields.

The second technique is to use templates, and to define one of the parameterizing types as a `friend` of the template, as in:

```
// form #1
template <typename T>
class Thing
{
  friend T; // Allow T to see inside Thing<T>
private:
  int m_value;
};
```

This seems like an eminently reasonable thing to do, does it not? Alas, it is not legal C++. The standard states that "within a class template with a template type-parameter T, the declaration ["]friend class T;["] is ill-formed" (C++-98: 7.1.5.3(2)). However, we're imperfect practitioners, not language lawyers, so that does not worry us, as long as what we're doing is sensible, which it is in this case.

The form shown above, which I'll call form #1, works with the following compilers: Borland (5.51 and 5.6), Comeau (4.3.0.1), Digital Mars, GCC (2.95), Intel (6 and 7), Watcom (11 and 12), and Visual C++ (4.2–7.1). It does not work with CodeWarrior (7 and 8) or GCC (3.2). Note that Comeau (4.3.0.1) works with this form, and all others, when in its Win32 default configuration. In strict mode (−A) it does not work with any, reflecting the fact that the technique in all of its forms is not legal C++. However, from version 4.3.3 onward, Comeau contains a `--friendT` option, which Greg Comeau kindly added after only a modest amount of badgering. Now we can use Comeau in strict mode, but still have this most useful construct. (We see exactly how useful in Chapter 35.)

Since `T` is a class—we're granting it friendship, so it can't exactly be an `int`—maybe we should be mentioning that fact to the compiler, as in:

```
// form #2
template <typename T>
class Thing
{
    friend class T; // Allow T to see inside Thing<T>
private:
    int m_value;
};
```

This is form #2. CodeWarrior, Digital Mars, and Watcom support this form. So a bit of compiler discrimination between forms #1 and #2 would cover most bases, but we're still not satisfying GCC 3.2.

Being someone that avoids `friend`ship like the plague,[2] I ran out of experience here and needed to consult with the kind people of the `comp.lang.c++.moderated` newsgroup, who suggested some alternatives. The suitable one I'll call form #3:

```
// form #3
template <typename T>
class Thing
{
    struct friend_maker
    {
        typedef T T2;
    };
    typedef typename friend_maker::T2    friend_type;
//  friend class friend_type;
    friend friend_type;
private:
    int m_value;
};
```

The complication here is we're back to the inconsistency seen in forms #1 and #2 between whether the `class` specifier should be used in the `friend` statement. GCC and Visual C++ both require that `class` is not used, whereas the other compilers require that it is used. But since GCC is the only one for which we (currently) require this third form, we'll omit the `class` specifier. Table 16.1 summarizes the support.

---

[2]I think that the `friend` keyword is way overused in the general development community. I'm not, of course, arguing that it should never be used. I think everything's got its place, even `goto`, but just that it's a very rare circumstance where `friend` is needed.

Table 16.1   Friendship support of various compilers

Compiler	Form #1	Form #2	Form #3
Borland C++ (5.51 & 5.6)	Yes	No	No
CodeWarrior (7 & 8)	No	Yes	Yes
Comeau (4.3.3)	with `--friendT`	with `--friendT`	with `--friendT`
Digital Mars (8.26 –)	Yes	Yes	Yes
GCC 2.95	Yes	No	No
GCC 3.2	No	No	Yes
Intel (6 & 7)	Yes	Yes	Yes
Visual C++ (4.2 – 7.1)	Yes	No	Yes
Watcom (11 & 12)	Yes	Yes	Yes

The language says it's illegal, so it's not surprising that there's variance in the compilers' "illegal" support. I really don't like macros as a rule, especially ones that generate code, but in this case it's probably necessary. Hence, we can define the macro DECLARE_TEMPLATE_PARAM_AS_FRIEND() as shown in Listing 16.3.

Listing 16.3

```
#if defined(__BORLANDC__) || \
    defined(__COMO__) || \
    defined(__DMC__) || \
    (  defined(__GNUC__) && \
       __GNUC__ < 3) || \
    defined(__INTEL_COMPILER) || \
    defined(__WATCOMC__) || \
    defined(_MSC_VER)
# define    DECLARE_TEMPLATE_PARAM_AS_FRIEND(T)    friend T
#elif defined(__MWERKS__)
# define    DECLARE_TEMPLATE_PARAM_AS_FRIEND(T)    friend class T
#elif defined(__GNUC__) && \
      __GNUC__ >= 3
# define    DECLARE_TEMPLATE_PARAM_AS_FRIEND(T)    \
  struct friend_maker                              \
  {                                                \
    typedef T T2;                                  \
  };                                               \
  typedef typename friend_maker::T2 friend_type;   \
  friend friend_type
#endif /* compiler */
```

It is then used as follows:

```
// form #2
template <typename T>
```

```
class Thing
{
  DECLARE_TEMPLATE_PARAM_AS_FRIEND(T);
private:
  int m_value;
};
```

Note that I've defined the macro so that it needs a terminating semicolon in the code where it is used; you may choose to do it otherwise. As I've made clear in the example code, the template friend technique can provide access to fields as well as methods, but it's not strictly legal even though it is very widely implemented. It also grants all-or-nothing access, rather than the fine-grained control I outlined at the start of the section.

This is one of a very few instances in this book where I advocate stepping outside the standard. I believe it's okay in this case for two reasons. First, almost all our compilers (see Appendix A) support it at the moment, and it seems *highly* unlikely that there'll be a mass change to break a potentially large existing code base. Second, it's a sensible thing to want to do, since it only apes perfectly legal behavior of nontemplate classes. The fact that the Comeau compiler—arguably the most compliant compiler in the industry—has seen fit to add the `--friendT` option to their latest version (version 4.3.3) is a good indicator that this is not a foolish thing to want to do.

The inheritance technique is legal, but requires new code for each composing class. Also, it cannot directly access fields; accessor methods are required, which further increase the new code that needs to be written, with the concomitant increase in maintenance and testing.

16.4   explicit(_cast)

The perils of implicit conversion operators have been very well documented in recent years ([Sutt2000, Meye1996, Dewh2003, Stro1997]), and can lead to all kinds of unintended consequences—both semantic and performance—in the manipulation of types. Item 36 from [Dewh2003] and Item 5 from [Meye1996] illustrate some of the problems.

Consider the gauche class shown in Listing 16.4, which provides a number of implicit conversion operators. Very few people would write a class such as this. But in some respects it is reasonable, since date/time manipulations do come in a variety of types, and a useful time class will be compatible with all such types as are needed.

Listing 16.4

```
class Time
{
  operator std::time_t () const;
  operator std::tm () const;
#if defined(UNIX)
  operator struct timeval () const;
#elif defined(WIN32)
  operator DATE () const;
  operator FILETIME () const;
  operator SYSTEMTIME () const;
#endif /* operating system */
};
```

But we're imperfect practitioners! Tenet #2 (see Prologue) states that we wear a hairshirt, so we certainly don't want implicit conversions. But tenet #4 states that we do not accept the limitations placed upon us, so let's seek out a solution.

explicit is already a keyword in C++, having the function of preventing the constructor to which it is applied from taking part in an implicit construction of the given class, known as *conversion construction* (see section 2.2.7). We'll look here at another potentially very useful application of the keyword, which is sadly missing from the language. Consider the rewritten pseudo-C++ form in Listing 16.5.

Listing 16.5

```
class Time
{
  explicit operator std::time_t () const;
  explicit operator std::tm () const;
#if defined(UNIX)
  explicit operator struct timeval () const;
#elif defined(WIN32)
  explicit operator DATE () const;
  explicit operator FILETIME () const;
  explicit operator SYSTEMTIME () const;
#endif /* operating system */
};
```

The explicit keyword marks the two conversion operators as being invalid for consideration for implicit conversion. What this means is that instances of Time would not be implicitly convertible to time_t, or struct timeval or any of the other time types, but they would be amenable to explicit conversions, as follows:

```
Time      t = . . .;
std::time_t v1 = t;                      // error - need explicit conv
#if defined(WIN32)
FILETIME    v2 = static_cast<FILETIME>(t);   // Explicit conv Ok!
#endif /* operating system */
```

The big win would be that multiple valid conversion operators could be supported, where currently one must eschew some or all of them due to ambiguities. Since the language does not provide this use of the explicit keyword, there are three solutions available to us.

16.4.1   Use Explicit Accessor Methods

The standard recommended approach [Meye1996] is to accept more typing and use normal method calls instead of the implicit conversion operators:

```
class Time
{
  . . .
```

```
    std::time_t get_time_t() const;
    std::tm      get_tm() const;

    . . .

    SYSTEMTIME  get_SYSTEMTIME() const;
#endif /* operating system */
};
```

We can give in to more typing, and simply write:

```
Time        t = . . .;
std::time_t v1 = t.get_time_t(); // Explicit method call: clear
```

The benefit of this approach is that, given meaningful accessor method names, it is clear what is being returned. This is the approach advocated by the standard library for its string type, as in:

```
std::string s("A string object);

puts(s);            // Error - no suitable conversion
puts(s.c_str());    // Return a c-style string
```

The main drawback of this approach is that it is highly fragile with respect to generality. It relies on all types that return a given value type using precisely the same name. If that works, then it is feasible to write generalized code—template or otherwise—that may be used with a variety of such types. But we all know how easy it is to get it wrong and have that mistake cemented by inertia. And that's before we consider differences of opinion over naming conventions: Is that get_time_t() or get_timet() or get_std_time_t()...?

Another drawback from my perspective is that the semantics (to a human, at least) are misleading. If I call a function get_XYZ() on something, I might resonably expect to be getting the XYZ that it owns, rather than receiving it as an XYZ. Granted that the difference is subtle, but subtlety is the eager precursor to confusion in this crazy game we play. Of course, one could call it as_XYZ(), but conventions dictate that get_ is the prefix for such methods, and flouting naming conventions is never a win-win game.

16.4.2   Emulate Explicit Casts

Since a compiler is only allowed to provide at most one implicit conversion in an expression, we can provide implicit conversion operators to an intermediate type, which is itself convertible to the actual result type. For example:

Listing 16.6

```
struct tm_cast
{
  tm_cast(std::tm v)
    : m_v(v)
  {}
```

```
    operator std::tm() const
    {
      return m_v;
    }
    std::tm m_v;
};

class Time
{
    . . .
    operator tm_cast() const;
    . . .
};

Time    t = . . .;
std::tm v1 = static_cast<tm_cast>(t); // Conversion via tm_cast
```

Now we have three types involved in each of our conversions, for example, `Time` => `tm_cast` => `std::tm`. To get the compiler to work out the second step in each conversion we need to give it the middle step and it can take it from there. Naturally, it would be much nicer if we could supply the third type, the one that is needed by the functions f1 and f2, and have the compiler provide the first conversion implicitly:

```
f1(static_cast<std::tm>(t));    // Illegal, but clearer to reader
```

Understandably, the compiler cannot have this level of intuition, as it would be too easy to tie it up in knots: What if both the intermediate types had the same implicit conversion type? The syntax does look very appealing though, doesn't it?

What if there was another way to achieve this? How about the following:

```
class Time
{
    . . .
    operator explicit_cast<std::tm>() const;
    . . .
};

Time    t = . . .;
std::tm v1 = explicit_cast<std::tm >(t); // correct & clear
```

It is relatively straightforward to create the `explicit_cast` template, and we look in detail at this in section 19.5. Note its more obvious syntax: it specifies precisely the type that we are explicitly casting to, rather than the intermediate type. It's pretty much self-documenting!

The other significant plus is that it is a general solution. We have one template, rather than the potentially limitless `tm_cast`, `DATE_cast`, `std_string_ref_const_cast`, and so forth intermediate types. In template code, a parameterizing type can be applied to the `explicit_cast` parameter, supporting type generality with aplomb.

As we see in section 19.5, this works really well for fundamental types, and for pointer types, but does not work well for `const` references and not at all for non-`const` references. As such, it is only a partial solution, for all its conceptual appeal.

16.4.3   Use Attribute Shims

The last alternative is to combine the explicit accessor method approach (see section 16.4.1) with attribute shims. A shim is a collection of one or more free function overloads that is used to elicit common attributes from instances of unrelated types; shims are a powerful generalizing mechanism. We learn all about them in Chapter 20, so I'll defer a detailed explanation of them until then. For the moment, let's just look at the two shims and the resultant client code:

```
// get_tm() attribute shim - uses Time::get_tm()
inline std::tm get_tm(Time const &t)
{
  return t.get_tm();
}
// get_time_t() attribute shim - uses Time::get_time_t()
inline std::time_t get_time_t(Time const &t)
{
  return t.get_time_t();
}
```

```
Time       t = . . .;
std::tm     v1 = get_tm(t);      // Calls get_tm() attribute shim
std::time_t v2 = get_time_t(t); // Calls get_time_t() attribute shim
f1(get_tm(t));     // Calls get_tm() attribute shim
f2(get_DATE(t));   // Calls get_DATE()attribute shim
```

This is the best general solution, and works correctly with all types and flavors (reference, pointer, `const` and/or `volatile`) thereof, without the drawbacks of the other approaches. As we see in Chapter 20 and later in the book, the use of shims is a great generalizing mechanism, albeit that it is somewhat verbose. (It also suffers the `get_` vs. `as_` naming, but no one's perfect!)

16.5   unique

We all know that any function declared `inline` is guaranteed to only have a single instantiation, don't we? In fact, that guarantee is about as strong as the one you get from a real estate agent that "compact and bijou" won't translate in actuality to "pokey and cramped." What's the problem?

Within a single source file or, rather, a single compilation unit, the compiler handles the business of ensuring that a function that is called in multiple places is only given one instance.

That's the basis of procedural programming, at which both C and C++ excel. Multiple definitions within a single source file are a language error, so the question of how to fold them into one does not arise.

Within a link unit, a given `inline` function notionally has only one instance, and the C++ language mandates that the compiler and linker should cooperate to ensure that this is true: "An inline function with external linkage shall have the same address in all translation units" (C++-98: 7.1.2; 4).

In other words, within any link unit (see section 9.2), there is only one instance. However, looking a little deeper, we see that the standard admits the force of reality, and actually only requires that an inline function "shall have the same address in all translation units." What this recognizes is that you could, for example, with the preprocessor, mess with the definition of an inline function, and produce different definitions of the "same" function, thereby violating the one definition rule. Hence the standard only requires that taking the address across compilation units reports the same value. It's a kind of "as much as we can do" measure, and you should be aware of it.

Once we step outside of link units, it is clearly impossible to mandate that only one instance of one function can exist in a given process. Even if the language provided lots of support, and we could ensure that every dynamic unit within a process did not contain any function that was defined in any other module (something that is impossible in practice), we would lose out at the operating system level. Where two or more processes, with arbitrarily large amounts of time (and versions) between their production, could share an operating system module, it would be impossible to ensure that neither contained a function that was already defined within any of their shared system modules. This is because these shared modules could have evolved during the span of the creation times of the processes and their specific subcomponents.

We saw some of the good and bad points of all this when we looked at shared contexts in Chapter 9. What we can say for now is that where it is not impossible/impractical, and where malicious action is not expected/tolerated, the `inline` specifier serves well as our `unique` keyword.

See section 12.1 for a discussion of other uses of `inline`.

16.6 final

When I had the original idea for this book, I wrote down a lot of my own opinions on the language, and I also solicited some from others. One of the popular ones suggested was C++'s lack of an equivalent to Java's `final` keyword. For those not familiar, it basically says, "nothing can inherit from me" when applied to a class.

This sounds great in theory, and would doubtless have saved many unwary souls from being caught out by the perils of nonvirtual overriding, as well as prevented those bad boys[3] who I've witnessed deriving from `std::string` in order to provide an implicit conversion operator. The advice is, roughly:

> "If your class should be inherited from, it should define a virtual destructor, or should derive from a class with a virtual destructor. If it does *not* define, or inherit, a virtual destructor, it should not be inherited from."

---

[3]You know who you are!

The reason for this is primarily because if you use a type polymorphically, it is possible to cause it to be deleted via a pointer to a base type. Without the virtual destructor, the derived parts would be left un-uninitialized, leading to resource leaks and/or program logic failure. There's also the "arrays of inherited types" issue, which we looked at already in section 14.5.

I think that this viewpoint is too narrow and, dare I say it, a little dated. It only really caters for the two programming paradigms of *Polymorphism* and *Abstract Data Types*, which doesn't really cover the full gamut. The new, powerful and (rightly) popular paradigm of *Generics* requires a whole new way of looking at types. In particular, types can be discriminated and manipulated by characteristics that have little or nothing to do with the C++ object model [Lipp1996], which means that applying adaptive veneers (see Chapter 21) that inherit from their parameterising type can be an appropriate and effective way of increasing flexibility and compatibility, while leaving the object model unchanged.

So we should be content with the freedom to do what we choose (i.e., no `final`), as long as we take the responsibility for our choices. (Experience, in other words!)

16.7   Unsupported Keywords

Since we live in the real world, where different compilers have different levels of support for various language features, we have to find mechanisms for working with and without support for keywords, especially those most lately introduced.

Imperfection: The introduction of new keywords into the language requires contingency mechanisms to maintain portability.

16.7.1   typename

Although the three keywords `mutable`, `explicit` and `typename` were introduced to compilers at the same time, `typename` still is not fully supported on some compilers in common use.[4]

There are four contexts within which `typename` is meaningful.

1. As a replacement for the class keyword in template parameter lists. In this guise `typename`, when provided, works correctly on all compilers that I am familiar with.
2. As a type qualifier [Aust1999] within template function bodies.
3. As a type qualifier in template function signatures and return types
4. As a type qualifier in template parameter default arguments.

Context 1, 2, and 3 look like the following:

```
template <typename /* 1 */ T>
typename /* 2 */ T::size_type get_sizeof(T const &t)
{
```

---

[4]Borland (including 5.6), Visual C++ 6, and Watcom.

```
  typename /* 3 */ T::size_type si = sizeof(t);
  return si;
}
```

Contexts 2 and 3 are used to inform the compiler that the particular identifier being qualified is a type of the given type, rather than, a member. This is because the default interpretation
prescribed by the language is that a qualified symbol is a member, rather than a type. In almost
all cases where the use of the keyword is supported in (2), it is in (3). However, it is only in very
recent compilers where (2) is mandated, as it should be. As of the time of writing, Visual C++
7.1 is the most correct, with CodeWarrior and GCC very close seconds.

The final case is the strangest. It looks like the following example

```
template< typename /* 1 */ S
        , typename /* 1 */ C = typename /* 4 */ S::value_type
        , typename /* 1 */ T = char_traits<C>
        >
class fast_string_concatenator;
```

This tells the compiler that `value_type` is a member type of `S`. Again there is much
equivocation on the validity of the use of `typename` in this context, though it does not detract
from a correct interpretation of the template—at last not with any that I have ever presented to
such a compiler—so the answer is to use compiler-dependent macros.

For example, the STLSoft libraries define the pseudokeyword preprocessor symbols
`ss_typename_param_k` (1), `ss_typename_type_k` (2) and (3), and `ss_typename_`
`type_def_k` (4) for these contexts, which are defined as `typename` for those compilers that
correctly support it, or as `class` (for 1) and nothing (for (2)–(4)). This allows library code to be
as neat as possible—which is not very neat when complex templates are involved—and local-
izes the environment specific features in one place. The names represent a compromise between
readability and uniqueness.

Syntax

I dreaded writing this chapter, because style wars on such topics are generally futile and cannot be won. I would bet my house on the proposition that it is impossible to write a chapter such as this that would elicit agreement from all, or even most, readers.

Hence, I'm not going to proselytize you with the virtues of my bracing style, or my exact conditional expression indentation, or even to convince you of the virtues of always putting expressions in braces. There are, however, parts of the C++ syntax that seem to positively invite errors, and those I am compelled to address, even though I expect some of you gentle readers to strongly disagree with my statements.

17.1   Class Layout

This item revolves around the way we lay out class declarations. C++ implements access specification on a last-known basis, as shown in Listing 17.1.

Listing 17.1
```
class ResourcePool
{
public:
  ResourcePool();                      // This is public
  ResourcePool(ResourcePool const &);  // This is public
  size_t GetCount() const;             // This is public
  Open(Rsrc *prsrc);                   // This is public
  void Close();                        // This is public
protected:
  ResourcePool(Rsrc *prsrc);           // This is protected
  virtual ~ResourcePool();             // This is protected
private:
  . . .
```

There's an undesirable tendency on the part of many developers[1] to clump members sharing the same access into related blocks, as shown above. The argument in favor of this policy is that the public interface of the class is in one place[2] and, therefore, readily accessible to the

---

[1]Even some of my august reviewers do this, or they used to, anyway!

[2]Hopefully at the start of the class! It was the fashion in the early days to put the member variables at the top of the class declaration, irrespective of their access, with the consequent results of unreadable code and practitioners of C++ who believe that member variables are more significant in class design than methods.

reader/user of the code. The kindest thing one can say about this is that it is naïve. Coding like this is a serious mistake, for both users and maintainers of the code.

First, it assumes that the public interface of the class encapsulates all the important aspects of the class design. This is not so. In the example above the `ResourcePool(Rsrc*)` constructor is protected, and this indicates that derived classes may acquire their own `Rsrc*` and pass this to the base class constructor. This is an important facet of the design of `ResourcePool` and should not be hidden lower down in the class declaration.

A second, more prosaic reason is that this practice reduces the maintainability of the code. If you want to change the access of a member, the member has to move a significant number of lines up or down within the class declaration; such changes are hard for the reader to track in a version control system (especially a non-GUI one).

Imperfection: Abuse of C++'s last-known access specifier mechanism leads to code that is hard to use and hard to maintain.

The solution is a very simple one: order the class members in functionally related sections. Furthermore, each and every one of these sections gets its own title comment and access control specifier, even when that specifier is the same as the previous one and functionally redundant. This dramatically reduces the likelihood of introducing—admittedly trivial, but annoying nonetheless—erroneous code breaking changes to the class definition. `ResourcePool` should have been written as shown in Listing 17.2.

Listing 17.2

```
class ResourcePool
{
// Construction
public:
  ResourcePool();
  ResourcePool(ResourcePool const &);
protected:
  ResourcePool(Rsrc *prsrc);
  virtual ~ResourcePool();
// Operations
public:
  void Open(Rsrc *prsrc);
  void Close();
// Attributes
public:
  size_t GetCount() const;
private:
  . . .
```

When we look at this class declaration, it is clear which operations are involved in the construction of the class, which are its operations, and so on. Rather than have the destructor and the third constructor skulking down at the end of the class definition with the member variables, they are collected together with the other construction members. In real code, the number of functional sections will include some or all of *Construction*, *Operations*, *Attributes*, *Iteration*, *State*, *Implementation*, *Members*, and my favorite, *Not to be implemented*. This last is the section, which I place at the very end of a class definition, that contains the items that are deliberately inaccessible (and undefined). We talked in Chapter 2 about the various ways to control the clients of one's class, such as hiding copy assignment operators, and these go in this section, as in:

```
  . . .
// Not to be implemented
private:
  ResourcePool &operator =(ResourcePool const &);
};
```

In fact, this violates my rule about all logically related parts being grouped together, and you would be quite right to point that out. I prefer it because there is a single place where all things banished reside, kind of like a method purgatory. However, I acknowledge the inconsistency, and you may choose to do differently in your own code.

Let's look at the benefit of this new approach. Suppose that we want to change the access of ~ResourcePool() so that ResourcePool hierarchy instances may be destroyed polymorphically. This involves the simple insertion of public: before the destructor, and protected: after it in order to retain the previous access for the remainder of the block (see Listing 17.3).

Listing 17.3

```
class ResourcePool
{
// Construction
public:
  ResourcePool();
  ResourcePool(ResourcePool const &);
protected:
  ResourcePool(Rsrc *prsrc);
public:
  virtual ~ResourcePool();
protected:
  . . .
```

It's now obvious what has happened, and why, when you look at the differences in a version control system. For readers of the code, the class structure is unchanged. The *construction* section still contains a list of constructors, followed by a single destructor. It is clear which are publicly accessible, and which are not, providing substantial self-documenting information. Remember: the *only* documentation that is guaranteed to be up-to-date is the code [Dewh2003, Kern1999].[3]

---

[3]A couple of friends, whose work I mostly respect, and occasionally ape, take this to the extreme. For them "the code *is* the documentation!"

Finally, I'd like to point out the obvious advantage of this approach. Because one quickly gets into the habit of having a single consistent structure, one is *far* less likely to forget to do the housekeeping tasks (e.g., ensuring that copy constructors and copy assignment operators are supplied or proscribed for types that manage resources; see Chapters 3 and 4) that good C++ practice dictates. Furthermore, writing parser scripts (in Perl, Python, or Ruby) to manipulate the code is much simplified.

A word of caution: if you find yourself persuaded by this, the very last thing you should do is go and apply it to all the code in your code base. You'll make history tracking of the existing code base virtually impossible, and your coworkers will murder you in your sleep! Always save wholesale application of any improved layout schemes to new code, and make gentle increments to extant code.

17.2 Conditional Expressions

17.2.1 Make It Boolean

C++ practitioners have inherited from C the propensity for expressing themselves tersely, sometimes extremely so. It's not uncommon to see such things as:

```
for(int i=23;i;−i)
  if(x) do{ . . . } while(j && p);
```

Of course there is a certain appeal in writing powerful code in as few lines/characters as possible, but in all but a very few cases [Dewh2003], the attraction is specious at best. There are three problems with this.

First, by relying on the compiler to convert any integer or pointer type to a Boolean expression, practitioners get in the mind-set that non-zero equates to true and zero equates to false for all types. This is correct for the vast majority of cases, but not for *all* cases. Needless to say, those minor cases cause many difficult-to-spot errors. Consider the Win32 type HANDLE: for most Win32 kernel objects a HANDLE value of 0 or NULL indicates a null handle. However, when dealing with file handles that is not the case. The symbol INVALID_HANDLE_VALUE (which has a value of 0xFFFFFFFF) represents a null handle; all other values represent valid handles. Thus the following code is entirely wrong:

```
HANDLE hfile = ::CreateFile( . . . );

if(hfile)
{
  . . .
}
```

The second problem is that using this syntax has inclined authors of user-defined types to provide certain implicit conversion operators (e.g., operator bool() const) in order to support this terse form. The classic horror in this regard is basic_ios::operator void *(), which returns a meaningless non-null pointer if the fail-bit has not been set on the stream. (We see a better way to represent `operator bool()` in Chapter 24.)

Imperfection: Implicitly interpreting non-Boolean (sub-)expressions[4] leads to failure to be mindful of the values of certain types, with a consequent propensity to overengineer user defined types.

The solution is to always make your expressions overtly Boolean. (Note that this does not mean they have to be explicitly coerced to Boolean type; that would be inefficient—see section 1.4.2). So our previous two examples would look like:

```
for(int i=23;i!=0;--i)
  if(x != 0) do{ . . . } while(j != 0 && p != NULL);
```

and

```
HANDLE hfile = ::CreateFile( . . . );

if(hfile != INVALID_HANDLE_VALUE)
{
  . . .
}
```

The customary exasperated sigh is followed by the cry of "it's more typing!" However, this fails to recognize the reality in software engineering that the vast majority of coding is in maintenance [Glas2003], so although it's more typing now, it's less in the long run. Frankly, such arguments are rarely heard from library writers or engineers that work on large projects with long lifetimes.

So that's accounted for simple types, but what about those user-defined types and their implicit operators? If we deprecate the use of implicit operators in implicit Boolean-interpreted expressions, we not only create more typing (now), which we know we can live with, but aren't we also reducing the flexibility of the code? For example, say we have some algorithms that work with "smart" and regular pointers. Our classes thankfully do not provide implicit conversion operators to their raw pointer equivalent (see Parts Four and Five for discussion of these issues), but they do provide `operator bool() const` and `operator !() const`. So if we dictate that our conditional algorithm expressions do not rely on implicit interpretation as Boolean for the raw pointers, and they cannot test against 0/NULL because such implicit pointer conversions are not provided for the smart pointers, we are left with the unpleasant choice of specializing our algorithms for pointer types and nonpointer types. Depending on the modernity of the compiler(s) we use, this will be two or more definitions. This seems like a convincing counterargument to my recommendation of explicit Boolean conditional expressions. The answer comes in the form of attribute shims (we meet the Shims concept in Chapter 20), such that the algorithm would contain shim-based tests, as in:

---

[4]For the purposes of this discussion, I'll attempt to use fewer trees, so where I say expression, it also means subexpression.

```
template <typename T>
size_t calc_something(T p)
{
  if(is_null(p))
  {
    return . . .;
  }
  return . . . ;
}
```

The is_null shim handles the differences in nature between the raw and smart pointer types automatically (by virtue of the appropriate shim definitions), the Boolean nature of the conditional is enforced by the shim's return type, and the algorithm is self-documenting because the shim does what it says—in this case it tests whether p "is null."

17.2.2   A Dangerous Assignment

This is such a simple item, but one that invites controversy. Many readers may have real problems with it, and accuse me of nannying; "I don't ever make that mistake!" . . . except that they do. We all do.

Consider the following code:

```
if ((options == (_ _WCLONE|_ _WALL)) && (current->uid = 0))
  retval = -EINVAL;
```

This code was a recent deliberate attempt [*http://lwn.net/Articles/57135/*] to introduce an exploitable flaw—a back door—into the Linux kernel code base.

If I'd also included several lines of surrounding code, and not given the game away by the portent in the section title, I'd bet that no more than 10 percent of you would have spotted the problem straight away. I'm not picking on you, because I'd be in that 90 percent group; I recently found one of these in some of my five-year-old code. It's just that human beings are pattern formers, and we often see what we expect to see.

The problem stems from the fact that C and C++ are able to interpret scalar expressions—integral, floating-point, and pointer types—as Boolean (C++-98: 6.4;4). Couple this with the ability to place assignment expressions in within conditional statements, and we have a recipe for disaster. All that it requires is an accidental—or deliberate—omission of the second = in the equality operator, and we end up with assignment. In the example, the author of the code has deliberately used the assignment operator rather than the equality operator to nullify the check of options. Usually these things happen by mistake, but it's an easy mistake to make, and it can be a killer.

Imperfection: The implicit interpretation of scalar types as Boolean in conditional statements facilitates erroneous assignment caused by syntax errors.

A simplistic answer to this would be to disallow assignment statements within expressions, as Python does. However, that really *would* be nannying; it'd never fly with the C/C++ community. But the language could be changed to enhance robustness, without losing any of the use-fulness of assignment within conditional expressions. All that would be needed would be to en-sure that when an assignment is in a conditional expression, the expression must be explicitly Boolean (as we discussed in the previous item). This would be a trifling imposition. After all, we're used to doing this in many cases anyway:

```
while((ch = getchar()) != EOF)
{
    . . .
```

Back in the world of the here and now, we have two options to avoid this problem. First is to set your compiler warnings high, and use more than one compiler on your code. Most good compilers will spot the blunder and warn you, but it's not a complete solution, because some do not, and some are not usable at their maximum warning level due to the volume of extraneous warnings in system and standard library headers.

Second, whenever either operand in the comparison is an *rvalue*—one which cannot be as-signed to—it should be placed on the left hand side of the equality operator. Then mistakenly using = rather than == will result in a compiler error, on *all* compilers. Note that this is not al-ways an option, because sometimes one will be comparing two *lvalues*.

If you're not persuaded by this, there's a much more compelling example. In Chapter 1 we looked at assertions and discussed the dangers of assert expression side effects. Consider the following code:

```
int i = . . .

assert(i = 1);
```

The assertion should have been written with ==, rather than with =, in which form it would have verified that i did indeed equal 1. Alas, in its current form the expression is an assignment. Since i = 1 evaluates to 1, the assertion will never fire, and the code will always appear to be correct. Because you have an assertion in there, you will have a false sense of security. Ouch! If it had been written assert(1=i);, the compiler would have balked immediately.

As well as being a complete solution for the erroneous assignment, it also makes expres-sions a lot more readable when testing the results of long function calls. Which one of the fol-lowing is easier to read?

```
if(long_function( argument1, argument 2, argument 3, argument 4,
                  argument5, argument6) == RETURN_CODE_3)
{
```

```
if(RETURN_CODE_3 == long_function( argument1, argument 2, argument 3,
                                   argument 4, argument5, argument6))
{
```

Consider what it's like when the return code is off the right-hand side of the visible area of your editor.

It's simple, it's dull, and it's a bit ugly. It also can be argued to be contrary to the way people think—we naturally think "the number of apples I have is 5" rather than "5 is the number of apples I have"—but it takes surprisingly little time to become accustomed to it.

This is not a debate over how many spaces you indent by, or other such fluff. There is a simple mechanism to improve the robustness of your code. It works. Use it.[5]

17.3 for

17.3.1 Initializer Scope

The rule-change for the `for` expression that was enacted in C++-98 is a porter's nightmare. Basically, the old rule was that a variable declaration in the initializer statement of a `for` statement would exist in the scope in which the `for` existed. Hence the code in Listing 17.4 is legal.

Listing 17.4
```
for(int i = 0; i < 10; ++i)
{
  . . .
}

i = 0; // i still exists here

for(i = 0; i < 10; ++i) // Re-use i here by old rule
{
  . . .
}
```

The rule change was to place the initialiser statement variables within the scope of the `for` statement, as in Listing 17.5.

Listing 17.5
```
for(int i = 0; i < 10; ++i)
{
  . . . // i is valid here
}

i = 0; // but does not exist here. Compile error

for(int i = 0; i < 10; ++i) // A different i by the new rule
{
  . . .
}
```

---

[5]One reviewer (who's not exactly a fan of the language) suggested that this is an argument for using lint, and that since lint doesn't work with C++, this is an argument why one shouldn't use C++ and should stick to C. Though I understand his point, I disagree, and presumably you do too, or you wouldn't be reading this book!

This rule change was to tighten up the scoping of the initializer variables, since it is possible under the old rule for variables declared in the initializer statement to be reused elsewhere within the containing scope, breaking locality of scope, and leading to unintended side effects and maintenance headaches.

Obviously these two rules can be completely contradictory for much reasonable existing code. Trying to maintain a simple code-base for various compilers is a challenge.

Imperfection: The contradiction between the old and new `for`-statement rules results in nonportable code.

Since portability (even so far as between versions of the same compiler) is a highly desirable attribute of software, we need a form that works with both old and new rules. One approach ([Dewh2003]) is to use a second enclosing scope, placing the entire `for` statement within a block:

```
{ for(int i = 0; i < 10; ++i)
{

  . . .

}}
```

This in effect forces any old-rule code to the new-rule way of doing things. Since the new rule is more sensible than the old in an absolute correctness sense, this technique has the beneficial side effect of preparing the code and its author for the new way of thinking.

The power of the little old } is quite something to behold, as we see throughout the book.

17.3.2   Heterogeneous Initializer Types

Unfortunately, that is not the only problem with the `for` statement. In fact, there is a far more irritating imperfection. The initializer statement allows for more than one variable to be declared and initialized, as in:

```
for(int i = 0, j = 10; i < j; ++i)
{

  . . .

}
```

However, one quickly runs aground of common sense when trying to do something such as

```
for(int i = 0, vector<int>::const_iterator b = v.begin(); i < 10 && b !=
v.end(); ++i, ++b)
{

  . . .

}
```

This is because only one type specifier is allowed in the initializer statement. I can't see why such multitype statements cannot be unambiguously parsed; although not being a compiler-writer, I concede there may be a sound objection. Whether there is or not, it is an inconvenience, and leads us straight back to the semantics of the old `for`-rule, since we must take all but one of the types out of the initializer statement, as in:

```
vector<int>::const_iterator b = v.begin();
for(int i = 0; i < 10 && b != v.end(); ++i, ++b)
{
    . . .
}
```

or:

```
int i = 0;
for(vector<int>::const_iterator b = v.begin(); i < 10 && b != v.end(); ++i, ++b)
{
    . . .
}
```

or:[6]

```
int                      i;
vector<int>::const_iterator b;
for(i = 0, b = v.begin(); i < 10 && b != v.end(); ++i, ++b)
{
    . . .
}
```

Whichever form you choose, one or both of these variables will still exist outside the scope of the `for` statement, so we're pretty much back to square one.

Imperfection: `for` statements requiring initializers of two or more types render the new `for`-scoping rule irrelevant.

We saw with the simple `for` statement problem that adding an extra scope helped make old `for`-rule code compatible with the new. We will use it again here, this time to facilitate the intended semantics of the new `for`-rule for code for which the rule itself fail to do so. It's very simple, albeit perhaps not very beautiful:

```
{ int                      i;
  vector<int>::const_iterator b;
for(i = 0, b = v.begin(); i < 10 && b != v.end(); ++i, ++b)
{
    . . .
}} // i and b both cease to exist here.
```

---

[6]In this case, b is default constructed before copy assignment. For nonpointer iterators, this may be inefficient.

If you think that this rule is contrived, consider the case where you need to iterate through two or more containers, of different types, manually rather than using `std::for_each`; without this technique you are forced to use b_v, b_l, b_m (or begin_vec, begin_lst, begin_map) instead of using your customary b (or begin, or whatever). It makes the code hard to write, read, and maintain.

Note that this is not just a flaw of C++; several other languages—C#, D—exhibit precisely the same flaw with their loop constructs (`for`, `foreach`).

17.4   Variable Notation

This section is much less a didactic diatribe than an opportunity to explain my class member notation, so that it'll not be an issue through the rest of the book.

17.4.1   Hungarian Notation

I'm going to be as brief as possible since this subject is like opening Pandora's box! I don't believe that decorating a variable with its type is particularly helpful, and I do think that it is a porting nightmare. Hungarian is intended to provide readers of code with rich information regarding the variable, as in:

```
short       sMaxHandleIndex; // s prefix denotes short
char const **ppcszEnvBlock; // ppcsz denotes pointer to pointer to const
                            // char representing a zero terminated string
```

What happens when the code containing sMaxHandleIndex is ported to another architecture on which the maximum number of handles can be a larger range than can be expressed with `short`? The type might be changed to `long`, in which case the variable name decoration is now an outright lie.

```
long sMaxHandleIndex;
```

Clearly porting undermines the whole raison d'être of Hungarian notation. The other part of it is that knowing every little bit about a variable's type is often highly irrelevant, and can be quite detrimental to readability.

```
typedef map<string, map<string, int> > string_2_string_2_int_map_map_t;

string_2_string_2_int_map_map_t        s2s2immIncludesDependencyTree;
```

Don't laugh; I've seen this (with actual names changed, of course) in real code! s2s2imm is not really a help here, is it? This is incredibly brittle, not to mention almost impossible to read. Much better as

```
typedef map<string, map<string, int> > string_2_string_2_int_map_map_t;

string_2_string_2_int_map_map_t        includesDependencyTree;
```

or

```
typedef map<string, map<string, int> >  IncludeDependencyTree_t;

IncludeDependencyTree_t                  includesDependencyTree;
```

Most people now completely eschew any form of Hungarian notation as a consequence of these issues. However, being an upstream swimmer, I actually use a restricted form of prefixing in my own code, which you'll see throughout the book. I'm not going to recommend that you do the same, so this item is merely an explanation, and an attempt to save you the effort of e-mailing me to tell me how old-hat my code is.

Remember I said that knowing the type of a variable is superfluous and nonportable. However, I think it's often valuable to know the purpose of a variable. For example, when dealing with character strings, one can be dealing with different character types, for example, `char` and `wchar_t`. Most often, when quantifying the sizes of buffers of such types, functions take or return values measured in terms of the number of characters. However, sometimes they need to measure in terms of the number of bytes. Failure to be mindful of the difference between these two concepts can be very costly in terms of program (and career) crashes. Hence I use the prefixes `cb` and `cch`, which denote count-of-bytes and count-of-characters, respectively. The prefixes in no way indicate the type of such variables—they could be `int`, `short`, `long`, whatever—so there are no porting issues, but they do indicate their purpose, which improves readability.

I don't expect you to agree with this viewpoint and adopt these conventions, and I'm not even suggesting that they are "the best approach." Wherever possible, it's better to have the variable's type itself denote its purpose (e.g., I prefer `byte_t` over `unsigned char`; section 13.1), but there are times when a bit more information is needed.

17.4.2 Member Variables

Most people decorate member variables in some fashion to distinguish them from non-member variables. However, there are several schemes employed.

The most basic form is to not decorate at all, as in:

```
class X
{
public:
  void SetValue(int value)
  {
    this->value = value;
  }
private:
  int value;
};
```

I know several chaps who like this form, but I think it's an accident waiting to happen. It's far too easy to omit the `this` in code, and have situations such as:

```
  void SetValue(int value)
  {
```

```
    value = value; // Does nothing; "this" is unchanged
}
```

Since assignment of a variable to itself is allowed (except where it's prevented by proscribing access to the copy assignment operator; see section 14.2.4), the compiler will happily do what you say, and your code is buggy. Of course, it is possible to make the arguments const in the method implementation, as in:

```
void SetValue(int const value)
{
    value = value; // Compile error
}
```

But support for this from compilers is not universal, and it's really just answering an awful problem with an awkward solution.

I occasionally use the undecorated form in trivial structures where all the members are public and there are very few and simple methods (perhaps just a constructor), but in class types of any sophistication I would not do so.

There are four other schemes that I know of. The first is to prefix the member variables with an underscore, as in:

```
void SetValue(int value)
{
    _value = value;
}
```

However, the standard reserves identifiers with a prefix underscore in the name global namespace (C++-98: 17.4.3.1.2) and ::std, so I think using them anywhere just represents a bad habit (albeit one I've still not completely broken). An alternative to this is to postfix an underscore, as in:

```
void SetValue(int value)
{
    value_ = value;
}
```

which is legal. However, both these forms are too subtle for my tastes. I prefer the convention popularized by MFC,[7] which is to prefix with m_, as in:

```
void SetValue(int value)
{
    m_value = value;
}
```

---

[7]You see, there is something good about MFC!

This is similar to the old C `struct` member tagging, for example, `struct tm`'s members `tm_hour`, `tm_wday`, and so on, which were introduced because in early versions of C all member names were in a single namespace. However, it is generic, and therefore consistent. In fact, I like it so much that I use variations on the theme, `sm_` for static member, `g_` for global variables,[8] and `s_` for static variables, as in:

```
int InitOnce(int val)
{
    static int s_val = val;
    return s_val;
}

class Y
{
    . . .
    static int sm_value;
};
```

These are the notations you'll see used in code throughout the book.

---

[8]Of course, global variables are so evil that I only get to use this one about once a year.

## CHAPTER 18

Typedefs

The `typedef` specifier in C and C++ provides a new name for a given type. Two classic uses in C are in removing confusion when using function pointers and reducing typing effort when using structures. Consider the code without typedefs in Listing 18.1.

Listing 18.1

```
// Info.h
struct Info
{};
int process(int (*)(struct Info*, int*), int*);


// client_code.cpp
int process_forwards(struct Info*, int);
int process_backwards(struct Info*, int);


int main()
{
  struct Info info;
  int (*pfn[10])(struct Info*, int);

  . . .
  for(i = 0; . . .; ++i)
  {
    pfn[i] = . . .
```

Contrast that with the code in Listing 18.2 that uses structure and function pointer typedefs.

Listing 18.2

```
// Info.h
typedef struct Info {} Info_t;              // struct typedef
typedef int (*processor_t)(Info_t*, int*);  // fn ptr typedef
int process(processor_t , int*);


// client_code.cpp
int process_forwards(Info_t*, int);
int process_backwards(Info_t*, int);


int main()
{
```

```
    Info_t        info;
    processor_t pfn[10];

    . . .
    for(i = 0; . . .; ++i)
    {
      pfn[i] = . . .
```

I hope you'll agree that the latter form is far more readable. It is also legal (C++-98: 7.1.3,2) to redefine the name of any type (within the same scope) to the type to which it already refers. This is pretty pointless for many types—for example, `typedef int SInt; typedef SInt SInt;`—but it is very useful for removing the need to type `struct` or to remember the association between a given structure typedef and the actual structure for which it acts as a synonym:

```
typedef struct Info {} Info; // synonym of itself
. . .
int main()
{
    Info          info;
    . . .
```

In fact, C++ differs from C in not requiring that a class type be prefixed with its class key (the `class`/`struct`/`union` bit; C++-98: 9.1). This gives a cleaner and more succinct form without the typedef:

```
struct Info
{};
Info    info;
```

But if you want C compatibility, it's better to define a synonym via a typedef.

Where typedefs have really come into their own in C++ is in the fact that they can be used to define member types within classes and namespaces, which underpins a great deal of generic programming, including the traits mechanism, as shown in Listing 18.3.

Listing 18.3

```
template <typename T>
struct sign_traits;

template <>
struct sign_traits<int16_t>
{
    typedef int16_t    type;
    typedef int16_t    signed_type;
    typedef uint16_t   unsigned_type;
};
```

```
template <>
struct sign_traits<uint16_t>
{
  typedef uint16_t  type;
  typedef int16_t   signed_type;
  typedef uint16_t  unsigned_type;
};
```

This chapter takes a close look at `typedef`, at some of the dangers of its use, and distinguishes between the use of `typedef` for conceptual type definitions and contextual type definitions. Finally, it introduces the concept of *True Typedefs*, and illustrates a template-based implementation of it that can be used to provide a stronger degree of type safety than is afforded by the language as it stands.

18.1   Pointer Typedefs

Can you spot the error in the following code?

```
class X
{
public:
  X(const PBYTE );
};


X::X(const BYTE *)
{}
```

You've probably just said that the constructor declaration and definition have different signatures. Well, you may be right, and you may be wrong. The declaration uses a pointer typedef, `PBYTE`, whereas the definition uses the plain type (albeit another typedef, no doubt) `BYTE`.

If `PBYTE` is a typedef, defined (presumably) as

```
typedef BYTE *PBYTE;
```

then you're right, and the above class definition is wrong. However, if it is defined as

```
#define PBYTE  BYTE*
```

then you're wrong, and (post-preprocessing) the constructor declaration and definitions are the same.

I'm sure some of you are saying that no one would ever do such a thing. Bless you! You either work in a place where all is harmony and professionalism, or you live in an institution. In the real world this is all too common.

The reason pointer typedefs are used is twofold. Firstly, there are, or have been at least, architectures where there were different "natures" to pointers, specifically the nasty `far`, `near`,

stuff from 16-bit Windows and the mixed-mode Intel architecture. The other reason is that dealing with multilevel pointer types is very verbose, for example:

```
const int * const * *      p1;
int const * * const *      p2;
int const * const * *      p3;
const int * * const *      p4;
int * const * const *      p5;
int * const * * const      p6;

const int * * const * far  p7;
int * far const * const *  p8;
```

Is that nasty or what? Some would argue that it is easier to see what's going on in pointer
typedef form:

```
PPCPCInt p1;
PCPPCInt p2;
PPCPCint p3;
PCPPCInt p4;
PCPCPInt p5;
CPPCPInt p6;

FPCPPCInt p7;
PCPFCPInt p8;
```

I concede that the reduction in eye-traffic is borderline, though it is perhaps a bit more useful when Win16's far-near stuff was involved. What is advantageous about such a scheme is
that it normalizes naming for pointers, especially when given the flexibility of qualifier
placement.

```
int const * * const *p9;
const int * * const *p10;
PPCInt const      *p11;
const PPCInt      *p12;
```

These are actually all the same: PCPPCInt. For good or ill these things exist, and therefore
we are exposed to the conflicts described earlier. The answer is twofold: you should choose one
or the other convention in your own work, and you should remember this issue whenever you
see pointer typedefs.

When working with new libraries, aimed at a modern subset of compilers and operating
systems, I tend to favor the plain pointer form, because this is the normal way of doing things,
and therefore is easier to read and learn to new users and less likely to offend conventionalists.
The Synesis libraries take the other approach, because they've been around a long time (and so
had to coexist with all manner of funky memory-model cruft from the past), and have had to
work with a much broader range of compilers and target environments.

If you choose not to use pointer typedefs, then you need to add an extra level of precision in the placement of qualifiers. I go with Dan Saks [Saks1996, Saks1999], and always (well, when pointers are involved anyway) place the qualifier *after* the type, as in:

```
int const volatile *x;
```

rather than

```
volatile const int *x;
const int volatile *x;
const volatile int *x;
volatile int const *x;
```

Apart from being consistent, you can read backward from the variable to the beginning of the type definition and, no matter how convoluted the definition, get an unambiguously correct understanding of what type it is. If you use the second way, you have to do partial shuffling of the declaration in your head, which seems like far too much work to me, especially when many levels of indirection are involved.

18.2   What's in a Definition?

The use of typedef is ubiquitous throughout C++ (and C) code. However, little attention is drawn to the distinct uses of type definitions, so let's do that now by defining two typedef-related concepts.

18.2.1   Conceptual Type Definitions

Let's consider a class used in implementing IP-based communications. We might see something such as the following:

```
// Socket.h
typedef int    AddressFamily;
typedef int    SocketType;
typedef int    Protocol;

class Socket
{
public:
  Socket(AddressFamily family, SocketType type, Protocol protocol);

   . . .
```

Here we see the definition of three typedefs—AddressFamily, SocketType, and Protocol—which identify the three defining characteristics required for the creation of a socket [Stev1998]. In this context, typedef has been used to define three distinct *logical* types, albeit they are, in this case, the same actual type: int. Hence:

Definition: *Conceptual type definitions* define logically distinct types.

Clearly the `Socket` constructor is more self-documenting than if the three parameters were just defined as `int`. One advantage of conceptual type definitions is that they provide this (modest) degree of self-documentation.

Another advantage to conceptual type definitions is that they provide a degree of platform independence. Consider the standard types `size_t` and `ptrdiff_t`, which are usually defined as:

```
typedef unsigned int   size_t;
typedef int            ptrdiff_t;
```

When you see `ptrdiff_t` in code, you are immediately cognizant that something here is going to be evaluating pointer differences. The same mental highlight is not achieved by just seeing `int`, which more commonly makes one think of basic arithmetic or indexing operations. Similarly, `size_t` inclines one to think about number of bytes, as opposed to an arbitrary integral measure. However, such typedefs serve an additional, and very important, function. Because an (`unsigned`) `int` may not be the appropriate type to represent a number of bytes or a pointer difference on a given platform, an implementation may redefine these types as appropriate for its supported platforms and there will be no need for user code to be changed. This is exactly how the fixed-sized integers of C99 are made portable.

By the way, both C and C++ support multiple definitions of the same `typedef`, so long as all definitions are identical. However, it is not generally good form to redefine any `typedef` and you should avoid doing so. There should be a single point of definition, usually within a shared included file, rather than having independent definitions, which can lead to very unpleasant side effects. If divergent definitions eventuate in different compilation units that are linked together, especially when that linking is dynamic, things can get grim, as we saw in Chapter 9. Don't do it!

18.2.2   Contextual Type Definitions

Where conceptual type definitions define concepts independent of context (for a given platform), contextual type definitions do precisely the opposite: they (re-)define a well-known[1] concept in multiple contexts.

Anyone who's had even a sniff of C++ programming since 1998 should be aware of the Standard Template Library[2] (STL), and will probably have seen code similar to that shown in Listing 18.4.

Listing 18.4

```
template< typename C
        , typename F
```

---

[1]Well-known insofar as constructs external to the definition context expect such definitions to exist and to represent a known taxonomy of type and/or behavior.
[2]Actually it's now officially just part of the C++ standard library, but everyone still refers to it as the STL.

```
         >
F for_all_postinc(C &c, F f)
{
  typename C::iterator b = c.begin();
  typename C::iterator e = c.end();
  for(; b != e; b++)
  {
    f(*b);
  }
  return f;
}
```

This algorithm applies a caller-supplied function f to all the elements within the container c defined by the asymmetric range [Aust1999]: [c.begin(), c.end()). The iterators returned from the begin() and end() methods are stored in the variables b and e, and the range is traversed by applying the postincrement operator to b.[3] The important thing to note in this algorithm is the type of the iterator variables. They are declared as being of type C::iterator. This means the algorithm can be applied to any type C that defines this type. iterator is thus a member type, as shown in Listing 18.5.

Listing 18.5
```
class String
{
public:
  typedef char *iterator; // 'iterator' is a simple pointer
  . . .

namespace std
{
  class list_iterator;
  class list
  {
  public:
    typedef list_iterator iterator; // 'iterator' is an external class
    . . .
```

All the standard library containers (including std::vector, std::deque, std::string) supply the iterator member type,[4] and there are a whole host of third-party library components that similarly support this requirement. For all these types, the iterator member represents a promise to the external context—in this case the for_all_postinc() algorithm but potentially any code that needs to define iteration variables—of certain attributes and behavior.

The actual type which the iterator typedef aliases may vary enormously between its host containers: in some it will be a pointer, in others a complex class type providing an appropriate

---

[3]This is a test function I use when writing STL components to ensure that postincrement semantics, which are less efficient (and therefore less frequently used) and harder to emulate, are valid for supporting iterator types.
[4]In fact this is one of the requirements of the STL *Container* concept [Aust1999, Muss2001].

set of operations. However, each actual type conforms to a known concept—the Iterator concept [Aust1999] in this case—and it is the member type that provides the expected type (and its implied behaviors) to the external context. Indeed, member types may even be nested classes (or enums, though that would not work here in this case) and not `typedefs` at all.

```cpp
class environment_variable_sequence
{
public:
  class iterator // 'iterator' is a nested class
  {
    . . .
```

Hence, `iterator` is a contextual type definition because it (re-)defines a well-known concept in several contexts.

Definition: *Contextual type definitions* define types that correspond to well-known concepts, relative to specific contexts. Such types act as descriptions of the nature (type and/or behavior) of their host contexts.

Contextual type definitions are not limited to being provided in template classes or to being used by template algorithms. Also, they are not necessarily members of classes. They can also be members of namespaces or local definitions within functions or even within individual blocks.

As well as being a mechanism that supports generic programming (via the type lookup mechanism we've just seen), they can also be a great aid in portability. Consider a situation where you're implementing a library to enumerate the contents of directories within the host file-system. On a platform where the constant `PATH_MAX` is defined, you may assume that all paths are bounded to the length given by its value.[5] You might, therefore, decide to implement your library for your fixed path-length platform, within the `fsearch::fixed_platform` namespace, using a fixed string class, as in:

```cpp
namespace fsearch
{
  namespace fixed_platform
  {
    typedef acme_lib::basic_fixed_string<char, PATH_MAX>  string_t;
    class directory_sequence
    {
      . . .
      bool get_next(string_t &entry);
```

In this case `string_t` is a contextual typedef for the namespace `fsearch::fixed_platform`. Client code may look something like the following:

```cpp
using fsearch::fixed_platform::string_t;
using fsearch::fixed_platform::directory_sequence;
```

---

[5]On UNIX platforms that do not define `PATH_MAX` you must call `pathconf()` to get the path limit at runtime. The implementation of the UNIXSTL `basic_file_path_buffer<>` class, included on the CD, illustrates how this compile-time/runtime evaluation may be abstracted.

```
int main()
{
  directory_sequence ds("/usr/include");
  string_t           entry;
  while(ds.get_next(entry))
  {
    puts(entry.c_str());
  }
  . . .
```

Of course, our directory utility becomes so useful that we want to port it to other platforms. Another platform, BigOS, can have paths of any length, so using a fixed string is not appropriate. (Note that I'm electing to take this particular porting strategy to illustrate the contextual type definition concept; in real life there are several ways to implement cross-platform APIs, and choosing between them is a nontrivial balancing of many factors that is outside the scope of this book.[6]) The BigOS namespace might look something like this:

```
namespace fsearch
{
  namespace bigos_platform
  {
    typedef std::string   string_t;
    class directory_sequence
    {
      . . .
      bool get_next(string_t &entry);
```

The advantage now is that because both operating-system variants of the fsearch library have logically equivalent interfaces, the changes to client code are exceedingly minimal:

```
#ifdef __BIGOS__
 namespace fsearch_platform = fsearch::bigos_platform;
#elif defined(__unix__)
 namespace fsearch_platform = fsearch::fixed_platform;
#elif . . .
 . . .
#endif /* operating system */

using fsearch_platform::string_t;
using fsearch_platform::directory_sequence;

int main()
{
  . . .
```

---

[6]Maybe if you get all your friends to buy this one we can persuade the publisher to commission a book on porting.

The discrimination of the platform may well be placed in a library header, which means that client code can be entirely independent of the platform (excepting representational differences between the file systems, of course).

18.3 Aliases

The `typedef` keyword (C++-98: 7.1.3) has precisely the behavior we are looking for when it comes to contextual type definitions, in that it merely defines another name, relative to a given context, for a particular type. In effect it is an alias for the existing type. For example, the types `String::iterator` and `char *` are the same, and may be used interchangeably, which is a good thing.

```
void make_upper(char *begin, char *end);

void set_chars(String &s)
{
  make_upper(s.begin(), s.end());
}
```

However, conceptual type definitions are all about defining new types based on existing ones. The aliasing that is the very instrument of contextual type definitions causes conceptual type definitions to be, at best, a very weak mechanism for type distinction.

18.3.1 Erroneous Conceptual Type Interchange

If we look again at our `Socket` class, we can easily envisage code such as the following:

```
AddressFamily family   = AF_INET;
SocketType    type     = SOCK_DGRAM;
Protocol      protocol = IPPROTO_UDP;

Socket(type, family, protocol);
```

Ouch! `type` and `family` were reversed by an overworked programmer. Fortunately the first test of the system will reveal that there is a problem, since the socket will not be opened due to the invalid family and type requested.

Actually, that may not be true. There's an altogether nastier facet to this problem. On one of my systems `AF_INET` and `SOCK_DGRAM` actually have the same value: 2! So now we've got the appalling situation that this code will work as expected because we have a bug that is benign in a platform-dependent manner. It's not hard to envisage porting the application to another platform, on which `AF_INET` and `SOCK_DGRAM` have different values, and spending days in the (correctly) ported platform-dependent parts because the system no longer works.

In certain cases, it is possible for such invalid exchanges of instances of conceptual type definitions to fail to cause breaking changes but merely to hamper system effectiveness. Such errors can be *extremely* hard to find. In one real case I came across, a logging API was defined with functions similar to the following:

```
typedef int       TE_DbgLevel;
typedef uint32_t TE_Flags;

void TraceEntry(TE_DbgLevel level, TE_Flags flags, . . .);
```

There were many cases throughout the code base where the flags and the level had been mistakenly reversed. (The API had formerly had them the other way round, and an "improvement" by one developer had swapped them to the current definition. This breaks one of the cardinal maintainability rules, which is to avoid changing function definitions, and instead favor defining new functions and "retiring" the old ones.) By coincidence, the debugging levels were between 0 and 7, and the only commonly used trace flags were those three whose values were 0x1, 0x2, and 0x4. The effect on the system was that performance was compromised to a significant degree.

Imperfection: C++ provides no type safety for the use of conceptual defined types, except where such types have incompatible underlying types.

Once I had come across one of these reversals, I applied the technique we're going to talk about in section 18.4, and found over a hundred more. System performance was improved by over 50% once they'd all been corrected!

18.3.2   No Overloading on Conceptual type

There's another problem caused by (typedef) aliasing. Imagine we had a Network class that acted as a supervisor for socket-based communications within a process. Such a class might provide functions to shutdown all sockets based on particular criteria, as in:

```
class Network
{
public:
  void QuenchMatchingSockets(AddressFamily family);
  void QuenchMatchingSockets(SocketType type);
  void QuenchMatchingSockets(Protocol protocol);

  . . .
```

But our compiler will reject this class, since it rightly cannot provide three overloads with the same fundamental signature, which in this case is void QuenchMatching Sockets(int);. Even worse is where we're writing such overloaded methods using conceptual types whose fundamental types are different for a particular platform. When ported to another platform two of more of the underlying types may now be equivalent, and the code will no longer build.

Imperfection: C++ does not support overloading on conceptually defined types, except where such types happen to have different underlying types on a particular platform.

18.4 True Typedefs

If we look at typedefs as a transfer of type from one type name to another, we can see that we want to allow two-way transfer for contextual typedefs, but only a one-way transfer for conceptual type definitions. What we would like would be to have two distinct keywords to represent this concept. I would suggest that the `alias` keyword would represent the two-way transfer and would behave as `typedef` currently does. Hence:

```
alias int IntType;

int     i1;
IntType i2;

i1 = i2; // int and IntType are fully interchangeable, and
i2 = i1; // they are in fact the same type
```

The `typedef` would be the one-way transfer. Hence:

```
typedef int IntType;

int     i1;
IntType i2;

i1 = i2; // Invalid! Cannot convert IntType to int
i2 = i1; // Invalid! Cannot convert int to IntType
```

But this is the real world: `typedef` carries the former meaning, and there is *no way* we will be able to foist our idealization on 5 million developers and billions of lines of code.[7] So, this being a book about proactively addressing C++'s foibles, what can we do about it?

In the spirit of the imperfect practitioner, I applied tenet #4—*Never give up!*—and after many attempts around the problem arrived at the solution, in the form of the `true_typedef` template class (see Listing 18.6).

Listing 18.6
```
template< typename T
        , typename U>
class true_typedef
{
public:
  typedef T       &reference;
  typedef T const &const_reference;
// Construction
public:
  true_typedef()
```

---

[7]Actually, the new language D [Brig2002] uses exactly these definitions for these two keywords and, therefore, provides conceptual type definitions as a built-in feature of the language.

```
      : m_value(T())
  {}
  explicit true_typedef(T const &value)
    : m_value(value)
  {}
  true_typedef(true_typedef const &rhs)
    : m_value(rhs.m_value)
  {}
  true_typedef const &operator =(true_typedef const &rhs)
  {
    m_value = rhs.m_value;
    return *this;
  }
// Accessors
public:
  const_reference base_type_value() const
  {
    return m_value;
  }
  reference base_type_value()
  {
    return m_value;
  }
// Members
private:
  T  m_value;
// Not to be implemented
private:
  // Not provided, as the syntax is less ambiguous when
  // assignment from an explicit temporary is made
  true_typedef const &operator =(T const &value);
};
```

As you can see, it's pretty simple. It contains a single member of the primary parameterizing type T, which is called the *base type*. It is also parameterized by an unused type U, which is the *unique type*. The unique type ensures that the instantiated types are unique, as we can see in the new definitions of our socket API types:

```
acmelib_gen_opaque(AddressFamily_u)
acmelib_gen_opaque(SocketType_u)
acmelib_gen_opaque(Protocol_u)
```

```
typedef true_typedef< int
                    , AddressFamily_u>    AddressFamily;
typedef true_typedef< int
                    , SocketType_u>       SocketType;
```

```
typedef true typedef< int
                    , Protocol_u>        Protocol;
```

The opaque type generator macro `acmelib_gen_opaque()`—a unique type generator (see section 7.4.4)—is used to define a unique type. By convention, I apply the _u postfix.

Now when we attempt to construct a `Socket` with `family` and `type` parameters in the wrong order, the compiler informs us that they parameters are incompatible, and we can fix the bug immediately.

We can now also overload on logical type, irrespective of any commonality of the underlying types, so the `Network` class can be correctly defined as it was intended.

You're probably asking how easy *True Typedefs* are to use. By looking at the template definition given earlier, it is clear that to access the value we need to call `base_type_value()`. This can't be good, can it? Thankfully we can adopt some of Scott Meyer's magic, patented cure-all free-function snake oil [Meye2000] and make things a great deal simpler. The `true_typedef` header file contains (as of the time of writing) 73 template free functions such as those shown in Listing 18.7.

Listing 18.7
```
template< typename T, typename U>
true_typedef<T, U> const operator ++(true_typedef<T, U> &v, int)
{
   true_typedef<T, U>   r(v);
   v.base_type_value()++;
   return r;
}


template< typename T, typename U>
bool operator <=( true_typedef<T, U> const &lhs, T const &rhs)
{
    return lhs.base_type_value() <= rhs;
}


template< typename T, typename U>
true_typedef<T, U> operator ~(true_typedef<T, U> const &v)
{
    return true_typedef<T, U>(~v.base_type_value());
}


template< typename T, typename U>
true_typedef<T, U> const &operator <<=( true_typedef<T, U> &v
                               , true_typedef<T, U> const &rhs)
{
    v.base_type_value() <<= rhs.base_type_value();
    return v;
}
```

This means that instances of *True Typedefs* that are based on fundamental types can be used in almost all expressions that their fundamental types can. For example,

```
true_typedef<int, . . .>  i1 = 1000;
int                       i2 = 1001;
true_typedef<int, . . .>  i3 = i2;

i1 <<= 2;
i1 = ~i3;
i3 = i2 + i3;
```

Naturally this is not possible for class types, unless they have those operators defined, but access to the base type value is pretty straightforward, via `base_type_value()`. And it's just as valid to take a reference to the base type value, as it would be to take a reference to an instance of that type. What is important is that the types are implicitly treated differently.

Both `const` and non-`const` access is provided. It is valid to include modifying operations, since the intention behind *True Typedefs* is to create strongly typed types and not strongly valued types (e.g., enums).

True Typedefs can also be used for underlying types other than the fundamental types, including class types.

```
typedef true_typedef<std::string, . . .> Forename;
typedef true_typedef<std::string, . . .> Surname;

bool lookup_programmer( Forename const &fn
                      , Surname const  &sn
                      , int            &iq);

Forename  fn("Archie");
Surname   sn("Goodwin");
int       iq;
```

```
fn = sn; // Error - types are different
```

```
if(lookup_programmer(sn, fn, iq)) // Error: fn and sn reversed
{
  printf("%s %s: %d\n", sn.base_type_value().c_str()
                      , sn.base_type_value().c_str()
                      , iq);
  // and would be disappointing if it did work ...
}
```

The *True Typedefs* concept completely answers the problems of weak conceptual type definitions: It prevents types with identical base types from being implicitly interconvertible, and it facilitates overloading of logically distinct types. Furthermore, it does this without sacrificing any efficiency, since the implementation is light, and all methods are inline. (I've not yet found a compiler that generates any differences in performance between *True Typedef* code and the plain typedef equivalents. This is so even for nontrivial base types.)

Let's now have a recap of the problem of implicit integer conversion in the serialization component in section 13.2.1. Using *True Typedefs*, we can rewrite the `Serializer` class, as shown in Listing 18.8.

Listing 18.8

```
// serialdefs.h
acmelib_gen_opaque(sint8_u)
acmelib_gen_opaque(uint8_u)
acmelib_gen_opaque(sint16_u)
acmelib_gen_opaque(uint16_u)
acmelib_gen_opaque(sint32_u)
acmelib_gen_opaque(uint32_u)
acmelib_gen_opaque(sint64_u)
acmelib_gen_opaque(uint64_u)
typedef true_typedef<int8_t, sint8_u>      sint8_type;
typedef true_typedef<uint8_t, uint8_u>     uint8_type;
typedef true_typedef<int16_t, sint16_u>    sint16_type;
typedef true_typedef<uint16_t, uint16_u>   uint16_type;
typedef true_typedef<int32_t, sint32_u>    sint32_type;
typedef true_typedef<uint32_t, uint32_u>   uint32_type;
typedef true_typedef<int64_t, sint64_u>    sint64_type;
typedef true_typedef<uint64_t, uint64_u>   uint64_type;

// Serializer.h
class Serializer
{
  . . .
// Operations
public:
  void Write(sint8_type i);
  void Write(uint8_type i);
  void Write(sint16_type i);
  void Write(uint16_type i);
  void Write(sint32_type i);
  void Write(uint32_type i);
  void Write(sint64_type i);
  void Write(uint64_type i);
  // No need to define any other (proscribed) methods
  . . .
};

void fn()
{
  Serializer    s;
  sint8_type    i8(0);    // Must use initialisation syntax ...
```

```
uint64_type   ui64(0);  // ... rather than assignment syntax.
int           i    = 0;

s.Write(si8);
s.Write(ui64);
s.Write(i);   // Error, plain and simple - no ambiguity
s.Write(0);   // ERROR: Ambiguous call

uint64_t      ui = ui64.base_type_value(); // Must use method
}
```

Now we have 100 percent type enforcement. Admittedly using the integer true typedefs is a bit inconvenient—in that you have to use initialization syntax to construct one from a base type variable or literal, and `base_type_value()` if you need to convert back to the base type—but is a small price to pay. And when you're working with cross-platform serializing types, a bit of explicit rigor is often helpful, both when writing and when reading/maintaining the serialization code.

18.5   The Good, the Bad, and the Ugly

This chapter is looking at typedefs and, in the main, lauding the `typedef` specifier as a very useful tool. However, I'd just like to have a small soapbox moment and comment on some common mistakes that often befall the overeager `typedef` convert

18.5.1   Good typedefs

Good typedefs are those that reduce typing, increase portability, or increase flexibility, or all of these things at once. For example, it is a matter of habit when I define any class that inherits from another that I declare a typedef `base_class_type`, as in:

```
template< typename T
        , typename A = std::allocator<T>
        >
class acme_stack
  : protected std::vector<T, A>
{
private:
  typedef std::vector<T, A>  base_class_type;
public:
  typedef typename base_class_type::reference        reference;
  typedef typename base_class_type::const_reference const_reference;
  . . .
```

This has two advantages. First, whenever I want to implement a member type or function of `acme_stack` in terms of `std::vector<T, A>` I can type `base_class_type`. Now admitting that in this case there is not a great saving in terms of the number of characters typed, the typing is nevertheless easier because we do not have to handle the braces and those messy double colons! In many cases, though, there is a dramatic saving in typing; the longest base class that I could find in the Synesis code base is:

```
ComRefCounter< ComRefCounterBase<IFileUtil>
             , ComQI3< IFileUtil2
                     , &IID_IFileUtil2
                     , IFileUtil
                     , &IID_IFileUtil
                     , IDispatch
                     , &IID_IDispatch
                     , ComRefCounterBase<IFileUtil> > >
```

Try replicating that throughout a class's implementation without making at least one mistake! (And remember that if your class is itself a template, then any mistakes will not show up until the particular member function is called, which can be some time after you'd "completed" and released it if your unit tests are missing 100% code coverage, which of course they are [Glas2003].)

The downside of this is that sometimes you may have more than one base type. However, if you wisely eschew using heavy multiple inheritance [Stro1997]—that is, where more than one base type provides significant members and behavior—then in almost all cases there is one identifiable base class that your class has an *IsA* [Meye1998] relationship with, and the remaining base types are used to provide policy-based behavior or to declare interfaces.

The other great use of `base_class_type` is that it simplifies the task of changing a base class in an inheritance hierarchy. Let's forget all about templates for the moment, and just think about a plain polymorphic set of classes.

```
class Window
{
  . . .
};

class Control
  : public Window
{
  . . .
};

class FileListControl
  : public Control
{
  DECLARE_MESSAGE_HANDLERS(FileListControl, Control)

  . . .

// in FileListControl.cpp
bool FileListControl::Create(Window const &parent, . . .)
{
```

```
    . . . // modify other-parameters
  return Control::Create(parent, other-parameters);
}
```

As is the nature of such hierarchies, let's assume heaps of macros within the declaration and definition of these classes (we'll presume they're wizard generated and are correct at the time they're generated). There can be many tens, or even hundreds, of references to `Control` within the declaration and definition of `FileListControl`. Of course, in a next revision of the libraries, a new window class, `ThreeDEffectControl`, is introduced, which derives from `Control`. Your manager thinks the 3D effects of this new control are the cat's meow, wants to see it in the `FileListControl`—and the 30 or 40 other controls that your former coworkers left with you when they left the company to join a startup doing SOAP-based multimedia instant messaging J2EE XML Web Services over WAP—and instructs you to "make it so!" You're in a pickle. You could do a global checkout from source control, search for every `Control`, and replace it with `ThreeDEffectControl`, but there are hundreds of classes derived from `Control` that want to stay just the way they are. So you're left with a manual task. Well, you can at least locate the header files for the controls you need to change. You make the changes, and now `FileListControl` and its buddies all derive from `ThreeD EffectControl`. Alas, as you're about to begin the changes to all the corresponding implementation files, your friendly manager rings and tells you he's sending you to a client site for the next three days to help locate a bug, and "you leave in 20 minutes."

I'm sure you get the picture. You get back to the control update task early next week, and make all the changes to the implementation files. Alas, you missed one file, in a rarely used component, and a couple of months later you're on another client site trying to find an intermittent crash when the program has been running a long time. The problem is that the system contains one class that has methods that call up to an indirect base (`Control`) rather than its immediate base (`ThreeDEffectControl`), which leaves system resources unreleased, and they eventually run short and your process crashes.

How much easier would it have been if each class had declared a private `base_class_type` typedef and only ever referred to its base class by that name?

Let's look back at our original `acme_stack` template class. If we wanted to upgrade it to a faster vector than `std::vector`, then we could do so by making just two simple changes

```
template< typename T
        , typename A = std::allocator<T>
        >
class acme_stack
  : protected fastlib::vector<T, A>
{
private:
  typedef fastlib::vector<T, A>  base_class_type;
public:
  typedef typename base_class_type::reference        reference;
  typedef typename base_class_type::const_reference const_reference;

  . . .
```

18.5.2   Bad Typedefs

I've seen people get into `typedef`, and go then quite mad with the power. An example[8] of a bad `typedef` is something such as the following:

```
#if defined(UNICODE)
 typedef wchar_t                              char_t;
#else
 typedef char                                 char_t;
#endif // UNICODE
typedef std::string<char_t>                   string_t;
typedef std::vector<string_t>::iterator
                                    string_container_iterator_t;
typedef std::vector<string_t>::const_iterator
                                  string_vector_const_iterator_t;
```

The first two typedefs `string_t` and `string_container_t` are perfectly appropriate. It may not be entirely necessary to define `string_t`, but it does help to avoid the irritating chevron parsing error that catches template newbies:

```
typedef std::vector<std::string<char_t>>::iterator
string_container_iterator_t;
                          ^
 compiler thinks you're right shifting!
```

The problem with the above set of definitions is the `iterator` typedefs. The whole point of the STL container member type `iterator` is that it is a contextual typedef. If we then define and use another typedef to represent that, we move the context of the conceptual type definition from `std::vector<string_t>`, where it belongs, to the global namespace, where it most certainly does not. Imagine some client code:

```
void dump_to_debugger(std::vector<string_t> const &sv, char const *message)
{
  string_container_const_iterator_t begin = sv.begin();
  string_container_const_iterator_t end   = sv.end();
  for(int i = 0; begin != end; ++begin, ++i)
  {
    printf("%s, %d: %s\n", message, i, (*begin).c_str());
```

The definition of `string_container_const_iterator_t` is brittle. If we change the definition of `std::vector<string_t>` (e.g., if we want to use a faster vector), then `string_container_const_iterator_t` may no longer be compatible with the new vector template's `iterator` type. It's actually even worse if it is compatible, since this nasty wart gets hidden, and the programmer who uses it is not schooled against this bad technique.

---

[8]This is a real example code from a client's code base. I've changed all the names to spare blushes (and lawsuits!).

A slightly milder form of this problem, which I've also seen a fair bit of in the real world, is:

```
typedef std::vector<string_t>                    string_container_t;
typedef string_container_t::iterator
                                    string_container_iterator_t;
typedef string_container_t::const_iterator
                              string_container_const_iterator_t;
```

In this case, the code will continue to work when `string_container_t` is changed, but we're still masking the fact that `iterator` is a contextual type definition and propagating a bad habit. Also, if someone defines a class with a member type of type `string_container_t`, and implements some functionality in terms of `string_container_(const_)iterator_t`, then they'll end up back at the inconsistency problem as soon as they need to change their type from `string_container_t` to something else, for example, `string_list_t`.

```
class X
{
public:
//  typedef string_container_t container_t; // Was this,
    typedef string_list_t      container_t; // upgraded to this
    . . .

    void dump(constainer_t const &c) const
    {
        string_container_const_iterator_t begin = c.begin() // Broken!
```

The only time this lesser form of `typedef` is valid is within a function or template algorithm where the type of the containing type is known and the derivative types are visible within a limited scope, as in:

```
template <typename C>
void dump_container(C const &c)
{
    typedef typename C::const_iterator iter_t;
    iter_t begin = c.begin();
    . . .
}
```

18.5.3   Dubious Typedefs

Recommendation: Avoid making conceptual typedefs that are comprised of contextual typedefs.

As I mentioned in section 2.2, declaring (but not defining) private methods may be used to prevent copy construction and/or copy assignment. When dealing with templates, some older compilers (e.g., Visual C++ 4.0, if I remember correctly) had problems deducing the actual operand types when they were specified as follows:

```
template <typename T>
class X
{
// Construction
public:
  X();
  explicit X(int i);
// Not to be implemented
private:
  X(X const &); // Confusion here
};
```

The problem was that some compilers could deduce that X, as a type within the scope of X<T>, actually meant X<T>, which is the interpretation that all modern compilers must make. Others could not, and either had a compiler error, or treated X as another type (of what exact type I could never determine), which meant that in the earlier case the copy constructor would not be properly declared and would, therefore, be automatically generated (see section 2.2) by the compiler! The answer I came up with was pretty simple:

```
template <typename T>
class X
{
public:
  typedef X<T>  class_type;

  . . .


// Not to be implemented
private:
  X(class_type const &); // No more confusion
};
```

I've been in the same habit ever since, and I almost always define a class_type for every class. It means that I can write the canonical prohibited copy operations in the above form without thinking about it much. (Of course, that's probably not entirely a good thing.) It's also very helpful to maintainability when dealing with nested classes of templates. Consider the following big hairy beast, which we also discuss in section 20.5:

```
template< typename S /* string type, e.g string */
        , typename D /* delimiter type, e.g. char or wstring */
        , typename B = string_tokeniser_ignore_blanks<true>
        , typename V = S /* value type */
        , typename T = string_tokeniser_type_traits<S, V>
        , typename P = string_tokeniser_comparator<D, S, T>
        >
class string_tokeniser
```

```
{
public:
  typedef string_tokeniser<S, D, B, V, T, P> tokeniser_type;

  . . .

  class const_iterator
  {
    . . .

  // Members
  private:
    tokeniser_type *const m_tokeniser;

  }
};
```

In this case the `string_tokeniser` template provides a "class_type" member type in the form of `tokeniser_type`. This is then visible to the nested class `const_iterator`, which maintains a back pointer to the `string_tokeniser` instance for which it is an iterator, in order that it may access the tokenized string to advance its position and return token values. If the member type `tokeniser_type` was not defined, then the const_iterator nested class would have to stipulate `string_tokeniser<S, D, B, V, T, P>`, and you can imagine how easy it is to get that out of step.[9]

Finally, the `class_type` nested type can also be useful when one is using macros[10] within a class definition, and we'll see an excellent example of this in the discussion of properties in Chapter 35.

All the typedefs in this item so far have been pretty justifiable, but I want to finish on another dubious typedef, this one being much less justifiable than `class_type`. In a Java parsing tool I wrote—in C++, of course—I made the reporter and modifier components conform to an agreed binary standard (see Chapter 8), so I could execute different tools over a Java source tree. It works very well, and can spot unused variables, redundant imports, and inefficient string concatenation in source code trees. It can even change the bracing styles of source trees containing a million lines of code in just a few minutes, which is much quicker than it can take to debate such matters. Since each `Reporter`/`Transformer` derived class contains very similar code, insofar as one or both of two member functions are redefined, I was doing a great deal of copy and paste. It gets deadly dull making the same changes in file after file, and there wasn't quite enough justification to make a code generator [Hunt2000], so I used a somewhat nasty but highly effective technique.

At the head of each implementation file—one could never conscience such a thing in header files!—is a definition of a contextual typedef `LocalClass`, which is defined to be the class corresponding to the implementation file. For example:

```
// PackageDependency.cpp
#include . . .
```

---

[9] The original implementation didn't have the `typedef`, and suffered from precisely this problem in the early days of its development, during which time I was tuning the best order of the six (!) template parameters.

[10] Although I stress each time we mention macros that they're nasty, on occasion they do represent the best choice, and to eschew their use in such cases is just cutting off your nose to spite your face.

```
typedef PackageDependency LocalClass;

// BraceInserter.cpp
#include . . .
typedef BraceInserter    LocalClass;
```

All the remaining references to the particular implementation class are via the type `LocalClass`, which cuts down the repetitive effort. There are no code correctness problems because the headers were constructed manually, and with due care.

The other benefit was that it was really useful when using a visual differencing tool to compare the implementations of, say, the `JavaDocInserter` and the `DoxygenInserter` classes, since the only differences were functional ones. The class names prefixing the method definitions are all `LocalClass::`.

Anyway, I'm not going to try too hard to sell you on this one, but I thought it was worth drawing your attention to a further example of the power of `typedef`. Wield it carefully!

Cognizant Conversions

If the chapters in Part One were too easy, or those in Part Two were altogether too C-oriented for your tastes, or those in Part Three were too "in the small," fear not. Part Four will deliver on all counts. The material covered in these chapters is challenging, 100% C++, and covers some seriously "in the large" imperfections. To the cyclists among my audience, I would say: we're about to hit the Alps! In this part we enter the big mountains; I just hope you've taken on enough fluids and carbs,[1] as it'll be some time before we get any respite on some long descents in Parts Five and Six.

Much of C++ is about enforcing, manipulating, and converting type, and it can reasonably claim to be a strongly typed language. Alas, it's not perfect in this regard, and some of the most vexing problems one encounters in the language are about the ways in which the correct language interpretations are just a little bit different from what you *know* to be correct in a particular case.

Whenever one is trying to write generic code—whether template, or pre-processor customizable—one of the big bugbears is in the control of type, and the interconversion between types. The title of Part Four connotes the approach taken in most of the techniques described: that being a deliberate cognizance on the part of the programmer of what is going on and, often, an expression of that in the use of the techniques. In some cases this takes the form of using explicit constructs to manage or manipulate the conversions. In others, it simply entails giving a description of the issues, and providing recommendations as to the best approach(es) to take to avoid the potential pitfalls.

The four distinct concepts that we will examine in the first four chapters are *Casts* (Chapter 19), *Shims* (Chapter 20), *Veneers* (Chapter 21) and *Bolt-Ins* (Chapter 22), each addressing different aspects of type manipulation. Casts are used to change type or views of type. Shims aid in the (unambiguous) interpretation of type. Veneers allow layering of one type on another. Bolt-ins "bolt in" enhancing functionality over existing, and often complete, types. We will see that the notion of type conversion is not a simple one of just plain-old casts, but rather a rich continuum, exposing some powerful emergent properties.

The last chapter, Chapter 23, *Template Constructors*, describes a particularly vexing facet of C++'s template instantiation mechanism, encountered when deriving template classes and forwarding their constructor calls, as we do in *Veneers* and *Bolt-ins*.

---

[1] Since this is software engineering, and not cycling, you probably want to steer clear of the carbs, which might make you sleepy, and instead get come coffee down you. You'll need all your attention in this part.

Each chapter contains various examples of how these concepts can be put to use. Many of these examples highlight important fundamental techniques that underpin the later parts of the book, especially the use of Shims as a mechanism that underpins explicit generalization. Others are more esoteric, and perhaps less practically useful, but they are important as they demonstrate useful ways in which the language and compiler can be made to do what you require.

## CHAPTER 19

Casts

Cast: The form in which something is made or constructed.

19.1   Implicit Conversion

On our behalf, the C++ compiler will carry out a multitude of implicit conversions between types. Just because they're implicit, however, doesn't mean that they're trivial. Conversions between integral and floating-point types can involve significant work [Meye1996, Stro1997]; conversion between integral types of difference sizes can involve truncation or sign extension [Stro1997]; conversions between pointer types of virtually derived classes on an implementing instance involve pointer adjustment [Lipp1996]. The problems, from the point of view of accuracy, of conversions were mentioned in Chapter 13, and are described in detail in [Stro1997]. In this section, we examine what support we get from the compiler to perform these and other conversions, and how we can enhance that support.

The imperfect practitioner's tool kit doesn't contain anything useful for us in such cases, and it is not really the case that there is anything wrong here, excepting the integral truncation and extension issues. It would be a very verbose language indeed that would not allow implicit conversion from `int` to `double`, or from `123` to `int`.

Casts don't always involve converting something. A cast can also be a means of getting access to another nature of an entity, a nature that it already possesses. For an instance of a composite type, say a derived class, the compiler will—issues of access and ambiguity aside—implicitly convert the pointer or reference variable of its type to one of its base class(es).

Indeed, it is possible to access a nature of an entity that does not even directly possess that nature. This is achieved, for class types, by implementing an implicit conversion operator [Meye1996, Meye1998, Sutt2000, Stro1997]. In such cases, a genuine type change is involved, and this is something of which we should be aware when we use the technique. Naturally, the technique has great potential to be abused, and its use is not recommended in most circumstances [Meye1996, Sutt2000, Stro1997, Dewh2003].

19.2   Casting in C++

Where implicit conversion is not sufficient, we may find it necessary to explicitly direct the compiler as to what conversion to apply (not that it is guaranteed to listen, of course). Sometimes, all that is needed is to provide a placeholder variable of an intermediate type, as in Listing 19.1.

Listing 19.1

```
class A
{};

class B
  : public A
{};

class C
  : public A
{};

class D
  : public B
  , public C
{};


D *d = new D();
A *a = d;       // Error. Ambiguous conversion
B *b = d;       // first step (D* => B*) ok
A *a2 = b;      // second step (B* => A*) ok
```

The alternative to this is to use a cast. In C, you have the choice of the C-style cast only, which is a brute-force mechanism, to say the least.

```
A *a = (B*)d;   // hmm ...
```

If we subsequently changed the definition of D such that it no longer inherited from B, this code would still compile. Core dump, here we come!

C++ provides four cast operators [Stro1997] which practitioners are encouraged to use in preference to the C-style cast. These cast operators—static_cast, const_cast, dynamic_cast, and reinterpret_cast—present a separation of the casting functionalities provided by the traditional C-style cast, and are deliberately [Stro1994] strict about how they may be used.[2] The previous code could now be written as:

```
A *a = static_cast<B*>(d);   // ... much better!
```

This will correctly compile and translate the D* to A* for the original class relationship. Were the inheritance relationship between B and D severed, however, this would fail to compile, and we avoid finding out about our mistaken conversion at run time. The code demonstrates the syntax of the casts, which is cast-name<target-type>(operand). The syntax is eminently clear, and the uniformity is helpful: the cast, if successful, returns a view of type

---

[2]If Asimov had been a C++ programmer, his robots would presumably observe the law(s) and use the C++ casts. I suspect the C-style case would be the favorite instrument of Iain Banks's Culture's much more autonomous *Attitude Adjuster*, or one of its brethren.

`target-type` on `operand`. One thing to remember as we develop the ideas in this section is that `dynamic_cast` can throw exceptions (`std::bad_cast` in fact) if a cast for a reference type fails.

There are obviously many more features and significant aspects to the C++ cast operators, which you can read about in most good C++ sources [Dewh2003, Meye1996, Meye1998, Sutt2000, Stro1997]. For the moment we'll consider the case made for their being preferred in good quality code, and move on, though we touch on them again regularly.

19.3   The Case for C Casts

Despite all that we read about C-style casting, there are still circumstances where they are useful, but it's a very few: laziness and sloppiness don't count. There are only two legitimate uses that I can think of.

The first one is where the code has to be compilable under both C and C++, and consequently the only available cast operator is C's. This may be because it is in a macro, or is in a source file that is introduced via inclusion, either as an inline function (see Chapter 12) or one with internal linkage (see sections 6.4 and 11.1).

In actual fact, since we should prefer to go for more power whenever it is available, the Synesis libraries have a set of cast macros—SyCastStatic, SyCastConst, SyCast Volatile, SyCastDynamic, SyCastRaw, and SyCastC—that are plain-old C casts in C, and the appropriate C++ cast in C++. It's ugly, but it works, and this approach has caught countless inappropriate casts.

The second use is subtler. Because the C++ casts are particular about the relationships between their operand and target types, one can get into scrapes in template code with them. For example, despite being The Thing in our "Fancastic Four," `reinterpret_cast` will refuse to cast when a `const` (or `volatile`) change is required as part of the conversion. The following code illustrates:

Listing 19.2

```
template< typename T1
        , typename T2
        >
struct test_cast
{
  test_cast(T2 *p2)
  {
    m_p1 = static_cast<T1*>(p2);       // a
    m_p1 = reinterpret_cast<T1*>(p2); // b
    m_p1 = const_cast<T1*>(p2);        // c
    m_p1 = (T1*)p2;                    // d
  }
  operator T1 *()
  {
    return m_p1;
  }
// Members
```

```
protected:
  T1   *m_p1;
};

int main()
{
  test_cast<int , int >        tc1(NULL);   // 1
  test_cast<int , short >      tc2(NULL);   // 2
  test_cast<int , int const > tc3(NULL);   // 3

  return 0;
}
```

Of the first scenario (casting int* to int*), all four casts will work. Of the second (casting int* to short*), only reinterpret_cast and the C-style cast work. Of the third (casting int* to int const*), only const_cast and the C-style cast work. While it is possible in some circumstances to deduce the respective const-ness of the two types, and thereby cause the correct permutation of const_cast and reinterpret_cast to be invoked, this requires a degree of template sophistication lacking in some compilers. The portable answer (if a cast can ever be considered portable!) may therefore be to use a C-style cast. (Naturally, I am assuming I'm talking to an audience that is fully aware of the badness of C-style casts, and eschews their use as a matter of course—it takes technical maturity and a steely nerve to use C-style casts—but I believe in being aware of all ramifications before adhering to rules, even very good ones.)

Outside these circumstances, the use of C-style casts should be, avoided. The practical problem is that there is so much code containing them, and removal is very difficult because they just blend into the scenery; it is no accident that the C++ operators are so distinct, some say ugly [Stro1994]. Thankfully some compilers provide a little help in this regard. GCC provides the compiler option -Wold-style-cast to provide warnings at each C cast. Recent versions of the Digital Mars and Comeau compilers provide the same functionality with the -wc and -C_style_cast_warning options, respectively.[3]

Specifying the requisite flag to the Comeau (version 4.3.3 or later), Digital Mars (version 8.29 or later), or GCC compilers results in your receiving a warning for each and every C-style cast—another reason to use multiple compilers in your work.

19.4   Casts on Steroids

Using C++'s support for conversion operator member functions [Stro1997], it is possible to write classes that can act as casts. Furthermore, the casts involved may be between semantically distinct types. As is widely commented [Meye1996, Meye1998, Dewh2003], the use of such operators can cause a lot of problems, and they are much abused. But they are in the language because they can be very useful, and their use in casting classes is both appropriate and necessary. Consider the following class, which converts a (C-style) string to an integer.

---

[3]Both these vendors were kind enough to respond to my requests for these features in impressively short times. How's that for service?

Listing 19.3

```
class str2int
{
// Construction
public:
  explicit str2int(char const *s)
    : m_value(atoi(s))
  {}
// Operators
public:
  operator int() const
  {
    return m_value;
  }
// Members
private:
  int m_value;
};
```

Given a string, we can now "cast" it to an integer by using the following form:

```
int val = str2int("34");
```

or

```
int val = (str2int)"34";
```

or even

```
int val = static_cast<str2int>("34");
```

That seems kind of cool, although in this case we might as well call `atoi()`. With the advent of C++'s template support, this technique can be generalized to a considerable degree, with some pleasing and surprising results.

Consider now that we'd like to expand our number parsing a bit, and generalize it to all integral types (including `bool`). Clearly we need some templates. Perhaps surprisingly, the solution is very simple indeed. (Note that this is written for compatibility with Metrowerks CodeWarrior only, and so uses the `long long` type. Nor have I bothered to cater for unsigned types or character encodings other than `char`. A real-world implementation would, of course, use correct abstractions, that is, `int64_t`, and provide a more portable solution.)

Listing 19.4

```
template <typename I>
class str2int
{
// Construction
public:
  explicit str2int(char const *s);
```

```
// Operators
public:
  operator I() const
  {
    return m_value;
  }
// Members
private:
  I m_value;
};


template <typename I>
inline str2int<I>::str2int(char const *s)
  : m_value(static_cast<I>(atoi(s)))
{}
template <>
inline str2int<long long>::str2int(char const *s)
  : m_value(strtoll(s, NULL, 10))
{}
template <>
inline str2int<bool>::str2int(char const *s)
  : m_value(0 == (strcmp(s, "true"))
{}
```

A pleasing consequence of the implementation is that in using the cast class we emulate the syntax of the built-in casts.

```
short     s  = str2int<short>("34");
int       i  = str2int<int>("65536");
bool      b  = str2int<bool>("true");
long long ll = str2int<long long>("-9223372036854775808");
```

So we've seen how to masquerade in the clothes of C++'s built-in cast operators. That's nice. But is there a serious point? Well, I'm sure that the fact that we've also catered for `bool` and its non-numeric string representation (which could easily be expanded to handle other strings, such as "1" and "TRUE") has got you thinking, but you probably want to see something that answers a genuine problem. After all, `str2int` could just be implemented as a suite of related functions, `str2short`, `str2bool`, and so on.

19.5   explicit_cast

Now we know a lot more about casts, we can look closely at the `explicit_cast` that was mentioned in section 16.4. The problem was how to provide explicit casts—to `std::tm` and DATE—for our `Time` class while avoiding the problems of implicit conversions. The second option suggested was to use an `explicit_cast` component.

```
class Time
{
  operator explicit_cast<tm> () const;
  operator explicit_cast<DATE> () const;
};
```

Given what we've just learned about implementing cast operators as template classes, we can postulate an implementation of `explicit_cast` such as the following:

Listing 19.5
```
template <typename T>
class explicit_cast
{
// Construction
public:
  explicit_cast(T t)
      : m_t(t)
  {}
// Conversions
public:
  operator T () const
  {
    return m_t;
  }
// Members
private:
  T    m_t;
};
```

This works really well for fundamental and pointer types. Alas, this being C++, such a simple thing could never be the final solution. The problem is that m_t is a member variable, and gets copied from t in the cast constructor. When T is a fundamental type, this copying is usually fine. In fact, compilers easily optimize the whole shebang out of existence for fundamental and pointer types[4] (and references, subject to the limitations described below).

It seems to be pretty complete for fundamental types. How will it work for user-defined types? Well, if T is a type with a nontrivial cost to construction, such as a vector of strings, then you will pay a potentially unacceptable cost of copying.

```
class Path
{
```

---

[4]Of course, if you want to pass out a long double value (which is either 64 or 80 bits on most 32-bit compilers [Kaha1998]) on a 32-bit architecture, then you may opt to express it as the slightly more efficient form of explicit_cast<long double const &> rather than explicit_cast<long double>, since your client code may further pass on the value as a reference (to const); hence you avoid an extra copy. However, this has nothing directly to do with the efficiency of explicit_cast in this case, merely what your choice of cast type may affect elsewhere in your code.

```
public:
  operator explicit_cast<string> () const;
};
void ProcessPath(Path const &path)
{
  string  s = explicit_cast<string>(path); // multiple copies!
  . . .
```

In fact, in code like that above, there may be several copies in a single cast operation. Borland, Digital Mars, GCC, Intel, and Watcom all create three copies; CodeWarrior and Visual C++ (without Microsoft extensions) create four; Visual C++ (with Microsoft extensions) creates 5! (And that was when compiled with maximum speed optimizations.) Needless to say, this is something to be avoided. However, since all programmers should know that copying nontrivial types involves costs, we can arguably accept this as an acknowledged artefact of such return-by-value.

Another problem arises when using references. This is because the language does not allow a non-const reference to a temporary. This is an eminently sensible rule in general because, if it did so, a piece of code would be able to change a temporary, which could have the confused programmer wondering what happened to their change as it disappeared along with the temporary instance, never to be seen again. Item #30 in *Effective C++* [Meye1998] discusses this, and also explains very well why one should avoid returning non-const references to members from class methods. That goes double for being able to cast to non-const references, so I would say that even though the reference-to-non-const temporary would be valid in this case—since the temporary merely passes along a reference that it "validly" obtained—we should not be troubled where such uses do not compile.

```
class Path
{
public:
  operator explicit_cast<string &> (); // Danger!
};
void ProcessPath(Path &path)
{
  string &s = explicit_cast<string&>(path); // Not legal or nice
  . . .
```

So that just leaves us with casting to reference-to-const. There is no reason why our cast should not work; merely that it does not with some compilers. Actually the cast compiles, but the problem is that some compilers create intermediate temporary copies of the type of which a reference is being returned, and do so without issuing any warnings. Specifically, Intel 6.0, 7.0 and 7.1 and Visual C++ 6.0 and 7.0 each seem to create an extra temporary. Borland, Digital Mars, CodeWarrior, GCC, Visual C++ 7.1, and Watcom all behave as desired.

```
class Path
{
public:
  operator explicit_cast<string const &>() const;
};
```

```
void ProcessPath(Path const &path)
{
  // Works, but a temporary may be created here
  string const &s = explicit_cast<string const &>(path);
  . . .
```

To summarize: we have a missing language feature—explicit casts—that, though needed only rarely, is nonetheless useful. (We'll see some examples of such use in Part Six.) We have a component that provides ideal behavior with fundamental types and all types of pointers, but has problems with references. It does not work for references-to-non-`const`, but we're content with that because even if it did not violate the language rules, it would be an unwise and rarely useful capability. The component is flawed, however, insofar as it can create unwanted copies in some compilers and not others. Such inconsistencies in the behavior of code between compilers, even if the "fault" lies with some of the compilers themselves,[5] is not acceptable in quality software, so we need to do something about this. It's simply not acceptable to write a generic component and say that it can and should be used for some compilers, but not for others, given that it will compile without warning on the ones where it does not work as expected. People will rightly refuse to use it, and will probably be turned off all your other work as well.

What's to be done? Well, we need to prevent `explicit_cast` being used for references to user-defined types, while allowing it to be used for references to (`const`) fundamental types. There are two ways with which we can forcibly proscribe inappropriate use of this component: specialization and constraints.

The first way, using both partial and full specialization, looks like the following:

Listing 19.6

```
// Prohibit all reference types
template <typename T>
class explicit_cast<T &>
{
// Construction
private:
  explicit_cast(T &);
// Conversions
private:
  operator T & ();
};


// Explicitly allow specific (fundamental) types

template <>
class explicit_cast<char const &>
{
// Construction
public:
```

---

[5]Strictly, this is an optimization issue, rather than one of correctness, and pertains to a particular implementation's interpretation of the standard insofar as it elects to elide copy constructors. (See Chapter 18.)

```
    explicit_cast(char const &t)
      : m_t(t)
    {}
// Conversions
public:
  operator char const & () const
  {
    return m_t;
  }
// Members
private:
  char const &m_t;
};


. . . // repeat for bool, wchar_t
. . . // repeat for signed & unsigned char
. . . // repeat for (unsigned) short/int/long/long long
. . . // repeat for float, double & long double


// Enable for all pointer types
template <typename T>
class explicit_cast<T *>
{
// Construction
public:
  explicit_cast(T *t)
     : m_t(t)
  {}
// Conversions
public:
  operator T * ()
  {
    return m_t;
  }
// Members
private:
  T    *m_t;
};
```

The first partial specialization `explicit_cast<T&>` declares its constructor and implicit conversion operator private, which essentially prevents any references being used in explicit casts. This is good, but too powerful, since we want the fundamental types to work for reference-to-`const` casts. That's where the full specializations come in. The one shown is for `char`, and there are corresponding specializations for all the fundamental types.[6] The picture is

---

[6]On (nonconformant) compilers that do not support `wchar_t` as a distinct type, you'd have to have the appropriate preprocessor discrimination to hide that definition, since it is not legal to provide two specializations of the same type, even where the definitions are identical.

completed by the provision of a partial specialization for pointer types, to enable them to be used, as some compilers may get confused between the template itself and the reference special-ization when asked to instantiate for pointer types. (If in doubt, be explicit, if you'll pardon the pun.) With these specializations we have the precise behavior we want.

(Note that if you want the extra caution of prohibiting any pointers to non-const being re-turned, you can change the pointer specialization to use `private` access control in the same way as the reference one did, and then further specialize a pointer to const one, that is, `explicit_cast<T const *>` with public constructor and conversion operator. It's up to you.)

Alas, not all compilers in common use support partial specialization, so it's prudent to pro-vide a correspondingly restricted version of `explicit_cast` in such circumstances. This re-lies on constraints. We apply the `constraint_must_be_pod()` constraint (section 1.2.4) in the destructor, which means that the template cannot be used for non-POD types.

Listing 19.7

```
template <typename T>
class explicit_cast
{
  . . .

#ifndef ACMELIB_TEMPLATE_PARTIAL_SPECIALIZATION_SUPPORT
  // For compilers that don't support partial specialization we
  // enforce the constraint that only POD types may be used.
  ~explicit_cast()
  {
    constraint_must_be_pod(T);
  }
#endif /* ! ACMELIB_TEMPLATE_PARTIAL_SPECIALIZATION_SUPPORT */
  . . .
};
```

That's it! It's not perfect, because it does allow the template to be applied to nontrivial POD types, for example, large structures. However, since we've already decided that the cost of copying with by-value parameterization of the template is a matter of caveat emptor, in the rare cases where a compiler cannot optimize intermediate copies of the structure, it's your responsibility for electing to pass by value. What the constraint does buy us though—and remember that this is at compile time—is the rejection of any nontrivial user-defined types with potentially costly copying.

One great thing about `explicit_cast` is that it can be applied, in client code, both to types that express `explicit_cast` operators and to those that provide implicit conversion op-erators. This means that you can write generic code to both kinds of types—the cautiously writ-ten and the injudiciously written—in the same way `explicit_cast` can, therefore be the basis of a generic conversion mechanism, where the exercising of the choice of whether, and to what, to convert is in the hands of the programmer, rather than the compiler. That's where it should be.

19.6 literal_cast

Although the use of literal integer constants in our code is not the done thing, we nevertheless use named constants quite often. Sometimes it is possible to use a constant in an inappropriate way, and risk loss of information through truncation. Although most good compilers warn of constant truncation, several do not, or do not in their commonly used configurations. In any case it is still only a warning. I know that none of you gentle readers would let such a warning slip through your build/release process, but there are people who are less diligent, or who are forced to suppress some warnings, or who "inherit" such warning suppressions from poorly written third-party libraries. It would be nice to have a construct that detected truncation and forced a compile-time error.

Just such a construct is the template function `literal_cast`, shown in Listing 19.8.

Listing 19.8

```
#ifdef ACMELIB_64BIT_INT_SUPPORT
typedef int64_t    literal_cast_int_t;
#else /* ? ACMELIB_64BIT_INT_SUPPORT */
typedef int32_t    literal_cast_int_t;
#endif /* ACMELIB_64BIT_INT_SUPPORT */

template< typename T
        , literal_cast_int_t V
        >
inline T literal_cast()
{
  const int literal_cast_value_too_large =
                      V <= limit_traits<T>::maximum_value;
  const int literal_cast_value_too_small =
                      V >= limit_traits<T>::minimum_value;
  STATIC_ASSERT(literal_cast_value_too_large);
  STATIC_ASSERT(literal_cast_value_too_small);
  return T(V);
}
```

It uses a `limits_traits` template class that provides the member constants (see section 15.5.3) `minimum_value` and `maximum_value`. It works by treating the constant to be tested as a signed integer of the maximum size for the compiler—`literal_cast_int_t`; for example, 64 bits for 32-bit compilers. This is then tested against the cast type's minimum and maximum values in the static assertions (see section 1.4.8).

In the comparisons, all values are promoted to `literal_cast_int_t`, so for all types smaller than this, the case provides a comprehensive evaluation of the type's value. Assuming `literal_cast_int_t` is 64-bits, consider the following code:

```
const int I    = 200;
sint8_t   i8  = literal_cast<sint8_t, I>();   // Compile error
uint8_t   ui8 = literal_cast<uint8_t, I>();   // Compiles ok
sint16_t  i16 = literal_cast<sint16_t, I>();  // Compiles ok
```

There's a limitation in its application to casts to 64-bit types, by virtue of the fact that it uses the signed 64-bit type for the constant. If you specify `uint64_t` as the cast type, and pass in a value larger than the maximum positive signed value, you will get truncation or sign conversion. This is a flaw in the technique, to which the language can provide no remedy; we cannot escape the truth that there's no recourse to a larger type than the largest type available.

The only answer is to prevent the cast being used with the largest unsigned integer type. This is easy to do using partial specialization, but it requires that we transform the cast from a function to a class, as shown in Listing 19.9.

Listing 19.9

```
#ifdef ACMELIB_64BIT_INT_SUPPORT
typedef int64_t    literal_cast_int_t;
typedef uint64_t  invalid_int_t;
#else /* ? ACMELIB_64BIT_INT_SUPPORT */
typedef int32_t    literal_cast_int_t;
typedef uint32_t  invalid_int_t;
#endif /* ACMELIB_64BIT_INT_SUPPORT */

template< . . . >
class literal_cast
{
public:
  operator T () const
  {
    . . . // the rest of the previous implementation
  }
};


template<literal_cast_int_t V>
class literal_cast<invalid_int_t, V>
{
private:
  operator invalid_int_t () const
  {
    const int cannot_literal_cast_to_largest_unsigned_integer = 0;
    STATIC_ASSERT(cannot_literal_cast_to_largest_unsigned_integer);
    return 0;
  }
};
```

The specialization for the new `invalid_int_t` type, representing the largest unsigned integer type, hides the conversion operator, thereby preventing use of the cast with this type. For good measure, the operator contains a static assertion (see section 12.4.8), which will aid the unsuspecting developer a little better than the `"operator is inaccessible"` compile errors they would otherwise only receive.

Now you can cast literals to any type (except the largest unsigned integer type) in your code with complete confidence against truncation.

Before I complete this section, I'd like to mention that the Boost libraries contains a run time analog of this cast, called `numeric_cast`, written by Kevlin Henney. Whether you want compile time or run time detection of truncation, your bases are covered.

19.7   union_cast

In [Stro1997], Bjarne Stroustrup observes that it is possible to use a union to cast between unrelated types, even where such a conversion would not be supported by any of the C++ cast operators.

Listing 19.10
```
template< typename TO
        , typename FROM
        >
union union_cast
{
  union_cast(FROM from)
    : m_from(from)
  {}
  operator TO () const
  {
    return m_to;
  }
private:
  FROM  m_from;
  TO    m_to;
};
```

Bjarne's message is that such things are evil hackery and mark their users as naïve and/or dangerously cavalier. I couldn't agree more . . . except that sometimes it's helpful.

The two specific problems Bjarne describes are size and alignment. On some architectures the size of a pointer and an `int` are different, so conversion could result in dangerous truncation. Also, several architectures require that pointers have specific alignments, and attempting to dereference a misaligned pointer will result in something nasty, for example, a hardware exception.

```
long   l  = 3; // Not a likely address for a string . . .
string *ps = union_cast<string*, long>(l); // Eek!
```

Using `union_cast` offers no more guarantees than does `reinterpret_cast`, and in some aspects fewer, since it will perform some casts that `reinterpret_cast` will reject.

So if the picture's so bad, why are we even considering using union casts? There are two reasons, both eminently prosaic. First, as was noted in section 19.3, some conversions can require more than one cast, which leads to long-winded code that is hard to read and hard to maintain. Second, some compilers warn on the use of any casts, not just implicit casts and C-style casts, which can leave the adherent to the zero-warning philosophy tearing at his (or her!) beard.

There are widely used system architectures that simply force the use of casts. The most obvious one that springs to mind is the Windows API. Each message in the system is associated with two opaque data values of type WPARAM and LPARAM, which are, on Win32, uint32_t and sint32_t, respectively. These are used to pass all manner of things around, including system object handles, C-string pointers, and pointers to C++ objects. On Win32, therefore, it's useful to define constructs that help to enhance readability and maintainability, as well as to introduce as much type safety as is possible in such circumstances. Therefore, use of specific parameterizations of union_cast can be appropriate, as in:

```
typedef union_cast<LPARAM, wchar_t const*>  StrW2LPARAM;
typedef union_cast<HDROP, WPARAM>           WPARAM2HDROP;
```

Because union_cast is such a dangerous tool, we need to take some serious measures to curb its power before we can use it in good conscience. The first one is that it is *never* used in its raw form. If you were to grep my source control system, you would not find a single instance of union_cast in implementation code for any products or components. The only place it will be used is in the definition of specific typedefs in the header files of technology/operating system-specific libraries, such as the two shown above. Such typedefs may reasonably be presumed to have had more consideration than a single specific instantiation lurking deep within an implementation file.

The second measure used to minimize the risk of misuse is that there are several constraints built into the cast class, as can be seen in Listing 19.11. The first of these is that the conversion types are the same size. This removes the danger of truncation. The second constraint we would want is that the types must be POD, but since this is one of the things we use a union for, it's a done deal. For pedagogical purposes, the constraint constraint_must_be_pod() (see section 1.2.4) is applied to the two types, even though it is unnecessary: the constraint works by attempting to define a union containing the given type.

Listing 19.11

```
template< typename TO
        , typename FROM
        >
union union_cast
{
  explicit union_cast(FROM from)
    : m_from(from)
  {
    // 1. Sizes must be the same
    STATIC_ASSERT(sizeof(FROM) == sizeof(TO));
    // 2. Both must be of POD type
    constraint_must_be_pod(FROM);
    constraint_must_be_pod(TO);
# if defined(ACMELIB_TEMPLATE_PARTIAL_SPECIALIZATION_SUPPORT)
    // 3. Both must be non-pointers, or must point to POD types
    typedef typename base_type_traits<FROM>::base_type
                                    from_base_type;
```

```
    typedef typename base_type_traits<TO>::base_type
                                            to_base_type;
    constraint_must_be_pod_or_void(from_base_type);
    constraint_must_be_pod_or_void(to_base_type);
# endif /* ACMELIB_TEMPLATE_PARTIAL_SPECIALIZATION_SUPPORT */
  }
    . . .
};
```

The third concern is that a union cast should not allow casts to or from pointers to class type, because this would facilitate nonchecked down or cross casts that should properly be dealt with by `dynamic_cast`. This is policed by applying another constraint to the base types of the cast's types. In other words, in addition to ensuring that the manipulated types are POD, we also ensure that any types that are pointers—pointers are also POD, remember (see Prologue)—only point to POD (or to `void`). They do so by determining the base type and applying the `constraint_must_be_pod_or_void()` (see section 1.2.4).

For compilers that support partial specialization, the `base_type_traits` template is able to deduce the base type from any type. It is a simple template with appropriate (partial) specializations, as follows:[7]

Listing 19.12

```
template <typename T>
struct base_type_traits
{
  enum { is_pointer    =  0 };
  enum { is_reference  =  0 };
  enum { is_const      =  0 };
  enum { is_volatile   =  0 };
  typedef T  base_type;
  typedef T  cv_type;
};
 . . .  // Various cv & ptr/ref specialisations
template <typename T>
struct base_type_traits<T const volatile *>
{
  enum { is_pointer    =  1 };
  enum { is_reference  =  0 };
  enum { is_const      =  1 };
  enum { is_volatile   =  1 };
  typedef T  base_type;
  typedef T const volatile  cv_type;
};
```

We've now dealt with most of the problems raised by the `union_cast`, and any potential misuses are handled at compile time. The last issue is that the cast can be used to produce a mis-

---

[7]The full implementation of this and other constraints used in the book are provided on the CD.

aligned pointer (which `reinterpret_cast` can also do). Naturally this cannot be checked at compile time, but we can use the `base_type_traits` to help us here as well. In my implementation there's an assertion that is tested when the from-type is nonpointer and the to-type is pointer, which ensures that the from-value is aligned on the size of the to-type's base type. In other words, if the to-type is `uint64_t (const)(volatile)*`, then the from-value must be an integral of eight. You may choose to have an exception thrown in your own implementation.

With all four of these measures thrown in, it's arguable that `union_cast` is safer than `reinterpret_cast`, and the only cost in usability is that pointers to or from class types cannot be used. Since doing so represents the greatest danger to C++ programmers, I think this is a boon: the cast class handles (and validates) the benign conversions, leaving the scary ones to be done explicitly by the programmer.

Note that it does not prevent you casting from, say, `char const*` to `wchar_t*`, since it's the use of more than one cast we're trying to encapsulate. This represents a danger, hence my strict rule to only use it via typedefs, for example, `WPARAM2HDROP`, since creating and using such typedefs can be reasonably assumed to have been done in a thoughtful manner.[8]

19.8 comstl::interface_cast

Although it's good to keep examples nonproprietary, I think it might be time to get all technology specific. For those few who've not yet heard of COM, I'll give a whistlestop tour of the bits germane to this section. (If you want to get into it in depth there are many good books on the subject [Box1998, Broc1995, Eddo1998]; prepare for a lot of learning![9])

COM stands for component object model, and it does exactly what it says on the tin: It's a model for describing and implementing component software, for creating and managing component objects. It is based around the `IUnknown` interface, which has three methods. `AddRef()` and `Release()` are responsible for reference counting. `QueryInterface()` is the method whereby one can ask a COM object whether it has another nature—the one we're querying for—and request a pointer to that nature. The natures we are talking about are other interfaces derived from `IUnknown`, identified by unique interface identifiers (IIDs), which are 128-bit numbers.

Listing 19.13

```
interface IImpCpp
  : public IUnknown
{
  virtual HRESULT CanSupportOO(BOOL *bOO) = 0;
};
extern const IID IID_IImpCpp;
interface IImpC
  : public IUnknown
{
  virtual HRESULT CanSupportOO(BOOL *bOO) = 0;
```

---

[8]There's nothing much else that we can do to guard against potential Machiavellian behavior of programmers. At some point we have to rely on professionalism.

[9]I must confess that I'm very fond of COM. Not DCOM, MTS, OLE, ATL, or `__declspec(uuid)`, but pure boiled-down COM is great, despite its complexity.

```
};
extern const IID IID_IImpC;
```

Because a COM object can implement a number of interfaces, and because it is not pre-scribed that it inherits from any or all of them, it is not appropriate to cast COM interface point-ers as we might other inherited types. If we held a pointer to `IImpCpp` and wished to convert it to `IImpC`, we cannot cast, since they are not directly related; they only share a parent. (Other important rules within COM prevent the use of `dynamic_cast` to cross-cast [Stro1997] such a relationship.) In fact you can see from this simple example that if we wished to inherit from both `IImpCpp` and `IImpC`, we would have a deal of a time providing differential implementa-tions of their `CanSupportOO()` methods.[10]

When we want to access another nature of a COM object, therefore, we must ask—query—the current interface for whether it implements the required interface. Hence:

Listing 19.14

```
IImpCpp *ic =  . . .;
IImpCpp *icpp;
// Acquire a pointer to the IImpC interface
HRESULT hr = ic->QueryInterface(IID_IImpCpp,
                                reinterpret_cast<void**>(&icpp));
if(SUCCEEDED(hr))
{
  BOOL bOO;
  icpp->CanSupportOO(&bOO);
  icpp->Release(); // Release the interface
}
```

This is pretty much boilerplate for getting hold of another interface from an existing one. There are two problems associated with this mechanism. First, one must be sure to specify the right `IID` constant. The second problem is that it is easy to get the cast wrong, usually by for-getting the address of operator, instead passing in `reinterpret_cast<void**>(icpp)`. This only comes out in complete code coverage tests, which are very difficult to achieve in sig-nificant projects [Glas2003].

There have been numerous attempts at encapsulating this procedure, some of which involve "smart" pointers but it's not yet been done to (my) satisfaction. Since no one likes a critic who lacks a better alternative I'll put my head on the chopping block and show you my answer: the interface casts.[11]

19.8.1   interface_cast_addref

We'll look at one of these in action, and rewrite the example.

```
IImpC   *ic =  . . .;
IImpCpp *icpp = interface_cast_addref<IImpCpp*>(ic);
```

---

[10]Naturally both methods would return true, as was demonstrated in Chapter 8.

[11]These form part of COMSTL, an STLSoft subproject devoted to COM, and are included on the CD.

```
if(NULL != icpp)
{
  BOOL bOO;
  icpp->CanSupportOO(&bOO);
  icpp->Release(); // Release the interface
}
```

Since the interface identifier and the pointer to receive the acquired interface are related to the type of interface required, we deduce both of them from the interface type. We've lost the `QueryInterface()` call, and its associated gobbledegook, and removed the two common problems. A successful cast results in a non-`NULL` pointer, which the client code is responsible for releasing when it has finished with it.

This is a nice start, but we still have the remainder of the boilerplate, including the check on conversion success, and the manual release of the interface when we're finished with it.

19.8.2   interface_cast_noaddref

Sometimes all you want to do is make a single method call on an interface, as is the case in our example. In that case, the eight lines of code can be more than a little cumbersome. That's where the second interface cast comes in. Using this cast, we can rewrite it in three lines:

```
IImpC *ic =  . . .;
BOOL  bOO;
interface_cast_noaddref<IImpCpp*>(ic)->CanSupportOO(&bOO);
```

As its name suggests, this cast does not effect an `AddRef()` on the given interface. Actually, it does temporarily increase the object's reference count, via a call to `Query Interface()` to acquire the `IImpCpp` interface, but then it releases that interface again at the end of the statement: thus effecting no net reference count change on the object.

Since this cast performs the interface querying and makes the method call in a single statement, there is no opportunity for error testing in the client code, and so the cast throws an exception—defaulted to `bad_interface_cast`—if the interface cannot be acquired.

19.8.3   interface_cast_test

As we'll see in Part 7, whether you use exceptions or return values for error handling, you still must take responsibility for failure conditions somewhere along the way. So when using `interface_cast_addref` we must check for `NULL`, and when using `interface_cast_noaddref`, we need to catch `bad_interface_cast`. Because COM is a binary interface, we cannot throw exceptions out of the link unit (see Chapter 9), so we could be in for a lot of try-catch blocks around the place.

The rules of COM identity [Box1998] require that if an instance has ever returned a given interface in response to a `QueryInterface()` call, it must always do so throughout its lifetime. Therefore, the third component of this set, `interface_cast_test`, comes into play. Essentially this is a cast masquerading as a *Logical Shim* (see section 20.3), which is for use in conditional expressions. It can be used to ensure that a given use of `interface_` cast_noaddref will not throw an exception, or that an interface_cast_addref will not return NULL. But where it really comes into use is when combined with nontemporary interface_cast_noaddref, as in:

```
IUnknown  *punk =  . . .;
if(interface_cast_test<IThing*>(punk))
{
   interface_cast_noaddref<IThing*>  thing(punk);
   thing->Method1();
   . . .
   thing->MethodN();
} // dtor of thing will release the reference
```

Of course, the same could be achieved by creating the nontemporary thing instance, and catching an exception thrown if punk was not convertible to IThing*. But in practice, the creation of COM components is a lightweight exercise, and in some cases in environments where a C/C++ run time library is not available [Rect1999]. In such circumstances, the default exception used by interface_cast_noaddref can be set (via the preprocessor) to one that does not actually throw, allowing the above form to be succinct, safe, and yet lightweight. This may not be "proper" C++ but we're imperfect practitioners, and it's a pragmatic increase in code quality within the limitations of the technological environment.

I'm in the Kernighan and Pike camp [Kern1999] in believing exceptions should be reserved for truly unexpected conditions, so tend to prefer this approach in most circumstances.

19.8.4   Operator Implementations

By now you must be asking how these cast operators work, so let's take a look. All three classes inherit protectedly from the template interface_cast_base, but in slightly different ways. First, interface_cast_noaddref:

Listing 19.15

```
template< typename I
        , typename X = throw_bad_interface_cast_exception
        >
class interface_cast_noaddref
   : protected interface_cast_base<I, noaddref_release<I>, X>
{
public:
   typedef interface_cast_base<. . . >    parent_class_type;
   typedef I                              interface_pointer_type;
   typedef . . .                          protected_pointer_type;
public:
   template <typename J>
   explicit interface_cast_noaddref(J &j)
     : parent_class_type(j)
   {}
```

```
    explicit interface_cast_noaddref(interface_pointer_type pi)
      : parent_class_type(pi)
    {}
public:
  protected_pointer_type operator -> () const
  {
    return static_cast<. . .>(parent_class_type::get_pointer());
  }
// Not to be implemented
private:
  . . . // Inaccessible copy ctor & copy assignment op
};
```

The parent class is a specialization of interface_cast_base, based on the noaddref_release functor class and the given exception policy type. This functor is used to ensure that there is no net gain (or loss) to the reference count of the instance being cast, by releasing the interface acquired in the constructor.

The template constructor provides the flexibility to attempt a cast to any COM interface. Since that is an operation with a modest cost, the second constructor, which takes a pointer of the desired type, is implemented to efficiently call AddRef() on the given pointer. In both cases, the constructors defer to their corresponding constructors in the base class.[12]

The queried interface is accessible only via the operator ->() const method, which helps to ensure the safety of this cast. Since no implicit conversion operator is provided, the compiler will reject code of the following form, which would otherwise represent a dangerous potential dead reference:

```
IX *px = interface_cast_noaddref<IX>(py); // Compiler error
px->SomeMethod(); // Crash. Can't get here, thankfully!
```

This is classic hairshirt programming: protecting users of our types from misuse by compilers conspiring with the language to make things too easy. However, it does make the cast difficult to use in a scenario such as the following:

```
func(IX *px);
IY *py = . . .;
func(interface_cast_noaddref<IX>(p)); // Compile error
```

The rules of COM say that you don't take ownership of a reference passed to a function (except where that's the explicit semantics of a given function). So, although using interface_cast_addref here would compile, it would leave a dangling reference. interface_cast_noaddref is the one we need.

---

[12]All of the cast classes provide both constructor versions, rather than just the template one, in order to work correctly with compilers that do not support member template constructors correctly.

Of course, where there's a will, there's a way. If you're feeling perverse, you could always write

```
IStream *pi = interface_cast_noaddref<IStream, . . .>(p).operator ->();
pi->SomeMethod(); // Undefined behavior. May crash!
```

but then I'd have to call the C++ police, and it would be "No code for you! You come back: one year!" Naturally, because imperfect programming tells us to be respectful of the wishes of (experienced) developers, there is a solution to this. We can use the associated get_ptr() *Attribute Shim* (we meet the *Shims* concept in all its glory in the next chapter) as in:

```
func(get_ptr(interface_cast_noaddref<IX>(p))); // Ok
```

The implementations of the two other casts are similar to that of interface_cast_noaddref. interface_cast_test uses the inert exception policy type ignore_interface_cast_exception so that failure does not result in an exception being thrown and is, rather, represented by the Boolean implicit conversion operator.[13] interface_cast_test uses noaddref_release to ensure that there is no net reference count change.

Listing 19.16
```
template<typename I>
class interface_cast_test
  : protected interface_cast_base<I, noaddref_release<I>,
                                  ignore_interface_cast_exception>
{
  . . .
  operator bool () const
  {
    return NULL != parent_class_type::get_pointer();
  }
  . . .
```

interface_cast_addref similarly uses the inert exception policy, albeit as a defaulted template policy parameter, but uses addref_release to effect the necessary increase in the reference count. It provides access to the acquired interface via an implicit conversion operator.

Listing 19.17
```
template< typename I
        , typename X = ignore_interface_cast_exception
        >
class interface_cast_addref
    : protected interface_cast_base<I, addref_release<I>, X>
```

---

[13]This is not the real implementation of the Boolean operator. We see how to do this properly in Chapter 24.

```
{
  . . .
  operator pointer_type () const
  {
    return parent_class_type::get_pointer();
  }
  . . .
```

19.8.5   Protecting the Reference Count

You've probably noticed that `interface_cast_noaddref` returned a pointer to the acquired interface in the form of the `protected_pointer_type`. This is used to prevent client code from making pathological calls to an interface's `AddRef()` or `Release()`; since the cast manages the cast interface's lifetime, client code has no business calling these methods. Thus `protected_pointer_type` is defined in terms of the `protect_refcount` template,[14] which looks like the following:

Listing 19.18

```
template <typename I>
interface protect_refcount
    : public I
{
private:
  STDMETHOD_(ULONG, AddRef)()
  {
    I    *pi = static_cast<I*>(this);
    return pi->AddRef();
  }
  STDMETHOD_(ULONG, Release)()
  {
    I    *pi = static_cast<I*>(this);
    return pi->Release();
  }
};
```

The two methods are made inaccessible to client code of `interface_cast_noaddref`, while all the other interface-specific methods remain accessible.[15]

```
interface_cast_noaddref<IX>(py)->Release(); // Compile error!
```

---

[14]Since version 3.0, Microsoft's Active Template Library (ATL) has done the same thing, so it can't be all bad, eh?

[15]This guarantee is only for compilers that support partial template specialization. But if you regularly compile your source with multiple compilers, as you should, this won't be a problem.

19.8.6   interface_cast_base

The three cast classes merely parameterize the base class with appropriate policy classes, and render certain features accessible. All the action happens in `interface_cast_base`, shown in Listing 19.19.

Listing 19.19

```
template< typename I
        , typename R
        , typename X
        >
class interface_cast_base
{
protected:
  typedef I    interface_type;
  typedef R    release_type;
  typedef X    exception_policy_type;
protected:
  template <typename J>
  explicit interface_cast_base(J &j)
    : m_pi(do_cast(j))
  {}
  explicit interface_cast_base(interface_type pi)
    : m_pi(pi)
  {
    addref(m_pi);
  }
  ~interface_cast_base()
  {
    if(NULL != m_pi)
    {
      release_type()(m_pi);
    }
  }
  static interface_type do_cast(LPUNKNOWN punk)
  {
    interface_type  pi;
    if(NULL == punk)
    {
      pi = NULL;
    }
    else
    {
      REFIID  iid = IID_traits<interface_type>().iid();
      HRESULT hr  = punk->QueryInterface(iid,
                            reinterpret_cast<void**>(&pi));
      if(FAILED(hr))
      {
```

```
            exception_policy_type()(hr, iid);
        pi = NULL;
      }
    }
    return pi;
  }
  interface_type const   &get_pointer_();
  interface_type          get_pointer_() const;
private:
  interface_type const   m_pi;
private:
  . . . // Inaccessible copy ctor & copy assignment op
};
```

There are several points to note. First, all methods are protected, so it cannot be (mis)used directly; it can only be used via derived classes. Second, as was discussed earlier, the constructors are defined as a template and nontemplate pair, to support both generality and efficiency. Third, the interface pointer, if non-NULL, is released by the parameterizing release_type functor, thereby effecting the release (or not) as requested by the release_type policy type.

So that leaves the static method do_cast(), which is where all the action is. do_cast() is called from the template constructor in order to try to effect the cast. If the given interface pointer is non-NULL, QueryInterface() is called on it to obtain the required interface. If this succeeds, then the new interface is returned, otherwise the exception_ policy_type functor is called. After the exception_policy_type functor is called, the pointer is set to NULL in the cases where the exception_policy_type does nothing.

19.8.7   IID_traits

The only remaining query regarding the implementation is how the interface identifier is determined. Simply, we use the classic technique [Lipp1998] for accessing values from types: traits. The interface identifier traits class, IID_traits, is defined as follows:

```
template <class I>
struct IID_traits
{
public:
  static REFIID   iid();
};
```

Hypocrisy alert: on translators that support Microsoft's _ _uuidof()extension, I go the easy route and define the iid() method (for the general case) as:

```
template <class I>
inline /* static */ REFIID IID_traits<I>::iid()
{
```

```
    return __uuidof(I);
}
```

For those that do not, no definition is provided for the general case and individual special-izations (for both *Interface* and *Interface**) must be defined. A macro—COMSTL_ IID_TRAITS_DEFINE()—is provided for this purpose, and all the current standard interfaces are thus specialized in the header comstl_interface_traits_std.h, which is included in these circumstances, in the following manner:

```
#ifdef __IClassFactory_FWD_DEFINED__
COMSTL_IID_TRAITS_DEFINE(IClassFactory)
#endif  /* __IClassFactory_FWD_DEFINED__ */
```

Users of the casts whose compilers do not provide __uuidof() must define specializa-tions for their own interfaces in the same way. This is not exactly ideal, but it's not exactly onerous either, and it's pretty foolproof: the lack of a general case prevents any errors getting past the compile phase.

In an idealized sense it's vexing to have to relent from one's principles of eschewing pro-prietary extensions, but pragmatism wins out over idealism here (and in most other cases, I guess). We should be willing to use such things as long as we are not, and don't become, depen-dent on them. The goal is to have the highest quality software, not the purest soul!

19.8.8   interface_cast Coda

What a lot of COM! I would have preferred to have a non-technology-oriented example, but it is difficult to synthesize something meaningful to this degree.[16] We've made the querying of interfaces type safe, succinct, and even have policy-based error handling. So what's the catch?

Well it's not performance: everything is inline, and the code has no difference in perfor-mance from the original. There's definitely a significant gain in robustness: we've removed the complexity and buggish tendencies of QueryInterface(). Furthermore, we've reduced the opportunity for reference-count abuse by restricting the availability of the interface (and the AddRef() and Release() methods, as we'll see in a moment) to a functional minimum.

We've made the code clearer by reducing the amount of code and by using cast syntax. A reader of your code can quite clearly see what you're attempting to query for, and also whose responsibility it is to deal with any concomitant reference count increase.

Portability has improved, albeit that it's not perfect. When using custom interfaces for com-pilers that do not support the __uuidof() extension, one must provide an IID_traits spe-cialization. But the important thing is that, although the use of this extension makes our use of the casts easier, it is not necessary to have the extension, so we still have excellent portability.

It's now more maintainable, because the amount of code has shrunk, and the opportunity to introduce errors has been minimized.

---

[16]I have to admit that the interface casts hurt my brain while I was creating them!

To be honest, the only criticism that the casts get is their names. I recognize that the names are not exactly succinct, but it is very important that people who use the casts, and those who will maintain their code, are presented with as little ambiguity as possible. When we're dealing with reference counting, one too many or too few references can be a significant error. Therefore, I opted for the explicit but ugly naming conventions. I've had other names suggested, but none that preserve the unambiguous semantics of the casts, so it looks like they're staying.

19.9   boost::polymorphic_cast

Casts don't have to be, and rarely are, as complex as the interface casts. Often they are much less so.

In [Stro1997], Bjarne Stroustrup set an exercise to the reader, asking for an implementation of a template ptr_cast to work like dynamic_cast except that it should throw bad_cast for pointers as well as for references. Well, what he actually said was "Write a template ptr_cast that works like dynamic_cast, except that it throws bad_cast rather than returning 0." Nothing other than the name of the requested entity, ptr_cast, suggests that this works for pointer types only, but that's no doubt the interpretation that was meant and that is generally taken. Boost's polymorphic_cast has the following implementation:

```
template <class Target, class Source>
inline Target polymorphic_cast(Source* x)
{
  Target tmp = dynamic_cast<Target>(x);
  if ( tmp == 0 ) throw std::bad_cast();
  return tmp;
}
```

and is used in the following manner:

```
try
{
  Base    *b = new Base();
  Derived *d = boost::polymorphic_cast<Derived*>(a);
}
catch(std::bad_cast &x)
{
  . . .
}
```

It seems curious at first to have the argument x be declared as a pointer (i.e., x is Source* rather than Source, or Source &) when that could be deduced by the compiler. But this actually makes sense since by declaring it explicitly as a pointer the cast is constrained from being applied to nonpointer types.

What about if we were to take a stricter interpretation, that is, that ptr_cast can work with reference *or* pointer types and that in both cases it throws bad_cast when conversion fails? A quick search around the Internet reveals precious few `ptr_casts`, so I guess the problem must be pretty tricky. The best I could come up with in a morning's (very taxing) effort is shown in Listing 19.20.

Listing 19.20
```
template <typename T>
struct ptr_cast
{
public:
  typedef typename base_type_traits<T>::cv_type cv_type;
  typedef cv_type                               &reference;
  typedef cv_type                               *pointer;
public:
  template <typename Source>
  ptr_cast(Source &s)
    : m_p(&dynamic_cast<Target>(s))
  {
    // Nothing to do: dynamic_cast throws for reference types
  }
  template <typename Source>
  ptr_cast(Source *s)
    : m_p(dynamic_cast<Target>(s))
  {
    if(NULL == m_p)
    {
      throw std::bad_cast();
    }
  }
  ptr_cast(pointer_type pt)
    : m_p(t)
  {}
  ptr_cast(reference_type t)
    : m_p(&t)
  {}
public:
  operator reference () const
  {
    return const_cast<reference>(*m_p);
  }
  operator pointer () const
  {
    return const_cast<pointer>(m_p);
  }
protected:
  pointer m_p;
};
```

The cast uses the `base_type_traits` template (see section 19.7) to deduce the appropriate cv-qualified base type. This type is then used to derive the `pointer` and `reference` types, which are then used to define the implicit conversion operators needed to return the converted value back to the caller. The last part of the picture is that the result of the `dynamic_cast` applied to a pointer is tested, and `bad_cast` is thrown if the cast failed and returned `NULL`.

Now we can use it with pointers *and* references.

```
class X
{};
class D
{};
D d;
dynamic_cast<X&>(d);    // Throws bad_cast
ptr_cast<X&>(d);        // Throws bad_cast
dynamic_cast<X*>(&d);   // Returns NULL
ptr_cast<X*>(&d);       // Throws bad_cast
```

The implementation works only for compilers that support partial template specialization, so that rules out Visual C++ (6.0 and 7.0) and Watcom immediately. The real implementation has some workarounds to work with Borland, and has an ambiguity with GCC when passed pointers to intermediates rather than a separate variable. But with CodeWarrior, Comeau, Digital Mars, Intel, and Visual C++ 7.1, it works perfectly in all guises.

Of course it's nicer, where possible, to have a unified way of dealing with pointers and references, but given the almost-but-not-quite nature of this version, we cannot castigate the Boost implementation for constraining itself to deal only with pointers.

19.10   Casts: Coda

We've seen how casts can be implemented either as functions or as classes. The former represent the more straightforward approach, but are underpowered for many tasks. Using classes allows us to make specializations to factor out common code from several casts into a common parent class and to more easily constrain the potential uses of the casts. When implementing casts as classes, measures should be taken to minimize the potential for abuse of the class (cast) instances that must only be used as temporaries. These measures include restricting the set of class operators, the types returned by these methods, and clearly documenting the semantics of the classes.

We've also focused on cast failure. The C++ casts have fixed and well-defined behavior for failure to cast. Upon failure, `const_cast`, `static_cast`, and `reinterpret_cast` all fail to compile, while at run time `dynamic_cast` returns a null pointer for failed pointer casts or throws an instance of `std::bad_cast` for failed reference casts. When implementing a cast-like operator, the failure response must be carefully considered. Whenever possible, compile-time failure is preferred to run time failure. `explicit_cast` and `literal_cast` fail at compile time. `union_cast` fails primarily at compile time. The interface casts and `ptr_cast` necessarily fail at run time.

For run time failure, it can be unclear clear whether returning a null value or throwing an exception is the best choice. This is especially so when providing general-purpose and/or open-source libraries, where it is impossible to anticipate all the contexts in which your code will find itself and unhelpful to prescribe limitations. In such situations, it is nice to be able to use a parameterizable policy, as with `interface_cast_addref`.

Shims

Shim: A thin, often tapered piece of material, used to fill gaps, make something level, or adjust something to fit properly.

This entire chapter revolves around one rather important imperfection that C++ shares with pretty much any language you can think of, so I'm going to start with the imperfection itself.

Imperfection: Logically related types in C++ can, and usually do, have incompatible interfaces and operations, rendering a generalized approach to type manipulation sometimes difficult and often impossible.

Needless to say, this is a pretty bold claim, and a serious problem. The concept of shims described here and the broader concept of explicit generalization supported by it have evolved in two separate threads over several years.

Ironically, shims first came about as a result of my naïve irritation with the specification of the `std::basic_string` template, insofar as it's not providing an implicit conversion operator. Thankfully, I woke up to myself before doing something as heinous as deriving from it and implementing a conversion operator in the derived class.[1] The original shim technique developed to address that case has, through a couple of evolutionary steps, ended up as the `c_str_ptr` access shim, which we see in section 20.6.1.

The second was a continual frustration over the inconsistencies between so-called smart pointers and their raw pointer equivalents. The technique that has evolved provides a unified syntax for dealing with pointers, whether they are raw, simple, smart, or too-smart-for-their-own-good.

20.1 Embracing Change and Enhancing Flexibility

Unrelenting exposure to change is about the only constant thing in our industry. Whether writing application or systems software, it is inevitable that you will need to change existing code [Glas2003]. You want to know when you make a change that it can be done with as little pain as possible, with a consequent minimization of bugs. When writing open-source libraries, you need to make your libraries as flexible as is reasonably possible, because there's no chance that you'll anticipate all the weird uses to which people will put them. Let's familiarize ourselves with a couple of problems that change presents.

---

[1] In my consultative work I have seen this very thing on more than one occasion. <Sigh!>

Because it supports a wide variety of expression of basic concepts, C++ can sometimes suffer from providing too many choices for representing the same concept. The most obvious example of this is that there are many different ways to represent strings. Not only are there different fundamental encodings (i.e., `char` or `wchar_t`), but also there is a large number of string classes, many having mutually incompatible syntax. The introduction of the standard library's `basic_string` template has helped somewhat, but it has also drawn critics ([Henn2002]), and does not answer all requirements. Being a general solution, there are some cases it cannot cater for, and some efficiencies it cannot take advantage of.

Consider the following extract defining a class to scope the current directory. (We saw some of the power of scoping classes in Chapter 6.)

```
template<typename C, . . .>
class current_directory_scope
{
public:
  explicit current_directory_scope(C const *dir);


  . . .

};
```

This interface is fine, as far as it goes. But if we want to use `std::string` in our client code, we are required to call its `c_str()` method in the client code, as in:

```
current_directory_scope    scope(s.c_str());
```

This ties in the client code to a particular string type (or rather a string model, one where the underlying C-style string is retrieved, or synthesized, via a `c_str()` method). That may not seem too great a problem in application code, although I maintain it is an unnecessary and undesirable restriction. But if the use of `current_directory_scope` was inside template code, this would limit its generality to those string classes that provide `c_str()` (and whose `c_str()` returns a C-style string[2]).

Of course, if we had control or influence[3] over the author of the library, we might ask them to provide an overload for the constructor to take `std::string const &`. But again, this ties us to a specific string type, reducing the generality of our component needlessly.

A second source of consternation is in the use of pointers, and smart pointers, and their mixing, especially in conditional expressions. Most authors of smart pointers wisely eschew providing implicit conversion operators. But a consequence of this is that the writing of algorithms designed to work with raw pointers and smart pointers alike is complicated, or made impossible.

```
template <typename T>
void pass_to_API_if_non_null(T pt)
```

---

[2]Well, you never know!

[3]Library vendors are eminently receptive to sensible requests for changes; as well as being a great impetus for improvement, it's also a boost to your ego to know that someone's using your libraries.

```
{
  if(NULL != pt)
  {
    ::SomeGlobalApiFunction(pt);
  }
}
```

This function works fine with raw pointers. It will also work with smart pointers that provide implicit conversion to their contained pointer type—we don't like those types, of course. But it will not work for smart pointers that wisely keep their pointer hidden under a bushel. For that, we would have to overload the method:

```
template <typename T>
void pass_to_API_if_non_null(std::auto_ptr<T> &pt)
{
  if(NULL != pt.get())
  {
    ::SomeGlobalApiFunction(pt.get());
  }
}
```

What if we need to provide similar "safe" functions for a number of different global/API functions and/or for other smart-pointer types? It's a lot of mundane, repetitive work.

There are myriad such examples of how syntax gets in the way of semantics. Dealing with them is very irksome: it can feel like the compiler is a niggardly nitpicking nanny, rather than your batman. When I change from one type to a semantically similar type, I want the compiler to sort things out for me. Of course it can't, unless we can give it a hand, so let's put some shims in the gaps and make things fit together properly.

The access shim concept (see section 20.6.1; [Wils2003c]) addresses the issue of rigidity in current_directory_scope and its use. Such classes can be given a high degree of generality and made able to deal with virtually any string type without introducing coupling or sacrificing efficiency. We'll see several examples of this throughout the remainder of the book.

By using attribute and logical shims (see sections 20.2 and 20.3; [Wils2003c]), raw vs. smart-pointer type problems are voided, and the generality and robustness (since we now have to change them much less frequently) of the algorithms is significantly increased.

The classic answer to everything in software engineering is to add a layer of indirection. This is the essence of what the shims concept is all about. But the layer is a very efficient layer, in most cases it adds no cost; where cost is involved, it is predominantly the case that is no more than would be incurred by equivalent conversion in client code. In any case, it is explicit, so the compiler is not bulking up (and slowing down) your code without being asked.

20.2   Attribute Shims

Definition: *Attribute Shims*

Attribute shims retrieve attributes or states of instances of the types for which they are defined.

The names of attribute shims take the form get_xxx, where xxx represents the particular attribute being accessed (except where they form part of a composite shim concept).

The values returned from attribute shims are always valid outside the instance of the shim, in cases where the shim is implemented by the creation of a temporary object.

Consider an illustrative example. The get_ptr attribute shim is a suite of functions that retrieve the pointer attributes of the types to which they are applied. We may define some of its members as follows:

Listing 20.1

```
template <typename T>
inline T *get_ptr(T *p)
{
  return p;
}
template <typename T>
inline T *get_ptr(std::auto_ptr<T> &p)
{
  return p.get();
}
template <typename T>
inline T const *get_ptr(std::auto_ptr<T> const &p)
{
  return p.get();
}
template <typename T>
inline T *get_ptr(comstl::interface_ptr<T> &p)
{
  return p.get_interface_ptr();
}
```

The get_ptr shim allows us to generalize our use of pointers. Consider the scenario where we are writing a functor to work with a sequence of pointers to instances of Resource (or rather of its polymorphic derived classes) in order to preprocess them by a visual system before rendering. Our functor might look like this:

Listing 20.2

```
struct resource_prerenderer
  : public std::unary_function<Resource *, void>
{
  resource_prerenderer(VisualSystem *vs)
    : m_vs(vs)
  {}
  void operator ()(Resource *resource)
  {
    m_vs->PreRender(resource);
```

```
    }
private:
  Resource  *m_vs;
};
```

The visible resources can be stored in a `VisibleList` instance via raw pointer (perhaps in a `vector<Resource*>`), because their lifetimes are controlled separately in the `ResourceManager` singleton [Gamm1995], and the contents of the `VisibleList` instance are vouched by the documented semantics of the class (see section 5.1). This means that the `VisibleList` can be very efficient, as our requirements dictate. We may now effect prerendering of all visible objects in the following fashion:

```
std::for_each( visible.begin(), visible.end()
             , resource_prerenderer(g_vs));
```

However, the system is now to be ported to another architecture, and the `Resource` instance lifetimes are no longer to be centrally managed. On the new architecture, `VisibleList` will store them as reference-counting instances using, say, some class `Resource_ptr`. What should we do? Create a separate functor to handle reference-counted objects, selecting the correct one via the preprocessor? Maintain a single `resource_prerender` functor but conditionally compile different `operator ()()` methods? What if the specifications change again? It all sounds like far too much work for this little pixie!

The answer is that we rewrite `resource_prerenderer` just once,[4] and then we never have to change it again (at least not in respect of changes to the pointer type). It would now look like this:

```
template <typename R>
struct resource_prerenderer
{
  . . .
  void operator ()(R &resource)
  {
    m_vs->PreRender(get_ptr(resource));
  }
  . . .
```

Given the available definitions of `get_ptr` shown earlier, our code will work whether `Resource` instances are stored as raw pointers or reference-counted pointers. It would even work if they were stored as `std::auto_ptrs`, but I know that you know not to try to place `auto_ptr` in standard library containers [Meye1998, Dewh2003].

---

[4]I'm with James L. Brooks [Broo1995] on this one. You will always write two versions, so don't try to do the ultimate generic version in the first.

20.3   Logical Shims

Definition: *Logical Shims*

Logical shims are a refinement of attribute shims in that they report on the state of an instance to which they are applied.

The names of logical shims take the form of an interrogative coupled with the particular attribute or state being queried. Examples would be `is_open`, `has_element`, `is_null`.

An obvious, and widely compatible, logical shim is `is_empty()`, which generalizes the accessing of state on any container type (for which it has been defined).

In my opinion, the authors of the standard library made a mistake in selecting `empty()` for the name of methods on various types which answer the question, "Is this instance empty?" as opposed to those effecting the imperative "Make this instance empty!" Not only is this not natural, it is inconsistent, both with other elements of the standard library—`erase()` is an imperative—but also with extant libraries, where it is more common to see `IsEmpty()` or `is_empty()`.

Not one to sit on a problem, I quickly gave life to the `is_empty()` logical shim. Some definitions:

Listing 20.3
```
template <typename C>
bool is_empty(C const &c)
{
  return c.empty();
}
bool is_empty(CString const &s)
{
  return s.IsEmpty();
}
bool is_empty(comstl::interface_ptr const &p)
{
  return NULL == p.get_interface_ptr();
}
```

Note that because of the standardized nature, and the large and increasingly established role of the standard library, the `is_empty()` shim general case—the second one in the list above—is defined in anticipation of its being applied to the standard library containers. While this borders on the presumptuous, and makes me a little nervous, the argument to the shim function is `const`, so unless you have encountered a class with an `empty()` method that is `const` but yet has modifying semantics, applying the general case should be safe. Bear it in mind though, there is no limit to the perversity of the code that people will dream up (see Appendix B).

20.4 Control Shims

Definition: *Control Shims*

Control shims define operations that are applied to the instances of the types for which they are defined.

The names of control shims take the form of an imperative element coupled with the particular attribute or state being modified. Examples would be `make_empty`, `dump_contents`.

Control shims are less widely used than attribute and logical shims, because generalization of operations is less ubiquitous than the accessing of attributes or states. (We saw a pair of control shims in section 6.2 when we talked about state scoping.) Control shims are not only used for designing flexible policy-based general components; they are also exceedingly useful tools for assisting in maintenance, especially in porting code.

Consider having some nontrivial code that makes extensive use of instances of one or more container types. Say it's the source for a Linux PC game. You then have a requirement to port it to an embedded game platform. As such you want to change the container type(s) used, and make use of a highly optimized in-house container library, specifically written for the new platform. Unfortunately, the container library was written a long time before the Standard Template Library (STL) *Sequence* and *Associative Container* concepts [Aust1999, Muss2001] became a widely accepted form, and so does not conform. What do you do?

Well, you could insist that the container library be rewritten to conform to the STL. Regrettably, the original authors long since left the company, and although they left a very comprehensive test suite[5] that gives you confidence in the quality of the container library, no one in the company has much expertise in the internals of this library. The changes would be nontrivial, deadlines are tight, and you cannot justify the risk of wholesale changes.

Alternatively, you could populate the source with `#ifdefs`, specializing client-code use of the container libraries (remember we're now conceptually dealing with two) via the preprocessor. This is a workable solution in the short term, but as an experienced cross-platform developer, you know this is just setting yourself up for more grief down the line.

The classic advice in these scenarios is to abstract all platform-specific code into separate implementation files, and use link-time selection to keep the messiness to a minimum. While this is great for truly platform-specific areas—file systems, memory mapping, synchronization objects—in some cases it is hopelessly naïve. In this case it is a bad idea because:

- You don't have time. This is the real world and you're playing catch-up with marketing.
- The code is extremely well meshed with the existing container class library.
- The speed advantage of the embedded container library relies in large measure on the use of inline functions, intrinsics, and inline assembler. Adding function call overhead would reduce speed and increase size, and you can afford neither.

---

[5]I know how realistic this is, but hey, I'm having a fantasy here.

Given these choices, most of us would go for the second option, and build in all the `#ifdefs` under the sun. The product would ship on time, but would become a maintainer's nightmare.[6] As soon as the developer who handled the first port to the new platform left the company, moved to another project, or perhaps even just got a full night's sleep, it would be impossible to enhance without adding bugs to one or the other (or both) implementations. Never mind adding another target platform!

So what's the answer? Shims, of course: attribute shims to get hold of elements; logical shims to ascertain container and element states; control shims to change the contents of the containers. `make_empty()` to clear the container of its elements; `insert_element()` to insert an element; `remove_element()` to remove an element; `get_nth_element()` to access an element by index.[7]

You can have a single code base, with perhaps only a single preprocessor conditional to typedef the container types, and you write and use shims that are highly efficient and are inlined with no cost by the compiler. The code barely has to change, and does so in ways that are either meaning positive or neutral at worst—`make_empty(cont);` is a lot more obvious to a non-STL developer than `cont.erase(cont.begin(), cont.end());`—such that you can test with all existing test cases on the original platform, knowing that you have effected no semantic changes whatsoever. When it comes time to add new container types for your next platform, you can do so without changing a character of the valuable and fragile application code.

20.5 Conversion Shims

Definition: *Conversion Shims*

Conversion shims operate by converting instances of the range of compatible types to a single target type.

The names of attribute shims take the form `to_xxx`, where `xxx` is the name of, or represents, the target type, for example, `to_int`.

The values returned from conversion shims may be provided by intermediate temporary objects, so must only ever be used from within the expression containing the shim.

We're going to see a lot more about conversion in the next subsection, so we'll leave most of this for then. However, an interesting example—since it demonstrates an alternate shim implementation strategy—is to be found in the implementation of STLSoft's `string_tokeniser` template,[8] which we had a little peek at in section 18.5.3. This behemoth of a template takes a whopping six template parameters—the excuse for this is that it's *very* fast [Wils2004a, Wils2003e]—for stipulating various permutations of string tokenization, such as delimiter type, what to do with blanks, and so on. Thankfully, all but two of these parameters are defaulted;

---

[6]In my first job in the commercial sector I worked on a code-base—used to implement ISDN basic rate servers and clients and primary-rate servers—that had 13-way conditional compilation for three processor architectures, four operating systems, and three physical guises. I witnessed changes being implemented on up to 20 different branches at any one time! Anything you can ever imagine about source management problems, I've seen it. Never again!

[7]Be aware that shims are not the be all and end all. See section 10.11 for a note of realism/caution.

[8]This is available on the CD, along with sufficiently helpful and exemplifying test programs.

these two are the type used to store the copy of the string to be tokenized (S) and the type of the iterator's value_type (V).

```
template< typename S /* string type, e.g string */
        , typename D /* delimiter type, e.g. char or wstring */
        , typename B = string_tokeniser_ignore_blanks<true>
        , typename V = S /* value type */
        , typename T = string_tokeniser_type_traits<S, V>
        , typename P = string_tokeniser_comparator<D, S, T>
        >
class string_tokeniser;
```

Dereferencing the iterator via operator *() to obtain its current value entails the creation of an instance of V. Since it is a template parameter, the string_tokeniser needs a mechanism to create the strings, and uses a control shim to do it.

The traits parameter, T, is used to abstract the manipulation of the types S and V. One of its main responsibilities is to define a static method called create(), which takes two parameters (of type S::const_iterator) that must return an instance of V. Hence T::create() is a control shim, and is an example of a shim implemented via the traits [Lipp1998] mechanism.

It defaults to string_tokeniser_type_traits<S, V>, which assumes that S and V both conform to the standard library's *String* model (C++-98: 21.3). The implementation of its create() is as follows:

```
static V create(S::const_iterator f, S::const_iterator t)
{
  return V(f, t);
}
```

This default implementation works for *any* string type that can be constructed from a bounding iterator range. To implement the shim for another string type can be done either by specializing the string_tokeniser_type_traits template, or by providing a custom traits type. In either case, you have effectively expanded the shim definition to incorporate the new type.

Imagine for a moment that we wanted to use the string_tokeniser with MFC's CString.[9] This class does not define any member types, so at first glance it would seem like a bit of a job to make it work. We have two choices. First, we could specialize stlsoft:: string_tokeniser_type_traits for MFC's CString:

Listing 20.4

```
namespace stlsoft
{
  template <>
  struct string_tokeniser_type_traits<CString>
```

---

[9]You only have to imagine it. I'm not going to actually make you do it.

```
  {
    . . .
    static CString create(TCHAR const *f, TCHAR const *t)
    {
      return CString(f, t - f);
    }
  };
};
```

We could then use it to populate a Win32 list-box control with the contents of the INCLUDE environment variable, using a windows control inserter functor [Wils2003g, Muss2001], as in:

```
CString                                  include = . . .
stlsoft::string_tokeniser<CString, TCHAR>  tokens(include, ';');

for_each(tokens.begin(), tokens.end(),
              listbox_back_inserter(hwndListBox));
```

The alternative would be to define our own custom traits type:

```
stlsoft::string_tokeniser< CString
                         , TCHAR
                         , stlsoft::string_tokeniser_ignore_blanks<true>
                         , CString_tokeniser_type_traits
                         >  tokens(include, ';');
```

The latter is more verbose as shown, but you could wrap the tokenizer parameterization in a typedef, so there's no great hardship. The benefit is that you're not poking something into another namespace, which has practical and theoretical difficulties, as we see in section 20.8.

(There's actually a third alternative in this specific case, but this uses a technique we look at in the next chapter; see section 21.3.)

20.6 Composite Shim Concepts

Definition: *Composite Shims*

Composite shims are a combination of two or more fundamental shim concepts.

The names of composite shims do not have a fixed convention, but rather take a name indicative of their purpose.

Composite shims obey the most restrictive rule, or combination of rules, from their constituent shims.

We'll illustrate the composite shim concept with the first, and most well used, composite shim concept, the access shim.

20.6.1 Access Shims

Definition: *Access Shims*

Access shims are a combination of *Attribute* and *Conversion* shims, which are used to access the values of the instances of the types for which they are defined.

The values may have to be synthesized via conversion shims.

The values returned from access shims may be provided by intermediate temporary objects, so must only ever be used from within the expression containing the shim.

In order to illustrate the access shims concept, we'll need to revisit our `current_directory_scope` class. To answer the criticisms we had earlier, we now add another constructor with the following form:

Listing 20.5
```
template<typename C, . . .>
class current_directory_scope
{
public:
  explicit current_directory_scope(C const *dir)
  {
    init_(c_str_ptr(dir));
  }
  template <typename S>
  explicit current_directory_scope(S const &dir)
  {
    init_(c_str_ptr(dir));
  }
private:
  void init_(C const *dir);
  . . .
```

Both constructors[10] use the `c_str_ptr`[11] shim to convert their argument type to `C const*`, which is passed to the `init_()` method, so that the class can be used with any string type for which the `c_str_ptr` shim is defined and accessible. Given the following `c_str_ptr` shims definitions:

Listing 20.6
```
inline char const *c_str_ptr(char const *s)
{
```

---

[10]You might think that only the second, template, constructor should be required. In an ideal world that is so, but some compilers get confused. In practice, it is necessary to provide both for some compilers, and only the second one for others, by resorting to the preprocessor.

[11]The `c_str_ptr` shim was originally called just `c_str`, but it had to be changed since users found it too confusing, and it was difficult to search for it and/or the string class method of the same name. Hindsight suggests there could still be a better and yet similarly succinct name, perhaps `c_string`, but we're stuck with it now.

```
    return s;
  }
inline wchar_t const *c_str_ptr(wchar_t const *s);
{
    return s;
  }
template <typename T>
inline T const *c_str_ptr(std::basic_string<T> const &s)
{
    return s.c_str();
  }
template <typename T>
inline T const
      *c_str_ptr(stlsoft::basic_frame_string<T> const &s)
{
    return s.c_str();
  }
```

we are able to use the `current_directory_scope` class with any of the following types:

```
char const                     *dir1 = "/";
std::basic_string<char>         dir2("/");
stlsoft::basic_frame_string<char> dir3("/");

current_directory_scope<char>   scope1(dir1); // ok
current_directory_scope<char>   scope2(dir2); // ok
current_directory_scope<char>   scope2(dir3); // ok
```

20.6.2   Return Value Lifetime

The keen-eyed among you may have spotted that the four `c_str_ptr` shims we just looked at are all attribute shims. Why cannot `c_str_ptr` just be defined as an attribute shim? To understand this we need to look at a shim with a nontrivial implementation, whose proper use relies on adherence to the rule regarding return values.

One of the reasons that the standard library's *String* model (C++-98: 21.3) does not stipulate a conversion operator is to facilitate storage of the contained sequence without a null terminator. This is a well-known idea that can be found in a variety of libraries. One such is the Win32's Security API's `LSA_UNICODE_STRING` type, which is defined as follows:

```
typedef struct _LSA_UNICODE_STRING
{
  unsigned short  Length;
  unsigned short  MaximumLength;
  wchar_t         *Buffer;
} LSA_UNICODE_STRING;
```

The extent of the string described by the structure is defined not by a null-terminating character, but by the `Length` member. In fact `Buffer` may not contain a null terminator at all. Given this, how do we access a C-style string in a generic (i.e., via `c_str_ptr`) fashion?[12]

The answer lies in the use of a proxy class, an instance of which is returned by the `c_str_ptr` shim function for this type, as in:

```
inline c_str_ptr_LSA_UNICODE_STRING_proxy
    c_str_ptr(LSA_UNICODE_STRING const &s)
{
  return c_str_ptr_LSA_UNICODE_STRING_proxy(s);
}
```

To acquire a C-style string from this requires that the proxy class provides and instantiates an appropriate character buffer and, in order to support identical syntax to other `c_str_ptr` shims, implements an implicit conversion operator. A simplified definition of this class is shown in Listing 20.7.

Listing 20.7
```
class c_str_ptr_LSA_UNICODE_STRING_proxy
{
public:
  typedef c_str_ptr_LSA_UNICODE_STRING_proxy  class_type;
public:
  explicit c_str_ptr_LSA_UNICODE_STRING_proxy(
                                  LSA_UNICODE_STRING const &s)
    : m_buffer(new WCHAR[1 + s.Length])
  {
    wcsncpy(m_buffer, s.Buffer, s.Length);
    m_buffer[s.Length] = L'\0';
  }
  ~c_str_ptr_LSA_UNICODE_STRING_proxy()
  {
    delete [] m_buffer;
  }
  operator LPCWSTR () const
  {
    return m_buffer;
  }
private:
  LPWSTR  m_buffer;
// Not to be implemented
private:
```

---

[12]We can't simply write a terminating null character into the buffer because we have no idea what other code might be doing with it. Even if we did not care about that, sometimes we'll have to operate with `const` instances. And even if we were reckless enough to `const_cast` that away, sometimes there will be no spare space to accommodate any more characters (i.e., `Length == MaximumLength`); that's the whole point of this type.

```
    void operator =(class_type const &rhs);
};
```

When `c_str_ptr` is applied to an instance of `LSA_UNICODE_STRING`, the string contents are copied into a null-terminated buffer. The shim's value is retrieved via the implicit conversion operator. In this way, this `c_str_ptr` and the proxy class work together to synthesize and provide access to a C-style string, which is the expected type obtained from the `c_str_ptr` shim.

Now we can see the reason for the restriction regarding the use of its return value. The proxy object exists only for the lifetime of the expression within which the shim is used. If the return value of the shim was to be saved and used outside of this expression, then undefined behavior would ensue.

```
LSA_UNICODE_STRING  lsa = . . .;
wchar_t const       *s  = c_str_ptr(lsa);
wputs(s);                                    // Danger, Will Robinson!
```

We look at the issue of *Return Value Lifetime* in detail in Chapter 31.

20.6.3 Generalized Type Manipulation

By now you hopefully see the power of shims, and how easy they usually are to implement. We're now able to work with any kind of string type in a consistent and generic fashion. This is extremely useful stuff. But it's possible to extend this a lot further. Let's look at a different scenario.

UNIX provides two common ways of inspecting file-system contents. The `opendir()` API provides functions to open a directory for enumeration via its `readdir()` function. This function returns a pointer to a `dirent` structure, which is required to provide a single member `d_name`, a character buffer containing the name of the current entry. The other API is based on the very powerful `glob()` function, which returns to its caller an array of pointers to entries that match a given search criteria.

UNIXSTL[13] provides wrapper sequence classes for these two APIs in the form of the `readdir_sequence` and `glob_sequence` classes. The `value_types` for them are, respectively, `struct dirent const*` and `char const*`. Writing code for one or the other, including functors and algorithms, is straightforward. But because of the difference in their value type, writing code that works with both can be a real pain.

Let's imagine that we want to write an algorithm—`sub_dir_count`—that can count the number of subdirectories of a given directory in the file system and also record their names in a container. It might look something like this:

Listing 20.8
```
bool is_dir(char const *entry); // Deduces entry type

template< typename S
```

---
[13]The STLSoft subproject that maps UNIX APIs to STL concepts.

```
        , typename C
        >
size_t sub_dir_count(S const &s, C &c)
{
  typedef typename S::const_iterator  const_it_t;
  const_it_t  begin   =   s.begin();
  const_it_t  end     =   s.end();
  size_t      cDirs   =   0;
  for(; begin != end; ++begin)
  {
    if(is_dir(*begin))
    {
      c.push_back(*begin);
      ++cDirs;
    }
  }
  return cDirs;
}
```

It could be used like this:

```
void process_entry(string const &s);

findfile_sequence entries("/");
vector<string>     directories;

size_t cDirs = sub_dir_count(entries, directories);

printf("Number of dirs = %u\n", cDirs);
for_each(directories.begin(), directories.end(), process_entry);
```

This compiles without any complaint for `glob_sequence` because its value type is `char const*`. However, it does not compile for `readdir_sequence`. What can we do about it?

We could create a separate version of the algorithm for `readdir_sequence`, but this is Nightmare on Maintenance Street. Furthermore, it requires programming effort in linear proportion to the number of mutually incompatible types we require such an algorithm to support.

Wouldn't it be far nicer to centralize the generality and rewrite it only once? By using the `c_str_ptr` access shim, we can do just that and can create a version that will work for any type:

Listing 20.9

```
template< typename S
        , typename C
        >
size_t sub_dir_count(S const &s, C &c)
{
  . . .
```

```
    for(; begin != end; ++begin)
    {
      if(is_dir(c_str_ptr(*begin)))
      {
        c.push_back(c_str_ptr(*begin));
        ++cDirs;
      }
    }
    . . .
```

It can now work for both the glob_sequence and for the readdir_sequence by
virtue of the c_str_ptr shim for struct dirent.

```
inline char const *c_str_ptr(struct dirent const *d)
{
  return (NULL != d) ? d->d_name : "";
}
```

20.6.4   Efficiency Concerns

In the sub_dir_count function, there were actually two calls to the c_str_ptr shim.
For types, such as struct dirent, where the shim acts as an attribute shim, the cost of ob-
taining the c-string pointer is very low, and will be optimized out on most compilers. However,
where the shim acts as a conversion shim, as with LSA_UNICODE_STRING, there will be nontrivial amounts of processing. Although each one of these will be virtually equivalent to any
manual string access, doing it additional times hardly represents efficient coding. What we can
do is rewrite the algorithm.

Listing 20.10
```
template< typename CH
        , typename C
        >
size_t record_if_dir(CH const *entry, C &c)
{
  return is_dir(entry) ? (c.push_back(entry), 1) : 0;
}
template< typename S
        , typename C
        >
size_t sub_dir_count(S const &s, C &c)
{
  . . .
  for(; begin != end; ++begin)
  {
    cDirs += record_if_dir(c_str_ptr(*begin), c);
  }
}
```

```
    return cDirs;
}
```

Now there is only one possible shim, in the call to `record_if_dir()`, within which the C-string is used twice in the raw, with maximal efficiency.

20.7   Namespaces and Koenig Lookup

The picture I've painted of shims seems almost perfect:[14] we've enhanced maintainability (comprehensibility/readability and modifiability), generality (reuse), all without sacrificing performance (when used correctly, anyway). But this is the real world, and nothing's ever perfect. As well as the restriction in the use of access shims to immediate expressions, there is another small problem.

So far I've not made any mention of namespaces, and all the examples appear to be in the global namespace. If all the types for which the shim you're using is defined are user-defined types, and are defined within the namespaces of their "shimmed" type, and the compiler(s) you are using support(s) Koenig lookup,[15] then you do not need to specify any using declarations, and the whole thing works like a treat. *Got all that?*

Koenig lookup (C++-98: 3.4.2)—also known as Argument-dependent Lookup [Vand2003])—is the mechanism whereby symbols from other namespaces may be accessed in another namespace, without being introduced via `using` declarations or directives (or `typedef` declarations), by virtue of being associated with a symbol that has been introduced. For example, in the following code the function `f` is defined with namespace `ns` and is not introduced into the (global) namespace of the `g()` function. However, because the variable `s` is of type `S`, which is defined in the namespace `ns`, `f` can be looked up in the namespace of `S`.

Listing 20.11

```
namespace ns
{
  struct S
  {};
  void f(S &)
  {}
}
void g()
{
  ns::S s;
  f(s); // f looked up in same namespace as S
}
```

Unfortunately, this being the real world, several compilers do not fully implement Koenig lookup. Furthermore, we often want to define shims to include basic types and those defined within the global namespace. In such cases, we need to use `using` declarations between the

---

[14]At least I hope you think so!

[15]Digital Mars prior to v8.34, Visual C++ prior to v7.1, and Watcom do not support Koenig lookup

declaration of the types and the algorithms, classes, or client code that is implemented in terms of the shims. With the majority of the time this is simple both to do and to understand, but there are occasional confusions when dealing with heavily derivative code.

In the long run, it'd be nice for popular shims (such as `get_ptr`, `c_str_ptr`/`c_str_len`) to be declared and defined in the namespace along with their requisite types, including those in the `std` namespace, for example, `c_str_ptr(basic_string<T> const &)`. That is unlikely to happen soon, if at all, so you'll need to bear in mind that you may have to "use" them to use them.

Furthermore, several types for which we'd want to define shims exist in the global namespace (e.g., `char const*`, `struct dirent`, `LSA_UNICODE_STRING`). Because it is more than a little presumptuous to define shims in the global namespace or even in the `std` namespace,[16] I define all my shims within the `stlsoft` namespace. This serves the dual purposes of not polluting the global namespace and also of having a single namespace within which all the shims that I use are defined. For any components using the shims that are defined within the `stlsoft` namespace, or within any of its sub-namespaces [Wils2003b], they pick up the necessary shim definitions even when Koenig lookup does not apply (whether that is because the type is a fundamental type or whether the compiler does not support it).

For classes that I write that are not part of STLSoft, for example, application code, I simply define their shims along with the components—either in an application-specific namespace or within the global namespace—and then "use" them within the `stlsoft` namespace. Let's have a look how this works in practice.

Consider some client code, in the namespace `client`, which uses the third-party component `tp_string` that resides in the `third_party` namespace and the Win32 `LSA_UNICODE_STRING` type. In order to write our client code to select the `c_str_ptr` shim for either type, we need to ensure that the requisite shim functions are visible in the `client` namespace. Listing 20.12 shows one way that this is achieved.

Listing 20.12
```
// tp_string.h
namespace third_party
{
  class tp_string
  {
    . . .
    wchar_t const *c_str() const;
  };
  inline wchar_t const *c_str_ptr(tp_string const &s)
  {
    return s.c_str();
  }
}
// Client.cpp
```

---

[16]In fact, the standard prescribes that the only things you may add to the `std` namespace are specializations of templates that exist in `std`.

```
namespace Client
{
  using stlsoft::c_str_ptr;      // for LSA_UNICODE_STRING
#if !defined(ACMELIB_COMPILER_SUPPORTS_KOENIG_LOOKUP)
  using third_party::c_str_ptr; // for tp_string
#endif /* ! ACMELIB_COMPILER_SUPPORTS_KOENIG_LOOKUP */

  template <typename S>
  void puts(S const &s)
  {
    ::putws(c_str_ptr(s));
  }
}
```

The first using declaration is necessary because LSA_UNICODE_STRING type is defined in the global namespace, so Koenig lookup does not apply. The second using declaration is only needed when the compiler does not support Koenig lookup. But really we've got four lines of gunk when we only need one. The better way to do this is to add the following to the end of tp_string.h:

```
namespace stlsoft
{
  using third_party::c_str_ptr;
}
```

Now the preprocessor compiler discrimination and the third_party using declaration can be omitted, leaving us with a simple clean using stlsoft::c_str_ptr. In your own work, you should follow this convention: define the namespace within which your shims will reside, and then either define them in that namespace, or introduce them into that namespace via a using declaration. In any code, whether library or application, that uses the shims, you have one using declaration to introduce all potentially applicable shim functions.

Naturally, in the long run, I'd like to see shims incorporated into the standard library. What I'd suggest in that case, however, would be that shims are given their own namespace—std::shims—within which users would be free to define their own overloads of extant shims or to introduce their own shims.

20.8 Why Not Traits?

We've seen some shims implemented as traits, others can be implemented as functions, and others again as functions that return temporary instances of proxy classes. Throughout parts of this discussion, you may have wondered whether traits [Stro1997] could be used to provide similar generalization facilities to shims. Indeed, some commentators have suggested that shims should *only* be implemented using traits. There are a number of reasons why the traits technique cannot be the only implementation technique for shims.

First, functions have the capability to deduce type automatically, whereas traits, being template classes, must always be explicitly qualified. This is not only of syntactic significance. It means that traits can only be used in contexts in which type is known.

Second, shims can directly incorporate existing (or new!) C-functions without any C++ function or class wrapping.

Third, traits are not a good conceptual fit for this purpose. A shim concerns itself with only one particular facet, conversion, or manipulation on a (usually) loosely associated range of types. Conversely traits can, and usually do, define and associate a number of characteristics and operations with a (usually) closely related range of types. In this way, the classes and/or functions that constitute a particular shim do not become bloated with accreted unnecessary or unspecific baggage, which is something that (regrettably) happens to traits.

However, the most compelling reason for rejecting an exclusively traits-based implementation is to do with namespaces. If shims were based on traits, we would have two choices for the specialization. We could include the header in which the template definition resided into the header for our code, and then specialize within the main namespace in our own header. This would introduce a great deal of physical coupling [Lako1996], which I hate (and you do too, I'm sure).

Or we could forward declare the template in its original namespace within our header—still defining our specialization in the original namespace—to avoid the coupling. This fails in many ways. One such is that standard library constructs supply type definitions that are compatible with, but may not be identical to, the expected published definitions [Dewh2003]. The construct might be defined within a namespace that is actually defined (directly or indirectly) via a macro; if we did not include any headers within which this macro was defined, we would be specializing a template in the wrong namespace, and hence specializing something that does not exist.

20.9   Structural Conformance

Shims represent a distillation of what is known as structural conformance. Basically, this says that things that look the same (are expected to) act the same.

Classically (by which I mean pretemplate generics), C++ focused on what is sometimes called named conformance, which essentially refers to the situation whereby an overridden method in a derived class must conform to the method in the parent class. Naturally, this is based around *vtable* inheritance-based polymorphism.

Structural conformance is both more useful, and more fraught with problems. It usually pertains to template functions. As we saw in section 20.6.3, the `readdir_sequence` and `glob_sequence` classes exhibit structural conformance with respect to the `sub_dir_count` algorithm.

Simplistically speaking, structural conformance guarantees that types are compile-time compatible, whereas named conformance guarantees that they are run time compatible. However, there is a lot of gray in those distinctions. The weakness of structural conformance is that it is not difficult to have structurally conformant types that do semantically nonconformant things. What is often overlooked, however, is that it is not particularly hard to have semantically nonconformant classes that exhibit putative named conformance. The only difference is that the set of types to which one might apply generic code is potentially unbounded, whereas the set of types that will exhibit named conformance is bound to those that are related by inheritance. The second set is smaller, and more subject to the keen-eyed instincts of experienced C++ programmers,[17] and non-conformance is much more rare but it is still possible.

The question as to whether structural conformance (with the expectation of semantic conformance) is a good thing is another of those debates that rage endlessly: just do a quick search on the comp.* newsgroups, and give yourself a few days. Some hold the opinion that reliance on structural conformance is at once restrictive, prescriptive, and fragile. It locks us into a correspondence between syntax and semantics that often, in hindsight, would be better discarded or modified. Furthermore, the expectation that all parties will respect expressed, but not mandated, conventions in the unbounded set of types expressible to our generic components could be deemed impossibly optimistic.

I can certainly see the logic in that. When you look at the nastiness that is the naming of several standard library function methods, such as empty(), we see the conflict between conformance and freedom. It's rare to see a class these days with a method empty() that does not mean *is empty?* but that is only as a result of the standard library forcing its structural conformance on the whole development community. Previously, you would be able to find libraries where the naming was unambiguous.

Detractors argue that structural conformance represents brittleness at best and subversion at worst. They are largely correct. But what is the alternative? Pretty much every aspect of naming in C++ (and most other languages, for that matter) is reliant on convention, and it is absolutely necessary for comprehensibility. What are we to do about empty()? Should we maintain that it is ill named, stipulate that all our own libraries will use it to mean *make empty!* and supply a separate method is_empty() for the current semantic? All that will do is confine us to a backwater of our own making.

20.9.1   Semantic Conformance

Shims represent a convention whereby structural conformance is extended to include an explicit semantic for each shim. Naturally, this is only achieved by voluntary adherence to the semantics of a given shim. We must ensure that shims are named appropriately; hence the distinct naming conventions for the different shim concepts.

Where we compromise is in readability against potential ambiguity. Thus it can be argued that c_str_ptr() is mildly ambiguous and should have been called access_c_str(). However, I would struggle to see how is_null(), get_ptr(), or make_empty() are ambiguous in any reasonable estimation.

Overall, I acknowledge the problems of structural conformance, but don't see a better alternative. Using shims provides a significant boost toward avoiding the problems of structural conformance, but they are not a complete solution, since such cannot exist.

---

[17]It's conceivable that as the next generation of C++ programmers grow up seeing dynamic (*vtable*) and static (template) polymorphism as equally natural mechanisms, this differential will lessen. But it's hard for the old dogs to call this one, since we've already been through our learning process.

20.10   Breaking Up the Monolith

One of the biggest problems in object-oriented design, for most object-oriented languages, but especially for C++, is the business of determining the level of encapsulation of the operations for a given type. For some types it can be impossible to come to an optimal balance between the requirements of encapsulation and usability. Consider the example of a file.

If we encapsulate a system file handle within a class, we will provide operations to open, close, read-from, and write-to the file. What if we then want to interface with another API that uses a file? For example, we might want to use memory-mapped I/O. We have two choices. One option is to include memory-mapping operations in our file class. We're then on a slippery slope. We might subsequently want to, say, use the file handle on Win32 in combination with an IO Completion Port [Rich1997]. Soon our file class is becoming more of an I/O class. What's next—methods for opening sockets and manipulating IP addresses?

A second approach is to have a class framework, and to declare various classes as friends, so `MemoryMap` and `CompletionPort` classes would be declared as friends of our `File` class. I barely need to comment that this increases the physical coupling [Lako1996] and the logical fragility of the entire framework. Not to mention the nightmare that becomes the binary distribution of the framework. We've seen notable examples of just how bad this approach can get in the real world. This problem's not just restricted to C++. Although there are several good examples of this bad situation in C++ libraries, there are better examples in languages that are supposed evolutionary successors of C++.

A third approach is to have the underlying resource handle be publicly accessible. The problem here, of course, is that it is far too easy to break the encapsulation, since the only thing keeping it is the assumption that all developers will understand the details of any such direct access that they make, and will not make any mistakes. Since even the best developers make simple mistakes, this is a reckless approach.

The final approach is to have read-only implicit conversion operators. This is no less horrible than the others. You can close a file handle behind the back of the File class instance. Need I say more?

There's no wonder, when you consider these options, that many programmers favor using C-APIs, or prefer to stick to standard C++ where all these egregious interdependencies are "hidden" inside, or at least not commented upon. The fact is, there is no right approach here, and I'm not going to try to pretend that there is one. Wherever possible, you are going to have more success by keeping your classes small and simple. But there will inevitably be compromises.

What I can tell you, though, is that shims are *extremely* helpful in this regard. Using shims you can write classes that can interoperate, but that do not need to be aware of each other's natures in any way. You do not need to write monolithic classes, or monolithic class frameworks (i.e., you can leave the `friend` declarations at home); you do not need to make members publicly accessible; you do not need to provide implicit conversion operators. You will still have to compromise and make the underlying resource handles accessible, but this can be via shims whose invocation is never implicit. Thus, I would write a `File` class that had a simple set of operations and that provided its internal handle—int on UNIX; HANDLE on Win32—via a `get_handle()` shim. Then the `MemoryMap` class would be defined with a template constructor that uses the `get_handle()` shim to elicit the file handle associated with its argument, as in:

```
class MemoryMap
{
public:
  template <typename F>
  explicit MemoryMap(F f)
    : m_f(get_handle(f))
  {
    . . .
```

And so the classes can interoperate without knowing anything about each other:

```
File        f("/ImperfectsC++/readme.txt");
MemoryMap   mm(f);
```

Naturally, there's nothing stopping someone from making pathological calls:

```
File        f("/ImperfectsC++/readme.txt");
close(get_handle(f)); // Now f's dtor will crash!
```

But then there's nothing stopping anyone from casting an int to a vector<string>* when you get down to it; if you want to have an elephant in your drawing room, I'm not going to tell it to pack its trunk!

20.11 Shims: Coda

I hope you're convinced of the utility and power of shims, and I encourage you to incorporate them in your work and take advantage of the low-cost and easily comprehensible generalization that they afford. But before any of the early adopters among you go away and start making everything use shims for everything, I'd like to make a note of caution. As with anything else in software engineering (and, waxing philosophical, in life, too), they are not a panacea, and they can be used to excess. They are not intended to be the prime mechanism of object manipulation. Notwithstanding the practical issues with respect to namespaces, if every second line in your code uses a shim, you've pretty much left the object-oriented world behind[18] and started a new realm of attribute-based, almost declarative, programming. Too many shims can make your code virtually unreadable.

We've seen that there is a downside to using conversion shims, or any composite shim comprising the conversion shim concept, wherein the return values can only be used within the lifetime of the expression containing the shim. A consequence of this is that one may be required to make multiple shim calls within a function or, where possible, restructure the function to only require one call to the shim. These issues are eminently surmountable in practice, but nonetheless require a level of cognizance of the particular shim concept that one is using, in much the same way that one must be mindful of the particular iterator concept when using a given STL sequence and its iterators.

To my mind, shims are, when used correctly, a powerful adjunct to "normal" C++ programming, and represent an excellent addition to the imperfect practitioner's tool kit.

---

[18]Of course, some would say that's not a bad thing.

## CHAPTER 21

Veneers

Veneer: A thin leaf or layer of a more valuable or beautiful material for overlaying an inferior one.

Veneers are used to layer type, functionality, or both, over existing types in a fine-grained manner. A veneer is often used to add that "final touch" to an existing, substantial type. It may also be a way to bind specific behavior to a simple type. Think of veneers as being a jar of fine polish in your cognizant-conversion toolbox.

Definition: *Veneers*

A veneer is a template class with the following characteristics:

1. It derives, usually publicly, from its primary parameterizing type.

2. It accommodates, and adheres to, the polymorphic nature of its primary parameterizing type. This means that a veneer cannot define any virtual methods of its own, though it can override those defined by its primary parameterizing type.

3. It may not define any nonstatic member variables.

The consequence of 2 and 3 is that a veneer may not change the memory footprint of its primary parameterizing type, and this is achieved by virtue of the *Empty Derived Optimization* (EDO; see section 12.4), a very widely supported optimization. In other words, instances of a veneer composite have the same size as the primary parameterizing type.

These constraints distinguish the veneer concept from similar concepts and are provided to ensure that it is legitimate for veneer types to do two things that are normally proscribed by accepted C++ good practice: passing arrays of inherited types by pointer and deriving from non-polymorphic types.

We saw the problem of arrays of inherited types in Chapter 14, along with the `array_proxy` template class, which may be used by libraries to protect themselves against inappropriate use. The `array_proxy` enforces the rejection of unsuitable types being passed as arrays, while specifically allowing the expected/defining type of the array and any derived types that have the same memory footprint. Veneers represent the other side of the solution to this problem, in that they help enforce design decisions and provide a measure of protection when used with functions that are not protected by `array_proxy` or an equivalent mechanism.

Before I introduce the second, more commonly applied characteristic of veneers, I want to reiterate what was said in Chapter 14 about using arrays of inherited types: *Don't do it!* It's a

hazardous thing to do, often indicates bad (or at least hasty) design, and will get you cutting re-
marks in code reviews unless you can justify why you've done so. Given that, however, you
may have cause to occasionally define such functions, and I've no doubt that you'll come across
them, so one aspect of the veneer concept is to give you some measure of protection when you
must work in this fashion.

The second feature of veneers, whose use is significantly less contentious, is in the requirement to respect the polymorphic nature of the parameterizing type, which legitimizes the application of veneers to, and hence the inheritance from, nonpolymorphic types, a practice that is
normally frowned upon.

Veneers have a broad conceptual scope. Where one constraint pertains to the classic virtual
function based polymorphic capabilities of C++, the other finds utility in C++'s generic programming capabilities. Veneers can be put to a wide variety of uses, sometimes quite surprising
ones, and this chapter illustrates both aspects of the concept by demonstrating some of these
uses.

21.1 Lightweight RAII

Sometimes we may find that a particular class does almost everything we want, but lacks that
last little feature. This is the classic circumstance in which one chooses to inherit.

The STLSoft libraries define a performance counter class model. The UNIXSTL and Win-
STL subprojects each define a class—performance_counter—that implements the functionality prescribed by the model. The classes have two epoch variables, representing the start
and end of the measured interval. For efficiency reasons the member variables are not initialized
in the constructor but are set via the start() and stop() methods, respectively. Under certain circumstances, however, it would be helpful to have the member state initialized upon
construction.

This can easily be achieved using the STLSoft performance_counter_initialiser
veneer. It is defined as follows:

Listing 21.1

```
template <typename C>
class performance_counter_initialiser
    : public C
{
public:
  performance_counter_initialiser()
  {
    C::start(); // Initialise interval start member
    C::stop();  // Initialise interval end member
  }
};
```

The implementation is obvious and a classic veneer. It derives from its parameterizing type,
and it adds nothing to the size of the parameterizing type. Instead it enhances the functionality
provided by the parameterizing type: in this case initializing both epoch member variables to

ensure that all subsequent calls on the instance will yield meaningful intervals. It can be applied to any class that conforms to a simple set of constraints, which is that the parameterizing type has a `start()` method and a `stop()` method, both of which take no nondefault parameters.

```
#ifdef WIN32
  typedef winstl::performance_counter            base_counter_t;
#else
  typedef unixstl::performance_counter           base_counter_t;
#endif /* operating system */
typedef performance_counter_initialiser<base_counter_t>
                                               counter_t;
```

The functionality is provided in the constructor, wherein the method calls are qualified with the base class type C. This is to ensure that the parameterizing type has these methods. If the calls were not qualified in this way, the template could be applied to any type given the presence of free functions `start()` and `stop()`.

21.2   Binding Data and Operations

When using data structures and a (C-)API (see section 3.2), it is common practice to create wrapper classes for the data structures and to take advantage of C++'s built-in support for resource cleanup through the mechanism of object destruction. As we know all too well from experience, it is also common to quickly accrete functionality for doing "just that one extra feature" and end up with a bloated class with lots of dependencies.

As we saw in Chapters 3 and 4, life in C++ is thankfully a lot richer than some instructional texts would have us believe, where types exist either as plain-old-data (POD; see Prologue), or as rich classes with tight access control and fully fledged semantics. Often what is needed is something in the middle of the spectrum. For now, let's assume we only need to be part way along.

The COM VARIANT type is a discriminated union, in the form of a 16-byte structure that is used to contain, or hold pointers to, C and COM types. Because COM is not C++-specific, VARIANT is a C-compatible type. Hence the VARIANT API is a set of C functions that initialize, copy, and uninitialize the structures. Obviously such an arrangement—raw structures (sometimes) holding allocated resources—is a leading candidate for wrapping in the safety of a C++ class, and there have been several developed, such as CComVariant (Active Template Library), COleVariant (Microsoft Foundation Classes), _variant_t (provided with the Visual C++ compiler), and my own Variant. While there are legitimate criticisms of all these classes, I'm not necessarily saying that any particular ones are bad or shouldn't be used. What we're going to do is see if they are necessary, and in so doing exemplify another kind of veneer.

The work I'm going to describe is an extensible type-safe generic logging subsystem, based on previous work of a lesser scope that I designed for a medium-traffic application server a couple of years ago. The requirements were:

• Message-based—facilitate multiple language support
• Instance-oriented—messages are associated with application instances

- Pluggable—the ability to plug in different log recipients (file, network, memory) at run time
- Efficient—minimum amount of data traveling; minimum call cost in the calling code
- General—can accommodate a wide (though limited) range of types
- Extensible—new message ids can be added without breaking existing code
- Type safe—no `printf(...)`-like opacity; must break at compile time if a message definition is changed such that the argument list is changed

To cater for these requirements, the foundation of the API is the `ILog` interface, which looks like the following:

```
struct ILog
{
  virtual void Log( AIID_t const  &instanceId,
                    MsgId_t const &msgId,
                    size_t        cArgs,
                    VARIANT       args[]) = 0;
};
```

Different implementing instances could be plugged in—via a `SetLog()` function—even chained together, at the will of the implementer of the given client process. The current active log was accessed via the free-function `GetLog()`. Hence one could issue a log entry by the following:

```
GetLog()->Log(instId, msgId, 2, &args[0]);
```

That seems to give us the message-based, instance-oriented, pluggable, and general characteristics, but we're still some way from a foolproof (and attractive[1]) system.

21.2.1   pod_veneer

If we want to have a type safe yet general approach to the types of the arguments, it suggests that templates are going to be involved. The first template we need is the `pod_veneer` template, which applies immutable RAII (see section 3.5) to POD types.

Listing 21.2
```
template< typename T
        , typename CF // Constructor function
        , typename DF // Destructor function
        >
class pod_veneer
  : public T
{
```

---

[1]Software is a lot like maths. Oftentimes if your solution doesn't feel elegant, it's likely not ready.

```
    typedef pod_veneer<T, CF, DF>   class_type;
public:
  pod_veneer()
  {
    CF()(static_cast<T*>(this));   // Construct the pod
  }
  ~pod_veneer()
  {
    constraint_must_be_pod(T);
    constraint_must_be_same_size(class_type, T);
    DF()(static_cast<T*>(this));   // Destroy the pod
  }
};
```

The veneer takes a POD-type parameter, from which it inherits, along with two functor types. In the constructor it executes the constructor function type on itself, and in the destructor it executes the destructor function type on itself; in effect it binds operations to the raw (POD) data. Note also that it uses two constraints. The constraint_must_be_pod() is used to ensure that its primary parameterizing type is POD. The constraint_must_be_same_size() (see section 1.2.5) is used to ensure that the parameterization of the template has obeyed EDO. So how does this help us with our logging API?

Clearly we're going to use the pod_veneer on the VARIANT type. We could define the following construction and destruction functors:

Listing 21.3
```
struct variant_init
{
  void operator ()(VARIANT &var)
  {
    ::VariantInit(&var);
  }
};
struct variant_clear
{
  void operator ()(VARIANT &var)
  {
    ::VariantClear(&var);
  }
};
```

These functors simply translate the requisite functions from the VARIANT API into a form digestible to the template; because pod_veneer is a class template, we cannot use the VariantInit() and VariantClear() functions to instantiate it as we would if it was a function template.

21.2.2 Creating Log Messages

The generated class MSG_BASE is used to provide the translation from a generic set of parameters to a call to Log::Log(). To do this it takes the arguments, packs them into an appropriately sized array of pod_veneer<VARIANT, . . .>, and writes that array to the log.

Listing 21.4

```
typedef pod_veneer< VARIANT
                  , variant_init
                  , variant_clear
                  >       VARIANT_veneer;

class MSG_BASE
{
public:
  template <typename T1>
  MSG_BASE(AIID_t const &aiid, MsgId_t const &msgId, T1 const &a1)
  {
    VARIANT_veneer  args[1];
    InitialiseVariant(args[0], a1);
    STATIC_ASSERT(dimensionof(args) == 1);
    GetLog()->Log(aiid, msgId, dimensionof(args), args);
  }
  template <typename T1, typename T2>
  MSG_BASE(AIID_t const &aiid . . ., T1 const &a1, T2 const &a2)
  {
    VARIANT_veneer  args[2];
    InitialiseVariant(args[0], a1);
    InitialiseVariant(args[1], a2);
    STATIC_ASSERT(dimensionof(args) == 2);
    GetLog()->Log(aiid, msgId, dimensionof(args), args);
  }
  template <typename T1, typename T2, typename T3>
  MSG_BASE(AIID_t const &aiid . . . T1 const &a2, T1 const &a3)
  {
    VARIANT_veneer  args[3];
    InitialiseVariant(args[0], a1);
    InitialiseVariant(args[1], a2);
    InitialiseVariant(args[2], a3);
    STATIC_ASSERT(dimensionof(args) == 3);
    GetLog()->Log(aiid, msgId, dimensionof(args), args);
  }
  . . . // Constructors with more parameters
// Not implemented
private:
  . . . // Hide copy ctor/assignment op
};
```

The `InitialiseVariant` functions are a suite of overloaded `inline` free functions that initialize a `VARIANT` from a set of types and that do not throw any exceptions.

```
void InitialiseVariant(VARIANT &var, char const *v);
void InitialiseVariant(VARIANT &var, wchar_t const *v);
void InitialiseVariant(VARIANT &var, uint16_t v);
void InitialiseVariant(VARIANT &var, sint32_t v);
void InitialiseVariant(VARIANT &var, double v);
. . .
```

21.2.3 Reducing Waste

In fact, there's actually inefficiency in the picture I just painted. Because the overload conversion functions initialize the `VARIANT` before instantiating it, we don't need to initialize the variant in the array construction; we can do nothing, knowing that the initialization functions will handle this for us. The actual implementation uses `noop_function<VARIANT>`, which does surprisingly little.

Listing 21.5
```
template <typename T>
struct noop_function
    : public std::unary_function<T const &, void>
{
  void operator ()(T const & /* t */)
  {} // A minimalist functor
};


typedef pod_veneer< VARIANT
                  , noop_function<VARIANT>
                  , variant_clear
                  >     VARIANT_veneer;
```

Now we've actually taken a step back from RAII to RRID (see section 3.4). This is appropriate in this instance because the log API does not throw exceptions, nor do the initialization functions: if they cannot allocate some resources to initialize the `VARIANT` with the appropriate value, they are guaranteed to initialize it to `VT_EMPTY`. This is an artifact of the execution context dictated by the requirements of the logging subsystem. In the general case you may choose to throw allocation failure exceptions in the initialization functions (though that does leave the question as to who's going to log the failure of the log), in which case you would use `variant_init` as originally described.

There are two important features to note about what we've done. First, we've ensured that the initialized `VARIANT` array instances are destroyed, no matter what, because the destructor of the `pod_veneer` will call the function operator of `variant_clear` for each constructed instance. The language guarantees that this will happen. Of course, this would be the case with a full-fledged `VARIANT` class. However, we *know* that an array of `pod_veneer<VARIANT, ...>` is safely convertible to `VARIANT*` because `pod_veneer` guarantees this to be the case.

Another variant class may exhibit the same behavior, but it may not. You won't find out at compile time (see section 1.4), and there's nothing to stop an update to the class implementation from changing it even if it currently works.

The second feature is an issue of efficiency. Because in the actual implementation we guaranteed that the `InitialiseVariant()` functions do not throw, and null initialize the variants on failure, we chose to have `pod_veneer` do no work in its constructors. This was achieved by parameterizing it with another type, a type that could be a member type of `MSG_BASE`. Hence we can stipulate behavior by policy, and that policy type can be centralized. This provides a great deal of flexibility when the API is put to use on another project or the assumptions of the current project change. The only ways to change policy in the same way when using `VARIANT` wrapper classes from external sources are either to place them in parameterizable veneers or to select different wrapper classes by policy. Neither of those options is attractive from either a maintenance or effort point of view. Remember that there is no reason other than automatic destruction for having fully fledged `VARIANT` wrapper classes in this context. We must use the `InitialiseVariant()` functions, in order for the generic log-argument mechanism to work. Hence, the only functionality we need wrapped up in objects is resource initialization and resource destruction. We've got all the power we need, and none of the dependencies or costs (i.e., inefficiencies) we don't need.

21.2.4   Type-safe Message Classes

We've seen the point of the `pod_veneer`, but I'd like to just finish off the discussion by describing how it all fits together, with all the requirements fulfilled. The message ids are maintained in a database, from which two files are produced. One is a binary file for use with a fast message lookup mechanism when the logs are being inspected (either at run time or offline). The other is a header with definitions of generated message classes such as the following:

Listing 21.6

```
class MSG_RESOURCE_NOT_FOUND
  : public MSG_BASE
{
public:
  MSG_RESOURCE_NOT_FOUND(UINT id)
    : MSG_BASE(AIID_NULL, MSGID_RESOURCE_NOT_FOUND, id)
  {}
  MSG_RESOURCE_NOT_FOUND(AIID_t const &instanceId, UINT id)
    : MSG_BASE(instanceId, MSGID_RESOURCE_NOT_FOUND, id)
  {}
};
class MSG_BAD_CAST
  : public MSG_BASE
{
public:
  MSG_BAD_CAST(char const *expression, int level)
    : MSG_BASE(AIID_NULL, MSGID_BAD_CAST, expression, level)
  {}
```

```
   MSG_BAD_CAST(AIID_t const &instanceId, char const *expr, int level)
     : MSG_BASE(instanceId, MSGID_BAD_CAST, expr, level)
   {}
};
```

Messages are logged by using temporaries of these classes, as in:

```
if(!resmgr.Contains(rsrcId))
{
  MSG_RESOURCE_NOT_FOUND(rsrcId);
}
```

So how does it square up? Have we achieved the things—over and above those provided by the `Log` interface API—that were stipulated in our requirements?

- Type safety: It is as type safe as it is possible to get with C++, that is, 100 percent but for a few implicit integer conversions, and possible confusion over 0 (although we could use safer `NULL` now, which would help).
- Extensibility: New messages are defined in the database, and their type-safe wrapper classes, with exact arguments, are generated automatically.
- Generality: It works with any `VARIANT`-compatible type.
- Efficiency: Everything that can be inlined is inlined, and we are able to parameterize our veneer to prevent unnecessary work being done.

21.3   Rubbing Up to Concepts

When we looked at conversion shims, we saw that one answer to making `CString` work with our string tokenizer (see section 20.5) was to specialize the traits template and provide the necessary types. While this solution worked perfectly well, we've run into one of the problems with the traits technique. It's great if all we want to use the `CString` for is with one tokenizer type. But consider now that we want to use Acme Web Software's template, `html_link_parser`, which parses HTML documents and places all the hyperlinks in a container of strings. As is the case with the string tokenizer, `acmeweb::html_link_parser` is parameterized by the string type and uses an `html_string_traits` template to deduce string characteristics.

The default definition of `acmeweb::html_string_traits` reasonably requires that its parameterizing string type conforms to the standard library's *String* model (C++-98: 21.3) and assumes most cases will use `std::string`. However, this is not always possible or optimal. So to use `CString` with `html_link_parser`, what are our alternatives?

We could simply go the hard-coded route, and specialize `html_string_traits` for `CString`. But we've already done a specialization for the string tokenizer. Good sense, programming lore, and the instinctive apathy of all good software engineers tells us that this is wrong. Good software engineering practice involves doing things twice, once to learn, once to generalize. If we come across a third processing class from Job Creation Incorporated, do we define a third specialization? A one-time only alternative to this is to give `CString` a serious promotion into the big league, and let it parade around in team colors. Sounds like a problem for a veneer.

It's really simple, and it looks like this.

Listing 21.7

```
class CString_veneer
  : protected CString
{
public:
  typedef TCHAR         value_type;
  typedef TCHAR        *iterator;
  typedef TCHAR const *const_iterator;
  typedef TCHAR        *pointer;
  typedef TCHAR const *const_pointer;
  typedef size_t        size_type;
// Construction
public:
  explicit CString_veneer(const_pointer s);
  explicit CString_veneer(const_pointer from, const_pointer to);
// Iteration
public:
  const_iterator  begin() const;
  const_iterator  end() const;
// Access
public:
  const_pointer c_str() const;
};

inline TCHAR const *c_str_ptr(CString_veneer const &s) // Shim
{
  return s.c_str();
}
```

You might be saying "But it's missing some methods: I can't see some constructor over-loads, and operators, or the find_kitchen_sink_last_not_of_where_next_to_larder() method." Well that's perfectly fine. What we have here is a beautifully contained playpen in which to mess around. We know the starting point: the embarrassingly naked (from the STL point of view of, anyway) CString. We know the end point: the types, variables (actually variable, npos), and methods of the standard library's *String* model (C++-98: 21.3). We're not going to go outside that, unless we deliberately choose to be perverse, but that doesn't mean we have to complete it until we need to. How's that for facilitating lazy tendencies: you can complete it at your leisure, and there's no downside. (For those of you who defend the std::basic_string template against accusations that it has too many methods, I challenge you to create a veneer in the manner we are talking about, use it throughout all your work, populate it only as need dictates, and write to me when it matches the dictates of the *String* model. Note that by 2030 I expect to be living in a bubble on the lower slopes of Olympus Mons, so you'll have to send it care of Addison-Wesley Mars Division.)

You might also be saying "But you've derived from a class that doesn't have a virtual destructor, and everyone knows you shouldn't do that!" Well the classic advice when using inheritance is to "make sure base classes have virtual destructors" [Meye1998]. This advice is 100 percent correct when you are dealing with polymorphic types, and failure to do so will leave you an unhappy chappy. The rationale is that if your derived classes have a nontrivial destructor, and the virtual destructor mechanism is not employed to ensure correct destruction, resources will leak when they are deleted polymorphically (via a pointer to a base class).

Grown-ups know, however, that this advice is not germane when dealing with nonpolymorphic classes, although, to be fair, this knowledge is usually couched within the caveat that non-polymorphic classes should not be used as bases. Since veneers are constrained to respect the polymorphic nature of their primary parameterizing types, they will be polymorphic (and, therefore, safe for destruction via base pointer) if their primary parameterizing type is, and will not be (and, therefore, not safe for destruction via base pointer) if their primary parameterizing type is not. Furthermore, users of a parameterization of your veneer have no business misusing its polymorphic (or lack of) nature. In plain English, if someone wraps your veneer around something that lacks a virtual destructor, it is their responsibility to ensure they follow the rules, and do not attempt to destroy it virtually. If they have not read your documentation, then give them a gentle reminder. If you didn't document your veneer (including a reference to the rules of veneers), then you'd better start baking that Humble Pie.

21.4 Veneers: Coda

The idea of veneers came about through a desire to fine polish existing classes, but has evolved into a concept that finds wide application. Veneers can be used to inject behavior into a hierarchy of classes, to round off encapsulation, to adapt types, to manage conversion. They might add new methods, perform additional processing during construction and/or destruction, or might specify new member types. Veneers do all these things in a lightweight manner, according to a set of rules that many of their applications rely upon. In the next chapter, we look at more substantial type adaptation, in the form of bolt-ins.

Bolt-ins

Bolt: A strong pin, of iron or other material, used to fasten or hold something in place, often having a head at one end and screw thread cut upon the other end.

The term *bolt-in* was originally coined, to the best of my knowledge, by my friends and former colleagues Leigh and Scott,[1] who have a software consultancy based in Sydney, Australia. Generally speaking, bolt-ins "bolt in" significant enhancing functionality around existing classes. This sounds similar to the concept of veneers, and indeed bolt-ins can be considered a closely related concept. However, they are a whole lot more substantive, and they have fewer constraints than veneers.

Definition: *Bolt-ins*

Bolt-ins are template classes with the following characteristics:

1. They derive, usually publicly, from their primary parameterizing type.

2. They accommodate the polymorphic nature of their primary parameterizing type. Usually they also adhere to the nature, but this is not always the case, and they may define virtual methods of their own, in addition to overriding those defined by the primary parameterizing type.

3. They may increase the footprint of the primary parameterizing type by the definition of member variables, virtual functions, and additional inheritance from nonempty types.

There is a significant gray area between veneers (see Chapter 21) and bolt-ins, but they have different intents. Where veneers are, by and large, concerned with polishing existing types, bolt-ins are concerned with significantly changing or completing the behavioral nature of (often partially defined) types.

22.1 Adding Functionality

The primary purpose of bolt-ins is to add or enhance functionality. There are three ways in which this can be achieved. First, it may be new functionality, which is then accessible to derived classes and/or client code of the composite type.

---

[1]The impossibly tall Perry brothers.

Second, it may be the replacement of existing functionality. This can be via the well-known C+ mechanism of run time polymorphism [Stro1997], whereby derived class may override the virtual methods of their parent class(es). However, it is also possible to override nonvirtual functions. This is known as function hiding, which usually constitutes an abuse of the class whose methods are being hidden, and is a likely source of bugs [Meye1998, Dewh2003]. However, there are some circumstances in which it is safe and quite reasonable to do this, which we cover in this chapter.

Last, it may be providing functionality that does not yet exist. This can be achieved by two obverse techniques: run time polymorphism of abstract types and simulated compile-time polymorphism (see section 22.5). Where the former prescribes behavior that must be provided by inheriting classes, the latter prescribes behavior that must be supplied by the inherited class.

If this is all as clear as vegetable soup, worry not: it will be strained to a light consommé in this chapter.

22.2 Skin Selection

As we've mentioned earlier, one of the uses of bolt-ins is to finish off an incomplete class. Microsoft's Active Template Library (ATL) framework provides a number of examples of this. You define your class, which inherits from one or more COM interfaces, but do not define your reference-counting boilerplate. Specifically you do not implement the pure virtual methods of IUnknown (see section 19.8). Your class is, therefore, an abstract class, and you cannot instantiate instances of it.

However, you can define composite types, using one of ATL's predefined bolt-ins—CComObject, CComAggObject, CComObjectStack, and so on—or one of your own, and it is this composite type that is instantiated and that handles the IUnknown method implementations for us.

```
class MyServer
  : public IMyServer
  , public . . .
{};

new MyServer;          // error -  abstract type
new CComObject<MyServer>; // Ok; make me a normal COM object

MyServer                ms1; // error - abstract type
CComObjectStack<MyServer> ms2; // Ok; make me a stack COM object
```

Hence, bolt-ins are a way of applying functionality to partially defined types, for example, implementing an interface. This means that the implementation of certain parts can be abstracted and generalized into a suite of related bolt-ins, which allows design decisions to be delayed and/or revised without the need for any (significant) coding effort. Not only does this help with the flexibility and reusability of software components, but it allows designs to be fixed at a later stage in the development process, which means that external change can be accommodated [Beck2000] at lower cost: a kind of software utopia.

Naturally this mechanism lends itself to the overriding of any virtual functions, not just those for which a vtable entry does not yet exist. Skinning completes abstract classes and/or changes the nature of concrete polymorphic classes. Next we'll look at the modification of non-virtual functionality.

22.3 Nonvirtual Overriding

When writing bolt-ins (and veneers also, on occasion) that are aimed at a general model of primary parameterizing type, it can be the case that you may be hiding, rather than overriding, for some of the targeted types. Overriding nonvirtual functions is usually a much frowned-upon activity, and quite rightly, too. Doing so can cause the instance of a class to have different behavior depending on where it is used. Consider the `TradingRegister` class in Listing 22.1, which has not been designed to act as a base class because it's `Add()` method is nonvirtual.

Listing 22.1

```
class TradingRegister
{
public:
  void Add(Trade const &trade); // Adds a trade to the trading reg
};

void DoTrade(TradingRegister &reg, Trade const &trade)
{
  reg.Add(trade);
}
```

Subsequently, someone has need to override the functionality provided in the guise of the `LoggingTradingRegister`, shown in Listing 22.2. Unfortunately, passing the `LoggingTradingRegister` instance to `DoTrade()` causes an error, in that the `Add()` method from `TradingRegister` is the one that is called.

Listing 22.2

```
class LoggingTradingRegistr
  : public TradingRegistr
{
public:
  void Add(Trade const &trade); // Adds a trade and logs it
};

Trade                   trade;
LoggingTradingRegister  ltr;
```

```
DoTrade(ltr, trade); // Nasty. Trade doesn't get logged
```

This is the result of C++'s type resolution and inheritance mechanisms working together to be able to interpret instances of a type as that type, or as any of its publicly derived parent types.

Without these mechanisms, C++ would be a pretty useless language, but it does mean that we should avoid overriding nonvirtual mechanisms in general.

However, where there is no chance of the type being used via its parent type, there is no problem with non-virtual overriding. This is the case when using templates. Consider if `DoTrade()` was expressed as a template:

```
template< typename T
        , typename U
        >
void DoTrade(T &reg, U const &trade)
{
  reg.Add(trade);
}
. . .
```

```
DoTrade(ltr, trade); // Fine. Trade is logged
```

This form of `DoTrade()` does not, and in fact cannot, know about the parent class(es) of T. Hence, the instantiation of `DoTrade()` knows only that `ltr` is of type `LoggingTradingRegister`, so it can only call `LoggingTradingRegister::Add()`.

Although using them with templates is safe, types that employ nonvirtual overriding can also be used in other nontemplate contexts, in which case they still represent a danger. The problem with any technique that employs template derivation—whether that be veneers or bolt-ins or any similar mechanisms—is that experience shows that it can be very easy to break the rule against hiding when you're designing templates with a large potential set of parameterizing types. This is a significant flaw in these techniques, and one must be mindful of it when using them. In practice, users must treat such components as a white box just as they must when using libraries based on run time polymorphism.[2]

22.4 Leveraging Scope

An interesting side effect of the template resolution mechanism is that the symbols that are resolved within a bolt-in template needn't necessarily be part of the template or of its parameterizing class(es). This can be a flaw (and an obscure source of head-scratching consternation), but on occasion may be used to provide a more flexible template.

The Synesis libraries contains a suite of cooperating templates that bolt in reference counting logic to classes that may already be defined in terms of a reference counting interface, as well as those that may not.[3] The templates are based around a set of bolt-ins—`Synesis Std::RefCounter` and its several skinning (see section 22.2) peers—which take the following form:

---

[2]The current (2003) intensity of the debate regarding implementing the `export` keyword seems to miss this point. Anachronistically, my opinion is that the only components that even approximate a black box are those hidden behind a compiler-independent library C-API.

[3]These classes have not changed substantially since the mid 1990s, and are therefore looking a bit decrepit. Please bear that in mind; I'd almost certainly design them differently now, but I'm using them here as they illustrate the point.

```
template< typename T
        , typename S = Sync
        , typename C = InitialCount<1> >
class RefCounter
  : public T
  , public S
{
   . . .
```

The bolt-in derives from the primary parameterizing type T and from the mixin policy type S, which defines the synchronization policy. The third parameter, C, defines the initial count policy. The synchronization policy defines locking functionality and atomic integer operations with the following interface:

```
struct S
{
// Atomic operations
  static int AtomicDecrement(int volatile &);
  static int AtomicIncrement(int volatile &);
// Locking operations
  void Lock();
  void Unlock();
};
```

There are four synchronization policy classes defined: SyncST, SyncMTNoLock, SyncMT, and the template SyncMTOuterLock, and preprocessor discrimination is used to define the typedef Sync to either SyncST or SyncMT depending on whether the compile environment is multithreaded. The last of the four policy types implements its locking by deferring to the composite class, which allows the bolt-ins to work with classes that already provide their own locking functionality, thereby saving space and potentially expensive synchronization objects. It is defined in Listing 22.3.[4]

Listing 22.3

```
template <class O>
struct SyncMTOuter
    : public SyncMTNoLock
{
  SyncMTOuter()
    : m_po(0)
  {}
  void Lock()
  {
    m_po->O::Lock();
  }
```

---

[4]Note that this uses nonvirtual overriding (see section 22.3), but in these circumstances it is entirely safe since the template is used as a parameter to the RefCounter bolt-in template.

```
  void Unlock()
  {
    m_po->O::Unlock();
  }
  void InitSync(O *po)
  {
    m_po = po;
  }
  void UninitSync(O *po)
  {
    m_po = NULL;
  }
private:
  O *m_po;
};
```

The `InitSync()` and `UninitSync()` methods are then called within the bolt-in constructors and destructor, as shown in Listing 22.4:

Listing 22.4
```
template< typename T
        , typename S = Sync
        , typename C = InitialCount<1> >
class RefCounter
    : public T
{
  RefCounter::RefCounter()
    : m_cRefs(C::Count)
  {
    InitSync(this);
  }
  RefCounter(RefCounter const &rhs)
    : ParentClass(rhs)
    , m_cRefs(C::Count)
  {
    InitSync(this);
  }
  ~RefCounter()
  {
    UninitSync(this);
  }
  . . .
```

That's great for `SyncMTOuterLock`, but what about the other synchronization policies? Well, one option would be to have them define `InitSync()` and `UninitSync()` methods, but that seems a bit ugly. The option I chose was to rely on the template resolution mechanisms and define the two free functions within the same namespace as the bolt-in classes:

```
inline void InitSync(void *)
{}
inline void UninitSync(void *)
{}
```

The template picks them up from outside its class definition (which includes all the types from which it is defined, including the synchronization mixins), and only "sees" the free functions when it cannot locate them internally. Now you can add any kind of synchronization class that you like and only define InitSync() and UninitSync() when you need to.

22.5   Simulated Compile-Time Polymorphism: Reverse Bolt-ins

This is another of those techniques, like the Schwarz counter (see section 11.2.3), that seems to get invented again and again. It also has several names. Let's have a look at it first, before we try to arbitrate between the different names. Consider the following template:

```
template <typename T>
struct RecursiveBoltIn
{
  void DoIt()
  {
    static_cast<T*>(this)->Do();
  }
};
```

RecursiveBoltIn is a not a bolt-in, because it doesn't derive from its parameterizing type. In a sense, though, it's a *Reverse Bolt-in,*[5] as we'll see. At first glance, it appears to be pretty simple and operates a constraint on its parameterizing type, requiring it to have a method Do(). Looking a little more closely, of course, we see that it's actually casting itself (this) to its parameterizing type. But it doesn't derive from the parameterizing type, so how can this work?

As we know, the virtual function mechanism supports polymorphism by dereferencing the virtual function table pointer to access the virtual function table for the particular class [Lipp1996].[6] This occurs at run time. The lookup we see in RecursiveBoltIn, is performed in reverse bolt-ins at compile time, avoiding the cost of indirection at run time. For this reason, I like to call it *Simulated Compile-time Polymorphism.*

The first documentation of this technique that I'm aware of was by James Coplien [Lipp1998] in which he called it the *Curiously Recurring Template Pattern* (CRTP). It is used throughout Microsoft's Active Template Library (ATL), wherein it is called *Simulated Dynamic Binding* [Rect1999], and it is suggested in [Rect1999] that the ATL development team discovered it. The authors also suggest that this technique is not necessarily a supported part of the lan-

---

[5]In the absence of a better name, that's what I'm calling the concept.

[6]This is not prescribed by the standard (see Chapters 7 and 8), but is the common implementation mechanism.

guage, but I have not been able to locate a compiler that is unhappy with it as demonstrated in the two cases shown here; even Comeau in strict mode accepts it without question. (It's extremely useful, and so probably worth using despite the potential nonconformance.)

We can easily see how it works by looking at an example of a class that uses it.

```
class RecChild
  : public RecursiveBoltIn<RecChild>
{
public:
  void Do()
  {}
};
```

Now we see how the `static_cast` can work. `RecChild` derives publicly, and nonvirtually, from `RecursiveBoltIn<RecChild>`, so within the instantiation of `Recursive BoltIn<RecChild>, this` can be statically cast to `RecChild`. Granted it seems more than a little strange, but it works, and is quite useful in applying a constraint to the parameterizing type of the bolt-in.

Note that the technique is not limited to functions; it is also possible to require a parameterizing derived class to provide nonfunction members, that is, member variables and enum members.

22.6   Parameterized Polymorphic Packaging

The classic trade-off between efficiency and flexibility has no clearer case than in whether to make a class polymorphic. It's an argument that can't be won, and it would be far nicer not to have to make the decision. Using bolt-ins, we can do just that in many cases, such that the decision may be postponed to where it belongs: at the manifestation of the programmer's design.

Consider a class used for locking via mutual exclusion between the threads of a single process, shown in Listing 22.5.

Listing 22.5
```
class ThreadMutex
{
public:
  ThreadMutex();
  ~ThreadMutex();
// Operations
public:
  void Lock();
  void Unlock();
// Members
private:
  . . . // platform-specific data
};
```

For efficiency, no methods are declared virtual, and the `Lock()` and `Unlock()` methods are inlined. That works fine, and is maximally efficient, but it constrains the behavior of the code that uses `ThreadMutex` to the decisions made when the class was written. There is still a lot of flexibility in this model, for example, you might also define `ProcessMutex` and `Noop Mutex` classes, but the flexibility is at compile time, leveraged by selecting one or the other of the types, perhaps via preprocessor selection.

Alternatively, if you needed run time flexibility, you could define an interface `IMutex`, wherein `Lock()` and `Unlock()` would be declared virtual, as in:

```
struct IMutex
{
  virtual void Lock() = 0;
  virtual void Unlock() = 0;
};
```

You would then code in the following way:

```
IMutex   *mx = FastLookupMutex(API_ID_XYZ);
mx->Lock();
XYZFunction(); // from the XYZ API
mx->Unlock();
```

Now the actual concrete mutex class would be locked and unlocked via the *vtable*. (In the real world, we'd scope the `Lock()` and `Unlock()` calls; see section 6.2). But now we've got two versions of code. While some operating systems have simple and obvious synchronization APIs, others do not, so it's maintenance headache time.

(By the way, I know—from bitter personal experience—that using synchronization objects polymorphically is likely to have a nontrivial overhead. Pondering this might help you avoid the embarrassment I had a few years when I foisted a similar polymorphic version of this on an unsuspecting client: it accounted for 15 percent of processor time until I realized my error and switched it. They were very happy and congratulated me for my expertise; I was most embarrassed to admit what I'd done. Some consultant![7])

So what's to be done? How can we get polymorphic flexibility when we want it, and efficient inflexibility when we want it? Answer: bolt-ins and a dash of EBO (see section 12.3).

We can redefine our `ThreadMutex` class to be a template, thus:

```
template <typename I>
class ThreadMutex
  : public I
{
  . . .
```

[7]They actually appreciated my honesty in coming clean. Lesson: always be honest; it can earn you friends in this industry where responsibility takers are few and far between.

Now `ThreadMutex` derives from `I`, whatever `I` may be; nothing else in the class definition changes. If we want to have a thread mutex that is polymorphic with respect to `IMutex`, we use the `ThreadMutex<IMutex>` parameterization.

If we want a nonpolymorphic version, we would parameterize with a null type such as `boost::null_t`, which adds no data, no methods, and no *vtable/vptr* (see Chapters 7 and 8). Since most compilers employ EBO very well, we'll have a type that is physically identical to the original definition of `ThreadMutex`. Even with those few that do not (see Table 18.3), it is a benign flaw, since it's the run time cost of *vtable* indirection that we're most concerned about; we're hardly likely to be creating thousands of `ThreadMutex<boost::null_t>` instances.

This is as big a bolt-in as you can get. In the composite type `ThreadMutex<boost::null_t>`, `ThreadMutex<>` provides everything: data, methods, and type (apart from the fatuous ability to cast to `boost::null_t&`).

22.7   Bolt-ins: Coda

Whatever you call them, the bolt-in clearly represents a very powerful mechanism for significantly enhancing existing types; the most widely used framework for building COM components—ATL—is virtually all bolt-ins. In my own work I've found them to significantly enhance reuse. Where classic inheritance is able to provide modest reuse gains in related classes, and template, especially STL, techniques are able to provide reuse in implementation and algorithms, bolt-ins provide us with a way to combine the benefits of both.

Template Constructors

An obvious disadvantage of bolt-ins, veneers, and other templates that derive from their para-meterizing type(s), is that they hide that type's constructors. Consider the hypothetical classes in Listing 23.1.

Listing 23.1

```
class Double
{
public:
  typedef double  value_type;
public:
  Double();
  explicit Double(double d);
public:
  double GetValue() const;

  . . .
};


template <typename T>
class Wrapper
  : public T
{
  . . .
};


typedef Wrapper<Double>  Double_t;

Double_t  d1;
Double_t  d2(12.34); // Error!
```

Wrapper has effectively hidden the second constructor of Double, so the attempt to non-default construct it is an error.

The method of solving this problem for Microsoft's Active Template Library (ATL) is to avoid it. CComObject has a single constructor with the following signature, as do most of its brethren (some others have a default constructor only):

```
CComObject(void *pv = NULL);
```

This constructor is used to pass all kinds of things into the (your) bolted class, including interface pointers, pointers to containing classes, and so on. Recently this restrictiveness caused me to have to write two specific classes and two new templates just to create a component that could utilize an STL container held in the component's containing object; frustrating to say the least! There should be a better approach.[1]

The answer to the problem in general would be to use template constructors. For our example, we could add the following template constructor:

Listing 23.2

```
template <typename T>
class Wrapper
  : public T
{
  . . .
public:
  Wrapper()
  {}
  template <typename T1>
  explicit Wrapper(T1 t1)
    : base_class_type(t1)
  {}
  . . .
```

The first thing to note is that we've had to add a default constructor. If we didn't do so, then the first object in our example program would be illegal. As we saw in section 2.2, whenever you define a nondefault constructor in the absence of a default constructor, the default constructor is effectively hidden. I should also point out that template constructors are never used to generate copy constructors [Dewh2003], so if you have a bolt-in that allocates resources you need to be careful about its definition in this regard, and either provide a copy constructor and copy assignment operator, or hide them (see section 2.2).

The main play is in the template constructor, which seems quite straightforward. The constructor simply takes a single argument of its template type T1. For `Wrapper<Double>` the constructor passed the `double` value through to `Double`'s constructor. What could be simpler?

Alas, that's the best we can expect. As soon as we want to handle class types, or references, the fun starts.

23.1   Hidden Costs

Let's look at another class, `String`:

```
class String
{
```

---

[1]To be fair to the implementers of ATL, much of the initialization of an ATL object is done outside its constructor because ATL is designed to be independent of a C/C++ standard library and, therefore, exceptions. As is often the case in the real world, you can't have everything.

```
public:
  typedef std::string const  &value_type;
public:
  explicit String(std::string const &value);
  explicit String(char const *value);
public:
  std::string const &GetValue() const;

  . . .
```

We can use this as we did `Double`, with the current definition of `Wrapper`:

```
typedef Wrapper<String>  String_t;

std::string      ss("A std::string instance");
String_t         s1("A c-style string"); // Ok
String_t         s2(ss);                  // Ok, but . . .
```

Both the constructors compile, and the code works as expected, but there is a hidden gotcha. The construction of `s2` results in the creation of two copies of the string `ss`, where we only expect and want one. The extra copy is created because compilers instantiate a template based on the types of the arguments expressed *to it*, without any consideration as to how they might be used *within it*. Thus, the construction of `s2` is actually done by a constructor equivalent to the following:

```
Wrapper<String>::Wrapper(String s)
  : m_value(s)
{}
```

***

Imperfection: The C++ template mechanism instantiates a template based on the arguments to it, and takes no account of how, or in what form, those arguments are subsequently used within the templates. This can lead to the generation of inefficient and/or erroneous code since temporary instances of class type may be created during the forwarding of arguments through the template.

***

23.2   Dangling References

To accommodate the `Double` and `String` classes, we can change the nondefault constructor of `Wrapper` to take `T const&`, rather than just `T`. This enables the string instance to be passed through the template to the underlying type without the unnecessary copy, and it passes the double by `const`-reference rather than by value. If anything, this is possibly more efficient in theory, since the `double` is probably 64 or 80 bits, and the reference is 32 or 64 bits; in practice it will probably make no difference since compilers will be able to optimize the outer call to the inner initialization without any trouble.

```
template <typename T>
class Wrapper
```

```
  : public T
{
  . . .
  template <typename T1>
  explicit Wrapper(T1 const &t1)
    : base_class_type(t1)
  {}
  . . .
```

Naturally, you'll be wondering now about what happens when we need to pass through a non-`const` reference, as required by the constructor for our next class, `StringModifier` (Listing 23.3).

Listing 23.3
```
class StringModifier
{
public:
  typedef std::string const   &value_type;
public:
  explicit StringModifier(std::string &value)
    : m_value(value)
  {}
public:
  std::string const &GetValue() const;
  void SetValue(std::string const &value);
private:
  std::string &m_value;
};
```

For the current definition of the `Wrapper`, the answer is that it won't work.

```
typedef Wrapper<StringModifier>  StringModifier_t;

std::string      ss("A std::string instance");
StringModifier_t  s1(ss);      // Error!
```

What's worse is that many compilers will actually compile this,[2] without warning, with the first version of the `Wrapper`, This leaves `s1` holding onto a non-`const` reference to a temporary that, once the constructor returns, no longer exists! Buenas noches, Señor Core-Dump!

23.3 Template Constructor Specialization

That's okay, you say, because we have specialization. We can specialize the template for by-value, by-reference and by-`const`-reference. Unfortunately, that's not the case. The constructors are member templates and are, therefore, function templates. The language does not

---

[2]None of our compilers (see Appendix A) could be persuaded to even give a warning about this, never mind an error.

(yet[3]) support the specialization of function templates. What we might do, therefore, is to provide overloads for the constructor, as in:

Listing 23.4

```
template <typename T>
class Wrapper
  : public T
{
  . . .
  template <typename T1>
  explicit Wrapper(T1 t1) // by-val
    : base_class_type(t1)
  {}
  template <typename T1>
  explicit Wrapper(T1 &t1) // by-ref
    : base_class_type(t1)
  {}
  template <typename T1>
  explicit Wrapper(T1 const &t1) // by-const-ref
    : base_class_type(t1)
  {}
  . . .
```

Unfortunately, we're so far away from civilization with this stuff that we're just about to sail off the edge of the C++ world. Combining the three examples so far—which test `double`, `char const*`, `std::string const&` and `std::string&`—we get the unpromising spectrum of behavior from a range of compilers shown in Table 23.1.

When CodeWarrior and Comeau agree, I'm tempted to believe them even when they are at odds with GCC, Intel, and Visual C++ 7.1. But whether they're right or wrong is immaterial

Table 23.1

Compiler	by-val & by-ref & by-const-ref	by-ref & by-const-ref
Borland (5.6)	Ambiguity error	OK
CodeWarrior (8.0)	OK	OK
Comeau (4.3.3)	OK	Ambiguity error
Digital Mars	Ambiguity error	Compiles, with warnings
GCC (2.95)	OK	OK
GCC (3.2)	Ambiguity error	OK
Intel (7.1)	Ambiguity error	OK
Visual C++ (6.0)	Ambiguity error	Ambiguity error
Visual C++ (7.1)	Ambiguity error	OK

---

[3]This is one of the issues currently under discussion for the next standard [Vand2003].

because we have some serious contradictions to deal with. This is a truly foul problem, and neither of the two answers to it are ideal.

Since all the compilers, or all the latest versions at least, support what we are trying to achieve in one form or another, one answer would be to use preprocessor discrimination in order to provide our bolt-ins and similar template classes with the appropriate constructors. The fly in this particular ointment is the combinatorial explosion. We have to support either two or three permutations for each argument. Since template constructors are used in types that, by definition, do not generally know of all the types to which they will be applied, we necessarily have to anticipate a large number of potential applications. In other words, we need to write these templates to provide template constructors up to a large number. In my own work I consider eight as a more than generous upper limit: a constructor with more than six parameters is getting pretty silly. Even restricting ourselves to only two parameter types for a template with eight constructors would still require 510 constructors, and this is without factoring in `volatile` and `const volatile` references!

23.4   Argument Proxies

The first solution, which can be made to work fully but is largely more horrible than the problem, uses what I call argument proxies. There are several types of argument proxies, corresponding to the various permutations of const/non-const, volatile/non-volatile and pointer/reference/value, although not all of them need to be defined. I'll demonstrate by showing just two of them.

We can make our bolt-in work with all four parameter types by providing only by-value template constructor arguments and using them with argument proxy classes. The two argument proxies we'd need for the example are the `reference_proxy` and the `const_reference_proxy`. The definition of `reference_proxy` is shown in Listing 23.5. `const_reference_proxy` is identical save that all references are `const`.[4]

Listing 23.5
```
template <typename A>
class reference_proxy
{
public:
  explicit reference_proxy(A &a)
    : m_a(a)
  {}
  reference_proxy(reference_proxy<A> const &rhs)
    : m_a(rhs.m_a)
  {}
// Accessors
public:
  operator A&() const
```

[4]I don't doubt that I could generalize these various classes into a single definition, as they're pretty ancient in C++ template terms. But it's so rarely used, and so undeserving of any glorification, that I just haven't got around to it.

```
   {
      return m_a;
   }
// Members
private:
   A &m_a;
// Not to be implemented
private:
   . . . // Prevent copy assignment
```

There's no rocket science here. The important part of each of the templates is that the implicit conversion operator is `const` in all cases—so that it can be called on the temporary instance that eventuates inside the template constructor calls—and yet returns the full "type" of the type, that is, a non-`const` reference for `reference_proxy` and a non-`const` pointer for `pointer_proxy`. They could be used in our previous examples as follows:

```
String_t          s2(const_reference_proxy<std::string>(ss));
```

```
StringModifier_t  s1(reference_proxy<std::string>(ss));
```

No extra copy is made in the first case, and the non-`const` reference is passed through to the `StringModifier_t` instance in the second case. It works 100 percent correctly.

It is also possible to use forwarding functions, as we saw with the `array_proxy` in sections 14.4 and 14.6, as in:

```
template <typename A>
inline const_reference_proxy<A> const_ref_proxy(A &a)
{
   return const_reference_proxy<A>(a);
}
```

```
String_t          s2(const_ref_proxy(ss));
```

```
StringModifier_t  s1(ref_proxy(ss));
```

The Boost libraries define a similar set of components, whose forwarding functions are called `ref` and `cref`. I prefer the longer names shown here for the same reasons that the C++ casts (see section 19.2) have long and ugly names: they stand out clearly to the reader, are easily `grep`-able, and engender conscience-pricking discomfort when using them. This latter reason is especially important for argument proxies since they are a measure for dealing with a part of the language that is fundamentally flawed.

The problem is all too evident: The burden is on the *client code* to use them correctly in order to obviate the problems caused by the (broken?) template constructor mechanism.[5] This

---

[5]This is analogous to the situation with destruction/finalization in Java and .NET, whereby the onus is on the user of a class to remember to clean up its resources. Is that object oriented? I don't think so!

would be at least partially reasonable if the client code would otherwise always fail to compile. But as we've seen, this is only so for some cases. In others, compilers merrily generate code that is either inefficient or erroneous.

I do not recommend you employ these techniques for any client-facing code, or, rather, to rely on users of your templates to be familiar with the technique and rigorous in its application. It's largely impractical. The reason I've deigned to discuss them—beyond the pedagogical—is that there are limited circumstances in which they've proved useful, even essential, when using a template within the implementation of some library code, well away from any client code. Use with caution!

23.5   Argument Targeting

It's pretty disappointing stuff really, and something we can all hope the next standardization will address explicitly. In my opinion, compilers should be required to work correctly with all permutations (const/non-const, volatile/non-volatile, by-value/reference/pointer), and to select the most specialized as appropriate, rather than complaining about ambiguities. A former colleague once expressed disdain that compilers cannot work out what is needed on a case-by-case basis, but obliging compilers to look "through" a template to see how an argument is used within a given instantiation would be asking too much, I think.

The prosaic and incomplete solution to this is a targeted approach. Many bolt-ins and other deriving templates generally have a predictable subset of types that they must work with. In such cases, one can target the template constructors accordingly. For example, the veneer template sequence_container_veneer (see Chapter 21; included on the CD) designed to be parameterized by the standard library sequence containers—list, vector and deque[6]—would only need to provide for the following constructors:

```
// C = container; V = value type; A = allocator
explicit C(A const &al = A());
explicit C(size_type n, V const &v = V(), A const &al = A());
        C(C::const_iterator first, C::const_iterator last
                                , A const &al = A());
```

With types that really do have to be very widely applicable, you can resign yourself to your fate and wrap all the permutations in a macro, comforting yourself that it's not your fault.

23.6   Template Constructors: Coda

So where are we? Argument proxies are a perfectly good solution technically, but they are counter to the C++ ethos, whereby types, even those obtained by the parameterization of templates, should present a simple and robust interface and should manage things on behalf of their users. Requiring users of your templates to know when and where to use argument proxies is not practicable, so this technique is useful only in extreme cases in well-managed contexts.

---

[6]I'm not counting basic_string, although it too is a sequence container.

That leaves us with targeting argument types. It can hardly be considered a good solution, but it's preferable to forcing all composite types to be default constructed. Ever heard of RAII? The combinatorial problem is a pain, but it's a write-once thing, so I guess we can't complain (apart from those extended compilation times). These things are easily done with scripting langauges.

One thing I should point out, if it's not already obvious: The problem of passing arguments through templates is not limited to constructors. It's just that we don't usually need to provide forwarding functions for nonconstructor methods. The only time when this is an issue is when using nonpublic inheritance, which is unlikely to be encountered with bolt-ins and similar generic templates.

This is one of the few issues covered in this book where we're really just going to have to kill time until the standards committee decrees sensible behavior, and compiler vendors implement it, as the solutions discussed here are, at best, partial. Hmm, maybe I'll send my favorite vendors some more e-mails.

PART FIVE

Operators

One of the most powerful and important aspects of C++ is the ability to overload operators. It facilitates the extension of the language to user-defined types, enabling them to exhibit natural syntax and to be manipulable along with built-in types in generic code. Even before templates became a part of the language, the generalized approach afforded by operator overloading was invaluable. Now that we have templates, the possibilities are almost endless.

However, operator overloading has a dark side, which stems from several factors. Some programmers nonchalantly use overloads that contradict expected semantics.[1] Another problem is the fact that C++ is still living a dual life as a super-C, carrying with it all those implicit conversion rules that we've come to live with and depend on for the fundamental types, but that can cause all kinds of problems when combined with overloaded operators for user-defined types. Finally, some of the overloadable operators have subtly different semantics to their built-in equivalents that cannot be overcome.

In previous parts we've talked a little about operators, but not gone into much depth on the imperfections associated with their use, or how best to implement them when we determine that we need to do so. In this part we'll take a look at a variety of issues to do with operators. We begin, in Chapter 24, *operator bool()*, with the way in which operators can be used to indicate a notion of Boolean state, how this can be problematic due to unwanted conversions, and how it can be implemented in a maximally safe and portable way.

Next, in Chapter 25, *Fast, Nonintrusive String Concatenation*, we take an entirely upbeat look at string concatenation. In particular how we can achieve dramatic performance improvements by using a fast concatenation component that can be integrated with *any* string libraries in a nonintrusive fashion.

Then it's downbeat again in Chapter 26, *What's Your Address?* to look at the use—well, abuse, in the main—of the address of operator. We cover the several pitfalls with overloading this particular operator, but in the spirit of imperfect practitioners, we also look at some neat tricks to use if you choose to go ahead and overload.

The next chapter, Chapter 27, *Subscript Operators*, covers the debate between providing implicit conversion or subscript operators for array types, and provides some further insights into the imperfect relationship between arrays and pointers.

Chapter 28, *Increment Operators,* takes a brief but important look at the mechanism of overloading the increment and decrement operators, mounts the soapbox to berate the standard of education in our universities and ubiquitous inconsistency in professional practitioners, and

---

[1]See Appendix B.

then shows an efficient template-based return value monitor, which can be used to prevent abuse of your carefully crafted increment/decrement operators.

In the penultimate chapter, Chapter 29, *Arithmetic Types,* we catch up with our old friends the 64-bit integers from Chapter 1, and try and give them natural syntax. We ultimately fail, as we are wont to do, but we have some fun and learn some useful things in the process.

Finally, in the shortest chapter in the book, Chapter 30, *Short-circuit!,* we look at how overloading the logical operators tramples over C's short-circuit semantics, and recommend giving the practice a wide berth.

operator bool()

We saw in section 13.4.2 that conditional expressions are translated to an integral form (`int` in C; `bool` in C++) before evaluation. C and C++ are capable of applying implicit conversions from a variety of scalar types (see Prologue), including pointers, which allows for the somewhat useful constructs such as:

```
void *p = . . .;

if(p)    // Evaluates whether p is the null pointer
{}
if(!p)   // Evaluates whether p is not the null pointer
{}
```

There are occasions when it is necessary to allow instances of user-defined types to do the same. A good example is the idiomatic IOStreams extraction loop:

```
while(std::cin >> name >> salary)
{
  . . .
}
```

Smart pointers, such as `std::auto_ptr`, are another example, but there are many other cases where it's appropriate. Sometimes we can return an instance of a simple class by value, and want to have it "be" or "not be" rather than having to throw an exception. Whatever the motivation, not to mention the rights or wrongs of the matter, you'll come across such things quite often, and will occasionally want to provide such behavior for your own classes.

24.1   operator int() const

Prior to the introduction of the `bool` keyword to the language, the most obvious form of such a thing might have been to provide `operator int() const`, as in:

Listing 24.1
```
class ExpressibleThing
{
public:
  operator int() const;
};
```

```
ExpressibleThing  e;

if(e)   // Evaluates whether e "is"
{}
if(!e)  // Evaluates whether e "is not"
{}
```

The big problem with this is that an `int` is readily convertible to many other types, and it can be meaninglessly used in the construction of an entirely unrelated type:

```
ExpressibleThing    e;
std::vector<String> vs(e); // What on earth does this mean?!
```

This is meaningless, and also a potential source of undefined behavior. Since `Expressible Thing` need only return any non-zero value, it could be correctly implemented to return a different non-zero value each time it is called. This could result in a silent failure, or cause memory exhaustion, or, worse, could actually work correctly in most cases: `operator int() const` might return 1,000, which is always large enough for the subsequent uses of `vs`, throughout your testing but not enough when your product goes live.

24.2   operator void *() const

But we know that `int` is not the only type that can be used in expression evaluation (see section 15.3). In pre-C++-98 times, the `int` problems were somewhat ameliorated by providing `operator void*() const`. The original IOStreams `ios` class did so, and its modern template form `basic_ios` carries the same method.

Listing 24.2
```
class ExpressibleThing
{
public:
  operator void *() const;
};

ExpressibleThing  e;

if(e)   // Evaluates whether e "is"
{}
if(!e)  // Evaluates whether e "is not"
{}
```

Alas, the implicit conversion problem hasn't gone away, it's just been moved sideways. Now you can inadvertently convert to any pointer type through a simple cast. Even worse, the following is legal, though more than a little incorrect:

```
ExpressibleThing  e;

delete e; // Nasty!
```

Needless to say, this is not good enough.

24.3   operator bool() const

Since the operator we're after is logically representing a Boolean, what better to have than `operator bool() const`?

```
class ExpressibleThing
{
public:
  operator bool() const;
};
```

This is the approach commonly taken since the `bool` type was introduced in C++-98. Unfortunately, `bool` is implicitly convertible to `int`, so we've still got the integral promotion problems we saw in section 24.1, so that `ExpressibleThing` can take part in arithmetic expressions, as in:

```
ExpressibleThing  et1;
ExpressibleThing  et2;
int               nonsense = et1 + et2;
```

But there's worse news. All of our three solutions so far return a basic, publicly accessible, type, either `int`, `void (const)*`, or `bool`. This means that the types can take part in erroneous equality comparisons with *any* other type that provides conversions to our type's "Boolean" type, or any type to which that might be converted. Consider the following scary bunch of code:

```
class SomethingElseEntirely
{
public:
  operator bool() const;
};

SomethingElseEntirely set;
ExpressibleThing       et;

if(set == et)
{
  . . .
```

This is really not good.

24.4   operator !()—*not!*

Another strategy I've seen[1] espoused is to supply only logical negation via `operator !()` `const`. The corresponding idiom is to double negate to test for truth, as in:

Listing 24.3
```
class ExpressibleThing
{
public:
  bool operator !() const;
};


ExpressibleThing  e;

if(!!e) // Evaluates whether e "is"
{}
if(!e) // Evaluates whether e "is not"
{}
```

This is just too nasty to be taken seriously. Imagine the confusion on even moderately complex conditional expressions, and not just for novice programmers. The opportunities for errors to creep in during maintenance are too great. Last, it does not follow the normal look of code, which can only detract from its readability.

24.5   operator boolean const *() const

Since all integral types are out of the question, and `void*` is too generic, maybe a non-`void` pointer type would work, as in:

```
class ExpressibleThing
{
private:
  struct boolean { private: void operator delete(void*); };
public:
  operator boolean const *() const;
};
```

The reason that a `struct` is used is to allow it to be a private nested type. This can then be given a hidden `operator delete()` in order to preclude instances of `ExpressibleThing` being passed to `delete`. It also prevents the declaration of variables of the `operator`'s return type, `boolean const*`, and conversion to another pointer type will require two `static_cast` operator applications.

---

[1] A high degree of respect for the particular individuals prevents me from mentioning any names.

24.6 operator int boolean::*() const

The `operator boolean const *()` const technique has been my preferred way of doing things until the last few years, but most compilers have now improved to the point where they support a much more satisfying method [Vand2003] proposed by Peter Dimov on the Boost newsgroups. The problem with any of the pointer-based techniques is that they allow conversion to `void (const)*`, which means that a type providing this operator can undergo unwanted conversions. However, there is a class of pointer types—pointers to members—that cannot be converted, either implicitly or via casts, to a regular pointer type. This results in the following operator:

Listing 24.4

```
class ExpressibleThing
{
private:
  struct boolean { int i; };
public:
  operator int boolean ::*() const
  {
    return <condition> ? &boolean::i : NULL;
  }
};
```

This is great stuff, since it has all the attributes we require of an `operator "Boolean"`.

24.7 Operating in the Real World

Of course, when I said that compilers have improved to allow for the `operator int boolean::*()` const technique, they've not all come along in unison. As is always the case in the real world, there are significant differences to the support for such complex techniques.[2] For example, some cannot handle use of the operator in compound expressions, as in:

```
ExpressibleThing  et1;
ExpressibleThing  et2;

if(et1 && et2) // Error 'operator &&' not implemented for Ex ...
{
  . . .
```

The scariest behavior is of Visual C++ 6, which compiles all expressions involving this operator without a problem, but misinterprets the truth of (sub-)expressions at run time!

So although the vast bulk of the modern compilers handle the optimal technique with aplomb, if you care about portability, you must consider a mixed solution:

---

[2]Visual C++ 6.0 does not support this, nor does Borland (not even the latest 5.6.4). Interestingly, Watcom's compiler manages more support than Borland.

Listing 24.5
```
private:
  struct boolean { int i; private: void operator delete(void*); };
public:
#ifdef ACMELIB_OPERATOR_BOOL_AS_OPERATOR_POINTER_TO_MEMBER_SUPPORT
  operator int boolean::*() const
  {
    return m_b ? &boolean::i : NULL;
  }
#else
  operator Boolean const*() const
  {
    boolean b;
    return m_b ? &b : NULL;
  }
#endif ACMELIB_OPERATOR_BOOL_AS_OPERATOR_POINTER_TO_MEMBER_SUPPORT
```

But I'm sure you'd be as unhappy as me to see that stuff cluttering up all your lovely succinct classes. There was another of those think-about-it-for-several-days efforts to come up with
the solution, but I think you'll agree that the result is very nice indeed. Let's first look at it in
action:

```
private:
  typedef operator_bool_generator<class_type>   boolean_type;
public:
  operator boolean_type::return_type() const
  {
    return boolean_type::translate(m_b);
  }
```

The actual operator type, and the mechanism of providing the "true" and "not true" values
is provided by the operator_bool_generator template:

Listing 24.6
```
template <typename T>
struct operator_bool_generator
{
public:
  typedef operator_bool_generator<T>  class_type;
#ifdef ACMELIB_OPERATOR_BOOL_AS_OPERATOR_POINTER_TO_MEMBER_SUPPORT
  typedef int class_type::*return_type;
  /// Returns the value representing the true condition
  static return_type true_value()
  {
    return &class_type::i;
  }
private:
```

```
    int i;
#else
  typedef class_type const  *return_type;
  /// Returns the value representing the true condition
  static return_type true_value()
  {
    class_type  t;
    void    *p = static_cast<void*>(&t);
    return static_cast<return_type>(p);
  }
#endif // ACMELIB_OPERATOR_BOOL_AS_OPERATOR_POINTER_TO_MEMBER_SUPPORT
public:
  /// Returns the value representing the false condition
  static return_type false_value()
  {
    return static_cast<return_type>(0);
  }
  /// Does the ternary operator for you
#ifdef ACMELIB_MEMBER_TEMPLATE_FUNCTION_SUPPORT
  template <typename U>
  static return_type translate(U b)
#else /* ? ACMELIB_MEMBER_TEMPLATE_FUNCTION_SUPPORT */
  static return_type translate(bool b)
#endif // ACMELIB_MEMBER_TEMPLATE_FUNCTION_SUPPORT
  {
    return b ? true_value() : false_value();
  }
private:
  void operator delete(void*);
};
```

Now compilers that support `operator  int  boolean::*()  const` and those that merely support `operator Boolean const*() const` are catered for equally well by the `operator_bool_generator` template. It might look like a lot of guff, but all the nasty conditional compilation is hidden inside the template, rather than polluting your classes. And it's perfectly efficient: compilers easily optimize it all out to nothing but the fundamental Boolean test passed to `translate()`.

The template parameter is merely there to give the operator's return type uniqueness. The example uses the enclosing class's member type `class_type` (section 18.5.3), as that's my habit, but you could use the name of the enclosing class itself if you prefer. In fact, it could just as easily be an inner class, or any other class, but using the enclosing class does not require any additional type definitions.

Alas, that's not quite the final picture, nice as it is. Visual C++ (from versions 4.2 right up to the latest 7.1) has a peculiarity whereby it complains that it is illegal to have a `typedef` between the `operator` keyword and the operator type. Huh? Indeed, you may ask. Clearly it's a paradox inside an enigma, cleverly disguised as a bug, wrapped in a feature. Similarly, Borland gets discombobulated when an operator is defined with the scoping operator : : in the operator type.

The workaround for Visual C++—don't ask me to explain it—is to use some aspect of the class before the operator. The following does it:

```
private:
  typedef operator_bool_generator<class_type>    boolean_type;
  typedef boolean_type::return_type              operator_bool_type;
public:
  operator boolean_type::return_type() const
  {
    . . .
```

I was a bit glum about this for a while as it had uglified my solution. Thankfully a good night's sleep was the answer, and I realized that one way of declaring and using the type in one statement was to define the enclosing class's boolean_type from the instantiation of operator_bool_generator's own class_type, so it boils down to:

```
private:
  typedef operator_bool_generator<class_type>::class_type   boolean_type;
public:
  operator boolean_type::return_type() const
  {
    . . .
```

Alas, for Borland, this still doesn't cut it. When the enclosing type is a template itself, using its instantiation type—class_type—does not work, and we're forced to define the operator return type external to the operator itself, as in:

Listing 24.7
```
private:
  typedef typename
    operator_bool_generator<class_type>::class_type
                                operator_bool_generator_type;
  typedef typename operator_bool_generator_type::return_type
                                operator_bool_type;
public:
  operator operator_bool_type() const
  {
    return operator_bool_generator_type::translate(. . .
```

So, after all that, a macro is needed, which encapsulates the above typedefs, and looks like the following:

```
private:
  DEFINE_OPERATOR_BOOL_TYPES(class_type, bool_gen_type, bool_type);
```

```
public:
  operator bool_type() const
  {
    return bool_gen_type::translate(. . .
```

Actually, there are two macros to cater for the times when the operator is defined inside a template, in which case the `typename` keyword is needed for a type specifier, or not, in which case it's not. Examples of these two macros, `DEFINE_OPERATOR_BOOL_TYPES()` and `DEFINE_OPERATOR_BOOL_TYPES_T()`, are found on the CD.

And that's it! It's been a lot of effort for something so conceptually simple, but I hope you'll agree that having a maximally safe, unified technique for implementing a Boolean operator is worth it. We can now provide an operator that exhibits the required semantics in conditional expressions of arbitrary complexity, suffers from none of the dangerous implicit conversions that are evinced in the other forms, and is portable to a very wide variety of compilers with the maximal safety achievable with each.

24.8   operator!

We've seen how to implement operator `"Boolean"()` and relied on the fact that the compiler can apply a logical negation to an instance supporting our operator `"Boolean"()`.

```
ExpressibleThing  e;

if(!e) // Negates operator boolean_type::return_type() const
{}
```

With both the `T const *()` and the `int T::*()` forms, all compilers tested are able to apply negation, so there is no need to explicitly provide operator `!()` in addition to our operator `"Boolean"()`.

However, there are times when this is too coarse grained. A good example is when dealing with database types, such as VARCHAR, which can, like many string class implementations, have more than two-states: null, empty, and nonempty. Essentially, for VARCHAR, and for string classes, the logical negation—whether it is implicitly done by the compiler or via an operator `!() const` method—does not have enough information. Since it is useful with such types to be able to test against these multiple states, we need to find a mechanism to do so. Naturally we must use methods:

```
class varchar_field
{
public:
  bool is_empty() const;
  bool is_null() const;
};
```

But then we run up against a lack of genericity. If we want to use the code that is testing the database fields for something else, the `is_null()` or `is_empty()` methods may not be available. The answer here, of course, is to rely on our old friends the *Attribute Shims* (section 20.2). Hence,

```
bool is_null(varchar_field const &);
bool is_empty(varchar_field const &);
bool is_not(varchar_field const &);
```

The advantage to this is that we are not forced to make a preemptive, and irreversible, decision by binding the meaning of "is" or "is not" in the type, but can delay it until appropriate, in the client code. The disadvantage is that it makes the client code less succinct—although I'd argue it is more readable—and we have to take care to maintain consistency to avoid ending up with a large number of shims, leading to confusion on the part of the authors and maintainers of code.

Fast, Non-intrusive String Concatenation

A well-known inefficiency in Java [Larm2000] is in string concatenation. The way around it is to ensure that the concatenation is done within a single statement, which facilitates a compiler optimization in which the successive arguments to the + operator are silently translated into calls to a hidden `StringBuffer` instance, resulting in a more efficient construction of the string from its constituent parts. Hence,

```
String s = s1 + " " + s2 + " " + s3;
```

is automatically converted to

```
StringBuffer  sb = new StringBuffer();
sb.append(s1);
sb.append(" ");
sb.append(s2);
sb.append(" ");
sb.append(s3);
String        s = sb.toString();
```

This results in significant increases in performance [Wils2003e] compared with manual concatenation over several statements.

Most C++ libraries overload the semantics of `operator +()` for string concatenation, resulting in similar inefficiencies as a result of the generation of the intermediate objects required in the concatenation chains. The inefficiency of C++ string concatenation sequences stems from two factors.

First, the intermediate string associated with each intermediate concatenation (each + operator subexpression) will involve at least one memory allocation[1] to accommodate the total string contents of the concatenation's two parameters.

Second, every intermediate will copy the contents of its two arguments. For an expression with N concatenations (N + operator's), arguments 0 and 1 will be copied N times, argument 1 will be copied N-1 times, and so on.

---

[1]Except in the cases where the string class uses the small-string optimization (SSO) [Meye2001], and it is applicable. Of course, as soon as the combined length of the intermediates reaches the SSO internal capacity, it then becomes a pessimization.

Assuming that the following code is compiled with a compiler that supports NRVO (see section 12.2.1), there are still likely to be between 4 and 8 memory allocations, and 4, 3, and 2 copies taken of the contents of strings s3, s2 and s1, respectively.

```
String      s1  = "Goodbye";
char const  *s2 = "cruel";
String      s3  = "world!";
String      s   = s1 + ' ' + s2 + ' ' + s3;
```

In principle, since none of the intermediate results are used (or useful) outside of the statement, all that is required is one memory allocation and one copy of the contents of each source string. Ideally, we would like to see each individual concatenation subexpression resulting only in a record being taken of the arguments, and being passed "up" the chain, until the string needs to be generated, at which point the allocation of memory, and the copying into that memory of the individual pieces of the resultant string, can be done just once.

25.1 fast_string_concatenator<>

Even if you're like me and find most programming books impossible to digest whole, I'd advise you to have a copy of Bjarne Stroustrup's *The C++ Programming Language* [Stro1997] by your bed, or in the bathroom, or next to the goggle-box,[2] and idly dip into it every now and then. It's by far the best catalyst of new ideas I've come across in C++, probably because Bjarne makes only brief but pithy mention of an idea and then moves on. (I sometimes wonder whether this is a deliberate tactic, so that all we second stringers can feel like we're inventing things that he's already anticipated.)

Chapter 22 of [Stro1997] describes how several operators can be used in a chain to represent a single logical operation for matrix manipulation. This had me wondering about whether I could apply these principles to string concatenation to achieve performance improvements: the result is the fast_string_concatenator template.[3]

25.1.1 Working with Custom String Classes

Before we get into the details of the implementation of fast_string_concatenator, let's see how we might use it with a custom string class, String.

The canonical way to implement concatenation [Meye1998] is as a nonmember function that is implemented in terms of the member operator +=():

```
String operator +(String const &lhs, char const *rhs)
{
  String result(lhs);
  result += rhs;
  return result;
}
```

---

[2]What my dad used to call the television, mostly when he'd catch me watching cartoons at unearthly hours.

[3]Unusually for me, this one wasn't dreamt up in my sleep. It was more of an Archimedes moment . . .

There's an alternate form, if `operator +=()` returns a reference to the instance:

```
String operator +(String const &lhs, char const *rhs)
{
  return String(lhs) += rhs;
}
```

It's quite clear from this implementation where all the costly intermediate instances, allocation, and copying come from. There would be similar implementations for the four other overloads:

```
String operator +(String const &lhs, char rhs);
String operator +(char const *lhs, String const &rhs);
String operator +(char lhs, String const &rhs);
String operator +(String const &lhs, String const &rhs);
```

When using `fast_string_concatenator`, the five operators share a seemingly identical, simple definition:

Listing 25.1

```
fast_string_concatenator<String>
  operator +(String const &lhs, char const *rhs)
{
  return fast_string_concatenator<String>(lhs, rhs);
}
fast_string_concatenator<String>
  operator +(String const &lhs, char rhs)
{
  return fast_string_concatenator<String>(lhs, rhs);
}
fast_string_concatenator<String>
  operator +(String const &lhs, String const &rhs);
fast_string_concatenator<String>
  operator +(char lhs, String const &rhs);
fast_string_concatenator<String>
  operator +(String const &lhs, String const &rhs);
```

The most obvious difference is that they no longer return instances of `String`, instead returning instances of `fast_string_concatenator<String>`. The implementation of each operator is simply to pass the two arguments to the constructor of the anonymous concatenator instance, which will be subject to RVO (see section 12.2).

25.1.2   Tying the Concatenators Together

Since each `operator +()` returns a concatenator, we clearly need more if we're going to make multipart concatenation sequences. This is facilitated by a number of standard `operator`

+() overloads that are defined along with the class. The first three we'll look at each take a concatenator instance as their left-hand parameter:

```
template <typename S, typename C, typename T>
fast_string_concatenator<S, C, T>
  operator +(fast_string_concatenator<S, C, T> const &lhs, S const &rhs);
. . .
  operator +(fast_string_concatenator<S, C, T> const &lhs, C const *rhs);
. . .
  operator +(fast_string_concatenator<S, C, T> const &lhs, C const rhs);
```

Since the + operator is left-to-right associative, these three operators enable the result of the left-most concatenation to be bound with the next, and so on. Looking at our example, "Goodbye" and ' ' are concatenated to form a concatenator instance using one of the custom String operator +()s, which is then concatenated with "cruel" via the second of the standard ones shown earlier.

In this way, any permutation of character, C-style string and string class can be combined in a concatenation sequence, resulting in a final fast_string_concatenator instance. There's more to it, such as concatenation seeding (see section 24.4) and pathological bracing (see section 25.5), but that's essentially it for the operators in normal circumstances.

25.1.3 The Concatenator Class

Now it's time to look at the concatenator class itself. We've already seen that it is a template, and that it takes three template parameters. The three parameters S, C, and T represent the string type, the character type, and the traits type, respectively

```
template< typename S
        , typename C = typename S::value_type
        , typename T = std::char_traits<C>
        >
class fast_string_concatenator;
```

In the definition of the class, C defaults to S::value_type, and T defaults to std::char_traits<C>. These are provided as default parameters rather than just assumed to allow wider application of the template.

In most cases, therefore, one only has to be concerned about the string type, and leave the rest to the defaults. Since most modern string classes define a value_type member type, it works swimmingly. For those that do not, it is not difficult to stipulate both first and second types in the concatenator instantiation, or to use a type veneer (see Chapter 21) to provide the necessary member types for the string.

We've seen that all the operator +() implementations follow precisely the same form by returning an anonymous instance of the concatenator, constructed from the left and right hand parameters to the operator. This is reflected in the public interface of the class, as shown in Listing 25.2.

Listing 25.2
```
template< . . . >
class fast_string_concatenator
{
public:
  typedef S                               string_type;
  typedef C                               char_type;
  typedef T                               traits_type;
  typedef fast_string_concatenator<S, C, T> class_type;
// Construction
public:
  fast_. . . (string_type const &lhs, string_type const &rhs);
  fast_. . . (string_type const &lhs, char_type const *rhs);
  fast_. . . (string_type const &lhs, char_type const rhs);
  fast_. . . (char_type const *lhs, string_type const &rhs);
  fast_. . . (char_type const lhs, string_type const &rhs);

  fast_. . . (class_type const &lhs, string_type const &rhs);
  fast_. . . (class_type const &lhs, char_type const *rhs);
  fast_. . . (class_type const &lhs, char_type const rhs);
// Conversion
public:
  operator string_type() const;

  . . .
```

You'll also note the only other public method of the class, which is an implicit conversion operator to the string_type. (You see, I told you there were rare occasions when it's good to have such a thing!) Now you can see how we get back the resultant string from the concatenator. This method has a simple implementation:

```
template< . . . >
fast_string_concatenator<S, C, T>::operator S() const
{
  size_t     len = length();
  string_type result(len, '~');
  write(&result[0]);
  assert(len == traits_type::length(result.c_str()));
  return result;
}
```

The concatenator's length() method is called, then a string instance result is created of the given length, using the standard library's *String* model's constructor (C++-98: 21.3.1) that takes a length and the character to assign to all elements. This is how we achieve the single memory allocation for the entire concatenation sequence. You could use any character here—the code shown uses '~' as an eye-catcher—since they will all be overwritten. In fact, this represents a possible future optimization of the technique, whereby one could have a private constructor of the string class, to which the concatenator had access, which would allocate and zero terminate the string contents but not otherwise initialize its contents. (Though as we'll see later, the excellent performance of the current solution probably makes this unnecessary.)

Next the `write()` method is called, passing the address of the start of `result`'s internal memory. This method walks the concatenation sequence and writes the contents into the given memory. When it returns, `result` contains the result of the concatenation and is returned. If your compiler supports NRVO, then `result` will actually be the variable receiving the result of the concatenation sequence in the client code.

25.1.4   Internal Implementation

Before we look at the implementation of the `length()` and `write()` methods, I'll show you the remainder of the class definition—Listing 25.3—so you'll see how the arguments to the individual concatenation operators are represented as a network.

Listing 25.3

```
template< . . . >
class fast_string_concatenator
{
  . . . // Public interface
private:
  struct Data
  {
    struct CString
    {
      size_t        len;
      char_type const *s;
    };
    union DataRef
    {
      CString         cstring;
      char_type       ch;
      class_type  const *concat;
    };
    enum DataType
    {
        seed     // Argument was the seed type
      , single  // Argument was a single character
      , cstring // Argument was a C-string or string object
      , concat  // Argument was another concatenator
    };
    Data(string_type const &s);
    Data(char_type const *s);
    Data(char_type ch s);
    Data(class_type const &fc);
    Data(fsc_seed const &fc);
```

```
    size_t    length() const;
    char_type *write(char_type *s) const;

    DataType const  type;
    DataRef         ref;
  };
  friend struct Data;
private:
  char_type *write(char_type *s) const;
private:
  Data            m_lhs;
  Data            m_rhs;
  . . .
};
```

The nested structure Data is a discriminated union of a single character ch, a character sequence cstring (of type struct CString), and a pointer to a concatenator concat. Each concatenator instance contains two instances of this structure, m_lhs and m_rhs, representing the two arguments to operator +(). Now it's clear how the network is represented. Except for single characters, all the other types—c-strings, string objects, and concatenator instances—are referenced by pointers.

This is perfectly valid because C++ requires that temporary objects remain alive (i.e., do not have their destructors called) until the end of the statement in which they are constructed. Hence, all the temporary objects in the concatenation sequence are still valid at the point that the final fast_string_concatenator<String> instance is used to create the final string instance.

In our original example, the network builds as follows:

```
// FC = shorthand for temporary fast_string_concatenator<String>
FC#1: lhs == c-string ("Goodbye"); m_rhs == character (' ')
FC#2: lhs == ptr to FC (FC#1);     m_rhs == c-string ("cruel")
FC#3: lhs == ptr to FC (FC#2);     m_rhs == character (' ')
FC#4: lhs == ptr to FC (FC#3);     m_rhs == c-string ("world!")
```

FC#4 is the instance on which operator string_type() const is called to return the result to the client code.

Given that we know how the network is constructed, the implementations of length() and write() are very straightforward. First length().

```
template< . . . >
size_t fast_string_concatenator<S, C, T>::length() const
{
  return m_lhs.length() + m_rhs.length();
}
```

The length of a given concatenator is simply the sum of the two arguments it represents. Hence it defers to its m_lhs and m_rhs members. The implementation of Data::length() switches on the data type, recursing in the concat case:

Listing 25.4

```
. . .
switch(type)
{
  case    seed:
    len = 0;
    break;
  case    single:
    len = 1;
    break;
  case    cstring:
    len = ref.cstring.len;
    break;
  case    concat:
    len = ref.concat->length();
    break;
}
. . .
```

Note that the normal wisdom of having a default case is not followed here. This is because tests showed that it cost 1 to 5% performance on several compilers involved in the test (see below). The actual code contains a run time assertion (see section 1.4) such as the following:

```
assert( type == cstring || type == single ||
        type == concat || type == seed);
```

The result of the outermost length() call is used in the implicit conversion operator to create a string of exactly the required size; hence only one allocation is needed.

But how do we achieve the single write operation? This starts out in the concatenator's write() method:

```
template< . . . >
C *fast_string_concatenator<S, C, T>::write(C *s) const
{
  return m_rhs.write(m_lhs.write(s));
}
```

The left-hand side writes out its contents into the buffer that is passed into the method via Data::write(), which returns the point at which it finished writing. This is then passed to the right-hand side, and the result of that is passed back to the caller.

The implementation of Data::write() follows a similar pattern to the length() method, in switching on the data type. Single characters are copied in and the write pointer advanced by one. The contents of string objects and C-style strings are copied into the buffer via memcpy(), and the pointer is advanced by the appropriate amount. For concatenators, the write() method is called and its return value returned.

Listing 25.5

```
template< . . . >
C *fast_string_concatenator<S, C, T>::Data::write(C *s) const
{
  size_t  len;
  switch(type)
  {
    case    seed:
      break;
    case    single:
      *(s++) = ref.ch;
      break;
    case    cstring:
      len = ref.cstring.len;
      memcpy(s, ref.cstring.s, sizeof(C) * len);
      s += len;
      break;
    case    concat:
      s = ref.concat->write(s);
      break;
  }
  return s;
}
```

Hence, write() copies in the requisite number of characters for the data type, and then passes back the address of the next location in which to write. That means that the reversed double call m_rhs.write(m_lhs.write(s)) in fast_string_concatenator<>::write() results in the string being written in correct order, and in a single pass.

It may seem like a lot of code, but you can be assured that good compilers make short work of such things. In optimized builds it is very efficient indeed.

It's worth noting that by using only standard expected public operations of a string classes, application of the concatenator to arbitrary string types is nonintrusive.

25.2   Performance

I've tested the concatenator with quite a number of different string classes, and it has the same excellent performance characteristics with all of them. We look at the performance of three string classes in particular.

The first, trivial_string, is a custom class written specifically for this test. It has two members, m_len (size_t) and m_s (char_type *), which hold the length and a dynamically allocated character buffer. It uses new and delete to allocate the memory, and stores

exactly the amount of memory required for the current contents and the terminating null character. In other words, it is a bog-standard string class.

The second string used is the standard library's `basic_string`. Since different compiler
vendors use different implementations, the performances between the different standard strings
will be representative as much of the library implementation as it is of the compiler. Despite this
likely variation, I've included this string since it represents, for many developers, *the* string
class; the other two strings here will clearly demonstrate compiler, rather than library, differences in application of the concatenator.

The third string is STLSoft's `basic_simple_string<>`, which stores its capacity and
length along with the string contents in a resizable dynamically allocated buffer and which performs optimistic allocation on a granularity of 32 characters.

The same test program was used for the three string types, measuring the performance of
concatenation sequences of 1, 2, 3, 4, 8, 16, and 32 with and without `fast_string_`
`concatenator`.[4] The results shown here represent the relative times, as a percentage, of the
`fast_string_concatenator` with respect to the normal `operator +()` implementations
provided with the given string class. Values lower than 100% indicate a superior performance
for the concatenator. The program was compiled and tested with Borland (v5.6), CodeWarrior
(v8), Digital Mars (v8.38), GCC (v3.2), Intel (v7.0), and Visual C++ (versions 6.0 and 7.1).

Table 25.1 shows the performances for the `trivial_string` class, Table 25.2 shows the
performances for `std::basic_string<char>`, and Table 25.3 shows the performances for
`stlsoft::basic_simple_string<char>`.

Before I conducted the tests, my expectation was that using the concatenator for sequences
of one or two concatenations would actually result in a performance hit, with only longer sequences feeling the benefit of the optimization. Thankfully, in most cases, it seems that I under-
estimated the effect of the optimization. Though the data points for 16 and 32 concatenations
are merely academic—if you're writing code with 32 concatenations, you probably need to take
a holiday—the savings to be had for up to, say, 8 concatenations are considerable, up to 80%.

With `trivial_string` (see Table 25.1), every data point demonstrates a superior performance for the concatenator, so using it for this class represents an unconditional win. Roughly

Table 25.1   Relative performance of the concatenator for the `trivial_string` class.

#Concats	Borland	CodeWarrior	Digital Mars	GCC	Intel	VC++ (6.0)	VC++ (7.1)	Average
1	90.8%	77.8%	87.8%	77.5%	64.8%	92.6%	99.6%	84.4%
2	47.8%	42.8%	47.9%	38.4%	36.8%	52.3%	52.8%	45.5%
3	35.2%	29.7%	34.5%	29.1%	25.9%	36.9%	37.0%	32.6%
4	29.1%	24.3%	28.4%	25.0%	23.9%	29.7%	29.6%	27.1%
8	24.2%	19.6%	24.0%	21.3%	19.1%	24.3%	23.6%	22.3%
16	13.3%	7.7%	13.8%	12.2%	11.0%	11.4%	10.7%	11.4%
32	9.6%	4.2%	8.9%	10.2%	7.7%	6.5%	7.7%	7.8%

---

[4]The test program and full results are all included on the CD.

Table 25.2 Relative performance of the concatenator for `std::basic_string<char>`.

#Concats	Borland	CodeWarrior	Digital Mars	GCC	Intel	VC++ (6.0)	VC++ (7.1)	Average
1	101.4%	89.4%	132.8%	91.3%	55.1%	188.1%	170.8%	118.4%
2	56.1%	57.4%	91.7%	52.9%	44.9%	108.7%	137.5%	78.5%
3	43.0%	44.2%	71.3%	39.0%	32.1%	76.2%	76.3%	54.6%
4	36.9%	33.8%	64.4%	35.2%	23.7%	59.5%	48.1%	43.1%
8	30.7%	30.6%	63.9%	31.8%	20.5%	49.0%	47.1%	39.1%
16	15.6%	14.3%	49.3%	25.3%	10.7%	26.2%	16.2%	22.5%
32	12.9%	10.2%	26.1%	16.7%	8.5%	19.6%	11.0%	15.0%

speaking, a concatenation sequence of length 2 is twice as fast, and one of length 3 is three times as fast. This is very encouraging, but the string implementation is quite rudimentary so perhaps we shouldn't count any chickens just yet.

With STLSoft `basic_simple_string` (see Table 25.3), the performance results are almost as encouraging, except that for a single concatenation CodeWarrior and Digital Mars both suffer a small performance penalty, of 27% and 2%, respectively. Despite that, I think it's clear that using the concatenator represents a definite win.

The results for `std::basic_string` (see Table 25.2) are somewhat less conclusive. Some standard library implementations use reference counting and copy-on-write, and this may affect the performance advantage of the concatenator. For a single concatenation, Borland and Digital Mars both suffer a small cost, although at 1% and 33%, they're not particularly off putting. Of more concern is that both Visual C++ versions exhibit a performance loss for concatenation sequences of length 1 *and* 2. Of course, we might simply surmise that the Visual C++ run time library has such a good string implementation that the concatenator cannot keep up until sequences of three or more elements. However, since the Intel performance was obtained with the Visual C++ 7.0 library, whose string implementation is virtually identical to that

Table 25.3 Relative performance of the concatenator for `stlsoft::basic_simple_string<char>`.

#Concats	Borland	CodeWarrior	Digital Mars	GCC	Intel	VC++ (6.0)	VC++ (7.1)	Average
1	98.6%	127.2%	102.1%	67.7%	50.8%	99.3%	99.7%	92.2%
2	62.4%	82.8%	98.8%	42.8%	33.9%	67.0%	65.4%	64.7%
3	50.3%	61.5%	74.7%	31.7%	29.4%	51.1%	49.8%	49.8%
4	44.6%	53.6%	66.3%	29.0%	27.6%	46.5%	41.2%	44.1%
8	37.6%	45.6%	55.3%	23.3%	23.8%	40.8%	35.6%	37.4%
16	21.8%	21.4%	25.7%	13.7%	15.6%	21.9%	18.0%	19.7%
32	17.9%	13.7%	15.2%	10.6%	13.7%	14.6%	13.8%	14.2%

Table 25.4

#Concats	VC++ (6.0)	VC++ (6.0) + concatenator	VC++ (7.1)	VC++ (7.1) + concatenator
1	143	269	226	386
2	263	286	275	378
3	408	311	476	363
4	543	323	761	366
8	665	326	969	456
16	2338	613	4116	667
32	5180	1016	9232	1011

for version 7.1,[5] that explanation doesn't really hold water. In other words, where Visual C++ has a relative performance of 171% and 138% Intel has a relative performance of 55% and 49%. This goes to show the effect that the template optimizing capabilities of the compiler can have on the use of such a scheme. It is my belief that as compilers continue to improve in their abilities to optimize templates, the exceptional levels of performance afforded by the concatenator with the Intel compiler will be more broadly applicable.

Notwithstanding potential future improvements in compilers, I would suggest that use of the fast concatenator with string libraries represents a net win, and a significant one at that, although it must be conceded that, for Visual C++ at least, performance profiling might be needed to prove this. To inform on that, it's interesting to take a look at the absolute concatenation times, in milliseconds, for the two compilers (see Table 25.4).

Using the concatenator does not linearize the time cost with respect to the number of concatenation elements, but it does flatten the exponential growth considerably. Hence, in any software where the average sequence length is greater than 2, there are likely to be significant savings even with Visual C++.

25.3   Working with Other String Classes

So far we've seen how the concatenator can be used with your own string class by implementing your `operator +()` overloads in terms of the `fast_string_concatenator<>`. In this guise, there are no problems of any kind, and it all simply works.

However, you might also wish to use the concatenator with other string classes, in which case there are several issues of which you need to be aware.

25.3.1   Incorporation into Standard Libraries

In order to ensure that the concatenator would be compatible with standard library implementations (see section 25.6), I hacked it into the standard library headers of all the compilers tested. Although it's not possible to include them on the CD for copyright reasons, I can assure you that it was simple and easy to do, and there were no surprises.

---

[5]Indeed, performing the same test using Intel 7.1 using Visual C++ 7.1 libraries shows virtually identical performance to the Intel 7.0 performance shown here.

25.3.2 Incorporation into Modifiable Extant Classes

The concatenation operators of extant string classes can be "upgraded" simply and safely by replacing the existing operators with equivalent versions incorporating the concatenator. If your organization has its own string classes, then you will be able to upgrade them and the only effect to any client code, once it's recompiled, will be that it will run faster: that's not something you often get to say in software engineering!

To test this out, I've done it to several existing string classes from different libraries, including MFC's `CString` and STLSoft's `basic_simple_string`.

25.3.3 Interoperation with Nonmodifiable Classes

This is where things get a little tricky. If you're using a third-party library, such as MFC's `CString`, you should not alter the headers that accompany the library. Any future update of the library will overwrite your changes. Even worse, some libraries, such as MFC, come in part in binary format, so any changes to the headers will not be reflected in the binary part of the library. At best you're going to get a crash in testing. Don't do it!

But we like the concatenation optimization, and we want to use it with third-party libraries. So what do we do?

If the string class you're interested in does not provide its own operators, then your task is comparatively easy. You can either define the new operators within the global namespace, which is appropriate on an application level, or within your own namespace if you'll be using these operators with your own libraries. Of course, if the string class comes in a third-party namespace, then you *could* define the operators in that namespace. To do that, however, you must have missed the "Namespaces Dos and Don'ts: 101" as it's a very foolish thing to add things into namespaces that you're not responsible for; conflicting things can be placed in that namespace at any time by the authors of the libraries.

If the string class comes with its own operators, you're in stickier waters. If it's a template class, then you can define your own operators *for specific instantiations* of the string template. In other words, if the string is `tp_string`, you can define your own operators for `tp_string<char>`, or `tp_string<wchar_t>`, or whatever, since a compiler can unambiguously select a nontemplate function over a template one. If it's not a template class, you're stuck. Even if you write your own concatenator-returning overloads in a "nearer" namespace, Koenig lookup (see sections 6.2 and 20.7) will ensure that the compiler can see multiple equivalent operators, and it will rightly fail to compile. For this we need concatenation seeding.

25.4 Concatenation Seeding

Since the + operator is left-to-right associative, the compiler takes its cue from the left-hand argument prior to looking at the right-hand argument. We can take advantage of this to lead it down the path we want it to follow.

In the same namespace as `fast_string_concatenator<>` is defined another class `fsc_seed`:

```
class fsc_seed
{};
```

We saw references to this in the constructor of the `Data` nested class and the `DataType` enum. This class extends the nonintrusive nature of the technique by allowing us to seed a concatenation sequence involving *any* string type to use fast concatenation:

```
String s = fsc_seed() + s1 + " " + s2 + " " + s3;
```

In this case, all we need to make it work is define a single `operator +()` overload:

```
fast_string_concatenator<String>
  operator +(fsc_seed const &lhs, String const &rhs)
{
  return fast_concat_t(lhs, rhs);
}
```

and the compiler does the rest. The result of the first concatenation is `fast_string_concatenator<String>`, so the next operator is deduced (via Koenig lookup) to be one of the standard ones in the concatenator's namespace. Naturally, such a thing is a little ugly, but it's better than messing around in the headers of third-party libraries, and it's a solution where otherwise none is available. It also allows you to explicitly use fast concatenation in some parts of your code and not others. It's analogous to `operator new(nothrow)` (C++-98: 18.4).

Although it hardly counts as a disadvantage, when writing templates you must follow the constraint that the first element in the sequence after the seed is of string class type, rather than a character or a C-style string, since there would be no way to deduce the string type from the character type in the corresponding `operator +()`:

```
template< . . . >
fast_string_concatenator<S, C, T>
  operator +(fsc_seed const &lhs, C const *rhs) // What is S??
{
  return fast_string_concatenator<S, C, T>(lhs, rhs);
}
```

The use of seeding does very little damage to the performance characteristics of fast concatenation.

25.5 Pathological Bracing

You might think you've spotted a flaw in the technique, whereby unnecessary, but perfectly legal, bracing could break the technique, or at least render it ineffective. In the following code, the application of the parentheses has reversed the order of evaluation.

```
String s = s1 + (" " + (s2 + (" " + s3)));
```

Although such things would likely only occur as a result of some helpful soul trying to demonstrate that fast concatenation could be broken, it's already been dealt with. We have more overloads to cope with all cases:

Listing 25.6

```
template < . . . >
fast_string_concatenator<S, C, T>
  operator +(fsc_seed const &, fast_. . .< > const &);
. . .
  operator +(fast_. . .< > const &, fast_. . .< > const &);
. . .
  operator +(S const &, fast_. . .< > const &);
. . .
  operator +(C const *, fast_. . .< > const &);
. . .
  operator +(C const &, fast_. . .< > const &);
```

and the corresponding constructors in the class:

```
fast_. . . (class_type const &lhs, class_type const &rhs);
fast_. . . (string_type const &lhs, class_type const &rhs);
fast_. . . (char_type const *lhs, class_type const &rhs);
fast_. . . (char_type const lhs, class_type const &rhs);
```

The interesting thing about the use of this bracing is that not only can it not break the legality of the code but, just as with seeding, it scarcely affects performance.[6]

25.6 Standardization

Since this technique brings only benefits, you may wonder whether it should be adopted as a standard mechanism. Not being a member of the standards committee, I cannot answer that, and it may be that there are ramifications precluding its adoption that I've not thought of. (The only thing I have been able to come up with is that one would not be able to declare pointers to functions such as S (*)(S const &, S const &) and assign to them the address of std::operator +(). I can't imagine any reason why anyone would do that, so it doesn't seem particularly dissuasive.)

Naturally it would be great if this mechanism were adopted, and I'm currently talking with compiler and library vendors to get their feedback; at least one vendor is keen so far. It's possible that you'll see fast_string_concatenator in a library near you in the future!

Whether that happens or not, though, there's no reason why you can't use it in your own string libraries, or apply it nonintrusively in your own client code, and take advantage of the performance improvements it confers.

---

[6]Full results for both seeding and pathological bracing are included on the CD.

What's Your Address?

Programmers who overload unary operator& should be sentenced to writing libraries that need to operate properly when fed such classes.

—Peter Dimov, esteemed Boost member, Boost newsgroup June 2002

Although that's very funny, it's also a pretty strong statement. Why is there such antipathy to the use of this operator?

In this chapter we look at some of the problems that overloading `operator &()` can cause. Our solution will be an unexciting one, simply the recommendation that you follow Peter's implicit advice, forswear any use of this overload for shortsighted gains, and avoid much grief down the line.

One thing I should make clear. Anytime in this chapter that I refer to `operator &()` it will be the unary form, which is the address of operator. The binary form, which is the bitwise OR operator, is an entirely different beast.

```
class Int
{
  Int operator &(Int const &);   // Bitwise operator
  void *operator &()             // Address-of operator
. . .
```

26.1   Can't Get the Real Address

Like most C++ operators, you're free to return anything you like from `operator &()`. This means that you can alter the value, or the type, or both. This can be a powerful aid in rare circumstances, but it can also cause you a world of trouble.

26.1.1   STL Containment

The standard library containers store contained elements via in-place construction. For instance, containers following the *Vector* model (C++-98: 23.2.4) maintain a block of memory within which each element is stored contiguously. Since they are resizable, there needs to be a mechanism to add and remove elements from this storage, which is provided by the allocators. The *Allocator* concept [Aust1999, Muss2001] includes the `construct()` and `destroy()` methods, whose canonical definitions are as follows:

```
template <typename T>
struct some_allocator
```

```
{
  . . .
  void construct(T* p, T const &x)
  {
    new(p) T(x);
  }
  void destroy(T* p)
  {
   p->~T();
  }
  . . .
```

The `construct()` method is used by containers to in-place construct elements, as in:

```
template <typename T, . . . >
void list::insert(. . ., T const &x)
{
  . . .
  Node *node = . . .
  get_allocator().construct(&node->value, x);
```

If the type, `T`, that you're storing in the list overloads `operator &()` to return a value that cannot be converted to `T*`, then this line will fail to compile.

26.1.2 ATL Wrapper Classes and CAdapt

One of the major beefs I have with Microsoft's Active Template Library (ATL)—which, like most frameworks, started out with high ideals—is the heavy overloading of `operator &`. There are quite a number of classes that overload it, including `CComBSTR`, `CComPtr` and `CComVariant`.

To account for the incompatibility between ATL types and STL containers, the designers of ATL introduced the `CAdapt` template, which attempts to solve the problem by containing an instance of its parameterizing type. It then provides implicit conversion operators and comparison operations to allow it to be used in place of its parameterizing type. Because `CAdapt<T>` does not overload `operator &()`, it can be used to mask the overload for any `T` that does.

Listing 26.1
```
template <typename T>
class CAdapt
{
public:
  CAdapt();
  CAdapt(const T& rSrc);
  CAdapt(const CAdapt& rSrCA);
  CAdapt &operator =(const T& rSrc);
  bool operator <(const T& rSrc) const
  {
```

```
    return m_T < rSrc;
  }
  bool operator ==(const T& rSrc) const;
  operator T&()
  {
    return m_T;
  }
  operator const T&() const;

  T m_T;
};
```

Unfortunately, this is just a Band-Aid on a broken arm. As we saw in Chapter 23, templates that inherit from their parameterizing type have a deal of trouble in unambiguously providing access to the requisite constructors of their parent class. The same problem exists for types such as CAdapt, which enhance their parameterizing type via containment rather than inheritance. All the constructors of T, except the default and copy constructors, are inaccessible. This clutters your code, reduces the applicability of generic algorithms, and prevents the use of RAII (see section 3.5).

26.1.3   Getting the Real Address

So is there a way to get at the real address? Since there is no equivalent overloadable operator for eliciting a reference from an object, we can use some dubious reference casting to get our address, along the lines of the following attribute shim (see Chapter 20):

```
template<typename T>
T *get_real_address(T &t)
{
  return reinterpret_cast<T*>(&reinterpret_cast<byte_t &>(t));
}
```

There are other complications, to account for const and/or volatile, but that's the essence of it. The Boost libraries have a nifty addressof() function, which takes account of all the issues.

But the use of reinterpret_cast is cause for some concern. The standard (C++-98: 5/2.10;3) says, "[T]he mapping performed . . . is implementation-defined. [Note: it is intended to be unsurprising to those who know the addressing structure of the underlying machine]." Since the result may conceivably not be valid, it's not possible to claim that this technique is truly portable. However, it's also pretty hard to imagine a compiler that would not perform the expected conversion.

We can now sidestep types with pathological operator &() overloads, but this would require peppering all our code with calls to the real address shim. But it's ugly, and its correctness is implementation defined. Do you want to use a standard library implemented with myriad reinterpret_casts?

26.2   What Actions Are Carried Out during Conversion?

Since it's a function like any other, the `operator &()` overload can do things other than simply return a converted value. This has serious consequences.

Imperfection: Overloading `operator &()` breaks encapsulation.

That's a bold statement. Let me illustrate why it is so.

As I've mentioned already, ATL has a large number of wrapper classes that overload `operator &()`. Unfortunately, there are different semantics to their implementations. The types shown in Table 26.1 all have an assertion in the operator method to ensure that the current value is NULL.

Don't worry about the specifics of the types TYPEATTR, VARDESC, and FUNCDESC—they're POD open type structures (see section 4.4) used for manipulating COM meta data. The important thing to note is that they have allocated resources associated with them, but they do not provide value semantics, which means that they must be managed carefully in order to prevent resource leaks or use of dangling pointers.

The operator is overloaded in the wrapper classes to allow these types to be used with COM API functions that manipulate the underlying types, and to be thus initialized. Of course, it's not an initialization as we RAII-phile C++ types know and love it, but it is initialization, because the assertion means that any subsequent attempt to repeat the process will result in an error, in debug mode at least. I'll leave it up to you to decide whether that, in and of itself, is a good way to design wrapper classes, but you can see that you are required to look inside the library to see what is going on. After all, it's using an overloaded operator, not calling a function named `get_one_time_content_pointer()`.[1]

The widely used CComBSTR class, which wraps the COM BSTR type, also overloads `operator &()` to return BSTR*, but it does *not* have an assertion. By contra-implication, we assume that this means that it's okay to take the address of a CComBSTR multiple times, and, since the operator is non-const, that we can make multiple modifying manipulations to the

Table 26.1

Wrapper Classes	Operator &() return type
CComTypeAttr	TYPEATTR**
CComVarDesc	VARDESC**
CComFuncDesc	FUNCDESC**
CComPtr / CComQIPtr	T**
CHeapPtr	T**

---

[1]Of course, in an ideal world one would only have to read the documentation to understand, and memorably absorb, the fine nuances of the libraries such as those mentioned in this section. However, this is anything but the case. Documentation is at least one conceptual step away from the code-face, out of date the moment it's written, and difficult to write (either by the author of the code, who knows too much, or by another party, who knows too little). In reality, the code is often the documentation [Glas2003].

encapsulated `BSTR` without ill-effect. Alas, this is not the case. `CComBStr` can be made to leak memory with ease:

```
void SetBSTR(char const *str, BSTR *pbstr);

CComBSTR          bstr;

SetBSTR("Doctor", &bstr);   // All ok so far
SetBSTR("Proctor", &bstr);  // "Doctor" is now lost forever!
```

We can surmise that the reason `CComBSTR` does not assert is that it proved too inconvenient. For example, it is not uncommon to see in COM an API function or interface method that will take an array of `BSTR`. Putting aside the issue of passing arrays of derived types (see sections 14.5; 33.4), we might wish to use our `CComBSTR` when we're only passing one string.

An alternative strategy is to release the encapsulated resource within the `operator &()` method. This is the approach of another popular Microsoft COM wrapper class, the Visual C++ `_com_ptr_t` template. The downside of this approach is that the wrapper is subject to premature release on those occasions when you need to pass a pointer to the encapsulated resource to a function that will merely be using it, rather than destroying it or removing it from your wrapper. You may think that you can solve this by declaring const and non-const overloads of `operator &()`, as in Listing 26.2.

Listing 26.2
```
template <typename T>
class X
{
  . . .
  T const *operator &() const
  {
    return &m_t;
  }
  T *operator &()
  {
    Release(m_t);
    m_t = T();
    return &m_t;
  }
}
```

Unfortunately, this won't help, because the compiler selects the overload appropriate to the const-ness of the instance on which it's to be called, rather than on the use one might be making of the returned value. Even if you pass the address of a non-const X<T> instance to a function that takes `T const *`, the non-const overload will be called.

To me, all this stuff is so overwhelmingly nasty that I stopped using any such classes a long time ago. Now I like to use explicitly named methods and/or shims to save me from all the uncertainty. For example, I use the sublimely named[2] BStr class to wrap BSTR. It provides the DestructiveAddress() and NonDestructiveAddress() methods, which, though profoundly ugly, don't leave anyone guessing as to what's going on.

26.3   What Do We Return?

Another source of abuse in overload operator &() is in the type it returns. Since we can make it return anything, it's easy to have it return something bad; naturally, this is the case for any operator.

We saw in Chapter 14 some of the problems attendant in passing arrays of inherited types with functions that take pointers to the base type. There's another dimension to that nasty problem when overloading operator &(). Consider the following types:

Listing 26.3

```
struct THING
{
  int i;
  int j;
};
struct Thing
{
  THING thing;
  int   k;

  THING *operator &()
  {
    return &thing;
  }
  THING const *operator &() const;
};
```

Now we're in the same position we would be if Thing inherited publicly from THING.

```
void func(THING *things, size_t cThings);

Thing things[10];

func(&things[0], dimensionof(things)); // Oop!!
```

By providing the operator &() overloads for "convenience," we've exposed ourselves to abuse of the Thing type. I'm not going to suggest the application of any of the measures described in Chapter 14 here, because I think overloading operator &() is just a big no-no.

---

[2]This was a definite case of not thinking before coding. The names BSTR and BStr are far too alike, and have caused me not a little bother.

A truly bizarre confluence of factors is the case where the operator is destructive—it releases the resources—and you are passing an array of (even correctly size) wrapper class instances to a function, as in Listing 26.4.

Listing 26.4

```
struct ANOTHER
{
  . . .
};


void func(ANOTHER *things, size_t cThings);
inline void func(array_proxy<ANOTHER> const &things)
{
  func(things.base(), things.size());
}


class Another
{
  ANOTHER *operator &()
  {
    ReleaseAndReset(m_another);
    return &m_another;
  }
private:
  ANOTHER m_another;
};
```

Let's assume you're on your best behavior and are using an array_proxy (see section 14.5.5) and translator method to ensure that ANOTHER and Another can be used together.

```
Another  things[5];

. . . // Modify things

func(things); // sizeof(ANOTHER) must == sizeof(Another)
```

Irrespective of the semantics of func(), in calling the function things[0] will be reset and things[1] – things[4] will not be affected. This is because the array constructor of array_proxy uses explicit array subscript syntax, as all good array manipulation code should (see Chapter 27). If you were to do it manually, you'd still need to apply the operator, unless Another inherited publicly from ANOTHER and you called the two parameter version of func() and relied on array decay (see section 14.2).

If func() does not change the contents of the array passed to it, then this supposedly benign call has the nasty side effect of destroying the first element passed to it. If func() modifies the contents of the array, then things[1] – things[4] are subject to resource leaks, as their contents prior to the call are simply overwritten by func().

26.4   What's Your Address: Coda

I hope I've managed to convince you that Peter was spot on. Overloading `operator &()` is just far too much trouble. Consider the amount of coding time, thinking time, and debugging time that is expended trying to understand and work with libraries that use it, I struggle to imagine how using it helps the software engineering community.[3]

In short, don't do it. In grepping through all my source databases at the time of writing, I found eleven uses of it. Of the three that were used in "proper" classes—that is, those that are not in utility or meta-programming classes—I can probably truly justify only one of them. I removed two immediately.[4] The third I cannot justify, but I'm keeping it for reasons of expediency. For grins, I'll describe this in the following subsection.

26.4.1   A Sensationalist Backflip!

I'm not going to try to justify this to you; you can make up your own mind whether its utility outweighs the many good reasons against overloading `operator &()`.

The Win32 API defines many nonstandard basic structures, oftentimes for closely related types. Further, since many Win32 compilers did not provide 64-bit integers in the early years of the operating system, there are several 64-bit structures that filled in the gap. Two such structures are `ULARGE_INTEGER` and `FILETIME`. Their structures are as follows:

```
struct FILETIME
{
  uint32_t     dwLowDateTime;
  uint32_t     dwHighDateTime;
};


union ULARGE_INTEGER
{
  struct
  {
    uint32_t  LowPart;
    uint32_t  HighPart;
  };
  uint64_t     QuadPart;
};
```

Performing arithmetic using the `FILETIME` structure is tiresome, to say the least. On little-endian systems, the layout is identical to that of `ULARGE_INTEGER`, so that one can cast instances of one type to the other; hence one can manipulate two subtract `FILETIME` structures by casting them to `ULARGE_INTEGER` and subtracting the `QuadPart` members.

---

[3]Keeping developers employed in remediation work doesn't count, since they'd be better off working on new projects, as would be their employers.

[4]There's another reason to write a book: you get to go through all your own code and learn how much you didn't used to know.

```
FILETIME ft1 = . . .
FILETIME ft2 = . . .
FILETIME ft3;

GetFileTme(h1, NULL, NULL, &ft1);
GetFileTme(h2, NULL, NULL, &ft2);

// Subtract them - yuck!
reinterpret_cast<ULARGE_INTEGER&>(ft3).QuadPart =
  reinterpret_cast<ULARGE_INTEGER&>(ft1).QuadPart -
  reinterpret_cast<ULARGE_INTEGER&>(ft2).QuadPart;
```

This also is pretty tiresome, so I concocted the `ULargeInteger` class. It supplies various arithmetic operations (see Chapter 29), has a compatible layout with the two structures, and provides an `operator &()` overload. The operator returns an instance of `Address_proxy`, whose definition is shown in Listing 26.5.

Listing 26.5
```
union ULargeInteger
{
private:
  struct Address_proxy
  {
    Address_proxy(void *p)
      : m_p(p)
    {}
    operator FILETIME *()
    {
      return static_cast<FILETIME*>(p);
    }
    operator FILETIME const *() const;
    operator ULARGE_INTEGER *()
    {
      return static_cast<ULARGE_INTEGER*>(p);
    }
    operator ULARGE_INTEGER const *() const;
  private:
    void  *m_p;
  // Not to be implemented
  private:
    Address_proxy &operator =(Address_proxy const&);
  };
  Address_proxy operator &()
  {
    return Address_proxy(this);
  }
```

```
Address_proxy const operator &() const;
. . .
```

It holds a reference to the `ULargeInteger` instance for which it acts, and it provides implicit conversions to both `FILETIME*` and `ULARGE_INTEGER*`. Since the proxy class is `private` and instances of it are only returned from the `ULargeInteger`'s address-of operators, it is relatively proof from abuse, though you'd be stuck if you tried to put it in an STL container. But it considerably eases the burden of using these Win32 structures:

```
ULargeInteger ft1 = . . .
ULargeInteger ft2 = . . .

GetFileTme(h1, NULL, NULL, &ft1);
GetFileTme(h2, NULL, NULL, &ft2);

// Subtract them - nice syntax now
ULargeInteger ft3 = ft1 - ft2;
```

CHAPTER 27

Subscript Operators

27.1   Pointer Conversion versus Subscript Operators

I mentioned earlier (see section 14.2.2) that one must choose between providing implicit conversion to a pointer (to the managed sequence) or subscript operators. In this section, we'll see why. Consider the code in Listing 27.1.

Listing 27.1

```
typedef size_t   subscript_arg_t;
typedef int      indexer_t;
struct DoubleContainer
{
  typedef size_t  size_type;
                operator double const *() const;
                operator double *();
  double const &operator [](size_type index) const;
  double       &operator [](size_type index);
  size_type    size() const;
};
. . .
DoubleContainer dc;
indexer_t       index = 1;
dc[index];   // S#1
dc[0];       // S#2
```

Most types that provide subscripting can only support non-negative indexes, so most such types define the subscript operator in terms of an unsigned type. The C++ standard (C++-98: 23.1) stipulates that the `size_type` of containers, including those providing subscript operators, is unsigned, and it usually resolves to `size_t`.

Many programmers, whether right or wrong, tend to write their indexing code in terms of `int`. Even if you use `size_t` for your indexer, unadorned literal integers will be interpreted as a signed integer, usually `int` (see section 13.2).

The problem we have with a class like `DoubleContainer` is that subscript syntax can also be applied to pointers. Depending on the types of the subscript operator argument and the indexer variable, our compilers (see Appendix A) exhibit slightly different, but very important differences, as shown in Table 27.1.

Table 27.1

Compiler	Operator [] () argument type	Indexer type	Ambiguous?
Visual C++ 6.0,	int	int	No
Visual C++ 7.1	int	size_t	Yes
	size_t	int	Yes
	size_t	size_t	No
Borland,	int	int	No
CodeWarrior,	int	size_t	No
Digital Mars,	size_t	int	No
Watcom	size_t	size_t	No
Comeau, GCC,	int	int	No
Intel	int	size_t	No
	size_t	int	Yes
	size_t	size_t	No

The most unpopular combination for our compilers—size_t for the subscript operator argument and int for the indexer—is the one we will most commonly encounter. Clearly, providing both implicit conversion and subscripting together is a nonportable proposition, and I strongly urge you not to bother trying it. Imagine the hassles you'll have if you're working with one of the four that work unambiguously with both and you gaily go ahead and define them. When you move to another compiler, you could have myriad small changes, each one of which will require you to think about the changes involved.

You may think you can be immune by setting the warning level of your compiler to high, to detect use of int for the indexer, and sticking to size_t. Alas, being a good citizen you'll be properly retrieving a pointer to a given array's elements in generic code via the form &ar[0] (see Chapter 33), in which the 0 will be interpreted as an int.[1] To make them work with types such as DoubleContainer, you'd need to rewrite such expressions as &ar[static_cast<size_t>(0)]. Naturally, this will then trip us up on some compilers if the code was applied to types whose subscript argument type was int. Aargh!

It is a habit of mine to define an index_type member type when writing array classes (see Chapter 33), which could be used in these cases—&ar[static_cast<C::index_type>(0)]—but it's nonstandard, so not of much use in code that needs to be widely applied. In any case, such casts are ugly beyond bearing.

Keep in mind that the use of implicit conversion operators is not a terribly good thing in general, and I'm not advocating otherwise here. But there are circumstances where they are

---

[1]Please note that I recognize the partial circularity of this argument. We use &ar[0] notation because we often do not wish to provide implicit conversion. One of the reasons for this is because of the ambiguities when combined with subscripting.

appropriate, and also where they'd be appropriate in concert with subscript operators. Better minds could probably explain why the subscript operator cannot take precedence over the in-built subscripting of an implicit conversion operator, but it's largely irrelevant. We're in the real world, and the only sensible solution is to refrain from ever trying to do it.

Imperfection: Provision of implicit conversion operator(s) to pointer type(s) along with subscript operator(s) is nonportable.

Note that the problem even occurs if the base class has the implicit conversion operator, and a derived class provides the subscript operator. This is the reason that `pod_vector` (see section 32.2.8) uses `auto_buffer` via composition, rather than via non-`public` inheritance, which was how I originally had it until trying to use the subscript operators. Note that the compilers still report an ambiguous conversion even when the inheritance is non-`public`, and the base class's implicit conversion operators are inaccessible to client code of the derived class.

27.1.1   Choose Implicit Conversion Operators

Given that we must choose, what are the circumstances in which we would choose implicit conversion over subscript operators? The only situation I know of is when one must accommodate the widely practiced array to pointer decay. This is why `auto_buffer` (see section 32.2) provides implicit conversion, since its intent is to be maximally compatible with built-in arrays.

27.1.2   Choose Subscript Operators

In almost all circumstances, I believe one should prefer subscript operators to implicit conversion operators. The reason is that the subscript operator receives the index to be applied from which it calculates the appropriate return value. In the case of implicit conversion, the compiler carries out the index offsetting itself. The advantage of having the index is that it can be validated.

```
double &DoubleContainer::operator [](size_type index)
{
  . . . // Validate the index
  return m_buffer[index];
}
```

How we choose to implement this validation is the subject of the next section.

27.2   Handling Errors

There are two things we need to do with indexing errors: detect them and handle them. But before we decide how to do either of these things, we need to decide whether to do them at all.

The standard library `deque`, `basic_string`, and `vector` sequence containers provide two ways of getting at individual elements: the subscript operator(s) and the `at()` method(s).[2] Given an invalid index, `at()` will throw a `std::out_of_range` exception, whereas the

---

[2]There are `const` and non-`const` versions of each. There are also `front()` and `back()` methods, which have the same behavior as the subscript operators.

subscript operator has "undefined behavior," which usually means that it does no checking.[3] In other words, it's your responsibility to pass a valid index to the subscript operator.

Clearly, there is a trade-off here. Detecting the error will incur a performance cost. Not detecting it places the burden on users of the classes to ensure that they supply valid indexes. (We'll also see an interesting twist on this tale in Chapter 33 when we need to efficiently acquire the elements of multidimensional array classes.)

For my part, I agree with the approach taken by the standard library and prefer to have the subscript operator maximally efficient. Naturally, even if I didn't agree, structural conformance (see section 20.9) would have molded the expectations of users of my containers such that not conforming to the STL container semantics would only result in their misuse, followed swiftly by disuse.

But there's more to it than throwing in `at()` and doing nothing in `operator [] ()`. We can use an assertion to check in `operator[]()` in debug mode, in which we're not concerned with the performance costs:

```
double &DoubleContainer::operator [](size_type index)
{
  assert(index < size());
  return m_buffer[index];
}
```

Look through the implementation of your favorite compiler vendor's standard library, however, and you're very unlikely to see such a thing. I think the reason for this is that one often wishes to pass an asymmetric range representing the managed sequence to an external function, as in:

```
void DumpDoubles(double const *first, double const *last);
. . .
DoubleContainer dc;
```

The most syntactically succinct and, in my opinion, elegant way to do this is as follows:

```
DumpDoubles(&dc[0], &dc[dc.size()]);
```

There are other ways to do it, such as the turgid:

```
DumpDoubles(&dc[0], &dc[0] + dc.size());
```

or, the indigestible:

```
DumpDoubles(&dc[0], (&dc[0])[dc.size()]);
```

---

[3]I'm not aware of a standard library implementation that provides equivalent behavior for subscript operator(s) and `at()` method(s), but since it's implementation defined, you'd be perfectly within your rights to do so in your own containers.

but I'd not wish to see either of those. Hence, the reason I suspect standard library containers eschew assertion-based index validation is to avoid mistakenly reporting errors in one-off-the end indexing. Since the second address is never dereferenced, the index is not actually invalid.

You might wonder why they don't check that the index is either valid, or equal to the one-off-the-end index, and I've wondered this myself. When writing container libraries, I always do exactly that, as in:[4]

```
double &DoubleContainer::operator [](size_type index)
{
  assert(!(size() < index));
  return m_buffer[index];
}
```

Tellingly, CodeWarrior's excellent MSL standard library implementation has a check in its `basic_string::operator []()` that provides this very semantic, so I figure I'm in good company.

27.2.1   Subscript Operators versus Iterators

As you hopefully well know [Meye2001], it is illegitimate to use the `begin()` method of a sequence container to attempt to obtain a pointer to the managed sequence of elements. Although it may work with some containers, for example, vector, on most implementations, it is not guaranteed to work with all, since the sequence containers are free to provide iterators of class types.

In the above example, the `DumpDoubles()` function takes a pointer range. This is a conceptually different beast from one that takes an iterator range, which, assuming Double Container provided a `const_iterator` member type, would be expressed as:

```
void DumpDoubles( DoubleContainer::const_iterator first
               , DoubleContainer::const_iterator last);
```

The confusion arises when the `const_iterator` is defined as `value_type const*`— that is, `double const*`—since there will, in that case, be only one `DumpDoubles()`. This is an inconsistency that you, as the user of the `DoubleContainer()` will have to live with. Just don't be seduced into using `begin()` (and `end()`), when you are conceptually dealing with pointers, rather than iterators. It will give you bad habits that will turn on you at inopportune moments (see section 14.2.2).

By the way, use of the `end()` method does not have the same potential problems as `&c[c.size()]`, since `end()` is explicitly intended to refer to the one-off-the-end element.

---

[4]The only reason I don't write `index <= size()` is that I'm obsessed with only using the < operator. Reducing one's dependence down to this one operator for all manner of comparison operations can be important in a minority of cases. Alas, I've just absorbed the rule and forgotten the motivating cases, as is my wont, so you'll have to research this yourself if you're motivated to find them.

27.3   Return Value

So we've decided on a reasonable strategy for index validation, but there still remains the issue of what we actually return from the subscript operator. Thankfully, the use of the canonical `&c[0]` makes this pretty simple. We must return something that, when subject to the address-of operator (unary `operator &`), will yield a pointer to the managed sequence. Hence `Double Container` returns `double&` or `double const &`, either of which will yield a pointer when subjected to the address of operator.

I don't know how many of you have done as I have in the past and written naïve pre-STL containers that returned by value, as in:

```
class DoubleContainer
{
  . . .
  double operator [](size_t index) const;
```

This is simply not good enough. If you return by value, you're introducing a disconnect between the managed sequence and the client code that may wish to meaningfully apply the address-of operator to get a pointer to the managed sequence.

That's not to say that you *must* return a reference. An alternative strategy is to return an instance that can act as a reference. For example, `DoubleContainer`'s `operator []()` could return an instance of `DoubleIndexProxy`:

```
class DoubleIndexProxy
{
  . . .
  double *operator &();
  double const *operator &() const;
```

As you can see, this goes against the advice of the last chapter, which is to eschew the overloading of `operator &()`. In this case, it's fine because no one in their right mind will be attempting to put a `DoubleIndexProxy` in a container, or indeed use it for any other purpose. In fact, it would be a private nested class within `DoubleContainer`, so no one can access it save the compiler, and she'll faithfully follow your access control dictates.

This seems a reasonable principle, but it falls on its face a bit when we try to use this with multidimensional arrays (see Chapter 33).

Chapter 28

Increment Operators

The built-in prefix and postfix increment and decrement operators are great shorthand. Rather than writing

```
x = x + 1;
```

we can simply write

```
++x;
```

or

```
x++;
```

Of greater significance, especially since the advent of the STL, is that these operators can be overloaded for class types. The prefix increment and decrement operators are defined for classes by the following functions:

```
class X
{
  . . .
  X &operator ++();    // pre-increment
  X &operator -();     // pre-decrement
  X operator ++(int);  // post-increment
  X operator -(int);   // post-decrement
  . . .
```

Although there's nothing forcing you to do so, the intent is that the return types of the prefix and postfix forms are as shown above, that is, that the prefix forms return a non-const reference to the current instance, and the postfix forms return a copy of the current instance prior to its value being changed. In other words, they should do as the ints do [Meye1996].

Although it may seem obvious to some, I've seen plenty of people struggle with the implementation of the postfix form, so I'll just show the canonical form:

```
X X::operator ++(int)
{
  X ret(*this);
```

```
  operator ++();
  return ret;
}
```

Throughout the STLSoft libraries, 18 of the 20 post-increment operators take exactly this form, and, unless you've got a special reason to do something else, this will serve you well.

28.1 Missing Postfix Operators

Since C++ lets you take responsibility for things—in contrast to some of the annoyingly nanny-ing more "modern" languages—you are allowed to define prefix methods without the postfix equivalents, and vice versa. The problem in this case is that compilers exhibit different behavior when an operator is missing. For example, if your class defines only the preincrement operator, and your client code places an instance of your class in a postfix increment expression, some compilers will issue an error, whereas others will only issue a warning. Table 28.1 summarizes the behavior for a range of compilers.

In my opinion, such a thing is unambiguously an error, and I cannot conceive of a reason such behavior would be implemented, unless it is to pander to sloppy application programmers who are too unprofessional to use the appropriate form. In the other direction—that is, substituting a prefix call with a postfix operator—all the compilers do the right thing and reject it outright. If anything, this adds weight to my supposition.

Clearly, there's danger here. The semantics of the two operators are significantly different. If your compiler substitutes one for the other, your program is incorrect. Thankfully the majority of compilers will reject outright the substitutions and those that allow it still issue a warning, but if you're working with one of the warning-only compilers and your coworkers have messed with the warning levels,[1] it's possible that it could slip through.

Table 28.1

Compiler	Behavior
Borland	Warning, and uses prefix operator
CodePlay	Error
CodeWarrior	Error
Comeau	Error
Digital Mars	Warning, and uses prefix operator
GCC	Error
Intel	Warning, and uses prefix operator
Visual C++	Warning, and uses prefix operator
Visual C++ (-Za)	Error
Watcom	Error

---

[1] I suggest your co-worker, since I know you'd never do such a thing.

Imperfection: Some C++ compilers will substitute prefix increment/decrement overloaded operators at the call site in place of absent postfix equivalents.

The solution here is pretty simple. You just declare the overload that you do not wish to use
with `private` access. No compilers will substitute the publicly accessible prefix in place of a
private postfix operator and vice versa.

This is actually the better solution anyway, since it's an overt expression of your design intentions; there's very little chance a maintenance programmer will mistake your intention if it's
`private` and festooned with a comment mentioning its intended inaccessibility.

28.2   Efficiency

Since postfix operators have to maintain the previous value in order to return it to the calling
context, they often have an efficiency cost over their prefix analogs. I remember many years
ago being told by a hardware guru[2] that Motorola chips were able to operate more efficiently
with prefix rather than postfix operations. Unless the hardware supports a postfix increment,
using one usually winds up consuming a temporary register, except when the compiler can deduce that the original value is not needed, in which case it would generate identical code to the
prefix form. However, when dealing with class types, it is almost always the case that there is
an efficiency cost for calling the postfix operator rather than the prefix operator.

Sadly, all too many teaching institutions must be failing to explain the ramifications, because there's still a lot of new code being written using postfix forms. I've encountered many
engineers who use the postfix form as a matter of convention, and who insist that they nevertheless use the prefix form for class types. Phooey!

This nonsensical stance fails for two reasons. First, humans are habit-forming creatures by
nature. Every time I've had this debate with engineers and they've been man enough to offer up
their code for inspection, I've found cases where they forgot, and their machine was executing
cycles it needn't have.

The second failing of this flummery is that it neglects genericity. Many times we use template algorithms that operate on fundamental types and on user-defined types, that is, nonpointer iterator types. Failing to observe correct prefix usage may be immaterial when such
algorithms are applied to fundamental types, but compilers may not be able to clean up after
you with other types.

28.2.1   Detecting Unused Postfix Operators

If, like me, you sometimes tire of debating correctness, robustness, and efficiency with people who can drive you to wonder whether they're in the right industry, then you may yearn for a
definitive proof of their folly. Wouldn't it be nice to be able to automatically detect inappropriate use of postfix operators? Thankfully, we can.

---

[2]Well, he said he was a guru, anyway.

I'm sure you'll not exactly fall off your chair to learn that there's a template-based solution to this. It is based around the unused_return_value_monitor class.

Listing 28.1

```
template< typename V
        , typename M
        , typename R = V
        >
class unused_return_value_monitor
{
public:
  typedef unused_return_value_monitor<V, M, R>  class_type;
public:
  explicit unused_return_value_monitor(R value, M monitor = M())
    : m_value(value)
    , m_monitor(monitor)
    , m_bUsed(false)
  {}
  unused_return_value_monitor(class_type const &rhs)
    : m_value(rhs.m_value)
    , m_monitorFn(rhs.m_monitorFn)
    , m_bUsed(rhs.m_bUsed)
  {
    rhs.m_bUsed = false;
  }
  ~unused_return_value_monitor()
  {
    if(!m_bUsed)
    {
      m_monitor(this, m_value);
    }
  }
public:
  operator V() const
  {
    m_bUsed = true;
    return m_value;
  }
private:
  R             m_value;
  M             m_monitor;
  mutable bool  m_bUsed;
// Not to be implemented
private:
  unused_return_value_monitor &operator =(class_type const &rhs);
};
```

It is easily integrated into your class's postfix operators, as can be seen in the following class:

Listing 28.2

```
class X
{
private:
  struct use_monitor
  {
    void operator ()(void const *instance, X const &value) const
    {
      printf( "Unused return value %s from object instance %p\n"
              , value.get_value().c_str(), instance);
    }
  };
public:
  X &operator ++()
  {
    . . . // Increment stuff
    return *this;
  }
#ifdef ACMELIB_DEBUG
  unused_return_value_monitor<X, use_monitor> operator ++(int)
#else /* ? ACMELIB_DEBUG */
  X operator ++(int)
#endif /* ACMELIB_DEBUG */
  {
    X ret(*this);
    operator ++();
    return ret;
  }
private:
  string_t  m_value;
};
```

Since this is an inefficiency detector, it's only appropriate to use it in debug builds, so I'd advise you to use preprocessor discrimination to select the raw return type in release builds, as shown in the example.

As for what your monitor function should do, I suggest that it should trace to the debugger or to a log file, rather than, say, throw an exception or abort(), since calling the inappropriate form of the operators is (or rather will be, unless strange things are happening) an efficiency error rather than a semantic error. But since it's parameterizable, you can do whatever you think is appropriate.

Arithmetic Types

In section 13.3 we looked at extending the integer types provided by C++ in the form of the uinteger64 and sinteger64 types. What we'll be trying to see is whether we can create a type that can genuinely and completely integrate into the language such that it can be used as we would use any of the built-in integer types. (The imperfect results of these efforts are included on the CD.)

29.1   Class Definition

Before we get stuck into the minutiae, we'll just take a look at the class definition. I decided, in order to avoid confusion with the two extant member variables lowerVal and upperVal, to use protected inheritance and derive a new type UInteger64. This is so we can cheat and use a union of uinteger64 and a uint64_t in order to perform the arithmetic. This relies on the correct layout of the two members in the structure, as follows:[1]

Listing 29.1
```
struct uinteger64
{
#if defined(ACMELIB_LITTLE_ENDIAN)
  uint32_t  lowerVal;
  uint32_t  upperVal;
#elif defined(ACMELIB_BIG_ENDIAN)
  uint32_t  upperVal;
  uint32_t  lowerVal;
#else
# error Need to discriminate further . . .
#endif /* endian */
};
```

This allows us to do the following monstrosity, which, as I said, is merely for expediency for this specific type, rather than a technique one would use for large integers in general:

Listing 29.2
```
class UInteger64
  : protected uinteger64
```

---

[1]Naturally there are implications for such a type in conversion to and from a byte stream, but they're the same for a built-in 64-bit integer.

```
{
public:
  typedef union
  {
    uint64_t      i;
    uinteger64   s;
  } ui64_union;
  ui64_union &get_union_()
  {
    uinteger64   *p1 = this;
    ui64_union   *p2 = reinterpret_cast<ui64_union*>(p1);
    return *p2;
  }
  ui64_union const &get_union_() const;
  . . .
```

It's not the way you'd start out and design a large integer class from scratch, where you'd not have the option of using a higher fundamental type in anything larger than 64 bits.

The test harness for this chapter consists of a template function within which a variety of numeric operations are performed. We'll go through them all, and see the ramifications for the design of our class.

29.2   Default Construction

This one's a no-brainer. I usually go for maximum speed here and do not initialize the member(s) of the integer type, consistent with the behavior for the built-in types. There's very little in it, though, and you'd be perfectly reasonable to decide to zero initialize the members.

One interesting strategy is to maintain an extra member, perhaps in debug builds only, which denotes an uninitialized integer, in much the same way as does the special value NaN for floating point types. Access of the values from uninitialized (i.e., default initialized) instances would result in a precondition violation assertion.

29.3   Initialization (Value Construction)

The next thing we need to do with our integer type is be able to initialize our type from another value. Given that the type is unsigned, we give it the ability to construct from a single uint32_t, as well as construct from two uint32_t values:

```
class UInteger64
{
  . . .
  UInteger64(uint32_t i) // The low 32-bits
  {
    this->lowerVal = i;
    this->upperVal = 0;
  }
```

```
UInteger64(uint32_t upper, uint32_t lower);
. . .
```

In this case, I've chosen to make it non `explicit`, so that it is a *conversion constructor* (C++-98: 12.3.1), because the type is to be a very simple type. We'll see that this seemingly innocuous decision has profound implications for the rest of the class design.

Now we can write the following normal looking statement:

```
UInteger64 i = 0;
```

Unfortunately, things get a little tricky now. Since it's a 64-bit integer, it's overwhelmingly likely that we'd want to be able to initialize it from a `uint64_t` when using the class with a compiler that supports that type.

```
class UInteger64
{
  . . .
  UInteger64(uint32_t i);
#ifdef ACMELIB_UINT64_T_SUPPORT
  UInteger64(uint64_t i)
  {
    get_union_().i = i;
  }
#endif ACMELIB_UINT64_T_SUPPORT
  . . .
```

However, now we're in trouble. Specifying an argument of any unsigned type smaller than 64 bits—again, we're assuming that int is 32 bits here—will resolve to the `uint32_t` overload. Specifying an argument of `uint64_t` will use that overload. But integer literals that do bear a modifying suffix (see section 15.4.2) are interpreted as `int` or `long` or, although it's not part of the standard, as `sint64_t` where supported. One option is to add a third constructor for `int`:

```
class UInteger64
{
  . . .
  UInteger64(uint32_t i);
#ifdef ACMELIB_UINT64_T_SUPPORT
  UInteger64(uint64_t i);
#endif ACMELIB_UINT64_T_SUPPORT
  UInteger64(int i);
```

There are two problems with this. First, now we can pass an `int` with a negative value. Although we can write the constructor to simply cast it to an unsigned value, this is semantically meaningless—you cannot represent a negative number in an unsigned quantity, merely use it as a repository for the bits to be placed back in a signed variable at a later stage. This factor alone rules out this as a sensible strategy.

There's also a practical objection. Say you want to be able to convert from unsigned long, unsigned int, unsigned short, and unsigned char, which is perfectly reasonable (assuming long is not larger than 64 bits), then you'll run into ambiguities. Because uint32_t may be implemented, on our range of compilers alone, as unsigned int, unsigned long or unsigned _ _int32 (see section 13.2), we will have to do a lot of preprocessor discrimination in order to have a portable class. You end up in a mess like that shown in Listing 29.3.

Listing 29.3

```
class UInteger64
{
  . . .
  UInteger64(uint32_t i);
#ifdef ACMELIB_UINT64_T_SUPPORT
  UInteger64(uint64_t i);
#endif ACMELIB_UINT64_T_SUPPORT
  UInteger64(int i);
if defined(ACMELIB_COMPILER_IS_BORLAND) || \
      . . . CodeWarrior, Comeau, Digital Mars, GCC
    defined(ACMELIB_COMPILER_IS_WATCOM)
  UInteger64(unsigned int i);
#elif defined(ACMELIB_COMPILER_IS_INTEL)
  UInteger64(unsigned long i);
#elif defined(ACMELIB_COMPILER_IS_MSVC)
  UInteger64(unsigned long i);
# ifdef ACMELIB_32BIT_INT_IS_DISTINCT_TYPE
  UInteger64(unsigned int i);
# endif /* ACMELIB_32BIT_INT_IS_DISTINCT_TYPE */
#endif /* compiler */
```

The answer is to use conditional compilation to select the best constructor whose type is supported by the current compiler. It's hardly beautiful, but it's unambiguous and a lot prettier than the alternative:

```
class UInteger64
{
  . . .
#ifdef ACMELIB_UINT64_T_SUPPORT
  UInteger64(uint64_t i);
#else /* ? ACMELIB_UINT64_T_SUPPORT */
  UInteger64(uint32_t i);
#endif ACMELIB_UINT64_T_SUPPORT
  . . .
```

In fact, you *must* provide the larger-type constructor, since it is all too easy to experience a truncation with the 32-bit constructor when given arguments of 64 bits. A significant minority of compilers will fail to warn about this, particularly inside template code.

Note that there's a small potential efficiency issue here. Even though inside either constructor there is a total of 64 bits being set by the compiler, and that therefore it is highly likely that they have exactly the same costs, in client code the `uint64_t` version will have to extend any 32-bit (or smaller) arguments to 64 bits. But even if this isn't made moot by compiler optimizations, it's a small price that's well worth paying to avoid all the ambiguities and countless overloads.

29.4   Copy Construction

This one's simple. The `UInteger64` class is a simple value type that does not manage any resources (see Chapters 3 and 4), so you can leave it to the compiler to provide a copy constructor by default, or you can explicitly define one and perform a memberwise copy. There's no compelling reason to do the latter, beyond consistency with your own coding standards.

```
UInteger64 i    = 0;
UInteger64 i2   = i; // Assignment syntax
UInteger64 i3(i);    // Constructor syntax
```

29.5   Assignment

This is actually reasonably easy if we choose to rely on conversion constructors. Again, because `UInteger64` is a value type that does not handle resources, we can leave the assignment operator for the compiler to define. What this means is that any expression containing assignment to an instance of `UInteger64` will succeed if the right-hand side expression can be converted to `UInteger64`, that is, it matches a constructor. Hence, the following all succeed, since the constructors also succeed.

```
UInteger64 i;
unsigned   i2 = . . .
uint64_t   i3 = . . .
UInteger64 i4;

i = 0;
i = i2;
i = i3;
i = i4;
```

29.6   Arithmetic Operators

Just as with assignment, we can rely on conversion construction to make our task here very simple. First, we need to define the member composite assignment operators [Stro1997]:

Listing 29.4
```
class UInteger64
{
  . . .
```

```
UInteger64 &operator +=(UInteger64 const &rhs)
{
  get_union_().i += rhs.get_union_().i;
  return *this;
}
UInteger64 &operator -=(UInteger64 const &rhs);
UInteger64 &operator *=(UInteger64 const &rhs);
UInteger64 &operator /=(UInteger64 const &rhs);
UInteger64 &operator %=(UInteger64 const &rhs);
UInteger64 &operator ^=(UInteger64 const &rhs);

. . .
```

The binary operators are then provided as nonmember functions, implemented in terms of the public interface of the class:

```
UInteger64 operator +( UInteger64 const &lhs
                     , UInteger64 const &rhs)
{
  return UInteger64(lhs) += rhs;
}
```

29.7   Comparison Operators

The comparison operators can be implemented in exactly the same way as the arithmetic operators, with nonmember binary operators implemented in terms of member functions:

```
bool operator ==( UInteger64 const &lhs
                , UInteger64 const &rhs)
{
  return lhs.IsEqual(rhs);
}
bool operator <( UInteger64 const &lhs
               , UInteger64 const &rhs)
{
  return lhs.Compare(rhs) < 0;
}
```

29.8   Accessing the Value

The only question remains is how do we extract the values from instances of UInteger64, when we need to store it, or transmit it, and so forth.

Remember that we're only using the 64-bit integers as an example, so although we might choose to have an accessor method or operator providing the value in a built-in 64-bit integer type for compilers that support it, in general we'd not have that option. This is a perfect case for explicit casts (see section 19.5) if only they were portably reliable and efficient with reference types. The alternative I would choose would be to provide const and non-const get_value() methods, which return const and non-const references to the underlying structure as follows:

```
class UInteger64
{
  . . .
  uinteger64        &get_value();
  uinteger64 const &get_value() const;
  . . .
```

Although the non-const version of cast or function will allow you to manipulate the contents of the instance outside of the public interface, you'll probably, in the general case, need to be able to provide such access to C-APIs. Since UInteger64 is a simple value type that manages no resources, we're not exactly letting the burglars at the crown jewels by doing so.

If you prefer to provide them as implicit conversion operators, then you may as well just derive publicly from uinteger64, and let the compiler convert where necessary. I prefer the cautionary aspect inherent in requiring an explicit function call: it requires an explicit choice on the part of the programmer and is also much easier to search for automatically.

29.9   sinteger64

The issues we've examine for uinteger64 / UInteger64 largely apply to the signed version, except that we no longer need to provide a dubious int overload in order to cater for literals. But this is moot since, as with UInteger64, we can simply provide a single constructor representing the largest possible built-in signed integer:

```
class SInteger64
  : protected sinteger64
{
  . . .
#ifdef ACMELIB_SINT64_T_SUPPORT
  SInteger64(sint64_t i);
#else /* ? ACMELIB_SINT64_T_SUPPORT */
  SInteger64(sint32_t i);
#endif ACMELIB_SINT64_T_SUPPORT
  . . .
```

Everything else just flows smoothly from this.

29.10   Truncations, Promotions, and Tests

The story so far looks pretty spanking good, methinks. However, we're not there yet. Even though we've discussed two possible mechanisms for retrieving the underlying values from large integer types when we need them, there're several operations of the built-in integer types that we're yet to address.

29.10.1 Truncations

Although we usually couch mention of truncation in negative terms, there are occasions when it is precisely what is required. Since the built-in integral types support truncation, we should try to provide it for our large integer types. For a 64-bit type, we'd naturally want to be able to truncate to 32-bit and smaller types. The only way we can facilitate this as part of the natural syntax is to provide an implicit conversion operator:

```
class SInteger64
{
  . . .
  operator sint32_t () const
  . . .
```

However, there's a very nasty problem here. If we provide this operator then, aside from the usual problems of implicit conversion, we will be facilitating a truncation without warnings. Even though it's *implementation defined*, compilers do provide truncation warnings for fundamental types, and we certainly want the same from our large integral types.

Given that neither of our two classes are templates, the truncation inside these operators will be detected at the epoch of compilation of the functions, rather than of their use. If the operators are inline, all client code of these types will be informed, in each client compilation unit, that the classes are flawed, which will serve only to disincline people from using them. If the operators are in separate implementation files, then no one's going to see the warnings anyway.

Another, slightly better, option is to use explicit casts (see section 19.5). Since we're talking about returning fundamental types by value, explicit casts will work perfectly well:

```
class SInteger64
{
  . . .
  operator explicit_cast<sint32_t>() const
  . . .
};

SInteger64  i64;
sint32_t    i32 = explicit_cast<sint32_t>(i64);
```

The problem here is that once again the client code will not receive a warning about the truncation. It's a little better than with the implicit conversion operator, since at least there's something eye-catching in the source, but I still don't think it's good enough.

The only solution I can think of is to copy the explicit cast mechanism to a new template—called a `truncation_cast`—that will work in the same way as explicit cast, but will provide a more obvious sign of the truncation by virtue of its name.

But I really think this is a step too far from sanity, so I'd content myself to have methods to perform the truncations:

```
class UInteger64
{
   . . .
   uint32_t truncate32() const;
   . . .
```

Note that there's still no truncation warning by the compiler, but that's not needed because we won't be using the large integer types in the same way as built-in types syntactically.

29.10.2 Promotions

As well as truncating values, sometimes we may also wish to promote the values to other numeric types, specifically `float`, `double` and `long double`. The obvious way to do this is to provide implicit conversion operators:

```
class SInteger64
{
   . . .
   operator float() const;
   operator double() const;
   operator long double() const;
   . . .
```

Unfortunately, this blows all our previous arithmetic operators out of the water. An expression such as the following now fails due to a conflict between the nonmember addition operator and the inbuilt arithmetic operator.

```
SInteger64  i1;
SInteger64  i2;
i1 = i2 + 100;
```

This is because the expression can be interpreted to mean either convert `100` to `SInteger64` and then add it to `i2`, or convert `i2` to `float` (or `double`, or `long double`) and add it to the `100`.

We cannot provide an implicit conversion to any numeric type, or we lose all our arithmetic operators. The only answer is to have explicit casts or conversion methods.

29.10.3 Tests

The last aspect of built-in integer operations is the ability to implicitly take part in Boolean conditional subexpressions. Even though I don't like to use such things for integers (see section 17.2.1), it is still a part of built-in integral type semantics, and so we should consider it for our large integer types.

We've just learned that any integral type cannot be used for our Boolean operator, so we'd need to use either the `void*()`, `T *()`, or `int T::*()` options we covered in Chapter 24. Naturally the best thing would be to use the "proper" Boolean generator macro.

Alas, the addition statement we've just seen would also cause ambiguities. It could be interpreted to mean either convert `100` to `SInteger64` and then add it to `i2`, or convert `i2` to `int operator_bool_generator< SInteger64>::*` and then increment that pointer by 100.

It sure makes you weep sometimes, doesn't it?

The answer here is to go back to our trusty friend the attribute shim (see section 20.2), and declare `is_true()` and `is_not()` shims:

```
inline bool is_true(SInteger64 const &i)
{
  return i != 0;
}
inline bool is_not(SInteger64 const &i) // or is_not_true()
{
  return i == 0;
}
```

This can then be used in the largely digestible form:

```
SInteger64 i = . . .

if(is_true(i))
{
  . . .
```

In my opinion, though, this is just one more nail in the coffin for the use of non-Boolean expressions and their implicit interpretation to Boolean, so if you stick to the advice in section 17.2.1 you'll never have to worry about such things.

```
if(0 != i) // What could be simpler?
{
  . . .
```

29.11   Arithmetic Types: Coda

I hope you've enjoyed this trip into the dark side of what seems on the surface to be a trivial matter. We've seen just how refreshingly easy it was to define our assignment, comparison, and arithmetic operations given that we chose to allow conversion (non-`explicit`) construction.

Alas, that's as far as we were able to go with our emulation of built-in syntax. Any support for implicit truncation, promotion, or Boolean testing invalidates the arithmetic operations, and so cannot be used. Explicit casts, accessor member functions, and shims all provide reasonable workarounds but they're neither seamless nor attractive, and we can hardly call their use an unqualified victory.

But those are the breaks. This great language does its best to support our intents, but it can only be persuaded to go so far.

Short-circuit!

The `&&` and `||` operators provide a Boolean evaluation of the two expressions, as in:

```
if(x && y) // Evaluates to true if both x and y are true
if(x || y) // Evaluates to true if either x or y are true
```

Both these operators have what is known as short-circuit evaluation semantics [Stro1997]. Since the `&&` operator provides a logical AND of the two arguments, there is no need to evaluate the second argument if the first is false. Conversely, for the `||` operator, which provides a logical OR of its arguments, the second argument does not need to be evaluated if the first is true. Since C is all about efficiency, the second arguments are only evaluated when they are needed. This is a very useful facility since it allows us to write succinct yet safe conditional expressions:

```
if( !str.empty() &&
    str[0] == '[')
```

However, the short-circuit nature of the operators is not respected when they are overloaded with one or both arguments being of class type. The following code might or might not print out its plaintiff cry, depending on whether the required overloaded `operator &&()` arguments are of type `bool` and `Y const&` or `bool` and `X const&`:

```
class X
{};

class Y
{
public:
  operator X() const
  {
    printf("Why am I called?\n");
    return X();
  }
};

Y y;
```

```
if(false && y)
{}
```

This is a fundamental change in semantics that is almost impossible to detect by looking at the code.

Imperfection: Overloading the && and || operators for class types represents an invisible breaking of short-circuit evaluation.

This is definitely one to be avoided. Thankfully the need to do so is very rare: I've not had occasion to do it, other than for research, in over ten years of C++ programming, and the chances are that you won't need to do so either. If you do, you must be aware of the potential side effects from the change in semantics.

# PART SIX

Extending C++

A bove all else, the most powerful aspect of C++ is its extensibility. The most clear and persuasive example of this is the Standard Template Library (STL), which has changed the way most of us use C++ and has become a major component of the C++ standard library. Covering the extensibility of STL would be a book in itself.

However, the STL is just one example. There are myriad ways in which this extensibility can manifest, and in this final part we'll cover just a few of the more interesting ones.

The first of the five chapters, Chapter 31, *Return Value Lifetime*, goes into the subject in some depth, via the implementation of a conceptually simple library component. We end up incorporating into the solution a practical treatment of several of the issues covered earlier in the book, including threading, statics, and efficiency. We end up finding a real value in garbage-collected systems that even the grand skeptics—such as me—cannot refute.

Chapter 32, *Memory*, looks at the various memory mechanisms in C/C++, and addresses the traditional, and often vexing, choice between speed and flexibility. It also looks at the costs and benefits of compile-time and run time allocator selection, and discusses ways in which all the different schemes may be optimally combined.

The next chapter, Chapter 33, *Multidimensional Arrays,* demonstrates several techniques for addressing the limited facilities in C++ for dynamically variable multidimensional arrays. As we so often find, there are imperfections with providing such multidimensional arrays as class types, but we learn that by wearing the hairshirt, and being good subscripting boys and girls, we can have our cake and eat it, too.

Chapter 34, *Functors and Ranges,* investigates some of the less usable aspects of the STL and modern C++ idioms, and describes some of the early stages of a project—RangeLib—in which I'm involved with some other C++ expansionists. The range concept is essentially a way of dealing with a range as a single entity rather than the now classic asymmetric pair. We'll take a look at some of the early work on the RangeLib project to see just how powerful this simple concept can be.[1]

The final chapter, Chapter 35, *Properties*, describes how C++ can be made to support properties in a time- and space-efficient manner. We'll see just how far we can stretch the language into some dark corners in our quest for high-level concepts at low (speed and memory) cost. This is one of my favorite chapters in the book,[2] and it really does speak strongly to how powerful and adaptable this language really is.

---

[1]Later versions of the RangeLib may well find their way onto the CD, and are also available from the RangeLib site at http://rangelib.org/.

[2]If you think that's because it's the biggest, and I'm just an old windbag, well . . . there may some merit in that.

## CHAPTER 31

Return Value Lifetime

This chapter contains much of the material from a series of installments of *Flexible C++*, my *C/C++ User's Journal Expert's Forum* column [Wils2003d, Wils2003f, Wilson2004b]. It revolves around the seemingly trivial problem of converting integers to strings in an efficient manner.

As it turns out, it's anything but a trivial issue when the details start to come out, and as well as illustrating some practical ramifications of many of the issues covered in the book so far, it brings into sharp focus the issue of *Return Value Lifetime* (RVL) which we discussed in the section on *Conversion Shims* (see sections 16.2 and 20.5).

Probably the most common way to convert integers to strings is via `sprintf()`, whether called directly in client code or indirectly, for example, within IOStream insertion manipulators [Lang2000]. However, this very powerful function is overkill for many simple conversions, and there is a performance penalty for its use. We'll look at a simple, highly efficient, template-based technique, and then enhance it in several different forms, exploring the issues thrown up by each of five imperfect solutions.

Each of these solutions to the integer to string conversions is flawed in one way or another, and examination of these flaws will highlight issues within C++ that tend to bite the unwary (and sometimes the wary).

31.1 A Taxonomy of Return Value Lifetime Gotchas

The issue of RVL comes about from the fact that not everything in C++ is a value type. Sometimes we refer to an entity by reference. This reference can, in C++, be either a pointer (e.g., X*) or a C++ reference (e.g., X&), but in either case it is effectively a simple value that denotes the location of the entity that it references.

The RVL problem comes about because it is possible for such a reference to become stale, by virtue of the fact that the entity that it references changes or ceases to exist. There are three main ways in which this problem can occur in C++, all of which will impact on our implementations for integer to string conversion.

31.1.1 Local Variables

Almost every C++ basic instructional or gotcha book [Dewh2003, Meye1998, Stro1997] contains a warning about returning the address of local variables, and I'm going to take it that you're aware of the dangers.[1] We'll refer to this as RVL-LV.

---

[1] If you're not at that level, then I certainly commend you on your grit in making it this far through this book.

31.1.2 Local Statics

As we've mentioned previously (see Chapter 11), the use of local statics can be either menace or godsend, depending on the circumstances in which they're used. In almost all circumstances in which a local static is involved in call-by-reference, it is a menace. We'll refer to this as RVL-LS.

31.1.3 Postdestruction Pointers

As we saw in section 16.2, and in the discussions of *Conversion* and *Access Shims* (see Chapter 20), it is all too easy in C++ to assign a pointer/reference to something that is held in an object instance and that is subsequently destroyed. We'll refer to this as RVL-PDP.

31.2 Why Return-by-Reference?

You may wonder why we should ever return by reference, given that it is so fraught with danger, as we've already seen (see sections 16.2, 20.6.1) and will see further in this chapter. Well, the reason we've used it a great deal in our discussions of shims has been that it affords us the ability to provide highly generalized code by using a fundamental type—for example, `char const*`—as our common type. Furthermore, since all of C++ is a wrapper to some degree, we eventually have to get down to the metal at some point—that's the reason `std::basic_string` has a `c_str()` method, after all—so there's no escaping these issues somewhere along the way.

The other reason, as we shall see in this chapter, is that it is more efficient than return by value, occasionally by a large margin.

31.3 Solution 1—integer_to_string<>

The basis of all five techniques is the suite of `integer_to_string()` template functions,[2] which are overloaded to select the appropriate implementation template functions `signed_integer_to_string()` and `unsigned_integer_to_string()`:

```
template <typename C>
C const *integer_to_string(C *buf, size_t cchBuf, sint8_t i)
{
  return signed_integer_to_string(buf, cchBuf, i);
}
. . . // and uint8_t, sint16_t, etc.
template <typename C>
C const *integer_to_string(C *buf, size_t cchBuf, uint64_t i)
{
  return unsigned_integer_to_string(buf, cchBuf, i);
}
```

---

[2]These are part of the STLSoft libraries. The full implementation, along with the test programs, supporting headers and full results, is provided on the CD.

Separate implementation functions are provided because signed conversion needs to take account of processing negative numbers and is therefore slightly less efficient than unsigned conversion, which does not. The unsigned version is shown in Listing 31.1.

Listing 31.1

```
template< typename C
        , typename I
        >
const C *unsigned_integer_to_string(C        *buf,
                                    size_t  cchBuf,
                                    I       i)
{
  C *psz  = buf + cchBuf - 1;    // Set psz to last char
  *psz = 0;                      // Set terminating null
  do
  {
    unsigned    lsd = i % 10;    // Get least significant digit
    i /= 10;                     // Prepare for next most
                                 // significant digit
    —psz;                        // Move back
    *psz = get_digit_character<C>()[lsd]; // Write the digit
  } while(i != 0);
  return psz;
}
```

The functions work by writing backward into a caller-supplied character buffer and returning a pointer to the converted form within the buffer. The least significant digit is calculated and written to the current end point within the buffer. Each digit is converted into its equivalent character value via the lookup table contained within get_digit_character()[3] shown in Listing 31.2.

Listing 31.2

```
template <typename C>
const C *get_digit_character()
{
  static const C  s_characters[19] =
  {
      '9', '8', '7', '6', '5', '4', '3', '2', '1'
    , '0'
    , '1', '2', '3', '4', '5', '6', '7', '8', '9'
  };
  static const C  *s_mid  =   s_characters + 9;
  return s_mid;
}
```

---

[3] As well as providing flexibility beyond the decimal digits (in anticipation of supporting the planned nonbase 10 implementations), this implementation will also work with any character encoding schemes that do not have contiguous ordering of the characters '0', '1' – '9'.

The convertee value is divided by 10, the end point moved backward, and the cycle repeated until 0 is reached, and the current end point is returned as a pointer to the converted string. Note that this may not be the start of the given buffer. For signed integers with a negative value, a minus sign is then prepended, and the function returns a pointer to that character. Using the functions is very simple:

```
uint64_t      i = . . .
wchar_t       buf[21];
wchar_t const *s = integer_to_string(buf, dimensionof(buf), i);
```

Because it does not use an internal buffer, the technique is thread safe (see Chapter 10). It is type safe and works with any integer type for which `integer_to_string()` overloads are defined, and with any character type. And it is very fast—as low as 10% of the cost of using `sprintf()` (see section 31.8).

However, there are two criticisms to be made. First, it is not very succinct: one needs to supply the length of the buffer along with the buffer pointer and the integer arguments.

Second, and more serious, it is possible to supply an incorrect value for the buffer length. This value—which represents length in characters rather than size in bytes—is used to determine the end point of the resultant string form, at which point the reverse writing begins. Since the implementation only does a debug run time assertion, it is possible for a buffer underrun to occur. It is beholden on the programmer to provide a buffer of sufficient length; this is one of the ways in which the technique derives its extra speed. Naturally, you'll do like I do and use `dimensionof()` (see section 14.3) or an equivalent mechanism to avoid any problems, but the fragility is there nonetheless.

Although the required sizes for buffers of the various types are both small and constant (see Table 31.1) and although developers who've used the function suite readily comprehend the idiom, it still has an uneasy sense of fragility. Furthermore, though no one who's used it has reported any error, there are many complaints regarding the verbosity of the client code.

There are a number of different options by which we can extend the technique to address these criticisms.

Table 31.1   Required buffer sizes for integer conversion.

Type	Size (in chars), including null terminator	Example
8-bit signed	5	"-127"
8-bit unsigned	4	"255"
16-bit signed	7	"-32768"
16-bit unsigned	6	"65535"
32-bit signed	12	"-2147483628"
32-bit unsigned	11	"4294967295"
64-bit signed	21	"-9223372036854775808"
64-bit unsigned	21	"18446744073709551615"

31.3.1 RVL

Solution 1 does not have any issues with respect to RVL-LS or RVL-PDP. It is susceptible to RVL-LV, but only in the same way as any other function—for example, `memset()`, `strcpy()`, and so forth—that returns a pointer that it is passed.

31.4 Solution 2—TSS

Two of the three parameters to the `integer_to_string()` functions are provided to ensure thread safety. If we could somehow arrange to have a thread-safe internal buffer, then we'd only need to supply the integer to be converted. Sounds like a job for some *Thread-Specific Storage* (TSS) (see section 10.5). Using TSS, we can extend the original functions in a new function, say `int_to_string()`,[4] which could be defined as:

```
template< typename C
        , typename I
        >
C const *int_to_string(I value)
{
  const size_t  CCH     = 21; // fits 64-bit + sign
  C             *buffer = i2str_get_tss_buffer<C, CCH>();
  return integer_to_string(buffer, CCH, value);
}
```

We make CCH = 21, to provide enough space for any integer type up to 64 bits (signed or unsigned). The implementation relies on the function `i2str_get_tss_buffer()` to return a buffer, of static storage, of the given character type C on a thread-specific basis.

31.4.1 _ _declspec(thread)

On the Win32 platform, TSS is available in two forms, as we saw in section 10.5.3. For executables and dynamic libraries that are explicitly loaded during application startup [Rich1997], several Win32 compilers provide the Microsoft extension `_ _declspec(thread)`, which declares a thread-specific variable. Using `_ _declspec(thread)` we can offer an implementation of `i2str_get_tss_buffer()` as follows:[5]

```
template< typename C
        , size_t   CCH
        >
```

---

[4]There are actually eight functions, corresponding to the eight `integer_to_string` functions, for each numeric integer type (signed and unsigned 8-, 16-, 32-, and 64-bit integers). It's more effort for the poor library writer (sigh), and occasionally inconvenient for the user, but this way helps ensure that other integral types, for example, `wchar_t` and `bool`, are not (mis-)used with these purely numeric functions (see section 19.4).

[5]Note that in the actual WinSTL implementation each of the eight `int_to_string<>()` functions use 21 as their buffer length. This actually saves space—both code and data—since the number of instantiations of `i2str_get_tss_buffer<>()` drop from a potential maximum of 8 to just 2. In addition, it also reduces time costs where the implementation of the function contains nontrivial logic, as we see with the next implementation.

```
C *i2str_get_tss_buffer()
{
  __declspec(thread) static C s_buffer[CCH];
  return s_buffer;
}
```

This implementation has extremely good performance characteristics, only marginally less than `integer_to_string()` itself (see section 31.3). Alas the restrictions to the use of `__declspec(thread)` (see section 10.5.3) mean we can't seriously consider it for our conversion library functions.

31.4.2   Win32 TLS

The other form of Win32 TSS is the TLS API, which we discussed in section 10.5.2. Using Win32 TLS, the implementation of `i2str_get_tss_buffer` becomes:

Listing 31.3
```
template< typename C
        , size_t   CCH
        >
C *i2str_get_tss_buffer()
{
  static Key<C, CCH>  s_key;
  Slot<C, CCH>        *slot = s_key.GetSlot();
  if(NULL == slot)
  {
    slot = s_key.AllocSlot();
  }
  return slot->buff;
}
```

All the work is done by the `Slot` (see Listing 31.4) and `Key` (see Listing 31.5) classes, in which we get to give our threading skills a good workout.

Listing 31.4
```
template< typename C
        , size_t   CCH
        >
struct Slot
{
  Slot(Slot *next)
    : next(next)
  {}
  ~Slot()
  {
    delete next;
  }
  C     buff[CCH];
```

```
    Slot  *next;
};
```

The `Key` class allocates a TLS key via `TlsAlloc()`, which is then used in its `GetSlot()` and `AllocSlot()` methods. `GetSlot()` simply returns the suitably cast return value from `TlsGetValue()`. `AllocSlot()` is a little more complicated, since it needs to allocate a `Slot` instance and add it onto `Key`'s linked-list of `Slot` instances, within a thread-safe block. This block only needs to guard the integrity of the linked-list—held by the the `m_top` member—and so does not incorporate the call to `TlsSetValue()`. (The `Slot` instances are all destroyed in `Key`'s destructor, which occurs at module/process shutdown and does not need to use any thread-safe measures.)

Listing 31.5

```
template< typename C
        , size_t   CCH
        >
struct Key
{
  typedef Slot<C, CCH>  Slot;
  Key()
    : m_key(::TlsAlloc())
  {
    if(TLS_OUT_OF_INDEXES == m_key)
    {
      . . . // throw an exception
    }
  }
  ~Key()
  {
    // Walk the slot list and free. This can be as slow as you
    // like, since performance is not important at this point.
    delete m_top;
    ::TlsFree(m_key);
  }
  Slot *GetSlot()
  {
    // NOTE: This does not need to be thread-safe
    return reinterpret_cast<Slot*>(::TlsGetValue(m_key));
  }
  Slot *AllocSlot()
  {
    Slot   *next;
    { // Protect linked-list manipulation
      lock_scope<thread_mutex>  lock(m_mx);
      m_top = next = new Slot(m_top);
    }
    ::TlsSetValue(m_key, next);
```

```
    return next;
  }
private:
  dword_t const m_key;
  Slot          *m_top;
  thread_mutex  m_mx;
};
```

There's a fair bit of code involved, here, but once the `Key` has been constructed the first time through the function (on any thread), and a `Slot` has been allocated the first time through for each thread, there is very little further cost as we'll see in section 31.8. The very observant among you may have noticed a potential race condition[6] in that there is no thread-serialization protection visible in `int_to_string()` for the static construction of the `Key` instance (see Chapter 11).

The solution in this case is that the constructor for the `Key` class is itself thread safe, via the use of spin mutexes—what else?—and you can find the full implementation on the CD.

So the DLL dynamic-loading issue has been addressed, but the garden's not all green. One problem is that the number of keys on a given Win32 system is finite. On later operating systems, this is not a big problem, but on earlier versions of Windows there are very few TLS keys available (see section 10.5.2). It's not difficult to imagine very sophisticated software having a great many components that utilize TLS, so it is quite conceivable that exhaustion may occur.

Another downside is that this form of TSS is slower (though not by much; see section 31.8) than `__declspec(thread)`. As noted earlier, making all the `int_to_string()` overloads use CCH set to `21` is efficient in space and time terms. However, there is another benefit. In light of what we now know about the potential scarcity of keys we can see that we will now use a maximum of two TLS keys—for `char` and `wchar_t`[7]—rather than up to eight, making the catastrophic failure to allocate a key significantly reduced.

Nonetheless, there is the issue of what to do if and when a TLS key is unavailable. From a practical point of view, one can ensure that both `char` and `wchar_t` variants of one of the conversion functions are called in the application initialization. While not proofing the application from failure, this will at least precipitate that failure sooner, so is a significant help with testing practical robustness. Naturally it does absolutely nothing to guarantee that exhaustion cannot happen. Where absolute robustness is required, we must take another approach.

31.4.3 Platform-Independent APIs

The previous two solutions were both variants of the same function(s) in the WinSTL project.[8] In my commercial incarnation as a consultant for Synesis Software, I implemented a platform-independent version of the int-to-string functions, which have been recently updated

---

[6]I'm sure that those of you who spotted it will have reasoned just how incredibly unlikely this race condition is to be encountered. However "incredibly unlikely" doesn't cut the mustard in multithreaded software development, so it must be rendered impossible.

[7]If you want to be perverse, you may say three, since you might, if you were brave enough, be doing variable length internationalized string handling on Windows 95/98 using the `unsigned char` type.

[8]The implementation defaults to the `TlsAlloc()` version, but allows you to specify the appropriately ugly `_WINSTL_INT_TO_STRING_USE_DECLSPECTHREAD_FOR_EXES` to use `__declspec(thread)`. If you do so in a DLL build, however, you'll receive some warnings strongly advising you not to do so.

to use the STLSoft `integer_to_string()` function(s). In one of the Synesis core DLLs exists the function `LongToStringA()`—along with its `unsigned`, Unicode and 64-bit siblings—defined within the `SynesisStd` namespace (see Listing 31.6).

It utilizes the platform-independent TSS library which we saw in section 10.5.4. The implementation of the library involves intraprocess mutual exclusion synchronization objects and ordered thread-identifier slot lists, so it shouldn't come as a great surprise that the disadvantage with this approach is that it performs substantially less well than the other two approaches.

Listing 31.6

```
PCAChar LongToStringA(Long value)
{
  const size_t  I2S_LIMIT = 0x7f;
  TssValue      value    = Tss_GetSlotValue(sg_hkeyA);
  PAChar        buffer;
  if(value == 0)
  {
    value = (TssValue)Mem_Alloc_NoTrack(
                          sizeof(AChar) * (1 + I2S_LIMIT)));
    . . .
    Tss_SetSlotValue(sg_hkeyA, value, NULL);
  }
  buffer = SyCastRaw(PAChar, value);
  return integer_to_string(buffer, 1 + I2S_LIMIT, value);
}
```

31.4.4   RVL

This solution is immune to RVL-LV and RVL-PDP. At first glance it also looks as if we've addressed the problem of RVL-LS by virtue of provided thread-safe buffers, albeit at a substantial increase in complexity. However, this RVL is tricky stuff, and we'll see in the next section that there are still problems with this solution.

31.5   Solution 3—Extending RVL

The advantages of the TSS-based approach of Solution 2 are that it is thread safe, works with any character type, and does not require a caller-supplied buffer. Naturally, it does not need a caller-supplied buffer length either, so there is no possibility of an insufficient buffer being passed through to `integer_to_string()`.

One slight inconvenience is that there is no longer any character-based parameter from which the compiler can deduce the character type, which means that the template function must be explicitly parameterized (C++-98: 14.8.1):

```
uint64_t      i = . . .
wchar_t const *result = int_to_string<wchar_t>(i);
```

However, there is another, more significant, drawback, which we're going to examine, and attempt to address in Solution 3. Consider the following example, in light of the implementation of Solution 2:

```
printf("%s %s", int_to_string<char>(5)
                , int_to_string<char>(10));
```

With our current `int_to_string()` function implementation, we may get `"5  5"` or `"10  10"`, but there's *no way* we're going to get the intended `"5  10"`. This is because the value returned by the two calls to `int_to_string()` are the same, that is, a pointer to the thread-specific buffer for the particular combination of character and integer type.

This is a twist on the RVL-LS problem, which can also occur in subtler cases:

```
int some_func(int, char **);

printf("%s %d\n", int_to_string<char>(argc)
                , some_func(argc, argv);
```

If `some_func()` calls `int_to_string<char>(int)`, whether directly or indirectly, then we're back to undefined behavior in our output.

For efficiency reasons the conversion functions return C-strings, rather than instances of `std::basic_string()` or similar. The problem is that a C-string is not a value type; it is a pointer type whose value is the address of the integer's string representation laid out in memory. This problem is not unique to `int_to_string()`: any function that returns a pointer to a structure can suffer from this, irrespective of whether or not they are, like `int_to_string()`, thread safe.

31.5.1   Solving Intrathread RVL-LS?

So what can we do about it? Let's assume that we are adamant that we want to return pointers to C-strings. Clearly we want to be able to return distinct buffers from a parameterization of `i2str_get_tss_buffer()` when the corresponding parameterization of `int_to_string()` is called multiple times within a single expression. Unfortunately, I think that that's pretty much impossible, or at least would have a heavy run time cost.

However, we don't actually need to know whether successive calls are from within a single expression; one option is simply to make sure that the likelihood is very low. Because of the nature of integer to string conversion—that is, there are fixed maximum lengths to the converted string form—we can approximate "impossible" by changing the implementation of `i2str_get_tss_buffer()` to the following:[9]

---

[9] Note that this is only the implementation for the `__declspec(thread)` version. As described in section 31.4, `__declspec(thread)` is suitable only for a limited number of development scenarios, so you'd probably have to use another form of TSS. In performance terms, both the `__declspec(thread)` version of this solution and the one based on the Tss Library (see section 10.5.4) have performances that are indistinguishable from their single-buffer variants described in section 31.4.

Listing 31.7

```
template< typename C
        , size_t    CCH
        >
C *i2str_get_tss_buffer()
{
  const size_t                     DEGREE  =   32;
  __declspec(thread) static C       s_buffers[DEGREE][CCH];
  __declspec(thread) static size_t  s_index;
  s_index = (s_index + 1) % DEGREE;
  return s_buffers[s_index];
}
```

By picking a number that we believe is large enough, we reduce the likelihood of overwrites. 32 buffers of thread-specific storage, each of size CCH (the size adequate for a converted integer), are declared along with a thread-specific indexing variable. Upon each call, the indexer is incremented, and is cycled back to 0 when it reaches 32. Thus, each of the 32 buffers is used in turn, this cycling occurring on a thread-specific basis.

Naturally 32 is a guess at the maximum number of integer to string conversions (remember that this is per-integer type, i.e., there are 32 for uint32_t, 32 for int16_t, etc.), and represents a compromise between desired "safety" and stack size. You would choose your own limit.

31.5.2   RVL

So we've ameliorated the RVL-LS problem. Sadly, we have *not* removed it, and I hope it is clear to you that it is theoretically impossible to do so. Of course we can practically remove it by selecting a sufficiently large degree of buffer array, but this is hackery gone nuts. Don't get me wrong; there are some circumstances where it's valid to go with practical, but not theoretical, correctness. I just don't think this is one of them. Interestingly, Bjarne Stroustrup discusses a similar use for this technique in a scenario in which failure to provide uniqueness would also represent a nonbenign condition. In his customary understated way, he observes that you'd be in trouble if you encountered conditions that precipitated nonuniqueness. I'd put it a lot more strongly than that.

I would suggest that this solution is actually less desirable than Solution 2, since at least in that case there is no attempt to give users of the function a false sense of security; any multiple-use of the return value *will* result in erroneous results. That's preferable to using a library that promises that "you're unlikely to encounter an error." This solution must be rejected completely.[10]

If we want to return a pointer to a buffer, it's looking like we're going to have to pass in the buffer ourselves.

---

[10]Actually, an approach such as this might be appropriate when the (rare) repeated use of an object would result in loss of efficiency, rather than breaking correctness, so it's not entirely without its place.

31.6   Solution 4—Static Array Size Determination

By now you may be despairing that these incremental solutions all represent retrograde steps. Thankfully that's not the case, and I suggest that solution 4 represents the optimal solution to the problem, given the current state of the language and the majority of its supporting compilers.

Getting back to the original `integer_to_string()` functions, the only aspect of them that drew any significant criticism is the ability for a caller to supply an invalid value for the buffer length. If the length is too small, then at least an assertion will fire in debug builds. If the length value stipulated is sufficient, but does not accurately represent the actual, undersized buffer length, then underrun will occur, which will result in corruption of either the stack or the heap.

But as we saw in section 14.3, most modern compilers can deduce the static size of arrays. Hence we can define overloads of the original `integer_to_string()` functions that take an array parameter rather than the pointer + size parameters:

```
template< typename C
        , size_t   N
        >
C const *integer_to_string(C (&buf)[N], int8_t i)
{
  return integer_to_string(buf, N, i); // Safely call ptr form
}
```

This eliminates the possibility of an erroneous buffer length being passed to the function. Even better, we can use compile-time checking, in the form of a static-assertion (see section 1.4.7), to ensure that the buffer length is sufficient.[11]

```
template< typename C
        , size_t   N
        >
C const *integer_to_string(C (&buf)[N], int8_t i)
{
  STATIC_ASSERT(!(N < printf_traits<int8_t>::size));
  return integer_to_string(buf, N, i);
}
```

Now there're no concerns about whether we'll run into a release-build bug that was not located via the assertion in debug-mode testing. If the given parameter is not sufficient, the code will not compile. Pretty spiffy, don't you think?

This solution is thread safe, is not susceptible to erroneous length specification, works with arbitrary character encodings, and does not require explicit instantiation. It is readily inlined into the function it is implemented in terms of, so it does not sacrifice efficiency. Furthermore,

---

[11]`printf_traits` is an STLSoft traits class that evaluates, at compile time, the maximum "printf-width" of a given integral type.

it is pleasingly simple and does not rely on any platform-specific functionality. And, finally, it leads to more succinct code, since we no longer have to specify the buffer size.

```
uint64_t      i = . . .
wchar_t       buff[12];
wchar_t const *result = integer_to_string(buff, i);
```

The only downside is that one must still supply a buffer.

31.6.1   RVL

The RVL ramifications of this are the same as for Solution 1, which is to say it is susceptible to RVL-LV.

31.7   Solution 5—Conversion Shims

The last solution is a departure from the previous four. Rather than returning a C-string pointer into a buffer passed to the function, or one provided by the library on a per-thread basis, this version returns an instance of a proxy object. In this way, it obviates the issues of RVL-LV and RVL-LS entirely. The proxy class—int2str_proxy—contains its own buffer as a member variable, and provides an implicit conversion to a C-string pointer. Integer to string conversion is, of course, carried out by integer_to_string() under the covers, as is the case with all the solutions. The implementations of the class and the assistor function, int2str(), are shown in Listing 31.8.

Listing 31.8
```cpp
template< typename C
        , typename I
        >
class int2str_proxy
{
public:
  typedef C    char_type;
  typedef I    int_type;
public:
  int2str_proxy(int_type i)
    : m_result(integer_to_string(m_sz, dimensionof(m_sz), i))
  {}
  int2str_proxy(int2str_proxy const &rhs)
    : m_result(m_sz)
  {
    char_type        *dest = m_sz;
    char_type const *src  = rhs.m_result;
    for(; 0 != (*dest++ = *src++);)
    {}
  }
  operator char_type const *() const
```

```
    {
      return m_result;
    }
private:
    char_type const * const m_result;
    char_type                m_sz[21];
// Not to be implemented
private:
    int2str_proxy &operator =(int2str_proxy const &rhs);
};


template< typename C
        , typename I
        >
int2str_proxy<C, I> int2str(I i)
{
    return int2str_proxy<C, I>(i);
}
```

To use it, one simply calls `int2str()`, stipulating the appropriate character type, as in `int2str<wchar_t>(101)`. `int2str()`, returns an instance of `int2str_proxy`, and is therefore a conversion shim (see section 20.5.)

31.7.1   RVL

The advantage of this technique is that it is immune to the return value lifetime problems inherent in Solutions 2–4. Hence an expression such as the following will yield correct results:

```
void dump_2_ints(char const *s1, char const *s2);

int i = . . . ;
int j = . . . ;

dump_2_ints(int2str<char>(i), int2str<char>(j));
```

However, in common with conversion shims, this one exposes a susceptibility to RVL-PDP:

```
int        i = . . . ;
char const *s = int2str<char>(i);
```

```
puts(s); // Eeek! s points into hyperspace
```

This code is bad. Although it *may* work, that will only be as an artifact of your compiler and the precise layout of your program. In principle, the behavior of the above code is undefined, and therefore it is broken. This is one of the caveats of conversion shims: the returned converted values must not be retained if they are pointers, but used immediately, or deep copies taken.

The efficiency we're buying is, in part, derived from the fact that we're trading in pointers, specifically C-string pointers. I think it's been amply demonstrated that the cost of such pointer-derived efficiencies are that the code is, if not dangerous, at least accompanied by a health warning. The way around this is to return something that is a value type, such as a string instance, as in:

```
std::string int_to_string_instance(int i)
{
  char  buffer[21];
  return std::string(integer_to_string(buffer, stlsoft_num_elements(buffer), i));
}
```

Naturally, the safety would be bought at the cost of a loss in efficiency.

31.8 Performance

Since the motivation for exposing ourselves to the RVL dangers inherent in these different conversion solutions is efficiency, it behooves us to quantify the potential payoffs so that we can judge whether it's worth all the inconvenience and complexity. In particular we're keen to discover whether the increases in usability in the later solutions has resulted in a significant loss of efficiency over Solution 1.

Since Solution 3 is a Dodo, I'm not including that in the performance test. Solutions 1, 2, 4, and 5 are compared with the standard C library function sprintf(), the popular C library extension function itoa(), and the int_to_string_instance() function described in the last section. These seven conversion mechanisms were tested for five popular Win32 compilers, all optimized for speed (see Appendix A). For each mechanism, 10 million 32-bit signed integer values are converted to string form. This is done twice, and the time of the second iteration is reported.[12] The results are shown in Table 31.2.

Table 31.2

	CodeWarrior	Digital Mars	GCC	Intel	Visual C++ 7.1	Average
sprintf	100.0%	100.0%	100.0%	100.0%	100.0%	100.0%
itoa	67.8%	44.8%	27.5%	26.8%	28.1%	39.0%
Solution 1	24.7%	18.8%	12.6%	12.0%	29.4%	19.5%
Solution 2	26.8%	20.4%	14.1%	12.7%	29.0%	20.6%
Solution 4	24.5%	19.6%	12.7%	11.8%	29.5%	19.6%
Solution 5	28.5%	18.9%	12.6%	11.8%	29.5%	20.3%
int_to_string_ instance	124.4%	37.4%	42.2%	28.1%	43.2%	55.1%

---

[12]All tests were carried out on a 2GHz 512MB Pentium IV machine in a single session with no other busy processes.

The results clearly show that the four custom conversion mechanisms represent a significant net performance win over `sprintf()` and `itoa()` for each of the compilers and their standard libraries, except for Visual C++ 7.1 where they are merely roughly on a par with its implementation of `itoa()`. Given that the Intel test was conducted with the Visual C++ 7.1 run time library, it's clear that the custom solutions do offer a significant performance advantage when paired with a compiler that is able to provide high levels of template optimisation. On average, the custom solutions are twice as fast as `itoa()`, and five times faster than `sprintf()`.

The four custom solutions provide virtually identical performance, so the choice between them can be made on the issues of ease-of-use, convenience, and the various strengths and weaknesses of their susceptibilities to RVL.

There's one last thing I should point out, though it may cost me some stars on my C++ good behavior chart. The performance for the value (`std::string`) returning option doesn't exactly set the world alight. In most cases it outperforms `sprintf()`, but despite the helping hand of being implemented in terms of `integer_to_string()`, the cost of the single memory allocation[13] and `strcpy()` involved in creating the return value means that this option does not fair well with respect to the custom solutions.

31.9   RVL: The Big Win for Garbage Collection

As someone who likes to have a modest mastery of several languages and can see the virtue in most of them,[14] one thing that dumbfounds me in the debate between languages that use garbage collection and those that do not is that the arguments for garbage collection are that it relieves the programmer from clearing up their own memory, or saves them from making the mistake of forgetting to release their memory. Politeness (and my editor) prevents me from saying what I really think about this argument, so I'll just say I think it's utter nonsense.

The first thing is, with C++ this is almost always a nonissue. If you are sensible, then you use RAII (see Chapters 3, 4, and 6), and therefore the problem largely disappears.

The second part of this that really irritates me is that proponents of such languages as, say, Java and .NET, always carp on about memory leaks, as if memory is the only kind of resource that can be leaked. At least as serious are leaks of other kinds of system resources, such as file handles, synchronization objects, and the like. The amazing thing is that these languages provide virtually no support for the automatic and exception-safe handling of such resources. One is left with a stinking big mess of `try-finally` blocks. Hideous stuff!

The irony is that these proponents never use the real issue in which garbage collection is indeed incontestably superior. When using garbage collection, the problems of RVL, as discussed in this chapter and in sections 16.2 and 20.6.1, simply disappear. Since garbage collection works by releasing memory only when there are no references to it in active code, it is axiomatic that a pointer to a heap-allocated memory block cannot be invalid while it is still needed. All we would need would be to return a new heap block containing the converted form. If there were efficiency issues with that, we could maintain a special memory pool of twenty-

---

[13]This assumes that all the compilers tested apply RVO in the `integer_to_string_instance<>()` function, which we saw that these five were able to do in Chapter 12.

[14]I can see no virtue in Visual Basic, and never have. Sorry.

one-character[15] heap blocks, which would be efficiently given out to the conversion functions for each conversion.

31.10   Potential Applications

The conversion functions described here could be well employed in the implementation of serialization libraries, since they convert much quicker than `sprintf()` for single variables. Furthermore, they are also useful in any situation where a function needs a pointer to char containing the (decimal) string form of an integer (e.g., when setting the text of a window in a UI). They do not conduct any kind of locale-sensitive conversion, such as the use of a comma as a thousands separator, but where plain conversion is needed, they represent a win that is hard to ignore.

31.11   Return Value Lifetime: Coda

I hope this chapter has provided you with a look into a different way of doing conversions, and that it's given you food for thought. In general, I think it's wise to profile the libraries you're using, even the standard libraries, and not just accept what you're given. It's interesting that some of the very best compilers are linked to lackluster libraries.

I also hope you've had a chance to ruminate about the subjects of threading and reentracy, and enjoyed the practical application of some of the threading techniques we learned in Chapter 10.

But most important, I hope you've enhanced or affirmed your knowledge about the problems of return value lifetime, and the trade-offs that we, as C++ practitioners, make in using this powerful and efficient language.

---

[15]The maximum number of characters in any 64-bit number is 20 (assuming no thousands-separator, or similar localization effects).

CHAPTER   3 2

Memory

32.1   A Taxonomy of Memory

We talked about some of the details of (local and nonlocal) static memory in Chapter 11, but we've not looked in any detail at the range of memory mechanisms supported by C and C++.

32.1.1   Stack and Static Memory

Stack variables are allocated from the executing thread's stack in the scope of the function within which they are defined by adjustment of the stack pointer on entering the scope of their declaration. Static variables are fixed in program global memory, allocated by reservation of space in the global memory area. For the purposes of this section, I focus on the implications of the use of stack memory, although some of the issues discussed also apply to global memory.

Because the allotment of memory for global and stack variables is carried out at compile time, there are both advantages and disadvantages. The main advantage is that there is no "allocation" actually happening, merely a manipulation of pointers or addresses; to all intents and purposes, the memory already exists. Consequently, this form of memory allocation is extremely efficient; in fact it is the most efficient form of memory allocation. An additional minor advantage is that one can determine, at compile time, the size of the allocated memory, by use of the sizeof operator.

The downside is that the memory can only be of fixed, predetermined, size. (The slight exception to this is the alloca() technique, which we cover in section 32.2.1.) This is often perfectly acceptable when, for example, dealing with file-system entity names, which have a fixed maximum on many platforms. When writing such code one may simply declare a buffer of the maximum potential size, confident that passing it to any function will not result in buffer overwrites. However, when dealing with APIs whose functions may use buffers of any lengths (e.g., the Win32 Registry API), one can never guarantee to have a fixed buffer of sufficient size.[1]

As was mentioned in Chapter 11, static variables have their storage initialized to 0. Stack variables are not automatically initialized and will contain random values until explicitly initialized.

---

[1] I am sure most of us have written RegXxx() code passing buffers of _MAX_PATH size, nonetheless!

32.1.2   Stack Expansion

I said above that stack memory already exists. However, this is only true as far as the C/C++ notional execution environment is concerned. In reality, the stack memory for a process may be as ephemeral as any other part of its virtual address space. It is up to the operating system to ensure that the stack memory exists when you need it.

On Win32 operating systems,[2] stack memory is committed on use on a per-page basis [Rich1997]. What this means is that if the current area of stack memory has not yet been committed, and an instruction touches that memory, the operating system will (attempt to) commit the page and then reexecute the instruction accessing the now valid memory. The next uncommitted page is called the guard page and bears a special guard attribute to facilitate stack expansion. However, the guard page attribute is only attached to the first uncommitted page, so that the touching of any other uncommitted pages beyond that results in a simple, terminal, access violation. Other operating systems operate analogous mechanisms.

The real-world problem for stack-memory (including `alloca()`; see section 32.2.1) is when the combined size of all variables within the local scope exceeds, or may potentially exceed, the system page threshold. In that instance the compiler is required to insert code in order to ensure that the stack memory is valid. The reason for this can be demonstrated with a simple example. Consider the following code:

```
void stack_func(size_t index)
{
    char    stack_buffer[4097];
    buffer[index] = '\0';
}
```

The code demonstrates the possibility of skipping a page in the manner described. If the page size is 4096 and the first byte of `stack_buffer` falls on the first byte of the guard page, then it is possible, with `index` equal to 4096, to skip the guard page and access the next uncommitted page. Since that page will not have the guard attribute, this will cause an access violation, and your process will be terminated. Although this example is contrived, it is common to see scenarios where several local buffers are declared and their total can even exceed the size of one or more pages, making the skipping of the guard page much more likely.

In order to ensure that all pages between the current last page and any and all required in any next block are valid, compilers must step in and shoulder some of the burden. The Visual C++ compiler inserts calls to the `chkstk()` function, which ensures that any pages that might slip through this window are touched in the correct order, thereby bringing them into committed memory in a coherent manner. Incurring this insertion has the two related disadvantages that it causes linking to the C run time library (which may be undesirable) and incurs a modest performance hit in the calling and execution of the `chkstk()` function.

---

[2]On Solaris, a similar scheme is operated: the stack is memory mapped using the MAP_NORESERVE flag; virtual memory is not allocated until the page is used. There is only one redzone per stack.

32.1.3 Heap Memory

Heap memory is the opposite of stack memory: it is obtained from *the* heap (sometimes referred to as the free store [Stro1994]), or from one of a set of heaps, at run time. Every heap API requires a function to allocate memory (e.g., `malloc()`) and, except where using garbage collection, a corresponding function to return it (e.g., `free()`).The advantage of heap memory is that the size of the buffer can be any practical size, within the limitations of the run time system (although some older memory APIs restrict the maximum size of individual buffers).

There are several disadvantages to the use of heap memory. First, heap allocations are considerably slower than stack/global allocations (due to the complexity of implementing the memory allocation schemes to reclaim and defragment freed memory). Second, it is possible that the request may not actually be satisfiable at run time, requiring client code to manage that eventuality (whether through exception handling or through testing the returned value against NULL). Third, you must explicitly return your memory when you no longer need it. If you forget to free allocated chunks, your process will likely die a slow death through memory exhaustion.

Additionally, heavy use of any heap can lead to fragmentation, whereby the free parts of the heap are spread around among many allocated sections. This can increase the likelihood of allocation failure, and can degrade performance due to the need to search through the free list to find areas of the appropriate size to match requests.

32.2 The Best of Both Worlds

Let's just put the minor problems of these memory schemes aside for a moment: stack expansion is handled for you by your compiler and operating system; heap allocation failure can often be left to an overarching processswide error handler; memory leaks can be avoided by using memory buffer management classes employing RAII (see section 3.5); and fragmentation can be minimized by using custom pools (see section 32.3). But there are two unavoidable issues when using memory as provided by C and C++. If you use stack memory, you'll have very high speed but will need to know the size of the memory required at compile time, and you will not be able to change it. Conversely, if you use heap memory you can determine the size, and change the size, at run time, but you will suffer from a performance hit that, with some heap managers, can be considerable.

To put it crudely:[3]

Imperfection: C and C++ make you choose between performance and flexibility when allocating memory.

Naturally, this conflict is not one that any developer relishes, nor one that they tend to accept. We'll look in this section at various mechanisms that have been developed to cheat the system.

---

[3]And bearing in mind that most other languages either have the same problems or don't have the guts to give developers access to stack memory.

32.2.1   alloca()

Since stack variable memory is "allocated" by adjustment of the stack pointer in accordance with the compiler's dictates, it seems reasonable to wonder whether the adjustment has to be of a fixed size. Although it is not possible on all architectures [Stev1993], an attempt to merge the speed of stack memory with the flexibility of heap memory is the `alloca()` function (and its analogues, e.g., Visual C++'s `_alloca()`). The function allocates memory, whose size is determined at run time, from the stack rather than from the heap, by simply adjusting the stack pointer. The memory is automatically "freed" when the enclosing scope exits. This is a very useful facility, and where available and applicable provides the best solution in most cases of automatic buffers. Unfortunately, its mechanism means it has rather a large set of restrictions and caveats, which severely restrict its utility.

There are several minor disadvantages. First, in common with heap-memory allocation, it cannot give compile-time size, and it requires a local variable to keep track of memory size in circumstances where that is needed. Second, it cannot reallocate memory in the same manner that `realloc()` (and its platform-specific analogs) can, so in that way does not represent a direct replacement for heap memory APIs. Third, it is nonstandard, so not guaranteed to be available with all platforms/compilers: the code using it is not portable. Fourth, it has varied failure behavior: on Linux it returns NULL if it fails to allocate the requested memory, whereas on Win32 a machine-dependent exception is generated. Fifth, in common with compile time stack allocation, `alloca()` requires the use of stack-checking code (see section 32.1.2). Finally, there are implementation-dependent restrictions to the context of its use. For example, the Win32/Microsoft C run time `_alloca()` variant cannot be used from within certain exception handling contexts, as it can cause the system to crash unpredictably.

The two major disadvantages are even more dissuasive. First, by virtue of its mechanism, `alloca()` cannot be used to hold memory outside the current execution context, so it cannot be used for allocating variable sized blocks inside object instances, nor wrapped in template or other functions, for example, it is not possible to write a `local_strdup()`.[4] Second, and most important, because of its adjusting of stack pointers within the current function context, it can easily cause stack exhaustion when used in a function that performs a number of allocation/ deallocation cycles. Indeed, the functions used to test the relative performances (see section 32.2.6) in this chapter quickly failed on both Linux and Win32 platforms for that reason. If it is not possible or practicable to move the `alloca()` call and the processing of the memory it returns into a separate function called within a loop—which may hurt performance too much to be useful anyway—then it should be avoided in such looping code.

32.2.2   VLAs

The C99 enhancements to the C-language specification included the new concept of *Variable Length Arrays* (VLAs) [Meye2001b], which (syntactically at least) addresses the issue of dynamically sized stack array variables. VLAs allow the dimensions of arrays to be determined at runtime, as in:

---

[4]Other than by using macros, that is.

```
void func(int x, int y)
{
  int ar[x][y];
}
```

At this time VLAs are not a part of C++, although some compilers do support them with C++ as an extension. Digital Mars and GCC both provide them, as does Comeau, if used with a back-end compiler that supports them.

VLAs will likely be implemented via either `alloca()` (or a similar technique) or via heap memory. Digital Mars uses `alloca()`. Comeau C++ currently uses whatever VLA mechanism its backend compiler provides, although they're considering directly implementing VLA in terms of `alloca()`; this would widen the support considerably. GCC uses a stack-based technique, but it does not appear to be `alloca()`, as we will see shortly. So although the syntax of the language will be clearer than current use of either `alloca()` or the heap, the implications for performance, robustness, and availability will largely be the same, as we'll see.

Support for non-POD types is implementation dependent. GCC is the only one of our compilers (Appendix A) that currently does so. VLA objects, for POD types at least, are uninitialized. The C standard (C-99: 6.2.4; 6) says that: "the initial value of object[s] [of variable length array type] is indeterminate."

There are two disadvantages of VLAs. The first is that they are not (yet) part of standard C++, and the support for them is scant. Second, they are subject to the same performance and robustness characteristics as their underlying mechanisms, which can differ widely between implementations, as we will see.

Note that `sizeof()` can be applied to VLAs, but the result is evaluated at run time.

32.2.3   auto_buffer<>

The proposed solution for efficient, variable-sized automatic buffers is the `auto_buffer` template class[5]—so named because of its primary intended use as automatic variables—as shown in Listing 32.1.

Listing 32.1
```
template< typename  T
        , typename  A
        , size_t    SPACE = 256
        >
class auto_buffer
  : protected A
{
public:
    . . . // Usual member type declarations
// Construction
  explicit auto_buffer(size_type cItems);
  ~auto_buffer();
```

---

[5]This is a part of the STLSoft libraries. The latest implementation, along with all test programs and full results, are available on the CD.

```
/// Operations
  bool   resize(size_type cItems);
  void   swap(class_type &rhs);
/// Operators
  operator      pointer ();
  pointer       data();
  const_pointer data() const;
/// Iteration
  // const / non-const, (r)begin() + (r)end() methods
/// Attributes
  size_type      size() const;
  bool           empty() const;
  allocator_type get_allocator() const;
/// Members
private:
  value_type  *m_buffer;          // Pointer to used buffer
  size_type   m_cItems;           // Number of items in buffer
  value_type  m_internal[space];  // Internal storage
// Not to be implemented
private:
  . . . // Prevent copy construction / assignment
};
```

The purpose of the class is to emulate the syntax and semantics of a standard array variable for POD types and to maximize the flexibility and performance of stack and heap memory. To achieve this it allocates from its internal buffer where possible, otherwise allocating from the heap via the allocator type.

To be as compatible as is possible with normal raw array syntax and to work in cases where array decay (see Chapter 14) was prevalent, it provides an implicit conversion operator rather than index operators (`value_type &operator [] ()`, and `const` version). This supports both conversion to pointer and (implicit) array indexing, whereas the index operator approach on its own allows only (explicit) array indexing.[6]

The implementation of the class is surprisingly simple. Almost all the action is in the constructor (see Listing 32.2). It takes a single argument: the requested number of elements in the array. This is tested against the size of the internal buffer, and if not larger, the `m_buffer` member is set to point to `m_internal`, the internal array. (This is fairly similar to the small string optimization [Meye2001].) If the requested size is larger, then a request is made to the allocator, setting `m_buffer` to the allocated block. (All accessor methods refer to `m_buffer`, in either case.)

Listing 32.2

```
  . . .
  explicit auto_buffer(size_type cItems)
    : m_buffer((space < cItems) ? alloc_(cItems) : &m_internal[0])
```

---

[6]Though index operators would afford the possibility of some simple index validation (e.g., `assert`, or even throw an exception), usability won over principle in this case.

```
    , m_cItems((NULL != m_buffer) ? cItems : 0)
  {
    STATIC_ASSERT(space != 0);
    STATIC_ASSERT( offsetof(class_type, m_buffer)
                  < offsetof(class_type, m_cItems));
    constraint_must_be_pod(value_type);
  }
  ~auto_buffer()
  {
    if(space < m_cItems)
    {
      assert(NULL != m_buffer);
      dealloc_(m_buffer, m_cItems);
    }
  }
  . . .
```

In the latter case, it is possible for the allocation to fail. Because an important requirement for the class, and for the STLSoft libraries as a whole, is to be as widely compatible as possible, the constructor is written to work correctly both in situations where allocation failures result in an exception being thrown, and in those where the `allocate()` method returns `NULL`. When an exception is thrown, it is propagated to the caller of the `auto_buffer` constructor, and the instance of the `auto_buffer` is not constructed. Some allocators do not throw exceptions when they fail to secure enough memory for the requested allocation, returning `NULL` instead. Also, when creating small programs it may be undesirable to compile/link in exception handling mechanisms, in which case one may deliberately plug in a `NULL`-on-failure allocator. In such circumstances it is prudent to leave the `auto_buffer` in a coherent state, therefore, the initializing condition for `m_cItems` discriminates on whether `m_buffer` is non-`NULL`. In the case where `NULL` is returned, the remaining construction of the `auto_buffer` instance results in initialization of the `m_cItems` member to 0, and thereby provides sensible and correct behavior for the use of this empty instance, namely, that `begin() == end()`, `empty()` returns `true` and `size()` returns 0.

Note that this uses the fragile technique of relying on the relative member (initialization) order of `m_buffer` and `m_cItems`. To that end there are assertions (static/compile time and dynamic/run time) in the constructor to guard against any maintenance edits that are not mindful of this requirement and might change this ordering, resulting in the discrimination against the value of `m_buffer` testing garbage and the classic undefined results (i.e., a crash). Such member ordering dependencies are not generally a good idea, but I chose to use the technique here as it allows me to declare `m_cItems` as const, and the assertions ensure that all is well.[7]

It is important to note that `auto_buffer`'s constructor performs only the allocation of memory, it does not in-place construct any elements, in common with built-in arrays (of POD

---

[7]Practice wins out over theory here. In principle `offsetof()` is undefined for non-POD types, so applying it here is not strictly valid. However, for all compilers supported by STLSoft it does what's required, so it is used. If STLSoft is ported to a compiler that lays out classes such that this would not apply, then `auto_buffer<>`, or the macro, will be rewritten accordingly.

type) and VLAs. Nor does its destructor destroy the elements. To ensure that it's not (mis)used with non-POD types, we use the constraint `constraint_must_be_pod()` (see section 1.2.4). While the `m_internal` array member would, in and of itself, prevent the compilation of parameterizations of `auto_buffer` with classes that do not provide publicly accessible default constructors, default-constructible class types could still be used, and so the constraint is necessary. Note that there's also a compile-time assertion to prevent someone from perversely parameterizing it with an internal size of `0`.

The constructor is `explicit` in common with good practice (though it's hard to conceive of an implicit conversion scenario against which to guard). The destructor has a straightforward implementation. By testing `m_cItems` against the size of the internal buffer, it determines whether `m_buffer` points to `m_internal` and, if not, frees the heap memory by calling the allocator's `deallocate()` method.

The class also provides basic STL container methods `empty()`, `size()`, `begin()` and `end()`. `begin()` and `end()` are added purely as a programmatic convenience and should not be taken to mean that `auto_buffer` is a full STL container. It is not, since it does not (currently) work with instances of non-POD types.

32.2.4 Using the Template

Using the template requires parameterization of the element type, the allocator type and, optionally, the size of the internal array (`m_internal`). As mentioned earlier, the class is designed such that it does not prescribe a particular memory allocation scheme to support its semantics, as long as the allocator supports the STL *Allocator* concept [Aust1999, Muss2001]. Any compliant allocator may be used, providing client code with maximal flexibility, conforming to STL good practice. The size of `m_internal`, measured in number of elements rather than bytes, is given by the third parameter, which defaults to 256. Client code can specify any size here to best match the most common required array size for maximum performance benefit.

```
int some_func(char *s, size_t len)
{
  typedef auto_buffer<char, std::allocator<char> > buffer_t;

  buffer_t buf(1 + len);
  strncpy(&buf[0], s, buf.size());
  . . .
```

Note that the use of `buf` in the call to `strncpy()` uses the `size()` method, to handle the case where allocation fails and the allocator returns `NULL` rather than throws an exception. In real cases, you'd have to do more than just not write anything in such a case, unless you wanted to surprise client code of `some_func()`.

32.2.5 EBO, Where Art Thou?

For all compilers other than Borland, `auto_buffer` derives from the allocator, and takes advantage of EBO (see section 12.3) when appropriate. However, with Borland this causes such significant performance degradation (actually worse than the `malloc()`/`free()` scenario in all cases) that an allocator is instead shared between all instances, as shown in Listing 32.3:

Listing 32.3

```
template< . . .

          >
class auto_buffer
#ifndef ACMELIB_COMPILER_IS_BORLAND
  : protected A
#endif /* !ACMELIB_COMPILER_IS_BORLAND */
{

  . . .

#ifdef ACMELIB_COMPILER_IS_BORLAND
  static allocator_type &get_allocator()
  {
    static allocator_type    s_allocator;
    return s_allocator;
  }
#else
  allocator_type        get_allocator() const
  {
    return *this;
  }

  . . .
```

Thankfully, the STL *Allocator* concept [Aust1999, Muss2001] dictates that allocators are not allowed to act as if they have per-instance data, and most actually do not, but if they did there's a very slight possibility of a multithreading race condition here, which is not pleasant. If you wished to be ultrasafe, you could apply a spin mutex here (see section 10.2.2).

32.2.6   Performance

The performance of `auto_buffer` was tested against the following memory allocation types: stack variables; heap using `malloc()/free()`; heap using `operator new/delete`; dynamic stack allocation using `alloca()/_alloca()`; VLAs; `std::vector`. For each allocation type, the program allocates a block, accesses a byte within it (to prevent the compiler optimizing away the loop), and then deallocates it. The operation is repeated for a given number of times determined by the second program parameter. Since the program's parameterization accepts the default 256 for the internal buffer size, the two sizes tested are above and below this, specifically 100 and 1,000 bytes, repeated 10 million times.[8]

Because `auto_buffer` does a test (comparing the size of its internal buffer against the requested buffer size), prior to making any heap allocation, in circumstances where it must allocate from the heap the performance will be less than going straight to the heap. Therefore the purpose of the performance test is to quantify the presumed superiority where it uses its internal buffer and the presumed inferiority where it allocates from the heap.

The test was carried out with our ten Win32 compilers (see Appendix A). The resultant times were normalized with respect to the time taken for `malloc()/free()` for each compiler, and are expressed in percentage terms.[9] Table 32.1 shows the performance for the internal

---

[8]Tests of 10 and 100 bytes with a 64-byte buffer size yielded virtually identical relative results for all compilers.

[9]The full results and test program are available on the CD.

Table 32.1   Performances (relative to `malloc()`) of schemes for 100-element allocations.

Memory	Slowest (Borland)	Fastest (Intel)	GCC	Average	Average (- Borland)
Automatic	2.2%	0.2%	0.3%	0.9%	0.7%
malloc()	100.0%	100.0%	100.0%	100.0%	100.0%
operator new	178.3%	98.6%	105.9%	109.3%	100.7%
vector<>	386.8%	335.3%	121.6%	153.2%	124.0%
auto_buffer<>	54.2%	1.2%	2.8%	8.6%	2.9%
alloca()	*	*	*	*	*
VLA	-	-	1.7%	-	-

allocation. The figures clearly show that a significant advantage can be gained when the size of the allocation is smaller than that of the internal buffer, with the cost being between 1% and 54% of that of `malloc()`/`free()`. The average cost was 8.6 percent, and discounting the very poor performance of Borland it falls to 2.9% —very close to that of stack memory.

For figures marked * it proved impossible to obtain meaningful performance figures due to stack exhaustion crashes on any useful level of loop repeats. This was the case for all `alloca()` implementations as well as VLAs with Digital Mars (which is expected given its implementation over `alloca()`). The interesting thing is that GCC's VLA did not suffer stack exhaustion (as its `alloca()` did), which implies it uses a different technique. Though slower than stack memory, it was nearly twice as fast as `auto_buffer`. My suspicion, therefore, is that it adjusts the stack pointer back when the scope, rather than the function, is exited, thus avoiding the exhaustion.

Table 32.2 shows the performance for allocation larger than the internal buffer size. In this case, performance ranges between 101% and 275%. The average is 123%, or just 104% if we remove Borland. Clearly, the wise programmer will be able to select a template size parameter such that the vast majority of allocations will fit within the internal size, which will result in significant net performance gains overall.

It's worth noting that the vector performance is up to 370% and up to 2500% (Intel, with Visual C++ standard library, not shown) for the two scenarios, so that there's no doubt that

Table 32.2   Performances (relative to `malloc()`) of schemes for 1000-element allocations.

Memory	Slowest (Borland)	Fastest (Digital Mars)	GCC	Average	Average (- Borland)
Automatic	2.0%	0.5%	0.3%	0.8%	0.6%
malloc()	100.0%	100.0%	100.0%	100.0%	100.0%
operator new	184.7%	101.8%	105.6%	112.0%	102.9%
vector<>	642.7%	614.8%	162.7%	608.5%	604.2%
auto_buffer<>	275.2%	101.4%	107.1%	122.7%	103.7%
alloca()	*	*	*	*	*
VLA	-	*	1.6%	-	-

`auto_buffer` is vastly more efficient than `vector`. But remember that `auto_buffer` does support non-POD types, and it does not initialize the memory it acquires. Furthermore it does not provide any of the insertion, removal, or other sophisticated operations of the *Vector* model (C++-98: 23.2.4). All of this is by design—I wanted one-time allocation,[10] and I wanted it fast—and so it's fair to draw a comparison with `vector` only in these circumstances. `auto_buffer` is not a replacement for `vector`, and is not intended to be.

It's worth noting that most operating systems provide a variety of memory allocators, which may provide more efficient or thread-friendly memory allocation, for example, libumem on Solaris, so it's possible that you may be able to get much better performance than `malloc()`. I doubt very much whether they'll provide performance comparable with `auto_buffer` and VLAs, but performance facts are only established by performance testing.

32.2.7 Heap vs. Stack vs. . . .

Including the quantitative results, we can draw up a table (Table 32.3) of the relative merits of the various schemes. Clearly, when used wisely, `auto_buffer` has the best mix of features of all the schemes for automatic arrays of fundamental and POD types.

In addition, `auto_buffer` can be used in composition, although care must be exercised in such circumstances. While it can provide similar performance advantages, it should only be

Table 32.3 Feature summary of the memory allocation schemes.

	Stack	Heap	alloca()	VLAs	vector<>	auto_ buffer<>
Size determinable at run time	No	Yes	Yes	Yes	Yes	Yes
Resizable	No	Yes	No	No	Yes	Yes
Prone to stack exhaustion	Yes	No	Yes	No	No	Not if used correctly
Precipitates stack checking	Yes	No	Yes	No	No	Not if used correctly
Possible failure to allocate	No	Yes	Yes	Yes	Yes	Yes
All platforms/compilers	Yes	Yes	No	No	Yes	Yes
Efficiency	Highest	Low	High	Low	Very low	High
Compiled-in memory size	Yes	No	No	No, but sizeof() is applied at run time	No, but size() is inline	No, but size() is inline
Can support non-POD class types	Yes	Yes	No	No	Yes	No
Usable in composition	Yes	Yes	No	No	Yes	Yes

---

[10]As `auto_buffer` has become more established and widely used, it's been upgraded with `resize()` and `swap()` methods (see Listng 32.1), which makes it much more useful when writing exception safe classes (that use construct-and-swap [Sutt2000]). These enhancements don't affect its performance and fundamental simplicity.

done in cases where the most common allocation size equals or is close to the internal buffer size. If the typical size is larger than the internal buffer, then most instances of the class will not use their internal buffer at all. If the typical size is significantly less than the internal buffer, then most instances of the class will not use most of their buffer. In either case, when the containing class is on the heap, then the auto_buffer and its internal buffer will also exist on the heap, potentially wasting a large amount of memory.

It's best to just stick to using it for auto variables. It is *auto*-buffer, after all!

32.2.8   pod_vector<>

Given the great performance savings but low-level nature of auto_buffer, it begs the question[11] whether we can apply the technique in a more general form. The answer is that we can, and it takes the form of the pod_vector template class (see Listing 32.4). pod_vector provides an implementation of the *Vector* model (C++-98: 23.2.4), restricted to POD types. Like auto_buffer, it uses an internal buffer of parameterizable size. In fact, it is implemented in terms of auto_buffer, requiring only a single additional member m_cItems, to represent the size() of the vector; the size of the auto_buffer member represents the capacity() of the vector.

Listing 32.4

```
template< typename  T
        , typename  A
        , size_t    SPACE = 64
        >
class pod_vector
{
/// Typedefs
private:
  typedef auto_buffer<T, A, SPACE>            buffer_type;
public:
  typedef typename buffer_type::value_type      value_type;
  typedef typename buffer_type::allocator_type  allocator_type;
  typedef pod_vector<T, A, SPACE>              class_type;

  . . .
/// Construction
  explicit pod_vector(size_type cItems = 0);
  pod_vector(size_type cItems, value_type const &value);

  . . .
/// Operations

  . . .
  void    resize(size_type cItems);
  void    resize(size_type cItems, value_type const &value);

  . . .
/// Members
private:
```

[11]Actually, Chris Newcombe posed the question and provided the impetus to develop pod_vector.

```
    size_type   m_cItems;
    buffer_type m_buffer;
};
```

pod_vector has two areas of potential performance advantage over standard library implementations of vector. First, it uses an auto_buffer to implement its storage. So long as it is parameterized and used appropriately, such that the net performance gains of auto_buffer are accessible, this will represent a significant optimization.

The other factor is that, because the vector contains only POD types, there is no requirement to destroy elements when they are removed from the vector. For example, the pop_back() method simply decrements m_cItems.

Despite these great potentials, the class will only provide significant performance advantages in certain circumstances, because misuse of auto_buffer results in performance costs. Table 32.4 shows the results from a set of tests—that I do not suggest are in any way exhaustive—written to help me performance tune the implementation. pod_vector<int,...,64> and std::vector<int> were each used in a series of operations, acting on 50 and 100 elements, to exercise the auto_buffer's internal threshold. As you can see, there are some significant performance gains to be had, even in some of the 100 cases. However, what is equally clear is that the relative performance of the two containers is strongly dependent on the type of operation, and also on the compiler used. Even if it may not be too surprising to see the Borland performance figures trailing a little, both CodeWarrior and GCC also have a few concerning data points. But it's also clear that there's great potential for performance gains.

My suggestion with a class such as pod_vector is to write your application using std::vector, and then plug in pod_vector during performance testing. Since it implements the STL *Vector* [Muss2001] model, as does std::vector, this will be as simple as changing a single line. This is one of the beauties of the STL.

Table 32.4 Performance of pod_vector<> relative to vector<>.

Test	Borland	CodeWarrior	GCC	Intel	VC 7.1
insert(begin()) - 50	69.1%	93.6%	70.6%	73.4%	64.2%
insert(begin()) - 100	78.9%	172.9%	92.5%	105.6%	89.5%
push_back - 50	132.4%	34.1%	37.8%	23.8%	12.3%
push_back - 100	188.4%	56.1%	72.2%	36.9%	22.7%
push_back + reserve - 50	331.5%	90.5%	168.6%	50.5%	27.8%
push_back + reserve - 100	374.2%	117.1%	266.2%	66.6%	38.4%
erase(begin()) - 50	22.9%	24.9%	50.2%	49.1%	31.9%
erase(begin()) - 100	15.7%	25.1%	30.6%	38.2%	26.0%
erase(&back()) - 50	59.4%	30.3%	86.7%	38.0%	28.2%
erase(&back()) - 100	78.2%	67.5%	188.9%	76.5%	79.6%
erase block - 50	78.5%	62.4%	72.7%	40.4%	34.6%
erase block - 100	85.5%	80.6%	88.0%	48.4%	44.9%

32.3 Allocators

We'll look now at another trade-off, between compile time and run time selection of allocators. Once again, this is a trade-off between efficiency and flexibility. We saw in Chapter 9 that passing memory between link units is an unappealing prospect whether we require all link units to share the same underlying allocator, or we require the client code of each link unit to return every allocated piece of memory from whence it came. The former approach is restrictive, and the latter can sometimes be hard to adhere to. In either case, the decision of the source of memory is made at compile time.

A third way to achieve this is to pass the allocator into the library, thereby saving the decision for run time. There is a cost to this, effectively the cost of a *vtable* call, although this is usually, but not always, insignificant compared with the cost of the allocation, and the use made of the block. But it also has a potentially large payoff.

First, it relieves the author of the library from having to care about making the decision regarding which memory allocation library to use. You may wonder why this is even an issue. If so, you should probably take a peek inside the C run time library of your favorite compiler. Most vendors go to some serious effort to tune the allocation of memory, often allocating from separate pools depending on the size of the memory allocations. The reason for this is that a single heap subject to a wide spectrum of block size requests will become seriously fragmented, and this can have a significant deleterious effect on performance. Second, you can plug in the allocator at run time, in response to conditions at the time. Third, you don't need to recompile the library in order to change allocators. Finally, you can de-/re-allocate in client code something that was allocated within the library, which can be a useful simplification in many circumstances.

There are different mechanisms for specifying allocators at run time, but most tend to boil down to the same thing:[12] specifying pointers to allocation and deallocation functions in a structure.

32.3.1 Function Pointers

The ubiquitous zlib library defines the two function typedefs:

```
typedef void *(*alloc_fn)(void *opaque, uInt items, uInt size);
typedef void (*free_fn)(void *opaque, void *address);
```

These function typedefs are used within the z_stream structure, which is used by the client to exchange information with the functions in the zlib API.

```
typedef struct z_stream_s
{
    . . .
```

---

[12]Another technique worth mentioning is interposing, or interpositioning [Lind1994], whereby a new library containing custom definitions of memory (or other) routines is linked in, and the calls to these libraries within the process are hooked into those from the new library. The author comments that "[o]ver the years we have seen no convincing examples where [it] was essential [and] the effect could not be achieved in a different . . . manner" and "[it is] only for people who enjoy a walk on the wild side." I couldn't agree more, and although I've used it on occasion, I think the techniques shown in this section represent the robust and maintainable choice.

```
    alloc_func zalloc;   /* used to allocate the internal state */
    free_func  zfree;    /* used to free the internal state */
    voidpf     opaque;   /* private data object passed to zalloc and zfree */
    . . .
} z_stream;
```

All you need do is set the `zalloc` and `zfree` members to point to your functions, and zlib will use them. If you don't have any special requirements, you can specify NULL, and zlib will use its own internal default allocation and deallocation functions.

32.3.2   Allocator Interfaces

An alternative, and more object-oriented, approach is to bind the functions into an interface. The extensible parser project I described in section 8.3 used this approach. The Synesis core libraries define an allocator `IAllocator`, with a portable interface (see section 8.2), which looks something like the following C++-ified version:[13]

```
struct IAllocatorVTable
  : public IRefCounter
{
  virtual LPVoid  Alloc(Size cb);
  virtual LPVoid  Realloc(LPVoid pv, Size cb);
  virtual void    Free(LPVoid pv);
  virtual Size    GetSize(LPCVoid pv) const;
  virtual void    Compact();
};
```

The advantages here are threefold. First, it puts all the functions in one place, which reduces the potential for erroneously specifying a mismatched pair. If you're really unlucky, such a combination might actually work with some compilers and/or operating environments, postponing maintenance conundrums for when your memory has faded and your timescales have shortened.

Second, by binding them in an interface, you can provide class instances for your allocators, which is by far the more convenient way to manipulate them (see Chapter 8).

Third, by using an interface you can feel free to provide more functions than are provided by just an allocation/deallocation function pair. Reallocation is an obvious choice, but there are others, as can be seen in `IAllocator`.

Finally if you supply a reference-counted interface, you can allow the library to hang on to it. We'll see how this can be useful shortly.

32.3.3   Per-library Initialization

Passing in the memory functions to each method, even via a structure or an interface, can still be tiresome and slightly inefficient if it requires an extra function parameter. One option is to supply it to the initialization function of the library API you intend to use.

---

[13]Any resemblance to the COM `IMalloc` interface can only be as a result of coincidence . . .

```
int AcmeLib_Init(IAllocator *ator);
void AcmeLib_Uninit();


void *AcmeLib_GiveMeBlock(size_t cb);
```

You can easily combine it with link-unit global state, and an allocator adapter, and happily use it with any STL classes within the library. An allocator adaptor would look something like that shown in Listing 32.5.

Listing 32.5

```
template< typename    T
        , IAllocator  *A
        >
struct IAllocator_adaptor
{
  typedef T           value_type;
  typedef value_type  *pointer;
     . . .
  typedef size_t      size_type;
  typedef ptrdiff_t   difference_type;

  static pointer allocate(size_type n, void const*)
  {
    return (pointer)(A->Alloc(sizeof(value_type) * n));
  }
  static void deallocate(pointer p, size_type)
  {
    A->Free(p);
  }
     . . .
```

It could be combined with an STL class as in the following:

```
IAllocator                          *s_ator;
typedef IAllocator_adaptor<int, s_ator> Acme_allocator;

void AcmeLib_DoOtherStuff(int i)
{
  std::vector<int, Acme_allocator>        v(i);
  std::basic_string<char, Acme_allocator>  s(. . .)'
  . . .
```

This is a convenient mechanism, but it has some serious flaws. First, it needs to be made reentrant, so it needs thread-safe link-unit global state, including the allocator pointer, initialization counter, and a locking object to protect the pointer.

Second, it is inconsistent with what we know about initializing APIs (see section 11.2)—that we like multiply-initializable APIs—if two calls stipulate different allocators. Both options—first wins and last wins—present problems. If first wins then the second initialization must fail, otherwise that client code will use the wrong allocator, the one specified in the first call. Conversely, if last wins then the relationship between the client code of the first initialization and the API will be broken. The only way such an API is usable is to make it singly-initializable.

Because of these problems, it is better to restrict use of this mechanism to a library that is only internally initialized in a link unit, and is not accessible to client code external to the authors of the library. In such contexts, however, it can be very useful, and I've used it to good effect on many occasions.

32.3.4   Per-Call Specification

We can obviate all the initialization, threading, and reentrancy issues of per-library initialization by doing as zlib does (see Appendix A), and passing the allocator along with every library API call. The downside to this is that the client code is responsible for maintaining the relationship between a memory block and its allocator. In most cases, the client code will only be using one allocator itself, so this is a no-brainer, but it's something you need to be aware of.

One interesting feature of this approach is that you can provide thread-specific allocators. Since most allocators are written to be thread safe, they must guard their internal structures with synchronization objects (see section 10.2). There are costs associated with such synchronization locking, and for a frequently used allocator they can be significant. One possible optimization is to use a different, nonlocking allocator for each thread, and per-call specification facilitates that.

32.4   Memory: Coda

This chapter has provided an introduction to a whole range of memory types, and we've discussed the trade-offs between efficiency and flexibility for the different types. We've also seen how the selection of allocators represents the same trade-off. A really good way to maximize flexibility and efficiency is to combine the techniques that have been presented. In other words, using a per-call dynamic specification of allocator along with `auto_buffer` can be a way to have all the flexibility you need with respect to your source of heap memory, while only going to the potentially expensive heaps in the minority cases.

Multidimensional Arrays

As we saw in section 14.7, C and C++ do not support multidimensional arrays of dynamic size, except where all but the most significant dimension is of constant size. In other words, you can do the following:

```
void f(int x)
{
  new byte_t[x];
}
```

but not:

```
void f(int x, int y, int z)
{
  new byte_t[x][y][z]; // Error
}
```

Creating a multidimensional array can only be in this form:

```
const size_t Y = 10;
const size_t Z = Y * 2;

void f(int x)
{
  new byte_t[x][Y][Z];
}
```

This can be quite a restriction. For example, a couple of years ago I was working on a multimedia product user interface where the layout of the interface was dynamically retrieved from a central server over the Internet. The layout could be any possible combination of video, text, dialog, image, and other visual controls within rectangles within rectangles to arbitrary depth sufficient to emulate an unstructured layout. All these levels of rectangles cried out "rectangular array," but because neither dimension was fixed or anticipatable, the built-in array support was not up to the job.

Imperfection: C/C++ does not support dynamically dimensioned multidimensional arrays.

You may not regard this as an imperfection, since one of the principles of C++ is to favor the provision of functionality by the addition of libraries rather than library features, and there exist such libraries, as we'll see later in this chapter. However, as I will demonstrate, it is not possible to *fully* emulate the syntax of the built-in arrays, although we can come pretty close.

Clearly the answer to this problem lies in custom containers. As we learned in section 14.7, the language supports the taking of slices, so this is eminently feasible. We'll look at several mechanisms for providing N-dimensional arrays in this chapter.[1]

33.1   Facilitating Subscript Syntax

We've already seen (see Chapter 14 and section 27.1) that we can facilitate subscripting for one-dimensional arrays by simply providing an implicit conversion to a pointer to the element type.

```
struct IntArray1D
{
  operator int *()
  {
    return m_elements;
  }
  int m_elements[3];
};


IntArray1D  ia;
ia[2] = ia[1] + 1;
```

We do not have the option to do this with arrays of any higher dimensionality, because the array decay that facilitates this shortcut is not available (see section 14.2). The following class has an implicit conversion to a pointer to a pointer to an `int`, which is quite a different thing to an implicit conversion to a two-dimensional array; if it were not, how would the compiler know how to calculate the most significant offset in the following case?

```
struct IntArray2D
{
  operator int **()
  {
    return m_elements; // Illegal
  }
  int m_elements[3][3];
};
```

---

[1]One or two chaps have suggested that such a study should include `std::valarray` in the comparison. Call me a pampered popinjay, but I simply can't bring myself to use a class which overrides `operator ==()` and returns, not a Boolean-indicating equality, but another `valarray` whose elements represent the equality of the individual elements of its two comperands!

```
IntArray2D  ia;
ia[2][2] = ia[2][1] + 1; // Compiler cannot deduce dimensions!
```

The only way for us to support natural syntax for multiple dimensions is to overload the subscript operator for the outermost dimension, and to have that return something that can be subscripted. In the case of a two-dimensional array, we could have the subscript operator return either a type that provides the subscript operator or one that provides an implicit conversion to a pointer. For any higher dimension, the type returned must be one that returns a type that overloads the subscript operator.

33.2 Sized at Run Time

Although we'll see some classes that provide multidimensional arrays of statically determined sizes later in the chapter, the need for such classes is not that great because built-in arrays provide most aspects of such classes for free. The most desirable types of multidimensional arrays are ones whose dimensions are specified at run time.

This is where C/C++'s array layout model serves us well, since all the intermediate instances can be implemented as slice proxies, which are quite efficient: there is no heap allocation, and only the initialization of a few member variables for each subdimension. The alternative would be for each intermediate instance to allocate their own storage, and copy in the values. Not only would this be horribly inefficient, it would also prevent the use of array elements as *lvalue*s.

33.2.1 Variable Length Arrays

As was mentioned in section 32.2.2, *Variable Length Arrays* (VLAs) provide dynamically sized built-in arrays. However, we learned that only three of our ten compilers (see Appendix A) support VLAs in any form, and only one of those, GCC, supports them for non-POD types.

Unless and until VLAs become a part of standard C++, we cannot count on them to answer our requirements. Even when they do, we'll have a long period where backward compatibility will require that we do not rely on them.

33.2.2 vector< ... vector<T> ... >

One solution I've seen used is to use std::vector to emulate the multiple dimensions, as in:

```
typedef std::vector<std::vector<int > >    intarray_2d_t;
```

Unfortunately, this does not create a two-dimensional array; it actually creates an array of arrays, which is quite a different beast. To create an array of 2×3, we would have to do the following:

```
intarray_2d_t  ar(2);
ar[0].resize(3);
ar[1].resize(3);
```

If we forget to do the additional two `resize()` calls, then any attempt to access the elements will result in undefined behavior. Worse than this, there's nothing stopping anyone from using different sizes and creating a jagged array:

```
intarray_2d_t  ar(2);
ar[0].resize(3);
ar[1].resize(2); // Better not use ar[1][2]!!
```

Clearly, this is an unacceptably fragile solution. Furthermore, it should be equally clear that there are multiple memory allocations occurring: one for the array itself and one for each of its array elements. This can have an important effect on performance, as we'll see in section 33.4.

The final nail in its coffin is that it is not possible to provide STL-like iteration throughout the entire range of elements, making it very difficult to apply all our treasured STL algorithms.

If we wanted to enumerate the contents, we'd have to write a special `for_each`, like:

```
template<typename T, typename A1, typename A2, typename F>
F for_each( std::vector<std::vector<T, A1>, A2>::iterator from
          , std::vector<std::vector<T, A1>, A2>::iterator to
          , F                                               fn)
{
  for(; from != to; ++from)
  {
    for_each((*from).begin(), (*from).end(), fn);
  }
  return fn;
}
```

How d'ya like them apples?

Frankly, this is where the mathematician's instincts need to kick in very strongly: it's not beautiful[2] and we can confidently deduce that it's bad. We're going to need some types that are specifically written for this purpose.

33.2.3   boost::multi_array

The Boost libraries have a dynamically sized array class, called `multi_array`.[3] It uses some heavy-duty template mechanisms to provide the ability to represent multiple dimensions within a single template.

Using `multi_array` requires that you instantiate the template with the element type and the number of dimensions, and then construct instances of your parameterization with the extent of the dimensions, as in:

```
boost::multi_array<int, 2>  intarray_2d_t(boost::extents[2][3]);
```

---

[2] And we've not even written the `const_iterator` version, which would also have to be explicitly provided!

[3] To be honest, I was going to submit the fixed and static arrays described in this chapter to Boost some time ago, but I dallied, and `multi_array` got in there first. This is a good lesson to anyone who wants to contribute to the development of open source libraries in C++, or indeed in any language; since it's just about impossible to have a novel thought in a community of about 3 million people, speed is of the essence.

As we'll see in section 33.5, the performance of `multi_array` is less than optimal, and this probably is an inevitable cost of its complexity and generality.

`multi_array` suffers from the same range iteration problem as does the `vector<…,` `vector<T>` …> solution. For me, this is a serious flaw, although I should concede that from some perspectives it may be that one would wish to deal with a multidimensional array each dimension at a time. Nonetheless, I think it would be better to have a separate mechanism for this, and that `begin()` and `end()` would return iterators to the entire range of managed elements, as they do with all the standard library containers, not just the sequence ones.

The news is not all bad, of course. Parameterizing the template is conceptually pleasing from the perspective of client code, insofar as one merely specifies the element type and the number of dimensions. The specification of the array extents is a little less elegant, in that it requires the use of the global `extents` object, but since it's wrapped up in a namespace and use of it does not result in any race conditions by virtue of its per-instance state, the usual gripes with global variables don't trouble us. `multi_array` is also resizeable.

Furthermore, the template can support Fortran ordering. In C the left-most dimension represents the largest stride in the array element memory; in Fortran the left-most dimension represents the smallest stride in the array element memory [Lind1994]. This is useful where one may wish to interface with Fortran link-units. The custom array classes I introduce shortly do not do that, although it would be a pretty simple addition.

I've not tested the performance of the Fortran ordering because there's (currently) nothing to test it against, and I don't really think it's likely to bring up significant differences in any case; the costs of reversing the offset calculations should be the same for `multi_array` as for any other multi-dimensional array class, unless the authors of one of them had a brain-freeze.

33.2.4   fixed_array_1/2/3/4d

Not surprisingly, the motivating factors that made me originally choose to write my own multidimensional arrays as a suite of cooperating template classes, one for each dimensionality, are precisely the things I disagree with in the design of Boost's `multi_array`. Not that I'm not saying that the approach of `multi_array` is wrong, merely that for my multidimensional requirements, and for my way of thinking, it is suboptimal. No doubt the authors of `multi_array` might have equally legitimate misgivings about my approach.

There are four templates, with startlingly original names: `fixed_array_1d`, `fixed_array_2d`, `fixed_array_3d`, and `fixed_array_4d`.

They're called "`fixed_array_*`" because each type implements a specific, fixed dimensionality. Naturally, this lends itself to a much simpler implementation than writing a single template to cater for any numbers of dimensions. (Not to mention being more efficient, as we'll see in section 33.5.).

The other functionality that `multi_array` has over `fixed_array` is that it is resizable. Again, this is not something that would be too difficult to add to the `fixed_array` classes, and it's very unlikely it would affect the performance of non-resizing operations, but I've not done so because I've simply never had call to resize a multidimensional array at run time. I'd rather not have to address the conceptually challenging, albeit technically simple, issues of what to do with new or discarded elements and determining what represents a legal resize and what does not.

There are no higher templates because I've never needed any higher. To be honest, I've never used `fixed_array_4d` in anger, but thought it prudent to go one higher than my needs, in case it's needed; it wouldn't be terribly good to introduce these "great fast, multidimensional array classes" to a client's project, and then to extend the component suite on site, only to bring down the system with untested code. Such is not the way to further your reputation, or the cause of open-source software.

There are several significant features of the `fixed_array` templates. First, each template maintains a pointer to a single-dimension block that contains its N-dimensional contents. We'll see how this is made to work safely and efficiently shortly.

Second, each class has a `dimension_element_type` member type. For the one-dimension case, this is the same as the `value_type`. However, for higher dimensions, it is a type defined from the template of the next lower dimension, as shown in Listing 33.1.

Listing 33.1

```
template< typename T           // Value type
        , typename A = . . .   // Allocator
        , typename P = . . .   // Construction policy
        , bool     R = true    // Owns data?
        >
class fixed_array_3d
  : public A
{
public:
  typedef fixed_array_3d<T, A, P, R>      class_type;
  typedef fixed_array_2d<T, A, P, false> dimension_element_type;
  typedef A                              allocator_type;
  . . .
private:
  fixed_array_3d( pointer data, index_type d0, index_type d1
                                            , index_type d2);
public:
  fixed_array_3d(index_type d0, index_type d1, index_type d2);
  fixed_array_3d(index_type d0, index_type d1, index_type d2
                                          , value_type const &t);
  ~fixed_array_3d();
  . . .
```

Third, the `begin()` and `end()` methods return iterators that represent the bounding range of the entire collection of controlled elements. That means that you can apply the same algorithm, for example, `for_each()`, to any of the array classes, irrespective of dimensionality. If you want to treat the arrays in per-dimension blocks that's easily achieved by taking a slice and applying standard algorithms to the slice.

Fourth, robustness and maintainability are maximized by using the same templates for the subdimensional slices as for the whole arrays. This means that all the subscript calculations, creation of new subdimensional slices, enumeration, and all other methods are shared. The only difference in behavior is how the memory is allocated and managed. If the ownership template parameter—R in the above declaration—is `true` then the standard constructor allocates the memory, and the destructor releases it. If it is `false`, then the slice constructor merely copies the pointer it's been given. Note that this behavior is selected at compile time, so there are no efficiency losses by testing for ownership at run time. Listing 33.2 shows two constructors and the destructor for `fixed_array_3d`, and also shows how static assertions are used to prevent misuse of the two flavors of the templates.

Listing 33.2

```
template<typename T, typename A, typename P, bool R>
fixed_array_3d<T, A, P, R>::fixed_array_3d( pointer data
                                          , index_type d0
                                          , index_type d1
                                          , index_type d2)
    : m_data(data)
    , m_d0(d0), m_d1(d1), m_d2(d2)
{
  STATIC_ASSERT(!R);
}
template <typename T, typename A, typename P, bool R>
fixed_array_3d<T, A, P, R>::fixed_array_3d( index_type      d0
                                          , index_type      d1
                                          , index_type      d2
                                          , value_type const &t)
    : m_data(allocator_type::allocate(d0 * d1 * d2, NULL))
    , m_d0(d0), m_d1(d1), m_d2(d2)
{
  STATIC_ASSERT(R);
  array_initialiser<T, A, P>::construct(*this, m_data, size());
}
template <typename T, typename A, typename P, bool R>
fixed_array_3d<T, A, P, R>::~fixed_array_3d()
{
  if(R)
  {
    array_initialiser<T, A, P>::destroy(*this, m_data, size());
    allocator_type::deallocate(m_data, size());
  }
}
```

Another aid to performance is that the construction policy parameter—P in the above code—is responsible for the determination for how to initialize the memory. This improves performance for basic, that is, POD, types in two ways, by using `memset()` rather than `std::fill_n()` to perform the initialization and by omitting the call of "destructors" prior to deallocation of the memory. Both these decisions are carried out inside the `array_initialiser` helper class, which is shared with the `static_array` templates we'll meet in section 33.3.2.[4]

---

[4]The source for all the `fixed_array` classes, the helper class, and the `static_array` classes discussed in the next section are all included on the CD.

The final aid to efficiency recognizes that even though the overloaded subscript operators are very efficient, there is still the non-zero cost of creating slice proxy objects involved. Therefore, each template is equipped with `at()` and `at_unchecked()` methods with the requisite number of parameters for each dimension.

```
template< . . . >
class fixed_array_3d
{
  . . .
public:
  reference at(index_type i0, index_type i1, index_type i2);
  reference at_unchecked(index_type i0, index_type i1
                                       , index_type i2);
  . . . // and const overloads
```

The `at()` methods follow the standard library practice of validating the index and throwing `std::out_of_range` if invalid. The `at_unchecked()` methods, however, provide a single unchecked method for accessing an element.[5] Rather than having three offset calculations and generating two intermediate slice object instances, these methods conduct one offset calculation. Naturally, this proves to be a very efficient mechanism, as we'll see in section 33.5.

Thus, all statements in the inner loop in Listing 33.3 are equivalent in semantics, but different in cost.

Listing 33.3
```
fixed_array_2d<int, . . .>  ar(10, 20); // Construct 10x20 array
int                     v = 0;
for(size_t i = 0; i < ar.dim0(); ++i)
{
  for(size_t j = 0; j < ar.dim1(); ++j, ++v)
  {
    ar[i][j]              = v;
    ar.at(i, j)           = v;
    ar.at_unchecked(i, j) = v;
  }
}
```

33.3   Sized at Compile Time

In discussing the various design decisions involved in creating dynamically sized multidimensional arrays, it behooves us to consider whether any of the characteristics of the various options make it worthwhile creating statically sized multidimensional classes.

Without question, the support in C++ (and C) for built-in multidimensional arrays of fixed size is extremely good. The main reason I think it's worthwhile to consider having a class type is to get a natural enumerable iterator range—that is, via `begin()` / `end()`—although it's not exactly hard to get hold of the one-past-the-end iterator of an array:

[5]Like operator `[]`, it performs DbC (see section 12.3) precondition testing via assertions in debug builds.

```
void print_int(int const &);

int ar[10][10];

std::for_each(&ar[0][0], &ar[10][10], print_int);
```

33.3.1   boost::array

Boost provides a one-dimension fixed-dimension array template, `boost::array`, which provides an STL *Sequence* concept [Aust1999, Muss2001] face to built-in arrays, including `begin()` and `end()`, `size()` and subscript operators. Using `boost::array` it's not difficult to synthesize multidimensional arrays:

```
boost::array<boost::array<int, 10>, 10>   ar;
```

But this doesn't really buy us anything over the built-in arrays, because we cannot use `begin()` and `end()` to enumerate over the elements (see section 33.2.2); they will return pointers to the next dimension down—in this case `boost::array<int>`. Similarly, the `size()` method will tell us the same lies as `boost::multi_array`, namely, only returning the number of elements in the most significant dimension of the instance on which it's called.

It's probably better to stick with built-in arrays than to try and force such types to masquerade as multidimensional array types.[6]

33.3.2   static_array_1/2/3/4d

My solution for statically sized multidimensional arrays is a suite of templates—`static_array`—that are very similar in concept to the `fixed_array` templates (see section 33.2.4). The main difference is that the array instances contain their array elements as a member array, rather than as a pointer to an allocated array; the subdimensional slices use the same mechanism of using a pointer into the requisite part of their containing instance's contents. Despite the similarities, I think the differences are worth pointing out, as they demonstrate some of the great things that you can do with templates in C++.

With `static_array` there is no allocation: an instance is either a proxy and holds only a pointer, or it *is* the array and contains the full N-dimensional built-in array of elements.

```
template< typename T          // Value type
        , size_t   N0         // Most significant dimension
        , size_t   N1         // Least significant dimension
        , typename P = . . . // Construction policy
        , typename M = T[N0 * N1]
        >
class static_array_2d;
```

---

[6]Note: this is not a specific criticism of `boost::array`, as I've never seen any documentation suggesting that it was suitable as, or intended to be, a composite type from which to build up multiple dimensions. I'm using it in that guise here for pedagogical purposes only.

But when `static_array_2d` is used as a subdimension slice, it is parameterized with `T*`, rather than the default `T[N0 * N1]`. This means that rather than defining its member `m_data` as an internal array it is defined as a pointer.

Listing 33.4

```
template< typename T
        , size_t N0
        , size_t N1
        , size_t N2
        , typename P  = . . . // Construction policy
        , typename M  =  T[N0 * N1 * N2]
        >
class static_array_3d
    : public null_allocator<T>
{
public:
  typedef static_array_3d<T, N0, N1, N2, P, M>  class_type;
  typedef static_array_2d<T, N1, N2, P, T*>       dimension_type;
  . . .
```

The only remaining part of the picture is the constructors and destructor, which are defined as follows:

Listing 33.5

```
template <typename T, . . . >
static_array_2d<. . .>::static_array_2d(T *data)
  : m_data(data)
{}
template <typename T, . . . >
static_array_2d<. . .>::static_array_2d(value_type const &t)
{
  array_initialiser<. . .>::construct(*this, m_data, size(), t);
}
template <typename T, . . . >
static_array_2d<. . .>::~static_array_2d()
{
  if(!is_pointer_type<M>::value) // Compile-time evaluation
  {
    array_initialiser<. . . >::destroy(*this, m_data, size());
  }
}
```

The first constructor is a slice constructor, and when that method is instantiated, it will be for a parameterization where `m_data` is a pointer, not an array. Conversely, the second constructor will be a parameterization when `m_data` is an array, so there is no need to "allocate" or initialize the member; the constructor merely initializes it, using our old friend the `array_initialiser`.

The destructor uses a meta-programming construct—is_pointer_type[7]—to determine whether the member type—M in the template parameter list—is a pointer. If it is, then the template instantiation is for a proxy, and no destruction need be performed. If not, then the parameterization is for a bona fide array, and the elements must be destroyed.

We have taken advantage of the ability of arrays and pointers to have similar syntaxes, since the access of the extents of the array's contents—&m_data[0] and &m_data [size()]—is the same in both cases.

Fundamentally, the static arrays are little more than a convenience, whose creation is a testament to the power and efficiency of templates. That's not to say that they do not provide useful facilities over and above built-in arrays; it's very nice to have sensible and meaningful values returned from the ubiquitous and important size(), begin(), and end() methods. It complicates the writing of generic code a great deal when these methods do not behave correctly with all types.

33.4   Block Access

One thing we commonly do with built-in arrays is to treat them en-bloc, and perform many operations on the elements of an array in a single statement or in a small number of statements. For example, it's easy to initialize them to zero by using memset(), as in:

```
byte_t  ar[10][10];

memset(&ar[0][0], 0, sizeof(ar));
```

or the lazy

```
memset(ar, 0, sizeof(ar));
```

or the dubious

```
memset(&ar, 0, sizeof(ar));
```

or the very dubious

```
memset(&ar[0], 0, sizeof(ar));
```

Unfortunately, it's all too easy to do this with class types that provide array semantics, as in:

```
fixed_array_2d<byte_t, . . . > fa2(10, 10);
boost::multi_array<byte_t, 3>  bma3(boost::extents[10][10][10]);

memset(&fa2[0][0], 0, sizeof(fa2)); // Wrong size!
```

---

[7]This is a template that simply contains an enumeration member—value—that is non-zero for pointer types. The definition of this, and many others, is included on the CD.

```
memset(&bma3, 0, sizeof(bma3));      // Wrong ptr; wrong size!
memset(&fa2[0], 0, sizeof(fa2));     // Wrong ptr; Wrong size!
```

Table 33.1 shows the permutations of using `memset()` and `sizeof()` for various one- and two-dimensional array types. A blank entry denotes that compilation and execution was correct. DNC denotes that the combination did not compile, which is a good thing. E denotes that it compiled and ran, but experienced erroneous behavior, either by writing too many or too few elements, or by overwriting the other member variables of the array instance; whatever the actual problem, E denotes a very bad thing.

There are two separate problems here. For one thing, it is possible to pass inappropriate things to `memset()`; since all it needs is a `void*`, it's all too easy to pass the wrong thing. This is especially dangerous since passing `&ar` actually works correctly in the case of a built-in array, but results in the overwriting of member data for class type instances.

It's no great surprise to learn that the dynamically sized array classes—`boost::multi_array` and `fixed_array`—experience run time problems when used with `memset()` and `sizeof()`. When their address is passed to `memset()`, the member variables are overwritten—E(O). When the address of their first element—`&ar[0]` for one dimension; `&ar[0][0]` for two dimensions—is passed, the wrong number of elements are written because the size of the instance does not (in the majority of cases) match the size of the managed elements—E(S).

If we want to write generic code that contains en-bloc manipulation of array types, we clearly have some work ahead of us.

33.4.1   Using std::fill_n()

Let's deal with the inappropriate pointer problem first. We can avoid this problem by using the more type-safe (and size-safe) standard library algorithm `std::fill_n()` instead of `memset()`. Rewriting our several examples, this roots out many of the problematic expressions.

```
byte_t                       ar[10][10];
fixed_array_2d<byte_t, . . . > fa2(10, 10);
boost::multi_array<byte_t, 3>  bma3(boost::extents[10][10][10]);

fill_n(&ar[0][0], dimensionof(ar), 0);    // Ok
fill_n(ar, dimensionof(ar), 0);           // Compile error!
```

Table 33.1   Compatibility of array types with `memset()` and `sizeof()`.

Array type	1-dimension			2-dimensions			
	ar	**&ar**	**&ar[0]**	**ar**	**&ar**	**&ar[0]**	**&ar[0][0]**
built-in							
boost::array	DNC			DNC			
static_array	DNC			DNC		E(O)	
boost::multi_array	DNC	E(O)	E(S)	DNC	E(O)	E(O)	E(S)
fixed_array	DNC	E(O)	E(S)	DNC	E(O)	E(O)	E(S)

```
fill_n(&ar, dimensionof(ar), 0);           // Compile error!
fill_n(&ar[0], dimensionof(ar), 0);        // Compile error!
fill_n(&fa2[0][0], dimensionof(fa2), 0));  // Wrong size!
fill_n(&bma3, dimensionof(bma3), 0);       // Compile error!
fill_n(&fa2[0], dimensionof(fa2), 0);      // Compile error!
```

Table 33.2 shows the permutations of using `std::fill_n()` and `dimensionof()` for various one- and two-dimensional array types. Note that we use `dimensionof()` (see section 14.3) rather than `sizeof()` because `fill_n()` takes the number of elements to modify, rather than the number of bytes.

You shouldn't worry about a loss of efficiency with `std::fill_n()`, because good standard library implementations will specialize for use of `memset()` with single byte types, and we can't use `memset()`—except where setting all bytes to 0—for larger types anyway.

With `std::fill_n()`, we turn almost all of the overwrite run time errors into compile-time errors. This is a compelling example of why we should prefer this to `memset()` as a general rule.

However, we are still specifying the wrong sizes for our dynamically sized arrays, `boost::multi_array` and `fixed_array`, which means either too few or too many bytes are likely to be overwritten—an error in either case.

33.4.2 array_size Shim

What we need is a single mechanism to determine the number of elements in any array type. The solution is an attribute shim (see section 20.2), the cunningly entitled `array_size()`. As with most shims, there are general definitions that handle most cases, along with specific definitions to handle the specific cases. The general definitions of `array_size()` are

```
template <typename T>
size_t array_size(T const &)
{
  return 1; // Not an array, so only one element
}
template <typename T, size_t N>
size_t array_size(T (&ar)[N])
{
```

Table 33.2 Compatibility of array types with `fill_n()` and `dimensionof()`.

Array type	1			2			
	ar	&ar	&ar[0]	ar	&ar	&ar[0]	&ar[0][0]
built-in		DNC		DNC	DNC	DNC	
boost::array	DNC	DNC		DNC	DNC	DNC	
static_array	DNC	DNC		DNC	DNC	DNC	
boost::multi_array	DNC	DNC	E(S)	DNC	DNC	DNC	E(S)
fixed_array	DNC	DNC	E(S)	DNC	DNC	DNC	E(S)

```
  return N * array_size(ar[0]); // N * number in next dimension
}
```

These two handle the potentially infinite dimensionality of built-in arrays and nonarray types. Hence, applying `array_size()` to `int ai[10][30][2][5][6]` will result in five calls to the second overload, and one call, the terminating case, to the first overload.

You may be wondering why we're not using compile-time techniques to work out the number of elements. The answer is that we also need to be able to apply to types whose dimensionality is not known until run time. Anyway, it's not a concern unless you want to use the value at compile time, because all decent compilers make mincemeat of the application of the shim to built-in arrays, and simply convert the run time result into a constant in optimized code.

So let's look at how we extend the shim to other types. Defined alongside the `fixed_array` and `static_array` classes are the requisite overloads of the shims:

```
template< typename T, typename A, typename P, bool R>
size array_size(fixed_array_4d<T, A, P, R> const &ar)
{
  return ar.size();
}
template< typename T, size_t N0, typename P, typename M>
size_t array_size(static_array_1d<T, N0, P, M> const &ar)
{
  return N0;
}
```

We can provide similar overloads for any other classes we wish to use, such as the Boost array classes:

```
template <typename T, size_t N>
size_t array_size(boost::array<T, N> const &ar)
{
  return N * array_size(ar[0]);
}
template <typename T, size_t N>
size_t array_size(boost::multi_array<T, N> const &ar)
{
  // NOTE: size() only returns most significant dimension
  return ar.num_elements();
}
```

Now we have a simple and general way to determine the number of elements in any array. The only gotcha is if you do not have a definition of the shim for your array type. But you'll pick this up in your comprehensive testing, won't you?

When used with `memset()`, we loose all the size-mismatch problems, although the address problems remain, as shown in Table 33.3.

Table 33.3   Compatibility of array types with `memset()` and `array_size()`.

Array type	1-dimension			2-dimensions			
	ar	&ar	&ar[0]	ar	&ar	&ar[0]	&ar[0][0]
built-in							
boost::array	DNC			DNC			
static_array	DNC			DNC		E(O)	
boost::multi_array	DNC	E(O)		DNC	E(O)	E(O)	
fixed_array	DNC	E(O)		DNC	E(O)	E(O)	

But, as shown in Table 33.4, when used with `std::fill_n()`, we achieve a perfect set of permutations. All the dubious pointer conversions do not compile, and the rest that do compile produce the correct results.

Recommendation: An array size shim should always be used when determining the sizes of arrays, as all other approaches do not generalize for both built-in and user defined array types.

33.5   Performance

We've looked at several different options for using multidimensional arrays in C++, which are adequate, elegant, or perfectly brilliant, depending on your point of view. But as with many aspects of software engineering, we must balance flexibility with performance, so we're going to finish the chapter by looking at the performance of various array types to inform on our balancing.

In the tests included here, the code executes N-inner loops, where N is the dimensionality of the array being tested, and assigns to and reads back from the `[i][j][k]`th elements in the loops. The values assigned are deterministically calculated, so that they are the same for each array type. Effectively, the test determines the costs of both read and write access to the elements. For the dynamically sized types, the cost of creation and destruction of the array storage are included within the timed sections.

Table 33.4   Compatibility of array types with `std::fill_n()` and `array_size()`.

Array type	1-dimension			2-dimensions			
	ar	&ar	&ar[0]	ar	&ar	&ar[0]	&ar[0][0]
built-in		DNC		DNC	DNC	DNC	
boost::array	DNC	DNC		DNC	DNC	DNC	
static_array	DNC	DNC		DNC	DNC	DNC	
boost::multi_array	DNC	DNC		DNC	DNC	DNC	
fixed_array	DNC	DNC		DNC	DNC	DNC	

The element types tested were `std::string`, `int` and `double`, but since the results indicated virtually identical relative performances in all cases, I'm just showing the results for `int`.

The times are expressed as percentages, relative to the slowest type for each dimension tested. All the test programs are included on the CD.

33.5.1   Sized at Run Time

Table 33.5 shows the relative performances obtained for `vector` of `vectors`, Boost's `multi_array`, and `fixed_array_1/2/3d`; all using index operator syntax. It also shows the costs for `fixed_array` using the `at()` and `at_unchecked()` direct method access (which circumvents the intermediates required for two or more dimensions).

There are several interesting things to note. First, the cost of the checked access provided by `at()` becomes less significant than that of the intermediates required by the subscript access at higher dimensions. When dealing with three dimensions, the `at()` access is approximately twice as fast as unchecked subscript access. This is because intermediates are not generated, and also because the entire offset calculation is done in one operation, rather than in three steps.

When `at_unchecked()` is considered, we can see that the benefits of skipping the intermediate calculations and the intermediate objects is compelling. It is on a par with `vector` and `fixed_array` subscript access in one dimension, with vector in two dimensions, and otherwise superior to all other schemes.

It's also equally clear that the flexibility of the design of Boost's `multi_array` has an impact on performance. At two and three dimensions, it is significantly less efficient than `fixed_array` and up to four times as slow. It fares worse than `vector` except in three dimensions where the cost of the large number of individual allocations required by the array of arrays of arrays created by the `vector` version begins to tell. Serious numerists may not wish to pay such costs.

I think we can fairly say that `fixed_array` has proven its worth, in performance. Sure, it's not terribly pleasing to have separate classes that do largely the same thing,[8] but to be able to sensibly enumerate *all* elements with `begin()`, `end()`, to have `size()` provide a meaningful result, and to have such great performance seals the argument for me. Of course, you may see it differently, and that's entirely proper; there isn't a black and white answer here, as we're deep inside one of C++'s imperfections.

Table 33.5   Relative performance of arrays sized at runtime.

int	1	2	3
vector< vector <. . .> >	39.1%	31.6%	100.0%
boost::multi_array	91.0%	100.0%	97.6%
fixed_array – [i][j][k]	41.0%	62.8%	77.7%
fixed_array – at	100.0%	53.8%	44.3%
fixed_array – at_unchecked	42.0%	31.6%	27.0%

---

[8]I've not given up on the notion of factoring out much of the repeated functionality, whilst maintaining the distinct nature of the `at()`, `at_unchecked()`, `begin()`, `end()` and `size()` methods. If you want to try this, you can find the classes on the CD; please email me with your results.

Table 33.6 Relative performance of arrays sized at compile time.

int	1	2	3
built-in array	50.9%	49.1%	35.6%
array< array<. . .> >	52.4%	48.3%	36.7%
static_array – [i][j][k]	54.2%	83.9%	100.0%
static_array – at	100.0%	100.0%	88.4%
static_array – at_unchecked	51.9%	49.0%	35.5%

33.5.2 Sized at Compile Time

Table 33.6 shows the relative performances obtained for built-in arrays, Boost's `array`, and `static_array_1/2/3d`, all using index operator syntax. It also shows the costs for `static_array` using the `at()` and `at_unchecked()` direct method access (which circumvent the intermediates required for two or more dimensions).

The picture's quite a bit different than the dynamically sized arrays. Simply, it's clear that subscript access of built-in arrays and `boost:array` and `at_unchecked()` access of `static_array` are all pretty much equivalent at all dimensions. Using subscript or `at()` for `static_array` is considerably more costly.

As was observed in section 33.3.1, building multidimensional arrays from `boost::array` is unsuitable because `begin()`, `end()` and `size()` all return meaningless values for two or more dimensions. But we can see from these performance results that `static_array`, even though it answers these concerns, imposed an unacceptable cost, except when using `at_unchecked()`, which is only able offer performance on par with built-in arrays.

Unlike `fixed_array`, then, I would say that `static_array` is not worth the bother. I would suggest that when using statically dimensioned arrays we are best to stick with the built-in arrays. They're the fastest, and although there is no direct support for treating them as STL containers, at least we're not facing types that give invalid answers to STL method questions.

33.6 Multidimensional Arrays: Coda

Hopefully you've had fun with this chapter, and learned some more ways in which C++ has flaws, but also a lot of power to correct them. We've seen that there are dangers in treating any arrays types in precisely the same way as we often (mis)use built-in arrays, but that by using `std::fill_n()` and the `array_size()` shim, we can safely write generic code that will work with all array types.

We've also seen how the sophisticated nature of dynamically sized types comes with a performance cost. Both `fixed_array` and `boost::multi_array` incur significant performance costs for higher dimensionality, requiring the use of unattractive, nonoperator methods of access. That's just the world we live in; flexibility and facilitating the emulation of built-in syntax can have a performance cost. Providing facilities such as `at_unchecked()` gives programmers the option of faster code, but at the loss of a more natural syntax. Such is life!

CHAPTER **3 4**

Functors and Ranges

34.1 Syntactic Clutter

Many of the standard library algorithms operate on ranges, where a range is defined as a pair of iterators [Aust1999]. This abstraction is very powerful, and has been exploited to the degree that much of the STL, and, therefore, much of modern C++, relies upon it.

An example of this might be in a simple program to read in integers into a vector:

```
std::fstream f("integers.dat", std::ios::in | std::ios::out);

std::copy( std::istream_iterator<int>(f)
         , std::istream_iterator<int>()
         , std::back_inserter(v2));
```

In this case, the second argument is a default-constructed iterator that acts as an indicator for the end of range. The two iterators are not connected in a physical sense; the implementation of istream_iterator is such that a default-constructed instance may be interpreted as the logic end point of the range.

Many times we use algorithms over a range of values acquired from a container or container-like, object as in:

```
struct dump_string
{
  void operator ()(std::string const &) const;
};

std::vector<std::string> >   strings = . . .;
std::for_each(strings.begin(), strings.end(), dump_string());
```

As such, it can become tedious, since we replicate the same calls to begin() and end() time and time again. This is miles away from being an imperfection—barely even a minor gripe—but there are circumstances in which it can be a pain. Consider the case when using (pseudo)containers such as glob_sequence (see section 20.6.3) that are only created in order to elicit their range.[1] Let's imagine we want to determine how many *Imperfect C++*

---

[1]Note that I'm kind of creating my own problem to solve in this specific case, because I tend to extend STL in this way. It is possible in many cases to follow the example of istream_iterator and encapsulate the start of the enumeration in the constructor of the nondefault iterator; Boost's file-system enumeration component works in this way. But this is a logical disconnect that troubles me too much to follow the lead—you may well see it differently.

header files are larger than 1024 bytes, because we want to really immerse ourselves in the magic:

```
struct is_large
  : public std::unary_function<char const *, bool>
{
  bool operator ()(char const *file) const
  {
    . . . // Return true if "file" > 1024 bytes
  }
};


glob_sequence gs("/usr/include/", "impcpp*");
size_t n = std::count_if(gs.begin(), gs.end(), is_large());
```

gs is not needed for any other purpose, and its presence otherwise serves only to pollute the local namespace.

An analogous situation occurs when we want to enumerate two or more ranges in the same scope. We can end up introducing several variables for the different begin and end conditions of each range into the current scope, as we saw in section 17.3.2, or using the double-scoping trick from section 17.3.1.

34.2   for_all() ?

Given the common enumeration of full ranges, it is a simple matter to create full-range equivalents of the standard algorithms. We might create a container-compatible version of std::for_each(), which we'll call for_all() for the moment:

```
template< typename  C
        , typename  F
        >
inline F for_all(C &c, F f)
{
  return std::for_each(c.begin(), c.end(), f);
}
```

This is a reasonable implementation for the general case of such an algorithm since most containers—standard and otherwise—provide begin() and end() methods.

As well as reducing the tedium of specifying the two iterator method calls, it can also further reduce the eyestrain when dealing with (pseudo)containers. Our glob_sequence can be declared as an anonymous temporary, giving us the pleasingly condensed:

```
n = std::count_if( glob_sequence("/usr/include/", "impcpp*")
                 , is_large());
```

When you're dealing with production code, such savings of syntactic clutter can be a real boost in readability.

Some critics may counter that the considerable amount of code involved in that single statement is another example of how C++ has strayed from the Spirit of C [Como-SOC]; it's certainly hard to argue "nothing is hidden." I would concede this point, but only as far as the functor is concerned. I think arguing that the "hidden" nature of the range access and enumeration is wrong is a specious argument; one may as well argue that we should all eschew the use of library functions and write everything in assembler. The STL *Iterator* concept [Aust1999, Muss2001] is designed to facilitate maximum efficiency of enumeration—usually the only way to "misuse" sequences is to use higher level *Iterator* concept [Aust1999, Muss2001] behavior, but `for_each()` requires only input iterators.

34.2.1   arrays

As we saw in Chapter 14, the fact that we've got two places of definition of the array size is a potential source of errors. Even when they both use the same constant, there are still, in effect, two definitions.

```
int    ari[10] = { . . . };

std::for_each(&ari[0], &ari[10], print_int);
```

We also saw that the foolproof way to deal with arrays is to use static array size determination in the form of `dimensionof()` or a similar construct.

```
std::for_each(&ari[0], &ari[dimensionof(ari)], print_int);
```

However, given our definitions of `for_all()`, we can easily specialize for arrays using the similar facilities, as in:

```
template< typename  T
        , size_t    N
        , typename  F
        >
inline F for_all(T (&ar)[N], F f)
{
  return std::for_each(&ar[0], &ar[N], f);
}
```

34.2.2   Naming Concerns

Let's now turn to the issue of the naming of such algorithms. I deliberately chose an unsuitable name, so that we wouldn't get comfy with it. The problem with the name `for_all()` is all too obvious: it doesn't transfer to other algorithms. Do we have a `fill_all()`, `accumulate_all()`, and so on? It's not an attractive option. Ideally we'd like to call it `for_each()`, so why not do that? Unfortunately, this is a bit of a conundrum: we must select from equally unpleasant options.

We are only allowed to specialize templates that already exist in the standard namespace for new types; we are not allowed to add any new template (or nontemplate) functions or types. I would say that the array form of `for_all()`, were we to call it `for_each()`, could not be reasonably classed as a specialization based on new types, although I confess the issue's hardly equivocal.

The alternative is to define it as `for_each()` within our own namespace. In that case, we must remember to "use" it, via a using declaration, whenever we want to use it outside our namespace. Unfortunately, we'll also have to remember to "use" `std::for_each()` whenever that's what's required, since any using declaration for our `for_each()` will mask out the `std` one. Failure to do this can lead to some very perplexing error messages. But despite this, the problems raised for writing generalized code when the algorithms are of different names are such that, in general, this approach should be seriously considered[2] despite the namespace "use" hassles.

We'll look at just one example of the namespace problems. Consider that you are using your own library components en masse via a using directive, `using namespace acmelib`. That's okay, you reason, because in this client code you'll be using heaps of things from the `acmelib` namespace. One of these is your array version of `for_each()`. You go along swimmingly with this for a while, and then need to use `std::for_each()` in some part of the implementation file, so you "use" that one function via a using declaration:

```
using namespace acmelib; // Using directive
using std::for_each;      // Using declaration

int   ai[10];

for_each(ai, print_int);
```

Now your code will not compile, because the specific introduction of `std::for_each()` via the using declaration takes precedence over the one "used" via the general introduction of the using directive. What's to be done: introduce `std::for_each()` via a using directive? What happens if there're conflicting definitions in the two namespaces of a given function or type that is being used in our code?

What we're forced to do is make an additional using declaration for `acmelib::for_each()`. Given that, why not simply use using declarations in the first place? It may be a little bit more work initially, but it's a big saving in the long run, and we all know that the cost of the initial coding phase of software is pretty irrelevant in comparison to its maintenance [Glas2003]. This is just one of the reasons why I refuse to use using directives under just about any circumstances.[3]

---

[2]This is the approach taken by John in his Boost-compatible implementation of RangeLib, although he relies more on the explicit qualification of the RangeLib algorithm namespace `boost::rtl::rng::for_each`.

[3]Much hard-won experience with Java's `import x.*` also contributes to my loathing for the indiscriminate introduction of names into namespaces. Herb Sutter and I have an ongoing difference of opinion on this point. Fortunately for Herb, he is vastly more knowledgeable and erudite on C++ than I am. Fortunately, for me, this is my book and I can write what I like.

In this case, our new `for_each()` and `std::for_each()` have different numbers of arguments, so we could not be writing generalized code that could work with both anyway. Hence, we could just call the algorithms `for_each_c()`, `fill_c()`, and so on.

We'll come back to the naming problem toward the end of this chapter.

34.3 Local Functors

So far our concerns have been largely syntactic. But there's a second, and more significant, troubling aspect of using STL algorithms, which represent a more serious imperfection. When you have a suitable function or functor available, then you can get code that is very succinct, as well as being powerful:

```
std::for_each(c.begin(), c.end(), fn());
```

However, as soon as you need to do something more sophisticated or specific to the elements in a range, you have two choices, neither of which is particularly attractive. Either you unroll the loop and provide the functionality yourself, or you wrap up that functionality in a custom function or functor.

34.3.1 Unrolled Loops

The normal option is to unroll the algorithm and do it longhand, as in the following code from an early version of the Arturius compiler multiplexer (see Appendix C):

Listing 34.1
```
void CoalesceOptions(. . .)
{
  . . .
  { OptsUsed_map_t::const_iterator  b = usedOptions.begin();
    OptsUsed_map_t::const_iterator  e = usedOptions.end();
  for(; b != e; ++b)
  {
    OptsUsed_map_t::value_type const &v = *b;
    if( !v.second &&
       v.first->bUseByDefault)
    {
      arcc_option option;
      option.name              = v.first->fullName;
      option.value             = v.first->defaultValue;
      option.bCompilerOption   = v.first->type == compiler;
      arguments.push_back(option);
    }
  }}
  . . .
```

Naturally, such things can get quite verbose; I could have grabbed another from the same file that was considerably longer.

34.3.2 Custom Functors

The alternative to unrolling loops is to write custom functors to provide the behavior you need. If the behavior is something that can be used in a variety of places that's great, but oftentimes you're writing a new class for just one, or a small number of cases.

Because it's a separate class, it will be physically separate from where it is being used, leading to the code being hard to comprehend and maintain. The best way you can handle this is to define the functor class in the compilation unit as the code that's going to be using it, preferably just before the function where it is used.

Listing 34.2

```
struct argument_saver
{
public:
  argument_saver(ArgumentsList &args)
    : m_args(args)
  {}
  void operator ()(OptsUsed_map_t::value_type const &o) const
  {
    if( !o.second &&
        o.first->bUseByDefault)
    {
      arcc_option option;
      . . .
      m_args.push_back(option);
    }
  }
private:
  ArgumentsList &m_args;
};


void CoalesceOptions(. . .)
{
  . . .
  std::for_each( usedOptions.begin(), usedOptions.end()
              , argument_saver(arguments));
  . . .
```

But the domain specific code encapsulated within the functor is physically separate from the only place(s) where it is used, and meaningful, and this is not ideal. The separation reduces maintainability and, worse, encourages overeager engineers to try and reuse it or to refactor it.

34.3.3 Nested Functors

One thing that could be done to improve the problem of separation of specific functors from their point of its use might be to allow them to be defined within the function in which they're used. For example, we might want `argument_saver` to be defined within `fn()`, as in:

```
void CoalesceOptions(. . .)
{
  . . .
  struct argument_saver
  {
    . . .
  };
  std::for_each( usedOptions.begin(), usedOptions.end()
              , argument_saver(arguments));
  . . .
```

Alas, local functor classes are not legal in C++. This is because a template argument must refer to an entity with external linkage (C++-98: 14.3.2).[4]

Imperfection: C++ does not support local functor classes (to be used with template algorithms).

Notwithstanding the illegality, some compilers do allow them: CodeWarrior, Digital Mars, and Watcom. Furthermore, Borland and Visual C++ can be tricked into supporting it by the simple rouse of encapsulating the next class within another nested class, as in

Listing 34.3
```
void CoalesceOptions(. . .)
{
  . . .
  struct X
  {
    struct argument_saver
    {
      . . .
    };
  };

  std::for_each( usedOptions.begin(), usedOptions.end()
              , X::argument_saver(arguments));
  . . .
}
```

Table 34.1 summarizes the support for both forms for several popular compilers. Comeau, GCC, and Intel do not supported nested functions in either guise.[5]

If you're using only one or more of Borland, CodeWarrior, Digital Mars, Visual C++, and Watcom, then you might choose this approach. But it's not legal, and your portability will be compromised if you do so.

---

[4]This applies to all templates, not just template algorithms and functors.

[5]If those three tell you your code is wrong, the odds are good that you're doing something wrong.

Table 34.1

Compiler	Local class	Nested local class
Borland	No	Yes
CodeWarrior	Yes	Yes
Comeau	No	No
Digital Mars	Yes	Yes
GCC	No	No
Intel	No	No
Visual C++	No	Yes
Watcom	Yes	Yes

34.3.4   Legally Bland

The only legal way I know of to make such things work is turgid beyond bearing. Since the template's parameterizing type must be an external type, we define the function type outside the function. Given that we want to specialize the behavior in a local class, we must relate the internal and external classes. Since we cannot use templates, we can fall back on the old C++ workhorse: polymorphism. The local class `argument_saver` inherits from the external class `argument_processor`, and overrides its `operator ()() const`, as in:

Listing 34.4

```
struct argument_processor
{
public:
  virtual void operator ()(OptsUsed_map_t::value_type const &o) const = 0
};

void CoalesceOptions(. . .)
{
  . . .
  struct argument_saver
    : argument_processor
  {
    virtual void
        operator ()(OptsUsed_map_t::value_type const &o) const
    {
      . . .
    }
  };
```

That doesn't seem so bad, I suppose. However, to use it in a template algorithm requires that the parameterization be done in terms of the external (parent) class. And since the parent is an abstract class, the functor must be passed as a (`const`) reference, rather than by value.

Further, `std::for_each()` takes the functor type as the second template parameter, so it is necessary to explicitly stipulate the iterator type as well. Thus, using the "convenient" `for_each()` isn't very succinct, or general, and it certainly isn't pretty:

```
for_each< OptsUsed_map_t::const_iterator
        , argument_processor const &>( &ari[0], &ari[10]
                                     , argument_saver());
```

You'd have to agree that manual enumeration would be preferable. There's one last gasp at making this prettier, which is to define a `for_each()` equivalent that takes the template parameters in the reverse order so that the function type can be deduced implicitly:

```
template< typename F
        , typename I
        >
inline F for_each_1(I first, I last, F fn)
{
  return std::for_each<I, F>(first, last, fn);
}
```

which brings us to the final barely chewable form:

```
for_each_1<argument_processor const &>( &ari[0], &ari[10]
                                      , argument_saver());
```

But for my money this is still nowhere near good enough. Imagine the poor maintenance programmer trying to follow this stuff![6]

34.3.5   Generalized Functors: Type Tunnelling

If we can't make functors more local, maybe we can improve the situation by making them more general? Let's look at an example where we can expand the generality of the `is_large` functor (see section 34.1). We can use this with a sequence whose `value_type` is, or may be implicitly converted to, `char const*`, such as `glob_sequence`. Unfortunately, it can *only* be used with such types. If we want to use the same function with a type that uses Unicode encoding and the `wchar_t` type, it won't work.

One answer to this is to make `is_large` a template, parameterizable via its character type, as in:

```
template <typename C>
  : public std::unary_function<C const *, bool>
struct is_large
{
```

---

[6]There were a few weeks between starting this chapter and doing the final version. In that short time I forgot how this worked, and I wrote it!

```
  bool operator ()(C const *file) const;
};
```

Now this will work with sequences using either `char` or `wchar_t` (using the fictional Unicode `globw_sequence`), so long as we stipulate the appropriate instantiation:

```
glob_sequence  gs("/usr/include/", "impcpp*");
n = std::count_if(gs.begin(), gs.end(), is_large<char>());
```

```
globw_sequence gsw(L"/usr/include/", L"impcpp*");
n = std::count_if(gsw.begin(), gsw.end(), is_large<wchar_t>());
```

That's a lot more useful, but it's still not the full picture. Looking back to section 20.6.3, we also looked at another file system enumeration sequence `readdir_sequence`, whose `value_type`—`struct dirent const*`—is not implicitly convertible to `char const*`. The solution for the problem in that section was to use *Access Shims* (see section 20.6.1), and we can apply them here to the same end. However, it's a little more complex now, because we've got templates involved, as shown in Listing 34.5.

Listing 34.5

```
template< typename C
        , typename A = C const *
        >
struct is_large
       : public std::unary_function<A, bool>
{
  template <typename S>
  bool operator ()(S const &file) const
  {
    return is_large_(c_str_ptr(file)); // apply c_str_ptr shim
  }
private:
  static bool is_large_(C const *file)
  {
    . . . // determines whether large or not
  }
};
```

The function-call operator—`operator ()() const`—is now a template member function, which attempts to convert whatever type is applied to it via the `c_str_ptr()` shim to `C const*`, which is then passed to the `static` implementation method `is_large_()`. Now we can use the functor with any type for which a suitable `c_str_ptr()` definition exists and is visible, hence:

```
readdir_sequence  rs("/usr/include/");
n = std::count_if(rs.begin(), rs.end(), is_large<char>());
```

I call this mechanism *Type Tunneling*.

Definition: *Type Tunneling* is a mechanism whereby two logically related but physically unrelated types can be made to interoperate via the use of *Access Shims*. The shim allows an external type to be *tunneled* through an interface and presented to the internal type in a recognized and compatible form.

I've used this mechanism to great effect throughout my work over the last few years. As well as facilitating the decoupled interoperation of a large spectrum of physically unrelated types via C-string forms, there is also the generalized manipulation of handles, pointers, and even synchronization objects. Type tunneling (and shims in general) goes to town on the principal of making the compiler one's batman. We saw another example of type tunneling in section 21.2, whereby virtually any COM-compatible type can be *tunneled* into the logging API through the combination of generic template constructors and `InitialiseVariant()` overloads, which combine to act as an access shim.

34.3.6   A Step too Far, Followed by a Sure Step Beyond

You may be wondering whether we can take this one further step, and remove the need to stipulate the character type. The answer is that we can, and with ease, as shown in Listing 34.6.

Listing 34.6
```
struct is_large
  : public std::unary_function<. . ., bool>
{
  template <typename S>
  bool operator ()(S const &file) const
  {
    return is_large_(c_str_ptr(file));
  }
private:
  static bool is_large_(char const *file);
  static bool is_large_(wchar_t const *file);
};
```

It is now simpler to use, as in:

```
n = std::count_if(rs.begin(), rs.end(), is_large());
n = std::count_if(gs.begin(), gs.end(), is_large());
n = std::count_if(gsw.begin(), gsw.end(), is_large());
```

However, there's a good reasons why we don't do this. This functor is a predicate—a functor whose function-call operator returns a Boolean result reflecting some aspect of its argument(s). One important aspect of predicates is that they may be combined with adaptors [Muss2001], as in the following statement that counts the number of *small* files:

```
n = std::count_if( gs.begin(), gs.end()
                 , std::not1(is_large<char>()));
```

In order for adaptors to work with predicates, they must be able to elicit the member types
`argument_type` and `result_type` from the predicate class. This is normally done by deriving from `std::unary_operator`. Now we can see why the final refinement shown in
Listing 34.6 cannot be done. There's no way to specify the argument type, other than to define
the predicate class as a template with a single template parameter to define the predicate. But
this would have to be provided in every use as there's no sensible default, which would be onerous to use and confusing to read.

This is why the actual functor definition is a two-parameter template, where the first parameter `C` represents the character type and the second parameter `A`, which defaults to `C
const*`, represents the `argument_type` of the predicate.

```
template< typename C
        , typename A = C const *
        >
struct is_large
        : public std::unary_function<A, bool>
{
    . . .
```

Now when we want to use this with an adaptor and a sequence whose `value_type` is not
`C const*`, we do something like the following:

```
n = std::count_if( rs.begin(), rs.end() // rs: readdir_sequence
        , std::not1(is_large<char, struct dirent const*>()));
```

It doesn't have beauty that will stop a man's heart, but it's bearable considering the fact that
the combination of sequence and adaptor that necessitates it is low incidence, and the advantages of the generality and consequent reuse are high. It also facilitates a high degree of generality, since we can write a template algorithm that would be perfectly compatible with any
sequence, and maintain the type tunneling, as in:

```
template< typename C // character type
        , typename S // sequence type
        >
void do_stuff(. . .)
{
  S s = . . .;
  size_t n = std::count_if( s.begin(), s.end()
        , std::not1(is_large<C, typename S::value_type>()));
    . . .
```

Okay, before you think I've gone completely cracked, I confess that this is hardly something that gambols into the brain through the merest wisp of rapidly clearing mental fog. It's
something that you definitely have to think about. But there are times when we simply *have* to

have complex bits of code; check out some of your friendly neighborhood open-source C++ libraries if you don't believe me.

The point is that we have a mechanism for writing highly generalized—reusable, in other words—components, which are very digestible—in that they follow accepted idiomatic forms—in most cases where they are used. This generality is bought for the acceptable, in my opinion, cost of requiring the specification of the given sequence's `value_type` when used with adaptors.

34.3.7   Local Functors and Callback APIs

Just because local functors are not allowed for STL algorithms does not mean that they cannot find use in enumeration. In fact, when dealing with callback enumeration APIs, local classes are eminently solutions. Consider the implementation of the function `FindChildById()` (see Listing 34.7), which provides a deep-descendent equivalent to the well-known Win32 function `GetDlgItem()`. `GetDlgItem()` returns a handle to an immediate child window bearing the given id. `FindChildById()` provides the same functionality, but is able to locate the id in *any* descendent windows, not just immediate children.

Listing 34.7

```
HWND FindChildById(HWND hwndParent, int id)
{
  if(::GetDlgCtrlID(hwndParent) == id)
  {
    return hwndParent; // Searching for self
  }
  else
  {
    struct ChildFind
    {
      ChildFind(HWND hwndParent, int id)
        : m_hwndChild(NULL)
        , m_id(id)
      {
        // Enumerate, passing "this" as identity structure
        ::EnumChildWindows( hwndParent,
                            FindProc,
                            reinterpret_cast<LPARAM>(this));
      }

      static BOOL CALLBACK FindProc(HWND hwnd, LPARAM lParam)
      {
        ChildFind &find = *reinterpret_cast<ChildFind*>(lParam);

        return (::GetDlgCtrlID(hwnd) == find.m_id)
                 ? (find.m_hwndChild = hwnd, FALSE)
                 : TRUE;
      }
```

```
        HWND       m_hwndChild;
        int const m_id;

      } find(hwndParent, id);

      return find.m_hwndChild;
    }
}
```

The class `ChildFind` is declared within the function, maximizing encapsulation. The instance `find` is passed the parent window handle and the id to find. The constructor records the id in the `m_id` member, and sets the search result member `m_hwndChild` to NULL. It then calls the Win32 callback enumeration function `EnumChildWindows()`, which takes the parent window handle, a callback function, and a caller-supplied parameter. The instance passes the static method `FindProc()` and itself as the parameter. `FindProc()` then responds to each callback by determining whether the desired id has been located, and, if so, it records the handle and terminates the search.

When the construction of `find` is complete, it will either contain the requested handle, or NULL, in the `m_hwndChild` member. In either case this is returned to the caller of `Find-ChildById()`. The entire enumeration has been carried out in the constructor of the local class, whose definition is not accessible to any outside context. `FindChildById()` perfectly encapsulates the `ChildFind` class.

34.4   Ranges

We've seen that there are two issues in the enumeration of ranges and the use of functors. First, we have a desire to avoid the general, though not universal, repeated stipulation of the `begin()` and `end()` methods for sequence types. Second, we have a need to avoid writing overly specific "write-once, use nowhere else" functors.

In a discussion with my friend John Torjo,[7] we discovered that we've had similar disenchantments with these issues, and wanted a better solution. We came up with the *Range* concept. Naturally, he and I see the issue slightly differently;[8] the concept definition and component implementations presented here primarily reflect my view.

34.4.1   The Range Concept

The range concept is quite simple.

Definition: A *Range* represents a bounded collection of elements, which may be accessed in an incremental fashion. It encapsulates a logical range—that is, a beginning and end point, along with rules for how to walk through it (move from the beginning to

---

[7]John was also a one of the reviewers for this book.

[8]You can fit more angels on the head of a pin than you can find software engineers who wouldn't argue over a blade of grass. Notwithstanding that, John and I are in a reasonable state of agreement. You can see the differences in our interpretation of the concept, and understand the different design principles and implementation mechanisms in our implementations, because John's expansive and impressive Boost-compatible implementation of the Range concept is included on the CD along with my own STLSoft version.

the end point)—and embodies a single entity with which client code may access the values contained within the range.

Sounds almost too simple to be meaningful, doesn't it? Well, the salient part of the definition is that it's a single entity. The canonical form of use is:

```
for(R r = . . .; r; ++r)
{
  f(*r);
}
```

or, if you don't go for all that operator overloading:

```
for(R r = . . .; r.is_open(); r.advance())
{
  f(r.current());
}
```

There's noticeable brevity of form, which is part the raison d'être of ranges. A range has the characteristics shown in Table 34.2.

Let's look at a couple of ranges in action:

```
// A range over a sequence
glob_sequence gs("/usr/include/", "impcpp*");
for(sequence_range<glob_sequence> r(gs); r; ++r)
{
  puts(*r); // Print the matched file entry to stdout
}

// A "notional range"
for(integral_range<int> r(10, 20, 2); r; ++r)
```

Table 34.2 Characteristics of a *notional range*.

Name	Expressions	Semantics	Precondition	Postcondition
Dereference	*r or r.current()	Returns the value of represented at the current position	r has not reached its end condition	r is unchanged
Advance	++r or r.advance()	Advances r's current position	r has not reached its end condition	r is dereference-able or has reached its end condition
State	r or r.is_open()	Evaluates to true if r has reached its end condition, false otherwise	-	r is unchanged

```
{
  cout << *r << endl; // Print int value at current point
}
```

There's no way any pointer can fit the range syntax[9] so we don't have to worry about catering for any fundamental types; this provides us with a lot of extra flexibility in the implementation. In other words, we can rely on all range instances being of class types, and therefore we can rely on the presence or absence of class type characteristics in order to specialize behavior for the algorithms that operate on ranges (see section 34.4.4).

The way this works is similar to the implementation of algorithms that manipulate Iterators [Aust1999], only simpler. My implementation of ranges simply relies on the specific range types deriving from the appropriate range type tag structure:

```
struct simple_range_tag
{};

struct iterable_range_tag
  : public simple_range_tag
{};
```

We'll see how these are used in the next sections.

34.4.2 Notional Range

Sometimes you don't have a concrete range, that is, one defined by two iterators; rather you have a notional range. It might be the odd numbers between 1 and 99. In this simple case you know that the number of odd numbers is 49 (1–97 inclusive), and so what you might do in classic STL is as shown in Listing 34.8:

Listing 34.8
```
struct next_odd_number
{
  next_odd_number(int first)
    : m_current(first - 2)
  {}
  int operator ()()
  {
    return ++++m_current; // Nasty, but it fits on one line ;/
  }
private:
  int m_current;
};

std::vector<int>  ints(49);
std::generate(ints.begin(), ints.end(), next_odd_number(1));
```

---

[9]Except if we were to point it high into the top of memory and then iterate until it reached 0, but this would result in an access violation on many platforms, so the issue is moot.

Books on STL tend to show such things as perfectly reasonable examples of STL best practice. That may indeed be the case, but to me it's a whole lot of pain. First, we have the creation of a functor that will probably not be used elsewhere.

Second, and more significantly, the technique works by treating the functor as a passive producer whose actions are directed by the standard library algorithm `generate()`, whose bounds are, in turn, defined by the vector. This is very important, because it means that we need to know the number of results that will be created beforehand, in order to create spaces for them in the vector. Hence, we need a deep appreciation of how the producer—the functor—works. In this simple case, that is relatively straightforward—although I must confess I did get it wrong when preparing the test program! But imagine if we were computing the members of the Fibonacci series up to a user-supplied maximum value. It would be impossible to anticipate the number of steps in such a range other than by enumerating it to completion, which would be a drag, not to mention inefficient.

What we want in such cases is for the producer to drive the process, in accordance with the criteria stipulated by the code's author. Time to crank out my favorite example range, the `integral_range` template, whose simplified definition is shown in Listing 34.9:

Listing 34.9

```
template <typename T>
class integral_range
  : public simple_range_tag
{
public:
  typedef simple_range_tag   range_tag_type;
  typedef T                  value_type;
// Construction
public:
  integral_range( value_type first, value_type last
               , value_type increment = +1)
  ~integral_range()
  {
    // Ensure that the parameterising type is integral
    STATIC_ASSERT(0 != is_integral_type<T>::value);
  }
// Enumeration
public:
  operator "safe bool"() const; // See Chapter 24
  value_type operator *() const;
  class_type &operator ++();
// Members
  . . .
};
```

The `integral_range` performs enumeration over its logical range via member variables of the given integral type, `T`.

We can now rewrite the instantiation of the vector with odd numbers as follows:

```
std::vector<int>  ints;
ints.reserve(49); // No problem if this is wrong.
r_copy(integral_range<int>(1, 99, 2), std::back_inserter(ints));
```

Note that the call to `reserve()` is an optimization and can be omitted without causing any change to the correctness of the code. `r_copy()` is a range algorithm (see section 34.4.3) that has the same semantics as the standard library algorithm `copy()` [Muss2001]. Now the producer, the instance of `integral_range<int>`, drives the process, which is as it should be. We could easily substitute a `Fibonacci_range` here, and the code would work correctly and efficiently, which cannot be said for the STL version.

34.4.3 Iterable Range

The *Iterable* range is an extension of the *Notional* range, with the additional provision of `begin()`, `end()` and `range()` methods, allowing it to be fully compatible with standard STL algorithms and usage (see section 34.4.4).

Iterable ranges usually maintain internal iterators reflecting the current and past-the-end condition positions, and return these via the `begin()` and `end()` methods. The `range()` method is provided to allow a given range to be cloned in its current enumeration state, although this is subject to the restrictions on copying iterators if the range's underlying iterators are of the *Input* or *Output* Iterator concepts [Aust1999, Muss2001]: only the *Forward* and "higher" models [Aust1999, Muss2001] support the ability to pass through a given range more than once.

It is possible to write iterable range classes, but the common idiom is to use an adaptor. In my implementation of the *Range* concept, I have two adaptors, the `sequence_range` and `iterator_range` template classes. Obviously the `sequence_range` adapts STL *Sequence*s, and the `iterator_range` adapts STL *Iterator*s.

Given a sequence type, we can adapt it to a range by passing the sequence instance to the constructor of an appropriate instantiation of `sequence_range`, as in:

```
std::deque<std::string> d = . . . ;

sequence_range< std::deque<std::string> > r(d);
for(; r; ++r)
{
   . . . // Use *r
}
```

Similarly, an `iterator_range` is constructed from a pair of iterators, as in:

```
vector<int> v = . . . ;

for(iterator_range<vector<int>::iterator> r(v.begin(), v.end()));
```

```
   r; ++r)
{
  . . . // Use *r
}
```

Iterable ranges at first glance appear to be nothing more than a syntactic convenience for reducing the clutter of unwanted variables when processing iterator ranges in unrolled loops. I must confess that this in itself represents a big attraction to draw for me, but the concept offers much more as we'll see in the next couple of sections.

34.4.4   Range Algorithms and Tags

All the examples so far have shown ranges used in unrolled loops. Ranges may also be used with algorithms. That's where the separation of *Notional* and *Iterable* range concepts comes in.

Consider the standard library algorithm `distance()`.

```
template <typename I>
size_t distance(I first, I last);
```

This algorithm returns the number of elements represented by the range `[first, last)`. For all iterator types other than *Random Access* [Aust1999, Muss2001], the number is calculated by iterating `first` until it equals `last`. But the template is implemented to simply and efficiently calculate `(last - first)` for random access iterators. We certainly don't want to lose such efficiency gains when using algorithms with ranges.

The answer is very simple: we implement the range algorithms in terms of the standard library algorithms where possible. The range algorithm `r_distance()` is defined as shown in Listing 34.10:

Listing 34.10

```
template <typename R>
ptrdiff_t r_distance_1(R r, iterable_range_tag const &)
{
  return std::distance(r.begin(), r.end());
}
template <typename R>
ptrdiff_t r_distance_1(R r, simple_range_tag const &)
{
  ptrdiff_t d = 0;
  for(; r; ++r, ++d)
  {}
  return d;
}
template <typename R>
inline ptrdiff_t r_distance(R r)
{
  return r_distance_1(r, r);
}
```

`r_distance()` is implemented in terms of `r_distance_1()`,[10] which has two definitions: one for the iterable ranges that defers to a standard library algorithm, and one for notional ranges that carries out the enumeration manually. The two overloads of `r_distance_1()` are distinguished by their second parameter, which discriminate on whether the ranges as simple or iterable.

We use run time polymorphism (inheritance) to select the compile-time polymorphism (template type resolution), so we need to pass the range to `r_distance_1()` in two parameters, to preserve the actual type in the first parameter while at the same type discriminating the overload in the second. Since compilers can make mincemeat of such simple things, there're no concerns regarding inefficiency, and the mechanism ably suffices. We saw in section 34.4.2 that the `integral_range` template inherited from `simple_range_tag`. Iterable ranges inherit from `iterable_range_tag`. Hence the implementations of all range algorithms unambiguously select the most suitable implementation.

We can now come back and address the algorithm name problem (see section 34.2.2). Since we're clearly distinguishing between iterator-pair ranges and instances of a range class, we're never going to need the same name to facilitate generalized programming because the former ranges come as two parameters and the latter as one. Therefore, we can avoid all the namespace tribulations and just use algorithms with an `r_` prefix.

34.4.5   Filters

Another powerful aspect of the *Range* concept abstraction is that of filters. This aspect of ranges is only just developing, but is already promising great benefits. I'll illustrate with a simple filter `divisible`, which we'll apply to our `integral_range`.

Listing 34.11
```
template <typename R>
struct divisible
      : public R::range_tag_type
{
public:
  typedef R                          filtered_range_type;
  typedef typename R::value_type   value_type;
public:
  divisible(filtered_range_type r, value_type div)
    : m_r(r)
    , m_div(div)
  {
    assert(div > 0);
    for(; m_r && 0 != (*m_r % m_div); ++m_r)
    {}
  }
```

---

[10]This is a general implementation naming policy, which helps to avoid clashes that can occur when the "outer" function and the implementing "inner" functions have the same name, and there are multiple overloads of the "outer" function. Different compilers have different aptitudes for resolving such things, so the simplest solution is to avoid it, and name the implementing "inner" functions unambiguously.

```
public:
  operator "safe bool"() const; // See Chapter 24
  {
    . . . // implemented in terms of m_r's op safe bool
  }
  value_type operator *() const
  {
    return *m_r;
  }
  class_type &operator ++()
  {
    for(; m_r && 0 != (*++m_r % m_div); )
    {}
    return *this;
  }
private:
  filtered_range_type m_r;
  value_type          m_div;
};
```

When combined with `integral_range`, we can filter out all the odd numbers in a given range to only those that are wholly divisible by three, as in:

```
std::vector<int>    ints;
integral_range<int> ir(1, 99, 2);
r_copy( divisible<integral_range<int> >(ir, 3)
      , std::back_inserter(ints));
```

Naturally range filters can be a lot more sophisticated than this in the real world.

34.4.6   Hypocrisy?

As someone who is against the abuse of operator overloading,[11] I am certainly open to accusations of hypocrisy when it comes to the operators that ranges support. Clearly it can be argued, if one wished to be terribly uncharitable, that the unrealistic combination of operators provided by ranges is an abuse.

I can't really defend the concept in any purist sense, so I can fall back on the Imperfect Practitioner's Philosophy, and state that the fact that it works so well, and so simply, is worth the pricked conscience.

If you like the range concept, but don't want to go for the operator overloading, it is a simple matter to replace some or all of the operators with methods. The semantics and efficiency will be the same; only the syntax will be slightly heavier.

```
for(R r = . . .; r.is_open(); r.advance())
{
```

---

[11]Although you'll have noted that I managed to overcome my squeamishness in Chapter 25.

```
    . . . = r.current();
}
```

34.5   Functors and Ranges: Coda

This chapter has been taking a somewhat meandering tour of what is at best a mild, often unnoticed, gripe with having to make too many keystrokes, but at worst can be a serious detriment to maintainability.

We've looked at the trade-offs between unrolled loops and functors, and some of the imperfections in the language in terms of the difficulties of using local functors.

We've also seen how we can maximize the generality of functors, by making them compatible with a wider variety of types, via character type parameterizations, type tunneling, and adaptor argument type parameterization. The combination of these techniques represents a substantial resolution of the issues raised in the early part of the chapter.

Last, we looked at the *Range* concept. Not only do ranges provide a nice syntactic convenience, but they also facilitate the unified manipulation of iterator-bound ranges and what we might call purely logical ranges. Furthermore, the application of range filters, to both kinds of ranges, represents a powerful but simple-to-use mechanism for criteria-driven manipulation of ranges.

Update: The latest work on Ranges has incorporated callback enumeration APIs (in the form of the Indirect Range)—something that cannot be handled by STL iterators. See http://www.rangelib.org/ for the latest details.

CHAPTER 35

Properties

Member variables (also known as fields) are data that are part of an object or, in the case of `static` member variables, belong to a class. Methods are functions that belong to object instances or, in the case of `static` methods, to a class. Several modern languages (C#, D, Delphi) support the concept of a property. Though using a property is syntactically the same as accessing member variables, properties are different to C++ member variables in that using them may actually involve a function call. For example, property definitions might look like[1] the `Date` class shown in Listing 35.1.

Listing 35.1
```
class Date
{
public:
  enum WeekDay { Sunday, Monday, ... };
public:
  property WeekDay      get_DayOfWeek() const;
  property int          get_DayOfMonth() const;
  property void         set_DayOfMonth(int day);
  property int          get_Year() const;
  static property Date  get_Now();
private:
  time_t  m_time;
};
```

There are several nice attributes that properties have over member variables. First, they can be read-only, write-only, or read-write. This provides finer grained control than is possible in C++, where a `public` member variable can be changed by any client code, unless it is made `const`:

```
Date          date    = Date::Now;      // calls get_Now();
Date::WeekDay weekday = date.DayOfWeek; // calls get_DayOfWeek();

date.DayOfMonth = 31; // calls set_DayOfMonth();
```

Second, they can be used as an overt, and readily comprehensible, conversion between internal and external types. Our `Date` class uses a field of type `time_t`, but its public interface is expressed in straightforward and usable concepts.

---

[1]Note that the keyword `property` and the `get_`/`set_` prefixes are just inventions of mine to illustrate what might be, they do not represent any particular compiler extensions, or proposals for language enhancements.

Third, properties can provide validation. You might define a `Date` type, which contains a read-write `Day` property. It is easy to implement the underlying property `set_DayOf Month(int day)` method so as to provide range validation, for example, restricting the value to be between one and the maximum number of days for the given month and throwing an exception otherwise.

Listing 35.2
```
void Date::set_DayOfMonth(int day)
{
  struct tm   tm = *localtime(&m_time);
  if(!ValidateDay(tm, day))
  {
    throw std::out_of_range("The given day is not valid for the current month");
  }
  tm.tm_mday = day;
  time_t   t = mktime(&tm);
  if(static_cast<time_t>(-1) == t)
  {
    throw std::out_of_range("The given day is not valid for the current month");
  }
  m_time = t;
}
```

Fourth, they separate interface from implementation. It is possible that one class may have a property that is simply a view to a member variable. Another class could provide a property that actually made an out-of-instance call to some shared system state. The caller neither knows nor cares about these details, only that the public interfaces of the types it is using are meaningful. The static property `Now` yields a `Date` instance representing the current time. The implementation of `get_Now()` could, if you wished, actually communicate via NTP (Network Time Protocol) to a time server and synchronize the local system time prior to returning the `Date` instance.

Fifth, they increase usability (read "success") of your classes, since there's less typing and fewer obfuscatory prefixes. We didn't have to write `date.get_Month()`, just `date .Month`. Hence, properties help to distinguish accessor methods from operational methods, which can represent a substantial help in the understanding of the public interfaces of nontrivial classes. Of course, this can be, should be, and usually is done by prefixing one's methods with `get_` or `Get` in existing class definitions, but this necessary ugliness wouldn't be missed by anyone but the masochists, I would hope.

Sixth, they provide a means to enforce invariants (see section 1.3), while maintaining the syntactic compatibility—structural conformance (see section 20.9)—with existing types and client code.

Finally, they provide a modest boost to genericity (see section 35.7.1), since complex class types can be made to look like simple structures.

Having used a lot of different languages in the last year or two, I've come to really like properties, and believe that they represent a very useful abstraction. As such, I'm going to suggest that:

Imperfection: C++ does not provide properties.

35.1   Compiler Extensions

Although properties are not part of the language at this time, a few compilers do provide them as an extension (e.g., Borland C++'s `__property` and Intel / Visual C++'s `__declspec(property)`), as in:

Listing 35.3
```
class Date
{
public:
  WeekDay get_DayOfWeek() const;

  . . .
#if defined(ACMELIB_COMPILER_IS_BORLAND)
  __property WeekDay DayOfWeek = {read = get_DayOfWeek};
#elif defined(ACMELIB_COMPILER_IS_INTEL) || \
      defined(ACMELIB_COMPILER_IS_MSVC)
  __declspec(property(get = get_DayOfWeek)) WeekDay DayOfWeek;
#else
# error Property extensions not supported by your compiler
#endif // compiler

  . . .

};
```

Obviously the main problem is that property extensions are nonstandard, and only available on a few compilers. Even those that do support them, support only instance properties, and not class (static) properties.[2] We need something more powerful and more portable.

35.2   Implementation Options

What we're after is the syntactic appearance of a member variable, but with the resultant access translating to method calls. Well, thankfully C++, as we've proven many times in this book already, has the supporting infrastructure we need, in the form of implicit conversion operators, user-definable assignment operators, references, and templates. (We use some less noble parts of the language as well, but I don't want to spoil a good story just yet.)

35.2.1   A Taxonomy of Property Implementation Options

I'd first like to highlight the options with which one might approach the implementation of properties. First, to achieve the syntax of a member variable, we need a member variable. After all, `operator .()` is not overloadable [Stro1994]. Beyond this, however, there are several alternatives.

In some cases, the property's *notional* value is backed up by an *actual* member variable (field) within the containing class: these are called *Field Properties* (see section 35.3), and provide read or write access control only. Conversely, the value may be implemented in terms of

---

[2]Visual C++ helpfully suggests that "property methods can only be associated with non-static data members." Borland C++ (5.6) has an internal compiler error.

arbitrarily complex methods, providing validation and/or proxying behavior; these are called *Method Properties* (see section 35.4). Naturally, the two can be combined (see section 35.4).

Where properties are backed by actual member variables, there are two further refinements. The member variable may be provided within the property member itself; these are *Internal Properties*. Alternatively, the member variable may already exist as part of the containing class, and therefore outside the property variable; these are *External Properties*.

The permutations of read and/or write, field and/or method, internal or external, will be examined in the sections that follow. They represent various trade-offs between portability, (space and time) efficiency, and even legality.

35.2.2 EMO?

Before we get stuck into the details of the various implementations, I want to discuss an issue that underpins the imperfect nature of some of these property solutions.

We saw in section 12.3 the officially recognized *Empty Base Optimization*, and the unofficial, but widely implemented, *Empty Derived Optimization*. Consider the following case, where empty classes are used as member variables.

```
struct empty
{};

struct emptyish
{
  empty e1;
  empty e2;
  empty e3;
  int   i1;
};
```

Since `e1`, `e2`, and `e3` are empty, it would be nice if the compiler could allocate the storage for instances of `emptyish` based on the nonempty fields, such that `sizeof(emptyish) == sizeof(int)`. This would be an *Empty Member Optimization* (EMO).

At first glance it seems like this shouldn't be a problem. After all, since they're empty, they don't need any space. Further, having no member variables, it wouldn't really matter if the address of any of the `empty` members were the same. However, consider what would happen in the following case:

```
struct emptyish2
{
  empty ae[3];
  int   i1;
};
```

The three `empty` members are now in an array. Clearly to allocate zero storage to them will now lead to a contradiction: `&ae[0] == &ae[1] == &ae[2]` just doesn't make sense. So, we have the rule that the members of any aggregate have non-zero storage.

35.3 Field Properties

There are four kinds of field properties, representing read or write access, and internal or external implementation. These are represented in the four classes, `field_property_get`, `field_property_set`, `field_property_get_external`, and `field_property_set_external`, which we'll look at now. Obviously there's no point combining field property get and set accesses, for example, `field_property_getset` and `field_property_getset_external`, since that is semantically equivalent to a public variable, and would be a grand waste of effort.

35.3.1 field_property_get

Let's look at how we might implement a read-only field property. Consider that we have a linked list class, and we want to provide a `Count` property, to indicate how many items are in the list. In any sane list implementation,[3] the count of items is maintained as a member variable, as opposed to conducting a count by walking the list. Since it makes no sense to assign to the count of a list, `Count` will provide a read-only view onto a `private` integer member variable. We could implement this as shown in Listing 35.4.

Listing 35.4

```
class ListElement;
class LinkedList;

class LinkedListCountProp
{
public:
  operator int() const
  {
    return m_value;
  }
private:
  friend class LinkedList; // Allow LinkedList access to m_value
  int m_value;
};

class LinkedList
{
// Properties
public:
  LinkedListCountProp    Count;
// Operations
public:
  void Add(ListElement *e)
  {
    . . .
```

---

[3]For an insane one, refer to more of my misdemeanors in Appendix B.

```
    ++Count.m_value; // Update the count
  }
};
```

The property `Count` is defined as of type `LinkedListCountProp`, and is a `public` member variable of `LinkedList`. It looks a little strange, since there's no `m_` prefix,[4] and it's uppercase. This is my naming convention for properties, in order that they are disambiguated from member variables; you're free to choose your own. For example, if you need them to appear as public member variables, for generalization, then they'd be defined according to the convention of the type(s) you're emulating.

Client code can refer to the `Count` member of instances of `LinkedList`, and in that way access the (`int`) value, via the implicit conversion operator. Client code cannot change the value of `LinkedListCountProp::m_value` because it is `private`, but the `friendship` declaration means that it can be altered by `Rectangle`. Simple really, isn't it?

The downside is all too clear. `LinkedListCountProp` is a purpose-written class, and an equivalent would be required for every containing class and every value type. Unless we want a lot of typing, code-bloat, and maintenance headaches, we want a generalized solution. Naturally, templates are the answer, in the form of `field_property_get`, which is shown in Listing 35.5.

Listing 35.5

```
template< typename V   /* The actual property value type */
        , typename R   /* The reference type */
        , typename C   /* The enclosing class */
    >
class field_property_get
{
public:
  typedef field_property_get<V, R, C> class_type;
private:
  // Does not initialize m_value
  field_property_get()
  {}
  // Initialises m_value to given value
  explicit field_property_get(R value)
    : m_value(value)
  {}
  DECLARE_TEMPLATE_PARAM_AS_FRIEND(C);
public:
  /// Provides read-only access to the property
  operator R () const
  {
    return m_value;
```

---

[4]Which may not be much of a loss to most of you. It's not exactly a popular notation, though I suspect that's for political more than technical reasons (see Chapter 17).

```
  }
private:
  V m_value;
// Not to be implemented
private:
  field_property_get(class_type const &);
  class_type &operator =(class_type const &);
};
```

The template takes three parameters: the type of the internal member variable, the reference type by which its value may be accessed, and the type of the containing class. The separation of value type and reference type increases flexibility and efficiency. For example, if you were using `std::string` as the value type, you would likely choose to use `std::string const&` as the reference type.

As with the specific case of `LinkedListCountProp`, read-only access is achieved by making the member variable `m_value` and the constructors `private`, but providing a `public` implicit conversion operator to the reference type.

Note that the default constructor does not perform explicit initialization of the member variable. This is in common with my personal predisposition to making efficiency a high priority, and that unnecessary initialization is a waste of time. Initialization of the value is achievable by the nondefault constructor. You may take a different point of view, and therefore implement the default constructor to also explicitly default construct the member variable.

```
  field_property_get()
    : m_value(V())
  {}
```

As before, the containing type needs write access to the member variable, which is provided by granting it `friend`ship of the template using the technique we saw in section 16.3.

Using this general class template, we can now define `LinkedList` as:

```
class LinkedList
{
// Construction
public:
  . . .
// Properties
public:
  field_property_get<int, int, LinkedList>   Count;
};
```

There's an added bonus in that the declaration of the property `Count` is also self-documenting: it is a field-based read-only (get) property, whose value and reference types are both `int`.

Client code expressions are also readable and unambiguous:

```
LinkedList   llist(...);
for(. . .)
{
   . . . // Add items to the list
}
int          count = llist.Count; // Gives the count of items

llist.Count = count + 1;    // Error! Write access denied
```

The copy constructor and copy assignment operator are hidden to prevent nonsensical use such as the following:

```
field_property_get<int, int, Count>  SomeProp(llist.Count); // Copy ctor

llist.Count = llist.Count;   // Copy assignment
```

Hopefully you'll agree that we've achieved read-only access in a very simple fashion. On all the compilers (Appendix A) tested, the `field_property_get` template causes no speed or space overhead, so it is 100 percent efficient. The only downside is that it uses the currently nonstandard, though very widely supported, mechanism of granting friendship to a template's parameterising type.[5] But we're imperfect practitioners, and we want something that works (and is portable). This does (and is).

35.3.2   field_property_set

I must say that I cannot think of any use for a write-only field property, but we're going to look at the mechanism for pedagogical purposes, as this will inform on our implementation of the write-only method properties (see section 35.4), which do have valid applications.

Write-only properties are the semantic opposite of read-only, so the `field_property_set` template replaces the `public` implicit conversion operator with an assignment operator, as in:

Listing 35.6
```
template< typename V    /* The actual property value type */
        , typename R    /* The reference type */
        , typename C    /* The enclosing class */
    >
class field_property_set
{
public:
  typedef field_property_set<V, R, C> class_type;
private:
  field_property_set()
  {}
```

---

[5]The other downside, for the code aesthetes, is the use of a macro. I really don't like doing so, but in this case it is the preferred option, since it allows the class definition to be succinct and readable, and therefore comprehensible and maintainable.

```
  explicit field_property_set(R value)
    : m_value(value)
  {}
  DECLARE_TEMPLATE_PARAM_AS_FRIEND(C);
public:
  /// Provides write-only access to the property
  class_type &operator =(R value)
  {
    m_value = value;
    return *this;
  }
private:
  V  m_value;
// Not to be implemented
private:
  field_property_set(class_type const &);
  class_type &operator =(class_type const &);
};
```

This template has the same efficiency, portability, and legality attributes as its read-only brother. Everything gets inlined, and it's conformant code apart from the (highly portable) friend relationship.

35.3.3   Internal Fields Properties: Coda

We've now seen the core aspects of the property technique. Read-only access is achieved by providing a public implicit conversion operator in the property class, and hiding the copy constructor and copy assignment operators to prevent misuse. The containing type is made a friend of the property so that it can set the value, which is otherwise inaccessible due to being declared private.

Write-only access is achieved by providing a public assignment operator, and not providing an implicit conversion operator. The containing type is once again made a friend, this time so it can access the value of the property. For the ultra-cautious (which includes me) it is tempting to declare, but not define, a private implicit conversion operator. We'll see why this is not wise shortly.

For the remaining permutations we'll take these aspects as read (pardon the pun!) and focus on the individual mechanisms.

35.3.4   field_property_get_external

The internal field properties are the best option if we have full control over the implementation of the containing class to which we are adding the properties. However, sometimes this is not the case, and what we seek to do is augment a class with properties based on existing member variables. This is achieved using a reference. Hence, field_property_get_external is defined as:

Listing 35.7
```
template< typename V   /* The actual property value type */
        , typename R   /* The reference type */
    >
class field_property_get_external
{
public:
  field_property_get_external(V &value) // Takes a reference
    : m_value(value)
  {}
// Accessors
public:
  /// Provides read-only access to the property
  operator R() const
  {
    return m_value;
  }
// Members
private:
  V  &m_value;
};
```

Ostensibly, this property looks simpler than the internal equivalent. `field_property_get_external` is parameterized with the value type and the reference type to the variable, and holds a reference to the value type, which is passed in its constructor.

Since the property object holds a direct reference to the member variable for which it acts, it does not need to know, or be `friends` with, the containing class. Hence, the template is 100 percent language compliant. Furthermore, it presents no challenge to even very template-deficient compilers; even Visual C++ 4.2 compiles this!

In terms of speed efficiency, the template is amenable to even cautious optimization, such that the notional indirection through the reference can be optimized into a direct reference. The downside is that the reference results in space inefficiency: on 32-bit machines, the reference costs 4 bytes per property. Furthermore the property is a little more complex to use, since it must be initialized with a reference to the variable for which it will act.

Listing 35.8
```
class LinkedList
{
// Construction
public:
  Rectangle(. . .
    : Count(m_count)
    , . . .
// Properties
public:
```

```
  field_property_get_external<int, int, LinkedList>    Count;
// Members
private:
  int m_count;
};
```

At first glance, this looks like a member initializer list ordering problem (see section 2.3), but in fact it's not. The reason is that Count is passed m_count as a reference, not as a value. Hence, the only way in which this could itself be an ordering problem would be if Count was being used in another initializer, which would be an ordering problem all its own and doesn't have anything to do with the property per se. Nonetheless, it's worth pointing out, since member ordering dependencies are in principal bad things, and you should be mindful of the pitfalls whenever you (think you) see them.

35.3.5   field_property_set_external

field_property_set_external provides the semantics of field_property_set with the same reference mechanism as field_property_get_external.

35.3.6   Hacking Away

When we look at method properties in the next section we're going to see that there's a way to hack away at the space inefficiencies by using esoteric techniques. While it's possible to do the same for external field properties, I've not done so simply because they are so very rarely used. Of course, they may be so rarely used because they have the space cost, but we're getting philosophical, so you take the chicken and I'll take the eggs, and we'll move on.

35.4   Method Properties

The picture gets a whole lot more complex when we look at method properties, so you might want to take a short nap or get a cup of your caffeine delivery system of choice before continuing.

There are six kinds of method properties, representing the permutations of internal or external, and read and/or write. The first three we examine, the internal read, write, and read/write, actually represent a hybrid of field and method properties, since they contain within themselves the field that backs up the property's value. I'm dealing with them first since they have the more straightforward implementation and are the most commonly used.

The last three represent the external read, write, and read/write situations, and are purely method based. As with external field properties, there is a waste of space, and it is in chasing this down to a minimum that we have some fun at the dark edges of the language.

35.4.1   method_property_get

A read-only internal method property has the following characteristics:

- An internal field that backs up the property's value
- Access to the private internals of the property to the containing class via a friendship declaration

- An implicit conversion operator
- A pointer to an instance (nonstatic) method of its containing class to which is delegated the value access of the implicit conversion operator
- A pointer (or reference) to the containing class instance on which to apply the delegated function

Providing the internal field and the friendship are boilerplate to us now. However, the other three represent something more of a challenge. A straightforward implementation could pass pointers to the containing instance and the member function in the constructor, and then call them from within the conversion operator, as in:

```
template < . . . >
class method_property_get
{
  . . .
  operator R() const
  {
    return (m_object->*m_pfnGet)();
  }
  . . .
};
```

However, a quick mental arithmetic will tell us that this will triple (at least) the size of the property. In fact, some compilers require several machine words to represent a pointer to a member function, so this can lead to considerable space penalties. It's a shame, of course, since such an implementation would be simple, whereas the one we have is not at all. It is highly portable and very efficient though, so do keep reading.

Let's look more closely at the two overheads that we want to eliminate: the containing-class pointer and the member-function pointer. Since a property field will be located within the containing class, why not simply deduce the class pointer from the this pointer of the property? Passing the offset to the property instance would simply add a member variable, however, which defeats the purpose of eliding space inefficiencies. One way around this would be as a static member of the property class. However, this would mean that each property would have to be a separate class. Unless we want to do a lot of repetitious coding, we'd have to use macros. And even if using macros we'd need to define the static offset member in an implementation file, which just adds to the hassle in using the properties.

How much better would it be if we could make the offset part of the type itself? Well, since we're using templates, wouldn't it be great if we could instead use the offset as part of the template parameterizations, as in:

Listing 35.9

```
class Date
{
public:
```

```
WeekDay get_DayOfWeek() const
{
   return WeekDay.m_value;
}
public:
  method_property_get<WeekDay
                   . . .
                   , offsetof(Date, DayOfWeek)
                   . . .
              >                                    DayofWeek;
```

The parameterizing method `get_DayOfWeek()` needs to be declared `public`, but this is a perfectly acceptable situation. There's no reason why the client code should be prevented from using the method for which the property merely acts as a syntactic proxy, so we don't have to worry about declaring it `private`. This looks nice and neat.

Alas, the real world nips at our hamstrings here. Neglecting the strict legality and portability issues of `offsetof()` (see section 2.3.3) for the moment, the fact is that it cannot deduce the offset of an incomplete type in its enclosing type. At the time of instantiation of `method_property_get<WeekDay, ..., offsetof(Date, DayOfWeek)>` it is not complete. Hence, its offset cannot be determined. Hence it cannot be used to instantiate the template. Hence . . . well I think you get the idea. So our elegant—well I think it's elegant, anyway—notion is invalidated. Thankfully there's a very simple alternative: static methods. Now we can break the instantiation and the offset calculation into two phases:

Listing 35.10

```
class Date
{
public:
  WeekDay get_DayOfWeek() const;
private:
  static ptrdiff_t  WeekDay_offset()
  { return offsetof(Date, DayOfWeek); }
public:
  method_property_get<WeekDay
                   . . .
                   , &WeekDay_offset
                   . . .
              >                                    DayofWeek;
```

Since the instantiation is now carried out on a function pointer, there is no need to attempt to calculate the offset at the time of instantiation, so it all works just fine. The function is called at run time (notionally at least; see below) to elicit the offset, which is then used to adjust the `this` pointer to get hold of a pointer to the containing class on which the member function is called. Which brings us to the last part of the puzzle.

Since we've parameterized the template on a method for the offset, why can't we just do the same for the function that actually implements the property access? Well, the answer is that we can, at least on modern compilers.

The offset method is a class (static) method, and is accepted as a template parameter by a very wide range of compilers. As far as we're concerned here, class methods are equivalent to free functions. Instance (nonstatic) methods are a different kettle of fish altogether [Lipp1996]. Although nonvirtual instance methods are treated by the linker in the same way as class methods and free functions, to C++ client code the this pointer of the instance on which the method is called is passed implicitly. It is this additional complication that seems to stymie the template interpretation of several compilers. Borland (5.5, 5.6), CodeWarrior 7, Visual C++ 7.0 and earlier, and Watcom all fail to compile such constructs. However, CodeWarrior 8, Comeau, Digital Mars, GCC, Intel, VectorC, and Visual C++ 7.1 all compile them without qualms.

Enough chat; let's look at the class (shown in Listing 35.11).

Listing 35.11

```
template< typename V              /* The actual property value type */
        , typename R              /* The reference type */
        , typename C              /* The enclosing class */
        , ptrdiff_t (*PFnOff)()   /* Pointer to fn providing offset of property
in container */
        , R (C::*PFnGet)() const  /* Pointer to a const member function
returning R */
        >
class method_property_get
{
public:
  typedef method_property_get<. . .>  class_type;
private:
  method_property_get()
  {}
  explicit method_property_get(R value)
    : m_value(value)
  {}
  DECLARE_TEMPLATE_PARAM_AS_FRIEND(C);
// Accessors
public:
  /// Provides read-only access to the property
  operator R() const
  {
    ptrdiff_t offset  = (*PFnOff)();
    C         *pC     = (C*)((byte_t*)this - offset);
    return (pC->*PFnGet)();
  }
// Members
private:
```

```
  V m_value;
// Not to be implemented
private:
  // This method is hidden in order to prevent users of this class from
  // becoming familiar with using operator = on the property instances
  // from within the containing class, since doing so with
  // method_property_getset<> would result in an infinite loop.
  class_type &operator =(R value);
};
```

The template has five parameters. V, R, and C represent the value type, the reference type, and the containing class type. The fourth parameter is the function that provides the offset of the property. It's simply declared as taking no parameters and returning a value of type ptrdiff_t. Note that we do not use size_t here, even though that's the type of the result of offsetof(), because we're deducing an offset back into the containing class from the property member. Applying a unary minus to an unsigned variable gives an unsigned result, which would point our class instance somewhere at the top of memory; not the desired result, to say the least! I've taken an early intervention approach here, mandating the offset functions return ptrdiff_t, rather than having to remember to cast appropriately in the property implementation(s).

The fifth parameter, which at first glance is the type of inscrutable gobbledygook that often gets C++ a bad name, is actually quite straightforward. It merely declares that PFnGet is a pointer to a const member function of C, which takes no arguments, and returns a value of type R.

We can now revisit our notional Date type described at the start of the chapter, and start plugging some real techniques into it. Let's imagine for this case that Date caches the values of the various date/time components in each of its properties. We'll see the single-member/multiple-properties version when we look at external properties (see sections 35.4.5–35.4.7).

Listing 35.12
```
class Date
{
public:
  WeekDay get_DayOfWeek() const
  {
    return DayOfWeek.m_value;
  }
private:
  static ptrdiff_t  DayOfWeek_offset()
  { return offsetof(Date, DayOfWeek); }
public:
  method_property_get<WeekDay, WeekDay
                  , Date
                  , &DayOfWeek_offset, &get_DayOfWeek
                  >                           DayofWeek;
  . . .
};
```

I've defined a `private static` offset method, `DayOfWeek_offset`, which provides the necessary offset. The `DayOfWeek` property is defined as a `method_property_get`, which has value and reference type of `WeekDay`, uses the offset method, and implements read access via the `get_DayOfWeek` method. Though this is now a reasonably portable solution, and all the requisite pieces are defined within close proximity, it leaves a bit to be desired in the amount of mess surrounding the property definition.

But make no mistake. The cost of this technique is only in developer effort, and readability. The proof of such techniques is in their performance. And it performs very well indeed. On all compilers tested, the space penalty is zero. In terms of speed, all the compilers are similarly able to optimize out both the call to the offset method and the nonvirtual member function, so there's no speed cost either. It is 100 percent efficient.

Most compilers are content with this syntax, but Digital Mars and GCC have a brain-freeze with it. Digital Mars cannot use a private method to parameterize the property template, and GCC must have the fully qualified method names, so you'll need to use the following form if you want to be portable:

Listing 35.13
```
class Date
{
public:
  WeekDay get_DayOfWeek() const;

  . . .
public:
  static ptrdiff_t  DayOfWeek_offset() { return offsetof(Date, DayOfWeek); }
public:
  method_property_get<WeekDay
                , WeekDay
                , Date
                , &Date::DayOfWeek_offset
                , &Date::get_DayOfWeek
                >                                DayofWeek;
```

Even the former version is hardly what one could call succinct, and this one's even worse. Given that the definition of the offset method is, to users of the containing class, nothing but a distraction, one answer to all this is to use a macro (with a suitably heavy heart, of course).

Listing 35.14
```
#define METHOD_PROPERTY_DEFINE_OFFSET(C, P) \
                                            \
  static ptrdiff_t P##_offset##C()          \
  {                                         \
    return offsetof(C, P);                  \
  }

#define METHOD_PROPERTY_GET(V, R, C, GM, P) \
```

```
                                               \
     METHOD_PROPERTY_DEFINE_OFFSET(C, P)        \
                                               \
     method_property_get<   V                   \
                          , R                   \
                          , C                   \
                          , &C::P##_offset      \
                          , &C::GM              \
                          >           P
```

Now using the property is quite clean:

```
class Date
{
public:
  WeekDay get_DayOfWeek() const;
  . . .
public:
  METHOD_PROPERTY_GET(WeekDay, WeekDay, Date, get_DayOfWeek, DayOfWeek);
  . . .
```

Note that the macro does not affect the access of the offset method. I know it seems quite popular these days to do so—mentioning no names, you understand—but I don't like placing access control specifiers into macros. Macros are bad enough at hiding things; masking access control seems way beyond the pale. It's possible, though not likely, that you might wish to make a property `protected`, so to stipulate `public` in the macro would be a mistake. In any case, making hidden accessibility changes violates the principles outlined in section 17.1. The slight downside is that the offset method will be public, and on some code sensing development environments this will clutter the containing class "interface," but that's insufficient motivation to make hidden access control changes.

It could even be made a little bit clearer, if we were to use the `class_type` idiom from section 18.5.3 to replace the macro parameter C, as this would obviate the need to specify the class type to the macro:

```
class Date
{
public:
  typedef Date class_type;
  . . .
  METHOD_PROPERTY_GET(WeekDay, WeekDay, get_DayOfWeek, DayOfWeek);
```

Despite this improvement, the fuller definition is the one used. Even though I religiously define a `class_type`, it's not a widely accepted practice, and METHOD_PROPERTY_GET will be less intrusive if it does not make extra demands on its user to change other parts of their classes.

35.4.2   method_property_set

There's really very little to say about the write-only version, given what we've seen with `field_property_set` and `method_property_get`, so I'll just show you the definition of the `method_property_set` template:

Listing 35.15

```
template< typename V              /* The actual property value type */
        , typename R              /* The reference type */
        , typename C              /* The enclosing class */
        , ptrdiff_t (*PFnOff)() /* Pointer to fn providing offset of property
          in container */
        , void (C::*PFnSet)(R ) /* Pointer to a member function taking R */
        >
class method_property_set
{
  . . .
public:
  /// Provides write-only access to the property
  class_type &operator =(R value)
  {
    ptrdiff_t offset = (*PFnOff)();
    C         *pC     = (C*)((byte_t*)this - offset);
    (pC->*PFnSet)(value);
    return *this;
  }
// Members
private:
  V m_value;
};
```

It employs the same mechanism of using static offset method and instance assignment method.

35.4.3   method_property_getset

We know that a combination of the read-only and write-only field properties is a waste of time, but the same cannot be said of method properties, where the read and/or write methods can provide translation and validation. Hence the logical step is to combine the definitions of the `method_property_get` and `method_property_set` templates, into the `method_property_getset` template, as shown in Listing 35.16.

Listing 35.16

```
template< typename V              /* The actual property value type */
        , typename RG             /* The get reference type */
        , typename RS             /* The set reference type */
        , typename C              /* The enclosing class */
        , ptrdiff_t (*PFnOff)()   /* Pointer to function providing offset */
```

```
       , RG (C::*PFnGet)() const /* Pointer to a const member function
       returning R */
       , void (C::*PFnSet)(RS)   /* Pointer to a member function taking R */
     >
class method_property_getset
{
  . . .
// Accessors
public:
  /// Provides read-only access to the property
  operator RG () const
  {
    ptrdiff_t offset  = (*PFnOff)();
    C         *pC     = (C*)((byte_t*)this - offset);

    return (pC->*PFnGet)();
  }
  /// Provides write-only access to the property
  class_type &operator =(RS value)
  {
    ptrdiff_t offset  = (*PFnOff)();
    C         *pC     = (C*)((byte_t*)this - offset);
    (pC->*PFnSet)(value);
    return *this;
  }
// Members
private:
  V m_value;
};
```

Other than the fact that there are two instance method pointers, in addition to the single off-set class method pointer, the other notable difference is that there are two reference type parameters, one for writing and one for reading. This is the case where the value is to be assigned as one type and accessed by another, as was mentioned when we discussed method_property_get.

The corresponding convenience macro is defined thus:

```
#define METHOD_PROPERTY_GETSET(V, RG, RS, C, GM, SM, P) \
                                                        \
  METHOD_PROPERTY_DEFINE_OFFSET(C, P)                   \
                                                        \
  method_property_getset< V                             \
                        , RG                            \
                        , RS                            \
                        , C                             \
                        , &C::P##_offset                \
                        , &C::GM                        \
```

```
                      ,   &C::SM                        \
                 >           P
```

Let's look at another property for our `Date` class, one that uses a read/write property:

Listing 35.17

```
class Date
{
public:
  int    get_DayOfMonth() const
  {
    return DayOfMonth.m_value;
  }
  void   set_DayOfMonth(int day)
  {
    if(!ValidateDay(. . ., day)) // Do some validation
    . . .
  }
  . . .
  METHOD_PROPERTY_GETSET(int, int, int, Date, get_DayOfMonth, set_DayOfMonth,
  DayOfMonth);
  . . .
};
```

I hope by now you're starting to see how kind of neat this stuff can be.

35.4.4   Loop the Loop!

One point worth noting is that in the original versions of the `field_property_set` and `method_property_set` templates I defined a `private` implicit conversion operator, in order that the containing class implementation could have the convenience of access to the property's internal value, as in:

Listing 35.18

```
template <. . .>
class method_property_set
{
private:
  operator R () const
  {
    return m_value;
  }
  . . .
};

class Container
{
public:
```

```
      method_property_set<int, . . .>    Prop;
public:
   void SomeMethod()
   {
      int pr_val = Prop; // Uses the implicit conversion operator
   }
   . . .
};
```

I'm sure you've guessed the gotcha. When using the `method_property_getset`, such a call would call back into the containing class to acquire the proxied value. If the implicit conversion was inside that method, we're in an infinite loop. Naturally, it seemed prudent to remove this facility from all other classes, in which it was harmless, for consistency. The same thing could apply in the reverse case so the assignment operator is also removed from get property templates.

35.4.5   method_property_get_external

External method properties are used when the containing class needs to represent the public face of its internal data in a different form. Our original `Date` class is a very good example of this. The implementations of the external method properties borrow the same offset and member function techniques from the internal equivalents, but are simplified since they do not have any fields themselves. We'll use that fact to our advantage later.

The `method_property_get_external` property template is defined as follows:

Listing 35.19
```
template< typename R              /* The reference type */
        , typename C              /* The enclosing class */
        , ptrdiff_t   (*PFnOff)() /* Pointer to fn providing offset of property
          in container */
        , R (C::*PFnGet)() const  /* Pointer to a const member function
          returning R */
        >
class method_property_get_external
{
public:
   typedef method_property_get_external<R, C, PFnOff, PFnGet>  class_type;
public:
   /// Provides read-only access to the property
   operator R () const
   {
      ptrdiff_t offset  = (*PFnOff)();
      C         *pC     = (C*)((byte_t*)this - offset);
      return (pC->*PFnGet)();
   }
// Not to be implemented
private:
```

```
  // This method is hidden in order to prevent users of this class from
  // becoming familiar with using operator = on the property instances
  // from within the containing class, since doing so with
  // method_property_getset<> would result in an infinite loop.
  class_type &operator =(R value);
};
```

This can be plugged into the original version of the Date class, using the appropriate macro, as in:

Listing 35.20

```
class Date
{
public:
  . . .
  WeekDay get_DayOfWeek() const
  {
    return static_cast<WeekDay>(localtime(&m_time)->tm_wday);
  }
// Properties
public:
  METHOD_PROPERTY_GET_EXTERNAL(WeekDay, Date, get_DayOfWeek, DayOfWeek);
private:
  time_t  m_time;
};
```

The property has no fields of its own, and delegates access to Date's get_DayOfWeek() method. get_DayOfWeek() uses the m_time member to convert to the day of the week. (Remember, this is for illustrative purposes; it's not exactly an efficient way of implementing a date/time class.)

External method properties are very flexible, by virtue of the fact that they implement a decoupling between the containing class's fields and its public (property) interface. They are just as speed efficient as internal method properties, since the mechanism is virtually identical. The one problem is that, as we discussed earlier in the chapter, they have non-zero size, even though they have no member variables—there's no EMO (see section 35.2.2). The minimum size that the compiler can give them is, of course, one byte. Hence, our Date class increases by 1 byte per property. This is not appealing.

However, remember that we saw in section 1.2.4 how a union can be used to constrain types to be POD (see Prologue). We can use this in reverse. Since our parameterized external method templates have no members, and do not derive from any other types (which might have various non-POD attributes), we are free to place them in a union. Hence,

```
class Date
{
// Properties
public:
```

```
union
{
  METHOD_PROPERTY_GET_EXTERNAL(WeekDay, Date, get_DayOfWeek, DayOfWeek);
  METHOD_PROPERTY_GET_EXTERNAL(int, Date, get_Year, Year);
  . . .
};

};
```

There's still a price to be paid, since the union itself cannot be given a zero size. But the price is minimal—1 byte, of course—and is paid once, irrespective of how many properties there are. It's not perfect, but it's pretty close[6].

There's one slight complication—isn't there always?—in that the macro-union composition shown above would not work. Remember that the macros contain within themselves the offset function. Clearly, it is not valid to define the offset function within the union, as it will then be a member of the union, and not the containing class. Since the union is anonymous, we'd have a hell of a time determining its name for the other parts of the macro in a portable way. This can be solved by separating the offset function definition and the property definition into two macros. We saw the METHOD_PROPERTY_DEFINE_OFFSET() macro in section 35.4.1, and the other is defined as follows:

```
#define METHOD_PROPERTY_GET_EXTERNAL_PROP(R, C, GM, P)  \
                                                         \
  method_property_get_external< R                        \
                              , C                        \
                              , &C:: P##_offset##C()      \
                              , &C::GM                    \
                              >        P
```

Armed with these macros the Date class can be rewritten as:

Listing 35.21
```
class Date
{
// Properties
public:
  METHOD_PROPERTY_DEFINE_OFFSET(Date, DayOfWeek)
  METHOD_PROPERTY_DEFINE_OFFSET(Date, Year)
  union
  {
    METHOD_PROPERTY_GET_EXTERNAL_PROP(WeekDay, Date, get_DayOfWeek, DayOfWeek);
    METHOD_PROPERTY_GET_EXTERNAL_PROP(int, Date, get_Year, Year);
    . . .
  };
```

---

[6]In fact, you could share the union with *one* of the enclosing class's members, as long as it is of POD type (see Prologue), and thereby achieve zero overhead.

```
     . . .
};
```

And that's it! It's speed efficient, and it only wastes 1 byte per containing class, irrespective of the number of properties.

35.4.6   method_property_set_external

Once again, we've seen enough in the previous property types to comprehend the implementation of `method_property_set_external`, so I'll just show it to you:

Listing 35.22

```
template< typename R              /* The reference type */
        , typename C              /* The enclosing class */
        , ptrdiff_t (*PFnOff)() /* Pointer to function providing offset in
          container */
        , void (C::*PFnSet)(R ) /* Pointer to a member function taking R */
        >
class method_property_set_external
{
public:
  typedef method_property_set_external<R, C, PFnOff, PFnSet>  class_type;
public:
  /// Provides write-only access to the property
  method_property_set_external &operator =(R value)
  {
    ptrdiff_t offset  = (*PFnOff)();
    C         *pC     = (C*)((byte_t*)this - offset);

    (pC->*PFnSet)(value);

    return *this;
  }
};
```

Although we've struggled to think of a real use for the previous write-only property types, this type may well have a compelling application. When dealing with container types, it is often the case that the container maintains two separate concepts regarding its element storage. The size of the container indicates how many elements it contains, whereas the capacity indicates how much memory is allocated for actual and potential element storage. Although most modern container libraries that provide public access to the capacity provide both read and write access (e.g., `std::vector`'s `reserve()` and `capacity()`), there's a school of thought that says that allowing client code access to the amount of storage of a container it is using is a breaking of that container's encapsulation and a coupling of the client code and the container's internal implementation. One (somewhat contrived, I admit) way to enable the client code to advise the container of the demands of its context, without becoming dependent on the advice, would be to implement a write-only `Capacity` property, using the `method_property_set_external` template, as in:

Listing 35.23

```
class Container
{
public:
  size_t get_Size() const;
  void   set_Capacity(size_t minElements);
// Properties
public:
  union
  {
    METHOD_PROPERTY_GET_EXTERNAL_PROP(size_t, Container, get_Size, Size);
    METHOD_PROPERTY_SET_EXTERNAL_PROP(size_t, Container, set_Capacity,
    Capacity);
  };
};
```

There are other, diagnostic, uses of write-only properties, which we'll see at the end of the chapter.

35.4.7   method_property_getset_external

As with `method_property_getset`, `method_property_getset_external` is a combination of its get and set brethren, and has corresponding macros `METHOD_PROPERTY_GETSET_EXTERNAL()`, which defines the property and its offset function, and `METHOD_PROPERTY_GETSET_EXTERNAL_PROP()`, which defines only the property itself.

Listing 35.24

```
template< typename RG            /* The reference type */
        , typename RS            /* The reference type */
        , typename C             /* The enclosing class */
        , ptrdiff_t (*PFnOff)()  /* Pointer to function providing offset in
          container */
        , RG (C::*PFnGet)() const /* Pointer to a const member function
          returning R */
        , void (C::*PFnSet)(RS ) /* Pointer to a member function taking R */
        >
class method_property_getset_external
{
  . . .
public:
  /// Provides read-only access to the property
  operator RG () const
  {
    ptrdiff_t offset  = (*PFnOff)();
```

```
      C           *pC      = (C*)((byte_t*)this - offset);
      return (pC->*PFnGet)();
    }
    /// Provides write-only access to the property
    class_type &operator =(RS value)
    {
      ptrdiff_t offset   = (*PFnOff)();
      C           *pC      = (C*)((byte_t*)this - offset);
      (pC->*PFnSet)(value);
      return *this;
    }
};
```

We'd use this in our `Date` class for read/write properties:

Listing 35.25

```
class Date
{
// Properties
public:
  METHOD_PROPERTY_DEFINE_OFFSET(Date, DayOfWeek)
  METHOD_PROPERTY_DEFINE_OFFSET(Date, DayOfMonth)
  METHOD_PROPERTY_DEFINE_OFFSET(Date, Year)
  union
  {
    METHOD_PROPERTY_GET_EXTERNAL_PROP(WeekDay, Date, get_DayOfWeek, DayOfWeek);
    METHOD_PROPERTY_GET_EXTERNAL_PROP(int, Date, get_Year, Year);
    METHOD_PROPERTY_GETSET_EXTERNAL_PROP(int, int, Date, get_DayOfMonth
                                    , set_DayOfMonth, DayOfMonth);
    . . .
  };
  . . .
};
```

You can see that we're just about done providing our putative `Date` class with all the properties that the original notional definition had. The only thing remaining is to implement class (static) properties.

35.5   Static Properties

As was observed at the start of this chapter, even those compilers that support properties as an extension do not provide class (static) properties. So even if you don't need to use the templates discussed in the intervening sections, you may still need to use the following techniques.

As with instance properties, static properties come in field and/or method flavors.

35.5.1   Static Field Properties

Implementing static field properties can be done in exactly the same way as, for instance, field properties, using the `field_property_get/set` templates, as in:

Listing 35.26

```
// SocketBuffer.h
class SocketBuffer
{
// Construction
public:
  SocketBuffer(. . . )
  {
    ++NumInstances.m_value; // Note: not thread-safe
  }
// Properties
public:
  static field_property_get<int, int>    NumInstances;

  . . .
};


// SocketBuffer.cpp
/* static */ field_property_get<int, int>    SocketBuffer::NumInstances(0);
```

This is used just as any other static field would be:

```
void monitor_proc(. . .)
{
  int bufferCount = SocketBuffer::NumInstances;

  . . .
}
```

35.5.2   Internal Static Method Properties

The instance method property mechanisms do not transfer to static method properties, since a static method property clearly cannot operate on an instance. Thankfully, this results in much simplified definitions.

I'm only going to show you the read/write versions, as the ground's been pretty much covered in previous sections. The internal version looks like:

Listing 35.27

```
template< typename V
        , typename RG
        , typename RS
        , typename C
        , RG (*PFnGet)(void)
        , void (*PFnSet)(RS )
        >
class static_method_property_getset
{
  . . .
// Accessors
```

```
public:
  operator RG() const
  {
    return (*PFnGet)();
  }
  static_method_property_getset &operator =(RS value)
  {
    (*PFnSet)(value);
    return *this;
  }
// Members
private:
  V m_value;
};
```

We might use an internal static method property in the Date class to count the number of instances created, as in:

Listing 35.28

```
class Date
{
public:
  Date(Date const &rhs)
    : m_time(rhs.m_time)
  {
    ++InstanceCount.m_value; // Note: not thread-safe
  }
public:
  static int get_InstanceCount()
  {
    return InstanceCount.m_value;
  }
public:
  static static_method_property_get<int, int, Date, &get_InstanceCount>
  InstanceCount;
  . . .
};
```

Since the property is static, it needs to be defined:

```
static_method_property_get<int
                          ,  int
                          ,  Date
                          ,  &Date::get_InstanceCount
                          >       Date::InstanceCount;
```

The constructors are public, since it has to be used at file scope. Since you are the one who'll be calling the constructor for the properties of your containing class, this doesn't represent any lack of security. The full qualification of the method name is mandatory, since it's outside the context of the class definition.

Because we're not concerned about the size of static properties, the only advantage to using internal method properties over field properties is the opportunity for validation and translation of the actual field to and from the client code.

35.5.3 External Static Method Properties

When we don't need internal fields, we get the simplest of all the method properties. Again, I'm only showing the read/write version for brevity:

Listing 35.29
```
template< typename RG
        , typename RS
        , RG (*PFnGet)(void)
        , void (*PFnSet)(RS )
        >
class static_method_property_getset_external
{
// Accessors
public:
  operator RG() const
  {
    return (*PFnGet)();
  }
  static_method_property_getset_external &operator =(RS value)
  {
    (*PFnSet)(value);
    return *this;
  }
};
```

`static_method_property_get_external` and `static_method_property_set_external` correspond to the read and write two halves of this type's implementation. Now we can at last define the Now property for Date:

Listing 35.30
```
class Date
{
public:
  static Date get_Now()
  {
    return Date(time(NULL));
  }
public:
  static static_method_property_get_external<Date, &get_Now>  Now;
```

```
    . . .
};
```

```
static_method_property_get_external<Date, &get_Now>    Date::Now;
```

and would be used as follows:

```
Date   date = Date::Now;
```

   With both the static method properties I've shown, I've not used macros, since they were not necessitated by any offset functions. However, for consistency you may wish to use them.

35.6   Virtual Properties

This simple mechanism does not allow us to have virtual properties directly, but it's very easy to provide them. As we saw with the `Container::set_Capacity` method, we would define a nonvirtual method that provided the correct syntax, and this would then call a virtual method. Any deriving classes would override the virtual method, and the property would act virtually.

Listing 35.31
```
class Super
{
  . . .
public:
  int get_Thing() const
  {
     return get_ThingValue();
  }
public:
  method_property_get_external<int, Super, . . .>    Thing;
protected:
  virtual int get_ThingValue() const = 0;
};

class Sub
  : public Super
{
protected:
  virtual int get_ThingValue() const
  {
     . . .
  }
};

Sub    sub;
Super &super = sub;
int    i = super.Thing; // Uses Sub::get_ThingValue()
```

This technique can also be used to adapt existing nonvirtual read or write methods to make them compatible with the function signature requirements of the method property templates, so your property access methods simply act as shims (see Chapter 20).

35.7   Property Uses

At this point you may be thinking: nice technique, but is it anything more than syntactic sugar, with an occasional 1-byte tariff for the luxury? Well, yes and no. It is mainly syntactic nicety, although not to be discounted for that, but there are other uses for properties that have more weight, and where properties can do things that other techniques cannot. Indeed, it is the very fact that they translate semantic complexity into syntactic simplicity that can be a very powerful tool.

35.7.1   Genericity

Consider that you work with two kinds of simple rectangle structures:

```
struct IntRect
{
   int left, right, top, bottom;
};
```

```
struct FloatRect
{
   double left, right, top, bottom;
};
```

You may use several complex templates to work with these structures, whose implementations rely on the public accessibility of the fields `left`, `right`, `top`, and `bottom`. Now you need to define a class that notionally represents a rectangle, but whose coordinates are defined in a different manner, perhaps as the two points top-left and bottom-right, or whose values are only obtainable via a method call. In this case, you would need to rewrite your algorithms, either to use traits or shims (see Chapter 20). But they may not be your templates, or the potential for introducing error into them is just too risky at your stage in the project. Either way, it can represent an unattractive amount of effort, and you need a much quicker solution. One alternative is to use properties. Simply enhance your new rectangle, say `DynRect`, type, and give it `left`, `right`, `top` and `bottom` properties.

```
class DynRect
{
   . . .
   union
   {

      METHOD_PROPERTY_GET_EXTERNAL_PROP(int, DynRect, get_left, left);
      METHOD_PROPERTY_GET_EXTERNAL_PROP(   . . . // right, top, bottom
};
```

```
      . . .
};
```

Even if you have to use external properties, and paying the 1-byte space cost is not justifiable in the long run, you have a robust and, except for a potential additional memory cost, efficient short-term solution to take you past your next milestone. (Of course, this being the real world, you then run the risk of it never being retro-optimized, but maybe a successful suboptimal product is the best of the alternatives open to your company at that time.)

35.7.2   Type Substitution for Diagnostics

As a diagnostic measure, consider the case where you have a *lot* of legacy code that uses struct tm and that there are occasional date/time errors cropping up in your testing. It would not be hard to create your own tm-like type, where the "fields" are replaced by validating properties (see Listing 35.32), and then to plug this into your existing code.

Listing 35.32

```
class tm_spy
{
  . . .
  method_property_getset_external<int, int
                         , tm_spy
                         , &sec_offset
                         , &get_sec
                         , &set_sec
                         >                        tm_sec;
  . . .
  method_property_getset_external<int, yday
                         , tm_spy
                         , &yday_offset
                         , &get_yday
                         , &set_yday
                         >                        tm_yday;
};
```

If it's your source, then all you'll have to do is make a single typedef change in a root header, right? However, even if it's someone else's code, and struct tm is dotted all around the place, you've several tractable, though not pretty, options. You could do a global search and replace to a single common typedef. This would probably be a nice idea anyway, since it would break nothing, and would facilitate any future changes with ease. Alternatively, you can define your class as a struct, and then #define tm tm_spy. Hokey stuff, indeed, but we're talking about diagnostics, rather than production code.

Anyway, I digress. The point is that once you've got your new type plugged in, you can run up the offending application, and your "smart" struct tm can detect any erroneous date manipulations. What you do when you catch them—logging to a file, printing to stderr, throwing an exception, assert()—is up to you. Thus, even in the cases where external properties are not the development solution due to their space inefficiency, they represent a useful diagnostic tool.

Alternatively, you may have a more benign requirement, which is simply to instrument the modifications to your structure. Again, properties can be the answer: just implement the write methods to log the activity.

35.8   Properties: Coda

It's been a big chapter, the biggest in the book, and I'm sure most of you will have been challenged one way or another. I know when creating these templates I had many brain aches, and coming back to them to document them here was also somewhat bewildering. I had several "why did I do that?" and "I can't remember writing this!" moments.

If you don't comprehend all the complexity in the method property implementations, I'm confident that you will at least appreciate the simplicity in the use of the templates, and to see how useful properties can be. I invite you to experiment with these templates and, fully informed of their strengths and caveats, to use them in your own work.

You should take care to note that it relies on the *friendly template* technique (see section 16.3), which is a not 100% standards compliant. I'm not playing down the significance of this nonstandard aspect, since you step outside the standard at your (future) peril. But all compilers (see Appendix A) support it apart from the widely respected and most highly standards compliant Comeau compiler in strict mode. And Comeau has recently added a compiler option—`friendT`—specifically to support this technique in strict mode, so I think we're safely hitching a ride on a train that can't be stopped.[7]

So, stick properties in your imperfect tool kit, and cross your fingers that the standards committee add them as a bona fide feature in the language, such that all this template flummery will eventually be moot.

---

[7]This is a case of *caveat emptor*. I'm not providing any guarantees, and I do not have inside knowledge of whether the standards body will legitimize friendly templates in C++-0x, merely a strong hunch.

APPENDIX A

Compilers and Libraries

A.1 Compilers

I used the following compilers from nine organizations in the research for the book:

- Borland C/C++ versions 5.5(1), 5.6 and 5.64
- CodePlay's VectorC version 2.06
- Comeau C++ versions 4.3.0.1 and 4.3.3
- Digital Mars C/C++ versions 8.30–8.38
- GCC versions 2.95 and 3.2
- Intel C/C++ versions 6.0, 7.0 and 7.1
- Metrowerks' CodeWarrior versions 7 and 8
- Microsoft's Visual C++ versions 6.0, 7.0, and 7.1
- Watcom version 12.0 (also known as Open Watcom 1.0)

Of these, the following are completely freely available:

- Borland (version 5.5(1))—available from *http://www.borland.com*
- GCC (all versions)—available from several sources; see *http://gcc.gnu.org/install/binaries.html*
- Watcom—available from *http://www.openwatcom.org/*

The following are freely available in some form:

- Digital Mars (all versions)—command-line tools only; from *http://www.digitalmars.com/*
- Intel (recent versions)—Linux versions only; *http://www.intel.com/*
- Visual C++ (version 7.1)—command-line tools only; *http://www.microsoft.com/*

The following are commercially available:

- CodePlay's VectorC—from *http://www.codeplay.com/*
- Comeau—from *http://www.comeaucomputing.com/*
- Metrowerks' CodeWarrior—from *http://www.metrowerks.com/*

Even when not freely available in some form, most of these vendors also offer free trials. I'm not going to offer any comparative advice in this forum, as there are plenty of comparison articles to be found by even halfhearted searches on the net. You've probably already picked up my impressions of most of them from the discussions throughout the book. In any case, I'm a big believer in using several compilers in your work, rather than sticking to just one (see Appendix D); every one of these compilers has offered useful warnings that all the others missed.

I'd like to thank all these vendors for being kind enough to supply me with their tools for use in the preparation of the book. It's great to see such a supportive spirit evinced by the smallest compiler teams (the smallest is one man: Digital Mars's Walter Bright) all the way up to some of the world's largest IT companies. It's much appreciated.

A.1.1   Compiler Optimizations

Wherever the performance of code has been measured, rather than just verifying correctness, all compilations have been conducted with maximum speed optimization and targeted (as much as is possible) at the host system processor, a Pentium IV. The settings for the compilers on Win32 were as follows:

Compiler	Optimization settings
Borland 5.6	-O2 -6
CodePlay VectorC 2.06	-nodebug -optimize 10 -max -target p4
Comeau 4.3.0.1 (Visual C++ 6.0 backend)	/O2 /Ox /Ob2 /G6
Digital Mars 8.38	-o+speed -6
GCC 3.2	-O7 -mcpu=i686
Intel 7.0	-Ox -O2 -Ob2 -GS -G7
Metrowerks CodeWarrior 8	-opt full -inline all,deferred -proc generic
Microsoft Visual C++ 6.0	-Ox -O2 -Ob2 -G6
Microsoft Visual C++ 7.1	-O2 -Ox -Ob2 -GL -G7
Watcom 12.0 (Open Watcom 1.0)	-oxtean -ei -6r -fp6

A.2   Libraries

Wherever possible, I've tried to use examples that are independent of any particular library. However, as the main author of the STLSoft libraries, I've naturally drawn many examples from that source. In most of those cases, I've attempted to keep their heritage quiet, not through some insincere modesty, but rather because I don't like to read books that are thinly veiled marketing vehicles for the author's own work. This is especially irritating when you're required to ingest a large quantity of substantive and interrelated components to understand each new topic discussed.

I have made the real nature of any libraries clear when I'm comparing implementations in performance terms, since I must facilitate any independent verification of the results that you readers may wish to make. They wouldn't be very trustworthy otherwise.

Other parts come from the libraries of my employer, Synesis Software *(http://
synesis.com.au/)*,[1] or from the Boost libraries (*http://boost.org/*), which is an open-source community of many of the leading names in C++. The remainder are repackaged (to avoid enmity)
mistakes I have witnessed in work for various clients, or are plucked from the ether as necessary
to illustrate the points.

A.2.1 Boost

Boost is the preeminent C++ library of recent times, and contains in its ranks many notable
figures in C++. It contains some very powerful components, a massive contributor base, and is
already seen as a de facto standard. It is likely that many of the new features of the next release
of the standard library will come from Boost.

The Boost libraries are included on the CD, and are also freely available online from the
Boost Web site at *http://www.boost.org/*.

A.2.2 STLSoft

STLSoft started life several years ago as a couple of STL-like sequence containers wrapped
around file-system enumeration and Win32 registry APIs. Its libraries have grown steadily over
the last few years and now cover a number of technology and operating system areas. Many of
the parts of the libraries are derived from proprietary Synesis Software code, so it has a lot of
years behind it. The focus of STLSoft is efficiency, robustness, and portability, all the while
keeping faith with the rule of 100 percent header-only source. It has fewer members than Boost.

I don't know whether any STLSoft features will make it into the next standard library, but
then I've not made that a focus up to this point. One of the reviewers of Imperfect C++ is on the
standards committee, and has invited me to make some submissions, so who knows?

The STLSoft libraries are included on the CD, and are also freely available online from the
STLSoft Web site at *http://www.stlsoft.org/*.

A.2.3 Others

There are a few other useful libraries that I think are worth mentioning.

Open-RJ (*http://www.openrj.org/*) is a small, simple, structured file reader library, for the
Record-JAR [Raym2003] format, written by Greg Peet and myself. It's implemented in C, but
provides a host of mappings, including C++, D, Ruby and STL. It's a very simple format—the
library compiles to less than 5KB—but surprisingly useful.[2]

PThreads-win32 (*http://sources.redhat.com/pthreads-win32/*) is a GNU library that provides almost all the PTHREADS specification for the Win32 platform. It's extremely useful
when you are writing for UNIX and need to work on a Windows machine. Of course, if your

---

[1]This code base has been building since my Ph.D. work in 1992–95. As such, there is a *lot* of unpleasant and arcane
stuff in there. If you have significant criticisms of any Synesis code shown in the book or included on the CD, please
temper your tendency toward any triumphant bug reporting with the caveat that I probably already know about it, have
put it on a to-do list, and have eschewed any reproduction of such affront in any newer software (such as STLSoft).
Being a chatty kind of chap I am, of course, happy to hear from you, but you may want to save yourself the effort.

[2] The Open-RJ website, and the HTML content of the Imperfect C++ CD, was generated by Ruby scripts from Open-RJ
content files. It's also used for configuration data for the Arturius compiler multiplexer (see Appendix C).

laptop dual boots Linux, then you may not need it for that reason, but it can still be useful for writing tools for both platforms with single code sets.

RangeLib (*http://www.rangelib.org/*) is the home of the Ranges concept, as developed by John Torjo and myself. The Ranges concept is still developing and, along with Boost and STL-Soft implementations, it may also slip across to other languages. But we'll have to wait and see on that one (see Epilogue).

recls (*http://www.recls.org/*)—for *rec*ursive *ls*—is a platform-independent recursive file-system search library of mine that I originally wrote due to constant frustration at endlessly coding the same old boilerplate every time I needed to conduct recursive searches. It has become an exemplar for my *C/C++ Users Journal* column, "Positive Integration," which describes techniques for integrating C and C++ with other languages and technologies. The library is implemented (using the STLSoft libraries) in C++, but provides a C interface to the outside world (see Chapters 7 and 8). It continues to evolve into other recursive searching areas, and has mappings to COM, D, Java, .NET, Ruby, and STL among an ever-growing list.

zlib (*http://www.zlib.org/*) is probably the most famous freely available compression library. It's very easy to use, and thankfully accepts external memory allocators (see section 32.3), of which I heartily approve.

A.3 Other Resources

All of the following resources are useful for C++ programmers and/or have proved useful to me during the research and writing of this book.

A.3.1 Journals

BYTE (*http://www.byte.com/*)
C/C++ Users Journal (*http://www.cuj.com/*)
CVu (*http://www.accu.org/*)
Dr. Dobb's Journal (*http://www.ddj.com/*)
Overload (*http://www.accu.org/*)
The C++ Source (*http://www.artima.com/cppsource/*)
Windows Developer Network (*http://www.windevnet.com/*)

A.3.2 Other Languages

D (*http://www.digitalmars.com/d*)
Java (*http://java.sun.com/*)
.NET (*http://microsoft.com/net/*)
Perl (*http://cpan.org/; http://perl.org/*)
Python (*http://python.org/*)
Ruby (*http://ruby-lang.org/*)

A.3.3 Newsgroups

comp.lang.c++.moderated
comp.std.c++

"Watch That Hubris!"

When I'd dodged real work (so I could spend more time cycling, actually!) for as long as I could muster, and finished my Ph.D., I went to work in "the real world." At the time, I can remember being confounded by potential employers who were neither particularly impressed with my list of qualifications, nor noticeably keen to offer the levels of remuneration—that's "compensation" to my friends in the United States—that my ego had in mind.[1] The problem seemed to be a lack of what they called "experience." I was dumbfounded at the shortsightedness, and railed against all the injustices for several weeks of job hunting. Why can't they just see I'm so damn clever, and give me lots of money?

Of course, these years of hard-won experience later, I absolutely appreciate the importance of experience. I've worked with highly qualified people who had nary a practical bone in their body, and with people with few or no qualifications who were brilliant engineers. I am forced to work on occasion with people who don't care about doing a quality job, and aren't in the slightest bit interested in learning anything new or better. These folks are a blot on our profession. The shabby nature of the software development industry cannot be entirely laid at the door of ignorant managers, tricky marketers, and impatient users. A lot of it is people who would be better off counting paper clips and looking out the window in an industry where their malpractice would do less harm—not in the building of the most complex creations of human imagination.

Ho hum. As my mum has been wont to say far too many times to me over the years: "Watch that hubris!" So here we go. In the spirit of humility, and just to plain amuse you, I'm going to detail some of the more pitiful casualties of my progression from hapless neophyte to someone that knows a little bit about a couple of things. If you recognize any of your own crimes in my experiences, shush! Just keep quiet, and let me take the heat.

B.1 Operator Overload

One of the first things new C++ programmers get turned onto is operator overloading, which is ironic because it's probably one of the most pervertible parts of the language.

My first string class had an enormous public interface, of which the following extract details only the very worst bits:

```
class DLL_CLASS String // Exports all members indiscriminately
  : public BaseObject // A polymorphic string . . . ?
```

---

[1] I learned a hard lesson in negotiation when accepting the job I chose. The manager said, "How much are you looking for?" I summoned my most devious cunning and countered with "somewhere between £20,000 and £25,000," and before my heart had pulsed another beat he'd replied with a final "We'd like to offer you the job for £20,000." I've never done that again.

```
{
    . . .
    // Makes the string nInitLen length, filled with cDef
    String &Set(int nInitLen, char cDef = '\0');
    . . .
    Bool    SetLowerAt(int nAt); // Returns true if was upper
    Bool    SetUpperAt(int nAt); // Returns true if was lower
    . . .
    String &operator =(int nChopAt); // Set length to nChopAt
    . . .
    String &operator +=(int nAdd); // Increase length by nAdd
    . . .
    String &operator -=(int nReduce); // Reduce length by nReduce
    // Reduces length to last matching character
    String &operator -=(char cChopBackTo);
    . . .
    // Rotate (with wrap) the string contents left/right
    String &operator >>=(int nRotateBy);
    String &operator <<=(int nRotateBy);
    . . .
    String &operator --();    // Makes all characters lower case
    String &operator --(int); // Makes all characters lower case
    String &operator ++();    // Makes all characters upper case
    String &operator ++(int); // Makes all characters upper case
    . . .
    // Returns a local static with converted value
    static String NumString(long lVal);
    . . .
    operator const char *() const; // Implicit conversion to c-str
    . . .
    operator int() const; // Implicit conversion, returning length
    . . .
    // Returns an element by value
    const char operator [](int nIndex) const;
    . . .
    String &operator ^=(char cPrep);          // Prepend char
    String &operator ^=(const char *pcszPrep); // Prepend string
    . . .
};
```

It'd be hard to imagine doing a worse job—a case of can be done, will be done. I'll be terribly saddened if your reaction to this was anything but violently antipathetic. Amazingly, I managed to get the addition operators correct: defined as free functions and implemented in terms of `operator +=()` (see section 25.1.1).

```
String operator +(const String &String1,const String &String2);
String operator +(const String &String1,const char *pcszAdd);
```

```
String operator +(const char *pcszAdd,const String &String2);
String operator +(const String &String1,char cAdd);
String operator +(char cAdd,const String &String1);
```

Scarily, recent postings on one of the newsgroups I follow, from a couple of people who are generally impressively cluey, said they thought "`operator ++()` means make upper" was a good idea! Let's hope they just hadn't thought it through.

B.2 DRY Rued Yesterday

Around the time I wrote the string class, I also wrote my first C++ linked-list. I just loved the idea of encapsulation. Alas, my enduring love for the *Don't Repeat Yourself* (DRY) principal [Hunt2000], which dictates that no item of information should be kept in more than one place, was naively misapplied in this class since I implemented the `GetCount()` method to do a count from the head to the tail every time it was called. Not exactly *O(1)*.

I dare not even talk to you about the self-balancing tree!

B.3 Paranoid Programming

One of the constant paranoias in software engineering is the protection of intellectual property, and I've fallen under this particular spell in the past. Here's a little slice of horror.

The Win32 GUI programmers among you will be well aware of the features and shortcomings of the List-View common control. My first stab at enhancing them was done via MFC, multiple inheritance, and some truly evil tricks. The extended features—colored subitem text and background; per subitem user-data and images; 2D walking edit fields; and so on—were provided by the mixin class `CColouredList`.[2]

```
class DLL_CLASS CColouredListView
  : public CListView
  , public CColouredList
{
  . . .


class DLL_CLASS CColouredListCtrl
  : public CWnd
  , public CColouredList
{
  . . .
```

Without having any idea as to whether this component would even be desirable to any potential clients, I nonetheless spent great effort in hiding the implementation of the ever-so-smart control enhancements, by virtue of a delightful artifice:

---

[2]Note the naïve use of the `CClassName` convention. I've heard that this was created to disambiguate the MFC core classes from any that users would create, but no one bothered to mention it to users or the folks writing the "How to write industrial strength applications in MFC in 24 hrs" books. This horrible convention persists in some areas to this day.

```
class _CLCInfoBlock; // Forward declaration
#define _CLC_RESBLK  (208)

class DLL_CLASS CColouredList
  : public COwnerDrawCtrl
{
  . . . // Many, many methods
// Members
protected:
  HWND            &m_hWnd;             // HWND reference.
  _CLCInfoBlock   &m_block;            // Info block.
private:
  BYTE            m_at[_CLC_RESBLK];   // reserved.
};
```

I'm sure you've guessed the rest: the class `_CLCInfoBlock` is defined within the implementation file of the `CColouredList` class. In the constructor of `CColouredList`, an instance of `_CLCInfoBlock` is placement constructed into the `m_at` storage:

```
CColouredList::CColouredList(HWND &hWnd)
  : m_hWnd(hWnd)
  , m_block(*new(m_at) _CLCInfoBlock)
{}
```

Never mind the fact that an array of bytes is not guaranteed to have correct alignment for the in-place construction of a user-defined type, why on earth 208? The whole thing's just so awful. This amounts to malpractice in any reasonable estimation, and I can't conceive of anyone purchasing anything that looks like `CColouredList`.

B.4   To Insanity, and Beyond!

Several years ago, I was tasked with writing a general-purpose library to supplant the standard library IOStreams, strings and containers for an existing, specific custom-database subsystem, and to then rewrite the existing solution to use the new classes, without changing the design or public interface of the subsystem—which had never shipped outside the development team— one iota.

By the end of our efforts on the project, we'd got ourselves so tangled up that we reached the nutty situation of having to have a separate include file for every standard library function, for example, `fprintf.h`, and contextual typedefs (see section 18.2.2) for every conceivable thing relative to every conceivable permutation of standard versus custom library component.

My mistake was a simple but crucial one. I should have said that the design was poor, the initial implementation was poor, and the idea of rewriting a great many standard components to work with the performance-related constraints was a bad one that, even if done well, would take several months. Instead, I allowed my working relationship and personal friendship with the original implementer, who was also the development lead for the client, to cloud my judgment, and I just busied myself with getting on with the task. I did what we programmers tend to do all too readily, which is to get stuck into the challenge without working out whether the challenge is a worthy one. Kind of like spending five hours in a gym, when what you should be doing is a three-col climb in the French Alps or staying at home and having pizza with your kids!

I'm sure the story is all too familiar. What was supposed to be a three-week job was still only halfway finished nearly three months later, by which time our working relationship had soured, I was deeply troubled by the work itself and severely demotivated, and my colleague was ruining his previously second-to-none reputation within the company. My contract was up for review, and I was relieved to be no longer required as the project got the can. My erstwhile colleague left his employer of several years soon after, and was out of work for many months.

The lesson here's simple: if the Emperor's not wearing any clothes, then for heaven's sake say something! Don't stay silent and work in swill because you'll end up regretting it anyway.

Arturius

A few years ago, when I started to focus more on code portability, I conceived of a tool that would act as a compiler, but which would actually dispatch a requested compilation among a group of real compilers, to provide the best overall coverage of warnings and errors.

Thus was Arturius born. The name is an Old English form of Arthur, of Round Table fame. The idea is that the suite of one's installed compilers would represent a round table of wise knights, who would collectively proclaim wisdoms to which any single compiler could only hope to aspire.[1]

The Arturius project has had a number of partially completed forms in that time. Since the inception of the *Imperfect C++* idea, I have intended to make the Arturius project available along with the book, and once it was decided that the book would include a CD, Arturius was the first thing I thought to put on it.

It's ironic that in the writing of the book, I've had chance to review a great many of my own works, and Arturius itself was left looking more than a little shabby. Since the writing of the book will be completed two to three months before the completion of the CD, I plan to spend a good deal of this time rewriting Arturius such that it will be a fitting exemplar of the practices and techniques I have been banging on about. As such, therefore, the form that you will get on the CD will not reflect its current form, so I'm not going to set us both up for confusion by describing features now that will not reflect what you will find on the CD.

What I can do now, though, is describe my broad plans for the project. My current plans include the following:

- A command-line form that acts as a compiler-multiplexer for a configurable set of compilers
- A customizable input filter that will be able to translate a standard command-line option format to the compiler-specific equivalents
- A customizable output filter that will be able to translate the compiler-specific error and warning message formats into a standard format
- An output filter that will be able to coalesce semantically equivalent messages to ensure that redundant information is not passed to the end user
- A plug in for popular IDDEs that will enable use of the command-line version and/or compilers from other vendors

If the CD does not contain the realization of all these plans, you will be able to obtain them online—at *http://arturius.org/* or via *http://www.imperfectcplusplus.com/*—sometime soon, probably before the book is actually published.

---

[1] I admit it's a bit twee, but *Hey!* the domain name was available.

A P P E N D I X   D

The CD

When the publisher suggested I provide a CD along with the book, I had a sinking feeling. Now I'd have to show in full the techniques I'd merely described snapshots of in the book. People would be able to see my code in all its majesty, or conspicuous lack thereof, and there'd be no hiding behind "for brevity I have elided the remainder of the class" and similar statements.

Having thought about it for a while, though, I decided that it was actually a great opportunity. There are several advantages to me, the author, and to you, the reader. The CD contains space for me to include libraries, sample projects, the full suite of test programs used in the book research, some free C/C++ compilers, the Arturius project (see Appendix C), and several of my published articles that detail issues that only briefly touched on in the book.

Bearing in mind that the preparation of the CD will happen a month or two after the final version of the book, it is my intention that it will contain the following items:

- The Arturius compiler multiplexer—See Appendix C.
- Compilers—If you've currently only got access to one compiler, you'll be a bit stumped in testing out Arturius. Thankfully, several vendors have agreed to provide free and/or time-limited versions of their compilers, so you can get busy subjecting your code to the prognostications of a collective. I've also provided links to other useful free compilers that you can download.
- Libraries—Many of the components described in the book are gleaned from existing libraries—particularly the Boost and STLSoft libraries—so they're included here in their latest forms, along with distributions for some other libraries with which I've been involved (see Appendix A). I've also included links to other libraries that I think are worth your looking into.
- Articles—A selection of articles, kindly provided by CMP publishing, that expand on material covered in the book.
- Example and test programs—The full suite of test programs and makefiles used in the research for the book. This code is not pretty, but it exercises the various topics covered.
- Tools and scripts—Miscellaneous system/development tools and code manipulation scripts.

Please see the index.html in the root directory of the CD for the final details of the contents.

Epilogue

And that's it! Our journey is over, for the moment at least. If you've found it easy, then I hope that reflects the effort my editors and reviewers have expended in turning my interminable blither into something readable. If you've found it hard, then at least I hope you've enjoyed yourself along the way. In either case, you can take some light relief in Appendix B, when I get all confessional and show you some of my most heinous gaffes.

I hope that you'll take three things from this book:

1. That C++ is not perfect, but it is *very* powerful. Just selecting a few of the items at random—portable vtables, properties, ranges, true-typedefs, type tunnelling—we can plainly see some of the immense intrinsic power. For all its faults, there is clearly a *long* way to go before we exhaust the possibilities of this remarkable language.

2. That, for just about any problem, there exists a solution that is simple, powerful, efficient, flexible, or robust, or some combination thereof. The challenge to the Imperfect Practitioner is in choosing the right combinations.

3. That you can, by using appropriate discipline, libraries, and techniques, truly make the compiler your batman, and avoid falling afoul of the majority of C++'s imperfections. For the remainder, you'll just have to read more (books), write more (code), and build your experience. That's what the rest of us are doing.

And for those few crazy critters who might just want more . . .

Matthew Wilson will return in *Extended STL*.

Bibliography

Naturally, when writing a book that adopts such strong stances on a variety of issues, it'd be foolish not to have any giants on whose shoulders to stand. The books, articles, and online resources referenced here represent a partial but representative sample of many of the authoritative sources in the industry.

Books
Devour Whole

As I think I've mentioned occasionally throughout the book, I'm a doer rather than a reader. I also tend to think in pictures rather than in words; kinetic, more than visual or auditory, if you like. I was the irritating kid in school who did well in exams, but always seemed to be a dunce in class by virtue of always asking the teacher all the *what-if?* questions every lesson. Very few things get through my cranium from words alone.

As such, I consider that the books in this section, which are the only ones I've managed to read whole, have been written by authors who not only know a huge amount about their subjects, but are also extremely good communicators. The fact that most of these chaps represent some of the most famous thinkers in the business cannot be a coincidence.

[Asim1972] Isaac Asimov, *The Gods Themselves*, Granada. From the master of science fiction, this book is top-notch, thought-provoking science fiction, pleasingly unabashed by its own gently absurd concepts. Time-kettles, indeed! It also has a compelling analysis of time-travel cause and effect.

[Broo1995] Frederick P. Brooks, *The Mythical Man-Month*, Addison-Wesley. Someone talking sense, for a change. (I just love realists.)

[Dewh2003] Steve Dewhurst, *C++ Gotchas*, Addison-Wesley. I was reviewing this great book for Addison-Wesley during the early phases of planning *Imperfect C++*. Thankfully, Steve and I disagree on enough things that no one can reasonably suggest that I've stolen any of his ideas. In fact, I was able to take a counterpoint to Steve on several issues. No doubt the truth will lie somewhere between our positions.

[Glas2003] Robert L. Glass, *Facts and Fallacies of Software Engineering*, Addison-Wesley. This is the first book I ever read that truly said to me: "It's ok, you're not mad." The author takes to task much of the nonsense to which we are subject in our industry, and against which we often have nothing more than an instinctive recoil.[1] I'd advise anyone going for an interview for any software engineering post to ask their prospective managers whether they've read this book, and make the decision as to whether to accept the role accordingly.

[Hunt2000] Andrew Hunt and David Thomas, *The Pragmatic Programmer*, Addison-Wesley. More sense. (I also love pragmatists.)

[Kern1999] Kernighan and Pike, *The Practice of Programming*, Addison-Wesley. An effective and unpretentious guide to effective and unpretentious programming: brilliant!

---

[1] Wouldn't you love to share a carriage on a long rail-journey with Robert L. Glass and Fred P. Brooks?

[Krug1995] David J. Kruglinski, *Inside Visual C++, Volume 4*, Microsoft Press. This may seem a strange book to include, but it's just really well written, and helped me master the heaving leviathan that is MFC, in the days when people thought that was still a useful thing to have on one's CV.

[Lind1994] Peter van der Linden, *Deep C Secrets*, Prentice Hall. This is a great and funny book. It's the only book I've found that truly explains what's going on with pointers and arrays. The opinions on C++ are hopelessly out of date, if indeed they ever were valid, but it's a book on C, and as such it's the best one I've read. It's also very amusing, and contains a number of highly entertaining asides, along with a worthy tribute to Theakstone's Old Peculiar. Despite its age, I would recommend you buy it.

[Lipp1996] Stanley Lippman, *Inside the C++ Object Model*. This is *the* book from which to learn about multiple inheritance. And when you've done that, make sure you give it a wide berth henceforth.

[Meye1996] Scott Meyers, *More Effective C++*, Addison-Wesley; **[Meye1998]** Scott Meyers, *Effective C++,* 2nd edition, Addison-Wesley. These books are must-reads for any C++ practitioner, and rightly so. They may skip or skim over the gnarlier issues of C++ (e.g. threads, dynamic libraries, etc.) but they manage to cover so many other fundamental issues that one can forgive that. You won't get a job in most development teams if you've not read these two books, and for good reason.

[Stro1994] Bjarne Stroustrup, *The Design and Evolution of C++*, Addison-Wesley. I bought this on a shopping trip with my wife, and I'd read a third of it by the time we got home. My lack of forthcoming opinion failed to affect any of my wife's purchasing decisions, so there was no harm done. If you ever wondered *Why?* about C++, this book's probably got the answers. Let's hope he's planning a second edition soon, so we can find out what happened with `vector<bool>`!

[Sutt2000] Herb Sutter, *Exceptional C++*, Addison-Wesley. This is my favorite C++ book ever! It explains very complicated things in simple terms, and it's really short, as all good books should be. If I were as didactically efficient as Herb, *Imperfect C++* would probably be the size of a pocket street directory.

Help Yourself to Generous Portions

The books in this category may not have been read cover to cover by little old me, but I have digested them in large parts, and they are still good books, both technically and in terms of their ability to communicate their concepts.

[Aust1999] Matthew Austern, *Generic Programming and the STL*, Addison-Wesley. This was one of the first books on the STL, and is still one of the best. It explains everything in simple and accessible language, and is a pleasure to read. It could be more substantial, and it probably needs updating in light of changes over the last five years, but it's still well worth the price.

[Beck2000] Kent Beck, *Extreme Programming Explained*. There are many interesting ideas in this book. I've done pair programming on several occasions in the past and, with the right partner, it can be an incredibly productive thing. I'm not as convinced about some other aspects of XP, but it still makes for a stimulating read.

[Box1998] Don Box, *Essential COM*, Addison-Wesley. This is the definitive guide to COM, in all its naked splendor (without all those obfuscatory wrapper frameworks).

[Broc1995] Kraig Brockschmidt, *Inside OLE,* 2nd edition, Microsoft Press. Probably caused the biggest brain strain I ever had. Only a couple of years into C++ programming, I swallowed this beastie almost whole, and barely recovered. A useful, though incredibly hard to read, book.

[Bute1997] David R. Butenhof, *Programming with POSIX Threads*, Addison-Wesley. A great source of PTHREADS information, and surprisingly digestible, too.

[Gamm1995] Gamma, Helm, Johnson, Vlissides, *Design Patterns*, Addison-Wesley. If you ever want to be cruel to an experiential learner, give them this book and tell them there's a test at the end of the week. Despite my personal pain, I cannot but recommend this book heartily to you.

[Gerb2002] Richard Gerber, *The Software Optimization Cookbook*, Intel Press. If you ever wondered about the weird and wonderful goings-on inside processors, caches, pipelines, and the like, this book provides an excellent insight, from the perspective of the Intel architecture.

[Lako1996] John Lakos, *Large Scale C++ Software Design*, Addison Wesley. Despite being written before dynamic libraries, templates and threading achieved their current importance in the industry, this book contains a wealth of still-relevant information regarding physical coupling and large system design and production.

[Larm2000] Larman and Guthrie, *Java 2 Performance and Idiom Guide*, Prentice Hall. Whatever you feel about Java as a language/technology, this is a good book containing a great amount of information in a small size. If only the same could be said of … [snip].

[Lian1999] Sheng Liang, *The Java Native Interface*, Addison-Wesley. A great little book, describing the mechanism by which Java connects to C, and thereby to the outside world. It's the only bit of Java I like, although only a mother could love its syntax and performance characteristics.

[Meye1997] Bertrand Meyer, *Object-Oriented Software Construction*, Prentice Hall. The origin of *Design by Contract* (DbC) and a whole lot more. He may censure one of my friends, but I'd still recommend it to you. Like *The C++ Programming Language*, I can't imagine digesting it whole,[2] but it's a great reference.

[Raym2003] Eric Raymod, *The Art of UNIX Programming*, Addison-Wesley. With contributions from thirteen UNIX pioneers, this is a grand tour of UNIX programming philosophy and practice. An absolute must read for anyone, whatever operating system they inhabit.

[Rect1999] Brent Rector and Chris Sells, *ATL Internals*, Addison-Wesley. The definitive guide to ATL. Sure, it fails to make any real criticism of a many-flawed technology, but does a fair job of showing ATL's good sides, which are also many.

[Rich1997] Jeffrey Richter, *Advanced Windows*, Microsoft Press. This is a great source of Win32 system programming information. It's conspicuously silent about security, but addresses just about any other area of core Win32 you can think of.

[Stev1993] W. Richard Stevens, *Advanced Programming in the UNIX Environment*, Addison-Wesley. This is a great reference book that presents heaps of useful information in an outrageously readable style.

---

[2]If you've done so, please let me know, and I'll take my hat off to you (though not while descending the French Alps on the holiday I'm hoping to pay for with my first year's royalties . . .).

[Stev1998] W. Richard Stevens, *UNIX Network Programming, Volume 1,* 2nd edition, Addison-Wesley. Another must-have from the UNIX expert, just as readable and useful as *Advanced Programming in the UNIX Environment*.

[Stro1997] Bjarne Stroustrup, *The C++ Programming Language, Special Edition*, Addison-Wesley. As I mentioned in Chapter 25, this book contains an enormous number of important issues, nonchalantly suffused within the workaday progression through the vast areas of the language. Buy it; keep it in your bathroom; derive regular inspiration for new designs.

[Sutt2002] Herb Sutter, *More Exceptional C++*, Addison-Wesley. Maybe not *quite* as enjoyable as its predecessor, but it's still a must-have, must-read book.

Sprinkle Lightly

These books provide stimulating content and/or are clear and accessible references. Even if you agree with me that they're a little hard on the gums, they are well worth the investment, and contain information that is invaluable in anyone's quest to become an *Imperfect Practitioner*. Get your manager to buy them; you can tell him I said it was ok.

[Alex2001] Andrei Alexandrescu, *Modern C++ Design*, Addison-Wesley.

[Bulk1999] Dov Bulka and David Mayhew, *Efficient C++*, Addison-Wesley.

[Eddo1998] Guy Eddon and Henry Eddon, *Inside Distributed COM*, Microsoft Press.

[Hans1997] David R. Hanson, *C Interfaces and Implementations*, Addison-Wesley.

[Knut1997] Donald E. Knuth, *The Art of Computer Programming, Volume 1: Fundamental Algorithms*, Addison-Wesley.

[Lang2000] Angelika Langer and Klaus Kreft, *Standard C++ IOStreams and Locales,* Addison-Wesley.

[Lipp1998] Stanley Lippman (ed.), *C++ Gems*, Cambridge University Press.

[Joss1999] Nicolai Josuttis, *The C++ Standard Library*, Addison-Wesley.

[Kern1988] Brian Kernighan and Dennis Ritchie, *The C Programming Language*, Prentice Hall.

[Meye2001] Scott Meyers, *Effective STL*, Addison-Wesley.

[Muss2001] David R. Musser, Gillmer J. Derge, Atul Saini, *STL Tutorial and Reference Guide,* 2nd edition, Addison-Wesley.

[Rich2002] Jeffrey Richter, *Applied Microsoft .NET Framework Programming*, Microsoft Press.

[Robb2003] John Robbins, *Debugging Applications for .NET and Windows*, Microsoft Press.

[Rubi2001] Allessandro Rubini and Jonathon Corbet, *Linux Device Drivers,* 2nd edition, O'Reilly.

[Schm2000] Douglas Schmidt, Michael Stal, Hans Rohnert and Frank Buschmann, *Pattern-Oriented Software Architecture, Volume 2*, Wiley

[Sedg1998a] Robert Sedgewick, *Algorithms in C, Parts 1-4,* 3rd edition, Addison-Wesley.

[Sedg1998b] Robert Sedgewick, *Algorithms in C++, Parts 1-4,* 3rd edition, Addison-Wesley.

[Sedg2002] Robert Sedgewick, *Algorithms in C++, Part 5,* 3rd edition, Addison-Wesley.

[Vand2003] Daveed Vandevoorde and Nicolai Josuttis, *C++ Templates: The Comprehensive Guide*, Addison-Wesley.

Articles

Journal Articles

These are articles from in-print magazines, some of which are also available online via the given URLs.

[Alli1993] Chuck Allison, *Bit Handling in C++, Part 1,* C/C++ Users Journal, Volume 11 Number 12, December 1993; *http://www.freshsources.com/19930352.HTM*

[Alli1994] Chuck Allison, *Bit Handling in C++, Part 2,* C/C++ Users Journal, Volume 12 Number 5, May 1994; *http://www.freshsources.com/19930352.HTM*

[Brig2002] Walter Bright, *The D Programming Language,* Dr Dobb's Journal, #332, February 2002; *http://www.ddj.com/documents/s=2287/ddj0202c/*

[Meye2001b] Randy Meyers, *The New C: Why Variable Length Arrays?*, C/C++ Users Journal, Volume 19 Number 10, October 2001.

[Henn2002] Kevlin Henney, *String Things Along*, Application Development Advisor, Volume 6 Number 6, July/August 2002; *http://www.two-sdg.demon.co.uk/curbralan/papers/StringingThingsAlong.pdf*

[Jagg1999] Jon Jagger, *Compile Time Assertions in C*, CVu, Volume 11 Number 3, March 1999; *http://www.jaggersoft.com/pubs/CVu11_3.html*

[Lang2002] Angelika Langer and Klaus Kreft, *Secrets of Equals*, Java Solution, C/C++ Users Journal Supplement, April 2002.

[Same2003] Miro Samek, *An Exception or a Bug?,* C/C++ Users Journal, Volume 21 Number 8, August 2003; *http://www.quantum-leaps.com/writings.cuj/samek0308.pdf*

[Saks1996] Dan Saks, *C++ Theory and Practice: Mixing const with Type Names*, C/C++ Users Journal, Volume 14 Number 12, December 1996.

[Saks1999] Dan Saks, *Programming Pointers: const T vs. T const*, Embedded Systems Programming, Volume 12 Number 2, February 1999.

[Meye2000] Scott Meyers, *How Non-member Functions Improve Encapsulation*, C/C++ Users Journal, Volume 18 Number 2, February 2000; *http://www.cuj.com/documents/s=8042/cuj0002meyers/*

[Wils2001] Matthew Wilson, *Generating Out-of-Memory Exceptions*, Windows Developer's Journal, Volume 12 Number 5, May 2001.

[Wils2003a] Matthew Wilson, *Win32 Performance Measurement Options*, Windows Developer Network, Volume 2 Number 5, May 2003; *http://www.windevnet.com/documents/win0305a/*

[Wils2003b] Matthew Wilson, *Open-source Flexibility via Namespace Aliasing*, C/C++ Users Journal, Volume 21 Number 7, July 2003.

[Wils2003c] Matthew Wilson, *Generalized String Manipulation: Access Shims and Type Tunnelling*, C/C++ Users Journal, Volume 21 Number 8, July 2004; *http://www.cuj.com/documents/s=8681/cuj0308wilson/*

[Wils2003g] Matthew Wilson, *Inserter Function Objects for Windows Controls*, Windows Developer Network, Volume 2 Number 11, November 2003; *http://www.windevnet.com/wdn/issues/*

[Wils2004a] Matthew Wilson, *C/C++ Compiler Optimization*, Dr Dobb's Journal, #360, May 2004.

Online Articles and Other Material

These are articles and specifications available via the given URLs.

[Como-POD] *http://www.comeaucomputing.com/techtalk/#pod*

[Como-SOC] *http://www.comeaucomputing.com/faqs/genfaq.html#betterCgeneral*

[Como-SOP] *http://www.comeaucomputing.com/faqs/genfaq.html#whatcando*

[Itan-ABI] Itanium C++ ABI; *http://www.codesourcery.com/cxx-abi*

[Kaha1998] Kahan and Darcy, *How Java's Floating-point Hurts Everybody Everywhere*, *http://http.cs.berkeley.edu/~wkahan/JAVAhurt.pdf*

[Otto2004] Thorsten Ottosen, *Proposal to Add Design by Contract to C++*, 2004; *http://anubis.dkuug.dk/jtc1/sc22/wg21/docs/papers/2004/n1613.pdf*

[Schm1997] Schmidt, Harrison and Pryce, *Thread Specific Storage: An Object Behavioral Pattern for Accessing per-Thread State Efficiently*, 1997, *http://www.cs.wustl.edu/~schmidt/PDF/TSS-pattern.pdf*

[Stro2003] Bill Venners, *The C++ Style Sweet Spot: A Conversation with Bjarne Stroustrup, Part 1*, Artima Developer; *http://www.artima.com/intv/goldilocks.html*

[Stro-Web] Bjarne Stroustrup's FAQ; *http://www.research.att.com/~bs/bs_faq.html#really-say-that*

[Torj2003] John Torjo and Andrei Alexandrescu, *Enhancing Assertions*, C/C++ Users Journal Experts Forum, August 2003; *http://www.cuj.com/documents/s=8464/cujcexp0308alexandr/*

[WB-Email] Walter Bright, private email communication, 2003.

[Wils2003d] Matthew Wilson, *Flexible C++ #1: Efficient Integer To String Conversions, Part 2*, C/C++ Users Journal Experts Forum, September 2003; *http://www.cuj.com/documents/s=8840/cujexp0309wilson/*

[Wils2003e] Matthew Wilson, *C# Performance: Comparison with C, C++, D and Java, Parts 1 & 2*, Windows Developer Network, Special Online Supplement, Fall 2003; *http://www.windevnet.com/wdn/webextra/2003/0313/*

[Wils2003f] Matthew Wilson, *Flexible C++ #2: Efficient Integer To String Conversions, Part 3*, C/C++ Users Journal Experts Forum, November 2003; *http://www.cuj.com/documents/s=8906/cujexp0311wilson/*

[Wils2004b] Matthew Wilson, *Flexible C++ #3: Efficient Integer To String Conversions, Part 4*, C/C++ Users Journal Experts Forum, January 2004; *http://www.cuj.com/documents/s=8943/cujexp0312wilson/*

Index